T0201275

FUNDAMENTALS OF COMPLEX NETWORKS

FUNDAMENTALS OF COMPLEX NETWORKS
MODELS, STRUCTURES AND DYNAMICS

Guanrong Chen

City University of Hong Kong, China

Xiaofan Wang

Shanghai Jiao Tong University, Shanghai, China

Xiang Li

Fudan University, Shanghai, China

HIGHER EDUCATION PRESS

Library of Congress Cataloging-in-Publication Data

Chen, G. (Guanrong)
  Fundamentals of complex networks : models, structures, and dynamics / Guanrong Chen, Xiaofan Wang, Xiang Li.
    pages cm
  Includes bibliographical references and index.
  ISBN 978-1-118-71811-7 (cloth)
  1. System theory. I. Wang, Xiaofan, 1967– II. Li, Xiang, 1976 February 8– III. Title.
  Q295.C4524 2015
  003′.72 – dc23

                                                                                    2014034304

Typeset in 10/12pt TimesLTStd by Laserwords Private Limited, Chennai, India
Printed and bound in Singapore by Markono Print Media Pte Ltd

1   2015

Contents

About the Authors

Guanrong Chen is Chair Professor and Founding Director of the Centre for Chaos and Complex Networks at the City University of Hong Kong. He was awarded the 2011 Euler Gold Medal, Russia, and was conferred Honorary Doctorate by the Saint Petersburg State University, Russia in 2011 and by the University of Le Havre, France in 2014. He is a member of the Academia Europaea.

Xiaofan Wang is Distinguished Professor of the Department of Automation at Shanghai Jiao Tong University, China. He received the 2002 National Science Foundation Award for Distinguished Young Scholars and the 2008 Distinguished Professorship from the Chang Jiang Scholars Program by the Ministry of Education, China. He is the 2014–2017 Chair of the IFAC Technical Committee on Large-Scale Complex Systems.

Xiang Li is Full Professor and Head of Department of Electronic Engineering, Fudan University, China. He received the 2005 Guillemin-Cauer Best Paper Award from the IEEE Circuits and Systems Society and the 2014 National Science Foundation Award for Distinguished Young Scholars, China.

Preface

The extensive study of complex networks is pervading sciences and engineering today, from physical, technological, biological, to social sciences. Their impacts on engineering and technology, in particular, are prominent and their influence is deemed to be far-reaching. Familiar complex networks include the Internet, the World Wide Web, wireless communication networks, biological neural networks, power grids, social relation and scientific cooperation networks, and so on. Research on fundamental properties and dynamical behaviors of various complex networks has recently become overwhelming.

The field of complex networks is indeed developing so fast and so wide that most newcomers typically find it quite difficult to know where to start their learning and research on the subject. Although there are some well-written textbooks and research monographs that can be adopted for studies by newcomers, these references are generally too advanced or too broad for those readers to comprehend, especially in a relatively short period of time; they are not easily used as textbooks for a short course on the subject either. Driven by such teaching and learning demands, this book has been designed to serve as a concise textbook for newcomers to the field. It is written as a one-semester introductory text for upper-division undergraduate or first-year graduate students in natural science, mathematics and engineering, or as an edited volume for self-study, or as a handy reference for research.

The book title retains the adjective "complex" to reflect the historical perspective and to emphasize the nature of the subject, which is in line with the common phrases of complex systems and complex dynamics alike, and therefore should not be seen as redundant.

The style of writing in this book is intended to be informal, emphasizing basic ideas and methodologies with elementary and sometimes heuristic mathematical arguments, easily readable by anyone having minimal knowledge of calculus, linear algebra and ordinary differential equations. In this regard, and to be self-contained, a preliminary chapter on graph theory, probability and statistics as well as dynamical systems is included after the first overview chapter. The book is divided into two parts: Part I *Fundamental Theory* is a detailed text consisting of three chapters, presenting background information and basic materials needed to learn the subject, with a variety of exercises for illustrating fundamental concepts and familiarizing related modeling and analysis techniques. Part II *Applications – Selected Topics* contains several selected application-oriented topics, which are all independent of each other, in the sense that one can choose any chapter to teach or to learn individually without referring to the contents of the other chapters in this part. Of course, the current arrangement of chapters would also be a logical ordering if one decided to read through this whole portion of the book. The last chapter of this part provides only outlines of several emerging topics which are believed important and promising, with sufficient numbers of key references provided for interested readers' future studies.

This book is a slightly modified and extended version of the same authors' earlier version of the book entitled *Introduction to Complex Networks: Models, Structures and Dynamics*, published by the Higher Education Press, Beijing in 2012. The basic materials of this book have been used in teaching a postgraduate course on *Complex Networks: Modeling, Dynamics and Control* at the City University of Hong Kong since 2007, received valuable feedback from students which has made the present version better suited to a text for both teaching and learning.

Owing to the introductory nature of the book, it does not cover the most advanced developments in the field, especially those in the last five years or so. It is the authors' hope that after learning this elementary text, readers are ready to read recent literature so as to pursue state-of-the-art research in the field of network science and engineering. For Chinese readers, there is a complementary volume written in Chinese by the same authors, entitled *Network Science: An Introduction* (Higher Education Press, Beijing, 2012), which has very little overlapping with the present book and hence should be fairly referential and informative.

Guanrong Chen
City University of Hong Kong

Xiaofan Wang
Shanghai Jiao Tong University

Xiang Li
Fudan University

Summer 2014

Acknowledgements

The authors would like to express their appreciation to their families for their long-term strong support and their great patience and understanding.

The authors also wish to thank those colleagues who have provided many helpful comments and suggestions to enhance the contents or to improve the descriptions of the book, especially Zhengping Fan (Section 3.6.4), Jun-An Lu and Housheng Su (Section 8.2), and Shi Zhou (Section 3.2.3), as well as the following individuals who have provided basic information and materials for Chapter 10, "Brief Introduction to Other Topics": Lin Wang (Section 10.2), Yuting Liu and Zhiming Ma (Section 10.3), Tao Zhou (Section 10.4), Linyuan Lu (Section 10.5), and Luonan Chen (Section 10.6). In addition, the authors would like to thank their students Jing Cui, Jingyuan Zhan and Yiqing Zhang, for their assistance.

The authors appreciate the courtesy of the following publishers in granting them permission to use various simulation and illustration figures from their journals, which have mostly been modified and have all been cited and acknowledged: The American Association for the Advancement of Science, American Physical Society, Association for the Advancement of Science, American Association for Computing Machinery Inc., Cambridge University Press, Elsevier, Europhysics Letter, IEEE, IOP Publishing, Macmillan Publishers Ltd (Nature), National Academy of Sciences U.S.A., Springer Science and Business Media, Society for Industrial and Applied Mathematics, University of Chicago Press, Wiley, and World Scientific Publishing.

The authors would also like to thank the following individuals for permission to use some of their artistic drawings or figures: L. Backstrom, J. Byer, B. Karrer, D. Krioukov, C. Marlow, I. Matta, A. Medina, V. Paxson, S. Sinha, S. Staniford, J. Ugander, N. Weaver, and Cliff C. Zou.

The authors are especially grateful to Ms Ying Liu, Editor of the Higher Education Press, Beijing, for her kind assistance and friendly cooperation throughout the process of the preparation and production of the book.

Finally, the authors acknowledge the Ministry of Education and the National Natural Science Foundation of China, and the Hong Kong Research Grants Council, for the long-term continuous research grants support for their research projects closely-related to the topics of this book.

Guanrong Chen
City University of Hong Kong

Xiaofan Wang
Shanghai Jiao Tong University

Xiang Li
Fudan University

Summer 2014

Part One

Fundamental Theory

1

Introduction

1.1 Background and Motivation

Between two randomly selected persons in the world, roughly how many friends are there connecting them together? When searching from one webpage to another through the World Wide Web (WWW), how many clicks are needed on average? How can computer viruses propagate so fast and so wide through the Internet? How are people infected by epidemics such as AIDS, SARS, and Avian Influenza all over the world? How do rumors spread in human societies? How does a regional financial recession trigger a global economic crisis? How does an electric power blackout emerge from a small local system failure through the huge-scale power grid? How can the human brain work so efficiently while every brain cell is relatively so simple? ... All these seemingly different issues have something to do with "networks" – Internet, WWW, social relationship networks, viruses and rumors propagation networks, economic trading and competition networks, power and traffic flow networks, wired and wireless communication networks, biological neural networks, ecosystem networks, and so on. Noticeably, and most important above all, these apparently different networks have a lot in common.

Since the 1990s, the rapid growth of the Internet as an icon of the high-tech era has led our life to an age of networks. The influence of various complex and dynamical networks is currently pervading all kinds of sciences, ranging from physical to biological, even to social sciences. Its impact on modern engineering and technology is prominent and will be far-reaching. There is no doubt that we are living in a networked world today. On the one hand, networks bring us convenience and benefits, improve our efficiency of work and quality of life, and create tremendous advantages and opportunities which we never had before. On the other hand, however, networks also generate harm and damage to nature and human societies, typically with epidemic spreading, computer virus propagation, and power blackouts, to name just a few. Therefore, the increasing demand for networks and networking also requires a correct view and a serious investigation of the complex properties of various networks and the dynamic mechanisms of networking. For a long time in history, studies of communication networks, power networks, biological networks, economic networks, social networks, etc., were carried out separately and independently. However, recently there has been some rethinking of the general concept and theory of complex dynamical networks towards a better understanding of the intrinsic relations, common properties and shared features of all kinds of networks in the real world, which are not isolated but actually networked together – network of systems and, more generally, network of networks. The new intention and desire of studying the fundamental properties and dynamical behaviors of most if not all complex networks, both qualitatively and quantitatively, is important and timely, although very challenging technically. The current research along this line has been considered as a "new science of networks" [1, 2], or network science and engineering, and has become overwhelming today.

Fundamentals of Complex Networks: Models, Structures and Dynamics, First Edition.
Guanrong Chen, Xiaofan Wang, Xiang Li.
© Higher Education Press. All rights reserved. Published 2015 by John Wiley & Sons Singapore Pte Ltd.
Companion Website: www.wiley.com/go/chen/complex

Life science is perhaps the most exciting revolutionary area of scientific research in this new century. The mainstream of research in life science in the last century was reductionism-based molecular biology. The fundamental principle of reductionism is that, within different levels of the structure of a biosystem, high-level dynamical behaviors are completely determined by those at the lower levels. There was a common belief that if the individual basic ingredients of life (e.g., DNA, RNA and proteins) could be well understood, then the activities and behaviors of cells at the higher level could be comprehended, while the interactions among these basic elements even among molecules could be neglected. Yet, this traditional reductionism has been seriously challenged at the beginning of the new century due to the many significant discoveries of the importance and essence of networking interactions and interactive dynamics between different levels of life structure and among large numbers of tiny ingredients. Barabási pointed out [3]: "Reductionism, as a paradigm, is expired, and complexity, as a field, is tired. Data-based mathematical models of complex systems are offering a fresh perspective, rapidly developing into a new discipline: network science."

All these have led to a new paradigm of network science, and more recently engineering and technology as well, not just about biology but literally about almost everything.

A *network* is a diagrammatical representation of some physical system or structure. A network consists of some *nodes* (vertices) connected by some *edges* (links) in a certain topology (structure). A *graph*, on the other hand, is a mathematical notion that represents only the structure of a network without physical meanings. Throughout the textbook, however, these two terms are often used for descriptive convenience without precise distinction. Likewise, the terms of *structure* and *topology* of a network or a graph are often arbitrarily used without distinction.

Real-work networks are generally complex, and the complexity of networks may be viewed from different perspectives:

1. *Structural complexity*: A network usually appears structurally complicated, which may even be seemingly messy and disordered (Figure 1.1). The network topology (i.e., structure) may vary in time (e.g., the WWW has new webpages to join and old websites removed everyday). Moreover, the edge connections among nodes may be directed and weighted (e.g., brain cells can be stimulated or restrained and the connections among cells can be strong or weak).
2. *Node-dynamic complexity*: A node in a network can be a dynamical system, which may have bifurcating and even chaotic behaviors (e.g., gene networks and Josephson lattices, which have dynamically evolving nodes). Moreover, a network may have different kinds of nodes (e.g., a power grid has electric generators and also has loads such as motors and machines).
3. *Mutual interactions among various complex factors*: A real-world network is typically affected by many internal and external factors (e.g., if the coupled brain cells are repeatedly excited by certain stimuli then their connections will be strengthened, which is considered the basic reason for learning and memorization). Furthermore, the close relations among networks or subnetworks make the already-complicated behaviors of each of them become much more complex and intrinsic (e.g., the blackout of a huge-scale power grid may lead to chain reactions in human lives and industrial productions, which may also slowdown the activities of other related networks such as traffic, communication and financial transactions). These are referred to as interdependent networks, which have received increasing attention recently.

In the intensive study of nonlinear science and dynamical systems, on the other hand, networked systems have been one of the focal topics for research since the mid-twentieth century. However, most such coupled dynamical systems were placed in a fixed and regularly connected network model for investigation, where the main interest was the complexity caused by the node dynamics but not that by the network topology. Typical examples of this type are coupled map lattice (CML) [4] and cellular neural (or nonlinear) networks (CNN) [5], which can generate rich spatiotemporal patterns. By assuming a network with a regular topology, one can focus on the effects of the node dynamics on the collective behaviors of the network in interest, setting aside the troublesome influence of the network structure. Moreover, the networked elements in a regular topology can be easily implemented by integrated circuits, which is a main concern in commercial applications of networked devices, systems and infrastructures.

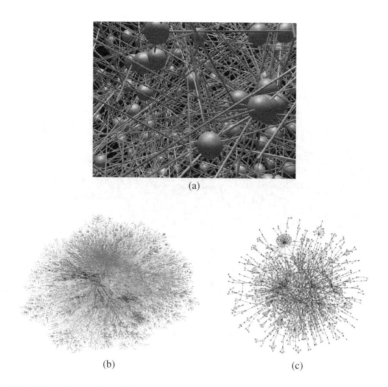

Figure 1.1 Three illustrative graphs with complex structures (from the Internet): (a) Illustrative graph of a social relationship structure in Canberra, Australia (Alden S. Klovdahl, Australian National University); (b) illustrative graph of some IP addresses on the Internet (William R. Cheswick, Lumeta Corporation, New Jersey, USA); (c) illustrative graph of interactions among proteins (Hawoong Jeong, Korea Advanced Institute of Science and Technology)

1.2   A Brief History of Complex Network Research

1.2.1   The Königsburg Seven-Bridge Problem

Complex network research has a long history. The recent study of complex networks has directed most interests to the modeling and understanding of various complex networks, especially the relations between the complexity of the network topology and the behaviors of the network dynamics.

To describe the common properties and characteristic features of different types of networks, a rigorous and efficient analytic tool is needed, which has been introduced in the form of graph theory in mathematics. A network can be viewed as a *graph* consisting of *nodes* connected by *edges* according to a certain rule or form, in which the nodes and edges do not necessarily have physical meanings in the discussion of graphs.

Representing a physical problem by a graph and then solving it by mathematical analysis and computation is not a new idea. This approach can be traced back to as early as the eighteenth century when the great mathematician Leonhard Euler (1707–83) studied and solved the famous seven-bridge problem in a town named Königsburg, which is now in the territory of Russia. As shown in Figure 1.2 [6], there is a river named Pregel passing through the town Königsburg, and there are seven bridges over the river. In the old days, the residents always wondered whether someone could walk through all seven bridges and then return to the starting point without going over any bridge more than once.

In 1736, the young Euler had a good idea to describe this real-world problem by an abstract graph, using four points *A, B, C, D* to represent the four pieces of lands separated by the river in town, with lines *a, b, c, d, e, f, g* to represent the seven bridges that connected the four points together (Figure 1.3 [6]).

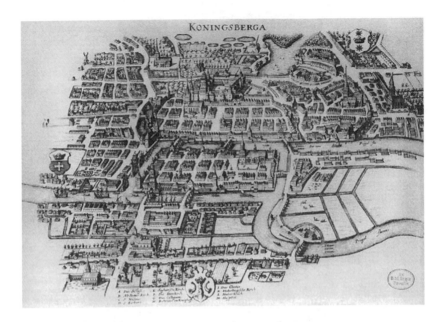

Figure 1.2   The town Königsburg and the seven bridges in 1736 [6]

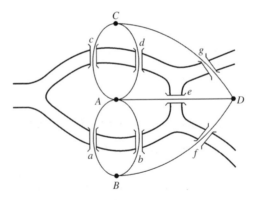

Figure 1.3   Graph of the Königsburg seven-bridge problem

Thus, Euler was able to convert the physical problem to the following mathematical problem: In the graph shown in Figure 1.3, starting from any point, is there a possible loop leading back to the starting point such that it passes all seven lines once and once only? Here and throughout, by "once and once only," it means not to miss any line and not to repeat any line.

Euler furthermore derived a necessary and sufficient condition for the existence of such a loop, thereby proving that the Königsburg seven-bridge problem has no solutions. More precisely, Euler observed that in order to have such a loop, if a point (A, B, C, or D in Figure 1.3) has one incoming edge then it should also have one outgoing edge; therefore, it is necessary for each point to have an even number of edges. However, the graph shown in Figure 1.3 does not satisfy this condition, therefore the problem has no solution. More significantly, Euler also proved that this condition is sufficient as well.

The contribution of Euler had gone far beyond this simple seven-bridge problem – it has opened up a new branch of mathematics: graph theory. Thereafter, Euler has been named the father of graph theory, and the picture shown in Figure 1.3 was called a Eulerian graph, an example of general Eulerian graphs to be further studied in Chapter 2. As a matter of fact, this simple graph is a foundation stone of modern mathematical graph theory, which has led to extensive studies of complex networks today.

1.2.2 Random Graph Theory

The development of graph theory had a very slow start after Euler solved the Königsburg seven-bridge problem. The first monograph on graph theory was not published until exactly 200 years later, in 1936, interestingly by a Hungarian mathematician named Dénes König [7]. Nevertheless, the theory was developed quite rapidly thereafter. The foundation of the now-famous "random graph theory" was laid by two Hungarian mathematicians, Paul Erdös (1913–96) and Alfréd Rényi (1921–70), in the late 1950s [8], which is considered the first rigorous and complete notion of modern graph theory.

Erdös and Rényi defined a random graph as N nodes connected by n edges, which are randomly chosen from the $N(N-1)/2$ possible edges.

The way to generate an ER random graph is to start with the N given nodes, from which every possible pair of nodes is being connected, once and once only, with probability p ($0 < p < 1$). More specifically, to generate an ER random network, one may start with N isolated nodes, pick up every possible pair of nodes, once and once only, from a total of $N(N-1)/2$ pairs of nodes, and then with probability p connect the pair with an edge.

Here, "with probability p" can be performed as follows: run a pseudorandom number generator to generate a "1" with probability p or a "0" with probability $1 - p$: at a step, if the generator yields a "1" then connect the pair of nodes by an edge; otherwise, the generator yields a "0," so do nothing.

Since every possible pair of nodes is picked up once and once only, there will not be multiple edges between any pair of nodes and, moreover, no node has self-connected edges.

It can easily be seen that in such an ER random graph of N nodes, the expectation value of the total number of edges will be $pN(N-1)/2$, which may not be an integer but is a random variable because p is so. Erdös and Rényi systematically studied many asymptotic properties, as $N \to \infty$, of such graphs and their relations with the edge-connectivity probability p. If a graph has a property P with probability 1 as $N \to \infty$, then they consider almost every ER random graph has property P. One of their most important and also quite surprising discoveries is that many properties of ER random graphs emerge suddenly but not gradually, in the sense that for a given edge-connectivity probability p, either almost every ER random graph has a certain property P or almost every such graph does not have property P [9].

As a historical remark, Paul Erdös is one of the most distinguished and leading mathematicians of the twentieth century, "the man who loves only numbers" [10]. Erdös was legendary; he had published more than 1600 research papers with more than 500 co-authors, and he had made very fundamental contributions in modern mathematics such as number theory, Diophantine equations, combinatory mathematics, probability theory, real and complex analysis, in addition to the random graph theory. Erdös was always excited when he met and worked with other mathematicians. When he met a colleague, he often said "My brain is open"; when he left one coworker to meet with another, he used to say "Another roof, another proof" [11]. In fact, he had devoted his entire life to the beloved mathematics. His stories and contributions will be revisited again and again throughout this textbook.

1.2.3 Small-World Experiments

1.2.3.1 Milgram's Social Experiment

A social network is a family of individuals and communities, connecting one another according to certain relationships. The human relationships in a social network can be friends, coworkers, marriages, partners, etc., or business cooperation between companies. Figure 1.1(a) illustrates one case of a social relationship in Canberra, Australia, based on real data from 5000 residents in 2005.

Take human friendship as an example. Many people have had the experience, when talking to a stranger for the first time, that both sides easily find a common friend in between, and so they yell surprisingly: "What a small world!" In general one may wonder, between two randomly selected persons in the world, how many intermediate friends are there connecting them together? In the 1960s, a psychologist at Harvard University, Stanley Milgram, did a survey in the United States and found that the average number of friends in between two randomly selected persons was only 6! This was the famous discovery of "six degree of separation."

Milgram's social experiment was carried out as follows. He first chose two targeted persons, the wife of a graduate student in a theological college in a small town called Sharon in Massachusetts, and a stockbroker in the big city Boston, unknown to the public in the experiment. He then called for two groups of volunteers in Kansas and Nebraska, respectively. He asked the volunteers each to send a letter to a friend and then ask that friend to forward the letter to another friend, and so on, towards one of the two targeted persons respectively in Sharon and Boston. In the May 1967 issue of *Psychology Today*, [12], Milgram reported his finding – it took only five times of forwarding, on average, to reach a target. In particular, one surprising example is that a letter from Kansas was first mailed to a priest and the priest forwarded it to his friend in Sharon and then the letter reached the target at the third step! Although not all letters were forwarded in such a short path, Milgram was able to statistically reach a conclusion of "six degree of separation."

Whether or not this number 6 was accurate is actually not important, which is not the point. In fact, the Facebook Data Team announced [13], on November 21, 2011, that this number should be 4.74 according to their survey of over 721 million active Facebook users (more than 10% of the global population), with 69 billion friendships among them. In this regard, what is important is the fact that this number is an extremely small number relative to the very large populations of the region, the country, or even the whole world. This indicates the so-called "small world" property of our huge-sized human society. Milgram's idea and experiment have had a great impact on later investigations and analyses of social science and social network research (of which more will be seen below).

1.2.3.2 Bacon's Oracle

To further verify Milgram's "six degree of separation," several social experiments were carried out later, among which was the quite interesting "Oracle of Bacon," also known as Six Degrees of Kevin Bacon or Bacon's networking game. Kevin Bacon (1958–) is a Hollywood actor who has featured in more than 60 movies to date and therefore has had quite a large number of intervening partners in these movies.

The game starts with the following numbering. Bacon himself has number 0. If an actor or an actress has been in a movie with Bacon, then he or she will be given the Bacon number 1; if an actor or actress does not co-show in a movie with Bacon directly but is a partner of someone with Bacon number 1, then this person has Bacon number 2, and so on. Thus, everyone who plays in a movie will have a Bacon number, big or small, indicating that he or she is a node in the network of movie stars starting from Bacon.

There is a database of movies and movie stars established in the Computer Science Department, University of Virginia [14], containing information of near half a million movies with near 1.7 millions of actors and actresses (Table 1.1, as of January 1, 2014). As a simple example, by inputting the name of the Hong Kong movie actor Stephen Chow, one finds his Bacon number to be 2. A prominent feature of this table of statistics is that amongst the very large number of near 1.7 million actors and actresses, the average Bacon number is very small – only about 3 – a small world of movie stars indeed!

1.2.3.3 Erdös Numbers

As mentioned above, Paul Erdös published more than 1600 research papers with more than 500 coauthors. Staring from Erdös, who has a number 0, one can build a network of coauthorships: if someone (likely a mathematician) has a joint paper with Erdös, then he or she will be given an Erdös number 1; if a

Table 1.1 Bacon numbers of actors and actresses (as of January 1, 2014) [14]

Bacon number	Number of actors/actresses
0	1
1	2 799
2	313 045
3	1 078 865
4	276 680
5	22 296
6	2 361
7	251
8	24

Total number of linkable actors: 1 696 322
Average Bacon number: 3.006

person does not coauthor a paper with Erdös directly but is a coauthor of someone with an Erdös number 1, then this person has an Erdös number 2, and so on [15]. Thus, sooner or later, every scientist who has a joint paper with someone in the fields of mathematics, physics, engineering and even social science will be a node in this coauthorship network, since mathematicians, scientists and engineers usually work in groups and frequently publish papers together.

As a simple example, Charles K Chui was a friend of Paul Erdös and they published one paper together; therefore Chui has an Erdös number 1 [16]. His former PhD student Guanrong Chen, first author of the present textbook, has an Erdös number 2 [17]. All the coauthors of Chen, such as Xiaofan Wang and Xiang Li, coauthors of this textbook, who did not have joint publications with Erdös and Chui, have a small Erdös number 3 [18] – once again, "what a small world"!

1.2.3.4 Experiments over the Internet

From a statistical point of view, although the networks of Bacon and Erdös can easily be computed, they are nevertheless too small to be conclusive. Knowing this, Duncan J Watts and his group of researchers at the Department of Sociology at the University of Columbia, who is now a Chief Scientist at Yahoo, set up a "Small World Project" on their website in 2001 [19], trying to carry out a large-scale international experiment to verify the hypothesis of "six degree of separation." They selected some targeted people and some volunteers, with different ages, races, professions and financial statuses. Once logged in, a volunteer would be given a piece of information and asked to pass on this information by email to a friend towards an unknown targeted person, in a way similar to Milgram's experiment. They reported their findings in *Science* in 2003 [20], showing that within more than one year they had more than 60 000 volunteers from 166 countries participated in this game targeting 18 selected people in 13 countries, and 384 emails eventually arrived at some targets through 5–7 people in between on average. Although there were some uncontrollable factors such as discontinuity of forwarding emails, just like Milgram's letters game, the experimental results agree quite well with Milgram's conclusion – six degree of separation – what a small world!

The largest experiment ever carried out was the one performed by the Facebook Data Team, mentioned above [13]. On November 21, 2011, they reported that according to their survey of over 721 million active Facebook users with 69 billion friendships among them, the average degree of separation was only 4.74, revealing that our world is not only small but today has actually become even smaller!

1.2.4   Strengths of Weak Ties

How do most people find their jobs? Namely, do they rely on their close relatives, or send out letters of application at random, or try the job fairs?

In the late 1960s, Mark Granovetter, then a graduate student of Harvard University, started his research based on the simple question referred to above. He interviewed around 100 people in the greater Boston area, and sent out more than 200 questionnaires, investigating a variety of technical people who had either just been offered a new job or had just lost the old job. Surprisingly Granovetter found that in people's job hunting, usually not those close family ties but new friends or even occasionally encountered strangers linked them to the new job positions. This means that, more often than not, weak connections lead to strong interactions (here, the results of getting jobs). In the language of network science, a long-range connection may lead to a stronger interaction between two nodes than that from short connections of neighboring nodes. From a social science point of view, this can also be easily understood: your relatives and best friends typically have the same groups of common friends; therefore, they usually do not provide new connections and additional information to your own knowledge.

One can easily find many cases from the real world. Here is one typical example provided by Granovetter in his research report [21]: Edward once met a young girl in a gathering in their high school, where he got to know the boyfriend of this girl's elder sister. This man was 10 years older than Edward. Three years later, when Edward lost his job, by chance he met that man again at a party. In conversation, Edward heard that his company was looking for a graph drawer and consequently he got that new job. This example showed once again, "What a small world!" And, moreover, how powerful a weak tie could be!

As a side note, Granovetter submitted his paper "Strength of Weak Ties" to the *American Sociology Review* in August 1969, but it was rejected after four months. His paper was set aside for four years, but then was resubmitted to the *American Journal of Sociology,* consequently being accepted and published [21, 22]. Interestingly enough, this paper has turned out to be one of the few important research papers that have had the highest impact in the field of social sciences today.

1.2.5   Heterogeneity and the WWW

The small-world property of many real networks reflects the essential homogeneity of such networks, in the sense that all nodes in a network have about the same number of connections to the others, which means that every one is equally important regarding their roles in the network. On the contrary, there are also many heterogeneous networks in which a small number of nodes have very large numbers of connections while the majority of nodes have very few connections each. If the number of connection represents the degree of importance of a node, then clearly the hub nodes with large numbers of connections play more significant roles in the network.

1.2.5.1   80–20 Rule

In 1906, Italian economist Vilfredo Pareto observed that about 80% of the land in Italy was owned by about 20% of the population. He then carried out some surveys on a number of other countries and found, to his surprise, that all the distributions are quite similar. Reportedly, he further verified the universality of the 80–20 phenomenon by observing that 20% of the pea pods contained 80% of the peas in his garden [23].

Thereafter, many events and phenomena support that 80–20 rule, which was then termed the Pareto principle, saying that for many events roughly 80% of the effects come from 20% of the causes. For instance, in the 1992 United Nations Development Program Report, it shows that the distribution of global income were very uneven, with the richest 20% of the world's population controlling 82.7% of the world's income. As another example, Microsoft noted that by fixing the top 20% most reported bugs, 80% of the errors and crashes would be eliminated [24]. Reportedly, in business roughly 80% of profits come from 20% of buyers, 80% of complaints come from 20% of customers, 80% of sales come from 20% of products, 80% of the sales come from 20% of the clients, and so on.

1.2.5.2   1% Rule

In Internet culture, there is a so-called 1% rule, known also as 90-9-1 rule, hypothesizing that more people will lurk than will participate in a virtual community.

The 1% rule is often used to refer to participation inequality in the context of the Internet; for example, the number of people who create content on the Internet represents approximately 1% of the people who actually view that content. For every forum posted by a user, generally about 99 other people are only viewing the forum but not posting any. The 90-9-1 version of this rule states that 1% of people create content, 9% edit or modify that content, and 90% only view the content without contributing anything to it.

It is noted, however, that according to a report in a 2012 BBC online briefing [25], about 83% of the population could properly be classified as lurkers, while 17% of the population could be classified as intense contributors of content which, instead, is closer to the 8020 rule discussed above.

1.2.5.3   World Wide Web

The World Wide Web (WWW) is a large-scale directed graph with nodes (vertices) being documents and edges (links) being URLs which point from one document to another. In 1999, Réka Albert, Hawoong Jeong and Albert-László Barabási from the University of Notre Dame, published a report in *Nature* on the connectivity topology (structure) of the WWW [26], showing that the connectivity distribution of the web is heterogeneous which follows a power law for both incoming edges and outgoing edges. This is also supported by the data analysis of Bernardo Huberman and Lada Adamic from the Xerox Palo Alto Research Center, reported in the same issue of *Nature* [27]. That means a small number of nodes have very large numbers of connections while the majority of nodes have very few connections each. Another important discovery in [26] about the WWW is that, although the web size was about 8×10^8 in that time, the average distance (number of hops) between any pair of nodes is only 18.59, namely with 19 clicks one can reach from any document to any other document on this huge web. This proves that the WWW is a small world. The web is also scale-free, since if the web were to increase 1000 percent in the same way it developed, the average distance would only increase from 19 to 21, in the sense that this and some other properties are basically independent of the scale of the network.

1.3   New Era of Complex-Network Studies

Since the 1960s, the theory of ER random graphs [8, 9] has been dominating academic research in network science, which was the only rigorous mathematical model that can describe the early small-scale telephone networks and the infant Internet the like. However, it was also aware of the fact that most real-world complex networks are not completely random, i.e., they are not generated by a completely random process. For instance, whether or not two persons are friends, whether or not two routers in the Internet are connected by optical fibers, whether or not two businessmen make a deal by signing an agreement, etc., are not totally random – these are not determined by simply tossing a coin. Besides, most natural and manmade networks are rapidly growing networks with evolutionary dynamics, very different from the fundamental framework of the ER random graphs, which is static and nongrowing, therefore more realistic network models are desirable.

The end of the twentieth century was a turning point in network science research: networks were being revisited from a physical rather than purely mathematical viewpoint by scientists, particularly applied physicists, computer scientists, engineers and biologists alike, with a new focus on the global behaviors, complex topologies, and evolving dynamics of various networks in interest.

Table 1.2 Some inferential historical markers in network science

Year	People	Event
1736	Euler	Seven-bridge problem
1959	Erdös and Rényi	Random graph theory
1967	Milgram	Small-world experiment
1973	Granovetter	Strength of weak ties
1998	Watts and Strogatz	Small-world network model
1999	Barabási and Albert	Scale-free network model

There were two groundbreaking research papers on complex networks published at the very end of the last century, opening up a new era of complex network studies. In June 1998, Duncan J. Watts, then a PhD student, and his advisor Steven H. Strogatz at Connell University, published an article in *Nature* on the so-called small-world networks [28], followed by another article in *Science* on the so-called scale-free networks by a Hungarian physicist Albert-László Barabási and his then PhD student Réka Albert from the University of Notre Dame in October 1999 [29]. These two seminal articles revealed the most fundamental characteristic of the small-world property and the defining feature of the scale-free property of various complex networks. They have stimulated a large number of new publications in diverse areas of applied physics, mathematics, computer and biological sciences, engineering and technologies, as well as social and economic sciences in the following years, on what is confronting us the most today – complex networks.

The aforementioned three network models, namely the ER random-graph network model, the WS small-world network model and the BA scale-free network model, will be studied in detail in the following chapters of this textbook (for more related information, see [30]).

To this end, a short list of inferential markers in the network science history is summarized in Table 1.2.

Scientific research on complex networks had very significant progress during the crossing time of the two centuries, attributing to basic natural science and several high-tech developments in engineering: (i) the tremendous supercomputing power and the broad-spanned Internet embedded with a vast volume of databases, enabling researchers to collect and process huge amount of real data of different kinds; (ii) fast and wide overlapping of even seemingly unrelated fields of research, leading to many new findings in a broad spectrum of interdisciplinary areas; (iii) recent breakthroughs in the study of complexity, from reductionism to global and structural understanding, spurs a renewal of interest and a rethinking of the network science, leading the contemporary research focus to move from local to global, from lower level to higher level, and from steady to dynamic.

Due to the restriction of large-scale computational ability and the nonavailability of sufficiently large amount of real data, the network study in the past was typically limited to a few hundred or even just a few dozens of nodes in a physical network model. However, we are facing with networks having millions or even billions of nodes and edges such as the Internet, power grids, cash dollars in world economics, human populations in worldwide social studies, biological neural networks at the cell level, biosystems at the gene level, crystals in nanoscale, and so on. Many traditional theories, methodologies and techniques, meaningful and efficient for small-scale computation and analysis, are no longer applicable to such giant networks. The interactions among nodes and between different levels of the complex structure of a huge network generate many unexpected or unpredictable behaviors, such as emergence and chaos, going much beyond the traditional thinking of networks as simple and steady graphs. Consequently, the traditional approaches to network research have to be drastically modified and advanced, or even completely changed. New viewpoints, new theories, new models, and new methods for investigating complex networks are all needed. We have, indeed, already entered a new era of complex network studies.

At present, studies of complex networks may be roughly categorized as follows:

1. *Discovering*: To reveal the global statistical properties of a network and to develop measures for these properties.

2. *Modeling*: To establish a mathematical model of a given network, enabling better understanding of the network statistical properties and the causes for their appearance.
3. *Analysis*: To find out the basic characteristics and essential features of nodes, edges, and the whole network, connected in a certain topology, to develop fundamental mathematical theories that can describe and predict network dynamical behaviors.
4. *Control*: To develop effective methods and techniques that can be used to modify and improve network properties and performances, suggesting new and possibly optimal network designs and utilizations, particularly in regard to network stability, synchronizability, and data-traffic management.
5. *Applications*: To apply and utilize some special and fundamental properties and characteristics of complex networks to facilitate the design and applications of network-related problems, such as data-flow congestion control on the Internet and traffic control for city transportations, optimal integrated circuit design for chip fabrication, better decision-making of policy and strategy for commercial trading and financial management, etc.

It is clear that, accomplishment notwithstanding, complex dynamical networks as a promising and profound research subject is merely at the beginning of a foreseeable far-reaching as well as long-sustainable research endeavor. The scientific research along this line has been considered as "network science", and "network science and engineering" more recently. New discoveries, developments, enhancements and improvements are still yet to come.

Exercises

1.1 In the Königsburg seven-bridge problem shown in Figure 1.3, if the requirement is to go through every bridge once and once only, but not necessarily return to the starting point, is the problem solvable? If so, show one solution; if not, explain why.

1.2 Name and briefly describe a few real-world examples of random-graph networks, small-world networks, and scale-free networks.

1.3 How many people will connect you to Paul Erdös, Kevin Bacon, Albert-László Barabási, and Barack Obama?

1.4 Give some real-world examples of strong interactions generated by weak connections, namely, a long-range connection leads to a stronger interaction between two nodes than those short connections of neighboring nodes.

1.5 Show some examples where the minority rules the majority (both in terms of numbers) in their social activities, cooperation, competition, business, etc. Also, show some other examples where majority rules the game.

References

[1] Barabási, A-L. (2002) *Linked: The New Science of Networks*. Massachusetts: Persus.
[2] Watts, D.J. (2004) The "new" science of networks. *Annual Review of Sociology*, **30**: 243–70.
[3] Barabási, A-L. (2012) The network takeover. *Nature Physics*, **8**: 14–16.
[4] Kaneko, K. (1992) *Coupled Map Lattices*. Singapore: World Scientific.
[5] Chua, L.O. (1998) *CNN: A Paradigm for Complexity*. Singapore: World Scientific.
[6] http://www-groups.dcs.st-andrews.ac.uk/history/Miscellaneous/Konigsberg.html (last accessed August 7, 2014).
[7] König, D. (1936) *Theorie der endlichen und unendlichen Graphen*. Teubner, Leipzig.
[8] Erdös, P. and Rényi, A. (1960) On the evolution of random graphs. *Publications of the Mathematical Institute of the Hungarian Academy of Sciences*, **5**: 17–60.
[9] Bollobás, B. (2001) *Random Graphs*. New York: Cambridge University Press.

[10] Hoffman, P. (1998) *The Man Who Loved Only Numbers*. New York: Hyperion.

[11] Schechter, B. (1998) *My Brian is Open: The Mathematical Journeys of Paul Erdös*. New York: Touchstone.

[12] Milgram, S. (1967) The small world problem. *Psychology Today*, May, 60–7.

[13] http://www.telegraph.co.uk/technology/facebook/8906693/Facebook-cuts-six-degrees-of-separation-to-four .html (last accessed August 13, 2014).

[14] http://oracleofbacon.org/cgi-bin/center-cgi?who=Kevin+Bacon (last accessed August 7, 2014).

[15] http://www.oakland.edu/enp/(last accessed August 7, 2014).

[16] Borosh, I., Chui, C.K. and Erdös, P. (1978) On changes of signs in infinite series. *Analysis Mathematica*, **4**(1): 3–12.

[17] Chui, C.K. and Chen, G. (1987, 2009) *Kalman Filtering with Real-Time Applications*. Berlin: Springer-Verlag, 1st edn 1987, 4th edn 2009.

[18] Wang, X.F., Li, X. and Chen, G. (2006) *Complex Networks: Theory and Applications* (in Chinese). Beijing: Tsinghua University Press; Wang, X.F., Li, X. and Chen, G. (2012) *Network Science: An Introduction* (in Chinese). Beijing: Higher Education Press; Chen, G., Wang, X.F. and Li, X. (2012) *Introduction to Complex Networks: Models, Structures and Dynamics*, Beijing: Higher Education Press.

[19] Watts, D.J. (2003) *Six Degrees: The Science of a Connected Age*. New York: Norton.

[20] Dodds, P., Muhamad, R. and Watts, D.J. (2003) An experimental study of search in global social networks. *Science*, **301**(5634): 827–9.

[21] Granovetter, M. (1973) The strength of weak ties. *American J. of Sociology*, **78**(6): 1360–80.

[22] Granovetter, M. (1983) The strength of weak ties: A network theory revisited. *Sociology Theory*, **1**: 201–33.

[23] http://en.wikipedia.org/wiki/Pareto_principle (last accessed August 7, 2014).

[24] Rooney, P. (2002) (Microsoft CEO): 80–20 rule applies to bugs, not just features, October 3.

[25] http://en.wikipedia.org/wiki/1%25_rule_(Internet_culture) (last accessed August 7, 2014).

[26] Albert, R., Jeong, H. and Barabási, A-L. (1999) Diameter of the World-Wide Web. *Nature*, **401**: 130–1.

[27] Huberman, B.A. and Adamic, L.A. (1999) Growth dynamics of the World-Wide Web, *Nature*, **401**: 131.

[28] Watts, D.J. and Strogatz, S.H. (1998) Collective dynamics of "small-world" networks. *Nature*, **393**(6684): 440–2.

[29] Barabási, A-L. and Albert, A. (1999) Emergence of scaling in random networks. *Science*, **286**(5439): 509–12.

[30] http://www.ee.cityu.edu.hk/~gchen/ComplexNetworks.htm (last accessed August 7, 2014).

2

Preliminaries

2.1 Elementary Graph Theory

2.1.1 Background

A *network* is a diagrammatical representation of some physical structure such as a circuit (Figure 2.1(a)), a computer web (Figure 2.1(b)), or some kind of human relationship (Figure 2.1(c)), etc. A *graph*, on the other hand, is a mathematical notion that represents only the structure of a network without physical meanings, which will be studied in detail in this part of the chapter. A network consists of some *nodes* (vertices) connected by some *edges* (links) in a certain topology (structure). Throughout this textbook, the two terms of network and graph are often used without precise distinction, and likewise the two terms of structure and topology of a network or a graph are often used to mean the same.

As mentioned in Chapter 1, the idea of representing a physical network by a mathematical graph and then solving it by analysis and computation may be traced back to the eighteenth century when the great mathematician Leonhard Euler (1707–83) studied and solved the seven-bridge problem in a town named Königsburg in Russia.

In Königsburg, there is a river named Pregel passing trough the town and there are seven bridges over the river, as shown in Figure 1.2, or again in Figure 2.2 [1]. The then residents were always intrigued by the possibility of being able to walk through all the seven bridges once and once only and finally returning to the starting point.

In 1736, Euler had a new idea to describe this real-world problem with an abstract graph, using four points A, B, C, D to represent the four pieces of lands separated by the river in town and using curves a, b, c, d, e, f, g to represent the seven bridges that connect the four points together (Figure 2.3 [1]). Thus, Euler converted the physical problem to a mathematical problem: In the graph shown in Figure 2.3, starting from any point, is there any possible way leading back to the starting point such that it passes all the seven curves once and once only? This interesting seven-bridge problem will be revisited later, after a brief introduction to some basic concepts and notations of elementary graph theory.

2.1.2 Basic Concepts

2.1.2.1 Simple Graphs

Let G be a nonempty graph with at least one *node* (or, *vertex*). In a nonisolated case, G has at least one *edge* (or, *link*), where the edge is not allowed to have an open end without connecting to any node; therefore every edge has two end nodes by convention. Let $N(G)$ and $E(G)$ denote the sets of its nodes and edges, with number of nodes $N = |N|$ and number of edges $M = |E|$, respectively. Only a finite

Fundamentals of Complex Networks: Models, Structures and Dynamics, First Edition.
Guanrong Chen, Xiaofan Wang, Xiang Li.
Companion Website: www.wiley.com/go/chen/complex

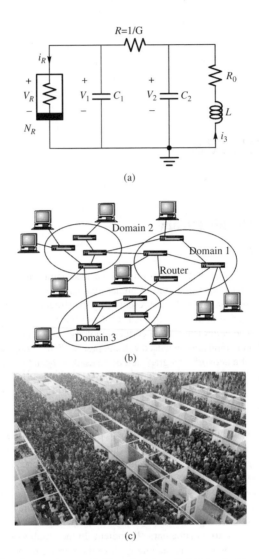

(a)

(b)

(c)

Figure 2.1 Some examples of network or graph (from the Internet): (a) circuit; (b) computer network; (c) social network

setting is considered, where $N(G)$ is a nonempty finite set of distinct nodes and $E(G)$ is a finite set of unordered pairs of distinct nodes in $N(G)$. Such a nontrivial pair $(N(G), E(G))$ is referred to as an *undirected graph*. In the trivial case where $E(G)$ is an empty set, the graph has only isolated nodes; it is a totally disconnected graph called a *null graph*. In most of this part of the section, only undirected graphs are discussed, therefore by a graph it refers to an undirected one, while directed graphs will be reviewed at the end of the section. Clearly, for a graph with N nodes, the maximum possible number of its edges is $N(N-1)/2$. If its existing number of edges is M, then, the ratio $D_M = 2M/N(N-1)$ can be used as a measure of the *density* of the graph. Clearly, $0 \leq D_M \leq 1$.

Figure 2.4 is an example of a nontrivial graph G with four nodes $N(G) = \{A, B, C, D\}$ and four edges $E(G) = \{AB, AC, BC, CD\}$, in which AB denotes an edge joining node A and node B, and so on. Every well-defined portion of a graph is a *subgraph* of that graph. For example, in Figure 2.4, the triangle ABC is a subgraph of the whole graph, and so are the node D, the edge AB, the piecewise line BCD, etc. Here, a

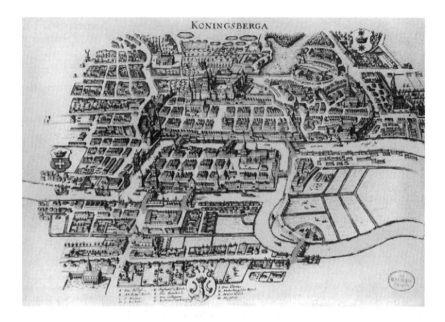

Figure 2.2   The town Königsburg and the seven bridges in 1736 [1]

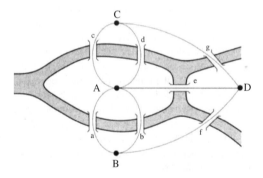

Figure 2.3   Graph of the Königsburg seven-bridge problem

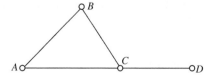

Figure 2.4   An example of a nontrivial graph

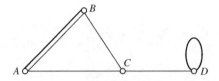

Figure 2.5   An example of a general graph

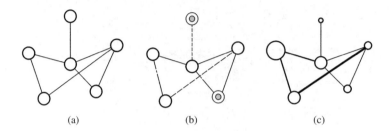

(a)   (b)   (c)

Figure 2.6   A few examples of different types of graphs: (a) an undirected and unweighted simple graph with same type of nodes; (b) an undirected and unweighted graph with different types of nodes and edges; (c) an undirected but weighted graph with weights on both nodes and edges

closed connection like the triangle *ABC* is called a *circuit* (or *cycle*) in the graph. A connected subgraph, if it is unconnected to the other parts of the same graph, is called a (*connected*) *component* of the graph. Figure 2.4 has only one component, while Figure 2.17(a) and Figure 2.20(b) shown below, each has two.

If two nodes are allowed to have more than one edge joining them, or a node can have a *self-loop*, i.e., an edge joining the same node at both ends, as shown in Figure 2.5, then the graph is called a *general graph*, which is considered not *simple*. On the other hand, if every edge (or, every node) is associated with a weight value, then the network is called a *weighted network*; otherwise, it is an *unweighted network*. Of course, an unweighted network can be viewed as a weighted network with all weight values identically equal to unity. In addition, a network may have different kinds of nodes. For example, in a human relationship network, different nodes may represent individuals with different races, ages, genders, professions, nationalities, etc. Such networks are not simple at all. A few examples of different types of networks are illustrated in Figure 2.6.

Figure 2.6 differentiates and illustrates different types of graphs. Throughout this textbook, only simple unweighted graphs are considered. So, from now on, a *graph* always refers to an undirected and unweighted simple graph, until later sections on directed or weighted graphs, or if otherwise indicated.

Note that in this and all other figures throughout, as a convention in drawing, two edges are not crossed if there is no node at the "crossing point." Thus, there are no crossings in between the upper-right node and lower-left node in Figure 2.6(a)–(c).

2.1.2.2   Degree and Degree Distribution

The concept of degree is the most fundamental character and measure of a node in a network, which may be defined in different ways. Here and throughout, the *degree* of node i in an undirected network is simply defined to be the number k_i of its existing edges. Thus, an isolated node has degree zero, while in Figure 2.4, $k_A = 2$, $k_B = 2$, $k_C = 3$ and $k_D = 1$. Sometimes, for clarity it may be more precisely referred to as *node degree*. The *average degree* of a graph is the average value of all such node degrees k_i over the entire graph, and is denoted by $\langle k \rangle$.

In a directed graph, however, there is a distinction between *in-degree* and *out-degree*, describing the numbers of incoming edges and of outgoing edges, respectively.

Since in a graph every node has a degree value, some large and some small, the distribution of nodes in the graph is an important concept, which may be of great concern in applications. The *degree distribution* is defined by a probability function, $P(k)$, which can be understood as the probability that a randomly picked node has degree k, where each node has an equal probability to be picked:

$$P(k) = \text{Probability that a node has degree } k,$$

$$\text{where the node is picked at random uniformly.} \tag{2.1}$$

It can be easily seen that the degree distribution $P(k)$ of a fully connected graph, called *complete graph*, is a discrete delta function. For example, in a fully connected network of 100 nodes, each node has degree 99; therefore, $P(99) = 1$ but $P(k) = 0$ for all $k \neq 99$ (i.e., for all $k = 0, 1, 2, \ldots, 98, 100, 101, 102, \ldots$). Other common degree distribution functions include uniform distribution, exponential distribution, power-law distribution, Poisson distribution, Pareto distribution, Gaussian distribution, etc., which will be frequently encountered and further studied later.

It is clear that

$$\sum_{k=0}^{\infty} P(k) = \sum_{k=0}^{k_{max}} P(k) = 1 \tag{2.2}$$

and

$$\langle k \rangle = \sum_{k=0}^{\infty} kP(k) = \sum_{k=1}^{k_{max}} kP(k) \tag{2.3}$$

where k_{max} is the maximum node degree on the graph.

The probability that a randomly picked node has degree at least k is given by the *cumulative degree distribution*, defined by

$$P_k = \sum_{k'=k}^{\infty} P(k'). \tag{2.4}$$

It can be verified that if the node-degree distribution is exponential of the form $P(k) \sim e^{-k/\sigma}$ with a constant $\sigma > 0$, then $P_k = \sum_{k'=k}^{\infty} e^{-k'/\sigma} \sim e^{-k/\sigma}$, and that if the node-degree distribution is a power law of the form $P(k) \sim k^{-\gamma}$ with a constant $\gamma > 0$, then $P_k = \sum_{k'=k}^{\infty} (k')^{-\gamma} \sim k^{-(\gamma-1)}$. Here and throughout, the notation $P_k \sim f(k)$ means $P_k = Cf(k)$ for a constant $C > 0$ which is not in concern.

The *joint degree distribution* is defined by a probability function, $P(k_1, k_2)$, being the probability that a randomly picked edge has one end-node with degree k_1 while another with k_2, which is equal to

$$P(k_1, k_2) = M(k_1, k_2)/M, \tag{2.5}$$

where $M(k_1, k_2)$ is the total number of edges having one end-node with degree k_1 while another with k_2, and M is the total number of edges, on the graph. The degree distribution and the joint degree distribution are related via

$$P(k) = \frac{\langle k \rangle}{k} \sum_{k_2=1}^{k_{max}} \frac{P(k, k_2)}{2 - \delta_{kk_2}}, \tag{2.6}$$

where $\delta_{kk_2} = 1$ if $k_2 = k$ but $= 0$ otherwise.

2.1.2.3   Distance and Average Path Length

The *distance* between two nodes, labeled i and j, can be defined by any metric, denoted as d_{ij}. The commonly used simplest definition is adopted in this textbook: the distance between two nodes is equal to the total number of edges that connect them through a shortest route.

The *diameter* of a network, denoted by D, is defined to be the largest of all distances in the graph; that is,

$$D = \max_{i,j} d_{ij}. \tag{2.7}$$

The *average distance*, or *average path length*, of a graph is defined to be the average value of all distances over the graph:

$$L = \frac{2}{N(N-1)} \sum_{i<j} d_{ij}. \tag{2.8}$$

Here, N is the size of the graph, i.e., the total number of nodes in the graph.

Example 2.1 Figure 2.7 shows another simple example of a network with 5 nodes and 5 edges, where $D = d_{45} = 3$ and $L = 16/10 = 1.6$, since

$$
\begin{array}{llll}
d_{12} = 1 & d_{13} = 1 & d_{14} = 2 & d_{15} = 1 \\
           & d_{23} = 1 & d_{24} = 1 & d_{25} = 2 \\
           &   & d_{34} = 2 & d_{35} = 2 \\
           &   &   & d_{45} = 3.
\end{array}
$$

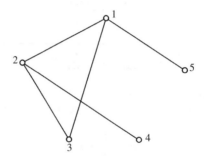

Figure 2.7   A simple graph with 5 nodes and 5 edges

2.1.2.4   Clustering Coefficient

In a friendship network, two friends of someone may or may not be friends themselves. This is characterized by the concept *clustering*.

In a graph, let i be a node with k_i edges connecting to other k_i nodes, which are called *neighbors* of node i. It is easy to verify that there are at most $k_i(k_i - 1)/2$ edges among these k_i neighbors. Let E_i be the number of the actual edges existing among these k_i nodes. Then, the ratio between the actual and the possible numbers of edges in the cluster of these k_i nodes is defined to be the *clustering coefficient* of node i, denoted as C_i; namely,

$$C_i = \frac{2E_i}{k_i(k_i - 1)}. \tag{2.9}$$

Consider the example shown in Figure 2.7 again, where

Node-1 has 3 neighbors, $E(1) = 1$, so $C_1 = 2 \times 1/(3 \times 2) = 1/3$;

Node-2 has 3 neighbors, $E(2) = 1$, so $C_2 = 2 \times 1/(3 \times 2) = 1/3$;

Node-3 has 2 neighbors, $E(3) = 1$, so $C_3 = 2 \times 1/(2 \times 1) = 1$;

Node-4 has 1 neighbor, $E(4) = 0$, so $C_4 = 0$;

Node-5 has 1 neighbor, $E(5) = 0$, so $C_5 = 0$.

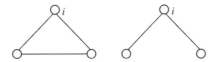

Figure 2.8   A complete triangle and a triangular graph

Therefore, their average, denoted $\overline{C}$, is

$$\overline{C} = (1/3 + 1/3 + 1 + 0 + 0)/5 = 1/3.$$

From a geometric point of view, this is equivalent to

$$C_i = \frac{\textit{number of complete triangles with corner } i}{\textit{number of triangular graphs with corner } i}, \qquad (2.10)$$

as visualized by Figure 2.8, where the complete triangle (left) is counted in both the numerator and the denominator, but the open triangular graph (right) is counted only in the denominator, in (2.5).

Once again, consider the example shown in Figure 2.7. Since

Node-1 has 1 complete triangle and 3 triangular graphs, so $C_1 = 1/3$;

Node-2 has 1 complete triangle and 3 triangular graphs, so $C_2 = 1/3$;

Node-3 has 1 complete triangle and 1 triangular graph, so $C_3 = 1$;

Node-4 has 0 complete triangles, so $C_4 = 0$;

Node-5 has 0 complete triangles, so $C_5 = 0$.

Hence,

$$\overline{C} = (1/3 + 1/3 + 1 + 0 + 0)/5 = 1/3.$$

The clustering coefficient C of the whole graph is the averaged value of all such clustering coefficients C_i of node i, for all i over the entire graph. Obviously, $0 \leq C \leq 1$, and $C = 0$ if and only if all neighbors are unconnected for any node in the graph (e.g., a star-shaped graph and a set of isolated nodes) and $C = 1$ if and only if all nodes are connected each other (i.e., a complete graph).

It has been a common observation that most real-world networks have a clustering coefficient C in the order of $C = O(1)$, satisfying $O(N^{-1}) \ll C \ll 1$. This also shows that most real-world networks are not completely random nor completely regular, as will be further discussed in the following chapters of the textbook.

2.1.2.5   Coreness and Closeness

For graphs (networks), there are various measures of the so-called *centrality* of a node within a graph, which determine the relative importance of the node in the graph; for example, it measures how important a person is within a social network and how well a router is being used within a local area network (LAN), etc. In other words, a centrality of a node is a measure of the structural importance of the node in the network. Generally, a more "central" node has a stronger influence on other nodes in the same network.

The *k-core* in a graph is defined to be the remaining subgraph after all the nodes with degrees $\leq k - 1$ have been removed successively, during which:

(i) when a node is removed, all its adjacent edges will also be removed;
(ii) after a node of degree $\leq k - 1$ is removed, in the remaining graph all the remaining nodes with a new degree $\leq k - 1$ also need to be removed.

If a node belongs to a k-core but not the $(k + 1)$-core of the graph, this node is said to have *coreness k*. The largest coreness in a graph is called the *coreness of the graph*.

Example 2.2 Consider some simple graphs.
First, a single isolated node has coreness 0, and a complete graph of size N has coreness $N - 1$. Second, consider a star-shaped graph:

1. the 1-core of the graph is the graph itself;
2. all nodes, including the central node, have coreness 1;
3. the coreness of the graph is 1.

Finally, consider a simple ring-shaped graph:

1. the 1-core of the graph is the graph itself;
2. the 2-core of the graph is the graph itself;
3. all nodes have coreness 2;
4. the coreness of the graph is 2.

The main purpose of introducing the concept of coreness is to reflect the fact that a higher core is more important than a lower core, and a higher-coreness node is more important than a lower-coreness node, in a graph against node-removal. This can reveal the hierarchical structure of a graph, where higher cores and higher-coreness nodes belong to higher-levels of the hierarchical graph. Clearly, the star-shaped and ring-shaped graphs do not have prominent hierarchical structures.

The main implication of the concept of coreness, on the other hand, is that a graph with a higher coreness will have better robustness against intentional attacks by means of node removal. Apparently, both star-shaped and ring-shaped graphs are fragile to intentional attacks.

Example 2.3 In the graph shown in Figure 2.9, the 1-core of the graph is the graph itself; the 2-core of the graph is Triangle 1-2-3. Node 4 and Node 5 have coreness 1, while Nodes 1, 2 and 3 have coreness 2. The coreness of the graph is 2.

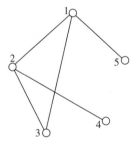

Figure 2.9   An example for calculating coreness

In a graph, a useful concept is closeness centrality. The *farness* of a node in the graph is defined as the sum of its distances to all other nodes, and its *closeness* is defined as the inverse of the farness. For example in Figure 2.9, Node 1 has farness $1 + 1 + 2 + 1 = 5$ and closeness $1/5$. The *average farness* and *average closeness* of the graph are defined to be the averages of all node farness and node closeness, respectively.

Thus, the more central a node is, the lower its total distance to all other nodes. Closeness can be regarded as a measure of how fast it will take to spread information from a node to all other nodes sequentially.

2.1.2.6   Betweenness and Information Centrality

In a graph of size N, the *node-betweenness* of node i is defined by

$$B(i) = \sum_{j \neq l \neq i} \frac{L_{jl}(i)}{L_{jl}}, \tag{2.11}$$

where L_{jl} is the number of all existing shortest paths from node j to node l, and $L_{jl}(i)$ the number of all shortest paths from node j to node l that actually pass through node i.

The node-betweenness may be normalized by dividing with the total number of pairs of nodes not including node i as an end-node, which is $(N-1)(N-2)/2$.

For an edge e_{ij} connecting node i and node j, the *edge-betweenness* of e_{ij} is similarly defined:

$$B(e_{ij}) = \sum_{(l,q) \neq (i,j)} \frac{L_{lq}(e_{ij})}{L_{lq}}, \tag{2.12}$$

where L_{lq} is the number of all existing shortest paths from node l to node q, and $L_{lq}(e_{ij})$ the number of all shortest paths from node l to node q that actually pass through edge e_{ij}. The edge-betweenness can also be normalized, by dividing with the total number of edges not including e_{ij}, which is $\frac{1}{2}N(N-1) - 1$.

Example 2.4 Consider the graph shown in Figure 2.10.

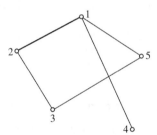

Figure 2.10   An example for calculating betweenness

The betweenness of Node 1 is:

$$B(1) = \frac{(5,1,4)}{(5,1,4)} + \frac{(5,1,2)}{(5,1,2)+(5,3,2)} + \frac{(4,1,2,3)+(4,1,5,3)}{(4,1,2,3)+(4,1,5,3)} + \frac{(4,1,2)}{(4,1,2)}$$

$$= 1 + \frac{1}{2} + 1 + 1 = \frac{7}{2}$$

or $B(1) = \frac{7/2}{(N-1)(N-2)/2} = \frac{7}{12}$ after normalization, where (i,l,q,j) is the path from Node i to Node j passing though Node l and Node q successively.

The betweenness of Edge e_{12} is:

$$B(e_{12}) = \frac{(5,1,2)}{(5,1,2)+(5,3,2)} + \frac{(4,1,2,3)}{(4,1,2,3)+(4,1,5,3)} + \frac{(4,1,2)}{(4,1,2)} + \frac{(3,2,1)}{(3,2,1)+(3,5,1)}$$

$$= \frac{1}{2} + \frac{1}{2} + \frac{1}{1} + \frac{1}{2} = \frac{5}{2}$$

or $B(e_{12}) = \frac{5/2}{N(N-1)/2-1} = \frac{5}{18}$ after normalization.

The importance of the node- and edge-betweenness centralities can easily be understood from Figure 2.11, where the bridging node has very small degree yet very large node- and edge-betweeness, while generally big nodes have large betweenness.

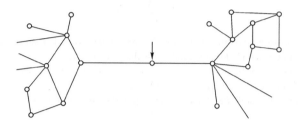

Figure 2.11   The importance of a node with a large betweenness value

The concept of information centrality of a graph, as its name suggested, is useful for measuring the information traffic over networks, which is very useful, for example, in finding the community structure of a network.

The *information centrality* of a network (graph) G of size N is defined to be the mean information flow rate over the network:

$$E_G = \frac{1}{N(N-1)} \sum_{i \neq j \in G} \varepsilon_{ij} = \frac{1}{N(N-1)} \sum_{i \neq j \in G} \frac{1}{d_{ij}}, \qquad (2.13)$$

where the *network efficiency* ε_{ij} of channel information transmission between node i and node j is defined to be inversely proportional to their shortest distance d_{ij}: $\varepsilon_{ij} = 1/d_{ij}$. If there is no edge between node i and node j in the network, then $d_{ij} = \infty$, so $\varepsilon_{ij} = 0$.

2.1.3   Adjacency, Incidence and Laplacian Matrices

For a graph G with N nodes, labeled as $N(G) = \{1, 2, \dots, N\}$, its *adjacency matrix* A is defined to be the $N \times N$ constant matrix those ijth entry is 1 if node i and node j are connected, and is 0 otherwise, with $a_{ii} = 0$ for all $i = 1, \dots, N$. An adjacency matrix is always symmetrical. If the edges of the graph are labeled as $E(G) = \{1, 2, \dots, M\}$, then the *incidence matrix* B of the graph is defined to be the $N \times M$ constant matrix whose ijth entry is 1 if node i connects edge j; and is 0 otherwise. An incidence matrix usually is nonsquare, unless the number of nodes is equal to the number of edges. Thus, for the graph shown in Figure 2.12, one has

$$A = \begin{bmatrix} 0 & 1 & 0 & 1 \\ 1 & 0 & 1 & 1 \\ 0 & 1 & 0 & 1 \\ 1 & 1 & 1 & 0 \end{bmatrix} \quad \text{and} \quad B = \begin{bmatrix} 1 & 0 & 0 & 1 & 0 \\ 1 & 1 & 0 & 0 & 1 \\ 0 & 1 & 1 & 0 & 0 \\ 0 & 0 & 1 & 1 & 1 \end{bmatrix}.$$

Some basic properties of the adjacency matrix A:

1. All main diagonal elements are 0; all the other elements are either 1 or 0; the sum of the ith row (or ith column) equals the degree of the ith node, k_i.
2. Let $A^2 = [\alpha_{ij}]$. Then, $\alpha_{ii} = \sum_{j=1}^{N} a_{ij}^2 = \sum_{j=1}^{N} a_{ij} = k_i$ and $\langle k \rangle = tr(A^2)/N$.

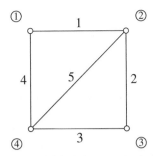

Figure 2.12   An example for the adjacency and incidence matrices

3. Let $A^n = [\beta_{ij}]$, $n \geq 1$. Then, β_{ij} = number of edges l_{ij} which is the shortest path of length n that connects nodes i and j.
4. For a graph with m components, $A = [A_1, A_2, \ldots, A_m]$, where A_l is the adjacency matrix of the lth component, $l = 1, 2, \ldots, m$; in particular, if $m = 1$, then A is called irreducible, corresponding to a connected graph.
5. Let $d_{ij}^m = 1$ if the shortest path length between node i and node j is m, and $= 0$ otherwise; let $h(x) = 1$ if $x > 0$, and $= 0$ otherwise; let $\delta_{ij} = 1$ if $i = j$, and $= 0$ otherwise; denote $A^n = [a_{ij}^n]$: then $d_{ij} = \sum_{m=1}^{D} m d_{ij}^m$, where D is the diameter of the graph and $d_{ij}^m = (1 - \delta_{ij} - d_{ij}^{m-1} - d_{ij}^{m-2} - \cdots - d_{ij}^1) \cdot h(a_{ij}^m)$ which can be calculated iteratively starting from $d_{ij}^1 = a_{ij}^1 = a_{ij}$.

Some basic properties of the incidence matrix B:

1. The sum of the ith row equals the degree of node i.
2. The sum of every column equals 2.
3. For a graph with m components, $B = [B_1, B_2, \ldots, B_m]$, where B_l is the incidence matrix of the lth component, $l = 1, 2, \ldots, m$.

For a graph, another important concept is the *Laplacian matrix* (also called *admittance matrix* or *Kirchhoff matrix*), denoted $L = [L_{ij}]$, which is defined as follows:

$$
L_{ij} = \begin{cases} k_i & if & i = j \\ -1 & if \quad i \neq j, & v_i \quad adjacent \quad v_j, \\ 0 & & otherwise \end{cases} \tag{2.14}
$$

where k_i is the degree of node v_i, $i, j = 1, \ldots, N$. By denoting $D = diag(k_1, \ldots, k_N)$, one has $L = D - A$. Thus, for the graph shown in Figure 2.12, the corresponding Laplacian matrix is

$$
L = \begin{bmatrix} 2 & -1 & 0 & -1 \\ -1 & 3 & -1 & -1 \\ 0 & -1 & 2 & -1 \\ -1 & -1 & -1 & 3 \end{bmatrix} = \begin{bmatrix} 2 & 0 & 0 & 0 \\ 0 & 3 & 0 & 0 \\ 0 & 0 & 2 & 0 \\ 0 & 0 & 0 & 3 \end{bmatrix} - \begin{bmatrix} 0 & 1 & 0 & 1 \\ 1 & 0 & 1 & 1 \\ 0 & 1 & 0 & 1 \\ 1 & 1 & 1 & 0 \end{bmatrix} = D - A,
$$

where the diagonal matrix has all node degrees on the diagonal and A is the adjacency matrix of the graph given above.

Some useful properties of the Laplacian matrix L :

1. L is always symmetrical and semipositive definite;
2. L has real eigenvalues $\lambda_1 \leq \lambda_2 \leq \cdots \leq \lambda_n$, with $\lambda_1 = \cdots = \lambda_q = 0$ where q is the number of disjoint subgraphs in the graph, therefore if the graph is connected, i.e., $q = 1$, then $0 = \lambda_1 < \lambda_2 \leq \cdots \leq \lambda_n$.

In the above, λ_2 is called the *algebraic connectivity* of the graph or the *spectral gap* of the corresponding Laplacian matrix.

2.1.4 Degree Correlation and Assortativity

The degree distribution of a graph is an important topological characteristic which, however, cannot be used as a unique measure of the essence of a graph because two graphs with the same degree distribution can have very different properties. Thus, to further describe and characterize the topology of a graph, more structural information with higher-order topological features are needed to be considered.

Here, only undirected graphs are discussed.

All graphs with N nodes and M edges have the same average degree, $\langle k \rangle = 2M/N$, which can be viewed as the zero-th order degree distribution, since it only shows how many edges there are, but does not give further information such as how they are distributed, therefore from which one cannot distinguish different graphs with the same numbers of nodes and edges.

On the other hand, the degree distribution, $P(k) = n(k)/N$ where $n(k)$ is the number of nodes with degree k, can be viewed as the first-order degree distribution, which describes the percentage of nodes with a certain degree in a graph. If one node is chosen at random, then the probability that this node has degree k is equal to $P(k)$. Clearly, this degree distribution contains the information about the average degree, because

$$\langle k \rangle = \sum_{k=0}^{\infty} kP(k) \tag{2.15}$$

2.1.4.1 Joint Probability Distribution

The joint probability $P(j, k)$ of degrees is defined to be the probability that a randomly chosen edge has two end-node degrees being j and k, respectively:

$$P(j, k) = \frac{m(j, k)\mu(j, k)}{2M}, \tag{2.16}$$

where $m(j, k)$ is the number of edges that has two end-nodes with degrees j and k, respectively, in which if $j = k$ the $\mu(j, k) = 2$, otherwise $\mu(j, k) = 1$.

Equation (2.16) shows the percentage of the number of edges with two end-node degrees j and k in the graph. This formula has the following properties:

Symmetry

$$P(j, k) = P(k, j), \quad \forall j, k \tag{2.17}$$

Normalization

$$\sum_{j,k=k_{\min}}^{k_{\max}} P(j, k) = 1 \tag{2.18}$$

Excess degree distribution

$$P_n(k) = \sum_{j=k_{\min}}^{k_{\max}} P(j, k), \tag{2.19}$$

where $k_{\max}$ and $k_{\min}$ are the maximum and minimum node degrees in the graph, and $P_n(k)$ is the probability that a randomly chosen neighbor of a randomly chosen node from the network has degree k. In general, $P_n(k) \neq P(k)$. In particular, if a network has isolated nodes then $P_n(0) \equiv 0 < P(0)$, because it is not possible to reach an isolated node from any other node in the graph.

Next, denote

$$p_k = P(k), \qquad q_k = P_n(k), \qquad e_{jk} = P(j, k). \tag{2.20}$$

Then,

$$p_k = \frac{\langle k \rangle}{k} \sum_{j=k_{\min}}^{k_{\max}} e_{jk} = \frac{\langle k \rangle}{k} q_k. \tag{2.21}$$

This shows that the second-order degree distribution contains information of the first-order degree distribution.

If, in a graph, a randomly chosen edge has its two end-node with random numbers of degrees, then these two end-node degrees are uncorrelated, hence

$$e_{jk} = q_j q_k, \qquad \forall j, k. \tag{2.22}$$

In this case, the graph is said to have no degree correlations (or, neutral), otherwise, the graph has degree correlations.

For a graph with a nonzero correlation coefficient, if nodes with large degrees tend to connect to nodes also with large degrees on average, the correlation coefficient will be positive, thus the graph is said to be assortative; but if nodes with large degrees tend to connect to nodes with small degrees on average, the correlation coefficient will be negative, thus the graph is said to be disassortative. Figure 2.13 shows that, graphs having the same degree sequence (hence the same degree distribution) can have very different degree correlations.

Table 2.1 shows two real networks – astrophysics coauthorship network and yeast protein–protein interaction (PPI) network – their joint probability distributions $[e_{jk}]_{k_{\max} \times k_{\max}}$, where the notation $\langle k_{nn} \rangle$ will be defined in the following subsection. A close look at them reveals that the former is assortative while the latter is disassortative. It can be seen from Figure 2.14 that in the yeast PPI network there are five prominent cycles, showing the tendency of big nodes connecting to small nodes. In general, however, to find the joint probability distribution by visual inspection is impractical, especially for large-sized networks, which often leads to vagueness, undeterminism and even controversy. Therefore, efficient methods are needed for determining if a network is assortative or disassortative, and the levels of such properties.

2.1.4.2 Excess Average Degree

Define the conditional probability $P_c(j|k)$ to be the probability that a randomly chosen node has degree k and, under this condition, it has one neighbor with degree j. This conditional probability is related to

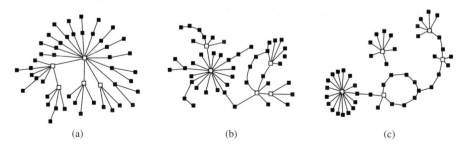

| (a) | (b) | (c) |

Figure 2.13 Three graphs with the same degree sequence: (a) assortative graph; (b) neutral graph; (c) disassortative graph

Table 2.1   Two real networks and their degree correlations (Courtesy of A-L. Barabasi)

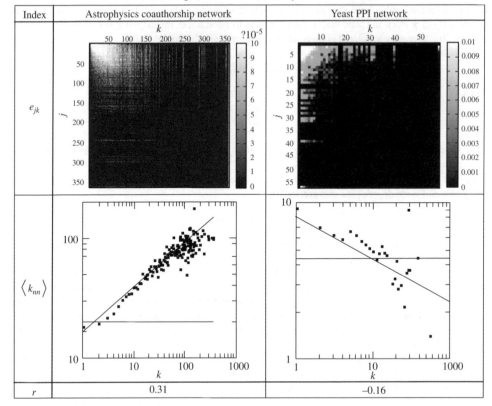

the joint probability via the following formula:

$$P_c(j|k)P(k) = P(j,k). \tag{2.23}$$

Furthermore, if the conditional probability depends on the degree k, then it implies that the node degrees have correlations, consequently the graph may have a hierarchical structure. But, if the conditional probability is independent of the degree k, then the graph does not have node-degree correlations.

Since the probability of an edge connecting to a node is proportional to the degree of that node, the conditional probability of a degree-uncorrelated graph is given by

$$P_c(k'|k) = P_c(k') = \frac{k'P(k')}{\langle k \rangle}. \tag{2.24}$$

Another, yet more concise, approach to computing the degree correction is to calculate the average degree of all neighbors, which is also called the *excess average degree*, of the node of degree k, denoted $\langle k_{nn} \rangle(k)$. More precisely, let the degree of the k_ith neighbor of node i be $k_{i_j}, j = 1, 2, \ldots, k_i$. The excess average degree of node i is the average degree $\langle k_{nn} \rangle_i$ of k_i neighbors of node i, given by

$$\langle k_{nn} \rangle_i = \frac{1}{k_i} \sum_{j=1}^{k_i} k_{i_j}. \tag{2.25}$$

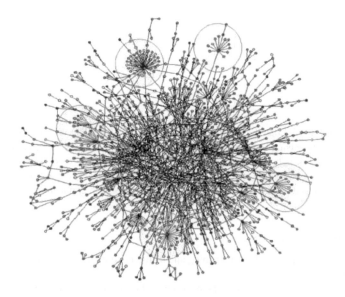

Figure 2.14   A yeast PPI network

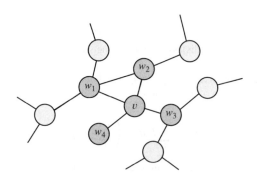

Figure 2.15   Example for computing the excess average degree

For example, in Figure 2.15, node v has excess average degree $\langle k_{nn} \rangle_v = \frac{4+3+3+1}{4} = \frac{11}{4}$. In general, if the nodes having degree k are $v_1, v_2, \ldots, v_{i_k}$, then the excess average degree of any node of degree k is

$$\langle k_{nn} \rangle(k) = \frac{1}{i_k} \sum_{i=1}^{i_k} \langle k_{nn} \rangle_{v_i}. \tag{2.26}$$

Note that the relation between $\langle k_{nn} \rangle(k)$ and the conditional probability and joint probability is given by

$$\langle k_{nn} \rangle(k) = \sum_{k'=k_{\min}}^{k_{\max}} k' P_c(k'|k) = \frac{1}{q_k} \sum_{k'=k_{\min}}^{k_{\max}} k' e_{kk'}, \tag{2.27}$$

where $q_k = P_n(k)$ and $e_{jk} = P(j,k)$, as defined in (2.20).

If $\langle k_{nn} \rangle(k)$ is an increasing function of k, then it follows that, on average, big nodes tend to connect to big nodes, namely the network is assortative. Conversely, if $\langle k_{nn} \rangle(k)$ is an decreasing function of k, then it follows that, on average, big nodes tend to connect to small nodes, thus the network is disassortative. If the network does not have degree correlation, then $\langle k_{nn} \rangle(k)$ is a constant independent of k:

$$\langle k_{nn} \rangle(k) = \frac{\sum\limits_{j} j e_{jk}}{\sum\limits_{j} e_{jk}} = \frac{\sum\limits_{j} j q_j q_k}{q_k} = \sum\limits_{j} j q_j = \sum\limits_{j} j \frac{j p_j}{\langle k \rangle} = \frac{\langle k^2 \rangle}{\langle k \rangle}. \tag{2.28}$$

It can be seen from Table 2.1 that the excess average degree $\langle k_{nn} \rangle(k)$ of the astrophysics coauthorship network is basically an increasing function of k, showing that this network is assortative; while the $\langle k_{nn} \rangle(k)$ of the yeast PPI network is basically a decreasing function of k therefore is disassortative. Compared to the joint probability distribution function (matrix) $[e_{jk}]_{k_{max} \times k_{min}}$, the excess average degree $\langle k_{nn} \rangle(k)$ is more intuitive but not as easy to apply to different kind of networks in applications.

2.1.4.3 Assortativity Coefficient

Now, a unified index is introduced for describing and distinguishing the assortativity and the disassortativity of a graph.

According to (2.22), if a network is of degree correlated then e_{jk} and $q_j q_k$ may not be equal. Thus, their difference may be used to describe the level of (dis)assortativity of the graph. More precisely, one may define

$$\langle jk \rangle - \langle j \rangle \langle k \rangle = \sum\limits_{jk} jk(e_{jk} - q_j q_k). \tag{2.29}$$

Generally, for a large-sized graph the absolute value of (2.29) will be relatively large, which can be normalized such that the levels of (dis)assortativity of networks of different sizes can be reasonably compared.

When a graph is totally assortative, with $e_{jk} = q_j q_k$, which maximizes (2.29), giving the variance of the excess average degree distribution of q_k as follows:

$$\sigma_q^2 = \sum\limits_{k} k^2 q_k^2 - \left(\sum\limits_{k} k q_k \right)^2. \tag{2.30}$$

Thus, a normalized assortativity coefficient can be obtained, as follows:

$$r = \frac{1}{\sigma_q^2} \sum\limits_{j,k} jk(e_{jk} - q_j q_k). \tag{2.31}$$

Clearly, $r \in [-1, 1]$. If $r > 0$ then the graph is assortative; if $r < 0$ then it is disassortative. Therefore, the value of $|r|$ describes the level of (dis)assortativity of a graph. Table 2.1 compares the levels of (dis)assortativity of two real networks.

The *assortativity* of a graph can also be defined via the Pearson correlation coefficient, as

$$r = \frac{M^{-1} \sum\limits_{e_{ij} \in E(G)} k_i k_j - \left[M^{-1} \sum\limits_{e_{ij} \in E(G)} \frac{1}{2}(k_i + k_j) \right]^2}{M^{-1} \sum\limits_{e_{ij} \in E(G)} \frac{1}{2}(k_i^2 + k_j^2) - \left[M^{-1} \sum\limits_{e_{ij} \in E(G)} \frac{1}{2}(k_i + k_j) \right]^2}, \tag{2.32}$$

where k_i and k_j are the degrees of the end nodes of edge $e_{ij} \in E(G)$, and M is the total number of edges in the graph. Clearly, $-1 \leq r \leq 1$. If $r > 0$ then the graph is *assortative*; if $r < 0$, then it is *disassortative*; if $r = 0$ then the node degrees in the graph are on average uncorrelated.

To describe the *closest-neighbor node degree* for node i, the following measure can be used:

$$k_i^{cn} = \sum_{j=1}^{N} a_{ij} k_j / k_i. \tag{2.33}$$

Thus, the *average closest-neighbor node degree* for all nodes of degree k in the graph is given by

$$k^{cn}(k) = \sum_{i=1, k_i=k}^{N} (k_i^{cn}/N)P(k), \tag{2.34}$$

where $P(k)$ is the degree distribution function. If $k^{cn}(k)$ is an increasing function of the degree variable k, then the graph is assortative; If $k^{cn}(k)$ is a decreasing function of k, then the graph is disassortative.

2.1.5   Some Basic Results on Graphs

Theorem 2.1 (Handshaking Lemma) *The total node degree of a graph is always an even number.*

Proof. Since every edge joins two nodes, this total node degree is twice the number of edges in any graph. ∎

Corollary 2.1 *In any graph, the number of nodes with odd degrees must be even.*

To introduce more results from graph theory, some new concepts are needed.

Two graphs G_1 and G_2 are said to be *isomorphic*, if there is a one–one correspondence between the nodes of G_1 and those of G_2 with the property that the number of edges joining any two nodes of G_1 is equal to the number of edges joining the two corresponding nodes of G_2. For example, the two graphs shown in Figures 2.13 (a) and (b) are isomorphic.

The graph G shown in Figure 2.16 (a) is quite special, in that all the nodes can be split into two disjoint sets, V_1 and V_2, in such a way that every edge of G joins a node in V_1 to a node in V_2. This kind of graph is called a *bipartite graph*. Another typical example of bipartite graph is the star-shaped graph, where the central node belongs to one set and all the other nodes belong to another.

For a given graph G, its *complementary graph* G^c is the graph containing all the nodes of G and all the edges that are not in G. For example, the complementary graphs of the two graphs in Figure 2.16 (a) and (b) are shown in Figure 2.17 (a) and (b), respectively. Clearly, the complementary graph of a connected graph may not be connected.

A graph in which every node has the same degree, i.e., the same number of connecting edges, is called a *regular graph*; if every node has degree r then the graph is called a regular *graph of degree r*, or r-regular

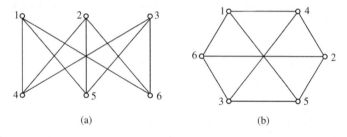

(a)   (b)

Figure 2.16   An example of two isomorphic graphs: (a) explicitly bipartite; (b) implicitly bipartite

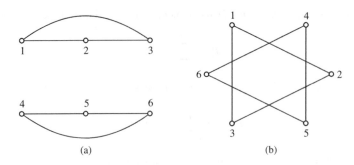

(a)   (b)

Figure 2.17 Two complementary graphs: (a) complementary graph of Figure 2.16a; (b) complementary graph of Figure 2.16b

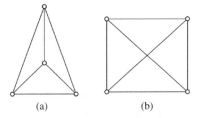

(a)   (b)

Figure 2.18 Examples of complete regular graphs of degree 3: (a) in triangular form; (b) in square form

graphs. For example, the graphs shown in Figure 2.16 are regular graphs of degree 3, or they are 3-regular graphs.

Theorem 2.2 *A regular graph of degree r with N nodes has rN/2 edges.*

Proof. Since every node connects with r edges, there are rN connecting edges. However, each edge has been doubly counted, so it should be divided by 2. ∎

For example, the two graphs in Figure 2.16 are regular graphs of degree 3, with 6 nodes, which both have $\frac{1}{2} \times 3 \times 6 = 9$ edges.

Of particular interest are the cubic (or trivalent) graphs, which are regular graphs of degree 3, such as those shown in Figures 2.16 and 2.18.

Denote a complete graph of N nodes by K_N. The two graphs shown in Figure 2.18 are isomorphic complete regular graphs, K_4.

Note that, in a graph like the one shown in Figure 2.18 (b), although two edges appear to be visually crossed they are actually not, as further explained and demonstrated by Figure 2.19 (b). Nevertheless, to avoid possible confusion it is much more convenient to show a graph on the plane or in the three-dimensional space, called the *Euclidean 3-space*, in such a way that no visual crossings will exist. This can be done, for example, by redrawing some edges, as illustrated by Figure 2.19. If a graph can be redrawn in such a way and then shown in the Euclidean 3-space without visual crossings, then it is said that the graph is being "embedded" into the Euclidean 3-space (including the plane, which as a special case is a Euclidean 2-space).

Before formally defining an embedding of a graph, recall the concept of a *Jordan curve* on the plane, which is a continuous curve with no self-crossings on the plane. Thus, all curves shown in Figure 2.19 (b) are Jordan curves on the plane, but the two in the middle of Figure 2.19 (a) are not.

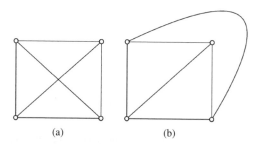

Figure 2.19 Illustration of avoiding visual crossings in a graph: (a) non-Jordan curves; (b) Jordan curves

Now, a graph G can be *embedded* in the Euclidean 3-space if it is isomorphic to a graph drawn in the space with points representing nodes of G and Jordan curves representing its edges (i.e., there are no crossings in the resulting graph diagram in the Euclidean 3-space).

Theorem 2.3 *Every simple graph can be embedded in the Euclidean 3-space.*

Proof. A constructive proof is given here. First, place all the nodes of the graph at distinct points of the x-axis of the Euclidean 3-space. Then, for each edge, choose a plane passing through the x-axis in such a way that distinct edges of the graph correspond to distinct planes. This is always possible, since there are only finitely many edges. Now, the desired embedding is obtained as follows: For each cycle of the graph, on the corresponding plane, draw a small circle passing through the relevant node; for each edge joining two distinct nodes, on the corresponding plane, draw a semi-circle connecting these two relevant nodes. Clearly, all these curves will not intersect since they lie on different planes. The resulting diagram is the embedded graph. ∎

Of particular interest are the *planar graphs*, which will be further discussed later. Here, it is mentioned that all planar graphs can be embedded on planes (within the Euclidean 3-space).

Theorem 2.4 *A simple graph is planar if and only if it can be embedded on the surface of a sphere.*

Proof. Let G be a graph embedded on the surface of a sphere. Place the sphere to sit on a horizontal plane in such a way that the "south pole" is the only point of contact. Then, connect the "north pole" to each node of the graph, which is on the surface of the sphere, and then extend the connection line outward until it intersects the plane on the base. Mark the intersection point as a new node on the plane, which is merely the stereographic projection of the original node on the plane. The desired planar representation of the original graph is then obtained by joining each pair of the new nodes with a new edge if there is an edge between the corresponding pair of nodes on the sphere. The converse can be similarly proved. ∎

Let $N(G) = \{v_1, v_2, \ldots, v_n\}$ be the set of the nodes of in a graph G. A finite sequence of edges in the form of $v_1 v_2, v_2 v_3, \ldots, v_{n-1} v_n$, if it exists, is called a *walk* in G. Such a walk is denoted by $v_1 \rightarrow v_2 \rightarrow \cdots \rightarrow v_n$ and the number of edges in the walk is called the *length* of the walk. A walk in which all edges are distinct is called a *trail*. A trail is called a *path* if all its nodes are distinct, except perhaps $v_1 = v_n$ which is called a *closed path*. A closed path is often called a *circuit* (or *cycle*), which contains at least two edges because no self-loop is allowed. A graph with no circuits is called a *tree*. Of particular interest are the circuits with an even number of edges.

Theorem 2.5 *In any bipartite graph, every circuit has an even number of edges in the path.*

Proof. Let $v_1 \rightarrow v_2 \rightarrow \cdots \rightarrow v_n \rightarrow v_1$ be a circuit in the bipartite graph $G = G(V_1, V_2)$. Assume, without loss of generality, that $v_1 \in V_1$. Then, since G is bipartite, one must have $v_2 \in V_2, v_3 \in V_1$, and so on. Finally, one must have $v_n \in V_2$ for a circuit, yielding an even number of path length. ∎

Theorem 2.6 *If a simple graph G with N nodes has K components, then the number M of edges of G satisfies*

$$N - K \leq M \leq \frac{1}{2}(N - K)(N - K + 1).$$

In particular, for a connected graph it reduces to

$$N - 1 \leq M \leq \frac{1}{2}N(N - 1).$$

Proof. To show that $M \geq N - K$, an induction on the number of edges of G may be used, as follows: If G is a null graph, the result holds trivially. Suppose that G has the smallest possible number of edges, say M_0. Then, removing any edge of G will increase the number of components by one, and the remaining graph will have N nodes, $K + 1$ components, and $M_0 - 1$ edges. It then follows from the induction hypothesis that $M_0 - 1 \geq N - (K + 1)$, implying that $M_0 \geq N - K$, as expected.

To show that $M \leq (N - K)(N - K + 1)/2$, consider the case where M is the largest possible, and assume that each component of G is a fully connected subgraph. Pick any two components, C_i and C_j, having N_i and N_j nodes, respectively, with $N_i \geq N_j > 1$. If these two components are replaced by two new ones having $N_i + 1$ and $N_j - 1$ nodes respectively, then the total number of nodes remains the same, but the number of edges is increased by

$$\frac{1}{2}\{N_i(N_i + 1) - N_i(N_i - 1)\} - \frac{1}{2}\{N_j(N_j - 1) - (N_j - 1)(N_j - 2)\} = N_i - N_j + 1,$$

which is a positive number. Thus, in order to attain the maximum number of edges, G must consist of a fully-connected component with $N - K + 1$ nodes and $K - 1$ isolated nodes. This yields the formula.

A connected graph has only one component, $K = 1$, so the result follows immediately. ∎

Corollary 2.2 *If a simple graph of N nodes satisfies $M > (N - 1)(N - 2)/2$ then it must be connected.*

Finally in this subsection, the important concept of *graph connectivity* is discussed. This tries to answer such questions as "how many edges or nodes must be removed in order to disconnect an originally connected graph?" By convention, if a node is removed, then all edges joining it will also be removed; but the converse may not be true.

For a given graph G, if after a set of edges, $E_0(G)$, is removed, G becomes unconnected, then $E_0(G)$ is called a *disconnecting set* of edges of the graph G. The smallest disconnecting set, i.e., no proper subset of which is a disconnecting set, is called a *cut-set*. In Figure 2.20, $E_0^1(G) = \{e_1, e_2\}$, $E_0^2(G) = \{e_1, e_2, e_5\}$ and $E_0^3(G) = \{e_3, e_6, e_7, e_8\}$ are disconnecting sets, in which both $E_0^1(G)$ and $E_0^3(G)$ are cut-sets.

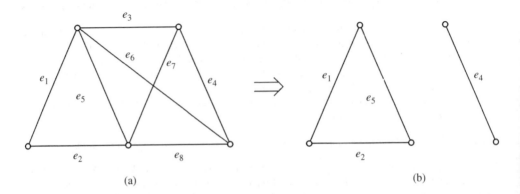

Figure 2.20 An example of disconnecting set and cut-set: (a) original graph; (b) disconnected graph

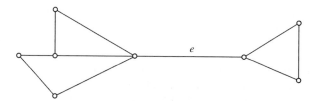

Figure 2.21   An example of bridge

A cut-set with only one edge is called a *bridge*, such as the cut-set {*e*} shown in Figure 2.21.

Theorem 2.7 *An edge is a bridge if and only if it does not belong to any circuit.*

Proof. If an edge is a bridge then its removal will disconnect the graph therefore this edge does not belong to any circuit because removing an edge from a circuit will not disconnect the graph. Conversely, if an edge belongs to a circuit, then removing this edge will not disconnect the circuit, hence will not disconnect the graph, therefore this edge is not a bridge. ∎

2.1.6   Eulerian and Hamiltonian Graphs

2.1.6.1   Eulerian Graphs

A simple connected graph is called a *Eulerian graph* if it has a closed trail (circuit) that traverses each edge once and once only. There may be more than one such trail, any of which is called a *Eulerian trail*. A graph is called a *semi-Eulerian graph* if it has a trail, need not be closed, that traverses each edge once and once only. Figures 2.22 (a), (b) and (c) show an Eulerian, a semi-Eulerian and a non-Eulerian graph, respectively.

Lemma 2.1 *If every node in a simple graph has degree larger than or equal to two, then this graph contains a circuit.*

Proof. Starting from any node v_0 of the graph, construct a walk $v_0 \rightarrow v_1 \rightarrow v_2 \rightarrow \cdots$ in such a way that v_1 is any adjacent node of v_0 and, for $i = 1, 2, \ldots, v_{i+1}$ is any (except v_{i-1}) adjacent node of v_i. Since every node has degree larger than or equal to two, such a node v_{i+1} exists. Since the graph has finitely many nodes, the walk eventually connects to a node that has been chosen before. This walk yields a circuit in the graph. ∎

Theorem 2.8 *A simple connected graph is Eulerian if and only if the degree of every node of the graph is an even number.*

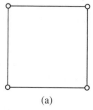
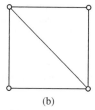
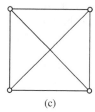

(a)   (b)   (c)

Figure 2.22   Examples of graphs: (a) Eulerian; (b) semi-Eulerian; (c) non-Eulerian graphs

Proof. Suppose that the connected graph G is Eulerian, containing a trail T. Since every edge connecting to a node in T must leave the node, the edge contributes a number two to the degree of the node. Since every edge in T is to be traversed once and once only, the degree of every node must be an integer multiple of two.

Conversely, suppose that the degree of every node in G is an even number. Since G is a connected graph, every node has degree at least two (i.e., even but nonzero), so it follows from Lemma 2.1 that G contains a circuit C. If C contains all edges of G, the proof is complete. If not, remove the edges of C from G, and denote the resulting (probably disconnected) graph by R. Since C does not contain all edges of G, only part of the edges of G have been removed, so R is not totally disconnected without any edge. Therefore, although R may contain some isolated nodes, it must contain at least one nontrivial component of G. It is clear that each component of R has at least one node in common with C and, more importantly, every node in R still has an even degree so that Lemma 2.1 implies that R contains a circuit. Thus, one can create a walk as follows: start from a common node of C and R, follow the edges of C until a nonisolated node in R is reached, trace an Eulerian trail in the component of R which contains that node, then continue along the edges of C until a node belonging to another component of R is reached, and so on, and finally stop when the walk returns to the initial node. This walk is a Eulerian trail, therefore G is a Eulerian graph. ∎

Corollary 2.3 *The seven-bridge problem of Königsburg shown in Figure 2.3 has no solutions.*

Proof. It follows from Theorem 2.8 that the graph of the seven-bridge problem of Königsburg shown in Figure 2.3 is not Eulerian, therefore it is impossible to traverse through each of its edges once and once only and finally return to the starting point. (See Exercise 2.23 for a more rigorous argument.) ∎

Corollary 2.4 (Fleury Algorithm) *In any given Eulerian graph G, an Eulerian trail can be found by the following procedure:*
Start from any node in G. Walk along the edges of G in an arbitrary manner, subject to the following rules:

1. *Erase the edges as they are traversed.*
2. *Erase the resulting isolated nodes.*
3. *Walk through a bridge only if there are no other alternatives.*

Proof. Basic idea can be gained from the proof of Theorem 2.8. A rigorous proof is tedious therefore omitted here. ∎

The Fleury algorithm is illustrated by the simple example shown in Figure 2.23.

2.1.6.2 Hamiltonian Graphs

A simple connected graph is called a *Hamiltonian graph* if it has a closed trail (circuit) that traverses each node once and once only. It is clear that the trivial case is a single node and a nontrivial Hamiltonian graph must be a circuit, called a *Hamiltonian circuit*. A graph is called *semi-Hamiltonian graph* if it has a trail, need not be closed, that traverses each node once and once only. Figures 2.24 (a), (b) and (c) show a Hamiltonian, semi-Hamiltonian and non-Hamiltonian graph, respectively.

Theorem 2.9 *Let G be a simple graph with N($\geq$3) nodes. If, for every pair of nonadjacent nodes v and u, their degrees always satisfy $k(v) + k(u) \geq N$, then G is a Hamiltonian graph.*

Proof. Suppose the assertion is not true. Then, by adding extra edges if necessary, which does not violate the inequality condition, one may assume that G is "only just" non-Hamiltonian in the sense that the

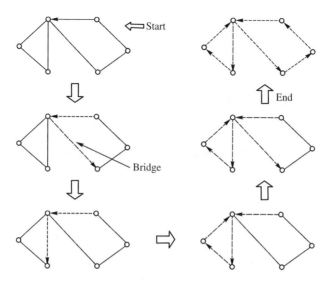

Figure 2.23 Illustration of the Fleury algorithm

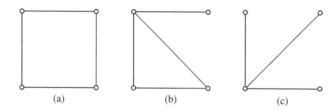

     (a)   (b)   (c)

Figure 2.24 Examples of graphs: (a) Hamiltonian; (b) semi-Hamiltonian; (c) non-Hamiltonian

addition of any more edge will result in a Hamiltonian graph. Let $v_1 \rightarrow v_2 \rightarrow \cdots \rightarrow v_n$ be a walk that traverses all nodes of G. Since G is non-Hamiltonian, the nodes v_1 and v_n will not be adjacent, and so by the assumption of the theorem one has $k(v_1) + k(v_n) \geq N$. Since $N \geq 3$, one must have $k(v_1) \geq 2$ or $k(v_n) \geq 2$. Suppose $k(v_1) \geq 2$. Then, other than v_2 there must be a node, denoted v_i, adjacent to v_1. However, if v_i is not adjacent to v_n then one has $k(v_i) + k(v_n) \geq N \geq 3$, so there must be another node, say v_j, adjacent to v_i. Since the graph has finitely many nodes, this process will stop at some node which appeared previously. This closed path yields a Hamiltonian circuit. ∎

Corollary 2.5 *Let G be a simple graph with N($\geq$3) nodes. If, for every pair of nodes v and u, their degrees always satisfy $k(v) + k(u) \geq N$, then G is a Hamiltonian graph.*

Note that the above only give some sufficient conditions. Unlike Eulerian graphs, there is no necessary and sufficient condition for Hamiltonian graphs, which remains to be an open problem in graph theory today.

2.1.7 Plane and Planar Graphs

A *plane graph* is one that can be drawn on the plane without crossing edges. A *planar graph* is one that is isomorphic to a plane graph. A plane graph is certainly a planar graph, but the main reason to

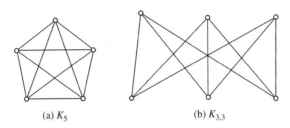

(a) K_5 (b) $K_{3,3}$

Figure 2.25   Two important examples of nonplanar graphs

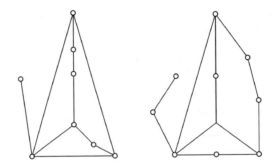

Figure 2.26   Example of two homeomorphic graphs

distinguish them will become clear later when the concept "face" is defined for plane graphs but not for planar graphs in general.

A triangle and a square are plane graphs, and a cube in the Euclidean 3-space is a planar graph. However, the two graphs shown in Figure 2.25 (a) and (b) are both nonplanar graphs (therefore no-plane graphs). These two nonplanar graphs, called K_5 and $K_{3,3}$ respectively, are very important graphs, as will be seen from Theorem 2.10 below.

Two graphs are said to be *homeomorphic* if they both can be obtained from the same graph by inserting new nodes of degree two into edges. Therefore, they are identical except possibly some nodes of degree two. For example, the two graphs shown in Figure 2.26 are homeomorphic.

Theorem 2.10 (Kuratowski) *A simple graph is planar if and only if it contains no subgraphs homomorphic to K_5 or $K_{3,3}$.*

Proof. A proof is mathematically involved [2], therefore omitted here. ∎

Now, one more new concept is introduced: *face*. In Figure 2.27, there are four faces: F_1, F_2, F_3 and F_4, where the last one is an infinite face.

Theorem 2.11 (Euler, 1750) *Let N, E and F be the number of nodes, edges and faces of a connected plane graph, respectively. Then,*

$$N - E + F = 2$$

Proof. Mathematical induction is applied to the number of edges of the graph as follows. If $E = 0$ then $N = 1$, since the graph is connected, and in this case $F = 1$, the infinite face. So the theorem is true. Suppose that the theorem is true for all graphs with at most $E - 1$ edges, and then consider a connected

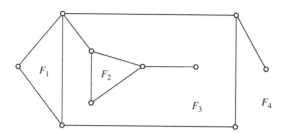

Figure 2.27   Example of a graph with four faces

plane graph with E edges. If the graph is a tree, then $E = N - 1$ and $F = 1$, the infinite face, therefore the theorem is true. If the graph is not a tree, then remove an edge E from any circuit in the graph. This will result in a connected plane graph with N nodes, $E - 1$ edges and $F - 1$ faces, so that $N - (E - 1) + (F - 1) = 2$ by the induction hypothesis, which gives $N - E + F = 2$. This completes the induction. ■

For example, the connected plane graph shown in Figure 2.27 has $N = 10$, $E = 12$ and $F = 4$, which verifies Theorem 2.11. As another example, consider a polyhedron. Any polyhedron can be projected on a sphere, where the resulting graph is called a *polyhedral graph*, which is isomorphic to a plane graph, therefore is a planar graph. Consequently, Theorem 2.11 holds for any polyhedron: $N - E + F = 2$, which is called the *Euler polyhedron formula*.

Finally, it is worth recalling Theorem 2.4 that a simple graph is planar if and only if it can be embedded on the surface of a sphere.

2.1.8   Trees and Bipartite Graphs

2.1.8.1   Trees

A graph containing no circuits is called a *forest*, while a connected forest is called a *tree*.

In other words, a forest is a family of trees. Some examples of forest are shown in Figure 2.28, where (b) and (c) are trees.

By the handshaking lemma (Theorem 2.1), in a tree the sum of degrees of all nodes is equal to two times the number of edges; that is, for a tree with N nodes, the number of its edges is $N - 1$ and the sum of all its node degrees is equal to $2(N - 1)$. It follows that if $N \geq 2$ then the tree always contains at least two end-nodes, as can be seen from Figures 2.25 (b) and (c).

Theorem 2.12 *Let T be a graph with N nodes. Then, the following statements are equivalent:*

1. *T is a tree.*
2. *T has $N - 1$ edges but no circuits.*
3. *T has $N - 1$ edges and is connected.*
4. *T is connected and every edge is a bridge.*
5. *Every pair of nodes in T are connected by exactly one path.*
6. *T contains no circuits, but the addition of any new edge creates exactly one circuit.*

Proof. Without loss of generality, assume $N \geq 2$.

1. $\Rightarrow$ 2. Since T is a tree, it contains no circuits. So, the removal of any edge will disconnect T into two subgraphs, each of which is a tree and each tree has one fewer edge than the number of its nodes. This implies that the total number of edges of T is $N - 1$.

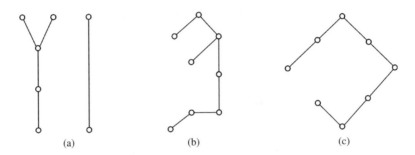

Figure 2.28   Examples of forest and tree: (a) forest; (b) tree; (c) another tree

2. ⇒ 3. If T is disconnected, then each component of T is a connected subgraph without circuits. Hence, by part (1), the number of nodes in each component has one more than the number of its edges. Consequently, in T the total number of nodes is more than the total number of edges at least by two, contradicting the fact that T has $N − 1$ edges.
3. ⇒ 4. The removal of any edge from T will result in a graph with N nodes and $N − 2$ edges, which must be disconnected according to Theorem 2.7.
4. ⇒ 5. Since T is connected, each pair of nodes is connected by at least one path. If a given pair of nodes is connected by two paths, then they enclose a circuit, contradicting the fact that every edge is a bridge.
5. ⇒ 6. If T contained a circuit, then any pair of nodes in the circuit would be connected by at least two paths, contradicting part (5). If an edge e is added to T, then since the nodes connecting with e are already connected in T, a circuit will be created. Moreover, this circuit is unique otherwise e would be the common edge of two circuits but then these two circuits remain to be a circuit without e, contradicting the fact that T contains no circuits at the beginning.
6. ⇒ 1. If T was disconnected, then by adding an edge to join any two components of T would not create a circuit. Therefore, T must be connected. Moreover, by assumption T contains no circuits, so it is a tree. ∎

Corollary 2.6 *A forest with N nodes and K components has N − K edges. Consequently, a tree with N nodes has N − 1 edges.*

Proof. Applying part 3 of Theorem 2.12 to each component of the forest leads to the first conclusion. The second conclusion follows from the fact that a tree has only one component, $K = 1$. ∎

Starting from a given graph, if it has a circuit, then remove one edge from the circuit. Clearly, the resulting graph remains to be connected. Repeat this procedure until no circuits are left. Then, the final resulting graph is a tree. This tree is called a *spanning tree* of the graph given at the beginning. More generally, if the graph has N nodes, M edges and K components, then one can carry out the above procedure on each component of the graph, resulting in a *spanning forest*. The total number of edges removed throughout this procedure is called the *circuit bank* number, which is equal to $M − N + K$.

Theorem 2.13 *Let T be any spanning forest of a graph G. Then,*

1. *Every cut-set of G has an edge in common with T.*
2. *Every circuit of G has an edge in common with the complementary graph of T.*

Proof.
1. Let C be a cut-set of G. Removing C will split one of the components of G into two subgraphs, G_1 and G_2. Then, since T is a spanning forest, it must contain an edge joining a node of G_1 to a node of G_2, which is the required edge.

2. Let C be a circuit of G that has no edges in common with the complementary graph of T. Then, C must be contained in T, which is a contradiction. ∎

Next, the important concept of spanning tree is discussed. In a connected graph, a tree that containing all nodes of the graph is called a *spanning tree*. The following obvious result guarantees the existence of a spanning tree, although spanning trees are generally not unique in a nontrivial graph.

Theorem 2.14 *Every connected graph has a spanning tree.*

2.1.8.2 Bipartite Graphs

Recall that if a *bipartite* graph G can be split into two disjoint sets of nodes, V_1 and V_2, where every edge of G joins a node in V_1 to a node in V_2. Let $n = |V_1|$ be the number of nodes in V_1 and $m = |V_2|$ be the number of nodes in V_2. Then, a bipartite graph is often specifically called an (n, m)-*bipartite graph*. In particular, if every node in V_1 has degree m and also every node in V_2 has degree n, then the graph is called a *complete (n, m)-bipartite graph*. In this textbook, only simple connected bipartite graphs are considered.

One simple example of bipartite graph is the star-shaped graph, where the central node belongs to one set and all the other nodes belong to another, which is a complete bipartite graph.

Another example is the two graphs shown in Figure 2.29, where the one in (a) is a (3,3)-bipartite graph while the one in (b) is a complete (2,3)-bipartite graph.

Theorem 2.15 *In a bipartite graph, every circuit has an even number of edges.*

Proof. Let G be an (n, m)-bipartite graph. For any circuit with nodes $v_1 \rightarrow \cdots \rightarrow v_{k+1} = v_1$ of length k, $v_1 \in V_1$ implies $v_2 \in V_2, v_3 \in V_1, \ldots, v_{2i} \in V_2, v_{2i+1} \in V_1$. Thus, the last node $v_{k+1} = v_1 \in V_1$, namely the index $k + 1$ is odd, therefore the circuit has an even number k of edges. ∎

2.1.9   Directed Graphs

So far, by a graph G, it refers to an undirected graph $(N(G), E(G))$, where $N(G)$ is the set of its nodes and $E(G)$ the set of its edges in which $(u, v) = (v, u)$ for all $u, v \in N(G)$.

2.1.9.1 Basic Concepts

In a graph, if some edges are ordered (directed, i.e., have directions), then the graph is called a directed graph, or simply, a *digraph*. Digraphs are classified into simple and general digraphs, similar to the

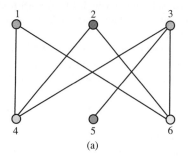 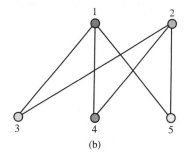

Figure 2.29 Examples of bipartite graphs: (a) (3,3)-bipartite; (b) complete (2,3)-bipartite

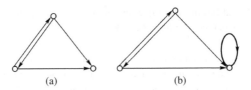

Figure 2.30   Examples of digraphs: (a) simple; (b) general

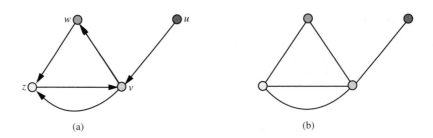

Figure 2.31   (a) A digraph; (b) its corresponding underlying graph

undirected setting, so the digraph shown in Figure 2.30 (a) is a *simple digraph* while the one in Figure 2.27 (b) is a *general digraph*.

In an undirected graph, $(u, v) = (v, u)$ and they are considered as one same edge in a graph. In a digraph, however, (u, v) and (v, u) are both well defined but different, and they can coexist in the same graph. More precisely, in a digraph, $(u, v) \in E(G)$ means node v is pointing to node u but not another way around, thus $(u, v) \neq (v, u)$. Figure 2.31 (a) shows an example of such a digraph.

For any digraph, the corresponding graph obtained by removing all direction arrows is called the *underlying graph* of the original digraph. Figure 2.31 (b) is the underlying graph of the digraph shown in Figure 2.31 (a). Two digraphs are isomorphic if their corresponding underlying graphs are so.

It is important to note that the digraph shown in Figure 2.31 (a) is a simple graph since bidirectional edges can coexist, as mentioned above, but its underlying graph is not a simple graph for it has double edges which are not allowed. This reveals that directed and undirected graphs may have very different properties.

A *directed path* in a digraph is an order sequence of edges: $\{(v_1, v_2), (v_2, v_3), \ldots, (v_{m-1}, v_m)\}$, where $1 < m \leq N$ with N being the size of the digraph, and it is possible to contain some cycles. For example, in Figure 2.31 (a), $\{(u, v)\}$, $\{(u, v), (v, w)\}$, $\{(u, v), (v, w), (w, z)\}$, $\{(u, v), (v, w), (w, z), (z, v)\}$, and $\{(u, v), (v, w), (w, z), (z, v), (v, z)\}$ are all directed paths.

A digraph is *weakly connected* (or simply, *connected*) if and only if its underlying graph is so, and a digraph is *strongly connected* if and only if there is a directed path from any node to any other node in the digraph. Thus, the digraph in Figure 2.31 (a) is connected but not strongly connected, unless there is an additional directed edge from node v to node u, or from node w to node u.

In a digraph, a *directed tree* consists of all directed paths without cycles. In Figure 2.31 (a), $\{(u, v)\}$, $\{(u, v), (v, w)\}$, $\{(u, v), (v, z)\}$ and $\{(u, v), (v, w), (w, z)\}$ are directed trees but $\{(u, v), (v, w), (w, z), (z, v)\}$, $\{(v, z), (z, v)\}$ and $\{(u, v), (v, z), (z, v)\}$ are not. Also, in a digraph, a node x is called a *root* if, for every node y in the digraph, there is a directed path connecting x to y. Clearly, node u is a root of the digraph shown in Figure 2.31 (a), which is the only root in this digraph. Also, $\{(u, v), (v, w), (w, z)\}$ is a *(directed) spanning tree* of the digraph, with root u.

In a digraph, the concept of node degree is twofold: in-degree and out-degree. For any node, its *in-degree* is the number of edges pointing to it while its *out-degree* is the number of edges pointing out from it. In Figure 2.31 (a), $k_{in}(u) = 0$, $k_{out}(u) = 1$ and $k_{in}(v) = 2$, $k_{out}(v) = 2$. Clearly, the sum of in-degree and out-degree of a node is precisely the degree of this node in the corresponding underlying graph. Moreover, a node has in-degree and out-degree being *balanced* if it satisfies $k_{in} = k_{out}$, and in this case its node *degree* is defined by $k = k_{in} + k_{out}$. Thus, in Figure 2.31 (a), $k(v) = 4$, but for all other nodes, their node degrees are undefined. If all nodes in a digraph are balanced then the digraph is said to be a *balanced digraph*. For *average in-degree* and *average out-degree*, one has

$$\langle k_{in} \rangle = \sum_{k=0}^{N} k P_{in}(k) = \sum_{k=1}^{k_{in}^{max}} k P_{in}(k) \tag{2.35}$$

and

$$\langle k_{out} \rangle = \sum_{k=0}^{N} k P_{out}(k) = \sum_{k=1}^{k_{out}^{max}} k P_{out}(k), \tag{2.36}$$

where $P_{in}(k)$ and $P_{out}(k)$ is the probability that a randomly picked node has in-degree k and out-degree k, while k_{in}^{max} and k_{out}^{max} are the maximum in-degree and maximum out-degree, respectively.

Similarly, the *cumulative in-degree distribution* and *cumulative out-degree distribution* are respectively defined by

$$P_k^{in} = \sum_{k'=k}^{\infty} P_{in}(k') \tag{2.37}$$

and

$$P_k^{out} = \sum_{k'=k}^{\infty} P_{out}(k'). \tag{2.38}$$

It can be verified that if the node in-degree (out-degree) distribution is exponential of the form $e^{-k/\sigma}$ with a constant $\sigma > 0$, then so is P_k^{in} (P_k^{out}), and that if the node in-degree (out-degree) distribution is a power law of the form $k^{-\gamma}$ with a constant $\gamma > 0$, then $P_k^{in} \sim k_k^{-(\gamma-1)}$ ($P_k^{out} \sim k_k^{-(\gamma-1)}$).

Define the *joint in/out-degree probability distribution function* $P_v(k_{in}, k_{out})$ be the probability of a randomly picked node v that has in-degree k_{in} and out-degree k_{out}. Clearly,

$$P_v(k_{in}, k_{out}) = N(k_{in}, k_{out})/N \tag{2.39}$$

where $N(k_{in}, k_{out})$ is the total number of nodes with in- and out-degrees (k_{in}, k_{out}).

Moreover, define the *degree-degree correlation coefficient* of a node v with in- and out-degrees (k_{in}, k_{out}) by

$$r_{vv}(k_v^{in}) = \sum_{i=1, k_i^{in}=k_v^{in}}^{N} (k_i^{out}/N) P_{in}(k_v^{in}) \tag{2.40}$$

where k_i^{in} (or k_i^{out}) is the in-degree (or out-degree) of node i, with $i = 1, \ldots, v, \ldots, N$. If the slope of the curve r_{vv} versus k_v^{in} is positive or negative, then k_v^{in} and k_v^{out} is positively or negatively correlated; if it is zero then they are uncorrelated.

The *adjacency matrix* of the digraph shown in Figure 2.31 (a) is

$$A_d = [a_{ij}] = \begin{bmatrix} 0 & 1 & 0 & 0 \\ 0 & 0 & 1 & 0 \\ 1 & 1 & 0 & 0 \\ 0 & 0 & 1 & 0 \end{bmatrix}.$$

Differing from undirected graphs, this adjacency matrix is asymmetric and, moreover, the adjacency matrix of its underlying network, given by Figure 2.31 (b), is even undefined.

Thus, with the above concepts defined, the following terminologies can be defined in an obvious way: *directed walk*, *directed trail*, *directed circuit*, *directed Eulerian graph* and *directed Hamiltonian graph*, and so on.

2.1.9.2   Basic Properties

The following are some basic properties of digraphs [2].

Theorem 2.16 *Let G be a connected (sub)digraph. If all its nodes have $k_{in} = 1$, regardless of their k_{out}, then G has one and only one directed circuit.*

Proof. Start from any node, say u. This node has one and only one incoming edge by assumption. Another end node of this incoming edge also has one and only one incoming edge by assumption. Keep moving backward this way. In the backward sequence of edges, since every node has one and only one incoming edge, the sequence will not hit any node of the sequence except possibly the very first one, u, and it will eventually do so because the network has finitely many nodes. ∎

Corollary 2.7 *Let G be a connected digraph. If all its nodes have $k_{out} = 1$, regardless of their k_{in}, then G has one and only one directed circuit.*

Theorem 2.17 *A connected digraph is a directed circuit if and only if all its nodes satisfy $k_{in} = k_{out}$.*

Corollary 2.8 *A connected digraph contains a directed circuit if and only if it has a subgraph with all nodes satisfying $k_{in} = k_{out}$.*

Theorem 2.18 *A connected digraph is directed Eulerian if and only if every node satisfies $k_{in} = k_{out}$.*

Theorem 2.19 *Let G be a strongly connected digraph with N nodes. If all nodes satisfy both $k_{in} \geq N/2$ and $k_{out} \geq N/2$, then G is a directed Hamiltonian.*

A graph is said to be *orientable* if its edges can be directed such that the resulting digraph is strongly connected. For example, it can be easily verified that the graph shown in Figure 2.32 (a) is orientable to that in (b), which obviously is not a unique solution, while the graph in (c) is not orientable.

Theorem 2.20 *A graph G is orientable if and only if each edge of the graph is contained in a circuit.*

Proof. Necessity. The G is orientable implies that every edge can be directed, so continuing a directed path will eventually return to a node in the path because the network has a finite number of nodes, which generate a directed circuit. ∎

Sufficiency. Choose an arbitrary circuit C and direct it cyclically. If $C = G$, done. If $C \subset G$, then consider any adjacent edge e. By assumption, e is in some circuit $e \in C^* \subset G$. Since C^* is a circuit, there is a path to come back to e. One can then direct this path cyclically. Repeating the procedure for all edges leads G to be orientable.

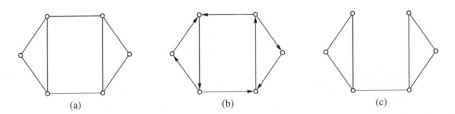

Figure 2.32   Orientable and not orientable graphs: (a) orientable to that in (b) ; (b) orientable to that in (a); (c) not orientable

2.1.10   Weighted Graphs

Traditional graph theory in mathematics does not focus on weighted graphs, namely edges have weight values in a graph, except the so-called "flows" studied in applied graph theory. In complex networks, however, weighted networks are very common due it their ubiquity in the real world.

First, a *weight* can be defined for an edge by associating the edge e_{ij}, which connects node i and node j, with a value w_{ij}. When all $w_{ij} = 1$, the weighted edges become the conventional unweighted ones.

Second, a weight can also be placed at a node, referred also to as *node strength*, which generalizes the concept of degree for undirected networks, as follows:

$$W_i = \sum_{j=1}^{N} a_{ij} w_{ij} = \sum_{j \in N_i} w_{ij}, \tag{2.41}$$

where $A = [a_{ij}]$ is the adjacency matrix of the graph, and N_i is the neighborhood of node i, namely all the nodes that connect with node i. When $w_{ij} = 1$ for all $j \in N_i$, one has $W_i = k_i$, the degree of node i.

For a digraph, usually $w_{ij} \neq w_{ji}$, but nevertheless, one always has

$$W_i = \sum_{j=1}^{N} a_{ij} w_{ij} = \sum_{j=1}^{N} a_{ji} w_{ji} \tag{2.42}$$

More precisely, one defines the in-weight and out-weight of a node respectively by

$$W_i^{in} = \sum_{j=1}^{N} a_{ji} w_{ji} \quad \text{and} \quad W_i^{out} = \sum_{j=1}^{N} a_{ij} w_{ij} \tag{2.43}$$

Clearly, $W_i = W_i^{in} + W_i^{out}$.

Furthermore, the above concepts can be normalized, as

$$U_i = W_i/k_i, \quad U_i^{in} = W_i^{in}/k_i^{in} \quad \text{and} \quad U_i^{out} = W_i^{out}/k_i^{out} \tag{2.44}$$

Weights may be correlated with node degrees, with edges, and with other weights, respectively.

First, for the correlation between weight and node degree, a measure called *weight-node correlation coefficient* is defined, for node i, by

$$C^{wd}(k) = \sum_{i \in N_i, k_i = k} (W_i/N) P(k) \tag{2.45}$$

where $P(k)$ is the degree distribution function defined in (2.1).

Similar formulas can be defined for W_i^{in} and W_i^{out} with respect to k_i^{in} and k_i^{out}, yielding four possible combinations.

Second, for the correlation between weight and edge, a measure called *weight-edge correlation coefficient* is defined, for node i, by

$$C_i^{we} = \sum_{j \in N_i} w_{ij} k_j / W_i = \sum_{j=1}^{N} a_{ij} w_{ij} k_j / W_i \tag{2.46}$$

If all nodes satisfy $C_i^{wd}(k) > k^{cn}(k)$, for all $k = 1, 2, \ldots, N$, where $k^{cn}(k)$ is defined in (2.33), then the heavier weights tend to connect to bigger nodes; if all nodes satisfy $C_i^{wd}(k) < k^{cn}(k)$, then the heavier weights tend to connect to smaller nodes.

Moreover, the *average weight-edge correlation coefficient* over the graph is defined by

$$C^{we}(k) = \sum_{i=1, k_i = k} (C_i^{we}/N) P(k) \tag{2.47}$$

where $P(k)$ is the degree distribution function defined in (2.1). If the slope of the curve of $C^{we}(k)$ versus the node degree k can be positive or negative, or zero, indicating the positive or negative correlation, or uncorrelated relations.

Third, for the correlation between weight and weight, a measure called *weight-weight correlation coefficient* is defined, for node i, by

$$C_i^{ww} = \sum_{j=1}^{N} a_{ij} w_{ij} W_j / W_i \tag{2.48}$$

Thus, the average of all nodes with weight value w, the *average weight-weight correlation coefficient* is given by

$$C^{ww}(w) = \sum_{i=1, W_i=w}^{N} (r_i^{ww}/N)P(w) \tag{2.49}$$

where $P(k)$ is the degree distribution function defined in (2.1).

Finally, *weighted clustering coefficient* can be introduced, which is defined by

$$C_i^w = \frac{1}{W_i(k_i - 1)} \sum_{j=1}^{N} \sum_{l=1}^{N} \frac{w_{ij} + w_{il}}{2} a_{ij} a_{jl} a_{li} \tag{2.50}$$

Another definition of the weighted clustering coefficient is given by the geometric mean:

$$C_i^w = \frac{1}{k_i(k_i - 1)} \sum_{j=1}^{N} \sum_{l=1}^{N} \left(w_{ij}^m w_{jl}^m w_{li}^m \right)^{1/3} \tag{2.51}$$

where $w_{ij}^m = w_{ij} / \max\{w_{ij}, w_{jl}, w_{li}\}$ is a normalization constant, which reduces to (2.9) when the graph is unweighted.

For both of the above formulas, the *average weighted clustering coefficient* is defined by

$$C^w = \frac{1}{N} \sum_{i=1}^{N} C_i^w \tag{2.52}$$

2.1.11 Some Applications

In this subsection, four typical applications of graph theory are discussed: A. the minimum connector problem; B. the minimum shortest path problem; C. the Chinese postman problem; D. the maximum flows problem. The networks under consideration are weighted graphs, and the last one is also directed.

2.1.11.1 Minimum Connector Problem

Suppose one wants to build a highway network connecting n given cities, in such a way that a car can travel from one city to another, but the total mileage of the highways is minimum. This is the so-called *minimum connector problem*.

Clearly, the graph formed by taking the N cities as nodes and the connecting highways as edges must be a tree because any more highways will be extra. The problem is to find an efficient algorithm to decide which of all the possible trees connecting these cities reaches the minimum total mileage, given that the distance between any pair of cities is known.

It should be noted that the numbers on the graph do not have to be "distances"; instead, they can be costs, weights, time, etc.

Just as the shortest path length problem, discussed above, one may reformulate this problem in terms of a weighted network, where the weight is the distance, and to find which tree has the minimum total weight. The resulting tree should be a minimum-weight spanning tree. It turns out that there is a simple and efficient algorithm, known as the *Kruskal (greedy) algorithm*, for solving this problem. The computational complexity of this algorithm is $O(M \ln M)$ for a network with M edges.

Theorem 2.21 (Kruskal Algorithm) *Let G be a connected graph with N nodes. Then, the following constructive scheme yields a solution to the minimum connector problem:*

1. *Let e_1 be an edge of G with the smallest weight.*
2. *Choose $e_2, \dots, e_{N-1}$ successively by choosing each edge e_i, not previously chosen, with a smallest weight, subject to the condition that it forms no circuit with all the previous edges $\{e_1, \dots, e_{i-1}\}$.*
3. *Repeat the above procedure for $i = 3, \dots, N$.*

The resulting graph is a spanning tree, the subgraph of G with edges $e_1, \dots, e_{N-1}$.

Proof. The resulting subgraph T is a spanning tree follows immediately from Theorem 2.12 (ii). It remains to show that the total weight of T, denoted $W(T)$, is minimum.

Suppose that S is a spanning tree of G such that $W(S) < W(T)$. If e_k is the first edge in the above sequence which is not contained in S, then the subgraph of G formed by adding e_k to S contains a unique circuit C that contains e_k. Since C must contain an edge e belonging to S but not to T, the subgraph obtained from S with e being replaced by e_k is still a spanning tree, denoted as S_0. But, by the construction, the edge weight $w(e_k) < w(e)$, therefore $W(S_0) \leq W(S)$, and S_0 has one more edge in common with T than with S. By repeating this procedure, it follows that one can change S into T at each step, with the total weight decreasing at each time. Consequently, $W(T) \leq W(S)$, which is a contradiction to the above assumption $W(S) < W(T)$. ∎

As an example, consider the graph shown in Figure 2.33. By the greedy algorithm, an optimal result can be found as follows:

1. Find an edge with the smallest weight, which is $e_1 = AB = 2$.
2. Find an edge with the smallest weight from the rest edges, which is $e_2 = DE = 3$.
3. Find an edge with the smallest weight from the rest edges, which is $e_3 = AD = 4$.
4. Find an edge with the smallest weight from the rest edges, which is $e_4 = BC = 7$, since any other choice will form a circuit, or will be longer than 7.
5. Stop, because a spanning tree has been obtained, i.e., adding any more edge will form a circuit.

The final result is given by $\{AB, AD, BC, DE\}$, as shown by the bold edges in Figure 2.33.

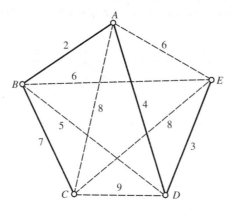

Figure 2.33   Example of the minimum connector problem

2.1.11.2 Shortest Path Length Problem

Consider the graph shown in Figure 2.34, where nodes $A - L$ denote cities, which are connected by roads (edges). If the distances (lengths) of the roads are as marked, what is the shortest path length from node A to node L?

A few remarks are in order. First, an upper bound for the shortest path can be easily found: arbitrarily connecting A to L certainly gives an upper bound, although may not be the largest upper bound. Second, the numbers shown in the figure do not necessarily refer to distances; they can be considered as other physical means such as time, cost, traffic flows, bandwidth, etc., and may be referred to as *weights*, giving a *weighted graph* in general. The problem is then to find a path from A to L with the minimum total weight. Finally, there are several different methods that can be used to solve the problem, while a typical one is the *Dijkstra algorithm* introduced below.

It should be noted that the Dijkstra algorithm is a *greedy algorithm*, namely, it searches through all possible ways to find a shorts path, therefore has very high computational complexity: for a network of N nodes and M edges, its complexity is $O(M + N \ln N)$.

A natural mathematical approach to solving the problem is to walk from A to L, associating each intermediate node V with a number $l(V)$ that is equal to the shortest path length from A to V. For example, when walking from A to J, one has $l(J) = l(G) + 5$ or $l(J) = l(H) + 5$ or even $l(J) = l(L) + 5$, whichever is shorter. Thus, the procedure is carried out as follows:

Starting from A with $l(A) = 0$, moving toward L, one has $l(B) = l(A) + 3 = 3$, $l(E) = l(A) + 9 = 9$ and $l(C) = l(A) + 2 = 2$; therefore node C is chosen with $l(C) = 2$.

Looking at the nodes adjacent to B, one has $l(D) = l(B) + 2 = 5$ and $l(E) = l(B) + 4 = 7$.

Looking at the nodes adjacent to C, one has $l(E) = l(C) + 6 = 8$ and $l(F) = l(C) + 9 = 11$. Here, $l(D) = 5$ is uniquely determined, but $l(E) = 7$, or $= 8$, or $= 9$, so node E is chosen with the shortest: $l(E) = l(B) + 4 = 7$.

Continuing this way, one finally found the shortest lengths of all nodes in the graph: $l(A) = 0$, $l(B) = 3$, $l(C) = 2$, $l(D) = 5$, $l(E) = 7$, $l(F) = 10$, $l(G) = 8$, $l(H) = 9$, $l(I) = 12$, $l(J) = 13$, $l(K) = 14$, $l(L) = 17$. This means that the shortest path length is 17, which cannot be further reduced. These also provide all the shortest lengths from A to any other nodes.

For the example shown in Figure 2.34, one solution is given in Figure 2.35. But it should be noted that such a possible path may not be unique, especially for a large-sized graph.

It should also be noted that the numbers on the graph do not have to be "distances"; instead, they can be costs, weights, time, etc.

2.1.11.3 Chinese Postman Problem

The problem of interest here is for a postman to deliver all letters in such a way that he passes every street at least once and finally returns to the starting point (the post office), traversing a shortest possible total path-length.

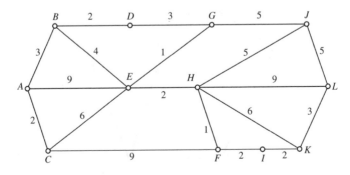

Figure 2.34 Example of the shortest path length problem

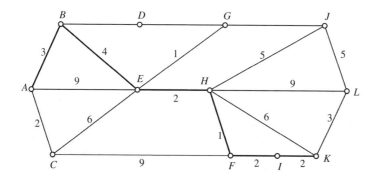

Figure 2.35   One solution to the shortest path length problem

Since it requires the postman to traverse through every street, this is a Eulerian-type of graph but it differs from a perfect Eulerian graph in that it allows multiple passing of some streets (otherwise the postman might not be able to return to the post office) and requires the total traveling path-length be minimal. This problem was solved in 1962 by a Chinese mathematician Professor Mei-ko Kwan (1934–) from Shanghai, China, thereby gaining the name as a "Chinese postman problem."

Clearly, if all nodes in such a graph have even degrees, then the graph is Eulerian; therefore the problem is trivially solved by the Fleury algorithm. It is also clear that if there are odd-degree nodes in the graph, the postman has to traverse through such nodes for one more time, which makes them of even degrees by means of adding one more edge to each of them. In so doing, however, some originally even-degree nodes would become of odd degrees instead, so that one more edge has to be added to each of the latter to make them even, until all nodes have even degrees. The question is how to do this, so that the total traveling path-length is minimal?

Theorem 2.22 (Kwan's Algorithm) *In any given connected graph G, a Chinese postman trail can be found by the following off-line procedure beforehand:*
Identify the initial node in G, and then do the following:

1. For each odd-degree node in G, add an edge to connect it to one of its neighboring node.
2. Repeat the above, until all nodes in G have even degrees.
3. Check all resulting reconfigurations – if the increment of the total path-length of every cycle is not longer than one half of the total path-length of the corresponding original cycle, then keep this cycle as a solution.

The Kwan algorithm is illustrated by the following example of postman route inspection problem.
Consider a postman route map shown in Figure 2.36 (a), where node A is the post office.
First of all, in order to be able to return to node A, one edge has to be added to it from node B, and for the same reason another one is added between node E and node F, as shown in Figure 2.36 (b).
After the above adding, however, the degrees of nodes B and E are changed from even to odd. Consequently, one more edge has to be added to node B and node E, respectively. There are three possible ways to do so, as shown in Figure 2.36 (c), (d) and (e), respectively.
A quick inspection of Figure 2.36 reveals the following:

1. There are three existing cycles:
    (i)   Total path-length of cycle B-C-E-D-B = 120 + 160 + 80 + 100 = 460
    (ii) Total path-length of cycle B-C-E-B = 100 + 80 + 200 = 380
    (iii) Total path-length of cycle B-D-E-B = 120 + 160 + 200 = 480

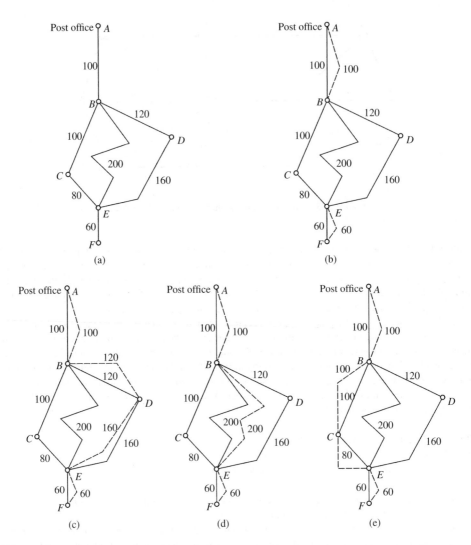

Figure 2.36 A postman route inspection problem: (a) the routing map; (b) making nodes A and F be of even degree; (c) possible route 1; (d) possible route 2; (e) possible route 3

2. Possible choices of routes are:

(i) Figure 2.36 (c): New increment of total path-length = 120 + 160 = 280, which is longer than one half of the corresponding cycle B-C-E-D-B = 460/2 = 230, and also longer than one half of the corresponding cycle B-D-E-B = 480/2 = 240. Hence, this is not a solution. (Note that the cycle B-C-E-B does not have new increment, so there is no need to compare to it. In a large-scale graph, typically there are many of such cycles without involving new increments therefore they are not needed to compute, revealing the advantage of Kwan's algorithm.)

(ii) Figure 2.36 (d): New increment of total path-length = 200, which is longer than one half of the corresponding cycle B-C-E-B = 380/2 = 190 (although not longer than one half of the corresponding cycle B-D-E-B = 480/2 = 240). Hence, this is not a solution.

(iii) Figure 2.36 (e): New increment of total path-length = 100 + 80 = 180, which is shorter than one half of the corresponding cycle B-C-E-B = 380/2 = 190, and also shorter than one half of the corresponding cycle B-C-E-D-B = 460/2 = 230. Hence, this is a solution, giving A-B-C-E-F-E-D-B-E-C-B-A.

Clearly, solutions are not unique; at least how to traverse a solution route is not unique.

2.1.11.4 Maximum Flow Problem

Consider the directional roadmap shown in Figure 2.37, where weights are profit values. Start from A and follow the directed roads to traverse to F. Repeated roads are not allowed. The objective is to find a path from A to F that can maximize the flow profits.

An algorithm is similar to the unidirectional Dijkstra algorithm for the shortest path length problem in Part B studied above. Specifically, one proceeds as follows:

$$l(A) = 0$$

$$l(B) = l(A) + 6 = 6$$

$$l(C) = l(A) + 10 = 10 \rightarrow l(B) = l(C) + 4 = 14 \rightarrow l(E) = l(B) + 7 = 21 \rightarrow l(F) = l(E) + 18 = 39$$

$$l(D) = l(C) + 1 = 11 \rightarrow l(E) = l(D) + 11 = 22 \rightarrow l(F) = l(E) + 18 = 40$$

$$l(F) = l(C) + 5 = 15$$

$$l(D) = l(A) + 10 = 10 \rightarrow l(E) = l(D) + 11 = 21 \rightarrow l(F) = l(E) + 18 = 39.$$

Thus, an optimal maximum flow solution is found as shown in Figure 2.38.

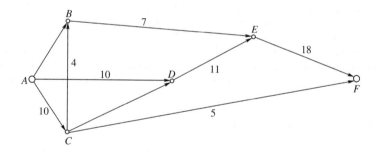

Figure 2.37 A directional road map

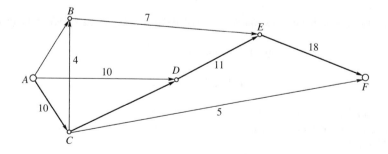

Figure 2.38 An optimal solution to the maximum flow problem

2.2   Elementary Probability and Statistics

2.2.1   Probability Preliminaries

Consider an experiment in which a fair coin is tossed such that on each toss either the head (denoted by H) or the tail (denoted by T) occurs. The actual result that occurs when the experiment is performed is called an *outcome* of the experiment and the set of all possible outcomes is called the *sample space* (denoted by S) of the experiment. For instance, if a fair coin is tossed twice, then each result of two tosses is an outcome, the possibilities are HH, TT, HT, TH, and the set $\{HH, TT, HT, TH\}$ is the sample space S. Furthermore, any subset of the sample space is called an *event* and an event consisting of a single outcome is called a *simple event*.

Example 2.5 In an urn, there are N balls, in which M are red and the rest are blue. If n balls are drawn out of the urn at random, but no one is put back to the urn, then what is the probability p that m red balls were drawn? Here, $1 \le m \le M \le n \le N$?

In the sample space, there are $\binom{N}{n} = \frac{N!}{n!(N-n)!}$ events. On the other hand, there are $\binom{M}{m}$ possibilities to draw out m red balls from the totally M ones, leaving the rest blue balls with $\binom{N-M}{n-m}$ possibilities, so that the probability of having m red balls and $n-m$ blue balls is $\binom{M}{m}\binom{N-M}{n-m}$. Consequently,

$$p = \binom{M}{m}\binom{N-M}{n-m} \Big/ \binom{N}{n}.$$

Since there is no way to predict the outcomes, we have to assign a real number P, between 0 and 1, to each event to indicate the probability that a certain outcome occurs. This is specified by a real-valued function, called a *random variable*, defined on the sample space. In the above example, if the random variable $X = X(s)$, $s \in S$, denotes the number of H's in the outcome s, then the number $P = P(X(s))$ gives the probability in percentage in the number of H's of the outcome s.

More generally, let S be a sample space and $X : S \to R^1$ be a random variable. For each measurable set $A \subset R^1$ (and in the above example, $A = \{0\}, \{1\}$, or $\{2\}$, indicating no H, one H, or two H's, respectively), define $P : \{events\} \to [0,1]$, where each event is a set $\{s \in S : X(s) \in A \subset R^1\} := \{X \in A\}$, subject to the following conditions:

1. $P(X \in A) \ge 0$ for any measurable set $A \subset R^1$;
2. $P(X \in R^1) = 1$;
3. for any countable sequence of pair-wise disjoint measurable sets A_i in R^1:

$$P\left(X \in \bigcup_{i=1}^{\infty} A_i\right) = \sum_{i=1}^{\infty} P(X \in A_i).$$

Then, P is called the *probability distribution* (or *probability distribution function*) of the random variable X.

If there exists a nonnegative integrable function f such that

$$P(X \in A) = \int_A f(x)dx \tag{2.53}$$

for all measurable sets A, then P is a *continuous* probability distribution and $f(\cdot)$ is called the *probability density function* of the random variable X. For any countable sequence of pair-wise disjoint measurable sets $A_i \subset R^1$, one has

$$\int_{\cup A_i} f(x)dx = \sum_i \int_{A_i} f(x)dx.$$

Note that if one defines $f(x)dx = d\tau$, where τ is a *measure* (e.g., a step function), then the discrete case such as the example of "tossing coins" can be also included.

2.2.1.1   Some Typical Probability Distributions

Example 2.6 If the probability density function $f(\cdot)$ is given by

$$f(x) = \frac{1}{\sqrt{2\pi}\sigma} e^{-\frac{1}{2\sigma^2}(x-\mu)^2}, \quad \sigma > 0, \ \mu \in R^1, \tag{2.54}$$

which is called a *Gaussian* (or *normal*) *probability density function*, then P is called a *Gaussian* (or *normal*) *distribution* of the random variable X, and denoted as $X \sim N(\mu, \sigma^2)$. For the Gaussian distribution, since $f(x) \geq 0$, for any measurable set $A \subset R^1$, one has $P(X \in A) = \int_A f(x)dx \geq 0$. By substituting $y = (x - \mu)/\sqrt{2}\sigma$, one has

$$P(X \in R^1) = \int_{-\infty}^{\infty} f(x)dx = \frac{1}{\sqrt{\pi}} \int_{-\infty}^{\infty} e^{-y^2} dy = 1.$$

If a random variable X only takes countably many values, for example integer values k, then it is called a *discrete random variable*.

Example 2.7 If the probability distribution function of a discrete random variable X is given by

$$P(k) = \binom{n}{k} p^k (1-p)^{n-k}, \quad k = 0, 1, \ldots, n, \tag{2.55}$$

then P is called a *binomial distribution* of $X (= k)$, denoted as $X \sim B(n,p)$. If the probability distribution function of a discrete random variable X is given by

$$P(k) = \frac{1}{k!} \lambda^k e^{-\lambda}, \ \lambda > 0, \quad k = 0, 1, 2, \ldots \tag{2.56}$$

then P is called a *Poisson distribution* of $X (= k)$, denoted as $X \sim P(\lambda)$.

As has been seen from the review of graph theory earlier, more precisely in the random-graph model, Poisson distribution is a limiting distribution of the binomial distribution.

Example 2.8 If the probability density function $f(\cdot)$ is given by

$$f(x) = \lambda e^{-\lambda x}, \ \lambda > 0, \ x \geq 0 \quad (\text{otherwise}, f(x) = 0). \tag{2.57}$$

which is called an *exponential probability density function*, then P is called an *exponential distribution* of the random variable X, denoted as $X \sim Ex(\lambda)$, and is given by

$$P(x) = 1 - e^{-\lambda x}, \ \lambda > 0, \ x \geq 0 \quad (\text{otherwise}, P(x) = 0). \tag{2.58}$$

If the probability distribution function of a discrete random variable X is given by

$$P(k) = Ck^{-\gamma}, \ \gamma > 0, \quad k = 0, 1, 2, \ldots \tag{2.59}$$

where $C > 0$ is a constant satisfying $\sum_{k=0}^{\infty} Ck^{-\gamma} = 1$, then P is called a *power-law distribution* of $X (= k)$, denoted as $X \sim Pw(\gamma)$.

Example 2.9 If a random variable X takes values in an interval $(a,b) \in R^1$ and its probability density function $f(\cdot)$ is given by

$$f(x) = \frac{1}{b-a}, \quad a < x < b \quad (\text{otherwise}, f(x) = 0), \tag{2.60}$$

which is called a *uniform probability distribution* of the random variable X, denoted as $X \sim U(a, b)$, and is given by

$$P(x) = \begin{cases} 0 & x \leq a \\ (x - a)/(b - a) & a < x < b \\ 1 & x \geq b \end{cases} \tag{2.61}$$

Example 2.10 If the probability density function $f(\cdot)$ is given by

$$f_r(x) = \alpha \frac{r^\alpha}{x^{\alpha+1}}, \quad x \geq r > 0 \quad (\text{otherwise, } f_r(x) = 0), \tag{2.62}$$

which is called a *Pareto probability density function* of the random variable X, then P is called the *Pareto probability distribution*, denoted as $Pa(x, r)$, and is given by

$$Pa(x, r) = 1 - \frac{r^\alpha}{x^\alpha}, \quad x \geq r > 0 \quad (\text{otherwise, } Pa(x, r) = 0). \tag{2.63}$$

Example 2.11 For a set of discrete events with N i.i.d. (independent identically distributed) random variables, in a power-law distribution $p(f) = \beta f^{-1-\alpha^{-1}}$ where $\beta > 0$ is a constant, if the probability function $f(\cdot)$ is given by

$$Z_f(k, \alpha, N) = \frac{1}{\sum_{n=1}^{N} n^{-\alpha}} k^{-\alpha}, \quad \alpha > 0, \ k = 1, 2, \ldots, N, \tag{2.64}$$

where k indicates the rank (frequency) of the random variables, then it is referred to as the *Zipf law*.

The simplest case of the Zipf law is the "$1/f$-function": given a set of Zipfian distributed frequencies, sorted from the most common to the least common, then approximately the second most common frequency will occur $1/2$ as often as the first. The third most common frequency will occur $1/3$ as often as the first. The nth most common frequency will occur $1/n$ as often as the first.

2.2.1.2 Basic Concepts and Properties of Probability Distributions

Let X be a random variable. The *expectation* of X indicates the *mean* (or, average) of the values of X, defined by

$$E(X) = \int_{-\infty}^{\infty} xf(x)dx. \tag{2.65}$$

Note that $E(X)$ is a real number for any random variable X with probability density function $f(\cdot)$. $E(X)$ is the *first moment* of the probability density function $f(\cdot)$. The *second moment* gives the *variance* of X, defined by

$$Var(X) = E(X - E(X))^2 = \int_{-\infty}^{\infty} (x - E(x))^2 f(x)dx. \tag{2.66}$$

This number indicates the dispersion of the values of X from its mean $E(X)$.

Example 2.12 For the Gaussian distribution, using the substitution $y = (x - \mu)/\sqrt{2}\sigma$ again, one obtains

$$\begin{aligned} E(X) &= \int_{-\infty}^{\infty} xf(x)dx \\ &= \frac{1}{\sqrt{2\pi}\sigma} \int_{-\infty}^{\infty} xe^{-\frac{1}{2\sigma^2}(x-\mu)^2} dx \\ &= \frac{1}{\sqrt{\pi}} \int_{-\infty}^{\infty} \left(\sqrt{2}\sigma y + \mu\right) e^{-y^2} dy \\ &= \mu \frac{1}{\sqrt{\pi}} \int_{-\infty}^{\infty} e^{-y^2} dy \\ &= \mu. \end{aligned} \tag{2.67}$$

Using the substitution $y = (x - \mu)/\sqrt{2}\sigma$, one has

$$
\begin{aligned}
Var(X) &= \int_{-\infty}^{\infty} (x - \mu)^2 f(x) dx \\
&= \frac{1}{\sqrt{2\pi}\sigma} \int_{-\infty}^{\infty} (x - \mu)^2 e^{-\frac{1}{2\sigma^2}(x-\mu)^2} dx \\
&= \frac{2\sigma^2}{\sqrt{\pi}} \int_{-\infty}^{\infty} y^2 e^{-y^2} dy \\
&= \sigma^2,
\end{aligned}
\tag{2.68}
$$

where the equality $\int_{-\infty}^{\infty} y^2 e^{-y^2} dy = \sqrt{\pi}/2$ has been used.

2.2.1.3   Random Vectors and Their Properties

Next, the concept of *random vector* is introduced. A random vectors has all components being random variables, denoted by $X = \begin{bmatrix} X_1 & \cdots & X_n \end{bmatrix}^T \in R^n$ where $X_i(s) \in R^1$ with $s \in S$, $i = 1, 2, \ldots, n$.
Let P be a continuous probability distribution function of X; that is,

$$
P(X_1 \in A_1, \ldots, X_n \in A_n) = \int_{A_1} \cdots \int_{A_n} f(x_1, \ldots, x_n) dx_1 \ldots dx_n,
\tag{2.69}
$$

where $A_1, \ldots, A_n$ are measurable sets in R^1 and $f(\cdot)$ is an integrable function, called a *joint probability density function* of X while P is called a *joint probability distribution (function) of X.
For each i, $i = 1, 2, \ldots, n$, define

$$
f_i(x) = \int_{-\infty}^{\infty} \cdots \int \int_{-\infty}^{\infty} f(x_1, \ldots, x_{i-1}, x_{i+1}, \ldots, x_n) dx_1 \ldots dx_{i-1} dx_{i+1} \ldots dx_n.
\tag{2.70}
$$

Then, it is clear that $\int_{-\infty}^{\infty} f_i(x) dx = 1$. Each $f_i(\cdot)$ is called the ith *marginal probability density function of* X corresponding to the joint probability density function $f(x_1, \ldots, x_n)$. Similarly, define $f_{ij}(\cdot)$ and $f_{ijk}(\cdot)$ by deleting the integrals with respect to x_i, x_j and x_i, x_j, x_k, respectively, etc., as in the definition of $f_i(\cdot)$, $i = 1, 2, \ldots, n$.

Example 2.13 If

$$
f(x) = \frac{1}{(2\pi)^{n/2}(\det R)^{1/2}} \exp\left\{-\frac{1}{2}(x - \mu)^T R^{-1}(x - \mu)\right\},
\tag{2.71}
$$

where μ is an n-dimensional constant vector, and R is a symmetric positive definite matrix, then $f(x)$ is called a *Gaussian* (or *normal*) *probability density function* of X. It can be verified that

$$
\int_{-\infty}^{\infty} f(x) dx := \int_{-\infty}^{\infty} \cdots \int_{-\infty}^{\infty} f(x) dx_1 \ldots dx_n = 1,
\tag{2.72}
$$

$$
\begin{aligned}
E(X) &= \int_{-\infty}^{\infty} x f(x) dx \\
&= \int_{-\infty}^{\infty} \cdots \int_{-\infty}^{\infty} \begin{bmatrix} x_1 \\ \vdots \\ x_n \end{bmatrix} f(x) dx_1 \ldots dx_n \\
&= \mu,
\end{aligned}
\tag{2.73}
$$

$$
Var(X) = E[(X - \mu)(X - \mu)^T] = R.
\tag{2.74}
$$

Indeed, since R is symmetric and positive definite, there is a unitary matrix U such that $R = U^T J U$, where $J = diag[\lambda_1, \ldots, \lambda_n]$ and $\lambda_1, \ldots, \lambda_n > 0$. Let

$$y = \frac{1}{\sqrt{2}} diag\left[\sqrt{\lambda_1}, \ldots, \sqrt{\lambda_n}\right] U(x - \mu).$$

Then

$$\int f(x)dx = \frac{2^{n/2}\sqrt{\lambda_1} \cdots \sqrt{\lambda_n}}{(2\pi)^{n/2}(\lambda_1 \cdots \lambda_n)^{1/2}} \int_{-\infty}^{\infty} e^{-y_1^2}dy_1 \cdots e^{-y_n^2}dy_n = 1.$$

Equations (2.73) and (2.74) can be verified by using the same substitution as that used for the scalar case (2.66) and (2.67).

Next, the concept of *conditional probability* is introduced. First, consider a simple example.

Example 2.14 In an experiment, balls are drawn one at a time from an urn containing m_1 white balls and m_2 black balls. What is the probability that the second ball drawn from the urn is also black (event A_2) under the condition that the first one is black (event A_1)? Here, one should sample without replacement; that is, the first ball is not returned to the urn after being drawn.

To solve this simple problem, one may reason as follows: since the first ball drawn from the urn is black, there remain m_1 white balls and $m_2 - 1$ black balls in the urn before the second drawing. Hence, the probability that a black ball is drawn is now

$$\frac{m_2 - 1}{m_1 + m_2 - 1}.$$

Note that

$$\frac{m_2 - 1}{m_1 + m_2 - 1} = \frac{m_2}{m_1 + m_2} \cdot \frac{m_2 - 1}{m_1 + m_2 - 1} \bigg/ \frac{m_2}{m_1 + m_2},$$

where $m_2/(m_1 + m_2)$ is the probability that a black ball is picked at the first drawing, and $[m_2/(m_1 + m_2)] \cdot [(m_2 - 1)/(m_1 + m_2 - 1)]$ is the probability that black balls are picked at both the first and second drawings.

In general, the *conditional probability* of $X_1 \in A_1$ given $X_2 \in A_2$ is defined by

$$P(X_1 \in A_1 | X_2 \in A_2) = \frac{P(X_1 \in A_1, X_2 \in A_2)}{P(X_2 \in A_2)}. \tag{2.75}$$

Suppose that P is a continuous probability distribution function with joint probability density function $f(\cdot)$. Then (2.75) becomes

$$P(X_1 \in A_1 | X_2 \in A_2) = \frac{\displaystyle\int_{A_1}\int_{A_2} f(x_1, x_2)dx_1 dx_2}{\displaystyle\int_{A_2} f_2(x_2)dx_2},$$

where $f_2(x_2) = \int_{-\infty}^{\infty} f(x_1, x_2)dx_1$ is the second marginal probability density function of $f(\cdot)$.

Let $f(x_1 x_2)$ be the probability density function corresponding to $P(X_1 \in A_1 | X_2 \in A_2)$. Then $f(x_1 x_2)$ is called the *conditional probability density function* corresponding to the conditional probability distribution function $P(X_1 \in A_1 | X_2 \in A_2)$. The *Bayes formula* is

$$f(x_1 | x_2) = \frac{f(x_1, x_2)}{f(x_2)}. \tag{2.76}$$

By symmetry, this formula can be written as

$$f(x_1, x_2) = f(x_1 | x_2)f_2(x_2) = f(x_2 | x_1)f_1(x_1). \tag{2.77}$$

Note that this formula also holds for random vectors X_1 and X_2.

Let X and Y be random n- and m-dimensional vectors, respectively. The *covariance* of X and Y is defined by the $n \times m$ matrix

$$Cov(X, Y) = E[(X - E(X))(Y - E(Y))^T]. \tag{2.78}$$

When $Y = X$, this reduces to the variance matrix, which is also called a *covariance matrix* of X, with $Var(X) = Cov(X, X)$.

It can be verified that the expectation, variance, and covariance have the following properties:

$$E(AX + BY) = AE(X) + BE(Y) \tag{2.79a}$$

$$E[(AX)(BY)^T] = A(E(XY^T))B^T \tag{2.79b}$$

$$Var(X) \geq 0 \tag{2.79c}$$

$$Cov(X, Y) = [Cov(Y, X)]^T \tag{2.79d}$$

$$Cov(X, Y) = E(XY^T) - E(X)E(Y)^T, \tag{2.79e}$$

where A and B are constant matrices.

X and Y are said to be *independent* if $f(x|y) = f_1(x)$ and $f(y|x) = f_2(y)$, and X and Y are said to be *uncorrelated* if $Cov(X, Y) = 0$. It is easy to see that if X and Y are independent then they are uncorrelated. Indeed, if X and Y are independent then $f(x, y) = f_1(x)f_2(y)$. Hence,

$$E(XY^T) = \int_{-\infty}^{\infty} \int_{-\infty}^{\infty} xy^T f(x, y) dx dy$$

$$= \int_{-\infty}^{\infty} x f_1(x) dx \int_{-\infty}^{\infty} y^T f_2(y) dy$$

$$= E(X)(E(Y))^T,$$

so that, by property (2.79e), $Cov(X, Y) = 0$. But the converse does not necessarily hold, unless the probability distribution is normal.

Example 2.15 Let

$$X = \begin{bmatrix} X_1 \\ X_2 \end{bmatrix} \sim N\left(\begin{bmatrix} \mu_1 \\ \mu_2 \end{bmatrix}, R \right),$$

Where

$$R = \begin{bmatrix} R_{11} & R_{12} \\ R_{21} & R_{22} \end{bmatrix}, \quad R_{12} = R_{21}^T.$$

And R_{11} and R_{22} are symmetric, and R is positive definite. Then, it can be verified that X_1 and X_2 are independent if and only if $R_{12} = Cov(X_1, X_2) = 0$.

Let X and Y be two random vectors. Similar to the definitions of expectation and variance, the *conditional expectation* of X under the condition of $Y = y$ is defined to be

$$E(X|Y = y) = \int_{-\infty}^{\infty} x f(x|y) dx \tag{2.80}$$

and the *conditional variance*, which is sometimes called the *conditional covariance* of X, under the condition of $Y = y$, to be

$$Var(X|Y = y) = \int_{-\infty}^{\infty} [x - E(X|Y = y)][x - E(X|Y = y)]^T f(x, y) dx. \tag{2.81}$$

Next, denote that

$$E\left(\begin{bmatrix} X \\ Y \end{bmatrix} \right) = \begin{bmatrix} \mu_x \\ \mu_y \end{bmatrix} \text{ and } Var\left(\begin{bmatrix} X \\ Y \end{bmatrix} \right) = \begin{bmatrix} R_{xx} & R_{xy} \\ R_{yx} & R_{yy} \end{bmatrix}.$$

Then, it follows from (1.25) that

$$f(x, y) = f\left(\begin{bmatrix} x \\ y \end{bmatrix}\right) = \cfrac{1}{(2\pi)^{n/2} \left(\det \begin{bmatrix} R_{xx} & R_{yx} \\ R_{xy} & R_{yy} \end{bmatrix} \right)^{1/2}}$$

$$\times \exp \left\{ -\frac{1}{2}\left(\begin{bmatrix} x \\ y \end{bmatrix} - \begin{bmatrix} \mu_1 \\ \mu_2 \end{bmatrix}\right)^T \begin{bmatrix} R_{xx} & R_{yx} \\ R_{xy} & R_{yy} \end{bmatrix}^{-1} \left(\begin{bmatrix} x \\ y \end{bmatrix} - \begin{bmatrix} \mu_1 \\ \mu_2 \end{bmatrix}\right) \right\}.$$

It can be verified that

$$f(x|y) = \frac{f(x, y)}{f(y)} = \frac{1}{(2\pi)^{n/2} \left(\det \tilde{R} \right)^{1/2}} \times \exp \left\{ -\frac{1}{2}(x - \tilde{\mu})^T \tilde{R}^{-1} (x - \tilde{\mu}) \right\}, \tag{2.82}$$

where

$$\tilde{\mu} = \mu_x + R_{xy} R_{yy}^{-1}(y - \mu_y) \quad \text{and} \quad \tilde{R} = R_{xx} - R_{xy} R_{yy}^{-1} R_{yx}.$$

Hence, by rewriting $\tilde{\mu}$ and $\tilde{R}$, one has

$$E(X|Y = y) = E(X) + Cov(X, Y)[Var(Y)]^{-1}(y - E(Y)) \tag{2.83}$$

and

$$Var(X|Y = y) = Var(X) - Cov(X, Y)[Var(Y)]^{-1}Cov(Y, X). \tag{2.84}$$

2.2.2   Statistics Preliminaries

First, a few basic concepts are introduced.

In a finite set of numbers (data), the *median* is the middle number arranged in numerical order. If the number of values in a set is even, then the median is the sum of the two middle values divided by 2. For example, the median of the set $\{1, 1, 1, 2, 2, 3, 3, 3, 200\}$ is 2, the 5th number in the set. The median is not affected by the magnitudes of the extreme (smallest or largest) values.

The *mean* of all values in a population of values is denoted by μ, while that of a sample, say $\{x_1, x_2, \dots, x_n\}$, is defined by the *arithmetic mean*:

$$\bar{x} = \frac{x_1 + x_2 + \cdots + x_n}{n}. \tag{2.85}$$

Unlike the median, the mean is sensitive to a change in any value, in the sense that the change of an extreme value may significantly affect the mean value. For example, the mean of the set $\{1, 1, 1, 2, 2, 3, 3, 3, 200\}$ is 24, although all but one member are very small (1, 2 or 3). To resolve this sensitivity problem, the *trimmed mean* may be used, where the smallest and largest quarters of the values are removed before taking the mean.

The *range* is the difference between the largest and the smallest values of a set of numbers. For example, the range of $\{1, 1, 1, 2, 2, 3, 3, 3, 200\}$ is 199. The *variance* is a measure of how some values are dispersed about their mean. The variance σ^2 of a whole population of N values is given by

$$\sigma^2 = \frac{\sum_{i=1}^N (x_i - \mu)^2}{N} = \frac{\sum_{i=1}^N (x_i)^2}{N} - \mu^2. \tag{2.86}$$

The variance s^2 of a sample of size n from the population is calculated differently, by

$$s^2 = \frac{\sum_{i=1}^n (x_i - \bar{x})^2}{n - 1} = \frac{\sum_{i=1}^n (x_i)^2}{n - 1} - \frac{(\sum_{i=1}^n x_i)^2}{n(n - 1)}. \tag{2.87}$$

The *standard deviation* σ (or, s for a sample) is the square root of the variance. The *relative variability* of a set of values is its standard deviation divided by its mean, which is useful for comparing several variances.

The so-called *z-score* of a specific value is defined by

$$z(x) = \frac{x - \mu}{\sigma}. \tag{2.88}$$

The mean $\bar{x}$ and variance s^2 defined above are the first moment and second moment of a random sample variable x, respectively, while the *kth moment* of x is defined by

$$M_k = \frac{\sum_{i=1}^{n}(x_i - \bar{x})^2}{n}, \qquad k = 1, 2, \ldots \tag{2.89}$$

Next, the concept of dispersion percentage is briefly reviewed.

The empirical rule states that for data with a "bell-shaped" curve, about 68% of the values lie within one standard deviation of the mean, about 95% lie within two standard deviations, and over 99% lie within three standard deviations of the mean. Since 99% of the data fall within a span of six standard deviations (z-scores of -1 to $+3$), the standard deviation of a set of values that are somewhat bell-shaped should be about $1/6$ of the range.

The *Chebyshev Theorem* states that for any set of data, at least $1 - 1/k^2$ of the values lie within k standard deviations of the mean; namely, with z-scores between $-k$ and $+k$.

In statistic testing and verification, very often one needs to decide if a certain claim is true or not. Such a claim is called a *hypothesis*. There are two basic hypotheses. The *null hypothesis* is a specific hypothesis to be tested in an experiment, which is usually labeled as H_0. The *alternative hypothesis*, labeled as H_a, is a hypothesis that is different from the null hypothesis, which one attempts to show to be true (thereby, the null hypothesis would be false). The alternative hypothesis needs to verify that some value is greater than or less than a *critical value*, c ($0 < c < 1$), which separates the null hypothesis "to reject" region from the "fail to reject" region.

More precisely, the null hypothesis is tested through the following procedure:

1. Determine the null hypothesis H_0 and an alternative hypothesis H_a.
2. Pick an appropriate sample $S = \{x_1, x_2, \ldots, x_n\}$ from the population.
3. Use measurements from the sample S to determine the likelihood of the null hypothesis H_0, against the critical value c, so as to decide either to accept H_0 or to reject H_0.

There could be two types of errors in the above determination.

Type I error. If the null hypothesis is true but the sample mean is such that the null hypothesis is rejected, then Type I error occurs. The probability that such an error will occur is referred to as the α-risk.

Type II error. If the null hypothesis is false but the sample mean is such that the null hypothesis cannot be rejected, then Type II error occurs. The probability that such an error will occur is called the β-risk.

2.2.3 Law of Large Numbers and Central Limit Theorem

Consider a set of i.i.d. random variables, $\{X_1, X_2, \ldots, X_n\}$, with a common finite mean μ and a common variance σ^2. Let $S_n = X_1 + X_2 + \cdots + X_n$. The average of S_n, denoted $\bar{X} = (X_1 + X_2 + \cdots + X_n)/n$, is also a random variable, with mean

$$E(\bar{X}) = [E(X_1) + E(X_2) + \cdots + E(X_n)]/n = \mu \tag{2.90}$$

and with variance

$$Var(\bar{X}) = [Var(X_1) + Var(X_2) + \cdots + Var(X_n)]/n^2 = \sigma^2/n. \tag{2.91}$$

The *Classical law of large numbers* is stated as follows. Consider a set of i.i.d. random variables, $\{X_1, X_2, \ldots, X_n\}$, with a common finite mean μ. For any $\varepsilon > 0$,

$$P\left(\left|\frac{S_n}{n} - \mu\right| \geq \varepsilon\right) \to 0 \quad (\text{as } n \to \infty). \tag{2.92a}$$

Or, equivalently,

$$P\left(\left|\frac{S_n}{n} - \mu\right| < \varepsilon\right) \to 1 \quad (\text{as } n \to \infty). \tag{2.92b}$$

The *Chebyshev law of large numbers* states that, for a set of independent random variables, $\{X_1, X_2, \ldots, X_n\}$, with uniformly bounded variances, for any $\varepsilon > 0$, one has

$$P\left(\left|\frac{S_n}{n} - \frac{M_n}{n}\right| \geq \varepsilon\right) \to 0 \quad (\text{as } n \to \infty). \tag{2.93a}$$

Or, equivalently,

$$P\left(\left|\frac{S_n}{n} - \frac{M_n}{n}\right| < \varepsilon\right) \to 1 \quad (\text{as } n \to \infty), \tag{2.93b}$$

where $M_n = m_1 + m_2 + \cdots + m_n$ with $m_i = E(X_i)$, $i = 1, 2, \ldots, n$.

The *Bernoulli law of large numbers* is about experiments. Let n_A be the number of occurrence of event A in n independent trials on the same experiment, and $p = p(A)$ be the probability of occurrence of event A. Then, for any $\varepsilon > 0$,

$$P\left(\left|\frac{n_A}{n} - p\right| \geq \varepsilon\right) \to 0 \quad (\text{as } n \to \infty). \tag{2.94a}$$

Or, equivalently,

$$P\left(\left|\frac{n_A}{n} - p\right| < \varepsilon\right) \to 1 \quad (\text{as } n \to \infty). \tag{2.94b}$$

For independent continuous random variables, $\{X_1, X_2, \ldots, X_n\}$, with a continuous density function $f(\cdot)$, a common finite mean μ and a common finite variance σ^2. Let $S_n = X_1 + X_2 + \cdots + X_n$. Then, for any $\varepsilon > 0$,

$$\lim_{n \to \infty} P\left(\left|\frac{S_n}{n} - \mu\right| \geq \varepsilon\right) = 0. \tag{2.95a}$$

Or, equivalently,

$$\lim_{n \to \infty} P\left(\left|\frac{S_n}{n} - \mu\right| < \varepsilon\right) \to 1. \tag{2.95b}$$

Example 2.16 Consider the experiment of randomly choosing n numbers from the interval $[0, 1]$ with uniform distribution. Let X_i be the ith chosen number, $i = 1, 2, \ldots, n$. Then,

$$\mu = E(X_i) = \int_0^1 x\,dx = \frac{1}{2}$$

$$\sigma^2 = Var(X_i) = \int_0^1 x^2\,dx - \mu^2 = \frac{1}{12}.$$

Thus,

$$E\left(\frac{S_n}{n}\right) = \frac{1}{2} \text{ and } Var\left(\frac{S_n}{n}\right) = \frac{1}{12n}.$$

Consequently, it follows from the Chebyshev inequality $P(|X - \mu| \geq \varepsilon) \leq \sigma^2/\varepsilon^2$ that

$$P\left(\left|\frac{S_n}{n} - \frac{1}{2}\right| \geq \varepsilon\right) \leq \frac{1}{12n} \to 0 \quad (\text{as } n \to \infty).$$

Here, the parameter ε plays the role of the amount of error which one would like to tolerate: if one choose $\varepsilon = 0.1$, for instance, then the chance for $|S_n/n - 1/2| < 0.1$ is larger than $1 - 100/(12n)$. Therefore, if one picks $n = 100$ then this chance is 0.92, if $n = 1,000$ then it is 0.99, and if $n = 10,000$ then it is 0.999.

Now, consider again a set of i.i.d. random variables, $\{X_1, X_2, \dots, X_n\}$, with a common finite mean μ and a common finite variance σ^2. Let $S_n = X_1 + X_2 + \cdots + X_n$. Then, as $n \to \infty$, the random variables $(S_n - n\mu)/\sqrt{n\sigma^2}$ converge in distribution to a normal distribution $N(0, \sigma^2)$. More precisely, the *central limit theorem* states that

$$\lim_{n\to\infty} P\left(a < \frac{S_n - n\mu}{\sqrt{n\sigma^2}} < b\right) = \frac{1}{\sqrt{2\pi}} \int_a^b e^{-x^2/2} dx. \tag{2.96}$$

2.2.4   Markov Chains

Consider a set of *states*, $S = \{s_1, s_2, \dots, s_n\}$, of a moving object (random variable), and the process starting in a specific initial state to move successively from one state to another. An initial probability distribution, defined on S, specifies the starting state.

Assume that the chain of motions is currently in state s_i, which moves to state s_j at the next step with a probability p_{ij}, called *transition probability*. Assume, importantly, that this probability does not depend upon which states the chain was in before the current state. The chain is allowed to remain in its current state, which occurs with probability p_{ii}, $i = 1, 2, \dots, n$. Putting together gives the matrix $P = [p_{ij}]$, which is called the *state transition matrix*, and the chain is called a *Markov chain*. The ijth entry of the product matrix $P^m = [p_{ij}^m]$ is given by

$$p_{ij}^m = \sum_{k=1}^m p_{ik} p_{kj},$$

which is the probability that the Markov chain moves from state s_i to state s_j in m steps.

Now, consider the long-term behavior of a Markov chain when it starts in a state chosen by a probability distribution on the set of states, $S = \{s_1, s_2, \dots, s_n\}$, which is also referred to as a (row) *probability vector*. A probability vector is a row vector whose components are nonnegative summing up to 1. Let u be the probability vector representing the initial state of the Markov chain. Then, the ith component of u represents the probability that the chain starts in state s_i, namely, $u = [s_1, \dots, s_n]$. It can be verified that the probability that the chain is in state s_i after m steps is the ith component of the vector

$$u^{(m)} = uP^m.$$

Furthermore, as $m \to \infty$, the powers P^m approach a limiting matrix W with all rows the same vector w. The vector w is called the *limiting probability vector*, which is a strictly positive probability vector (i.e., the components are all positive and they sum to one).

A Markov chain is called *ergodic*, if it is possible to go from every state to every state, not necessarily in one step. An ergodic Markov chain is also said to be *irreducible*. Moreover, a Markov chain is said to be *regular*, if some power of the transition matrix has only positive elements. In other words, for some m, it is possible to go from any state to any state in exactly m steps. It is clear that a regular chain is ergodic, but the converse may not be true, as shown by the following simple example.

Example 2.17 Let the transition matrix of a Markov chain be

$$P = \begin{bmatrix} 0 & 1 \\ 1 & 0 \end{bmatrix}.$$

Clearly, it is possible to move from any state to any state, so the Markov chain is ergodic. However, for an odd number m, it is impossible to move from state 0 to state 0 in exactly m steps; for an even number m, it is impossible to move from state 0 to state 1 in exactly m steps, so the chain is not regular.

For regular Markov chains, the following two results can be obtained. Let P be the transition matrix for a regular Markov chain.

1. As $n \to \infty$, the power matrices P^n approach a limiting matrix W with all rows being identical, denoted w. The row vector w is a strictly positive probability vector (i.e., the components are all positive and they sum up to 1).
2. For $W = \lim_{n \to \infty} P^n$, which is called the *fundamental limit*, with w being the common row and with c being the column vector of all components equal to 1:

$$Pw = w, \text{ and any row vector } v \text{ satisfying } vP = v \text{ is a constant multiple of } w;$$

$$Pc = c, \text{ and any column vector } u \text{ satisfying } Pu = u \text{ is a multiple of } c.$$

For any ergodic Markov chain, starting from any initial state, and for any real numbers $r < s$, one has the *central limit theorem*:

$$\lim_{m \to \infty} P\left(r < \frac{S_j^{(m)} - mw_j}{\sqrt{m\sigma_j^2}} < s \right) = \frac{1}{\sqrt{2\pi}} \int_r^s e^{-x^2/2} dx, \tag{2.97}$$

where $\sigma_j^2 = 2w_j z_{jj} - w_j - w_j^2$, with $[z_{ij}] = [I - P + W]^{-1}$ satisfying $Zc = c$.

2.3   Elementary Dynamical Systems Theory

2.3.1   *Background and Motivation*

A *nonlinear system* studied in this book is a set of nonlinear (algebraic, difference, differential) equations used to describe a physical model that otherwise cannot be well defined by a set of linear equations. Such a system may also depend on some variable parameters.

The theory of nonlinear dynamical systems has been greatly advanced since the pioneering work of Jules Henri Poincaré (1854–1912). Today, nonlinear dynamical systems are used to describe a vast variety of scientific and engineering phenomena ranging from physics, biology, and sociology alike to engineering and technology.

In this section, only those concepts and tools that are directly related to the contents of the book are briefly reviewed, leaving more concepts and content details to some relevant references.

2.3.1.1   Preliminaries

Most continuous-time nonlinear dynamical systems studied in this book are described by either a differential equation of the form

$$\dot{x} = f(x, t; p), \qquad t \in [t_0, \infty) \tag{2.98}$$

or a map,

$$M : x \to g(x, t; p), \qquad t \in [t_0, \infty), \tag{2.99}$$

where $x = x(t)$ is the *state* (vector) of the system belonging to a (usually, bounded) region $\Omega \subset R^n$, p is a vector of *system parameters* that may be allowed to vary within a prescribed (usually, bounded) interval $I^m \subset R^m$, often $m \leq n$, and $f(\cdot, \cdot)$ and $g(\cdot, \cdot)$ are continuous or differentiable nonlinear functions of comparable dimensions, which are explicitly given for a specified physical system.

It is always assumed that necessary conditions, such as the well-posed solvability conditions, are satisfied so that the system (or map) has a unique solution corresponding to any suitably given initial condition, $x(t_0) = x_0 \in \Omega$ at the initial time $t_0 = 0$ for convenience. In this book, the reverse processes of nonlinear dynamics are generally not considered, so the situation over the time interval $(-\infty, 0)$ is normally not discussed. The entire space $R^n \times [0, \infty)$, to which the system states belong, is called the *state space*.

For the discrete-time setting, a nonlinear dynamical system is described by either a difference equation of the form

$$x_{k+1} = f(x_k, k; p), \qquad k = 0, 1, 2, \ldots \tag{2.100}$$

or a map,

$$M : x_k \rightarrow g(x_k, k; p), \qquad k = 0, 1, 2, \ldots \tag{2.101}$$

where all notation are similarly defined. Given a current state, x_k, of a discrete-time system described by a map, M, repeatedly iterating the map backwards leads to

$$x_k = M(x_{k-1}) = M(M(x_{k-2})) = \cdots = M^k(x_0).$$

Here, the map M can also be replaced by a function, $f(\cdot)$, if the system is given via a difference equation such as (2.100), yielding

$$x_k = f^k(x_0) = \underbrace{f \circ \cdots \circ f(x_0)}_{m},$$

where and throughout, "$\circ$" denotes the composition of two subsequent mappings, functions, or iterations.

The dynamical system (2.98) is said to be *autonomous*, if the time variable, t, does not appear separately (independently) in the system function $f(\cdot)$; in this case,

$$\dot{x} = f(x; p). \tag{2.102}$$

Otherwise, as (2.98) stands, it is said to be *nonautonomous*. The same terminology may be used in the same way for discrete-time systems. Here, it should be noted that the state vector $x = x(t)$ is of course always a function of time.

A dynamical system is *deterministic*, if there is a unique consequence to every change of the system parameters or initial states. It is *random* or *stochastic*, if there is more than one possible consequence for a change in its parameters or initial states according to some probability distribution. This book essentially deals with deterministic systems, but occasionally, simple stochastic systems and deterministic systems that are subject to random noise (disturbances) are also discussed.

2.3.1.2 Nonlinear Dynamical Systems

In this section, only nonparametric systems (i.e., without the parameter vector p defined in (2.98), (2.99), or (2.100) are discussed. As an introduction, consider a general, two-dimensional, autonomous system,

$$\begin{cases} \dot{x} = f(x, y) \\ \dot{y} = g(x, y) \end{cases} \tag{2.103}$$

with given initial conditions (x_0, y_0) and two smooth nonlinear functions, $f(\cdot, \cdot)$ and $g(\cdot, \cdot)$. Here, (f, g) describes the *vector field* of the system.

The path traveled by the solution of system (2.103), starting from the initial state (x_0, y_0), is a *solution trajectory*, or an *orbit*, of the system. To distinguish a solution from the system state that produces it, and to indicate its dependence on the initial condition, a solution of system (2.103), with initial state (x_0, y_0), is usually denoted by $\varphi_t(x_0, y_0)$. The family of φ_t, $t \in [0, \infty)$, satisfies $\varphi_{t_1 + t_2} = \varphi_{t_1} \circ \varphi_{t_2}$, where $\varphi_{t_0}(x_0, y_0) = (x_0, y_0)$. Since, for autonomous systems, two different solution trajectories never cross each other (i.e., never intersect) in the x-y plane, any solution $\varphi_t(x, y)$ of an autonomous system, considered as a family of trajectories with different initial conditions, is called a *flow* in the x-y plane. However, to simplify the notation in this book, a solution, $\varphi_t(x_0, y_0)$, is generally not distinguished from its state, namely, $(x(t), y(t))$ represents both, which satisfies $(x(0), y(0)) = (x_0, y_0)$, unless otherwise indicated.

All the possible solution trajectories of an autonomous or nonautonomous system, plotted in the x-y plane corresponding to different initial conditions, constitute the *phase portrait* of the system solutions.

In this case, the $x–y$ plane is called the *generalized phase plane* as compared to the *standard phase plane* (i.e., the $x–\dot{x}$ plane) of a one-variable dynamical system. In a higher-dimensional case, it is called a *(generalized) phase space*.

Equilibria, or *fixed points*, of system (2.103), if exist, are the solutions that simultaneously satisfy the following two homogeneous equations:

$$f = 0 \quad \text{and} \quad g = 0$$

An equilibrium is usually denoted by (x^*, y^*) or $(\bar{x}, \bar{y})$. An equilibrium is *stable*, if all the nearby trajectories of the system, starting from any initial states, approach it; it is said to be *unstable*, if the nearby trajectories move away from it. Equilibria can be classified, according to their stabilities, as stable or unstable *node, focus, saddle point*, or *center*.

Let λ_1 and λ_2 be the eigenvalues of the system Jacobian

$$J = \begin{bmatrix} f_x & f_y \\ g_x & g_y \end{bmatrix}, \tag{2.104}$$

with $f_x = \partial f / \partial x$ and $f_y = \partial f / \partial y$ and so on, all evaluated at (x^*, y^*). Then, different equilibria and their stabilities, determined by these two eigenvalues, are summarized in Figure 2.39 [6].

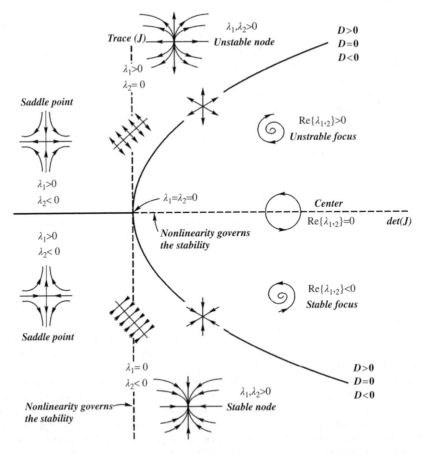

Figure 2.39 Classification of two-dimensional equilibria: stabilities are determined by eigenvalues. *Source:* Reprinted from Moiola, J.L. and Chen, G. (1996) *Hopf Bifurcation Analysis: A Frequency Domain Approach.* World Scientific Pub. Co., Singapore. Copyright (1996) World Scientific Pub. Co.

If the two eigenvalues of J satisfy $\mathrm{Re}\{\lambda_{1,2}\} \neq 0$, then the equilibrium (x^*, y^*), about which the linearization is taken, is said to be *hyperbolic*. The importance of hyperbolic equilibria can be seen from the following fundamental result on *local* dynamics, which holds for higher-dimensional dynamical systems as well [7].

Theorem 2.23 (Grobman-Hartman) *If (x^*, y^*) is a hyperbolic equilibrium of the nonlinear dynamical system (2.103), then the dynamical behavior of the nonlinear system is qualitatively the same as (i.e., topologically equivalent to) that of the linearized system.*

$$\begin{bmatrix} \dot{x} \\ \dot{y} \end{bmatrix} = J \begin{bmatrix} x \\ y \end{bmatrix}.$$

This theorem guarantees that, for the hyperbolic case, one can study the linearized system instead of the original nonlinear system, with regard to the local dynamical behavior of the system within a (usually, small) neighborhood of the equilibrium (x^*, y^*). In other words, there exist some *homeomorphic maps* that transform the trajectories of the nonlinear system into trajectories of its linearized system in a (small) neighborhood of the equilibrium. Here, a homeomorphic map, or a *homeomorphism*, is a continuous map whose inverse exists (so is one-to-one) and is also continuous. For the nonhyperbolic case, however, the situation is much more complicated, for which the above theorem is generally not valid.

In general, "dynamical behavior" includes basically all possible nonlinear phenomena such as stabilities and bifurcations, chaos and attractors, equilibria and limit cycles. System dynamics are further discussed later in this chapter, including the case where the system depends on additional parameters.

2.3.1.3 Periodic Orbits and Limit Cycles

In the general nonlinear dynamical system (2.98), a state $x(t)$ is a *periodic solution* of the given system if it is a solution of the system and satisfies $x(t + t_p) = x(t)$ for some constant $t_p > 0$. The minimum value of such $t_p > 0$ is called the *(fundamental) period* of the periodic solution, and this solution is said to be t_p-periodic. Clearly, a t_p-periodic solution always has (nonfundamental) periods $2t_p, 3t_p, \dots$.

The concept of a *limit cycle* of the two-dimensional nonlinear dynamical system (2.103) can be understood as a periodic solution of the system that corresponds to a closed orbit in the phase space, or phase plane for system (2.103), as shown in Figure 2.40 [6]. In this figure, (a) shows an *inner limit cycle*, (b) an *outer limit cycle*, (c) a *stable limit cycle*, (d) an *unstable limit cycle*, and (e) and (f), *saddle limit cycles*.

For an n-dimensional ($n \geq 2$) smooth dynamical system (2.98), there is the Poincaré-Andronov-Hopf *bifurcation theorem* [6, 7], providing the existence of limit cycles. For notational simplicity, the two-dimensional version of this bifurcation theorem is stated as follows, which is illustrated in Figure 2.41 [6].

Theorem 2.24 (Poincaré-Andronov-Hopf) *Suppose that the two-dimensional system (2.103) containing a constant parameter $\mu \in R$ has a zero equilibrium, $(\bar{x}, \bar{y}) = (0, 0)$, and that its associate Jacobian matrix has a pair of purely imaginary eigenvalues, $\lambda(\mu)$ and $\bar{\lambda}(\mu)$. If $dR\{\lambda(\mu)\}/d\mu|_{\mu=\varpi_0} > 0$ for some μ_0, then*

1. *$\mu = \mu_0$ is a bifurcation point of the system.*
2. *For close enough values $\mu < \mu_0$, the zero equilibrium is asymptotically stable.*
3. *For close enough values $\mu > \mu_0$, the zero equilibrium is unstable.*
4. *For close enough values $\mu \neq \mu_0$, the zero equilibrium is surrounded by a limit cycle of magnitude $O\left(\sqrt{|\mu|}\right)$.*

There is a concept of *resonance of frequencies* for periodic orbits. It can be easily illustrated by the simple equation

$$\ddot{x}(t) + p^2 x(t) = q\cos(t),$$

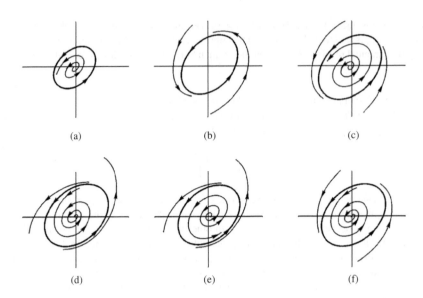

(a)   (b)   (c)

(d)   (e)   (f)

Figure 2.40   Classification of two-dimensional limit cycles [6]. (a) inner limit cycle; (b) outer limit cycle; (c) stable limit cycle; (d) unstable limit cycle; (e) and (f), saddle limit cycles *Source*: Reprinted from Moiola, J.L. and Chen, G. (1996) *Hopf Bifurcation Analysis: A Frequency Domain Approach*. World Scientific Pub. Co., Singapore. Copyright (1996) World Scientific Pub. Co.

where p and q are constants. This equation has the solution

$$x(t) = c\cos(pt + \phi) + q\cos(t)/(p^2 - 1),$$

where c and ϕ are constants determined by initial conditions, and the solution may be periodic with the same period as that of the forcing input term; that is, $x(t + 2\pi) = x(t)$. There are three possible cases for a solution: (i) *nonresonant*, or regular, if p is not an integer and, in this case, $x(t) = q\cos(t)/(p^2 - 1)$ is the unique 2π-periodic solution; (ii) *subresonant*, if $p = \pm k$ for some integer $k \neq 1$, where the two terms in the above solution formula have the same period, 2π, but the first term has also the least period, $2\pi/k$; (iii) *(frequency) resonant*, if $p = \pm 1$, then the equation does not have any 2π-periodic solution.

2.3.1.4   Limit Sets and Attractors

In the study of the general nonlinear dynamical system (2.98), one is often interested in the enduring phenomena of system solutions. *Steady states* of the system solutions refer to the asymptotic behaviors of the solutions as $t \to \infty$. Clearly, only those bounded steady states are meaningful. A solution trajectory between its initial state and steady state is called the *transient state*. Yet, there is generally no clear-cut line between transient and steady states, unless a transition point is specified.

For a given dynamical system, a point, y, in the state space is said to be an *ω-limit point* of an orbit, $x(t)$, of the system if, for every open neighborhood U_y of y, the trajectory of $x(t)$ enters U_y at a large enough but finite value of t. Consequently, the trajectory of $x(t)$ will repeatedly (infinitely many times) enter any given neighborhood of y, no matter how small it is, as $t \to \infty$. Here, ω is the last letter in the Greek alphabet, which is used here, following the tradition, to indicate the limiting process. The set of all ω-limit points of $x(t)$, denoted L_x, is called the *ω-limit set* of $x(t)$. An ω-limit set, L_x, is *attracting* if there exists an open neighborhood U_L of L_x, such that, if the trajectory of a system state enters U_L at some instant $t_1 \geq t_0$ then this trajectory will approach L_x arbitrarily closely, as $t \to \infty$. The *basin of attraction* of an attracting point is the union of all such open neighborhoods. An ω-limit set is *repelling* if the system trajectory always moves away from it.

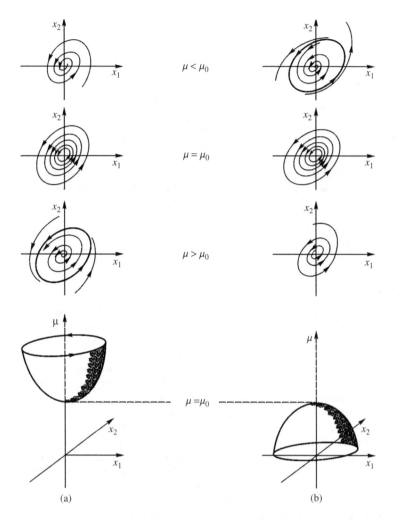

Figure 2.41 Two types of Hopf bifurcation illustrated in the phase plane [6]: (a) supercritical; (b) subcritical. *Source:* Reprinted from Moiola, J.L. and Chen, G. (1996) *Hopf Bifurcation Analysis: A Frequency Domain Approach.* World Scientific Pub. Co., Singapore. Copyright (1996) World Scientific Pub. Co.

Example 2.18 The simplest example of an attracting set is a stable equilibrium. A specific example of a physical system is the damped pendulum, described by

$$\begin{cases} \dot{x} = y \\ \dot{y} = -py - \sin(x) \end{cases}, \tag{2.105}$$

with a damping coefficient $p > 0$. This is a second-order autonomous system with infinitely many equilibria, $(x^*, y^*) = (k\pi, 0)$ for $k = 0, \pm 1, \pm 2, \ldots$. The equilibria with odd integers of k are attracting, and they altogether constitute an *attracting set*.

Figure 2.42 [8] shows the first few equilibria and part of their basins of attraction (the shaded area), where a boundary, that divides one basin from another, is called a *separatrix*.

For a given map, M, an ω-limit set is an invariant set of the map in the sense that $M(L_x) = L_x$, namely, starting from any point x_0 of the set, the orbit $x = x(x_0)$ will eventually return to the same set (but need not be the same point). Thus, an ω-limit set embraces both equilibria and periodic orbits.

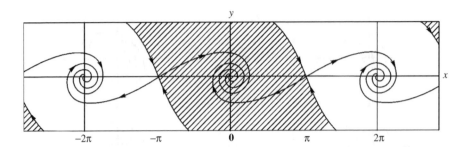

Figure 2.42 Phase portrait of the pendulum equation:the first few equilibria and their basins of attraction [8]. *Source:* Reprinted from Chen, G. and Dong, X. (1998) *From Chaos to Order: Methodologies, Perspectives and Applications.* World Scientific Pub. Co., Singapore. Copyright (1998) World Scientific Pub. Co.

An *attractor* is defined to be the union of all those points in an attracting set that is invariant under the iterations of the underlying map. In other words, an attractor is an ω-limit set, L_x, satisfying the property that all orbits near L_x have L_x as their ω-limit sets.

2.3.1.5 Poincaré Maps

Consider the general n-dimensional nonlinear autonomous system (2.102), and assume that this system has a t_p-periodic limit cycle, Γ, as shown in Figure 2.43. Let x^* be a point on the limit cycle and Σ be an $(n-1)$-dimensional hyperplane transversal to Γ at x^*. Here, the *transversality* of Σ to Γ at x^* means that Σ and the tangent line of Γ at x^* span the entire n-dimensional space.

Since Γ is a periodic orbit, the trajectory starting from the point x^* will return to x^* in one period of time, t_p. Any trajectory starting from a point, denoted x in Figure 2.43 [8], in a small neighborhood U_{x^*} of x^* on Σ, will return and hit Σ at a point, denoted $P(x)$, in the vicinity V_{x^*} of x^*. Therefore, a map, $P : U_{x^*} \to V_{x^*}$, can be uniquely defined by Σ along with the solution flow of the autonomous system. This map is called the *Poincaré map* associated with the system and the *cross-section*, Σ.

For different choices of the cross-section Σ, Poincaré maps are similarly defined. A suitably chosen cross-section can often reduce a huge amount of existing information about a dynamical model to a manageable level. A Poincaré map is only locally defined and is a *diffeomorphism*. A diffeomorphism is a differentiable map and has an inverse (so is one-to-one) that is also differentiable.

If a cross-section is suitably chosen, the aforementioned solution trajectory will repeatedly return and pass through the section, in which the Poincaré map together with the first-return trajectory is particularly important, and is called the *first-return Poincaré map*. Poincaré maps can also be defined for nonautonomous systems in a somewhat similar manner, each of which, however, depends on the initial time t_0 in a nonuniform fashion.

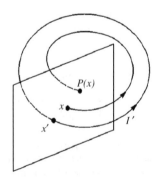

Figure 2.43 Schematic illustration of Poincaré map and a cross-section [8]. *Source:* Reprinted from Chen, G. and Dong, X. (1998) *From Chaos to Order: Methodologies, Perspectives and Applications.* World Scientific Pub. Co., Singapore. Copyright (1998) World Scientific Pub. Co.

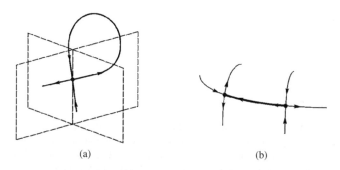

Figure 2.44   A schematic illustration of homoclinic and heteroclinic trajectories [8]: (a) homoclinic; (b) heteroclinic. *Source*: Reprinted from Chen, G. and Dong, X. (1998) *From Chaos to Order: Methodologies, Perspectives and
Applications*. World Scientific Pub. Co., Singapore. Copyright (1998) World Scientific Pub. Co.

2.3.1.6   Homoclinic and Heteroclinic Trajectories

Let x^* be a hyperbolic equilibrium of a diffeomorphism, $P : R^n \to R^n$, of unstable, center, or saddle type.
Let $\varphi_t(x)$ be a solution trajectory passing through x^*, and L_{x^*} be the limit set of $\varphi_t(x)$. The *stable manifold*
of L_{x^*}, denoted M_s, is the set of points, x, such that $\varphi_t(x)$ approaches L_{x^*} as $t \to \infty$. The *unstable manifold*
of L_{x^*}, denoted M_u, is the set of points, x, such that $\varphi_t(x)$ approaches L_{x^*} as $t \to -\infty$. In the case where
$L_{x^*} = x^*$, they reduce to the stable and unstable equilibrium point x^*, respectively.

Suppose that $\Sigma_s(x^*)$ and $\Sigma_u(x^*)$ are cross-sections of the stable and unstable manifolds of $\varphi_t(x)$, and
they intersect at x^*. Obviously, this intersection always includes one constant trajectory: $\varphi_t(x) = x^*$. A
nonconstant trajectory lying in the intersection is called a *homoclinic trajectory*. For two equilibria,
$x_1^* \neq x_2^*$, of unstable, center, or saddle type, a trajectory lying in $\Sigma_s(x_1^*) \cap \Sigma_u(x_2^*)$ or $\Sigma_u(x_1^*) \cap \Sigma_s(x_2^*)$,
is called a *heteroclinic trajectory*. As opposed to the homoclinic trajectories, shown in Figure 2.44 (a),
a heteroclinic trajectory approaches one equilibrium as $t \to \infty$ and approaches the other as $t \to -\infty$, as
shown in Figure 2.44 (b) [8].

It can be shown that if a stable and an unstable manifold intersect at a point $x_0 \neq x^*$, then they do so
at infinitely many points [9]. Denoted these points by $\{x_k\}_{k=-\infty}^{\infty}$, in which both forward and backward
indices are counted, including the point x_0. This sequence, $\{x_k\}$, is a *homoclinic orbit*, in which each x_k is
called a *homoclinic point*. This special structure is called a *homoclinic structure*. In this structure, the two
manifolds usually do not intersect transversally, so the structure is unstable in the sense that the connection can be destroyed by very small perturbations. However, if they intersect transversally, the transversal
homoclinic point will imply infinitely many other homoclinic points, which eventually leads to extremely
complicated stretching and folding of the two manifolds. Such stretching and folding of manifolds are key
to chaos, a concept to be further discussed later in this chapter. At this point, it is worth mentioning that a
transversal homoclinic point implies the existence of a *Smale horseshoe map*, embedded in the diffeomorphism P. Hence, the Smale horseshoe map, a special map with a horseshoe-like geometric shape, is also
an indication of chaos. The mathematical theory supporting this phenomenon is the following result [10].

Theorem 2.25 (Smale-Birkhoff)   *Let $P : R^n \to R^n$ be a diffeomorphism with a hyperbolic equilibrium
x^*. If the cross-sections of the stable and unstable manifolds, $\Sigma_s(x^*)$ and $\Sigma_u(x^*)$, intersect transversally
at a point other than x^*, then P has a horseshoe map embedded within it.*

Three-dimensional autonomous systems, that have an equilibrium with one real eigenvalue, λ, and two
complex conjugate eigenvalues, $a \pm jb$, are especially interesting. The case of $\lambda > 0$ and $a < 0$ gives a
Shilikov-type of homoclinic trajectory, with the following theoretical result [9].

Theorem 2.26 (Shilnikov)   *Let φ_t be the solution flow of a three-dimensional autonomous system that
has a Shilnikov-type homoclinic trajectory, γ. If $|a| < |\lambda|$, then φ_t can be perturbed to $\widetilde{\varphi}_t$, extremely
slightly, such that $\widetilde{\varphi}_t$ has a homoclinic trajectory $\widetilde{\gamma}$, near γ, of the same type, and the Poincaré map,
defined by a cross-section transversal to $\widetilde{\gamma}$, has a countable set of Smale horseshoes.*

2.3.2   Some Analytical Tools

Several useful mathematical tools are introduced here, which are frequently used in nonlinear systems analysis and design.

2.3.2.1   Center Manifold Theory

There are some efficient methods available for simplifying the representation of a solution trajectory of a nonlinear dynamical system, without any significant loss of important information about the solution, in a (small) neighborhood of a nonhyperbolic equilibrium. The *center manifold theory* is one such mathematical technique, which works for general higher-dimensional dynamical systems.

Essentially, the center manifold theory consists of three parts: the existence, approximation, and equivalence theorems.

To introduce this method, let x^* be an equilibrium (not necessarily of hyperbolic type) of the nonparametric nonlinear autonomous system

$$\dot{x} = f(x), \tag{2.106}$$

where $x \in R^n$ and $f(\cdot)$ is assumed sufficiently smooth. Also, let E_s, E_u, and E_c be the corresponding *generalized eigenspaces* associated with the Jacobian J of the system, defined by the real parts of the eigenvalues λ of J:

$$R(\lambda) = \begin{cases} < 0 & \text{defines} & E_s \\ = 0 & \text{defines} & E_c \\ > 0 & \text{defines} & E_u \end{cases}.$$

Then, there exist a *stable manifold*, M_s, an *unstable manifold*, M_u, and a *center manifold*, M_c, that are tangential to E_s, E_u, and E_c, respectively [7].

Here, the importance of a center manifold is that the asymptotic behavior of the overall dynamics of the nonlinear system is locally preserved by those trajectories on the center manifold, in a neighborhood of the equilibrium. More specifically, as $t \to \infty$, all trajectories converge exponentially in E_s, diverge exponentially in E_u, but behave in some complicated fashion within E_c (e.g., periodic or quasi-periodic orbits, strange attractors, bifurcations, and chaos).

The reduction of the system dynamics to those reproduced by the center manifold is the main subject of this theory. To characterize the trajectories of the reduced dynamics on the center manifold, one usually reformulates the system into a simpler form. To simplify the notation, without loss of generality, assume that the unstable manifold is empty. Then, system (2.106) can be decomposed as

$$\begin{cases} \dot{x}_c = J_c x_c + f_c\left(x_c, x_s\right) \\ \dot{x}_s = s_c x_s + f_s(x_c, x_s) \end{cases}, \tag{2.107}$$

where $x_c \in R^{n_c}$ and $x_s \in R^{n_s}$, with $n_c + n_s = n$. In this form, which is simpler than (2.106), the constant matrix J_c has n_c eigenvalues all with zero real parts, and J_s has n_s eigenvalues all with negative real parts. Moreover, the nonlinear functions f_c and f_s belong to C^2, and they vanish simultaneously with their first derivatives at the equilibrium x^*.

In system (2.107), x_c corresponds to the dynamics on the center manifold, and x_s, on the stable manifold. By the *existence theorem* [7], there is a center manifold, on which

$$x_s = h(x_c), \tag{2.108}$$

where h is a smooth nonlinear function. This center manifold is usually obtained numerically by applying the *approximation theorem* from the second equation of system (2.107). Then, substituting (2.108) into the first equation of system (2.107) yields

$$\dot{x}_c = J_c x_c + f_c(x_c, h(x_c)), \tag{2.109}$$

which is the *center manifold equation* associated with the nonlinear system (2.107). To this end, the *equivalence theorem* states that the asymptotic behavior of system (2.109) is topologically equivalent to that of system (2.107), in a neighborhood of the equilibrium x^*. In most cases, the reduced dynamics of the center manifold equation can be much more easily understood and solved [7].

2.3.2.2   Poincaré Normal Forms

Poincaré theory of *normal forms* provides an alternative approach to local dynamics analysis [7]. This technique, similar to the center manifold method, reduces a given nonlinear system to the simplest possible form that preserves the dynamics in a neighborhood of an equilibrium. The normal form theory can sometimes be combined with the center manifold method, to further reduce the local dynamics of a nonlinear system.

To briefly describe Poincaré normal forms theory, consider a system in the form

$$\dot{x} = Ax + f(x), \tag{2.110}$$

where A is a constant matrix in the Jordan canonical form, and $f(\cdot)$ is a smooth nonlinear function. Let the eigenvalues of A be $\{\lambda_1, \ldots, \lambda_n\}$. These eigenvalues are said to be (*eigen*) *resonant* if there is at least one index, $i : 1 \leq i \leq n$, such that $\lambda_i = \sum_{j=1}^{n} m_j \lambda_j$ with nonnegative integer coefficients, $\{m_j\}_{j=1}^{n}$, satisfying $\sum_{j=1}^{n} m_j > 2$. The following theorem characterizes the method of normal forms [7].

Theorem 2.27 (Poincaré) *If the constant matrix A in system (2.110) has no resonant eigenvalues, then the system can always be reduced to a locally topologically equivalent linear system of the form*

$$\dot{y} = Ay$$

by a series of suitable transformations of variables that yields $x \to y$.

2.3.2.3   Delay-Coordinates and Embedding

In practice, exact nonlinear mathematical models are often impossible to obtain, due to the complex and uncertain nature of the underlying dynamical processes and external random disturbances.

For observation data given in a time series form, obtained by sampling the input and output of a continuous-time finite-dimensional, linear dynamical system, there are many well-tested techniques for analysis, prediction, filtering, and control. A basic principle which supports this success is that the time-series data obtained from such systems can be characterized by a finite number of frequencies. However, these methods are generally ineffective in solving similar problems for time-series data measured from nonlinear dynamical systems.

Efficient methods for analyzing the time series produced by a nonlinear dynamical system constitute an important topic for research. In this regard, a technique for reconstructing a nonlinear dynamical system in a state space formulation from time-series data is the *delay-coordinates method*, and its underlying mathematical principle is called *embedology* [11].

To describe this technique, assume that the global dynamical equations of the system, $\dot{x} = f(x)$, are unknown, but the experimental time series, $z(t)$, can be measured from the system states. Then, a delay-coordinate vector, also called an *embedding vector*, is formed as

$$z_x = [z(t), z(t-\tau), z(t-2\tau), \ldots, z(t-(n_e-1)\tau)]^T,$$

where $\tau > 0$ is the *time-delay*, and n_2 the *embedding dimension*.

The embedding vector provides enough information for characterizing the dynamics of the system and can be used to obtain an experimental Poincaré map – generally a faithful one. For example, one may let the map be the equation of the first component of $z_x(t)$ being equal to a constant, $z(t_k) = $ constant, at

$t = t_k$. This yields the successive points

$$\xi_k = [z(t_k - \tau), \, \ldots \, , z(t_k - (n_e - 1)\tau)]^T$$

of the map, where ξ_k denotes the coordinates at the kth piercing of the surface of cross-section of the map, by the orbit of the vector $z_x(t)$, and t_k is the time instant at the kth piercing. It is then a straightforward process to locate the periodic orbits from $\{\xi_k\}$. The stable and unstable eigenvalues and manifolds of the surface of cross-section, at the chosen equilibrium of the map, may all be experimentally determined. Slightly varying a system parameter of interest, say p, and then observing how the desired equilibrium changes its position, one can also estimate the partial derivative of the map with respect to p.

It should be noted that both the delay time $\tau > 0$ and the embedding dimension n_e are very important in using the delay-coordinates technique to reconstruct a faithful dynamical model from time-series data [11].

A reasonable method of choosing a good value of τ, which has its root in statistical analysis, is to keep the coordinates more time independent. In other words, τ must be chosen to result in new points that are not correlated to previously generated points. Thus, a first choice of τ should be in terms of the decorrelation time of the time series in question. The decorrelation time may be defined via a straightforward procedure, by considering the decorrelation time equal to the lag time at which the autocorrelation function first attains the value zero. There are choices regarding the lag at which the autocorrelation function attains a certain value, such as 0.5 or 0.1, etc. Another suggestion is to use $\tau = t_p/n$, where $t_p > 0$ is the dominant period (revealed by Fourier analysis) and n is a chosen embedding dimension. A more sophisticated choice for $\$ \tau$ gives a criterion of more general independence. This is measured as the information in bits gained about $x(t + \tau)$ from the given time series $x(t)$. On the average, this is the mutual information function, and its first minimum can be a good estimate for τ. The mutual information method is a comprehensive method for determining a proper delay time. The main problem associated with this method is that it requires a large amount of data and is often computationally cumbersome [11].

According to the basic theory of embedology, if the chosen embedding dimension satisfies $n \geq 2n_e + 1$, then one can reconstruct a topologically equivalent trajectory in the state space form using a single, scalar time series [11]. But it is generally not true that a larger n yields a better reconstructed result in the state space. Since the reconstructed state space is used for identifying the unknown system, it is reasonable to believe that a suitable n must be the one that minimizes the total error between the identified model and the original system, for a suitably defined matching error criterion.

An alternative approach, which is applicable to most systems, uses the "correlation dimension" of the attractor [11], to be discussed in the next section. The computation of the correlation dimension starts from *the correlation function*

$$C(r) = \frac{1}{m(m-1)} \sum_{i,j=1}^{m} \theta(r - |x_i - x_j|), \tag{2.111}$$

where r is a real number, $\{x_i\}_{i=1}^{m}$ is the time series used, and $\theta(\rho)$ is the Heaviside step function defined by $\theta(\rho) = 1$ for $\rho \geq 0$ but $= 0$ for $\rho < 0$. From the correlation function, one can estimate the dimension of a chaotic attractor, discussed in the next section, by using the formula [11]

$$D = \lim_{r \to \infty} \frac{\ln C(r)}{\ln r}. \tag{2.112}$$

If the time delay τ and the embedding dimension n_e are known, the correlation dimension can be calculated. But, in general, the embedding dimension is still unknown, so $C(r)$ has to be computed for different values of m. It is known that the rate of $\ln C(r)/\ln r$ approaches a constant as $m \to \infty$.

2.3.3   Chaos in Nonlinear Systems

Nonlinear systems have various complex behaviors that have never been anticipated in the linear case. Before engaging in more serious discussion about chaos control, it is necessary to put chaos into perspective. While analytical and control tools for linear systems have been well established, nonlinear science is still mostly in the developing phase. As a result, nonlinear science appears to be rather difficult to divide into proper subfields. A simple fact is that, on rare occasions, a nonlinear system can be solved analytically. Moreover, the richness and complexity of the dynamics of nonlinear systems, in contrast to that of linear systems, can only augment the already daunting challenge. Chaos is just one of several closely related prominent complex behaviors of nonlinear dynamical systems.

2.3.3.1 What is Chaos?

There is no universally agreed definition of *chaos* in the current literature. Among a few definitions given in mathematical terms are two slightly different but well accepted ones, given respectively by Li and Yorke [12] and Devaney [13]. The first one formally initiates the use of the name "chaos" in the modern scientific and engineering literature, while the second is perhaps better known. The second definition states that a map, $M : S \to S$, where S is generally a compact and invariant set (under M) in R^n, is said to be *chaotic* if [13]:

1. M is *transitive* on S, in the sense that for any pair of nonempty open sets U and V in S, there is an integer, $k > 0$, such that $M^k(U) \cap V$ is nonempty;
2. the periodic points of M are *dense* in S;
3. M has a *sensitive dependence on initial conditions*, namely, there is a real number, $\delta > 0$, depending only on M and S, such that, in every nonempty open subset of S, there are a pair of points whose eventual iterates under M are separated by a distance of at least δ.

It has been noted lately, however, that these three conditions are somewhat redundant, especially the second condition may be removed from the definition.

From a physical point of view, a special principal feature of chaos is that it has apparently random-like dynamical behavior but is deterministic in nature.

2.3.3.2 Features of Chaos

Many distinct features about chaos have been repeatedly observed and well analyzed.

Extreme Sensitivity to Initial Conditions
A hallmark of chaos is its fundamental property known as *extreme sensitivity* (of the system dynamics) to initial conditions, in the sense that two sets of similar initial conditions can give rise to two dramatically different asymptotic states of the system trajectory. This is the well-known "butterfly effect," a term from atmospheric studies, meaning that a single flap of a butterfly's wings may alter the initial conditions of a weather dynamical system, leading to significantly different weather patterns at a future time. Poincaré was aware of this phenomenon. He informally used the word "chaos" and said [14], "It may happen that small differences in the initial conditions produce very great ones in the final phenomena. A small error in the former will produce an enormous error in the latter. Prediction becomes impossible." Therefore, for a dynamical system to be chaotic it must have a (large) set of such "unstable" initial conditions that cause divergence. No matter how precisely these initial points are measured, prediction of the subsequent motions of the initiated trajectory becomes unreliable after a relatively long period of time. Hence, there is this notion of "predictable unpredictability" of chaos. Note that in this context, the term "initial condition" is usually understood as the condition that exists when a disturbance or measurement error is introduced, not necessarily at time zero.

It is important to realize that, being deterministic, a chaotic system is short-term predictable given near-perfect knowledge of the initial conditions. And, in practice, it is always predictable for short times within a certain allowable small tolerance. However, the key distinction here is the long-term unpredictability for chaotic systems due to their extremely sensitive dependence on initial conditions. The possibility of unpredictability for a deterministic system, although chaotic, once came as a shock to many mathematicians and physicists, who had been used to a notion attributed to Laplace that given precise knowledge of the initial conditions it should be possible to predict the future of the universe. Yet, this has become the key point that distinguishes chaotic systems from linear or regular deterministic nonlinear systems.

Positive Leading Lyapunov Exponents

Although sensitive dependence on initial conditions does not necessarily require exponential growth of perturbations, this often is the case for chaotic systems. This exponential growth is related to the existence of at least one positive Lyapunov exponent. Among the main characteristics of chaos, positive leading Lyapunov exponent is perhaps the most convenient one to verify in engineering applications. Roughly speaking, positive Lyapunov exponents measure the rate of divergence of nearby orbits; in particular, the positive leading Lyapunov exponent is the time average logarithmic growth rate of the maximal distance between two nearby orbits. This leading exponent is generally the most important one, among other exponents, that indicates the sensitive dependence of the trajectory on initial conditions.

For example, if $\{x_k\}$ is a trajectory of a discrete-time dynamical system starting from an initial state, x_0, and, if it travels exponentially fast, then approximately, $||x_k|| \sim ||x_0||e^{\lambda k}$, for a constant λ, called the *Lyapunov exponent*. Consequently, $\lambda < 0$ if the trajectory is attracted by some attractors (stable points, orbits, sets) but $\lambda > 0$ if it diverges, and vice versa. Here, $|| \cdot ||$ denotes the Euclidean norm of a finite-dimensional vector. Thus, the system is sensitive to a very small perturbation of the initial state if $\lambda > 0$. Note, however, that a positive leading Lyapunov exponent alone is generally not sufficient to signify chaos since it may simply produce an unbounded system trajectory, and yet if the trajectories are bounded then the system is likely chaotic.

Conceptually, Lyapunov exponents are generalization of eigenvalues for linear systems, and are defined based on the multiplicative ergodic theorem [15]. To compute Lyapunov exponents, one can simply start with any two nearby points belonging to a system trajectory, and then evolve them in time, while measuring the growth rate of the distance between them. This is particularly useful when one has a time series rather than an analytic model. The problem is that the growth rate so obtained is really not a local effect as the two evolved trajectories separate in time. Another approach is to measure the growth rate of vectors tangent to the trajectory, which normally requires an accurate mathematical model for the underlying dynamical system.

To introduce the second method [8], consider a one-dimensional discrete-time dynamical system described by a smooth map,

$$x_{k+1} = F(x_k)$$

with two nearby initial positions, x_0 and y_0, in the phase space (with coordinates x_k-x_{k-1}). Let $x_k = f(x_{k-1}) = \cdots = f^k(x_0)$, and similarly, $y_k = f^k(y_0)$. If these positions, x_k and y_k, are separated exponentially fast in iterations, then

$$|y_k - x_k| = |y_0 - x_0|e^{\lambda k},$$

where $\lambda > 0$, and so

$$\frac{1}{k} \ln \frac{|y_k - x_k|}{|y_0 - x_0|} \to \lambda \quad (\text{as } k \to \infty).$$

In the case where the trajectory motion is within a bounded region, this phenomenon of exponential separation cannot occur unless the two initial positions are extremely close to each other. Thus, by letting $|y_0 - x_0| \to 0$ before taking the limit $k \to \infty$, a constant is induced:

$$\lambda = \lim_{k \to \infty} \frac{1}{k} \lim_{|y_0 - x_0| \to 0} \ln \left| \frac{y_k - x_k}{y_0 - x_0} \right|$$

$$= \lim_{k \to \infty} \frac{1}{k} \lim_{|y_0 - x_0| \to 0} \ln \left| \frac{f^k(y_0) - f^k(x_0)}{y_0 - x_0} \right|$$

$$= \lim_{k \to \infty} \frac{1}{k} \lim_{|y_0 - x_o| \to 0} \ln \left| \frac{d^k (x_0)}{dx_0} \right|$$

$$= \lim_{k \to \infty} \frac{1}{k} \sum_{i=1}^{k-1} \ln \left| \frac{df (x_i)}{dx_i} \right|. \tag{2.113}$$

This is the *Lyapunov exponent* of the trajectory $x_k = f^k(x_0)$, or, of the map f, starting from (hence, depending on) x_0.

For an n-dimensional, discrete-time dynamical system described by a smooth map, f, the ith Lyapunov exponent of the orbit $\{x_k\}_{k=0}^{\infty}$ is numbered in decreasing order of magnitude. This exponent, generated by the iterations of the map starting from any initial state x_0, is computed by

$$\lambda_i(x_0) = \lim_{k \to \infty} \frac{1}{k} \ln |\mu_i(J_k(x_k) \cdots J_1(x_1))|,$$

where $J_i = f'(x_i)$ is the Jacobian, $\mu_i(\cdot)$ denotes the ith eigenvalue of the matrix (numbered in decreasing order of magnitude), $i = 1, \ldots, n$; or

$$\lambda_i(x_0) = \lim_{k \to \infty} \frac{1}{2k} \ln |\mu_i(T_k^T T_k)|, \tag{2.114}$$

where $T_k = J_k(x_k) \cdots J_1(x_1)$ and $i = 1, \ldots, n$, which can guarantee the symmetry of the matrices therefore the realness of the eigenvalues in numerical computations.

In the continuous-time case, $\dot{x} = f(x)$, the largest Lyapunov exponent is defined by

$$\lambda(x_0) = \lim_{t \to \infty} \frac{1}{t} \ln ||z(t; x_0)||, \tag{2.115}$$

where $z = z(t; x_0)$ is the solution of

$$\dot{z} = J(z)z, \quad z(t_0) = x_0,$$

in which $J(\cdot) = f'(\cdot)$ is the Jacobian matrix.

Clearly, Lyapunov exponents are generalization of regular eigenvalues of linear time-invariant systems, and sensitively depend on the initial state of the system.

Lyapunov exponents provide a measure for the mean convergence or divergence rate of neighboring trajectories of a dynamical system. For an n-dimensional continuous-time system, depending on the direction (but not the position) of the initial state vector, the n Lyapunov exponents, $\lambda_1 \geq \cdots \geq \lambda_n$, describe different types of attractors [3]. For nonchaotic attractors (limit sets):

$$\lambda_i < 0, \qquad i = 1, \ldots, n \qquad \Rightarrow \qquad \text{stable equilibrium}$$
$$\lambda_1 = 0; \lambda_i < 0, \qquad i = 2, \ldots, n \qquad \Rightarrow \qquad \text{stable limit cycles}$$
$$\lambda_1 = \lambda_2 = 0; \lambda_i < 0, \qquad i = 3, \ldots, n \qquad \Rightarrow \qquad \text{stable two-torus}$$
$$\lambda_1 = \cdots = \lambda_m = 0; \lambda_i < 0, \quad i = m+1, \ldots, n \quad \Rightarrow \qquad \text{stable m-torus}$$

Here, a two-torus is a donut-shaped surface in three-dimensional space; an m-torus is its geometrical generalization in $(m + 1)$-dimensional space.

For a three-dimensional continuous-time dynamical system, the only possibility for chaos to exist is that the Lyapunov exponents of the system are

$$(+, 0, -) := (\lambda_1 > 0, \lambda_2 = 0, \lambda_3 < 0) \quad \text{and} \quad \lambda_3 < -\lambda_1.$$

Intuitively, this means that the trajectory of the system, in the phase space, expands in a certain direction but shrinks in another direction, yielding many complex (stretching and folding) dynamical phenomena within a compact (bounded) region.

For four-dimensional continuous-time systems, there are three possibilities for chaos to occur:

1. $(+, 0, -, -)$: $\lambda_1 > 0, \lambda_2 = 0, \lambda_4 \leq \lambda_3 < 0$
2. $(+, +, 0, -)$: $\lambda_1 \geq \lambda_2 > 0, \lambda_3 = 0, \lambda_4 < 0$
3. $(+, 0, 0, -)$: $\lambda_1 > 0, \lambda_2 = \lambda_3 = 0, \lambda_4 < 0$.

The discrete-time case is different, however. A simple example is the one-dimensional *logistic map*

$$x_{k+1} = 4px_k(1 - x_k), \quad 0 < p \leq 1, \quad x_0 \in (0, 1). \tag{2.116}$$

This map is chaotic but has only one positive Lyapunov exponent.

As mentioned above, for a map to be chaotic, having a positive Lyapunov exponent is only necessary but not sufficient: if the expanding orbit does not remain bounded in the phase space, it will diverge out to infinity and, hence, will never be able to produce chaos. There must be a stretching and folding mechanism within the system dynamics that is necessary to keep chaotic orbits in bound. An effective way to retain the boundedness of the trajectories of a map, which may help discover the existence of chaos, is to use *modular operations*. The mod-m operation, with a positive integer m, for a real number $r \geq 0$, is defined by

$$r \quad (\text{mod} \quad m) = c, \quad \text{if} \quad r = im + c,$$

where i is an integer and the residue $0 \leq c < m$. It can be verified that the chaotic logistic map

$$x_{k+1} = 4x_k(1 - x_k)$$

is actually equivalent to the *circle map*

$$x_{k+1} = 2x_k \quad (\text{mod} \ 1), \tag{2.117}$$

where $x_0 \in (0, 1)$, with $x_0 \neq 0.5$.

Simple Zero of the Melnikov Function

One theory that can be used to characterize chaos focuses on the saddle points of Poincaré maps of continuous flows in the phase space. Near such saddle points are the stable and unstable manifolds. The Melnikov function provides a measure of the distance between a stable and an unstable manifold. The Melnikov theory states that chaos is possible if these two manifolds intersect, which corresponds to that the Melnikov function has a simple zero.

The Melnikov function method is usually applied to conservative systems such as Hamiltonian systems. A system without energy dissipation (e.g., an idealized pendulum without friction) is a *conservative system*, while one with energy dissipation (e.g., a real pendulum with friction) is a *dissipative system*. A conservative system, when described by a map, has the property of *area preservation* or, *volume preservation* in higher-dimensional cases. This means that the map preserves the geometric area from domain to range. On the contrary, a dissipative map has the property of area or volume contraction. A *Hamiltonian system* usually refers to a conservative autonomous system in which the forces can be derived from an energy function. For a Hamiltonian system, when small nonlinearities are added to the linear part of the system, the regular motions of the original system, such as periodic oscillations, will continue to exist. This constitutes part of the *KAM theory*, named after Kolmogorov, Arnold, and Moser [7].

To introduce the Melnikov function [7], consider a nonlinear oscillator with small damping and force, described by

$$\begin{cases} \dot{p} = -\dfrac{\partial H}{\partial q} + \varepsilon f_1 \\[2mm] \dot{q} = \dfrac{\partial H}{\partial p} + \varepsilon f_2 \end{cases}, \tag{2.118}$$

where $f = [f_1(p,q,t), f_2(p,q,t)]^T$ with variables (p,q) and a small constant $\varepsilon > 0$. Also, $H = H(p,q) = E_K + E_P$ is the Hamilton function for the undamped, unforced oscillator (when $\varepsilon = 0$, in which E_K and E_P are the kinetic and potential energy of the system, respectively.

Suppose that the unperturbed (unforced) oscillator has a saddle point (e.g., the undamped inverse pendulum), and that f is periodic with phase frequency ω. If the forced motion is described in the three-dimensional phase space, $(p, q, \omega t)$, then the Melnikov function is defined by

$$M(d^*) = \int_{-\infty}^{\infty} [\nabla H(p^*, q^*)] f^* dt, \tag{2.119}$$

where $f^* = f(p^*, q^*, \omega t + d^*)$, $\nabla H = [\partial H/\partial p \, \partial H/\partial q]$, and (p^*, q^*) are the unperturbed homoclinic orbit solutions starting from the saddle point of the original Hamiltonian system. The variable d^* gives a measure of the distance between the stable and unstable manifolds near the saddle-node equilibrium. As mentioned above, for chaos to emerge, the Melnikov function must have a simple zero, i.e., $M(d^*) = 0$ at a single point, d^*.

2.3.4 Kolmogorov-Sinai Entropy

Another important characteristic of chaos and attractors is described by the Kolmogorov-Sinai (KS) entropy, based on Shannon's information theory [16].

To introduce the KS-entropy, first recall the *statistical entropy*:

$$E = -c \sum_k P_k \ln(P_k), \tag{2.120}$$

where c is a constant and P_k is the probability of the system state being at stage k. According to Shannon's information theory, this entropy, E, is a measure of the amount of information that is needed to determine the state of the system. Kolmogorov and Sinai used the same idea to define a measure for the intensity of a set of system states, which gives the mean loss of information on the state of a system when it evolves with time. This measure can also be used to characterize strange attractors and chaos.

To be more precise, let $x(t)$ be a trajectory of a dynamical system and partition its d-dimensional phase space into cells of a small volume, ε^d. Let $P_{k_0 \cdots k_i}$ be the joint probability that $x(t = 0)$ is in cell k_0, $x(t = t_s)$ is in cell $k_1, \ldots, x(t = it_s)$ is in cell k_i, where $t_s > 0$ is the sampling period. Then, according to Shannon, the information index

$$I_n := - \sum_{k_0, \ldots, k_n} P_{k_0 \cdots k_n} \ln(P_{k_0 \cdots k_n}) \tag{2.121}$$

is proportional to the information needed to determine the trajectory, if the probabilities are known. Thus, $I_{n+1} - I_n$ is the additional information needed to predict the next state if all the proceeding states are known. This difference is also the information lost during the process. The *Kolmogorov-Sinai entropy* is then defined to be

$$E_{KS} := \lim_{t_s \to \infty} \lim_{\varepsilon \to 0} \lim_{n \to \infty} \frac{1}{nt_s} \sum_{i=0}^{n-1} (I_{i+1} - I_i)$$

$$= \lim_{t_s \to \infty} \lim_{\varepsilon \to 0} \lim_{n \to \infty} \frac{1}{nt_s} \sum_{k_0, \ldots, k_{n-1}} P_{k_0 \cdots k_{n-1}} \ln(P_{k_0 \cdots k_{n-1}}). \tag{2.122}$$

This entropy, E_{KS}, quantifies degrees of *disorder*:

1. $E_{KS} = 0$ for regular attractors such as stable equilibria, limit cycles and tori;
2. $0 < E_{KS} < \infty$ for chaotic attractors;
3. $E_{KS} = \infty$ for totally random dynamics (which has no correlations in the phase space).

Therefore, E_{KS} can be used as a characteristic or measure of chaos.

There is a connection between the Lyapunov exponents and the KS-entropy, given by

$$E_{KS} \leq \sum_i \lambda_i^+, \tag{2.123}$$

where λ_i^+ are positive Lyapunov exponents of the same system [16].

2.3.5   Some Examples of Chaotic Systems

Chaos, as described above, is often associated with strange attractors or fractals, but there is no universally accepted and mathematically precise definition for it to date.

In addition to the aforementioned hallmarks of chaos: extreme sensitivity to initial conditions, existence of a dense set of unstable periodic orbits in its strange attractor, positive leading Lyapunov exponent, simple zero of Melnikov function, finite KS-entropy, etc., there are some other good criteria for chaotic characteristics, including the existence of a Smale horseshoe, positive topological entropy, continuous power spectrum and positive algorithmic complexity, ergodicity and mixing, and the statistical-oriented definition of Shilnikov.

Another note is regarding the minimum phase-space dimension required for chaos. A chaotic system must have at least one positive Lyapunov exponent. According to the Poincaré-Bendixson Theorem [7], a continuous-time autonomous system must have dimension three or higher to be able to display chaos. Discrete-time systems are quite different: the logistic map has only one positive Lyapunov exponent, but it can produce chaos.

The following are some representative examples of chaotic systems.

2.3.5.1   Continuous-Time Systems

Lorenz System
As an approximation (truncation) of a partial differential equation for fluid convection, where a flat fluid layer is heated from below and cooled from above, the Lorenz system is described by

$$\begin{cases} \dot{x} = a\,(y - x) \\ \dot{y} = bx - xz - y \\ \dot{z} = xy - cz \end{cases}, \tag{2.124}$$

where x represents the convective motion, and y and z the horizontal and vertical thermal variations, respectively. This is similar to the convection of the earth's atmosphere which is heated by the ground or ocean's absorption of sunlight and loses heat into space. The three positive parameters, a, b, and c, are proportional to the Prandtl number, the Rayleigh number, and the size of the region the behavior of which can be approximated by the model. When $a = 10.0$, $b = 28.0$, and $c = 8/3$, the system is chaotic, with the corresponding attractor shown in Figure 2.45.

The Lorenz system has the following basic properties:

1. It is a 3D autonomous system with only two quadratic nonlinear terms.
2. It has three equilibria: one saddle and two saddle-foci.
3. Its attractor is globally bounded.

Chen System
The Chen system is described by

$$\begin{cases} \dot{x} = a\,(y - x) \\ \dot{y} = (c - a)x - xz + cy \\ \dot{z} = xy - bz \end{cases}. \tag{2.125}$$

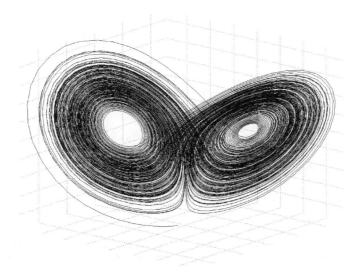

Figure 2.45 Chaotic attractor of the Lorenz system [8]. *Source:* Reprinted from Chen, G. and Dong, X. (1998) *From Chaos to Order: Methodologies, Perspectives and Applications.* World Scientific Pub. Co., Singapore. Copyright (1998) World Scientific Pub. Co.

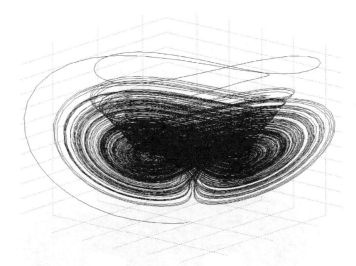

Figure 2.46 Chaotic attractor of the Chen system [18]. *Source:* Reprinted from Chen, G. and Dong, X. (1998) *From Chaos to Order: Methodologies, Perspectives and Applications.* World Scientific Pub. Co., Singapore. Copyright (1998) World Scientific Pub. Co.

When $a = 35$, $b = 3$ and $c = 28$, the system is chaotic, with the corresponding attractor shown in Figure 2.46.

The significance of the Chen system lies in its following:

1. It is a 3D autonomous system with only two quadratic nonlinear terms.
2. It has three equilibria: one saddle and two saddle-foci.
3. Its attractor is globally bounded.

4. It is nonequivalent to the Lorenz system.
5. It is *dual* to the Lorenz system in the sense of Celikovsky and Vanecek [17].
6. It has even more sophisticated dynamical behaviors than the Lorenz system, as can be realized by comparing their attractors.

More importantly, in between the Lorenz system and the Chen system, there are an infinite number of genetically-related chaotic systems, all of which constitute a family of one-parameter generalized Lorenz systems.

Lu System
The Lu system is described by

$$\begin{cases} \dot{x} = a\,(y - x) \\ \dot{y} = -xz + cy \\ \dot{z} = xy - bz \end{cases} . \tag{2.126}$$

When $a = 36$, $b = 3$ and $c = 20$, the Lu system is chaotic, with the attractor as shown in Figure 2.47.
The Lu system represents the transition in the duality between the Lorenz and the Chen systems.

Unified Chaotic System
The unified chaotic system encompasses both the Lorenz, the Lu and the Chen systems [20], which by nature is a convex combination of the Lorenz and Chen systems, and is described by

$$\begin{cases} \dot{x} = (25\alpha + 10)\,(y - x) \\ \dot{y} = (28 - 35\alpha)x - xz + (29\alpha - 1)y \\ \dot{z} = xy - (\alpha + 8)z/3 \end{cases} . \tag{2.127}$$

When $\alpha = 0$ it is the Lorenz system while with $\alpha = 1$ it is the Chen system, and moreover for any $\alpha \in (0, 1)$ the system remains to be chaotic, particularly when $\alpha = 0.8$ it is the Lu system.

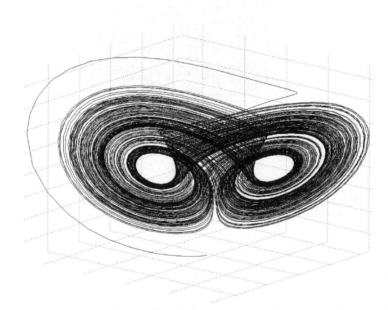

Figure 2.47 Chaotic attractor of the Lu system [19]. *Source:* Reprinted from Chen, G. and Dong, X. (1998) *From Chaos to Order: Methodologies, Perspectives and Applications.* World Scientific Pub. Co., Singapore. Copyright (1998) World Scientific Pub. Co.

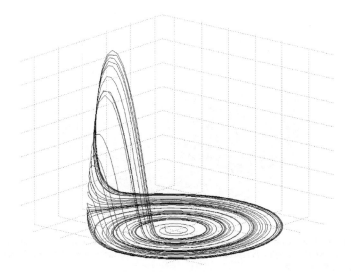

Figure 2.48 Chaotic attractor of the chaotic Rössler system [8]. *Source:* Reprinted from Chen, G. and Dong, X. (1998) *From Chaos to Order: Methodologies, Perspectives and Applications.* World Scientific Pub. Co., Singapore. Copyright (1998) World Scientific Pub. Co.

Rössler System
The Rössler system is simpler and is described by

$$\begin{cases} \dot{x} = -y - z \\ \dot{y} = x + ay \\ \dot{z} = b + z(x - c) \end{cases}, \tag{2.128}$$

where a, b, and c are real parameters. With $a = 0.15$, $b = 0.20$, and $c = 10.0$, the chaotic attractor is shown in Figure 2.48.

Duffing Oscillator
The forced and damped system

$$\ddot{x} + p_1\dot{x} + p_2x + p_3x^3 = q\cos(\omega t).$$

This represents a mass-damper-spring system with a hardening spring, where ω is a constant frequency, and other system parameters $p_1, p_3, q > 0$, but usually $p_2 < 0$. This equation describes the motion of a forced oscillator, such as a buckled beam undergoing forced lateral vibrations, when $p_1 < 0$, and the behavior of a charged particle in a periodic field, when $p_1 > 0$. This forced oscillator can be rewritten as

$$\begin{cases} \dot{x} = y \\ \dot{y} = -p_2x - p_3x^3 - p_1y + q\cos(\omega t) \end{cases}, \tag{2.129}$$

which produces some typical periodic and chaotic trajectories in the x-y phase plane: when $p_1 = 0.4$, $p_2 = -1.1, p_3 = 1.0$, $\omega = 1.8$, and $q = 1.800$ (chaotic orbit), as shown in Figure 2.49.

van der Pol Oscillator
The van der Pol oscillator is described by

$$\begin{cases} \dot{x} = x - (1/3)x^3 - y + p + q\cos(\omega t) \\ \dot{y} = c(x + a - by) \end{cases}, \tag{2.130}$$

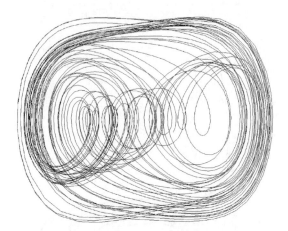

Figure 2.49 Chaotic attractor of the Duffing oscillator [8]. *Source:* Reprinted from Chen, G. and Dong, X. (1998) *From Chaos to Order: Methodologies, Perspectives and Applications.* World Scientific Pub. Co., Singapore. Copyright (1998) World Scientific Pub. Co.

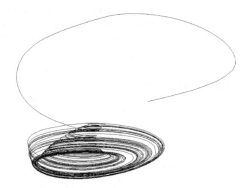

Figure 2.50 Chaotic attractor of the van der Pol oscillator [8]. *Source:* Reprinted from Chen, G. and Dong, X. (1998) *From Chaos to Order: Methodologies, Perspectives and Applications.* World Scientific Pub. Co., Singapore. Copyright (1998) World Scientific Pub. Co.

which is chaotic for a typical set of constants, $\omega = 1.0$, $a = 0.7$, $b = 0.8$, $c = 0.1$ and suitable parameters of p and q, such as $p = 0$ and $q = 0.74$, with a chaotic attractor as shown in Figure 2.50.

Chua's Circuit
Chua's circuit, shown in Figure 2.51, consists of one inductor L, two capacitors C_1, C_2, one linear resistor R, and one piecewise-linear resistor $g(\cdot)$. It possesses many different kinds of nonlinear dynamics, including bifurcations and chaos (double scroll, dual double scroll, double hook, etc.) [8].

The dynamical equation of Chua's circuit is described by

$$\begin{cases} \dot{x} = p\,(-x + y - f\,(x)) \\ \dot{y} = x - y + z \\ \dot{z} = -qy \end{cases}, \qquad (2.131a)$$

where $x(t) = v_{C_1}(t)$, $y(t) = v_{C_2}(t)$, $z(t) = Ri_L(t)$, $p = C_2/C_1 > 0$, $q = C_2R/L > 0$, $f(x) = Rg(v_{C_1}(t))$,
with

$$g(v_{C_1}) = m_0 v_{C_1} + (m_1 - m_0)(|v_{C_1} + 1| - |v_{C_1} - 1|)/2, \qquad (2.131b)$$

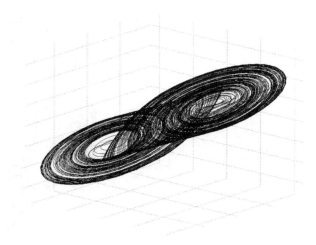

Figure 2.51 Chaotic trajectories of Chua's circuit [8]. *Source:* Reprinted from Chen, G. and Dong, X. (1998) *From Chaos to Order: Methodologies, Perspectives and Applications*. World Scientific Pub. Co., Singapore. Copyright (1998) World Scientific Pub. Co.

in which i_L is the current through the inductor L, v_{C_1} and v_{C_2} are the voltages across C_1 and C_2, respectively, with $m_0 < 0$ and $m_1 < 0$ being some appropriately chosen constants.

Chua's circuit can generate a double-scroll chaotic attractor, with $p = 15.6$, $q = 28$, $m_0 = -1.143$, and $m_1 = -0.714$, as shown in Figure 2.51. In the figures, the two equilibria inside the two scrolls are unstable.

2.3.5.2   Discrete-Time Systems

Logistic Map

The logistic map is described by (2.116), namely,

$$x_{k+1} = px_k(1 - x_k),\tag{2.132}$$

where $p > 0$ is a variable parameter. One of the early applications of this map is in biology as a model of population dynamics, in which x_k is the relative number of individuals of the kth generation [8].

As parameter p increases, $p_1 = 3.544090 \ldots$ to $p_2 = 3.568759 \ldots$ to $p_3 = 3.569891 \ldots$, and so on, a sequence of period-doubling bifurcations occur, leading to chaos, as shown in Figure 2.52. It is also interesting to note that the ratio $(p_{k+1} - p_k)/(p_{k+2} - P_{k+1}) \rightarrow 4.6692 \ldots$ as $k \rightarrow \infty$, which is universal, called a *Feigenbaum constant* [11].

Hénon Map

The Hénon map is given by

$$\begin{cases} x_{k+1} = -px_k^2 + y_k + 1 \\ y_{k+1} = qx_k \end{cases},\tag{2.133}$$

with real parameters p and q. When $p = 1.4$ and $q = 0.3$, the Hénon map has a chaotic attractor, as shown in Figure 2.53. The Hénon map confirms the universal Feigenbaum constant $4.6692 \ldots$ [11].

Lozi Map

The Lozi map, in some sense, is a simplified version of the Hénon map, and is described by

$$\begin{cases} x_{k+1} = -p|x_k| + y_k + 1 \\ y_{k+1} = qx_k \end{cases},\tag{2.134}$$

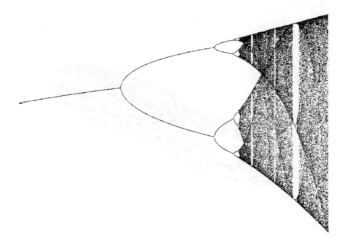

Figure 2.52   Period-doubling bifurcations leading to chaos in Logistic map [8]. *Source:* Reprinted from Chen, G. and Dong, X. (1998) *From Chaos to Order: Methodologies, Perspectives and Applications.* World Scientific Pub. Co., Singapore. Copyright (1998) World Scientific Pub. Co.

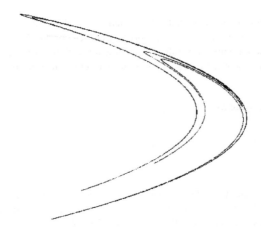

Figure 2.53   The chaotic attractor of the Hénon map [8]. *Source:* Reprinted from Chen, G. and Dong, X. (1998) *From Chaos to Order: Methodologies, Perspectives and Applications.* World Scientific Pub. Co., Singapore. Copyright (1998) World Scientific Pub. Co.

where p and q are real parameters.

As simple as it is, Lozi system is rife with chaotic phenomena. The determinant of the system Jacobian matrix, J, when evaluated at one of its equilibria, is $|J| = -q$. This implies that the dynamical behavior of the system depends sensitively on the parameter q. By varying the value of q, various patterns of a chaotic attractor' can be observed; a typical one is shown in Figure 2.54, where $p = 1.7$ and $q = 0.5$.

Arnold's Cat Map

Arnold's cat map is described by

$$\begin{cases} x_{k+1} = x_k + y_k \quad (\text{mod } 1) \\ y_{k+1} = x_k + 2y_k \quad (\text{mod } 1) \end{cases}, \tag{2.135}$$

which is defined on the two-torus (Figure 2.55).

The cat map has a special property – mixing – as the map is iterated it eventually spreads over the entire torus just like a drop of ink homogeneously distributed throughout a glass of water after being

Figure 2.54 The chaotic attractor of the Lozi map [8]. *Source*: Reprinted from Chen, G. and Dong, X. (1998) *From Chaos to Order: Methodologies, Perspectives and Applications*. World Scientific Pub. Co., Singapore. Copyright (1998) World Scientific Pub. Co.

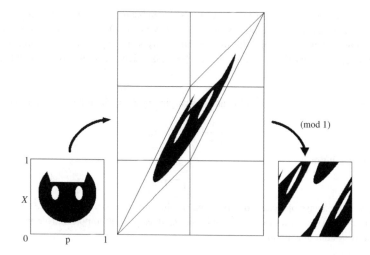

Figure 2.55 Arnold's cat map [8]. *Source*: Reprinted from Chen, G. and Dong, X. (1998) *From Chaos to Order: Methodologies, Perspectives and Applications*. World Scientific Pub. Co., Singapore. Copyright (1998) World Scientific Pub. Co.

stirred. In mathematical terms, *mixing* is defined as the situation where correlation functions decay to zero as $k \to \infty$.

2.3.6   Stabilities of Nonlinear Systems

Stability theory plays a central role in system engineering, with regard to both dynamics and control. Conceptually, there are various kinds of stabilities. For example, the concept of *bounded-input bounded-output stability* (or, *BIBO stability*), refers to the property of a system that any bounded input to the system produces a bounded output (through the system). However, since the stability of a system with respect to its equilibria and the structural stability of the system output trajectory are the main concerns in this book, only Lyapunov stabilities and the orbital stability are briefly introduced in this section [21].

2.3.6.1   Lyapunov Stabilities

Because the system parameters do not alter the concept of stabilities, they are dropped here for notational brevity.

Consider the general nonautonomous system

$$\dot{x} = f(x, t). \tag{2.136}$$

Without loss of generality, suppose that origin $x = 0$ is one of the system equilibria of interest. Lyapunov stability theory concerns various stabilities of this equilibrium of the system. Note that the autonomous system is a special case of the nonautonomous counterpart, especially regarding the notion of various stabilities.

Stability in the Sense of Lyapunov

The equilibrium, $x^* = 0$, of system (2.136) is said to be *stable in the sense of Lyapunov*, if for any $\varepsilon > 0$ and any initial time $t_0 \geq 0$, there exists a constant, $\delta = \delta(\varepsilon, t_0) > 0$, such that

$$\|x(t_0)\| < \delta \quad \Rightarrow \quad \|x(t)\| < \varepsilon \tag{2.137}$$

It should be emphasized that the constant δ generally depends on both ε and t_0. It is particularly important to point out that, unlike autonomous systems, one cannot simply assume the initial time $t_0 = 0$ for a nonautonomous system in a general discussion. The above stability is said to be *uniform*, with respect to the initial time, if this existing constant, $\delta = \delta(\varepsilon) > 0$, is independent of t_0 over the entire time interval $[0, \infty)$.

Example 2.19 Consider the following linear time-varying system with a discontinuous coefficient:

$$\dot{x}(t) = \frac{1}{1-t} x(t), \quad x(t_0) = x_0.$$

It has an explicit solution

$$x(t) = \frac{1-t_0}{1-t} x_0,$$

which is stable in the sense of Lyapunov about the equilibrium $x^* = 0$ over the entire time domain $[0, 1)$ if and only if $t_0 = 1$. This shows that the initial time, t_0, does play an important role in the stability of a nonautonomous system in general.

Asymptotic and Exponential Stabilities

The equilibrium, $x^* = 0$, of system (2.136) is said to be *asymptotically stable*, if it is stable in the sense of Lyapunov and, moreover, there exists a constant, $\delta = \delta(t_0) > 0$, such that

$$\|x(t_0)\| < \delta \quad \Rightarrow \quad \|x(t)\| \to 0. \tag{2.138}$$

This asymptotic stability is said to be *uniform*, if the existing constant δ is independent of t_0 over $[0, \infty)$, and is said to be *global*, if the convergence, $\|x(t)\| \to 0$, is independent of the starting point, $x(t_0)$, over the entire domain on which the system is defined (e.g., when $\delta = \infty$). If, furthermore,

$$\|x(t_0)\| < \delta \quad \Rightarrow \quad \|x(t)\| \leq ce^{-at} \tag{2.139}$$

for some constants $a, c > 0$, then the equilibrium is said to be *exponentially stable*. Clearly, exponential stability implies asymptotic stability, but the reverse need not be true.

Obviously, the concepts of (global) asymptotic stability are well defined for autonomous systems, while the latter is always uniform.

2.3.6.2 Orbital Stability

The orbital stability differs from Lyapunov stabilities in that it is concerned with the structural stability of a system orbit under perturbation.

Let $\varphi_t(x_0)$ be a periodic solution, of period $t_p > 0$, of the autonomous system

$$\dot{x} = f(x), \qquad x(t_0) = x_0 \tag{2.140}$$

and let Γ be the closed orbit of $\varphi_t(x_0)$ in the phase space, namely,

$$\Gamma = \{y | y = \varphi_t(x_0), \quad 0 \geq t < t_p\}.$$

If, for any $\varepsilon > 0$, there exists a $\delta = \delta(\varepsilon) > 0$ such that for any x_0 satisfying

$$d(x_0, \Gamma) := \inf_{y \in \Gamma} \|x_0 - y\| < \delta,$$

the solution $\varphi_t(x_0)$ of the system satisfies

$$d(\varphi_t(x_0), \Gamma) < \varepsilon, \qquad \text{for all } t \geq t_0,$$

then the t_p-periodic solution, $\varphi_t(x_0)$, is said to be *orbitally stable*. Furthermore, the concept of *asymptotical orbital stability* is defined by combining the two definitions of asymptotic stability and orbital stability.

Clearly, a periodic solution of (2.140) is never asymptotically stable by definition. Nevertheless, the following result can be established.

Theorem 2.28 (Andronov-Witt) *If the moduli of all multipliers (except one) of the periodic solution of this system are less than 1, then the trajectory of this periodic solution is asymptotically orbital stable.*

2.3.6.3 Lyapunov Stability Theorems

First, for the autonomous system (2.140), with a continuously differentiable function $f : D \to R^n$, the following criterion of stability is called the *first* (or *indirect*) *method of Lyapunov*. Let $J = [\partial f / \partial x]_{x=x^*=0}$ be the system Jacobian matrix evaluated at the zero equilibrium.

Theorem 2.29 (First method of Lyapunov) [for autonomous systems] *If all the eigenvalues of J have a negative real part, then the system (2.140) is asymptotically stable about $x^* = 0$.*

First, note that this and the following Lyapunov theorems apply to linear systems as well. Note also that the region of asymptotic stability given by the above theorem is local, which can be quite large for some nonlinear systems but may be very small for some others. However, there is no general criterion for determining the boundaries of such local stability regions when this and the following Lyapunov methods are applied.

Moreover, it is important to note that this theorem cannot be applied to a general nonautonomous system, since for general nonautonomous systems this theorem is either necessary nor sufficient.

Example 2.20 Consider the following linear time-varying system [21]:

$$\dot{x} = \begin{bmatrix} -1 + 1.5\cos^2(t) & 1 - 1.5 \sin(t) \cos(t) \\ -1 - 1.5 \sin(t) \cos(t) & -1 + 1.5\sin^2(t) \end{bmatrix} x(t).$$

This system has eigenvalues $\lambda_{1,2} = -1/4 \pm j\sqrt{7}/4$, both having negative real parts and being independent of the time variable t. If the above theorem is used to judge this system, the conclusion would be that the system is asymptotically stable about its equilibrium 0. However, the solution of this system is

$$x(t) = \begin{bmatrix} e^{t/2} \cos(t) & e^{-t} \sin(t) \\ -e^{t/2} \sin(t) & e^{-t} \cos(t) \end{bmatrix} \begin{bmatrix} x_1(t_0) \\ x_2(t_0) \end{bmatrix},$$

which is unstable, for any initial conditions with a bounded and nonzero value of $x_1(t_0)$, no matter how small this initial value is.

Next, introduce the concept of *class-K functions*:

$$K = \{g(t_0) = 0, \quad g(t) > 0 \quad for \quad t > t_0, \quad g(t) \text{ is continuous nondecreasing on } [t_0, \infty)\}.$$

Theorem 2.30 (Second method of Lyapunov) [for nonautonomous systems] *The system (2.136) is globally (over the entire domain D), uniformly (with respect to the initial time over the entire time interval $[t_0, \infty)$), and asymptotically stable about its zero equilibrium, if there exist a scalar-valued function, $V(x,t)$, defined on $D \times [t_0, \infty)$, and three functions $\alpha(\cdot), \beta(\cdot), \gamma(\cdot) \in K$, such that*

1. $V(0, t_0) = 0$;
2. $V(x,t) > 0$ *for all $x \neq 0$ in D and all $t \geq t_0$;*
3. $\alpha(\|x\|) \leq V(x,t) \leq \beta(\|x\|)$ *for all $t \geq t_0$;*
4. $\dot{V}(x,t) \leq -\gamma(\|x\|) < 0$ *for all $t \geq t_0$.*

In this theorem, the function V is called a *Lyapunov function*. The method of constructing a Lyapunov function for stability determination is called the *second* (or *direct*) *method of Lyapunov*.

Example 2.21 Consider the following nonautonomous system:

$$\dot{x} = Ax + g(x,t),$$

where A is a stable constant matrix and $g(\cdot, \cdot)$ is a nonlinear function satisfying both $g(0,t) = 0$ and $\|g(x,t)\| \leq c\|x\|$ for a constant $c > 0$ for all $t \geq t_0$. Since A is stable, the following matrix Lyapunov equation

$$PA + A^T P + I = 0$$

has a unique positive definite and symmetric matrix solution, P. Using the Lyapunov function $V(x) = x^T P x$, it can be verified that

$$\dot{V}(x,t) = x^T [PA + A^T P]x + 2x^T Pg(x,t) \leq -x^T x + 2\lambda_{\max}(P)c\|x\|^2,$$

where $\lambda_{\max}(P)$ is the largest eigenvalue of matrix P. So, if the constant $c < 1/(2\lambda_{\max}(P))$ and if the following class-K functions are used:

$$\alpha(\varsigma) = \lambda_{\max}(P)\varsigma^2, \quad \beta(\varsigma) = \lambda_{\max}(P)\varsigma^2, \quad \gamma(\varsigma) = [1 - 2c\lambda_{\max}(P)]\varsigma^2,$$

then conditions (3) and (4) of Theorem 2.30 are satisfied. As a result, the above system is globally, uniformly, and asymptotically stable about its zero equilibrium.

This example also shows that the linear part of a weakly nonlinear nonautonomous system can indeed dominate the stability.

Note that in Theorem 2.30, the uniform stability is guaranteed by the class-K functions α, β, γ stated in conditions (3) and (4), which is necessary since the solution of a nonautonomous system may sensitively depend on the initial time. For autonomous systems, these class-K functions (hence, condition (3)) are not needed. In this case, Theorem 2.30 reduces to the following simple form.

Theorem 2.31 (Second method of Lyapunov) [for autonomous systems] *The autonomous system (2.136) is globally (over the entire domain D) and asymptotically stable about its zero equilibrium, if there exists a scalar-valued function, $V(x)$, defined on D, such that*

1. $V(0) = 0$;
2. $V(x,t) > 0$ *for all $x \neq 0$ in D;*
3. $\dot{V}(x) < 0$ *for all $x \neq 0$ in D.*

Note that if condition (3) in the above theorem is replaced b

3. $\dot{V}(x) \leq 0$ for all $x \neq 0$ in D,

then the resulting stability is only in the sense of Lyapunov but may not be asymptotic.

Example 2.22 Consider a simple model of an undamped pendulum of length l described by

$$\begin{cases} \dot{x} = -(g/l)\sin(y) \\ \dot{y} = x \end{cases},$$

where $x = \theta$ is the angular variable defined on $-\pi < \theta < \pi$, with the vertical axis as its reference, and g is the gravity constant. Since the system Jacobian matrix at the zero equilibrium has a pair of purely imaginary eigenvalues, $\lambda_{1,2} = \pm\sqrt{-g/l}$, Theorem 2.30 is not applicable. However, if one uses the Lyapunov function

$$V = \frac{g}{l}(1 - \cos(y)) + \frac{1}{2}x^2,$$

then it can be easily verified that $\dot{V} = 0$ over the entire domain. Thus, the conclusion is that the undamped pendulum is stable in the sense of Lyapunov but not asymptotically, consistent with the physics of the undamped pendulum.

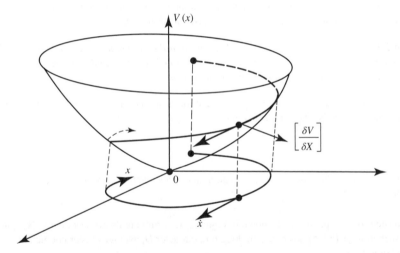

Figure 2.56 Geometric meaning of the Lyapunov function [21]. *Source:* Reprinted by permission of John Wiley & Sons Inc.

In Theorem 2.31, the geometric meaning of a Lyapunov function used for determining the system stability about the zero equilibrium may be illustrated by Figure 2.56. In this figure, assuming that a Lyapunov function, $V(x)$, has been found, which has a bowl-shape as shown based on conditions (1) and (2). Then, condition (3) is

$$\dot{V}(x) = \left[\frac{\partial V}{\partial x}\right]\dot{x} < 0,$$

where $[\partial V/\partial x]$ is the gradient of V along the trajectory $x(t)$. It is known, from Calculus, that if the inner product of this gradient and the tangent vector $\dot{x}$ is constantly negative, as guaranteed by condition (3) in Theorem 2.30, then the angle between these two vectors is larger than $90°$, so that the surface of $V(x)$ is monotonically decreasing to zero (this is visualized in Figure 2.56. Consequently, the system trajectory $x(t)$, the projection on the domain as shown in the figure, converges to zero as time evolves.

Now, consider again the autonomous system (2.136), and let $J = [\partial f / \partial x]_{x=x^*=0}$ be the system Jacobian matrix evaluated at the zero equilibrium.

Theorem 2.32 (Krasovskii) [for autonomous systems] *A sufficient condition for the autonomous system (2.136) to be asymptotically stable about its zero equilibrium is that there exist two real positive definite and symmetric constant matrices, P and Q, such that the linear matrix inequality (LMI)*

$$J^T(x)P + PJ(x) + Q \leq 0,$$

for all $x \neq 0$ in a neighborhood Ω of the origin. For this case, a Lyapunov function is given by

$$V(x) = f^T(x)Pf(x).$$

Furthermore, if $\Omega = R^n$ and $V(x) \to \infty$ as $\|x(t)\| \to \infty$, then this asymptotic stability is also global.

Finally, it is remarked that similar stability criteria can be established for discrete-time systems.

To this end, it is important to emphasize that all the Lyapunov theorems stated above only offer *sufficient* conditions for asymptotic stability. On the other hand, usually more than one Lyapunov function may be constructed for the same system.

For a given system, one choice of a Lyapunov function may yield a less conservative result (e.g., with a larger stability region) than other choices. However, no conclusion regarding stability may be drawn if, for technical reasons, a satisfactory Lyapunov function cannot be found. Nevertheless, there is a necessary condition in theory about the existence of a Lyapunov function [21].

Theorem 2.33 (Massera Inverse Theorem) *Suppose that the autonomous system (2.136) is asymptotically stable about its equilibrium x^* and $f(\cdot)$ is continuously differentiable with respect to $x(t)$ for all $t \in [0, \infty)$. Then a Lyapunov function exists for this system.*

Of course, how to find the existing Lyapunov function is another question, which usually depends on skillful techniques and also working experience.

Exercises

Note: An asterisk (*) following an exercise heading indicates that the exercise involves a problem that is more technically difficult.

2.1   Consider the simple network shown in Figure 2.57. Compute its average degree $\langle k \rangle$, joint degree distribution of $P(4, 5)$, average path length L, diameter D, average cluster coefficient C, coreness and closeness.

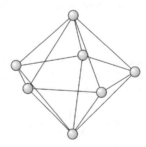

Figure 2.57   A simple graph. *Source*: Reprinted from Chen, G. and Dong, X. (1998) *From Chaos to Order: Methodologies, Perspectives and Applications*. World Scientific Pub. Co., Singapore. Copyright (1998) World Scientific Pub. Co.

2.2 Consider the simple networks shown in Figure 2.58 (a)–(f). Compute the average degree $\langle k \rangle$, average path length L, diameter D, average cluster coefficient C, coreness and closeness of each network.

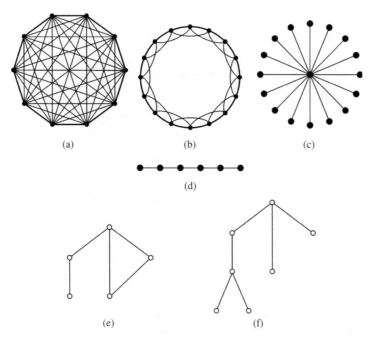

(a)	(b)	(c)

(d)

(e)   (f)

Figure 2.58 Simple examples of networks. *Source*: Reprinted from Chen, G. and Dong, X. (1998) *From Chaos to Order: Methodologies, Perspectives and Applications*. World Scientific Pub. Co., Singapore. Copyright (1998) World Scientific Pub. Co.

2.3 Consider the two networks shown in Figure 2.59 (a) and (b), respectively. Explain why the figure shown in (b), with only a few long-range edges, can gain a more prominent small-world feature than the one shown in (a).

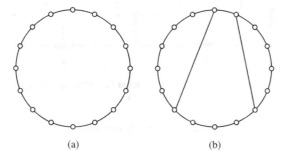

(a)   (b)

Figure 2.59 (a) Ring network; (b) small-world network. *Source*: Reprinted from Chen, G. and Dong, X. (1998) *From Chaos to Order: Methodologies, Perspectives and Applications*. World Scientific Pub. Co., Singapore. Copyright (1998) World Scientific Pub. Co.

2.4 Consider the following two questions:

   i. A network with a large clustering coefficient may have a long or a short average path length. Show (a) an example of a network with a *large* clustering coefficient (i.e., $C = 1$) and a *short* average path length (i.e., $L = 1$); (b) an example of a network with a relatively *large* clustering coefficient and also a relatively *long* average path length.

ii. A network with a small clustering coefficient may have a short or a long average path length. Show (a) an example of a network with a *small* clustering coefficient (i.e., $C = 0$) and a *short* average path length (i.e., $L = 1$); (b) an example of a network with a relatively *small* clustering coefficient and a relatively *long* average path length.

2.5 Walking through the graph shown in Figure 2.60, can one start from a certain node to go through all edges, once and once only, and finally return to the starting point? Why?

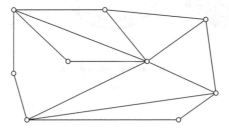

Figure 2.60 A simple graph. *Source*: Reprinted from Chen, G. and Dong, X. (1998) *From Chaos to Order: Methodologies, Perspectives and Applications*. World Scientific Pub. Co., Singapore. Copyright (1998) World Scientific Pub. Co.

2.6 In a laboratory shown by Figure 2.61, can you walk through every door once and once only, and finally return to the starting point? If so, how? If not, why?

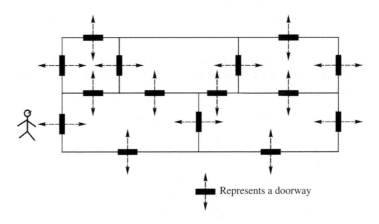

Represents a doorway

Figure 2.61 A lab with many doorways

2.7 A standard chessboard is shown in Figure 2.62 (a). Define a new "bishop-pawn" marked by a disc as shown in Figure 2.62 (b), which can move only "one step by one step" along the diagonal direction, as indicated in Figure 2.62 (b). Can this "bishop-pawn" start from a black block, somewhere on the chessboard, then move to visit every black block, once and once only, and finally return to the starting block? If so, how? If not, why?

2.8 Argue that Corollary 2.5 is correct.

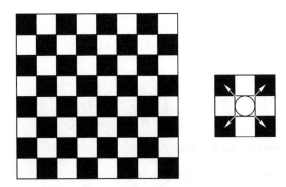

Figure 2.62   A new chessboard and game

2.9   Verify that the two graphs shown in Figure 2.63 have same node-degree sequence, average distance and node-betweenness. Are they isomorphic?

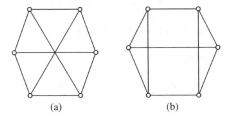

(a)   (b)

Figure 2.63   Two graphs. *Source*: Reprinted from Chen, G. and Dong, X. (1998) *From Chaos to Order: Methodologies, Perspectives and Applications*. World Scientific Pub. Co., Singapore. Copyright (1998) World Scientific Pub. Co.

2.10   Find the complementary graphs of the two graphs shown in Figure 2.63.

2.11   Can you find a disconnected graph such that its complementary graph is also disconnected? If so, show an example; if not, tell why.

2.12   Find the adjacency, incidence and Laplacian matrices of the graphs shown in Figure 2.63.

2.13   Consider the adjacency matrix, incidence matrix and Laplacian matrix of a given graph. If given any one of these three matrices, can you find the other two?

2.14*   Show that Laplacian matrix L has the following properties:
1. L is always semi-positive definite;
2. L has eigenvalues $\lambda_0 \leq \lambda_1 \leq \cdots \leq \lambda_n$, with $\lambda_0 = \cdots = \lambda_q = 0$ where q is the number of disjoint subgraphs in the graph; consequently, if the graph is connected, i.e., $q = 1$, then $0 = \lambda_0 < \lambda_1 \leq \cdots \leq \lambda_n$.

2.15*   Recall the clustering coefficient formula (2.9): $C_i = 2E_i/k_i(k_i - 1)$, where k_i is the degree of node i and E_i is the number of actual edges among the neighbors of node i. Recall also that the clustering coefficient of the whole network is the average of all such C_i over all i, namely $C = \sum_i C_i/N$. Verify that the number of edges among the neighbors of node i is equal to

$$E_i = \frac{1}{2}\sum_{jl} a_{ij}a_{jl}a_{li}$$

where $A = [a_{ij}]$ is the adjacency matrix of the network. Moreover, show that

$$C = \frac{1}{n} Trace\{A^3 \Delta\}$$

where matrix $\Delta = [\Delta_{ij}]$ is defined by

$$\Delta_{ij} = \begin{cases} \frac{\delta_{ij}}{k_i(k_i-1)} & if \quad k_i > 1 \\ 0 & otherwise \end{cases}$$

in which $\delta_{ij} = 1$ for $i = j$ and $\delta_{ij} = 0$ for $i \neq j$.

2.16 In the surface of the globe, use a node to represent a continent, so there are 7 nodes in total, labeled by A, B, C, D, E, F, G. Assume that there is an edge joining each pair of nodes, i.e., they are the nodes of a complete regular graph. Is this graph planar, and why? If so, draw an illustrative picture of this planar graph.

2.17 Verify Theorem 2.6 by an example of a graph with 3 components and 10 nodes, and by a tree with 10 nodes.

2.18 For an arbitrarily given graph of N nodes, what is the minimal number of edges you need to remove so that you can guarantee to obtain a new graph with at least 2 components? with at least 3 components? and, in general, with at least K $(2 \leq K \leq N)$ components?

2.19 Show all the cut sets in Figure 2.22 (b).

2.20 Distinguish Eulerian, semi-Eulerian and non-Eulerian graphs shown in Figure 2.64.

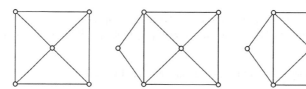

Figure 2.64 Distinguish the Eulerian, semi-Eulerian and non-Eulerian graphs

2.21 Show that if in a graph all nodes have degrees no less than 3 then this graph contains at least 2 circuits.

2.22 Argue that any two circuits are homeomorphic.

2.23 Based on the concept of homeomorphism, argue that Corollary 2.3 is perfectly correct.

2.24 Use the Fleury Algorithm (Corollary 2.4) to find a Eulerian trail in the Eulerian graph that you identified in Figure 2.64 in Exercise 2.20.

2.25 In 1856, the English mathematician William R. Hamilton studied a world navigation problem and considered a map with 20 nodes representing cities connected by sailing routes, as shown in Figure 2.65. He wanted to traverse through every city once and once only, and finally return to the starting city (His study eventually led to the establishment of the Hamiltonian graph theory). Can you find one solution too?

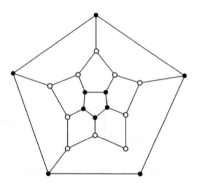

Figure 2.65   Hamiltonian world navigation problem

2.26   Are the graphs shown in Figure 2.66 Hamiltonian graphs?

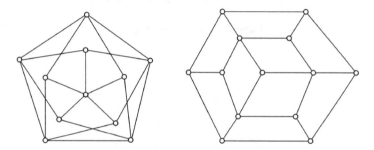

Figure 2.66   Two graphs

2.27   Are the following statements True or False? (To eliminate trivial cases, assume all networks have sizes $N > 3$.)
1. A fully-connected graph is Eulerian.
2. A fully-connected graph is Hamiltonian.
3. A bipartite network cannot be fully-connected.
4. A bipartite network cannot be a tree.

2.28   Verify that the two graphs shown in Figure 2.22 (a) and (b), namely, K_5 and $K_{3,3}$, are both nonplanar graphs. Then, show two more simple examples of nonplanar graphs.

2.29   Verify that the graph shown in Figure 2.67 corresponds to a polyhedron, and verify that the Euler polyhedron formula given in Theorem 2.11 holds for this graph.

2.30*   Verify that for any plane graph with N nodes, E edges, F faces and K components, it is always true that $N - E + F = K + 1$. [*Hint*: Apply Theorem 2.11 to each component separately, noticing that the infinite face should not be counted for more than once.]

2.31   Find all spanning trees in the graph shown in Figure 2.68.

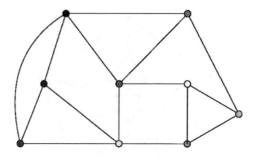

Figure 2.67   The polyhedral graph

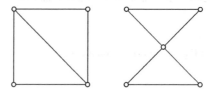

Figure 2.68   Find all spanning trees

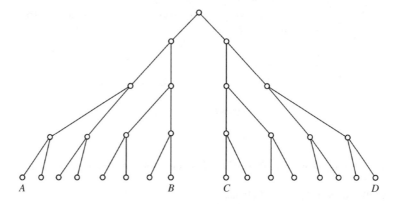

Figure 2.69   A binary-tree network

2.32 Are the following networks bipartite? Why?
1. a chain
2. a tree
3. a ring
4. a lattice
5. a star

2.33 The network shown in Figure 2.69 is called a *binary tree*.
   Starting from the top, there is $2^0 = 1$ node on the first layer, 2^1 nodes on the second layer, 2^2 nodes on the third layer, ... , 2^n nodes on the $(n + 1)$st layer. For a binary-tree network with m layers, (a) what is the total number of nodes in the network? (b) what is the total number of edges in the network?

In order to improve the overall robustness against various attacks on this binary-tree traffic network, you are allowed to add an edge either to connect node B with node C, or to connect node A with node D. Which connection is better, or they are the same, and why?

2.34 Apply the greedy algorithm (Theorem 2.21) to solve the minimum connector problem from point A to point B in the graph shown in Figure 2.70, where the numbers are costs.

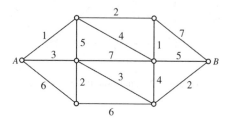

Figure 2.70   A minimum connector problem. *Source*: Reprinted from Chen, G. and Dong, X. (1998) *From Chaos to Order: Methodologies, Perspectives and Applications*. World Scientific Pub. Co., Singapore. Copyright (1998) World Scientific Pub. Co.

2.35 Consider a computer network in a lab, as shown by Figure 2.71, where each node is a computer (Router or PC) and the numbers indicate the lengths of optical fibers needed if the computers are connected.
  1. Design a best cost-effective Personal Area Network (PAN) by connecting all nodes together, so that every computer can communicate with every other one while the total optical fiber used is the shortest possible. Explain your steps, and what is the total length of optical fibers you need?
  2. Find the shortest path from computer A to computer B, which uses the shorter possible optical fiber. Show your reasoning.

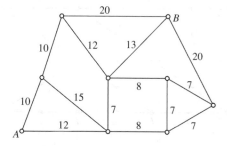

Figure 2.71   Computer network in a lab

2.36 Find a shortest path from A to G in Figure 2.72.

2.37 Find a solution of the Chinese postman problem for the postman route map shown in Figure 2.73.

2.38 Solve the maximum flow problem on the road map shown in Figure 2.74.

2.39 In an urn, there are N balls, in which M are red and the rest are blue, $1 \leq M \leq N$. Assume that one ball is drawn out of the urn at random, which is not put back to the urn, and then another ball is drawn out.
  1. What is the probability that the first ball was red?
  2. What is the probability that the two balls were both red?
  3. What is the probability that the first ball was red but the second was blue?

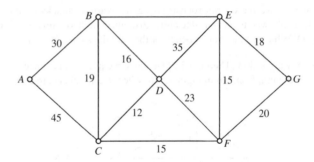

Figure 2.72   Find a shortest path length

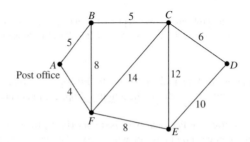

Figure 2.73   A Chinese postman problem

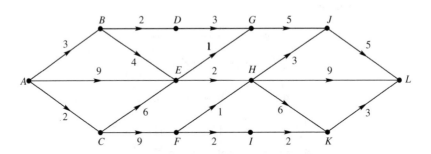

Figure 2.74   A maximum flow problem

2.40   Verify that $\int_{-\infty}^{\infty} y^2 e^{-y^2} dy = \sqrt{\pi}/2$.

2.41   Verify that two random variables with Gaussian distribution are independent if and only if they are uncorrelated.

2.42   Verify that for three events A, B, C, with positive probabilities,

$$P(A \cap B \cap C) = P(A)P(B|A)P(C|A \cap B)$$

2.43 Verify that for two events A and B occurring with positive probabilities, if $P(A|B) = P(A)$, then $P(B|A) = P(B)$.

2.44 Let X be a random variable uniformly distributed over a nontrivial interval $[c, d]$, and let $Y = aX + b$. For what choice of real constants a and b is Y uniformly distributed over $[0, 1]$?

2.45 Let X be a random event with probability p to occur, and denote $p_k = P(X = k)$, $k = 1, 2, \ldots$. Verify that $p_k = p^{k-1}(1 - p)$ and that $\sum_k p_k = 1$. Moreover, verify that $E(X) = 1/(1 - p)$.

2.46 Verify that for standard deviation: (i) $\sigma(X + c) = \sigma(X)$; (ii) $\sigma(cX) = |c|\sigma(X)$, where c is a constant.

2.47* Verify that the mean and variance of the Pareto probability distribution are given, respectively, by

$$E(X) = \frac{\alpha r}{\alpha - 1}, \text{ for } \alpha \leq 1 \quad \text{(or } \infty, \text{ otherwise)}$$

$$Var(X) = \frac{\alpha r^2}{(\alpha - 2)(\alpha - 1)^2}, \quad \text{for } \alpha > 2 \text{ (or } \infty, \text{ for } 1 < \alpha \leq 2; \text{otherwise undefined)}$$

2.48 Verify formulas (2.90) and (2.91).

2.49 Consider the Markov chain with transition matrix

$$P = \begin{pmatrix} 1/2 & 1/3 & 1/6 \\ 3/4 & 0 & 1/4 \\ 0 & 1 & 0 \end{pmatrix}$$

(a) Is this a regular Markov chain? Why?
(b) If the process starts from state 1, find the probability that it is in state 3 after 2 steps.
(c) Find the limiting probability vector w.

2.50 Is the Markov chain with the following transition matrix ergodic?

$$P = \begin{pmatrix} 1 & 0 & 0 \\ 1/2 & 1/2 & 0 \\ 0 & 1 & 0 \end{pmatrix}.$$

2.51 In system (2.103), suppose that an existing equilibrium, (x^*, y^*), is perturbed by increments $(\Delta x, \Delta y)$, and the nonlinear vector field, (f, g), is linearized at this equilibrium. Show that the approximate solutions for $(\Delta x, \Delta y)$ are given by

$$\begin{cases} \Delta x = c_1 e^{\lambda_1 t} + c_2 e^{\lambda_2 t} \\ \Delta y = c_3 e^{\lambda_1 t} + c_4 e^{\lambda_2 t} \end{cases},$$

where the constant coefficients, c_i, $i = 1, \ldots, 4$, are determined by the initial conditions of the system, and λ_1 and λ_2 are the eigenvalues of the system Jacobian

$$J = \begin{bmatrix} f_x & f_y \\ g_x & g_y \end{bmatrix},$$

with $f_x = \partial f/\partial x$ and $f_y = \partial f/\partial y$, etc., all evaluated at (x^*, y^*). Verify that

$$\lambda_{1,2} = \frac{1}{2}\left[trace\ (J) \pm \sqrt{D}\right],$$

where $trace\ (J) = f_x + g_y$, $D = [trace(J)]^2 - 4\det\ (J)$, and $\det\ (J) = f_x g_y - f_y g_x$.

2.52 Does the Grobman-Hartman Theorem (2.23) contradict the existence of chaos with an equilibrium point at the origin of a hyperbolic system? Explain why.

2.53 Figure 2.73 classifies inner limit cycle, outer limit cycle, stable limit cycle, unstable limit cycle, and saddle limit cycles on a plane. Can these concepts of different limit cycles be extended to the 3-dimensional space? Explain why and, if so, show how.

2.54 System (2.105) describes a dumped pendulum with a damping coefficient $p > 0$. Discuss the undamped pendulum with $p = 0$ therein (compare it with Example 2.0) and show its phase portrait (compare it with Figure 2.42).

2.55 Verify that the chaotic logistic map (2.116):

$$x_{k+1} = 4x_k(1 - x_k)$$

is actually equivalent to the circle map (2.117):

$$x_{k+1} = 2x_k \quad (\text{mod } 1),$$

where $x_0 \in (0, 1)$, with $x_0 \neq 0.5$.

2.56 Consider the damped pendulum

$$\begin{cases} \dot{x} = -(g/l)\sin(y) - (h/m)x \\ \dot{y} = x \end{cases},$$

where $x = \theta$ is the angular variable defined on $-\pi < \theta < \pi$, with the vertical axis as its reference, m is mass, h is the dumping coefficient and g is the gravity constant. Show that this pendulum is asymptotically stable about its equilibrium point $(0, 0)$.

References

[1] http://www-groups.dcs.st-andrews.ac.uk/history/Miscellaneous/Konigsberg.html (last accessed August 8, 2014).
[2] Wilson, R.J. (1985) *Introduction to Graph Theory*, 3rd edn. Longman House, England.
[3] Chui, C.K. and Chen, G.(2009) *Kalman Filtering with Real-Time Applications*. Springer, New York, 1st edn 1987; 4th edn 2009.
[4] Grinstead, C.M. (1997) *Introduction to Probability*. AMS, New York.
[5] Manoukian, E.B. (1986) *Modern Concepts and Theorems of Mathematical Statistics*. Springer-Verlag, New York.
[6] Moiola, J.L. and Chen, G. (1996) *Hopf Bifurcation Analysis: A Frequency Domain Approach*. World Scientific Pub. Co., Singapore.
[7] Wiggins, S. (1990) *Introduction to Applied Nonlinear Dynamical Systems and Chaos*. Springer-Verlag, New York.
[8] Chen, G. and Dong, X. (1998) *From Chaos to Order: Methodologies, Perspectives and Applications*. World Scientific Pub. Co., Singapore.
[9] Parker, T.S. and Chua, L.O. (1989) *Practical Numerical Algorithms for Chaotic Systems*. Springer-Verlag, New York.

[10] Guckenheimer, J. and Holmes, P. (1983) *Nonlinear Oscillations, Dynamical Systems, and Bifurcations of Vector Fields*. Springer-Verlag, New York.

[11] Sprott, J.C. (2004) *Chaos and Time-Series Analysis*. Oxford University Press, Oxford.

[12] Li, T.Y. and Yorke, J.A. (1975) Period three implies chaos, *American Mathematical Monthly*, **82**: 481–5.

[13] Devaney, R.L. (2003) *An Introduction to Chaotic Dynamical Systems*. Westview Press, |Boulder, CO.

[14] Crutchfield, J.P., Farmer, J.D., Packard, N.H. and Shaw, R.S. (1986) Chaos, *Scientific American*, **255**: 38–49.

[15] Boyarsky, A. and Góra, P. (1997) *Laws of Chaos: Invariant Measures and Dynamical Systems in One Dimension*. Birkhäuser, Boston.

[16] Dorfman, J.R. (1999) *An Introduction to Chaos in Nonequilibrium Statistical Mechanics*. Cambridge University Press, Cambridge.

[17] Čelikovský, S. and Vaněček, A. (1994) Bilinear systems and chaos, *Kybernetika*, **30**: 404–24.

[18] Chen, G. and Ueta, T. (1999) Yet another chaotic attractor, *International Journal of Bifurcation and Chaos*, **9**: 1465–6.

[19] Lu, J.H. and Chen, G. (2002) A new chaotic attractor coined, *International Journal of Bifurcation and Chaos*, **12**: 659–61.

[20] Lu, J.H., Chen, G., Cheng, D.Z. and Čelikovský, S. (2002) Bridge the gap between the Lorenz system and the Chen system, *International Journal of Bifurcation and Chaos*, **12**: 2917–26.

[21] Chen, G. (2004) Stability of nonlinear systems. In K Chang (ed.), *Encyclopedia of RF and Microwave Engineering*, John Wiley & Sons Inc., New York, pp. 4881–96.

3

Network Topologies: Basic Models and Properties

3.1 Introduction

In order to understand the relationships between the topology and dynamics of a complex network, it is necessary to study and comprehend the structural characteristics of real-world complex networks, thereby establishing appropriate mathematical network models. Since the discoveries of small-world networks by Watts and Strogatz [1] and scale-free networks by Barabási and Albert [2], many case studies on various real-world networks have been carried out and reported from different perspectives. Based on such insights and experiences, a number of new models of complex networks have been proposed, as summarized in [3–9]. This chapter introduces several basic network models, such as regular networks, random-graph networks, small-world networks, navigable networks, scale-free networks, hierarchical networks, and local-world evolving networks, and so on.

3.2 Regular Networks

The name regular network here does not necessarily refer to the mathematically defined concept of regular graph (Chapter 2). One of the most typical regular networks is a *fully-connected network* (complete graph). In such a network, between every pair of nodes there exists an edge connecting them together (Figure 3.1 (a)).

Theorem 3.1 *A fully-connected network has the average path length*

$$L_{full} = 1 \tag{3.1}$$

and the average clustering coefficient

$$C_{ful} = 1. \tag{3.2}$$

Also, a fully-connected network with N nodes has $N(N-1)/2$ edges. Moreover, the degree distribution of a fully-connected network is a discrete delta function.

Proof. They can be calculated directly based on the definitions. ∎

Note that among all networks with the same number of nodes, a fully-connected network has the shortest average path length, 1, and the largest clustering coefficient, 1.

Fundamentals of Complex Networks: Models, Structures and Dynamics, First Edition.
Guanrong Chen, Xiaofan Wang, Xiang Li.
© Higher Education Press. All rights reserved. Published 2015 by John Wiley & Sons Singapore Pte Ltd.
Companion Website: www.wiley.com/go/chen/complex

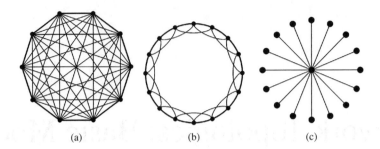

Figure 3.1 Some simple networks: (a) fully-connected network; (b) ring-shaped network; (c) star-shaped network

Note also that although fully-connected networks can describe the fact that many real-world networks possess high-clustering and small-world features, they are nevertheless too regular to be realistic. For example, a fully or almost fully-connected network with N nodes has the number of edges in the order of $O(N^2)$, but most real-world networks are known to be relatively sparse, with the number of edges only in the order of $O(N)$. A typical sparse regular network is a *nearest-neighbor coupled network*, where every node is connected to its nearest neighbors. In particular, such a network with a periodic boundary connectivity condition is a *ring-shaped network* (Figure 3.1 (b)).

Theorem 3.2 *Assume that in a large-scale ring-shaped network, with a large enough number N of nodes, if each node is connected to $2K$ nearest neighbors where $K > 0$ is an integer relatively small as compared to N, then the clustering coefficient can be asymptotically approximated by*

$$C_{ring} \approx \frac{3(K-1)}{2(2K-1)} \to \frac{3}{4} \ (K \to \infty). \tag{3.3}$$

Moreover, let M be the total number of edges of such a ring-shaped network. Then, the average path length can be asymptotically approximated by

$$L_{ring} \approx \frac{M(M+1) - 2(K-1)(M-K+1)}{2M} \to \infty \quad (M \to \infty). \tag{3.4}$$

Before giving a proof, it should be emphasized that formulas (3.3) and (3.4) are only asymptotic approximations, in the sense that the larger the K and M are, the more accurate the formulas are. The main reason is that when K becomes large (so that $2K$ is approaching N), the formula (3.3) becomes less accurate due to some multiple counting of common edges when such edges are connecting back towards the starting point along the circular path. Therefore, the formula is only a good approximation for relatively small N and relatively large K. Similarly, when K (hence, M) becomes large enough so that $2K$ (hence, M) is approaching N, the formula (3.4) becomes less accurate due to some multiple counting of common edges in the circular path; so the formula is only a good approximation for relatively large K (hence, relatively large M).

Proof. When $K = 1$, the resulting network is a ring, for which $C_{ring} = 0$. When $K = 2$, the resulting ring-shaped network is as shown in Figure 3.1 (b), from which it is also clear that $C_{ring} = \frac{1}{2}$, which verifies formula (3.3). Formula (3.3) can then be proved by mathematical induction.

To verify formula (3.4), first notice that when $K = 1$, namely, for a perfect ring, every node has the same average path length therefore one may only calculate a single node, denoted V_0, for its average path length in the ring, which is equal to the overall average path length: $L_{ring} = (1 + 2 + \cdots + M)/M$. Then, note that when $K > 1$, all distances to node V_0 are reduced by $K - 1$ each, except the $(K - 1)$ nearest-neighboring nodes of V_0; namely, the total reduction is $(K-1)(M-(K-1))$. Consequently, one has

$$L_{ring} = \frac{(1 + 2 + \cdots + M) - (K-1)(M-(K-1))}{M},$$

which is formula (3.4). ∎

Another typical regular network is the *star-shaped network*, which has a center, and all the other nodes are connected to, and only connected to the center (Figure 3.1 (c)).

Theorem 3.3 *For a star-shaped network of size N, counting the central node, the average path length is*

$$L_{star} = 2 - \frac{2}{N} \rightarrow 2 \quad (N \rightarrow \infty) \tag{3.5}$$

and the average clustering coefficient is

$$C_{star} = 0. \tag{3.6}$$

Proof. On one hand, regarding the total path length, first observe that the central node has a total path length $(N - 1)$. As to all the noncentral nodes, their total path length is equal to $(N - 1)(1 + 2(N - 2)) = (N - 1)(2N - 3)$. Thus, the total path length of the whole star-shaped network is given by $(N - 1) + (N - 1)(2N - 3)$.

On the other hand, regarding the total number of paths, notice that the central node has $(N - 1)$ paths. As to the noncentral nodes, each has $(1 + (N - 2))$ paths, giving a total of $(1 + (N - 2))(N - 1) = (N - 1)^2$ paths. Thus, there are $(N - 1) + (N - 1)^2 = N(N - 1)$ paths in total. As a result, one has

$$L_{star} = \frac{(N - 1) + (N - 1)(2N - 3)}{N(N - 1)} = 2 - \frac{2}{N}$$

Finally, it is obvious that $C_{star} = 0$. ∎

3.3   ER Random-Graph Model

The extreme opposite to the regular networks are completely random networks, where a typical model is the *random graph* introduced by Erdös and Rényi [9, 10].

An *ER random-graph network* is generated as follows:

1. Initialization: Start with N isolated nodes.
2. Pick up all possible pairs of nodes, once and once only, from the N given nodes, and connect each pair of nodes by an edge with probability $p \in (0, 1)$.

Statistically, the expectation of the number of edges of such a network is $pN(N - 1)/2$.

Generally, the larger the p is, the denser the resultant network will be, as illustrated by Figure 3.2. For $p = 0$, the initially isolate nodes remain to be isolated; for $p = 1$, one obtains a fully connected network.

Note that the above process of generating a random-graph network will not introduce multiple edges, nor self-loop at any single node; therefore the results are all simple graphs.

Note also that for different trials of the above generating algorithm with the same probability p, one obtains a somewhat different network due to the randomness of the connectivity probability p. Nevertheless, all resulting networks are similar in some sense (to be further explained later) and they share some common properties (to be further discussed below).

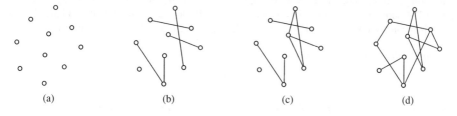

| (a) | (b) | (c) | (d) |

Figure 3.2   Some random graphs generated with different values of p: (a) $p = 0$; (b) $p = 0.1$; (c) $p = 0.15$; (d) $p = 0.25$

The main concern in studying ER random-graph networks has been the following: for what value(s) of p, will the resulting graph have certain specified properties? In the endeavor to search for answers, the most significant discovery of Erdös and Rényi is that many important properties of such random graphs *emerge* suddenly, in the sense that for a set of random graphs generated by a given probability p, either almost all these graphs possess a certain property P or almost all of them do not possess this property P. For instance, when p is larger than a certain threshold $p_c \sim \ln N/N$ (here and throughout the book, $a \sim b$ means "a is proportional to b" or "a is in the same order of b"), almost all random graphs generated by using this probability p in the above-described procedure will suddenly become connected, before which almost all such graphs were unconnected networks (i.e., had many pieces of isolated clusters).

ER random-graph networks have the following basic structural properties.

Theorem 3.4 *In an ER random-graph network, the average degree of nodes is*

$$\langle k \rangle_{ER} = p(N - 1) \approx pN, \tag{3.7}$$

the average path length is

$$L_{ER} \sim \ln N/\ln\langle k \rangle_{ER}, \tag{3.8}$$

and the average clustering coefficient is

$$C \approx \langle k \rangle_{ER}/N = p. \tag{3.9}$$

Proof. For any node, there are $N - 1$ other nodes for possible connections and each connecting edge has a probability p to appear; therefore, this node has a total of $p(N - 1)$ possible edges in expectation. On average each node has degree $\langle k \rangle_{ER}$, which is equal to the number of its edges, $p(N - 1)$. Usually, N is large so that $-p$ may be ignored. This is verified by formula (3.7).

For any node of degree $\langle k \rangle_{ER}$, the number of other nodes that it can connect to is $N_1 = \langle k \rangle_{ER}$. Then, moving forward from this node to the next one, the number of other nodes it can connect to in two steps will be $N_2 = \langle k \rangle_{ER} N_1 = \langle k \rangle_{ER}^2$, and so on. In general, $N_n = \langle k \rangle_{ER} N_{n-1} = \langle k \rangle_{ER}^n$, and this holds for every node in the network. On the other hand, the average distance between any pair of nodes is L_{ER}, therefore one can only go $n \sim L_{ER}$ steps forward from any node, and then has to stop. Consequently, the total number of nodes is equal to $N \sim \langle k \rangle_{ER}^{L_{ER}}$, which yields $L_{ER} \sim \ln N/\ln\langle k \rangle_{ER}$, which is (3.8).

To find the clustering coefficient of node i, notice that this node has $\binom{N-1}{2}$ different ways to pick two neighbors and with probability p connecting to each of them, therefore it has $p^2 \binom{N-1}{2}$ triangular graphs. On top of this, the probability that the two neighbors are connected to each other is p, which forms a complete triangle with node i. Consequently, the clustering coefficient defined by the geometric formula based on the ratio of complete triangles and triangular graphs is

$$C = p \cdot p^2 \binom{N-1}{2} \Big/ p^2 \binom{N-1}{2} = p = \langle k \rangle_{ER}/N,$$

which is (3.9), where the last equality comes from (3.7). ∎

It is a basic feature of the ER random-graph networks that they have relatively short average path length given by formula (3.8) in a logarithmic scale in the order of $O(\ln N)$. However, as seen from formula (3.9), the clustering coefficient of an ER random-graph network is fairly small: $C = p \approx \langle k \rangle_{ER}/N \ll 1$.

In the ER random graph theory, it has been proved that the degree distribution of a completely random network is a Poisson distribution [10]. Here, a simple heuristic proof is given for illustration.

Theorem 3.5 *The degree distribution of a random graph follows a Poisson distribution:*

$$P(k) = \frac{\mu^k}{k!} e^{-\mu}, \tag{3.10}$$

where μ is a constant parameter, referred to as the expectation value, $\mu = pN = \langle k \rangle_{ER}$.

Proof. First, notice that $P(k)$ is the probability that a randomly picked node happens to have degree k, which means that the node is connected to k other nodes in the network. Notice also that for a network of size N, there are $\binom{N-1}{k}$ different ways to pick k nodes from the rest $N-1$ nodes. Thus, the probability of a randomly picked node connecting to k other nodes (but not connecting to the rest $N-1-k$ nodes) is given by the binomial distribution

$$P(k|N') = \binom{N'}{k} p^k (1-p)^{N'-k},$$

where $N' := N-1$ and p is the probability that a pair of nodes is connected with an edge.

Now, introduce a parameter $\mu = N'p = \langle k \rangle_{ER}$ and fix it as a constant. Thus, viewing the above distribution as a function of μ, one can rewrite the distribution as

$$P_\mu(k|N') = \frac{N'!}{k!(N'-k)!} \left(\frac{\mu}{N'}\right)^k \left(1 - \frac{\mu}{N'}\right)^{N'-k}.$$

Consequently, as $N \to \infty$, one has $N' \to \infty$, so

$$
\begin{aligned}
P(k) &= \lim_{N' \to \infty} P_\mu(k|N') \\
&= \lim_{N' \to \infty} \frac{N'(N'-1)\cdots(N'-k+1)}{N'^k} \frac{\mu^k}{k!} \left(1 - \frac{\mu}{N'}\right)^{N'} \left(1 - \frac{\mu}{N'}\right)^{-k} \\
&= 1 \cdot \frac{\mu^k}{k!} \cdot e^{-\mu} \cdot 1.
\end{aligned}
$$

This completes the proof of the theorem. ∎

One illustrative example about the Poisson distribution of an ER random-graph network is shown in Figure 3.3 [11]. Clearly, the Poisson curve decays exponentially fast as k is moving away from the average value $\langle k \rangle$, which is the expectation value μ in the above Poisson distribution function, at which the function attains the maximum value. Similar to the above delta distribution, this implies that a node with a too-large or a too-small degree k can hardly be found, or actually does not exist in the network. In other words, in such a random network every node has about the same degree, at least in theory. This kind of network is referred to as a *homogeneous network*.

The classical ER random-graph network theory has already been applied, generalized and extended for better describing many real-world complex networks. For instance, for a given desirable node-degree

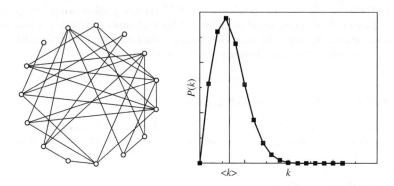

Figure 3.3 Illustration of ER random-graph networks. *Source*: Complex systems: analysis and models of real-world networks, in *Energy and Information Transfer in Biological Systems*. Crucitti, P., Latora, V., Marchiori, M., *et al.*, Copyright (2003) World Scientific Pub. Co.

distribution $P(k)$, which represents the proportion of nodes with degree k in the network, one can generate many degree sequences $\{k_i\}_{i=1}^n$, so as to obtain many networks with N nodes, in such a way that they all have the same node-degree distribution $P(k)$. The collection of all these networks is called a *configuration model*, useful for describing many real-world networks [7].

One of the most widely used configuration models was developed by Bender and Canfield in 1978 [12]. This configuration model is specified in terms of a degree sequence. More precisely, for a network of N nodes with a desired degree sequence $\{d_1, d_2, \ldots, d_N\}$, which specifies the degree d_i of node i, $i = 1, 2, \ldots, N$. For a given a degree distribution $P(d)$, one can generate the degree sequence for N nodes by sampling the degrees independently from the distribution $P(d)$, namely, $d_i \sim P(d)$. Thus, according to the law of large numbers (Chapter 2), the frequency of degrees $P^{(N)}(d) \to P(d)$ as $N \to \infty$.

3.4 Small-World Network Models

As mentioned above, a regular ring-shaped network has a large clustering coefficient and an ER random-graph network has a short average path length. Are there some kinds of networks that have both features of large clustering coefficients along with short average path lengths? The answer is *yes*, which are the so-called small-world networks discovered by Watts and Strogatz in 1998 [1], named WS small-world network model hereafter.

3.4.1 WS Small-World Network Model

A *WS small-world network* can be generated by the following algorithm (WS algorithm):

1. Start from a ring-shaped network with N nodes, in which each node is connected to its $2K$ neighbors, K nodes on each side, where $K > 0$ is a small integer.
2. For every pair of connected nodes in the ring-shaped network, rewire the edge in such a way that the beginning end of the edge is kept (i.e., this edge-end connection is unchanged) but the other end is disconnected with probability p and then reconnected it to a node randomly chosen from the network. This rewiring operation is performed edge by edge on the original ring-shaped network, once and once only, either clockwise or counterclockwise.

Here, at Step 2, the random rewiring operations follow a uniform distribution in the sense that every node has an equal probability to be picked, and self-loops and multiple edges are avoided (ignored).

Clearly, Step 2 will introduce some long-range connections, which are important as further discussed later. In the above algorithm, the case of $p = 0$ corresponds to a regular network (the original ring-shaped network) while the case of $p = 1$ corresponds to a kind of ER random-graph networks, except that it starts with a ring-shaped network as the initial condition and the total number of edges has been determined beforehand on the ring. By tuning the value of p, one can obtain a transition from a completely regular network to a random-like network, as illustrated by Figure 3.4 (a).

3.4.2 NW Small-World Network Model

Notice that the above WS algorithm may destroy the network connectivity during the rewiring process, yielding possibly some unconnected clusters (subnetworks). As a remedy, Newman and Watts [3] slightly modified the above algorithm, by replacing "random rewiring edges" with "random adding edges," as illustrated by Figure 3.4 (b).

The NW algorithm is as follows:

1. Start from a ring-shaped network with N nodes, in which each node is connected to its $2K$ neighbors, where $K > 0$ is an integer (usually small).

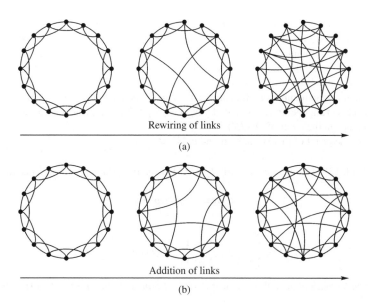

Figure 3.4 Illustration of two small-world network models: (a) WS small-world network model; (b) NW small-world network model

2. For every pair of originally unconnected nodes, with probability $p(0 < p \ll 1)$, add an edge to connect them.

In this process, between any pair of nodes there will not be multiple edges and no node will have self-loops.

In the *NW small-world model*, the case of $p = 0$ corresponds to the original ring-shaped network while $p = 1$ eventually yields a fully-connected network. By tuning the value of p, one can obtain a transition from a regular sparse network to a regular dense network, as illustrated by Figure 3.4 (b). For small enough values of p, though, the WS and NW models are about the same.

3.4.3 Statistical Properties of Small-World Network Models

For the WS network model, the clustering coefficient is redefined to be the ratio of the mean number of edges among the neighbors of a node and the number of all possible edges among the neighbors of the node:

$$C_{WS} = \frac{average\ number\ of\ neighboring\ edges}{total\ possible\ number\ of\ neighboring\ edges}. \tag{3.11}$$

Note that this definition differs from the original one only by a small amount in the order of $O(1/N)$, as further explained in the proof given below.

Theorem 3.6 [7, 14] *For large enough size N, the clustering coefficient of the WS small-world network model is given by* [14]

$$C(p) = \frac{3(K-1)}{2(2K-1)}(1-p)^3 \tag{3.12}$$

and the clustering coefficient of the NW small-world network model is given by [7]

$$C(p) = \frac{3(K-2)}{4(K-1)+4Kp(p+2)}. \tag{3.13}$$

Proof. An outline of the proof of (3.12) can be found in [11], as follows.

For $p = 0$, each node has $2K$ neighbors, so the number of edges among these neighbors is $N_0 = 3K(K-1)/2$, while the number of all possible edges among these nodes is $2K(2K-1)/2$; therefore, $C(0) = 3(K-1)/(2(2K-1))$. For $p > 0$, two neighbors of node i, which were connected at $p = 0$ are still neighbors of i and remain being connected with probability $(1-p)^3$, up to some terms in the order of $O(1/N)$. Thus, the mean number of edges among the neighbors of a node is $N_0(1-p)^3 + O(1/N)$. Consequently, the clustering coefficient is given by $N_0(1-p)^3/K(2K-1)$, which is formula (3.12), with a possible difference in the order of $O(1/N)$.

An outline of the proof of (3.13) can be found in [7]. ∎

Theorem 3.7 [3, 13] *The average path length of the WS small-world network model is given by* [13]

$$L(p) = \frac{2N}{K} f(2Np/K), \tag{3.14}$$

with

$$f(x) = \begin{cases} c & x \ll 1 \\ \ln x/x & x \gg 1 \end{cases} \quad (typically, \quad c = 1/4). \tag{3.15}$$

The average path length of the NW small-world network model is also given by (3.14), *with* [3]

$$f(x) \approx \frac{1}{2\sqrt{x^2 + 2x}} \tanh^{-1} \sqrt{\frac{x}{x^2 + 2x}}. \tag{3.16}$$

Proof. The proof of the first part can be found in [13], as follows.

For the WS network model, with p fixed, first perform the renormalization process (Figure 3.5) and let the number of sites of the resulting renormalized network be S. The average path length $L(p)$ is less than 1 and is increasing linearly as S gradually increases. But at some threshold value of S, denoted S^*, $L(p)$ will become bigger than 1. This leads to a phase transition, after which $L(p)$ will increase only logarithmically.

To be more precise, consider only the case of $K = 1$, namely, a perfect ring, and assume that $0 < p \ll 1$ and $S^* = 1/p$, thus $S^* \gg 1$. In this case, $L(p)$ should obey a finite-size scaling law of the form $L(p) = Sf(S/S^*) = Sf(pS)$, where $f(x)$ is given by (3.15). From the renormalized network, it can be seen that $S = 2N/K$; thus formula (3.14) follows.

For the NW network model, a proof of formula (3.16) is quite tedious, which can be found in [3]. ∎

Figure 3.6 depicts a typical evolutionary result on a small-sized network generated by the WS algorithm, where both values of the clustering coefficient and the average path length have been normalized for a better comparison. Clearly, the ring-shaped network ($p = 0$) has very high clustering ($C(0) \approx 3/4$ in this example) with a relatively long average path length (here, $L(0) \approx 2N/K \gg 1$). For a small p

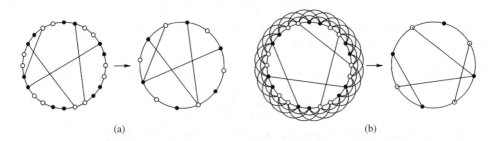

(a)   (b)

Figure 3.5 Renormalization of a small-world network model: (a) $K = 1$ (b) $K = 3$ [13]. *Source:* Reproduced with kind permission of Springer Science and Business Media

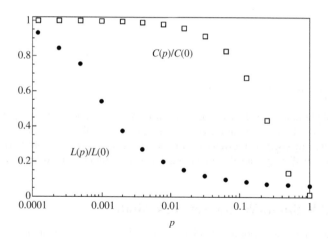

Figure 3.6 Clustering coefficient and average path length versus rewiring probability p in the WS small-world network model [1]. *Source*: Reprinted by permission from Macmillan Publishers Ltd: [Nature] (Watts, D.J. and Strogatz, S.H (1998) Collective dynamics of 'small-world' networks. *Nature*, **393** (6684): 440–2), copyright (1998)

$(0 < p \ll 1)$, the local properties of both the original network and the rewired network do not change by too much, therefore their clustering coefficients remain about the same $(C(p) \approx C(0))$; however, the average path length of the rewired network becomes much smaller than the original one $(L(p) \ll L(0))$. This implies that, after rewiring, the resulting network has become a small-world network with a large clustering coefficient and a small average path length.

Theorem 3.8 [7, 14] *The node-degree distribution of the WS small-world network model is given by* [14]

$$P_p(k) = \sum_{i=0}^{\min(k-K,K)} \binom{K}{i} (1-p)^i p^{K-i} \frac{(Kp)^{k-K-i}}{(k-K-i)!} \exp(-Kp) \ \ (k \geq K), \tag{3.17}$$

with $P_p(k) = 0$ for $k < K$; and the node-degree distribution of the NW small-world network model is given by [7]

$$P(k) = \binom{N}{k-K} \left(\frac{Kp}{n}\right)^{k-K} \left(1 - \frac{Kp}{N}\right)^{n-k+K} \ \ (k \geq K), \tag{3.18}$$

with $P(k) = 0$ for $k < K$.

Proof. The proof of formula (3.17) can be found in [14], as follows.

For the WS network model, with $p = 0$, each node has the same connectivity $2K$. For the nodes being rewired with probability $p > 0$, they introduce nonuniformity to the network while maintaining a fixed average node degree $\langle k \rangle = 2K$. Let this nonuniform probability distribution of network connectivity (degree) be denoted by $P_p(k)$. Since K of the initial $2K$ connections of each node are left unchanged by the construction, the degree of node i is $k_i = K + n_i$ with $n_i \geq 0$, where $n_i = n_i^1 + n_i^2$ in which $n_i^1 \leq K$ is the number of edges left unchanged (each one with probability $1 - p$) and n_i^2 is the number of edges that have been reconnected to some another node from node i (each one with probability p/N). Thus, one has

$$P_1(n_i^1) = \binom{K}{n_i^1} (1-p)^{n_i^1} p^{K-n_i^1}$$

$$P_2(n_i^2) = \frac{(Kp)^{n_i^2}}{n_i^2!} \exp(-Kp) \quad \text{for large } N$$

and, in general, one has

$$P_p(k) = \sum_{i=0}^{\min(k-K,K)} \binom{K}{i} (1-p)^i p^{K-i} \frac{(Kp)^{k-K-i}}{(k-K-i)!} \exp(-Kp) \text{ for } k \geq K.$$

For the NW network model, formula (3.18) can be found in [7]. ∎

Finally, it should be emphasized once again that ER random-graph networks typically have relatively short average path lengths given by formula (3.8) in a logarithmic scale in the order of $O(\ln N)$, and very small average clustering coefficient given by formula (3.9): $C = p = \langle k \rangle_{ER}/N \ll 1$. These qualitatively and also quantitatively distinguish ER random-graph networks from small-world networks.

3.5   Navigable Small-World Network Model

The Kleinberg navigable small-world network model [5, 15] is a generalization of the NW small-world network model. It was originally built on a planar lattice of N nodes, where for simplicity every crossed point of the lattice is placed a node which is connected to its direct neighbors: left, right, up and down.

Recall that in the NW small-world network model, each node on the given ring-shaped network has long-range edges connecting to some other nodes with a certain probability in such a uniform random manner that every other node has an equal probability to receive the new edge, excluding self-loops and multiple connections. Now, instead of assuming that new long-range connections are uniformly distributed over the whole network, Kleinberg argued [5] that intuitively it would be easer for a new edge to connect to a nearby neighbor than to the remote ones. He therefore assumed that the connecting probability is reversely proportional to the distance between the two nodes.

More specifically, it is assumed that the new connection from node u to any other node v in the given network, a lattice in the present discussion, is equal to

$$P(u, v) = \beta d_{uv}^{-\alpha}, \tag{3.19}$$

where d_{uv} is the distance between u and v with parameters $\alpha \geq 0, \beta > 0$ satisfying $\beta \sum_{(u,v)} d_{u,v}^{-\alpha} = 1$ as a probability measure. The edge-distribution mechanism is graphically illustrated by Figure 3.7, in which $d_{AB} = 1$ and $d_{AC} = 3$, so $P(A, B) = \beta \times 1^{-\alpha} > P(A, C) = \beta \times 3^{-\alpha}$. Clearly, when $\alpha = 0$, the new edge-addition probability is a constant, implying that every node has the same probability to receive the new edge, therefore the model reduces to the original NW small-word network model.

Now, the task is to deliver a message from a source, say S, to a target, say A, in as few steps as possible using only locally available information, while the programmer (player) is allowed to add m long-range edges anywhere within the lattice before the message is being transmitted out from the source. Here, the available local information includes:

1. Location of the target on the lattice
2. Locations and long-range neighbors of all nodes that had previously processed the message

Suppose, however, that every node does not have the second piece of local information listed above, namely, does not know the long-range neighbors of the other nodes that had not previously processed the message; otherwise, the problem would be easy to solve.

Since generally a small-world network has a short average path length, one may randomly add the m allowed long-range edges to the lattice so as to generate a NW-type small-world network, where all the long-range connections are chosen independently of the locations of the target and all related nodes on the lattice. This works fine to some extent, but Kleinberg showed [5, 15] that it takes $O(N^{2/3})$ time-steps for the message to reach the target on such a small-world network. Kleinberg then developed a generalized small-world network model and accordingly constructed an algorithm capable of finding a short path from the source to the target in only $O((\log N)^2)$ time-steps. He called such a network *navigable* if it requires at most *poly*$(\log N)$ time-steps to deliver a message to any target from any source on the network.

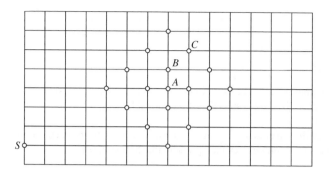

Figure 3.7   Illustration of the Kleinberg network model

Noticing that other algorithms may lead the message to go through some detours or even go back-and-forth in approaching the target, Kleinberg's idea was to find a way that guarantees the message to move at least one step closer to the target each time. He applied a greedy algorithm, where at every step the current message holder will pass the message to a neighbor who is as close to the target as possible. This explains why the local information of the target location is needed to know by the message holders.

As mentioned above, when $\alpha = 0$ the edge-addition probability is a constant, so the model is the original NW small-word network model. As α increases, a decentralized algorithm can take more advantage of the geographic structure with long-range connections. As α further increases, however, the number of long-range edges become very small therefore less useful for helping the message delivery. Therefore, there is a best value of α in between, and Kleinberg showed that this value is $\alpha = 2$, as illustrated by Figure 3.8. Precisely, Kleinberg established the following result in [15].

Theorem 3.9 *For $\alpha = 2$, there exists a constant β in (3.19), depending on m yet independent of N, such that the lattice is navigable at a rate $O((\log N)^2)$, but for all $\alpha < 0$ it is not navigable. For $0 \leq \alpha < 2$, it takes at least $O(N^{(2-\alpha)/3})$ time-steps for the message to complete a navigation from any source to any target on the given lattice; for $\alpha > 2$, however, it will be at least $O(N^{(\alpha-2)/(\alpha-1)})$.*

The basic idea for a proof of the theorem is outlined as follows. One starts from the target, and partitions the lattice into classes as follows: class 0 consists of the target only; class 1 consists of all nodes with distance 1 to the target; class 2 consists of all nodes with distances within the range of $2 \leq d \leq 4$, and so on,

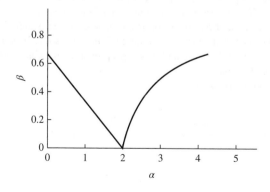

Figure 3.8   Relation between parameter α and the message delivery time $O(N^\beta)$ [5, 15]. *Source*: Reprinted by permission from Macmillan Publishers Ltd: [Nature] (Kleinberg, J. (2000) Navigation in a small world. *Nature*, **406**: 845), copyright (2000)

where class K consists of all nodes with distances within the range of $2^{K-1} \le d \le 2^K$, $K = 1, 2, \ldots$, with $K \le \log_2 N$ large enough to cover the whole lattice. Thus, by examining each class, with the best scenario where the message can find a long-range edge to jump into a lower class (closer to the target) through one of the m allowed long-range edges, Kleinberg derived a lower bound for the traveling time-steps; and with the worst scenario where the message has to move step by step along the grid of the lattice, he derived an upper bound instead. Thereby, Kleinberg completed the proof of the theorem.

Kleinberg also generalized the results to n-dimensional lattices, for which he proved that the graph is navigable if and only if $\alpha = n$.

Finally, it is noted that other than working on a lattice, for the same problem formulated in the original NW ring-shaped network setting, Newman gives an illustration in [8].

3.6   Scale-Free Network Models

A common feature of the ER random-graph networks and the WS/NW small-world networks is that their node-degree distributions are (exactly or approximately) described by the Poisson distribution, which peaks at the average degree $\langle k \rangle$ and then decays exponentially fast on both sides as $k \to 0, \infty$. In particular, nodes with very high degrees $k \gg \langle k \rangle$ almost do not exist. This kind of networks is referred to as *homogeneous networks;* sometimes, due to its two-sided decaying tails, they are also called *exponential networks.*

It has been found, however, that many real-world networks, including such typical ones as the Internet, WWW, metabolic networks, etc., are not homogeneous networks; instead, their connectivity is heterogeneous. More importantly, their node-degree distributions have a power-law form and are independent of the connectivity scale, therefore are referred to as scale-free networks, as will be further discussed below. At this point, it is remarked that as an example the Pareto distribution has a power-law form, $f(x) = Cx^{-\gamma}$, for some positive constants C and γ, which is linear (or affine) in a log–log plot, namely, $(\ln f) = -\gamma(\ln x) + \ln C$.

3.6.1   BA Scale-Free Network Model

It is noticeable that all the above-studied ER random-graph network model and WS/NW small-world network models do not grow in size, but most real-world networks grow and indeed grow very fast; for instance, journals have new papers being published every month and WWW has new websites being added every day. Furthermore, in the growth of such a network, a forthcoming node has the tendency to connect itself to some "big" nodes (with large degrees), which are more important therefore more attractive in some sense. This is referred to as *preferential attachment*, reflecting the so-called "rich gets richer" phenomenon, or Matthew effect; for example, a new paper is more likely to cite an already well-cited reference and a new web-site tends to link to famous sites like Yahoo or Google. Motivated by some observations like these, Barabási and Albert [2] proposed a new network model, known as the *BA scale-free network* model today.

The BA modeling algorithm is as follows:

1. *Growth*: Starting from a connected network of small size $m_0 \ge 1$, introduce one new node to the existing network each time, and this new node is connected to m existing nodes in the network simultaneously, where $1 \le m \le m_0$.
2. *(Linear) Preferential Attachment*: The above-referred incoming new node is simultaneously connected to each of the m existing nodes, according to the following probability: for node i of degree k_i,

$$\Pi_i = \frac{k_i}{\sum_{j=1}^{N} k_j}. \tag{3.20}$$

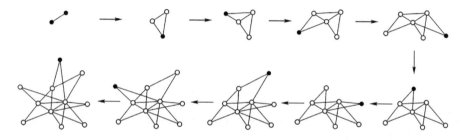

Figure 3.9 Illustration of the growth of a BA scale-free network [25]

Clearly, at the tth step of the node-adding process, the total number of existing nodes where $N = m_0 + t$, $t = 0, 1, 2, \ldots$. Thus, after t steps, the network will have $N = t + m_0$ nodes and $m\,t + m^*$ edges, where m^* is the number of initial edges. Thus, if the initial network is fully connected then $m^* = m_0(m_0 - 1)/2$. Figure 3.9 illustrates the evolving process of a BA scale-free network, with $m = m_0 = 2$, where the black nodes represent the new comers and the white nodes are the existing ones at each step.

Theorem 3.10 [17, 18] *The average path length of the BA scale-free network is given by*

$$L \sim \frac{\ln N}{\ln \ln N}. \tag{3.21}$$

Proof. A proof of this formula is rather mathematically involved [17, 18]. ∎

Note that this L actually is not very large, implying that the BA scale-free network model also has a certain small-world network feature – two randomly chosen nodes are connected by a fairly short path.

Theorem 3.11 *[19] The average clustering coefficient of the BA scale-free network model is given by*

$$C = \frac{m^2(m+1)^2}{4(m-1)} \left(\ln\left(\frac{m+1}{m}\right) - \frac{1}{m+1} \right) \frac{(\ln t)^2}{t}. \tag{3.22}$$

Proof. A proof of this formula is rather mathematically involved [19]. ∎

This result shows that the BA scale-free network model also has a certain random-graph network feature – the clustering property is not prominent.

Theorem 3.12 [2] *The average node degree of the BA network is approximately equal to 2m, and the node-degree distribution is approximately given by a power-law form*

$$P(k) \sim 2m^2 k^{-3}. \tag{3.23}$$

As a historical record, a heuristic proof [2] is outlined here, which is quite insightful. Other rigorous proofs can be found in, for example, [20, 21].

Proof. Let i be a node, which was added to the network at instant t_i, and let $p(k, t_i, t)$ be the probability that this node i has degree k when it is being picked up at time t $(t \geq t_i)$.

Imagine that k is a continuous variable, so that probability $\Pi(k_i) = k_i / \sum_j k_j$ may be viewed as a continuous rate of change of k_i; therefore,

$$\frac{\partial k_i}{\partial t} = a\Pi(k_i) = a\frac{k_i}{\sum_j k_j},$$

for some constant a. Since the new node brings in m new edges, which has degree m at time t_i, so the change of connectivity at t_i is m, implying that $a = m$. Also, at every step m new edges have been added, so the total node degree of the network at time t is $\sum_j k_j \approx 2mt$. Thus, since the number of nodes at this moment is t, the average node degree is approximately equal to $2m$. On the other hand, the above equation reduces to

$$\frac{\partial k_i}{\partial t} = \frac{mk_i}{2mt} = \frac{k_i}{2t}.$$

Solving this equation, with the initial condition that node i was added to the network at time t_i with connectivity $k_i(t_i) = m$, yields

$$k_i(t) = m\sqrt{\frac{t}{t_i}},$$

which gives

$$t_i = \frac{m^2 t}{k_i^2}.$$

On the other hand,

$$P(k_i(t) < k) = P\left(t_i > \frac{m^2 t}{k^2}\right).$$

Assuming that the new nodes are being added at equal time intervals, the time variables $\{t_i\}$ have a uniform distribution with $P(t_i) = \frac{1}{t+m_0}$, so that

$$P\left(t_i > \frac{m^2 t}{k^2}\right) = 1 - P\left(t_i \le \frac{m^2 t}{k^2}\right) = 1 - \frac{m^2 t}{k^2} \cdot \frac{1}{t + m_0}.$$

Consequently, the degree distribution $P(k_i(t) = k)$ can be obtained as

$$P(k) = \frac{\partial P(k_i(t) < k)}{\partial k} = 2\frac{m^2 t}{t + m_0} \cdot k^{-3} \approx 2m^2 k^{-3}.$$

This is the power law (3.22), in the form of $c \cdot k^{-\gamma}$ with $\gamma = 3$. ∎

It has been observed, for example in simulation, that as the network becomes less and less random (namely, more and more regular), the shape of the Poisson distribution curve will become narrower and narrower towards the delta function (completely regular).

Most of such distributions located in between Poisson and delta distributions are described by a power-law function of the form

$$P(k) \sim k^{-\gamma}. \tag{3.24}$$

Its log–log plot is shown in Figure 3.10 (a), where γ is a constant determined by the given network; for instance, for the BA network, $\gamma = 3$ in (3.23). Clearly, the logarithmic curve of a power-law distribution decays linearly, much slower than the Poisson curve, which decays exponentially.

As a historical remark, the following directed network model was initiated by de Solla Price in 1965 [23, 24]:

1. *Initialization*: Start from $m_0 \ge 1$ isolated nodes.
2. *Growth*: At every step, add one new node to the existing network, which brings in $m (m \le m_0)$ directed edges, each pointing to one existing node.
3. *Preferential Attachment*: for every node i with in-degree k_i^{in}, the above new node will connect to it according to the following probability:

$$\Pi_i = \frac{k_i^{in} + a}{\sum_j (k_j^{in} + a)} \qquad (a > 0 \text{ is a constant parameter}).$$

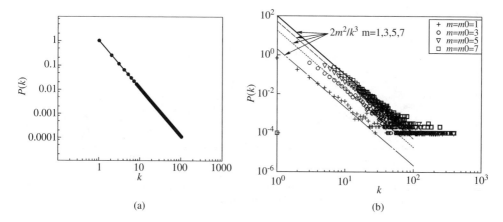

Figure 3.10 The node-degree distribution of a BA scale-free network model: (a) power-law distribution; (b) simulation results ($N = 1000$). *Source for (b)*: reproduced from Li, X. and Chen, G. (2003) A local-world evolving network model. *Physica A*, **328**: 274–86. Copyright (2003) Elsevier

It has been proved that the node-degree distribution of the above *Price model* is given by $P(k) \sim (k^{in})^{-\gamma}$ with $\gamma = 2 + a/m$.

It is noted that although the model starts from a set of "isolated nodes", due to the constant $a > 0$, even the isolated nodes will receive new connections, hence technically it is not a problem. It is clear that under a connected initial condition, and with $a = 0$, the undirected Price model yields the BA model, however with a different γ value caused by the different conditions.

The above power-law distribution is more commonly called a *scale-free* distribution, for they have the scale-independent property described by the following theorem.

Theorem 3.13 *Consider a continuously differentiable probability distribution function $f(x)$. If, for any given constant a, there is a constant b such that the following "scale-free" property holds:*

$$f(ax) = bf(x), \tag{3.25}$$

then, with the assumption of $f(1)f'(1) \neq 0$, the function $f(x)$ is uniquely determined by

$$f(x) = f(1)x^{-\gamma}, \qquad \gamma = -f'(1)/f(1). \tag{3.26}$$

Proof. Let $x = 1$ in (3.25). Then, one has $f(a) = bf(1)$, so $b = f(a)/f(1)$; therefore,

$$f(ax) = \frac{f(a)f(x)}{f(1)}.$$

Since this equality holds for arbitrary a and x, one may also consider a as a variable and take a derivative of the equality with respect to a, obtaining

$$\frac{df(ax)}{d(ax)}\frac{d(ax)}{da} = \frac{f(x)}{f(1)}\frac{df(a)}{da}.$$

In particular, letting $a = 1$ gives

$$x\frac{df(x)}{d(x)} = \frac{f'(1)}{f(1)}f(x),$$

which has a unique solution

$$\ln f(x) = \frac{f'(1)}{f(1)}\ln x + \ln f(1).$$

This is equivalent to (3.26), completing the proof of the theorem. ∎

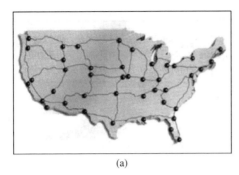 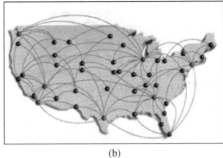

(a)   (b)

Figure 3.11 Comparison of a random network and a scale-free network [25]: (a) highway route map in USA; (b) airline route map in USA. *Source*: Reproduced from Scientific American

In a large-scale network with a power-law degree distribution, particularly if $2 \leq \gamma \leq 3$, most nodes have very low degrees (i.e., with very few edges) and yet there are a few nodes having very high degrees (i.e., with many edges). This kind of complex networks is referred to as *heterogeneous networks*, where the high-degree nodes are also called *hubs*.

A typical example of this kind is some USA airline route maps [25], shown in Figure 3.11 (b), in which a few airports are hubs (e.g., New York, Chicago, Atlanta, Dallas, etc.), while the majority of airports especially those in small towns have relatively very few flights each day. In comparison, the USA highway system, shown in Figure 3.11 (a), is a homogeneous network, simply because it is impossible for a particular city to have too many highways connecting it to other cities.

Table 3.1 [7] lists the statistical properties of some real-world complex networks, where N is the number of nodes, M is the number of edges, $\langle k \rangle$ is the average degree, L is the average path length, C is the clustering coefficient of a network, in which γ is the exponent of a power-law distribution function (for directed networks, both in- and out-degrees are given), and – means undefined or not applicable.

Figure 3.12 [7] shows the cumulative degree distribution functions of six examples, among others, given in Table 3.1 [7]. In Figure 3.12, the horizontal axes are the degree values (for the directed networks (b) and (c), they are in-degrees), and the vertical axes are cumulative degree distribution values. The curves in these figures correspond to: (a) a mathematical coauthorship network; (b) scientific citation index in 1981–87, provided by the Institute for Scientific Information; (c) a subnet of 0.3.billion nodes of the WWW in 1999; (d) the AS-level Internet in April 1999, where AS stands for autonomous systems; (e) a power grid in the Western USA; (f) protein reactions of a yeast metabolic network. It can be seen that curves in (c), (d) and (f) follow power laws, since their logarithmic curves are straight lines; curve in (b) follows a power law only near the end; curve in (e) actually follows an exponential distribution (a semi-logarithmic curve); curve in (a) looks like a combination of two power-law distributions with different exponents.

The curves in these figures correspond to: (a) a mathematical coauthorship network; (b) scientific citation index in 1981–87, provided by the Institute for Scientific Information; (c) a subnet of 0.3.billion nodes of the WWW in 1999; (d) the AS-level Internet in April 1999, where AS stands for autonomous systems; (e) a power grid in the Western USA; (f) protein reactions of a yeast metabolic network. Reprinted by permission of Society for Industrial and Applied Mathematics.

3.6.2   Robustness versus Fragility

In Greek mythology, Achilles was the son of Thetis and Peleus, the bravest hero in the Trojan war. According to the myth, when Achilles was born, his mother Thetis tried to make him immortal by dipping him in the river Styx. As she immersed him, she held him by one heel but forgot to dip him a second time

Table 3.1   Statistic data of some real networks [7]

	Network	Type	N	M	$<k>$	L	γ	C
Social science	Film actors	Undirected	449913	25516482	113	3.48	2.3	0.78
	Company directors	Undirected	7673	55392	14.4	4.6	–	0.88
	Math coauthorship	Undirected	253339	496489	3.92	7.57	–	0.34
	Physics coauthorship	Undirected	52909	245300	9.27	6.19	–	0.56
	Biology coauthorship	Undirected	1520251	11803064	15.5	4.92	–	0.6
	Telephone call graph	Undirected	47000000	80000000	3.16			
	Email messages	Undirected	59912	86300	1.44	4.95	1.5/2.0	0.16
	Email addresses books	Undirected	16881	57029	3.38	5.22	–	0.13
	Student relationships	Undirected	573	477	1.66	16	–	0
	Sexual contacts	Undirected	2810				3.2	
Information science	WWW nd.edu	Directed	269504	1497135	5.55	11.3	2.1/2.4	0.29
	WWW Altavista	Directed	203549046	2.13E+09	10.5	16.2	2.1/2.7	
	Citation network	Directed	783339	6716198	8.57		3.0/–	
	Roget's Thesaurus	Directed	1022	5103	4.99	4.87	–	0.15
	Word co-occurrence	Undirected	460902	1.7E+07	70.1		2.7	0.44
Technology	Internet (AS-level)	Undirected	10697	31992	5.98	3.31	2.5	0.39
	Power grid	Undirected	4941	6594	2.67	19	–	0.08
	Train routes	Undirected	587	19603	66.8	2.16	–	0.69
	Software packages	Directed	1439	1723	1.2	2.42	1.6/1.4	0.08
	Software classes	Directed	1377	2213	1.61	1.51	–	0.01
	Electric circuits	Undirected	24097	53248	4.34	11.1	3	0.03
	Peer-to-peer network	Undirected	880	1296	1.47	4.28	2.1	0.01
Biology	Metabolic network	Undirected	765	3686	9.64	2.56	2.2	0.67
	Protein network	Undirected	2115	2240	2.12	6.8	2.4	0.07
	Marine food web	Directed	135	598	4.43	2.05	–	0.23
	Freshwater food web	Directed	92	997	10.8	1.9	–	0.09
	Neural network	Directed	307	2359	7.68	3.97	–	0.28

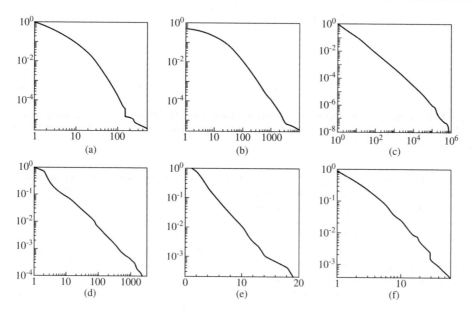

Figure 3.12   Cumulative degree distributions of six examples given in Table 3.1 [7]. *Source*: Reproduced by permission of Society for Industrial and Applied Mathematics

Figure 3.13   Achilles' heel and the Internet [16]: (a) Greek myth about Achilles' heel; (b) Achilles' heel of the Internet. *Source*: Copyright (1998) Macmillan Publishers Ltd [Nature]. Reprinted by permission

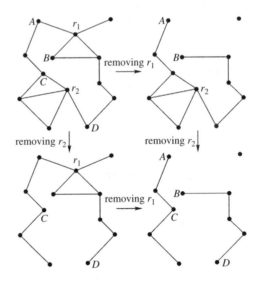

Figure 3.14   A connected network becomes unconnected due to removal of nodes [26]. *Source*: Complex networks: topology, dynamics and synchronization, *International Journal of Bifurcation and Chaos*. Wang, X.F. Copyright (2002) World Scientific Pub. Co.

to wet his other heel she held (Figure 3.13 (a)). Thus, as a result, the place where she held him remained untouched by the magic water of the Styx and that part stayed vulnerable. Achilles was killed in a battle by an enemy's arrow hit exactly at that very heel. Today, any weak point of a strong entity is called an "Achilles' heel." For instance, on July 27, 2000, *Nature* magazine had a story about the Internet's Achilles' heel, as shown in Figure 3.13 (b) [16].

For a given network of any kind, if one node is being removed at a time (consequently all the edges connecting it will also be removed), then at some point the network will be broken to become disconnected (Figure 3.14). If the network remains connected after some nodes have been removed, then the network is said to be *robust* against node-removal. Comparing two networks, when a certain number of nodes are removed and one network stays connected while another has lost connectivity, then the former is said to be more robust than the latter.

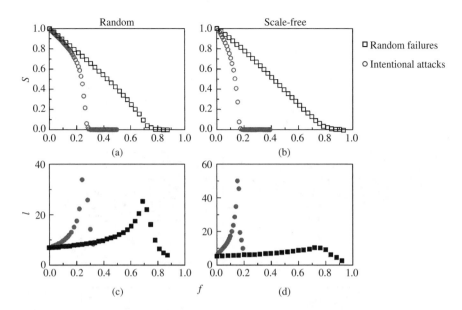

Figure 3.15 Robustness and fragility of ER random-graph and BA scale-free networks [6]: (a) and (c): ER random-graph networks; (b) and (d): BA scale-free networks;squares – random removal of nodes; circles – intentional removal of nodes. *Source*: Reproduced with permission from Albert, R. and Barabási, A-L. (2002) Statistical mechanics of complex networks. *Reviews of Modern Physics,* **74**: 47–97. Copyright (2002) American Physical Society

Now, compare the robustness of the ER random-graph networks and the BA scale-free networks in the sense described above: their maintenance of connectivity against node-removal.

Apply two strategies for node removal: random removal (uniformly randomly remove a node from the network) and intentional removal (selectively remove the highest-degree node from the network).

Let $\overline{L}$ be the average path length of a network, f be the fraction of nodes being removed, and S be the fraction of the largest connected subnetwork at the first time a network is disconnected due to node removal. Clearly, if there are several edges connecting node i and node j, then removing one edge between them will increase the distance d_{ij} between them, so that the average path length $\overline{L} = l$ of the whole network will increase. The distance between two unconnected nodes can be considered as ∞.

The simulation results shown in Figure 3.15 [6] show that the ER random-graph networks and the BA scale-free networks are very different in this respect: the BA scale-free networks are very robust against random removal of nodes: comparing to the ER random-graph network, the size S of the largest subnetwork in a scale-free network decreases to zero slowly and for a much larger fraction f of the removed nodes; yet its average path length grows also much slower.

The above-described robustness of scale-free networks against random removal of nodes is due to the heterogeneous distribution of nodes in the network: most nodes have very small degrees and only a few nodes have large degrees; thus, randomly removing a fraction of nodes will very likely remove some small nodes, which does not affect the network connectivity by too much. However, for exactly the same reason, any intentional removal of even a very small fraction of high-degree nodes will significantly affect the topology of the network, leading to drastic change of the network connectivity. Figure 3.16 [25] illustrates the robustness and fragility of the BA scale-free networks.

The Internet provides a typical example of the "robust yet fragile" phenomenon. The Internet has become an indispensable part of human life today. However, the Internet also faces various failures and attacks every day. Therefore, it is an extremely important issue to guarantee the robustness of the Internet against both random failures and intentional attacks, leaving a challenging technical issue for good solutions.

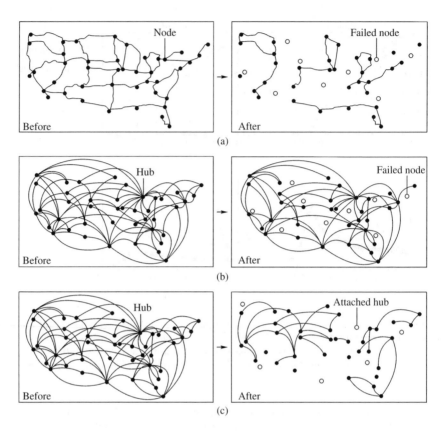

Figure 3.16 Comparison of robustness and fragility of ER random-graph and BA scale-free networks [25]: (a) effects on connectivity of ER networks due to random removal of nodes; (b) effects on connectivity of BA networks due to random removal of nodes; (c) effects on connectivity of BA networks due to intentional removal of nodes. *Source*: Reproduced from Scientific American

In a study of the Internet by Albert, Jeong and Barabási [6], a model of the Internet at the AS (Autonomous Systems) level with 6000 nodes, and a model of a subnet of the WWW with 326 000 nodes were investigated, showing that they behave in a way similar to the BA scale-free network (Figure 3.17). This implies that the Internet and the WWW have the "robust yet fragile" property, discussed above, due to their heterogeneous topologies. It is believed that this "robust yet fragile" property is an essential feature of various systems' complexity [27, 28].

As a side note, Broder *et al.* [29] studied the WWW and found that only when all nodes with a degree larger than 5 are removed can the WWW be disconnected, meaning that the WWW is quite robust against intentional attacks. Since the WWW is so large in size, the total number of degree-5 nodes is still a relatively small fraction of the entire huge network. This finding nevertheless is not conflicting with the observation reported in [16]. As to the Internet, Doyle *et al.* [30] argued that the Internet is a scale-free network but also is a highly optimized tolerance network, therefore its "robust yet fragile" property has to be measured from a somewhat different (i.e., technological) point of view. For more discussions on related issues, see [31–36].

3.6.3   Modified BA Models

The main contribution of the BA scale-free model is that it precisely captures the two essential features of many complex networks: growth and preferential attachment. Since complex networks are extremely

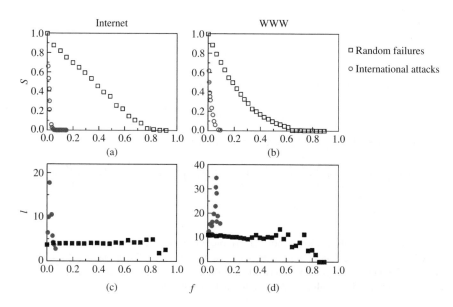

Figure 3.17 Robustness and fragility of the Internet and WWWagainst intentional attacks [6]: (a) and (c): Internet; (b) and (d): WWW;squares – random failures, circles – intentional attacks. *Source*: Reprinted with permission from Albert, R. and Barabási, A-L. (2002) Statistical mechanics of complex networks. *Reviews of Modern Physics,* **74**: 47–97. Copyright (2002) American Physical Society

complex, with many important parameters that can affect the network behaviors significantly, the BA model oversimplifies them thereby leading to some inconsistence with real-world complex networks. For example, in the BA model, the power-law form of degree distributions $P(k) \sim k^{-\gamma}$ has exponent $\gamma = 3$ (see Theorem 3.12 above), but real data show that most real-world networks have their exponents satisfying $2 < \gamma < 3$, and some satisfy $1 < \gamma < 2$ or $\gamma > 3$. Knowing this, some generalized and improved versions of the BA model were developed lately, among which the most popular is the following extended BA model, referred to as the *EBA Model*.

3.6.3.1 EBA Model

To allow for $2 < \gamma < 3$ in the power law $P(k) \sim k^{-\gamma}$ of the BA model, Albert and Barabási [4] extended the original BA model by incorporating the idea of "rewiring."

The following is the EBA modeling algorithm:

1. *Growth* and *Preferential Attachment*: Start from a connected network of small size $m_0 \geq 1$. At each step, with probability p a new node is added to the network and the new node brings $m(1 \leq m \leq m_0)$ new edges to the existing network: Simultaneously for the m new edges, the other end of each edge is selected from the existing node i of degree k_i according to the following probability:

$$\Pi_i = \frac{k_i}{\sum_{j=1}^{n} k_j},$$

where n is the total number of existing nodes at this step.
2. *Rewiring*: With probability q, $0 \leq q < 1 - p$, randomly rewire m existing edges: for each of the m edges, which connects a pair of existing nodes, with probability q reconnect one end of its edge to another node.

Clearly, in the extreme case with $p = 1$ as the first step with the second step removed, the EBA model reduces to the original BA model.

The EBA network model has the following properties.

Theorem 3.14 [4] *The node-degree distribution of the EBA model is approximately given by*

$$P(k) \sim [k + c(p, q, m)]^{-\gamma(p, q, m)}, \tag{3.27}$$

where $c(p, q, m) = 1 + A(p, q, m)$ *and* $\gamma(p, q, m) = 1 + B(p, q, m)$ *with*

$$A(p, q, m) = (p - q)\left[\frac{2m(1 - q)}{1 - p - q} + 1\right] \text{ and } B(p, q, m) = \frac{2m(1 - q) + 1 - p - q}{m}$$

in which $0 \le p < 1$ *and* $0 \le q < 1 - p$.

Proof. Here, for an insightful (though not very rigorous) proof [4], the degree k_i is considered as a variable, which is changing continuously with respect to time t, so that the probability $\Pi_i = \Pi(k_i)$ can be interpreted as the rate of change of k_i. Consequently, differentiation can be applied to it with respect to t. Thus, adding m new edges with probability p to the network yields

$$\left(\frac{\partial k_i}{\partial t}\right)_{(1)} = pC_1\frac{1}{n} + pC_1\frac{k_i}{\sum_{j=1}^{n} k_j},$$

where n is the current network size. The first term on the right-hand side corresponds to the random selection of one end of the new edge, while the second term reflects the preferential attachment probability used to select the other end of the edge. Since the total change in connectivity after one step is $\Delta k = 2m$, one has $C_1 = m$ at this stage.

Next, rewiring m edges with probability q gives

$$\left(\frac{\partial k_i}{\partial t}\right)_{(2)} = -qC_2\frac{1}{n} + qC_2\frac{k_i}{\sum_{j=1}^{n} k_j},$$

where the first term on the right-hand side incorporates the decreasing connectivity of the node from which the edge was removed, and the second term represents the increasing connectivity of the node to which the edge is reconnected. The total connectivity does not change during the rewiring process, however, so C_2 can be calculated by separating the two processes, resulting in $C_2 = m$ at this stage.

Moreover, adding a new node to the network with probability $1 - p - q$ leads to

$$\left(\frac{\partial k_i}{\partial t}\right)_{(3)} = (1 - p - q)C_3\frac{k_i}{\sum_{j=1}^{n} k_j},$$

where the number of edges connecting the new node to the existing nodes is m, giving $C_3 = m$ at this stage.

Now, by combining the contributions from the above three processes, one obtains

$$\frac{\partial k_i}{\partial t} = (p - q)m\frac{1}{n} + m\frac{k_i}{\sum_{j=1}^{n} k_j},$$

at this stage. To this end, notice that both the network size n and the total number of edges $\sum_{j=1}^{n} k_j$ are actually varying with time in the process, given by

$$n = m_0 + (1 - p - q)t \text{ and } \sum_{j=1}^{n} k_j = (1 - q)2mt - m.$$

Clearly, for large t, one may neglect the (relatively small) constants m_0 and m in the above two formulas. Consequently, a solution of the above differential equation, with initial condition that the connectivity of a node being added at time t_i is $k_i(t_i) = m$, is obtained as

$$k_i(t) = [A(p,q,m) + m + 1]\left(\frac{t}{t_i}\right)^{1/B(p,q,m)} - A(p,q,m) - 1,$$

where $0 \leq t_i \leq t$, and $A(p,q,m)$ and $B(p,q,m)$ are given as in the theorem.

Furthermore, notice that the probability that a node i has degree (number of connections) $k_i(t) < k$, denoted $P(k_i(t) < k)$, can be written as

$$P(k_i(t) < k) = P(t_i > C(p,q,m)\, t) \text{ with } C(p,q,m) = \left(\frac{m + A(p,q,m) + 1}{k + A(p,q,m) + 1}\right)^{B(p,q,m)}.$$

There are three cases to consider: (i) if $C(p,q,m) > 1$, then $P(k_i(t) < k) = 0$, thus for $P(k)$ to be nonzero the condition is $k > m$; (ii) if $C(p,q,m) > 1$ is not real, then $P(k_i(t) < k)$ is not well-defined, so in order to calculate $P(k)$ the condition must be $[m + A(p,q,m) + 1]/[k + A(p,q,m) + 1] > 0$ for all $k > m$, which can be satisfied when $m + A(p,q,m) + 1 > 0$; (iii) if $0 < C(p,q,m) < 1$, then $P(k)$ can be arbitrary, and in this case, one may define the time unit as one attempt of growth/rewire/edge-adding, where the probability density of t_i is $P_i(t_i) = 1/(m_0 + t)$, leading to

$$P(k_i(t) < k) = 1 - C(p,q,m)\frac{t}{m_0 + t},$$

which, together with $P(k) = \partial P(k_i(t) < k)/\partial k$, yields

$$P(k) = \frac{t}{m_0 + t}D(p,q,m)[k + A(p,q,m) + 1]^{1/(1+B(p,q,m))}$$

with $D(p,q,m) = [m + A(p,q,m) + 1]^{B(p,q,m)}B(p,q,m)$.

In summary, the degree (connectivity) distribution has the form of (3.27). ∎

It is easy to see that the biased (or shifted) power law (3.27) can generate scale-free networks with $2 < \gamma < 3$, which is a more practical situation than that with $\gamma = 3$, as has been verified by many simulated and real-world examples.

3.6.3.2 Fitness Model

Notice from the proof of Theorem 3.12 that, during the growth of the BA model, the degree of a node is also changing according to the following law:

$$k_i(t) = \sqrt{\frac{t}{t_i}}, \tag{3.28}$$

where $k_i(t)$ is the degree of node i at time t and t_i is the instant at which node i is being added into the network. This growth rate of the node degrees in the BA model implies that the older a node, the higher its degree. In real life, however, this is not always true. For instance, a young teenager can have more social connections than an elder man; a new website in WWW can have more links pointing to it than some old ones; a new scientific paper can receive more citations than many old articles, etc. All these depend on the importance or significance of the node in the network, which is referred to as the *fitness* by Bianconi and Barabási [37] in their modified version of the BA model, called the *fitness model*:

1. *Growth*: Start from a small connected network of size $m_0 \geq 1$ and introduce one new node to the existing network each time, which with probability $\rho(\eta)$ is given a fitness value, η_i, $0 < \eta_i < 1$.

2. *Preferential Attachment*: The new node is connected to $m (1 \le m \le m_0)$ existing nodes, according to a probability of connecting to node i of degree k_i with fitness value η_i given by

$$\Pi_i = \frac{\eta_i k_i}{\sum_{j=1}^{n} \eta_j k_j},$$
(3.29)

where $n = m_0 + t - 1$ is the total number of existing nodes at the $(t-1)$st step of the process.

Clearly, after t steps, the network will have a total of $n = t + m_0$ nodes and $mt + m^*$ edges, where m^* is the number of initial edges. This fitness model is the same as the BA model, except that in this model the preferential attachment is not only proportional to the degree (see (3.20)) but also proportional to the fitness value of the existing node. Consequently, a young node with a higher fitness value can obtain more new edges than an old node with a lower fitness value.

Depending on the form of the fitness probability $\rho(\eta)$, there are two behaviors of the fitness model [37]: if this probability distribution has a finite domain, then similar to the BA model this fitness model also has a power-law form of node-degree distribution; if this probability distribution has an infinite domain, then the node with the highest fitness value will attract a large portion of the total number of newly coming edges – known as the "winner takes all" phenomenon.

3.6.4   A Simple Model with Power-Law Degree Distribution

It should be noted that the property of a power-law degree distribution is not only pertaining to scale-free networks but to some other types of networks as well, even some special sparse random-graph networks [38]. A simple example is the following evolving random-graph type of network model formulated by Aiello Chung and Lu [39]:

1. *Initialization*: Start with nothing – no nodes, no links.
2. At each time-step, with probability p, one new node is added to the existing network.
3. In the current network at every time-step, for every pair of unconnected nodes, with probability $q = 1 - p$, one edge is added to connect them together.

Theorem 3.15 [39] *The degree distribution of the above network model has a power-law form, $P(k) \sim k^{-\gamma}$, where $\gamma = 1 + q^{-1}$. Consequently, if $1/2 < q < 1$ then $2 < \gamma < 3$.*

Proof. See [39]. ∎

Note that in this theorem, condition $1/2 < q < 1$ means that for any pair of two nodes in any current network, the chance to connect them together is larger than not to connect them. Consequently, this leads to $2 < \gamma < 3$.

3.6.5   Local-World and Multi-Local-World Network Models

In most network models that generate scale-free features by means of preferential attachment, the mechanism responsible for the emergence of the scale-free topology has a global feature; namely, the probability that an existing node receives a new edge is with respect to the total number of existing edges in the whole network. However, this is seldom the case in real life. For example, in the World Trade Web (WTW), it is reported [40] that the global preferential attachment mechanism does not work for those countries that have less than 20 trade connections with other countries. On the other hand, many countries are accelerating their economic cooperation in various regional economic-cooperative organizations, such as EU, ASEAN, and NAFTA. This indicates that very often preferential attachment mechanisms only exist

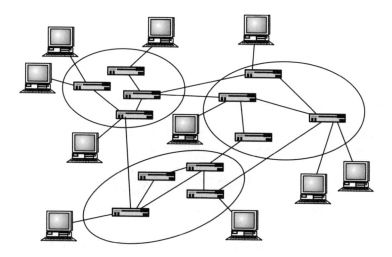

Figure 3.18 Illustration of Internet topology

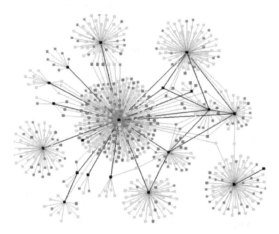

Figure 3.19 Illustration of topology of networks with localization feature

within local economy regions of the WTW. Another typical example, with local preferential attachment but not global preferential attachment, is the Internet. In the Internet, due to technical and economical limitations, a router in one autonomous system (AS) usually favors a shortest-path connection within the same AS when placing new edges. Therefore, the Internet can be divided into many subnetworks, and nodes in the same subnetwork are relatively densely connected while nodes in different subnetworks have very few connections. This is a prominent localization effect, as illustrated by Figure 3.18 for the Internet and Figure 3.19 in general.

Obviously, models with the mechanism of global preferential attachment, such as the BA, EBA and Fitness network models, do not fit well with the topological structures of networks with the localization feature. Motivated by this observation, Li and Chen [41] formulated a *Local-World* (*LW*) *network model*, followed by a somewhat more comprehensive model, the *Multi-Local-World* (*MLW*) *network model*, developed by Fan, Li and Chen [42–44].

3.6.5.1   Local-World Model

The algorithm of the LW model is outlined as follows [41]:

1. Start with a small connected network of m_0 nodes and e_0 edges.
2. At each time step $t \geq 1$, perform the following:
   (a) Select $M \leq m_0$ nodes at random from the existing network to form a "local world," denoted as LW_i.
   (b) Add a new node with $m \leq e_0$ edges, linking to m nodes in its local world formed at step (a), by following the preferential attachment with probability

$$\Pi_{local}(k_i) = \frac{M}{m_0 + t} \times \frac{k_i}{\sum_{j \in LW_i} k_j}, \qquad (3.30)$$

   where node $i \in LW_i$ with degree k_i, $i = 1, 2, \ldots$

Thus, the new coming node only connects to nodes within the corresponding LW model with preferential attachment but does not connect to any other nodes in the network, different from the global preferential attachment of the BA-type models.

Notice, furthermore, that in the LW model described above, a node that belongs to a certain local-world at the present time step may belong to another local-world at the next time step, since nodes in any local-world are selected randomly at every time step. However, in many real-world complex networks, for example on the Internet, after a newcomer (router) has been added to a certain local (regional) network, it will stay there unless it is removed from that particular local-world. Moreover, a real network usually consists of multiple local-worlds rather than only one. To model such networks with multiple local-worlds, a multi-local-world (MLW) model is proposed next, which will find an application for Internet modeling in the next chapter.

3.6.5.2   Multi-Local-World Model

The algorithm of the MLW model is outlined as follows [42, 43]:

1. Start with $m \geq 1$ isolated (small) sub-networks (each is referred to as a local-world), with m_0 nodes and e_0 edges in each local-world, where $1 \leq m_0 \leq m$ and $0 \leq e_0 \leq m_0(m_0 - 1)/2$.
2. At each time-step, perform one of the following five operations:
   (a) With probability p, a new local-world is created, which contains m_0 nodes and e_0 edges. Meanwhile, for convenience a unique name (e.g., A, B, C etc.) or number (e.g., I, II, III etc.) is generated to identify this new local-world.
   (b) With probability q, a new node is added to a randomly selected existing local-world, and the new node brings in m_1 edges connecting to some nodes within the same local-world. In doing so, first a local-world Ω is selected at random, and then a node to which the new node connects inside Ω is chosen with probability

$$\prod(k_i) = \frac{k_i + \alpha}{\sum_{j \in \Omega}(k_j + \alpha)}, \qquad (3.31)$$

   where Ω is the selected local-world, in which node i locates, and the parameter $\alpha > 0$ represents "attractiveness" of node i, which is used to guarantee a certain probability for "small" or "young" nodes to have a chance to receive new edges. This process is repeated m_1 times.
   (c) With probability r, m_2 edges are added to a randomly chosen local-world. To do this, first a local-world Ω is selected at random, and then one end of an edge is chosen randomly while the other end of the edge is selected from Ω with probability (3.31). This process is repeated m_2 times.

(d) With probability s, m_3 edges are deleted within a randomly chosen local-world, describing the death of some old edges during the growth of the network. In doing so, first a local-world Ω is selected at random, and then one end of an edge is chosen randomly while the other end of the edge is selected with probability

$$\Pi'(k_i) = \frac{1}{N_{\Omega}(t) - 1}(1 - \Pi(k_i)) \tag{3.32}$$

where $N_{\Omega}(t)$ represents the number of nodes within Ω at time step t, and $\Pi(k_i)$ is given by (3.28). (The negative terms are used to exclude selecting the other end of the edge from the same node i itself.) This process is repeated m_3 times.

(e) With probability u, m_4 edges are added between two randomly selected existing local-worlds. To do this, randomly select a local-world and a node in the local-world with probability given by (3.31). The selected node is used as one end of an edge, and then the another node of the edge, which is in another local-world chosen at random, is selected with probability (3.31). This process is repeated m_4 times.

In this MLW model, the probability parameters satisfy $0 < q \le 1$, $0 \le p, r, s, u \le 1$, and $p + q + r + s + u = 1$.

The whole procedure of the MLW model is illustrated by schematic diagram Figure 3.20 [42, 43]. In Figure 3.20 (a), the original network has $m = 3$ local-worlds (identified by the triangles A, B, and C), with $m_0 = 3$ nodes (represented by the black circles) and $e_0 = 2$ edges in each local-world. In Figure 3.20 (b), a new local-world D is created, depending on the probability p. This new local-world has $m_0 = 3$ nodes

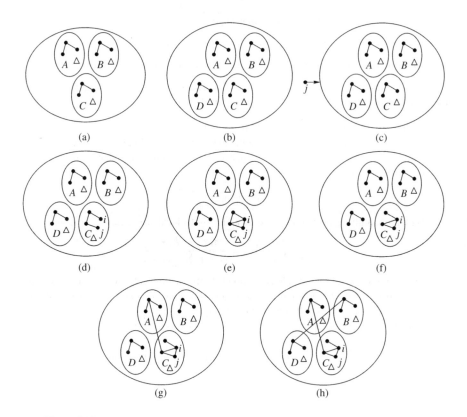

(a) (b) (c)

(d) (e) (f)

(g) (h)

Figure 3.20   Schematic illustration of the MLW model [42]. *Source*: Courtesy of Z. P. Fan

and $e_0 = 2$ edges. In Figure 3.20 (c–d), a new node j joins the network: first, it selects the local-world C in which it will locate, and then it connects to an existing node ($m_1 = 1$) inside this local-world with probability (3.31). In Figure 3.20 (e), $m_2 = 2$ edges are added to a randomly selected local-world. Here, for illustration, local-world C is selected. In so doing, one end of an edge is selected at random, and the other end of the edge is chosen with probability (3.31). In Figure 3.20 (f), a local-world is chosen at random, and then $m_3 = 1$ edge is deleted within this chosen local-world: an end of the edge is selected at random, and then the other end of the edge is chosen with probability (3.32). In Figure 3.20 (g), depending on the probability u, $m_4 = 1$ edge is added between two nodes located in two different local-worlds, respectively. Both ends of the edge are chosen with probability (3.31). In Figure 3.20 (h), at the next time step, one of the five possible operations listed above is performed, depending on the corresponding probability of occurrence. Here, for illustration, an edge is added between local-worlds B and D.

Theorem 3.16 [42] *The node-degree distribution of the MLW network model is approximately given by a biased power-law of the form*

$$P_t(k) = \frac{t}{a(3m + t(1 + 2p))}(m_1 + b/a)^{1/a}(k + b/a)^{-\gamma}, \qquad (3.33)$$

where $\gamma = 1 + 1/a$, *with*

$$a = \frac{qm_1}{c} + \frac{rm_2(q + m_0 p - p)}{(q + m_0 p)c} + \frac{sm_3 p}{(q + m_0 p)c} + \frac{2um_4}{c}$$

$$b = \frac{q\alpha m_1}{c} + \frac{rm_2}{(q + m_0 p)} + \frac{rm_2(q + m_0 p - p)\alpha}{(q + m_0 p)c}$$

$$+ \frac{sm_3 p\alpha}{(q + m_0 p)c} - \frac{2sm_3}{(q + m_0 p)} + \frac{2um_4\alpha}{c}$$

$$c = 2(pe_0 + qm_1 + rm_2 - sm_3 + um_4) + q\alpha$$

and all other probability parameters are defined as in the above-described algorithm.

Proof. [42] The following proof is similar to the proof of Theorem 3.14, in which the degree distribution of a node i in the local-world Ω is first derived, as outlined below.

Step (i) With probability p, a new local-world is created:

In this case, the degree of node i in the existing local-world Ω does not change over time, since the original nodes in the newly created local-world have no edges with any other nodes in the existing local-worlds. Thus,

$$\left(\frac{\partial k_i}{\partial t}\right)_{(1)} = 0.$$

Step (ii) With probability q, a new node is being added to the local-world Ω:

$$\left(\frac{\partial k_i}{\partial t}\right)_{(2)} = \frac{m_1 q}{m + tp}\frac{k_i + \alpha}{\sum_{j \in \Omega}(k_j + \alpha)}.$$

The term on the right-hand side corresponds to the random selection of a local-world, where a node is selected with probability (3.31). Since there are m_1 edges between the new node and the existing nodes, the coefficient is equal to m_1.

Step (iii) With probability r, m_2 edges are being added to the local-world Ω:

$$\left(\frac{\partial k_i}{\partial t}\right)_{(3)} = \frac{rm_2}{m + tp}\left[\frac{1}{N_\Omega(t)} + \left(1 - \frac{1}{N_\Omega(t)}\right)\frac{k_i + \alpha}{\sum_{j \in \Omega}(k_j + \alpha)}\right].$$

The first term on the right-hand side means the random selection of node i within the local-world Ω, which is also chosen at random; the second term represents the preferential selection of node i inside Ω.

Step (iv) With probability s, m_3 edges are being deleted from within a randomly chosen local-world Ω:

$$\left(\frac{\partial k_i}{\partial t}\right)_{(4)} = -\frac{sm_3}{m+tp}\left[\frac{1}{N_\Omega(t)} + \left(1 - \frac{1}{N_\Omega(t)}\right)\frac{1}{N_\Omega(t)-1}\left(1 - \frac{k_i + \alpha}{\sum_{j\in\Omega}(k_j+\alpha)}\right)\right].$$

The term on the right-hand side implies that the decrease of the degree of node i in the local-world Ω comes from two sources: one is that it acts as a randomly chosen end of a deleted edge, and the other is that it is the end of a deleted edge selected with probability (3.32).

Step (v) With probability u, m_4 edges are being added between two local-worlds in the network:

$$\left(\frac{\partial k_i}{\partial t}\right)_{(5)} = um_4\left[\frac{2}{m+tp}\frac{k_i+\alpha}{\sum_{j\in\Omega}(k_j+\alpha)} - \frac{1}{m+tp}\frac{1}{m+tp}\frac{k_i+\alpha}{\sum_{j\in\Omega}(k_j+\alpha)}\right].$$

Note that at time step t the total degree of any local-world Ω in the network, on average, is

$$\sum_{j\in\Omega} k_j = 2t(pe_0 + qm_1 + rm_2 - sm_3 + um_4)/(m+tp).$$

And the number of nodes in the local-world Ω, on average, is

$$N_\Omega(t) = m_0 + qt/(m+tp).$$

Fore convenience, let

$$c = 2(pe_0 + qm_1 + rm_2 - sm_3 + um_4) + q\alpha.$$

Now, by combining all related equations together, one obtains

$$\frac{\partial k_i}{\partial t} = \frac{qm_1}{c}\frac{k_i}{t} + \frac{qm_1\alpha}{c}\frac{1}{t} + \frac{rm_2(q+m_0p-p)}{(q+m_0p)c}\frac{k_i}{t}$$

$$+ \left(\frac{rm_2}{(q+m_0p)} + \frac{rm_2(q+m_0p-p)\alpha}{(q+m_0p)c}\right)\frac{1}{t}$$

$$- \frac{rm_2m}{(q+m_0p)c}\frac{(k_i+\alpha)}{t^2} + \frac{sm_3p}{(q+m_0p)c}\frac{k_i}{t} + \left(\frac{sm_3p\alpha}{(q+m_0p)c} - \frac{2sm_3}{(q+m_0p)}\right)\frac{1}{t}$$

$$+ \frac{sm_3m}{(q+m_0p)c}\frac{(k_i+\alpha)}{t^2} + \frac{2um_4}{c}\frac{k_i}{t} + \frac{2um_4\alpha}{c}\frac{1}{t} - \frac{um_4}{c}\frac{(k_i+\alpha)}{t(m+tp)}$$

$$= \left(\frac{qm_1}{c} + \frac{rm_2(q+m_0p-p)}{(q+m_0p)c} + \frac{sm_3p}{(q+m_0p)c} + \frac{2um_4}{c}\right)\frac{k_i}{t}$$

$$+ \left(\frac{q\alpha m_1}{c} + \frac{rm_2}{(q+m_0p)} + \frac{rm_2(q+m_0p-p)\alpha}{(q+m_0p)c}\right)\frac{1}{t}$$

$$+ \left(\frac{sm_3p\alpha}{(q+m_0p)c} - \frac{2sm_3}{(q+m_0p)} + \frac{2um_4\alpha}{c}\right)\frac{1}{t} \quad \text{(for large } t\text{)}.$$

Next, for convenience, define

$$a = \frac{qm_1}{c} + \frac{rm_2(q + m_0p - p)}{(q + m_0p)c} + \frac{sm_3p}{(q + m_0p)c} + \frac{2um_4}{c}$$

$$b = \frac{q\alpha m_1}{c} + \frac{rm_2}{(q + m_0p)} + \frac{rm_2(q + m_0p - p)\alpha}{(q + m_0p)c}$$

$$+ \frac{sm_3p\alpha}{(q + m_0p)c} - \frac{2sm_3}{(q + m_0p)} + \frac{2um_4\alpha}{c}.$$

Then, one has

$$\frac{\partial k_i}{\partial t} = a\frac{k_i}{t} + b\frac{1}{t}.$$

Since $a \neq 0$, using the initial condition $k_i(t_i) = m_1$, one can solve the above differential equation to obtain

$$k_i(t) = -\frac{b}{a} + \left(m_1 + \frac{b}{a}\right)\left(\frac{t}{t_i}\right)^a.$$

Furthermore, define the time unit in the above MLW model as (one local-world creation)/(one node increment)/(one edge deletion)/(one new edge within a local-world)/(one new edge between local-worlds). Then, the probability density of t_i is

$$P_i(t_i) = 1/(3m + t(1 + 2p)).$$

Consequently, one obtains

$$P(k_i(t) < k) = P\left(t_i > \left(\frac{m_1 + b/a}{k + b/a}\right)^{1/a} t\right)$$

$$= 1 - \frac{1}{(3m + t(1 + 2p))}\left(\frac{m_1 + b/a}{k + b/a}\right)^{1/a} t.$$

Since $P(k) = \frac{\partial(P(k_i(t) < k))}{\partial k}$, one has

$$P(k) = \frac{t}{a(3m + t(1 + 2p))}(m_1 + b/a)^{1/a}(k + b/a)^{-\gamma},$$

where $\gamma = 1 + 1/a$. ∎

To predict real-world networks, whose power-law exponents typically satisfy $2 < \gamma < 3$, the above MLW model can be applied, subject to the following conditions:

$$\begin{cases} (m_1 + b/a) > 0 \\ a < 1 \end{cases}.$$

Obviously, if one takes $rm_2 \geq 2sm_3$, then the above conditions are satisfied.

Note that the power-law exponent increases with the increase of the attractiveness α of nodes in the above MLW model, which indicates that the attractiveness of nodes in a network may play an important role although the underlying mechanism is somewhat complicated and ambiguous.

Now, consider the following special cases of the MLW model.

Case A: When $m = 1, q = 1$, and $p = r = s = u = 0$, the network has only one local-world, and the power-law exponent $\gamma = 3 + \alpha/m_1$. The MLW model reduces to the BA model.

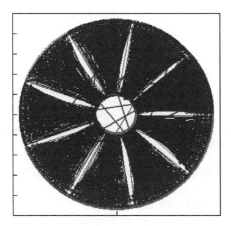

Figure 3.21   An example of a network generated by the MLW model [42]. *Source*: Courtesy of Z. P. Fan

Case B: If a network consists of only one local-world, and the evolution of the network only includes the events of adding node and edges, namely, if $m = 1, p = 0, s = u = 0$, then it becomes the local-world network model discussed in Section 3.6.5 above, with the exponent $\gamma = 3 + \alpha q/((m_1 - m_2)q + m_2)$. This indicates that the event of adding edges between two existing nodes in the network also has a significant impact on the scale-free feature of this evolving network. However, the exponent remains unchanged if one takes $\alpha = 0$, which may indicate that the attractiveness of nodes plays a more important role than the addition of edges in the evolution of the network.

Case C: If a network consists of a fixed number of local-worlds, and the events of addition and deletion of edges between two nodes in the same local-world do not occur, then one has $p = 0, \quad r = 0, \quad s = 0$. In this case, the degree exponent of the resulting network is $\gamma = 2 + (m_1 + \alpha)q/((m_1 - 2m_4) + 2m_4)$.

Case D: If $rm_2 = 2sm_3$, then $b = \alpha\ a$, so $P(k) \propto (k + \alpha)^{-\gamma}$, which is different from $P(k) \propto k^{-\gamma}$ in the BA model. This clearly indicates that the attractiveness of nodes is very important to the evolution of the network.

   To visualize the graph generated by the MLW model, a simple simulation is carried out as follows [42]: randomly assign a subregion to every local-world in the plane which the entire network occupies. Within the assigned subregion, nodes belonging to the same local-world are distributed randomly. Figure 3.21 shows such an example of a network generated by the MLW model, where the network consists of 500 nodes and includes 9 local-worlds. In this figure, nodes in the same local-world are relatively densely connected, while nodes between different local-worlds are connected sparsely.

Exercises

3.1   1. Let G be a random graph and G^c be its complementary graph. State three major properties of G^c.

   2. Let G be a scale-free graph and G^c be its complementary graph. State three major properties of G^c.

3.2   Show some real-world network examples that can be well described by the ER random-graph network model, the WS small-world network model, and the NW small-world network model, respectively.

3.3 Verify that every power law of the form $\alpha k^{-\gamma}$, where k is an integer variable and α, γ is a constant, satisfying the scale-free property $f(ax) = bf(x)$.

3.4 Start with a large-sized lattice. For every connected pair of nodes, with a certain probability rewire their edge to a randomly-picked third node in the lattice. Perform this operation on every directly connected node pair, once and once only, then stop. To that end, what kind of network will you obtain? Why?

3.5 Show some real-world examples of BA, EBA, Fitness and MLW networks and explain why you think they are such networks.

3.6 Consider the following four complex network models (A, B, C, D):

(a) Model A
   1. Start with a small-sized star-shaped network.
   2. At every step, add one node to the existing network. This new node is connected to every existing node according to the following preferential attachment probability, where k_i is the degree of node i:

$$\Pi_i = 1 - \frac{k_i}{\sum k_j}, \quad i = 1, 2, \ldots$$

   What kind of network will you obtain? Briefly explain why you think so.

(b) Model B
   1. *Initialization*: Start with a large-sized fully-connected network.
   2. *Process*: For every possible pair of nodes, with probability p ($0 < p < 1$) remove the edge between them. Remove all isolated nodes whenever they appear.
   3. *End*: After every possible pair of nodes has been operated once, and once only, stop.
      What kind of network will you obtain? Briefly explain why you think so.

(c) Model C
   1. *Initialization*: Start with a large-sized fully-connected network.
   2. *Process*: Pick up an edge: if removing it does not disconnect the whole network, then remove it; but if removing it will disconnect the network, then do nothing. Continue to pick up another edge from the resultant network and repeat the above possible edge-removal operation.
   3. *End*: After every possible edge has been operated once, and once only, stop.
      What kind of network will you obtain? Briefly explain why you think so.

(d) Model D
   1. *Initialization*: Start with a large-sized tree.
   2. *Preferential Attachment*: Pick up every possible pair of nodes from the tree. If this pair of nodes is directly connected already, do nothing; if this pair of nodes is not directly connected, then with a probability proportional to the degree of the larger node, add an edge between them.
   3. *End*: After every possible pair of nodes has been operated once, and once only, stop.
      What kind of network will you obtain? Is this resulting network a good model for an Internet-like network? If you think so, state three major advantages of this model; if you don't think so, state three major disadvantages of this model.

3.7 Consider two computer network models of the same large size, say 10 000 nodes: one scale-free network and one random-graph network.
   In each model, randomly pick 100 nodes as data sources, each generates and sends out one and only data packet. Also, randomly pick 100 nodes as destinations to possibly receive some coming packets. Assume that every packet traverses through the shortest path from its source to a destination (if there are more than one of such nearest destinations then the packet will randomly go to any one).

Now, in order to compare the traffic performance of the two networks, one can either wait until all packets have arrived at destinations and then count the total travelling time (the less the better); or, one can stop the process at a certain time instant and then count how many packets have arrived at destinations (the more the better).

1. Assume that all nodes and all edges have infinite betweenness. In this case, which network will likely have better traffic performance, and why?
2. Assume that all nodes and edges can only handle one packet at a time, so if two packets arrive at a node in the same time then they will have to form a queue, so one packet will be delayed to deliver by one time step. In this case, which network will likely have better traffic performance, and why?
3. Assume the data generation and transmission mechanism is changed to the following: Randomly pick one node as the data source to generate 100 packets, one at a time, and also randomly pick one node as the destination to receive all packets sequentially. In this new scenario, answer the above two same questions, in (1) and (2).

3.8   In a typical sensor network, each node is a sensor and there is a node which is the computing centre. Assume that all sensors are fixed in location and each node is equipped with a battery. When one sensor detects a moving target, it will send a massage to its immediate neighbor and the neighbor will then pass the message to the next, until the message finally reaches the computing centre. Meanwhile, every activated node will consumes some battery energy. In the design of such a sensor network, two key issues are the main concerns: detection coverage range and battery lifetime.

1. What kind of network structure will likely have the longest detection coverage range?
2. What kind of network structure will likely have the longest battery lifetime?
3. What kind of network structure will likely be optimal in the sense of having both a long detection coverage range and a long battery lifetime?

References

[1] Watts, D.J. and Strogatz, S.H (1998) Collective dynamics of 'small-world' networks. *Nature,* **393**(6684): 440–2.
[2] Barabási, A-L. and Albert, R. (1999) Emergence of scaling in random networks. *Science,* **286**(5439): 509–12.
[3] Newman, M.E.J. and Watts, D.J. (1999) Renormalization group analysis of the small-world network model. *Physics Letters A,* **263**: 341–6.
[4] Albert, R. and Barabási, A-L. (2000) Topology of evolving networks: local events and universality. *Physical Review E,* **85**(24): 5234–7.
[5] Kleinberg, J. (2000) Navigation in a small world. *Nature,* **406**: 845.
[6] Albert, R. and Barabási, A-L. (2002) Statistical mechanics of complex networks. *Reviews of Modern Physics,* **74**: 47–97.
[7] Newman, M.E.J. (2003) The structure and function of complex networks. *SIAM Review,* **45**: 167–256.
[8] Newman, M. E.J. (2010) *Networks: An Introduction.* Oxford University Press, Oxford, pp. 713–18.
[9] Erdös, P. and Rényi, A. (1960) On the evolution of random graphs. *Publications of the Mathematical Institute of the Hungarian Academy of Science,* **5**: 17–60.
[10] Bollobás, B. (2001) *Random Graphs.* Academic Press, New York, 2nd edn.
[11] Crucitti, P., Latora, V, Marchiori, M, and Rapisarda, A. (2003) Complex systems: analysis and models of real-world networks. In M. Francesco, L.S. Brizhik and M.W. Ho (eds), *Energy and Information Transfer in Biological Systems,* World Scientific, pp. 188–204.
[12] Bender, E.A. and Canfield, E.R. (1978) The asymptotic number of labeled graphs with given degree sequences. *Journal of Combinatorial Theory, Series A,* **24**: 296–307.
[13] Barrat, A. and Weigt, M. (2000) On the properties of small world networks. *European Physical Journal B,* **13**: 547–60.
[14] Newman, M.E.J. (2002) The structure and function of networks. *Computer Physics Communications,* **147**: 40–5.
[15] Kleinberg, J. (2000) The small-world phenomenon: An algorithmic perspective. *Proceedings of the 32nd ACM Symposium on Theory of Computing,* 163–70.
[16] Albert, R., Jeong, H. and Barabási, A-L. (2000) Error and attack tolerance of complex networks. *Nature,* **406**(6794): 378–82.

[17] Bollobás, B. and Riordan, O. (2003) Mathematical results on scale-free random graphs. In S. Bornholdt and H.G. Schuster (ed.), *Handbook of Graphs and Networks: From the Genome to the Internet.* Wiley-VCH, Berlin, 1–34.

[18] Cohen, R. and Havlin, S. (2003) Scale-free networks are ultrasmall. *Physical Review Letters,* **86**: 3682–5.

[19] Fronczak, A., Fronczak, P. and Holyst, J.A. (2003) Mean-field theory for clustering coefficients in Barabási-Albert networks, *Physical Review E*, **68**: 046126.

[20] Hou, Z., Kong, X., Shi, D. and Chen, G. (2009) Degree-distribution stability of growing networks. In J. Zhou (ed.), *Complex*, LNICST, 5: 1827–37.

[21] Dorogovtsev, S.N., Mendes, J.F.F. and Samukhin, A.N. (2000) Structure of growing networks with preferential linking. *Physical Review Letters,* **85**: 4633–6.

[22] Li, X. and Chen, G. (2003) A local world evolving network model. *Physica A*, **328**: 274–86.

[23] De Sola Price, D.S. (1965) Networks of scientific papers. *Science*, 149(3683): 510–15.

[24] De Sola Price, D.S. (1976) A general theory of bibliometric and other cumulative advantage processes. *Journal of the Association for Information Science,* **27**(5): 292–306.

[25] Barabási, A-L. and Bonabeau, E. (2003) Scale-free networks. *Scientific American*, May, 60–9.

[26] Wang, X.F. (2002) Complex networks: Topology, dynamics and synchronization. *International Journal of Bifurcation and Chaos*, **12**(5): 885–916.

[27] Carlson, J. and Doyle, J. (2000) Highly optimized tolerance: Robustness and power laws in complex systems. *Physical Review Letters*, **84**(11): 2529–32.

[28] Carlson, J. and Doyle, J. (2002) Complexity and robustness. *Proceedings of the National Academy of Sciences*, **99**(Suppl. 1): 2539–45.

[29] Broder, A., Kumar, R. and Maghoul, F. *et al.* (2000) Graph structure in the web. *Computer Networks,* **33**: 309–20.

[30] Doyle, J., Alderson, D., Li, L. *et al.* (2005) The "robust yet fragile" nature of the Internet. *Proceedings of the National Academy of Sciences*, **102**(41): 14497–14502.

[31] Callway, D.S., Newman, M.E.J., Strogatz, S.H. *et al.* (2000) Network robustness and fragility: Percolation on random graphs. *Physical Review Letters,* **85**(25): 5468–71.

[32] Cohen, R., Erez, K., ben-Avraham, D *et al.* (2000) Resilience of the Internet to random breakdowns. *Physical Review Letters,* **85**(21): 4626–8.

[33] Cohen, R., Erez, K., ben-Avraham, D *et al.* (2001) Breakdown of the Internet under intentional attack. *Physical Review Letters*, **86**(16): 3682–5.

[34] Valente, A.X.C.N., Sarkar, A. and Stone, H.A. (2004) Two-peak and three-peak optimal complex networks. *Physical Review Letters*, **91**: 118702.

[35] Bollobás, B. and Riordan, O. (2003) Robustness and vulnerability of scale-free random graphs. *Internet Mathematics,* **1**: 1–35.

[36] Holme, P., Kim, B.J., Yoon, C.N. *et al.* (2002) Attack vulnerability of complex networks. *Physical Review E,* **65**: 056109.

[37] Bianconi, G. and Barabási, A-L. (2001) Bose–Einstein condensation in complex networks. *Physical Review Letters*, **86**: 5632–5.

[38] Aiello, W., Chung, F. and Lu, L.Y. (2001) A random graph model for power law graphs. *Experimental Mathematics*, **10**: 53–66.

[39] Aiello, W., Chung, F. and Lu, L.Y. (2002) Random evolution of massive graphs. In J. Abello, P.M. Pardalos and M.G.C. Resende (eds), *Handbook on Massive Data Sets*, Kluwer Academic, pp. 97–122.

[40] Li, X., Jin, Y.Y. and Chen, G. (2003) Complexity and synchronization of the World Trade Web. *Physica A*, **328**: 287–96.

[41] Li, X. and Chen, G. (2003) A local-world evolving network model. *Physica A*, **328**: 274–86.

[42] Fan, Z.P. (2006) *Complex Networks: From Topology to Dynamics.* PhD Thesis, City University of Hong Kong, May.

[43] Chen, G., Fan, Z.P. and Li, X. (2005) Modeling the complex Internet topology. In G. Vattay and L. Kocarev (eds), *Complex Dynamics in Communication Networks*, Springer-Verlag, New York, pp. 213–34.

[44] Fan, Z.P., Chen, G., and Zhang, Y. (2009) A comprehensive multi-local-world model for complex networks. *Physics Letters A*, **373**: 1601–5.

Part Two

Applications -
Selected Topics

4

Internet: Topology and Modeling

4.1 Introduction

The Internet, initially developed in the 1970–80s for a small community of scientific researchers, has literally become the biggest manmade infrastructure, connecting about 2.7 billion users worldwide today.

The Internet contains roughly a trillion webpages, and transports about ten billion gigabytes of data every month on average. In 2013 alone, the Web grew by more than a third, with applications ranging from online videos to e-commerce and to cloud-computing, not to mention the continuous transmissions of massive scientific datasets, among many others. A good statistics source of the Internet is the "Internet World Stats" [1], in which most data are frequently updated.

By its very nature, the Internet is a computer network, or more precisely a network of heterogeneous computer subnetworks, such as *Local Area Network* (LAN), *Metropolitan Area Network* (MAN), and *Wide Area Network* (WAN), which are mutually interconnected in many different ways. LANs are used to connect *hosts* (sets of computers) within a relatively small local area such as a building or a college department, and employ technologies like Ethernet and token rings. MANs and WANs, on the other hand, are used to connect hosts scattered over a regional area such as a large company or a college campus, and use optical fibers, long-distance landlines, and even wireless satellite transmission channels.

On the Internet, every Personal Computer (PC), router, host, LAN and even MAN, can be considered as a node, and every kind of connection among them, such as optical fiber, wire, or wireless channel, can be considered as an edge. The ensemble of all these nodes and edges compose a heterogeneous and self-organized huge network, the biggest artificial network of its kind in the world. On the software side, Internet heterogeneity is reflected by its various protocols, such as Transmission Control Protocol (TCP) and Internet Protocol (IP protocol) suites consisting of a family of cooperative protocol software, and some others at the application level like Internet Control Message Protocol (ICMP), File Transfer Protocol (FTP), and Simple Mail Transfer Protocol (SMTP).

Although the Internet's infrastructure operates and grows without any central management, it nevertheless has been built by many dependent or independent designers according to their engineering considerations, possibly subject to some local optimization and technical constraints. As a result, the underlying structure of the entire Internet, or part of it, can be identified and described in an appropriate way. In fact, Internet modeling has gradually become a focal topic of the current scientific research. In order to predict and improve the performance of the Internet, it is very important to understand and model its topology. For this purpose, one approach is to study the Internet at the Autonomous Systems (AS) level, or at a much larger scale at the routers level, as illustrated by Figure 4.1 [2]. At the routers level, each node is a router and each edge is a physical link (e.g., optical fiber); while at the AS level, each AS (also called domain) is a subnet within which the information is routed using an internal

Fundamentals of Complex Networks: Models, Structures and Dynamics, First Edition.
Guanrong Chen, Xiaofan Wang, Xiang Li.

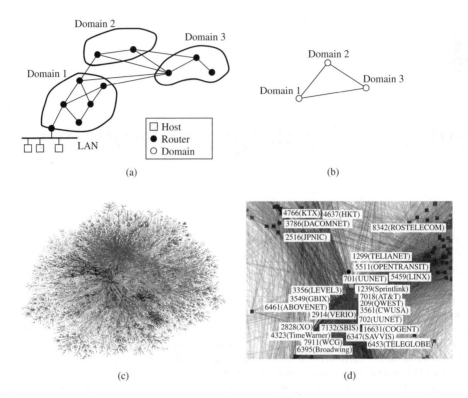

Figure 4.1 Two layers of the Internet: (a) Routers level [2]. (b) AS level [2]. (c) Illustration of an IP-address network at the router level (William R. Cheswick, Lumeta Corporation, New Jersey, USA); (d) Visualization of 12 979 AS nodes with 35 589 peering sessions (CAIDA Topology Mapping Analysis Team). *Source*: Reprinted by permission Faloutsos M, Faloutsos P, Faloutsos C. On power-law relationships of the Internet topology. *ACM SIGCOMM Computer Communication Review*, 1999, **29** (4): 251–262 © 1999 Association for Computing Machinery, Inc.

algorithm that may differ from the others used in other subnets. AS communicate each other using a specific routing algorithm – the Border Gateway Protocol (BGP). Thus, every AS approximately maps to an Internet Service Provider (ISP), which may consist of millions of routers linked together in some way.

The Internet is a typical complex network with large numbers of nodes and of edges processing huge amounts of information data growing rapidly and continuously. To model this extremely huge and complex network, or part of it, Internet topology generators are usually used. In the past, the study of Internet topology generators has gone through three stages of development:

1. The first generation includes the random topology generators, invented in the 1980s, with the Waxman generator [3] as its representative.
2. The second generation includes the structural topology generators, developed in the 1990s, with Tiers [4] and Transit-stub [5] generators being the most typical ones that have prominent hierarchical structures.
3. The third generation has been evolving since the year 2000, which is based on the node degrees, such as BRITE [6] and Inet [7], and more recently several others based on small-world and, in particular, scale-free network models [8–13].

4.2   Topological Properties of the Internet

Real AS-level Internet data can be obtained from the websites of the Oregon Route Views Project [14], the Internet Topology Collection [15], the National Laboratory for Applied Network Research (NLANR), and the Cooperative Association for Internet Data Analysis (CAIDA). Some of these websites are being updated, even within hours daily by taking snapshots from the routing tables of the Border Gateway Protocol (BGP). Figure 4.2 is the numbers of AS in the Internet from November 1997 to February 2002, from which one can see the trend of the AS expansion. Other useful information and data about the Internet, also at the AS level, mainly come from Skitter [16] and Whois [17] (see also [10–12]). Skitter provides the Internet topological measures by the CAIDA, using Traceroute (a computer network tool for determining the route taken by packets across an IP network), which is also continuously updated almost every day. Whois is a domain search tool and data base, identifying the owners and IP addresses of all domains, but it is not automatically managed; therefore information may not be updated in a timely way. Most data shown in the discussions below were actually taken from Oregon rather than Skitter and Whois. It is noted that Réseaux IP Européens (RIPE) [18] provides another important BGP data source. Recently, the Internet Research Lab of UCLA merges the data from different sources such as Oregon Route Views, RIPE, Abilene, CERNET, Looking Glasses, and Route Servers, into one single overall topology [19].

4.2.1   Power–Law Node-Degree Distribution

Based on a careful analysis of Internet statistical data from November 1997 to February 1998, for the first time in the literature the Faloutsos brothers observed some power–law types of distribution characteristics in 1999 [2] and then in 2003 using even more Internet data (from November 1997 to February 2002), both at the AS level [11]. They found that Internet topology satisfies the following four kinds of power–law distributions:

Power law I: $d_v \sim r_v^R$, where d_v is the degree of node v, r_v is the index of node v in decreasing order of all node-degrees, and R is a rank constant exponent (which is negative as shown below).

Power law II: $D_d \sim d^D$, where D_d is the percentage of nodes with degrees larger than d, and D is a degree constant exponent satisfying $D = 1/R$ (so it is negative).

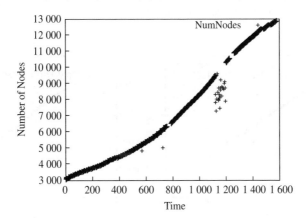

Figure 4.2   Numbers of Internet AS (November 1997–February 2002) [11]. *Source*: Reprinted with permission from Siganos, G, Faloutsos, M., Faloutsos, P. and Faloutsos, C. (2003) Power laws and the AS-level Internet topology. *IEEE/ACM Transactions on Networking*, **11**(4): 514–24. Copyright (2003) IEEE

Power law III: $\lambda_i \sim i^\varepsilon$, where λ_i is the *i*th eigenvalue in decreasing order of the network connectivity matrix, and ε is the characteristic constant exponent, satisfying $\varepsilon \approx 0.5D$ (therefore it is also negative).

Power law IV: $P(h) \sim h^H (h \ll \delta)$, where $P(h)$ is the number of node pairs of distance not larger than *h*, also referred to as the number of node pairs in the *h*-hop, including self-node pairs and counting twice of other node pairs, and *H* is a hop constant exponent satisfying

$$P(h) = \begin{cases} ch^H, & h \ll \delta \\ N^2, & h \geq \delta \end{cases},$$

where $c = N + 2M$, *N* and *M* are the numbers of nodes and edges, respectively, and δ is the diameter of the network.

Figures 4.3–4.6 plot the resulting curves calculated based on the real Internet data on May 26, 2001, and Figure 4.7 displays the four power–law curves calculated based on the data from November 1997 to February 2002 [11], where (a), (b), (c) and (d) depict the evolution of the exponents *R*, *D*, ε and *H*, respectively. It shows that all these parameters are changing rather slowly although the size of the Internet

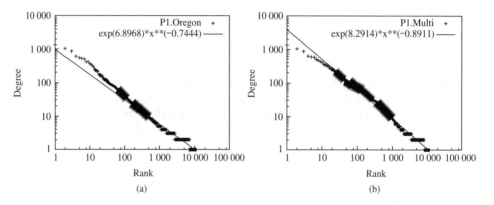

Figure 4.3   The log–log distributions of (a) d_v and (b) r_v [11]. *Source*: Reprinted with permission from Siganos, G, Faloutsos, M., Faloutsos, P. and Faloutsos, C. (2003) Power laws and the AS-level Internet topology. *IEEE/ACM Transactions on Networking*, **11**(4): 514–24. Copyright (2003) IEEE

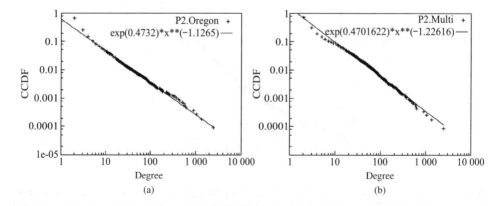

Figure 4.4   The log–log distributions of (a) D_d and (b) *d* [11]. *Source*: Reprinted with permission from Siganos, G, Faloutsos, M., Faloutsos, P. and Faloutsos, C. (2003) Power laws and the AS-level Internet topology. *IEEE/ACM Transactions on Networking*, **11**(4): 514–24. Copyright (2003) IEEE

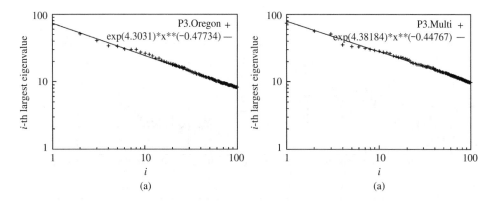

Figure 4.5 The log–log distributions of (a) λ_i and (b) i [11]. *Source*: Reprinted with permission from Siganos, G, Faloutsos, M., Faloutsos, P. and Faloutsos, C. (2003) Power laws and the AS-level Internet topology. *IEEE/ACM Transactions on Networking*, **11**(4): 514–24. Copyright (2003) IEEE

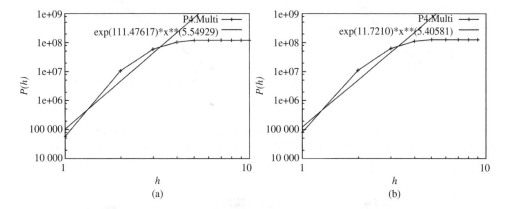

Figure 4.6 The log–log distributions of (a) $P(h)$ and (b) h [11]. *Source*: Reprinted with permission from Siganos, G, Faloutsos, M., Faloutsos, P. and Faloutsos, C. (2003) Power laws and the AS-level Internet topology. *IEEE/ACM Transactions on Networking*, **11**(4): 514–24. Copyright (2003) IEEE

grows very rapidly (for example, the total number of nodes within the six hops of the network increases from 3000 on November 8, 1997 to 13000 on February 28, 2002, as shown in Figure 4.7 (d)).

4.2.2 Hierarchical Structure

The Internet consists of a large number of interconnected Autonomous Systems (AS). Each AS may be considered as a *Stub domain* or a *Transit domain*. A Transit domain can be a Metropolitan Area Network (MAN) or a Wide Area Network (WAN), typically a regional or even a national Internet Service Provider (ISP). A Stub domain usually only processes the information starting and ending inside the domain, while a Transit domain has no such restriction. In fact, a Transit domain is typically used to link many nearby Stub domains together, such that the Stub domains do not need to be linked directly. Typically, a Stub domain consists of campus networks or some other interconnected Local Area Networks (LAN), depending on the respective Transit domain or some parts of the domain, to carry out information processing and communications [20]. The structure of the Internet at the AS level is illustrated by Figure 4.8 [13], and a simulated result is demonstrated in Figure 4.9 [14].

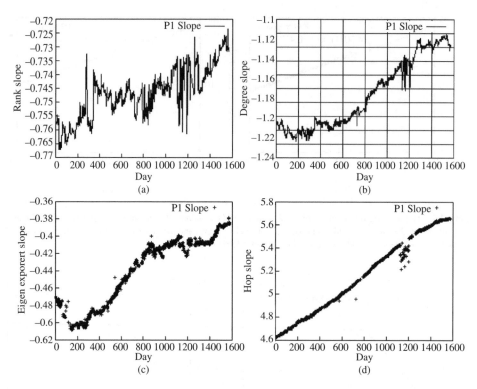

Figure 4.7 Evolutions of the four power–law distributions [11]. (a), (b), (c) and (d) depict the evolution of the exponents R, D, ε and H respectively. *Source*: Reprinted with permission from Siganos, G, Faloutsos, M., Faloutsos, P. and Faloutsos, C. (2003) Power laws and the AS-level Internet topology. *IEEE/ACM Transactions on Networking*, **11**(4): 514–24. Copyright (2003) IEEE

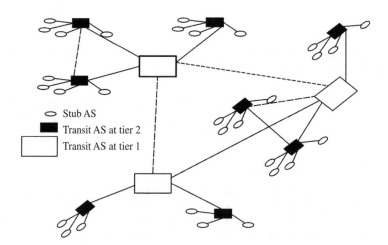

Figure 4.8 Structure of the Internet at the AS level [13]. *Source*: Reprinted with permission from Jaiswal, S., Rosenberg, A.L. and Towsley, D. (2004) Comparing the structure of power–law graphs and the Internet AS graph. *Proceedings of the 12th IEEE International Conference on Network Protocols*, 294–303. Copyright (2004) IEEE

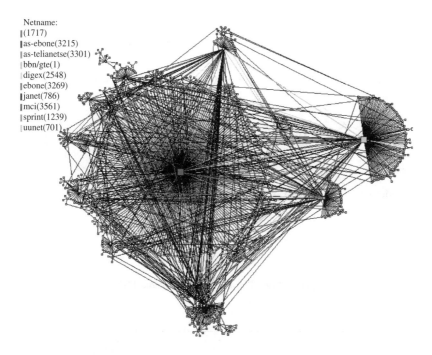

Netname:
|(1717)
|as-ebone(3215)
|as-telianetse(3301)
|bbn/gte(1)
|digex(2548)
|ebone(3269)
|janet(786)
|mci(3561)
|sprint(1239)
|uunet(701)

Figure 4.9   Internet at the AS level on 3 December 1998 (generated by Skitter) [14]

The concepts of Transit and Stub describes the structural inner-connections of the Internet at the AS level. A Transit as a node in the network connects one or more Stub nodes, where each path starting from or ending at a Stub node must go through those service-providing Transit nodes. With respect to other Transit domains, a Transit node can be a provider and also a customer; therefore, from such a provider-customer point of view, each AS on the Internet can be considered as some kind of *Tier*. An AS at the highest Tier belongs to the Transit domain, called Tier-1 provider. Those Transit and Stub domains at a lower Tier depend on the Transit nodes at a higher Tier to communicate with the other domains at their same level. On the other hand, a Transit domain can also communicate with other Transit domains through a certain peering relation at the same Tier, as illustrated by Figure 4.10 [21], where the average numbers of AS from Tier-1 to Tier-4 are 614.29, 19.30, 6.93 and 4.30, respectively, as shown in Figure 4.11 [13].

4.2.3   Rich-Club Structure

On the Internet, a few nodes have a large number of edges, called *hubs*, and they tend to connect to each other, as illustrated by Figure 4.12, leading to a structure called *rich club* [22]. A rich-club structure of the Internet at the AS level is illustrated by Figure 4.13 [23].

The rich-club phenomenon in an AS layer of size N can be described by the connectivity index $\Phi(r/N)$ of its first r biggest nodes defined by the ratio of the number M of their existing edges versus the number $r(r-1)/2$ of all possible edges among them; namely,

$$\Phi(r/N) = \frac{M}{r(r-1)/2} = \frac{2M}{r(r-1)}.$$

If $\Phi(r/N) = 1$, then the first r biggest nodes compose a fully connected subnetwork, as shown by Figure 4.14. Reportedly, some real data have verified that the connectivity index $\phi(r/N)$ follows a power–law form, $\Phi(r/N) \sim r^{-\gamma}$, with $\gamma = 1.1 \pm 0.2$ for the AS levels and $\gamma = 1.8 \pm 0.2$ for the router levels of the Internet [22].

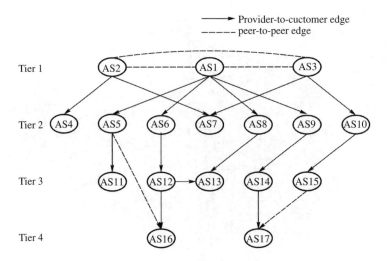

Figure 4.10   Tier structure of the Internet [21]

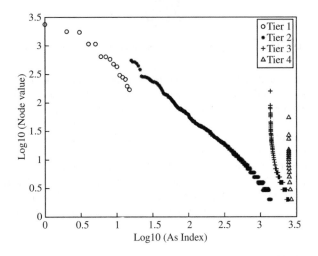

Figure 4.11   Degree distributions of AS at different Tiers [13]. *Source*: Reprinted with permission from Jaiswal, S., Rosenberg, A.L. and Towsley, D. (2004) Comparing the structure of power–law graphs and the Internet AS graph. *Proceedings of the 12th IEEE International Conference on Network Protocols*, 294–303. Copyright (2004) IEEE

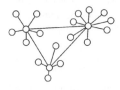

Figure 4.12   Structure of rich club [22]

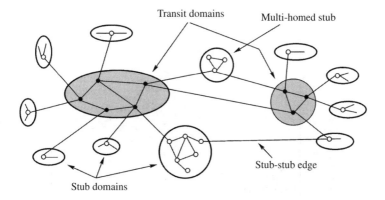

Figure 4.13 Rich-club structure of the Internet at the AS level [23]

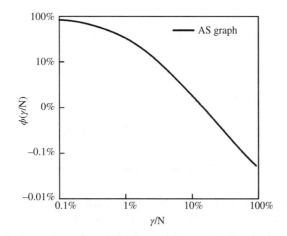

Figure 4.14 Rich-club phenomenon of the Internet at the AS level [33]. *Source*: Reprinted, with permission from Zhou, S. and Mondragon, R-J. (2004) The rich-club phenomenon in the Internet topology. *IEEE Communications Letters*, **8** (3): 180–2. © [2004] IEEE

4.2.4 Disassortative Property

As just mentioned, the Internet hubs are well interconnected. Since hubs are big nodes of high degrees, it is interesting to figure out what happens to the neighbors of such a hub.

It is quite phenomenal that most neighbors of a hub typically have small degrees. Analysis on the Internet data of April 2002, available at Traceroute [24], shows that nodes with degrees of 1, 2, and 3 were 26%, 38% and 14%, respectively, which together were about 80% of nodes in the whole network [25]. Quantitatively, Figure 4.15 shows that the *average neighboring connectivity* of a node, defined by

$$k_{nn}(k) = \sum_{k'} k' P(k'|k), \qquad (4.1)$$

where the conditional probability $P(k'|k)$ is the probability of nodes with degree k connects to nodes with degree k'.

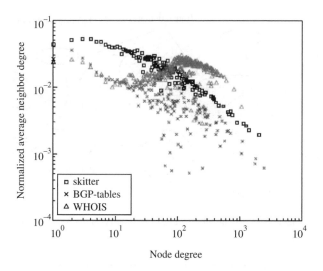

Figure 4.15 Distribution of average neighboring connectivity [12]. *Source*: Courtesy of arXiv.org, Cornell University Library, USA

The above phenomenon can be described by the *assortativity coefficient* [26], introduced in Chapter 2, defined by

$$r = \frac{M^{-1}\sum_i j_i k_i - \left[M^{-1}\sum_i \frac{1}{2}\left(j_i + k_i\right)\right]^2}{M^{-1}\sum_i \frac{1}{2}\left(j_i^2 + k_i^2\right) - \left[M^{-1}\sum_i \frac{1}{2}\left(j_i + k_i\right)\right]^2},$$ (4.2)

where k_i and j_i are the degrees of the end nodes of edge i, and M is the total number of edges in the network. If $r > 0$ the network is *assortative*; if $r < 0$, it is *disassortative*.

Geometrically, an assortative structure means hubs are mostly connected to hubs, while a disassortative structure reflects the opposite that hubs are mostly connected to small-degree nodes in a network.

Analysis of some real data from the Border Gateway Protocol (BGP), Skitter and Whois about the Internet at some AS levels shows that their assortativity coefficients on the Internet are -0.19, -0.24 and -0.04, respectively, implying that the Internet is disassortative [12].

In general, technological networks are disassortative, but social networks are assortative. This is probably due to the facts that social networks have prominent competition as well as cooperation behaviors, an interesting issue to be further studied.

4.2.5   Coreness and Betweenness

For graphs (networks), there are various measures of the *centrality* of a node within a graph, which determine the relative importance of the node in the graph; for example, it measures how important a person is within a social network, and how well a router is being used within a LAN, etc. In other words, a centrality of a node is a measure of the structural importance of the node in the network. These measures attempt to quantify the prominence of an individual node embedded in a network. Generally, a more "central" node has a stronger influence on other nodes in the same network.

Typical measures of the centrality include degree, betweenness, closeness, information, and flow-volume centralities. In network analysis and computation, the nodes may also be aggregated to obtain a group-level centrality. For example, centralization refers to the extent to which the network is concentrated on one group of nodes. For computational convenience, a network is sometimes reformulated to an equivalent one that has only one or a few nodes with considerably higher centrality values than the others in the network.

For the Internet topology, there are two particularly important centrality measures [27, 28]: *coreness centrality* and *betweenness centrality*, both introduced in Chapter 2.

The main purpose of introducing the concept of coreness is to reflect the fact that a higher core is more important than a lower core, and a higher-coreness node is more important than a lower-coreness node, in a network. This can reveal the hierarchical structure of a network, where higher cores and higher-coreness nodes belong to higher-levels of the hierarchical network. Clearly, the star-shaped and ring-shaped networks do not have prominent hierarchical structures.

The main implication of the concept of coreness, on the other hand, is that a network with a higher coreness will have better robustness against intentional attacks. Apparently, both star-shaped and ring-shaped networks are fragile to intentional attacks. Figure 4.16 shows the relations between node-degree and coreness of three sets of Internet data from Skitter, BGP and Whois: When the node-degree is relatively small, they have a power–law relation, with exponents 0.58, 0.68 and 1.07, respectively; while when the node-degree is larger than 100, their coreness values become saturated [12]. This implies that if those hub nodes continue to become bigger (with higher node degrees), it does not follow that they will become more important (with higher coreness) on the Internet, nor will the Internet become more robust against intentional attacks.

Another important measure of Internet topology is the betweenness centralities. Recall from Chapter 2 that in a network of size n, the *node-betweenness* of node i is defined by

$$B(i) = \sum_{j \neq l \neq i} \frac{L_{jl}(i)}{L_{jl}},\qquad(4.3)$$

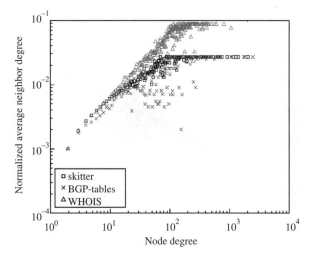

Figure 4.16 Relations between node-degree and coreness [12]. *Source*: Courtesy of arXiv.org, Cornell University Library, USA

where L_{jl} is the number of all existing shortest paths from node j to node l, and $L_{jl}(i)$ is the number of all shortest paths from node j to node l that actually pass through node i. The node-betweenness may be normalized by dividing with the total number of pairs of nodes not including node i, which is $(N-1)(N-2)/2$.

For an edge e_{ij} connecting node i and node j, the *edge-betweenness* of e_{ij} is similarly defined:

$$B(e_{ij}) = \sum_{(l,q)\neq(i,j)} \frac{\tilde{L}_{lq}(e_{ij})}{\tilde{L}_{lq}}, \tag{4.4}$$

where $\tilde{L}_{lq}$ is the number of all existing shortest paths from node l to node q, and $\tilde{L}_{lq}(e_{ij})$ is the number of all shortest paths from node l to node q that actually pass through edge e_{ij}. The edge-betweenness can also be normalized, by dividing by the total number of edges not including e_{ij}, which is $\frac{1}{2}N(N-1)-1$.

The importance of the node- and edge-betweenness centralities can be easily understood from the bridging nodes, which have very small degrees yet very large node- and edge-betweenness values.

Figure 4.17 shows the relations between node-degree and betweenness of three sets of Internet data from Skitter, BGP and Whois: For those from Skitter and BGP, their relations follow prominent power–law distributions with components 1.35 and 1.17, respectively [12]. It shows that larger nodes have larger node-betweenness in general.

Recall also from Chapter 2 that the *information centrality* of a graph G of size N is defined to be the mean information flow rate over the network:

$$E(G) = \frac{\sum_{i\neq j\in G} \varepsilon_{ij}}{N(N-1)} = \frac{1}{N(N-1)} \sum_{i\neq j\in G} \frac{1}{d_{ij}}, \tag{4.5}$$

where the *network efficiency* ε_{ij} of channel information transmission between node i and node j is defined to be inversely proportional to their shortest distance d_{ij} : $\varepsilon_{ij} = 1/d_{ij}$. If there are no edges in the graph, then $d_{ij} = \infty$, so $\varepsilon_{ij} = 0$.

The concept of information centrality is very useful in, for example, finding the community structure of a network [31].

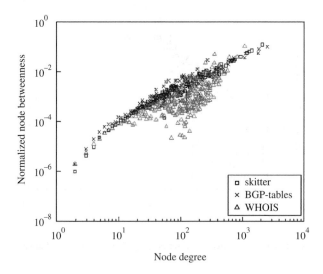

Figure 4.17   Relations between node-degree and normalized betweenness [12]. *Source*: Courtesy of arXiv.org, Cornell University Library, USA

4.2.6   Growth of the Internet

As seen above, there are some fundamental characteristics that have never changed, or basically do not change, during the evolution of the Internet, such as relatively small average path length, relatively large clustering coefficient, power–law distribution of node degrees, and so on, in the AS level or router level of the Internet, or some regional and local portions of it. Of most interest is the fact that despite the above-mentioned inherent properties, the Internet is actually a dynamically evolving complex network, which is rapidly and continuously growing and restructuring.

In this subsection, some historical data of the Internet will be examined, which were provided by the SCAN Project with a software named Mercator for the duration of October-November 1999 [32], by the Oregon route server (at the AS level), and by the Topology Project of the Computer Science Department of the Michigan University (at the Extended AS level), where the data obtained by the latter two projects were both from the same day May 26, 2001 [33].

Table 4.1 shows several average measures of the Internet at the Internet Router (IR), Autonomous System (AS), and Extended Autonomous System (EAS) levels [20], respectively, where N is the number of nodes, E is the number of edges, $\langle k \rangle$ is the average node degree, C is the average clustering coefficient, L is the average shortest path length, and B is the average node-betweenness centrality, of the network. It can be seen that $\langle k \rangle$ is small, implying that there are many nodes of small degrees in the network, and that L is small but C is large (relative to the ER random-graph model which typically has $C \approx 0.0001$), implying the small-world features of the Internet.

The real data collected from Oregon route server, the Looking Glass site, and the Internet Routing Registry (IRR), reveal that the Internet continuously has additions (births) and deletions (deaths) of AS and their peering relations, as shown in Figure 4.18 from November 1998 to November 2000 [33]. It can be seen that the birth rates of nodes and edges are both larger than their death rates, at least during this period of time.

Table 4.1   Some average measures of the Internet at the IR, AS, and EAS levels [20]

Level	N	E	$\langle k \rangle$	C	L	B
IR	228 263	320 149	2.8	0.03	9.5	5.3
AS	11 174	23 409	4.2	0.30	3.6	2.3
EAS	11 461	32 730	5.7	0.35	3.6	2.3

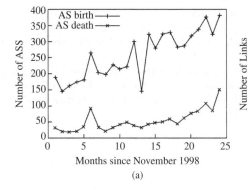
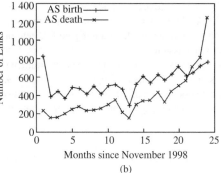

(a)   (b)

Figure 4.18   Monthly numbers of birth and death of the Internet at the AS level [33]: (a) nodes; (b) edges. *Source*: Reprinted with permission from Qian, C., Chang, H., Govindan. R. *et al.* (2002) The origin of power laws in Internet topologies revisited. *Proceedings of 21st Annual Joint Conference of IEEE Computer and Communication Societies*, **2**: 608–17. Copyright (2002) IEEE

Table 4.2 Total numbers of additions and deletions of the Internet at the AS level [33]

Degree	Number of additions	Number of deletions
1	5591	1184
2	816	204
3	23	22
4	4	6
5	1	4
6	1	1
7	1	1
9	0	1
10	1	0
11	1	0
12	0	1
14	1	0
48	0	1

Table 4.3 Monthly rate of new edges connecting old nodes to new and old ones [34]

Year	1998	1999
$E_{n,o}$	170	231
$E_{o,o}$	350	450
$E_{n,o}/E_{o,o}$	0.48	0.53

It is also interesting to observe from Table 4.2 [33] that during the same period of time, small-degree nodes (e.g., those connects to only one or two AS) have very high probabilities of change (more additions and also more deletions) while giant nodes (e.g., those connects to more than five AS) are quite robust with no or very few changes. It is likely due to the fact that small nodes represent small companies (service providers), which are frequently born and connected to giant companies but they also frequently die out of business.

On the other hand, Table 4.3 shows $E_{n,o}$, the numbers of new edge additions between new (incoming) nodes and old (existing) nodes, and $E_{o,o}$, the number of new edge additions between two old nodes at the AS level. It indicates that the Internet growth is significantly driven by the increase of wiring numbers (and bandwidths) among nodes, new or old, to meet the demand of continuously increasing data transmission.

Another observation is that there is a prominent rewiring phenomenon within the Internet [33], meaning that some AS shift their connections to other AS, from time to time during the evolution. This kind of rewiring not only change the figure of the existing edge addition $E_{o,o}$, but also implies the deletion (death) of some existing edges which, however, is not reflected by Table 4.3.

4.2.7 Router-Level Internet Topology

A common tool to represent the router-level Internet topology by a graph is the *traceroute* (Unix traceroute or Windows NT tracert.exe), or its IPv6 version, traceroute6 [35]. The traceroute uses hop-limited probe, which consists of a hop-limited IP (Internet Protocol) packet and the corresponding ICMP (Internet Control Message Protocol) response, to probe every possible IP address and record every reached router and the corresponding edges.

An earlier attempt in 1995 [36] was to use *traceroute* to trace 5000 hosts, selected from a network accounting database. After the 5000 destinations were selected, 11 of them were used as the new sources of routes to trace the remaining destinations. This eventually produced a graph of 3888 nodes and 4857 edges, excluding those routers that could not be traced due to transient routing or other technical problems. The analytical results show that more than 70% of the nodes have degree 1 or 2, and they do not belong to the core. The major limitation of this method is that it heavily depends on the choice of the destinations, namely, it needs to choose a certain number of destinations representing a subset of the Internet structure, to obtain the routing information before probing.

An intelligent heuristic technique was then introduced [37] to overcome this drawback, by using heuristic to decide whether the network includes a single node. This technique does not require an initial database of targets for exploring the network topology. Based on some careful analysis of the collected data, consisting of nearly 150 000 nodes (routers and interfaces) and almost 200 000 edges, it was found [38] that the degree distribution of nodes with degree less than 30 follows a power–law form. However, the distribution of nodes with degree larger than 30 turns out to be significantly different: it has a faster cut-off other than a power–law distribution, indicating that there may be another law governing the distribution of higher-degree nodes in the network. Moreover, it was found that the distribution of the numbers of node-pairs within a certain number of hops in the network follows neither exponential [39] nor power–law form. Some analysis on the real data collected during October and November of 1999 shows that the hierarchical characteristic nearly does not exist in the router-level of the Internet topology [40], where the node-degree distribution has a power–law behavior which however is smoothed out by a clear exponential cut-off. Therefore, the Weibull distribution, instead of the power–law distribution, can better fit the collected data, agreeing with the result reported in [38]. However, this approach could not give a complete map of the Internet topology since it fails to represent the details of the Stub subnets, although it can capture the topology of the Transit portion of the Internet. Therefore probing from a large number of sources may be able to improve the performance regarding the completeness of the traceroute-style probes [41].

Recently, Border Gateway Protocol (BGP) routing tables were examined to determine the destinations of a traceroute [42]. A directed probing technique was used to interpret BGP tables for identifying relevant traceroutes and pruning the remainders [42]. A path reduction technique can also be used to identify redundant traceroutes, so as to generate a router-level Internet topology. An advantage in using these two techniques is that it can significantly reduce the number of required traces without sacrificing the accuracy. Actually, compared to the brute-force all-to-all approach, this method of combining the directed probing and the path-reduction techniques can reduce the number of required traces significantly by three orders in magnitude. Some analytical results on the real data collected during December 2001 to January 2002 show that the Weibull distribution can better fit the complementary cumulative distribution function of router out-degree than the Pareto (power–law) distribution [42].

In general, however, because most Internet Service Providers regard their router-level topologies as confidential, and there exist some technical problems such as multiple interfaces leading to multiple IP addresses for a single router, it is still a challenge to build a relatively complete router-level Internet topology today.

4.2.8 *Geographic Layout of the Internet*

Due to the lack of topological information about the Internet with geographic layout of AS and routers, very little work has been done to explore the geometry of the Internet infrastructure to date.

One earlier work on this issue [43] used the NetGeo tool, developed by CAIDA [44], to identify the geographic coordinates of 228 265 routers of the *Mercator* map, aiming at investigating the fundamental driving forces that shape the Internet's evolution. The obtained Internet topology, embedded with geographic information of routers, allows one to analyze the physical layout of the Internet infrastructure. It was found that routers form a fractal set with fractal dimension $D_f = 1.5 \pm 0.1$, which strongly correlate with the population density around the world, as illustrated by Figure 4.19, where (a) is the router

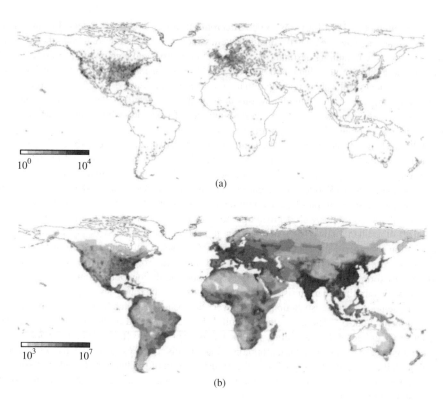

Figure 4.19 Router map density; (b) population density map [43]. *Source*: Yook, S., Jeong, H. and Barabási, A-L. (2002) Modeling the Internet's large-scale topology. *Proceedings of the National Academy of Sciences*, **99** (21): 13382–6. Copyright (2002) National Academy of Sciences, USA

distribution density of the geographic locations of 228 265 routers in the *Mercator* map, and (b) is the population density distribution calculated based on the CIESIN population data [45].

Two recent Internet maps are the *Mercator* map collected during August 1999, which consists of 268 382 routers and 320 149 edges, and the *Skitter* map collected from December 26, 2001 to January 1, 2002, which contains 704 107 routers and 1 075 454 edges [46]. The geographic information of routers in these two maps was obtained using two geographic mapping tools: IxMapper [47] and EdgeScape [48]. Some analysis on these two topologies, with geographic coordinates of routers, indicates that there is a correlation between the router interface and the population density, as shown in Table 4.4 [47] in various geographic areas of the world, including both developed and developing regions.

Table 4.4 shows that penetration of Internet infrastructure varies dramatically over different areas, indicating that the interface density is strongly correlated with the population density. This coincidence between the router interface and the population density is not surprising: higher population density in a wealthier region implies higher demands for Internet services, resulting in higher densities of routers and interfaces. More precisely, the correlation between the router or interface density R and the population density P are correlated as $R \sim P^\alpha$ with exponent $1.2 \leq \alpha \leq 1.7$, depending on the specific region of concern.

By examining a BGP table that matches IP addresses to their corresponding AS numbers, one can label routers or interfaces with the AS number to which they belong. In this way, geographic information of the AS-level Internet infrastructure can be obtained. It is found that the number of distinct locations spanned by an AS is strongly correlated with the degree of the AS [47]. For a small AS, these locations show

Table 4.4 Correlation between router interfaces and human population [47]

	Population (millions)	Interface	People per interface
Australia	18	18 277	975
Japan	136	37 649	3 631
Mexico	154	4 361	35 534
USA	299	282 048	1 061
South America	341	10 131	33 752
West Europe	366	95 993	3 817
Africa	837	8379	100 011

a wide variability in the geographic dispersal; however, for a large AS whose size exceeds a certain threshold, these locations are rapidly dispersed geographically.

Based on all the above observations and discussions, the geography-based BA model proposed in [43], referred to as the *GeoBA* model, is summarized as follows:

1. Consider a network on a plane of linear size L, and divide it into squares of size $l \times l$ with $l \ll L$.
2. Assign to each square a population density $\rho(x, y)$ with a fractal dimension, $D_f = 1.5$.
3. At each step, place a new node i into the network in such a way that the probability of the node being placed at position (x, y) is linearly proportional to $\rho(x, y)$. This new node will bring in m new edges. The probability of a new edge connecting to an existing node j of degree k_j at geographical distance d_{ij} from node i is

$$\Pi(k_j, d_{ij}) \sim \frac{k_j^\beta}{d_{ij}^\sigma},$$

(4.6)

where β and σ are constant parameters.

Note that β and σ govern the preferential attachment and the penalty of the node–node distance, respectively, such that increasing β favors the nodes with higher degrees and larger σ values discourage long-range connections. In comparison, L, l and m are less important parameters in the model.

4.3 Random-Graph Network Topology Generator

In the 1980s, the Internet started to be developed initially with a relatively small size. In 1988, Waxman proposed a simple model of the Internet [3], which was lately found to represent the Advanced Research Project Agency resource sharing computer network (ARPAnet) quite well.

The Waxman model is generated as follows:

1. Start with N nodes on a finite lattice.
2. At every step, one edge is being added to two randomly picked nodes, u and v, according to the following so-called *Waxman probability*:

$$\Pi(u, v) = \alpha e^{-d(u,v)/(\beta L_{\max})},$$

(4.7)

where $0 < \alpha, \beta \leq 1$, $d(u, v)$ is the Euclidean distance between node u and node v, α is the average number of edges (after normalization), $L_{\max}$ is the diameter of the network, and β is a parameter determined by the average path length.

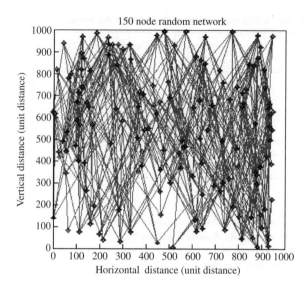

Figure 4.20   A typical Waxman network of 150 nodes, with $\alpha = 0.25$, $\beta = 0.3$ [4]. *Source*: Reprinted with permission from Doar, M.B. (1996) A better model for generating test networks. *Proceedings of IEEE Global Internet, London*, 86–93. Copyright (1996) IEEE

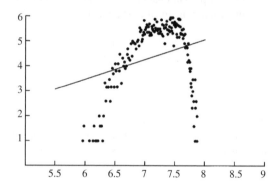

Figure 4.21   Distribution of the Waxman network: $N(k)$ versus k (log–log plot) [50] *Source*: *ACM SIGCOMM Computer Communication Review*, **29**(4): 251–62. Copyright (1999) Association for Computing Machinery, Inc. Reprinted by permission

It is clear from formula (4.7) that if α is increasing, then the growth probability of edges, $P(u, v)$, is also increasing; if β is increasing, then in the end relatively long edges become more than relatively short edges in the resulting network. Figure 4.20 is a typical Waxman network, and Figure 4.21 shows its degree distribution, where $N(k)$ (vertical axis) is the number of nodes of degree k (horizontal axis).

The Waxman network is a typical random graph, which has influences on some other random-graph-like models afterwards (for example, [49]). It can be seen that the probability of having an edge between two distant nodes is generally quite small, so that the probability of having a resulting connected graph is also small. Therefore, one usually studies the biggest connected subgraph of the Waxman network.

4.4   Structural Network Topology Generators

As the Internet becomes larger and more complex, and as the understanding of its topological features becomes deeper and more comprehensive, it has been realized that the Internet indeed is not a random graph in the classical sense, but has prominent hierarchical structures (as discussed in Section 4.2.2 above) and many other features. The first generation of Internet topology generators in the mid-1990s was based on the belief that the hierarchical structure is the main characteristic of Internet topology. Two representative hierarchical Internet models, the Tiers topology generator and the Transit–Stub topology generator, are briefly introduced here.

4.4.1   Tiers Topology Generator

This topology generator is used to represent Wide Area Networks (WANs), Metropolitan Area Networks (MANs) and Local Area Networks (LANs), as well as their connectivities [4].

To generate a network topology by Tiers, it is required to preassign the numbers of MANs and LANs, where all LANs have to be in star-shape. The main model parameters are:

N_W – number of WANs (usually, set $N_W = 1$ for simplicity)
S_W – number of nodes in a WAN
N_M – number of MANs ($N_M \leq S_W$, since every MAN connects to a node in a WAN)
S_M – number of nodes in a MAN
N_L – number of LANs ($N_L \leq S_M$, since there is one MAN node for each LAN)
S_L – number of nodes in a LAN

Total number of nodes is $N = S_W + N_M S_M + N_M N_L S_L$ (a typical example for a corporate Internet has $N_W = 5, N_M = 10$ with $S_M = 10$, and $N_L = 5$ with $S_L = 50$, given $N = 2605$).

The degree of intranetwork redundancy for WAN, MAN and LAN, defined as the number of directed edges from one node to another node of the same type (e.g., from LAN to LAN), is denoted by R_W, R_M and R_L, which are typically equal to 3, 2 and 1, respectively. The degree of intranetwork redundancy between a MAN and a WAN, or between a MAN and a LAN, is similarly defined, and is denoted by R_{MW} and R_{LW}, respectively.

The Tiers topology generator works as follows:

1. Generate one WAN:
    (a) Randomly put some nodes on a finite-sized lattice; if the new one happens to be too close to an existing one, then simply reject (ignore) the new one.
    (b) After putting in all pre-assigned nodes on the lattice, connect them as a spanning tree (see Chapter 2).
    (c) Check all nodes, in random order, to make sure that they all satisfy the redundancy $R_W = 3$ (if a node has more than R_W edges to its peer nodes then do nothing, but if it has less then add edges to its nearest nodes in the network, in increasing order of Euclidean distance).
2. Generate MANs:
    The procedure is similar to that for WAN above, but now in a smaller scale, with the exception of not rejecting the new MAN when it is too close to an existing one (since nodes in a MAN and in a LAN are much closer than those in a WAN), where typically $R_M = 2$, yielding a total of N_M MANs.
3. Generate LANs:
    Randomly select a node in a LAN as the center of a star-shaped network, and then connect it to every other nodes of the LAN by a single edge, where usually $R_L = 1$ (if $R_L > 1$ then do nothing), which yields a total of N_L LANs.
4. Connect all the above-generated WAN, MANs and LANs together:
    (a) Connect MANs to the WAN: Randomly select a group, denoted by A, of N_M nodes from among S_W nodes in the generated WAN; then, connect one node in A to one randomly selected node X in each MAN (thus, each MAN is connected to the WAN via one edge).
    (b) If $R_{MW} > 1$ then connect one node in each MAN (which can be X again) to a node in A, which is nearest to the node that was already connected to X.
    (c) Similarly to the above procedure, connect all the LANs to the MANs, where the node X to be chosen from a LAN is always the center of the star-shaped network.

An illustrative example of Tiers topology so generated is shown in Figure 4.22 [4].

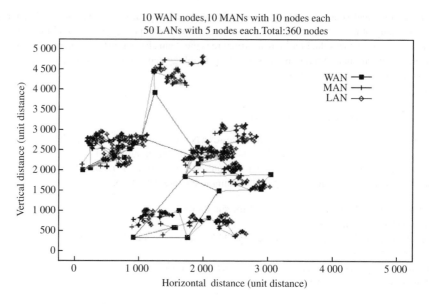

10 WAN nodes,10 MANs with 10 nodes each
50 LANs with 5 nodes each.Total:360 nodes

Figure 4.22 A typical Tiers topology [4]. *Source*: Reprinted with permission from Doar, M.B. (1996) A better model for generating test networks. *Proceedings of IEEE Global Internet, London*, 86–93. Copyright (1996) IEEE

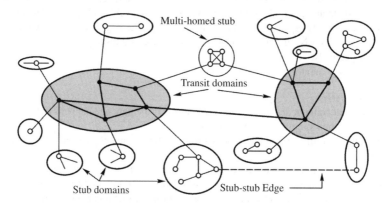

Figure 4.23 Illustration of network structure from Transit–Stub topology generator [5]. *Source*: Reprinted with permission from Calvert, K., Doar, M. and Zegura, E. (1997) Modeling Internet topology. *IEEE Communication Magazine*, **35**(6): 160–3. Copyright (1997) IEEE

4.4.2   Transit–Stub Topology Generator

The network structure generated by the Transit–Stub topology generator consists of three layers: the first one is the top layer, the Transit domain, followed by the Stub domain, and then the LANs. The nodes on each layer are restricted on a rectangular region, where each layer has a different rectangle and the smallest one is for the LANs, as illustrated by Figure 4.23 [5].

There are two groups of parameters that control the graph characteristics:

First group: This group of parameters controls the relative sizes of the domains.

T – number of Transit domains ($T \geq 1$)

N_T – average number of nodes in each Transit domain ($N_T \geq 1$)
S – average number of Stub domains in each Transit domain ($S \geq 1$)
N_S – average number of nodes in each Stub domain ($N_S \geq 1$)
L – average number of LANs in each Stub node ($L \geq 0$)
N_L – average number of hosts in each LAN ($N_L \geq 1$)
N_R – number of routers, satisfying $N_R = TN_T(1 + SN_S)$
N_H – number of hosts, satisfying $N_H = TN_TSN_SLN_L$.

Note that LANs are modeled as star-shaped networks with a router node at the center of each star and the host nodes each connected to the center router. This significantly reduces the number of edges in the generated network, and reflects the lack of physical redundancy in most LANs.

Second group: This group of parameters controls the connectivity of the domains.

E_T – average number of edges in each Transit domain ($E_T \geq 2$)
E_S – average number of edges in each Stub domain ($E_S \geq 2$)
E_{TT} – average number of edges in between Transit domains ($E_{TT} \geq 2$)
E_{ST} – average number of edges in between a Transit and a Stub domain ($E_{ST} \geq 1$)
E_{LS} – average number of edges in between a LAN and a Stub domain ($E_{LS} \geq 1$).

Note that E_T must be large enough so that the Transit domain is connected; E_S must be large enough so that the Stub domain is connected; E_{TT} must be large enough so that the Transit–Transit domains are connected; E_{ST} must be so large that every Stub connects to at least one Transit domain; finally, E_{LS} must be so large that every LAN connects to at least one Stub domain.

The Transit–Stub topology generator works as follows:

1. Generate all Transit domains within a desired region. To do so, any random-graph generation method may be used (usually, the Waxman algorithm is used). The resulting network must be connected, where each node represents a Transit domain.
2. Generate nodes in each Transit domain. To do so, place in N_T nodes around the Transit point, and then connect them with edges, where $N_T \geq 2$, $E_T \geq 2$.
3. Randomly select one node in each Transit domain and connect it to another Transit domain by one edge.
4. Generate Stubs for each Transit domain. To do so, select suitable locations for Stub domains, then generate N_S Stub domains in these locations, and finally connect them with edges.
5. Connect every Stub domain to a Transit domain. If $E_{ST} > 1$ then randomly select one node from a Stub domain and then connect this node to a Transit domain by an edge.
6. Generate LANs, all with star-shaped structures.
7. Connect every LAN to a Stub domain. If $E_{LN} \geq 1$ then connect the center of the LAN to a Stub domain.

Note that in the above modeling, typically Steps 1–5 are carried out while Steps 6–7 may be ignored.

An illustrative example of the out-degree (number of out-reaching edges) distribution of the resulting Transit–Stub network with 6660 nodes is shown in Figure 4.24 [49].

4.5   Connectivity-Based Network Topology Generators

In Section 4.4.2, two typical examples (Tiers and Transit–Stub models) of the first generation of Internet topology generators were introduced, which were developed based on the hierarchical structures of the Internet. Since the publication of the seminal paper [2], the main interest and emphasis have been gradually changed to the connectivity characteristics of the Internet. As a result, several connectivity-based Internet topology generators have been developed lately, which are briefly introduced in this section.

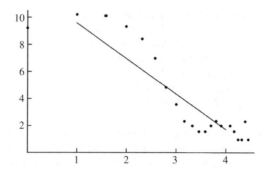

Figure 4.24 Out-degree distribution of a Transit–Stub network (log–log plot) [49]. *Source*: Proceedings of IEEE INFOCOM. Copyright (1993) IEEE

4.5.1 Inet

To reflect the power–law out-degree distribution of the Internet, coined in [2], researchers in the University of Michigan proposed a connectivity-based Internet topology generator, Inet 1.0, in year 2000. This model was then upgraded to Inet 2.0 followed by Inet 3.0 [7]. The new version 3.0 works as follows, where all node degrees are out-degrees [51]:

1. From the real data set, find the ratio ρ of degree-1 nodes over the total number of all nodes, which typically remains about $\rho \approx 30\%$.
2. Compute the number of months, t, over which the number of nodes of the Internet at the AS level has been increased from 3037 to N by using the following empirical formula:

$$N = \exp(0.0298t + 7.9842), \tag{4.8}$$

where according to the Oregon data [14] the number of AS nodes of the Internet in November 1997 was 3037 [51, 52] (as shown also in Figure 4.2). Clearly, there are a total of ρN nodes in V_1.
3. Let V_1 and V' be the set of degree-1 nodes and the set of the rest nodes, respectively, in the network. Use the t value obtained above in the following empirical formula to calculate the empirical complementary cumulative degree distribution of V':

$$f(d) = \sum_{i>d}^{\infty} k(i) = e^c d^{at+b}, \tag{4.9}$$

where $k(i)$ is the degree of node i, and a, b, c are some known constants previously determined by historical data.
4. Generate a spanning tree consisting of nodes with degree larger than 1. To do so, let G be the graph to be generated, starting from empty initial conditions; then, a node i of degree larger than 1 located outside G is connected to a node j inside G according to the following (preferential attachment) probability:

$$\Pi(i,j) = \frac{w_i^j}{\sum_{k \in G} w_i^k}, \tag{4.10}$$

where the Euclidean distance between two node degrees in the log–log scale of the d - $f(d)$ plot is used to set the weights, as

$$w_i^j = \text{Max}\left\{ 1, \sqrt{\left(\ln\left(d_i/d_j\right)\right)^2 + \left(\ln f\left(d_i\right)/f(d_j)\right)^2} \right\} d_j, \tag{4.11}$$

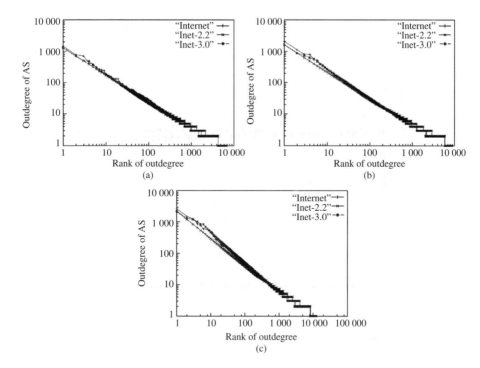

Figure 4.25 Outdegree distributions of the Internet [7]: (a) February 1, 2000; (b) February 1, 2001; (c) February 1, 2002

where d_i is the degree of node i, with $f(d_i)$ being the frequency (i.e., the total number of nodes) of degree d_i. Note that graph G grows in such a way that it includes more and more outside nodes as they are connected to it.

5. Connect all ρN nodes of V_1 to G, also according to the probability (4.10).
6. Connect high-degree nodes, in decreasing order, to those available nodes in G that do not have connections to V_1, also according to the probability (4.10).

Figure 4.25 shows the power–law distributions of out-degrees, the simulation results obtained by using Inet 3.0, based on the AS-level Internet data of 1 February 2000, 1 February 2001, and 1 February 2002, with 6700, 8880, and 12 700 nodes, respectively. Figure 4.26 further shows that the average path lengths of the Internet remained basically unchanged throughout the three years of time [7].

4.5.2 BRITE Model

BRITE (Boston university Representative Internet Topology gEnerator) [6] attempts to build a topology generation framework based on three basic design principles: representativeness, inclusiveness, and interoperability. Here, representativeness means synthesizing a topology that can accurately reflect most important aspects of the real Internet topology (e.g. its hierarchical structure and node-degree distribution); inclusiveness tries to combine the advantages of many good topology generators; interoperability provides interfaces to widely-used simulation applications such as Network Simulator (NS) and Scalable Simulation Framework (SSF).

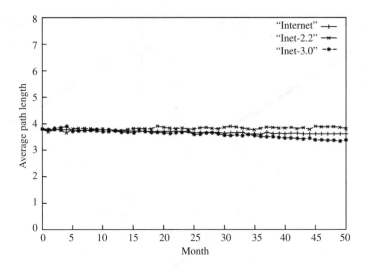

Figure 4.26 Average path lengths of the Internet [7]

BRITE generates a network topology in the following steps:

1. Divide a planar region into $HS \times HS$ squares, and then further divide each square into $LS \times LS$ smaller squares.
2. According to a uniform distribution, or a Pareto heavy-tailed distribution (see Chapter 2), determine the number of nodes to be placed in each large square. Then, in each large square, randomly pick a small square and assign at most one slot to a future node in the small square.
3. Now, place in nodes. Initially generate a random graph with m_0 nodes, and then add more nodes to the graph gradually. The way to connect nodes is determined by two parameters: Incremental Growth (*IG*) and Preferential Connectivity (*PC*). If $IG = 0$ then put m nodes onto the plane simultaneously, and randomly pick one node among them and then connect it to the other nodes; if $IG = 1$ then put one node onto the plane each time, and connect this new node to m existing nodes in the network. The way to establish connections is based on the *PC* parameter value: if $PC = 0$ then follow the Waxman probability (4.7) to connect the new node to the existing nodes; if $PC = 1$ then follow the BA linear preferential attachment probability (3.19), Chapter 3; if $PC = 2$ then use the following weighted preferential attachment probability:

$$\Pi(k_i) = \frac{w_i k_i}{\sum_{j \in C} w_j k_j},\tag{4.12}$$

where k_i is the degree of node i, w_i is the Waxman probability (4.7), and C is the set of all m nodes being connected to node i.

Clearly, choosing different parameter values of *IG* and *PC* will generate different topologies. In particular, with $IG = PC = 0$, it generates the Waxman topology. Simulations show that with $IG = PC = 1$, BRITE generates a topology that is closest to the real Internet with similar characteristics such as power–law degree distribution and average path length, etc.

Figure 4.27 [53] shows two examples with different node placements: uniform random distribution and Pareto heavy-tailed distribution; Figure 4.28 [54] shows a simulation example of 5000 nodes generated by BRITE, where $d(v)$ is the node degree and $f(d)$ is the frequency (total number) of nodes.

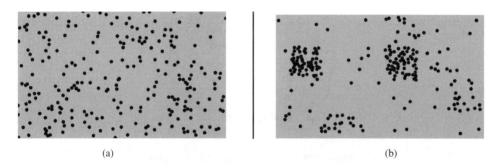

(a)   (b)

Figure 4.27   Node placements: (a) uniformly random (b) Pareto heavy-tailed [53]. *Source*: Courtesy of Boston University, USA

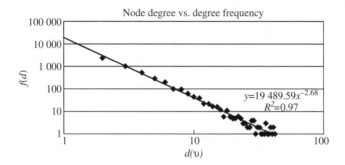

Figure 4.28   Log–log plot of node-degree distribution: a 5000-node BRITE network [54]. *Source*: Courtesy of University of Palermo, Italy

4.5.3   GLP Model

The so-called Generalized Linear Preferential (GLP) model tries to further improve the BA model [55], which is formed in the following steps:

Start with a connected network of m_0 nodes and $m_0 - 1$ edges.
Perform one of the following two operations:

1. With probability p, $0 \leq p \leq 1$, the existing network receives m ($0 \leq m \leq m_0$) new edges; one end of each new edge is connected to node i according to the following probability:

$$\Pi(k_i) = \frac{k_i - \beta}{\sum_j (k_j - \beta)}, \tag{4.13}$$

where k_i is the degree of node i, and $-\infty < \beta < 1$ is a tunable parameter, representing a certain bias in preferentially attaching to a more popular existing node, in which $\beta < 1$ gives degree-one nodes a chance to acquire new edges.
2. With probability $1 - p$, $0 \leq p \leq 1$, a new node is being added to the network, which brings in m ($0 \leq m \leq m_0$) new edges, each of which connects to node i according to probability (4.13).

Clearly, in the GLP model, the increments of new nodes and new edges are independent. The model generation procedure is illustrated by Figure 4.29.

The above GLP model also has a power–law node-degree distribution [55], for which the verification is similar to that of the BA model.

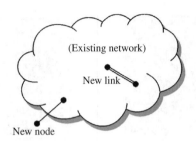

Figure 4.29   Generation of the GLP model [55]

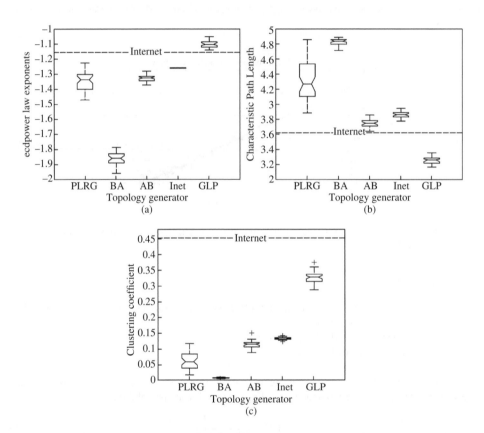

Figure 4.30   Comparison of several Internet AS models [55]: (a) ecd power law exponents; (b) characteristic path length; (c) clustering coefficient. *Source*: Reprinted with permission from Bu, T. and Towsley, D. (2002) On distinguishing between Internet power law topology generators. *Proceedings of INFOCOM*, **2**: 638–47. Copyright (2002) IEEE

In September 2000, the Internet at the AS level had $N = 8613$ nodes and $E = 18346$ edges. Using this set of real data, with $m = 1.13$, $p = 0.4695$ and $\beta = 0.6447$ in the GLP model, a comparison on the power–law exponent, average path length and clustering coefficient of several modes is demonstrated in Figure 4.30. This figure shows the average of 100 simulations, where PLRG refers to power–law random graph and AB is the EBA model of Albert and Barabási [56], introduced in Chapter 3.

4.5.4   PFP Model

The so-called Positive Feedback Preferential (PFP) model [25] is established based on the observation of the "rich club" phenomenon, discussed in Section 4.2.2 above. In this PFP model, the growths of new nodes and new edges are interactive [57], with a nonlinear preferential attachment scheme. In comparison to the so-called Interactive Growth (IG) model [57], it has a better match to the real Internet data.

In the PFP model, at each step a new node is being attached to an existing host in the network and, moreover, some new edges are being added between the host node and some other existing nodes. In looking for an existing node with degree k_i to attach, the following nonlinear preferential attachment probability is used:

$$\Pi(k_i) = \frac{k_i^{1+\delta \log_{10} k_i}}{\sum_j k_j^{1+\delta \log_{10} k_j}}, \quad \delta \in [0,1]. \tag{4.14}$$

More precisely, the model generation procedure is as follows:

1. With probability p, $0 \le p \le 1$, a new node is being added, which connects to a host; meanwhile, a new edge is being added between the host node and another node existing in the network.
2. With probability q, $0 \le q \le 1 - p$, a new node is being added to a host node; meanwhile, two new edges are being added between the host node and two existing nodes.
3. With probability $1 - p - q$, a new node is being added to two host nodes, respectively; meanwhile, a new edge is added between one of the host nodes and another existing node.

A comparison in the AS-level Internet of the PFP model with $p = 0.3$ and $q = 0.1$, against the IG and BA models, is shown in Table 4.5 [25].

Table 4.5   Comparison of network parameters among several models [25].

		AS graph	PFP model	IG model	BA model
Number of nodes	N	11122	11122	11122	11122
Number of links	L	30054	30151	33349	33349
Average degree	$<k>$	5.4	5.4	6.0	6.0
Exponent of power law	γ	2.22	2.22	2.22	3
Rich-club connectivity	$\phi(r/N = 0.01)$	0.27	0.30	0.32	0.045
Maximum degree	k_{max}	2839	2785	700	292
Degree distribution	$P(k = 1)$	26%	28%	26%	0%
Degree distribution	$P(k = 2)$	38%	36%	34%	0%
Degree distribution	$P(k = 3)$	14%	12%	11%	40%
Characteristic path length	l^*	3.13	3.14	3.6	4.3
Average triangle coefficient	$<k_t>$	12.7	12	10.4	0.1
Maximum triangle coefficient	$k_{t\ max}$	7482	8611	4123	64
Average quadrangle coefficient	$<k_q>$	277	247	105.4	1.3
Maximum quadrangle coefficient	$k_{q\ max}$	9648	9431	8780	527
Average k_{nn}	$<k_{nn}>$	660	482	103	20
Average betweenness	$<C^*_B>$	4.13	4.14	4.6	5.3
Maximum quadbetweenness	$C^*_{B\ max}$	3237	3419	1002	1064

4.5.5 T_{ANG} Model

The T_{ANG} model refers to the model generated by the Tel Aviv Network Generator, which combines the essential features of the Incremental Edge Addition (InEd) model and the Super-Linear Preferential Attachment (SLiP) model.

Start with a network of n_o nodes. At each step, one new node is being added along with m new edges connecting to m existing nodes, where the probability of an existing node i being chosen by the new node for connection is

$$\Pi(k_i) = \frac{k_i^{1+\varepsilon}}{\sum_j k_j^{1+\varepsilon}}, \qquad (4.15)$$

where $\varepsilon > 0$ is referred to as the super-linear preferential attachment parameter. Obviously, with $\varepsilon = 0$ the T_{ANG} model reduces to the BA model.

Figure 4.31 shows a comparison of the Complementary Cumulative Density Function (CCDF) of node degrees between the AS-level Internet and the T_{ANG} model with different values of ε [58].

Notice that connections in the Internet are generally not equivalent in the sense that more than 90% of connections represent customer-provider relationships, where information data flow from Internet Service Provider (ISP) to customers, therefore directed graphs are needed to describe the connections in reality. Based on geographic distribution of the Internet, the so-called $G_D T_{ANG}$ model was suggested, with a generation procedure as follows [59].

Define several different geographic regions for the Internet model. At each step, one new (customer) node is being added to the network along with m directed edges pointing from customer nodes to ISP nodes. In doing so, randomly select a region and a node i in that region, and the new customer node is connected by a directed edge to an ISP node i according to the following probability:

$$\Pi(y_i) = \frac{y_i}{\sum_j y_j}, \qquad (4.16)$$

where y_i is the out-degree (the number of out-pointing edges) of node i.

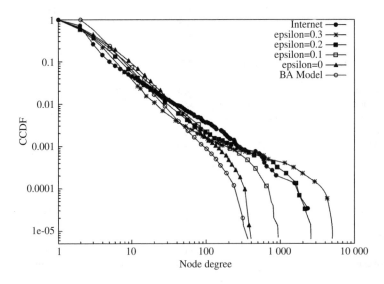

Figure 4.31   CCDF of node degrees of the T_{ANG} model (log–log plot) [58]. *Source*: Bar, S., Gonen, M. and Wool, A. (2004) An incremental super-linear preferential Internet topology model. *Proceedings of 5th Annual Passive and Active Measurement Workshop, LNCS* **3015**, 53–62. With kind permission from Springer Science and Business Media

Meanwhile, $m - 1$ edges are being added among the existing nodes: a customer node l is being selected according to the following probability:

$$\Pi(k_l) = \frac{k_l}{\sum_j k_j},\tag{4.17}$$

where k_l is the in-degree (the number of in-pointing edges) of node l; while any ISP node is being selected according to the probability (4.16).

This $G_D T_{ANG}$ model can generate various topological features closer to the Internet than the T_{ANG} model [59].

4.6 Multi-Local-World Model

Observe that at the Inter-domain level, the actual Internet hierarchy can be schematically divided into international connections, national backbones, regional networks, and local area networks. The nodes in the regional networks are tightly connected, yielding very high clustering coefficients within the networks. These highly clustered regional networks are then interconnected sparsely by national back-bones or international connections. This observation leads to an approach using the Multi-Local-World (MLW) model, introduced in Chapter 3, to describe the Internet structure [60].

4.6.1   Theoretical Considerations

When the MLW model is applied to model the Internet, some factors need to be carefully studied based on the collected Internet AS-level data.

4.6.1.1   Birth and Death of AS

Define an AS being "born" when a new ISP joins the Internet and being "dead" after it is disappeared. It has been found that the Internet on the basis of AS-level granularity continues to grow after it was born. For example, according to the data collected by the Oregon route server [15], the number of AS in the Internet was increased from 4320 in November 1998 to 9520 in November 2000. During this period, although there were so many dead AS in each time duration (e.g., month or year), the number of dead AS was always small as compared to the number of newly born AS within the same time interval. For example, the newly born AS number was about 200 in November 1998 while less than 50 AS died at the same month. It clearly indicates that the birth rate of AS is larger than its death rate. Therefore, it is reasonable not to consider the event of death of AS in the MLW model for simplicity of modeling and analysis.

4.6.1.2   Birth and Death of Edges

When a new AS is being added into the network, it creates a certain number of edges connecting the existing nodes. On the other hand, there may also appear new interconnections between the already existing nodes due, for instance, to the consideration of having redundancy for having fault tolerance or for avoiding possible traffic congestions. This is referred to as the birth of an emerging edge. Meanwhile, an edge between two nodes may be disconnected, for many obvious reasons, which is called the death of the (deleted) edge. The analysis on the AS-level Internet topology data shows that the event of death of edges should not be neglected, because the death rate of edges is comparable with its birth rate in reality. In fact, for the real Internet, in some cases the number of dead edges can even be larger than that of the newly born edges. For example, in November 2000, the number of dead edges was about 1300, which was 800 more than the newly born edges in that month. Therefore, both birth and death of edges should be considered in a realistic model of the Internet, at least at the AS level.

4.6.1.3 Rewiring

An ISP in the Internet may rewire one of its edges to connect to another node with a higher node-degree in order to gain more benefits in, for example, reducing the distance from it to other peer nodes in the network. However, a recent study [10] shows that the rewiring mechanism may not be a significant factor in the evolution of the AS-level Internet topology. Therefore, the rewiring mechanism for an Internet model is not very necessary, which may be ignored in the modeling.

4.6.1.4 Preferential Attachment

When a new node joins the network, an existing node i receives an edge from the new node according to a certain probability, which may depend linearly on the degree of node i, k_i, as in the BA model, in the form

$$\prod(k_i) = \frac{k_i}{\sum_j k_j} \tag{4.18}$$

or nonlinearly in the form

$$\prod(k_i) = \frac{k_i^\sigma}{\sum_j k_j^\sigma}, \tag{4.19}$$

where the parameter $\sigma > 0$.

A recent study on the real AS-level Internet topology data shows that the newly added nodes actually create new edges by a linear preferential attachment rule [34], which was lately confirmed by another study [43]. On the other hand, the edges attached to a node with a lower degree may more likely be removed, because ISPs always tend to delete those infrequently used edges so as to reduce the maintenance cost. Combining with the linear preferential attachment rule when adding an edge between two nodes, it is reasonable to assume that the probability of an edge attached to node i being deleted is

$$\Pi'(k_i) = \frac{1}{N(t) - 1}(1 - \Pi(k_i)), \tag{4.20}$$

where $N(t)$ is the number of nodes in the network at time step t. This term will be normalized such that $\sum_i \Pi'(k_i) = 1$.

4.6.1.5 Localization

As mentioned, at the AS level, the Internet hierarchy can be schematically divided into international connections, national backbones, regional networks (which contains some AS) and even local area networks. The nodes in a regional network are tightly connected, yielding a high clustering coefficient within the network. These highly clustered regional networks are then interconnected sparsely by national backbones or international connections. This observation is supported by real Internet data, shown in Table 4.6, where it can be seen that the number of intradomain edges is much larger than that of the interdomain edges, which is a prominent localization effect of the real Internet.

When a new node is to join a regional network, the nodes in other regional networks, even those with very large degrees, will have very little impact on the decision of receiving this new node. In other words, the ability that the node i in this regional network can capture a new edge from the newly added node may depend primarily on its position relative to the other nodes within the same regional network, but not to the entire multiregional Internet. Such a regional network is referred to as a *local-world*, while the

Table 4.6   Interdomain and intradomain edges of the Internet [46]

	Number of Interdomain edges	Number of Intradomain edges
US	77 367	354 593
Europe	15 365	99 023
Japan	3 651	44 701
World	146 936	715 997

entire Internet can be considered as an ensemble of many local-worlds. If one considers the Internet at the router level, then an AS may be regarded as a local world.

Combining the localization effect with the linear preferential attachment rule of the Internet, it is reasonable to assume that the probability with which a node i in a local-world Ω receives a new edge from the newly added node is in the form of

$$\prod(k_i) = \frac{k_i + \alpha}{\sum_{j \in \Omega}(k_j + \alpha)}, \tag{4.21}$$

where Ω denotes the Ω th local-world in which node i locates, and the parameter $\alpha > 0$ represents the attractiveness of node i, which is used to govern the probability for "young" nodes to receive new edges.

Similarly, the probability of an edge attached to node i being deleted can be rewritten as

$$\prod'(k_i) = \frac{1}{N_\Omega(t) - 1}(1 - \prod(k_i)), \tag{4.22}$$

where $N_\Omega(t)$ represents the number of nodes within the Ω th local-world in the network, and $\prod(k_i)$ is determined by (4.21).

All issues discussed in (i)–(v) above are then incorporated in the MLW model, introduced in Chapter 3, so as to describe the Internet structure [60]. The MLW modeling performance will be further discussed in the next subsection.

To this end, notice that the weight of each new incoming edge in the last step of the above MLW model is fixed to same value, say w_0, which is taken to be 1 in general. But, if the weights of the new edges between node i and node j, denoted w_{ij}, are considered to be variable:

$$w_{ij}(t + 1) = w_{ij}(t) + \delta \frac{w_{ij}(t)}{k_{ij}(t)}, \tag{4.23}$$

where $\delta \geq 0$ is a constant parameter, then an evolving weighted MLW model can be obtained [61, 62], which can be applied to modeling the Internet even at the router level [62].

4.6.2   Numerical Results with Comparison

As discussed in the previous sections, many models have been proposed to describe the Internet topology. Therefore, it is quite natural to compare their performances in characterizing the Internet. To do so, some real Internet data are first reviewed.

Since the early 1990s, the number of hosts in the Internet continues to grow exponentially, as shown in Figure 4.32 [63, 64]. For example, there are 376 000 hosts in January 1991 but 43 200 504 230 200 504 000 hosts in January 1999. Six years later in January 2005, there were even 317 200 504 646 200 504 084 hosts on the Internet, 634.3% increase comparing to that in January 1999.

Although the number of hosts on the Internet increases exponentially, some statistical parameters of the Internet do not change at all, or only have very small changes. For example, at the AS-level it was

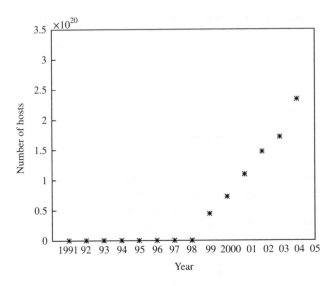

Figure 4.32   Number of hosts on the Internet [63]. *Source*: Courtesy of Z. P. Fan

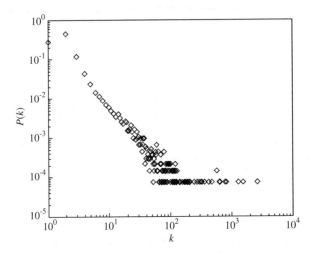

Figure 4.33   Degree distribution of the Internet on May 15, 2002 [63]. *Source*: Courtesy of Z. P. Fan

observed that the degree distribution of the Internet follows a power–law form with degree exponent $\gamma = 2.2$ on May 15, 2002, as shown in Figure 4.33 [63]. Yet, several years later, the degree distributions of the Internet, on every May 15, from the years 2004–2011, respectively, are still in the power–law form with the almost same degree exponent as shown in Figure 4.34 [63]. Therefore, the AS-level Internet is indeed a scale-free network. This invalidates the Waxman and Transit–Stub models in which the degree distribution follows a Poisson distribution.

On the other hand, the number of AS on the Internet grows linearly despite the fact that the number of hosts increases exponentially. Figure 4.35 shows the number of AS viewed from AS16517 during 2001–2005 [63, 64]. From this figure, one can see that the AS-level Internet is a linearly growing network. This observation is confirmed through analyzing the most completed datasets collected in [65].

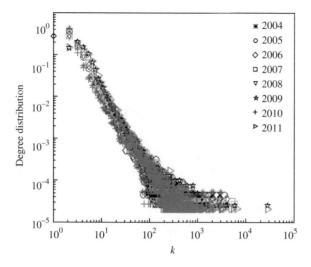

Figure 4.34   Degree distributions of the Internet on every May 15 in 2004–2011 [63]. *Source*: Courtesy of Z. P. Fan

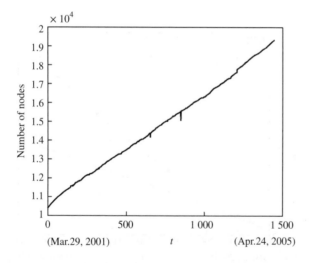

Figure 4.35   Number of AS viewed from AS16517 [63]. *Source*: Courtesy of Z. P. Fan

Figure 4.36 shows the number of AS on the Internet from January 1, 2004 to December 31, 2005. There are 16 571 AS on January 1, 2004, increasing to 24 340 on December 31, 2005. However, due to some unknown technical reasons, the collected number of AS on March 31, 2005 decreases sharply. For this reason, this set of data will not be considered later when the Internet topology models are simulated.

If one assumes that the Internet grows exponentially as in the so-called fluctuation- driven model [66], then the obtained number of AS will be much larger than the real number of AS, shown in Figure 4.37 [63]. Thus, the fluctuation-driven model will not be compared below for performance evaluation on different models of the AS-level Internet topology.

Therefore, only BA, EBA, Fitness, and MLW models will be further investigated as candidate models for the AS-level Internet topology, because they preserve at least two fundamental features, namely, the scale-free feature and the linear growth of the node numbers.

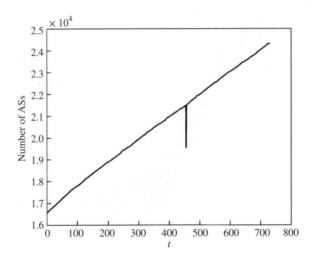

Figure 4.36   Number of AS on the Internet from January 1, 2004 to December 31, 2005 [63]. *Source*: Courtesy of Z. P. Fan

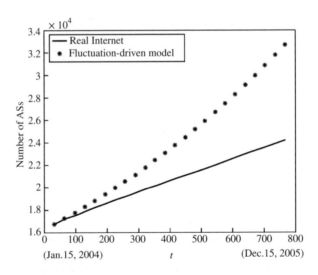

Figure 4.37   Comparison of numbers of AS between the real Internet and the prediction of the fluctuation-driven model [63]. *Source*: Courtesy of Z. P. Fan

To compare the BA, EBA, Fitness, and MLW models, the real AS-level internet data collected on May 15, 2005 is applied to fit to these candidate models. On this snapshot of the Internet, it has 21 999 nodes and 85 762 edges.

For the BA model, the number of edges is $E \approx Nm$. Therefore, the parameters in the BA model are chosen as $m = m_0 = 4$.

For the EBA model, the number of nodes is $N = m_0 + (1 - p - q)t$, and the number of edges is $E = m(1 - q)t - m/2$. Moreover, the degree exponent in the EBA model is $\gamma = 1 + \frac{2m(1-q)+1-p-q}{m}$. Therefore, in simulation, $\gamma = 2.2$ and $m = m_0 = 3$, which yield $p = 0.4$, and $q = 0.32$.

Similar to the BA model, the parameters in the Fitness model are selected to be $m = m_0 = 4$.

Table 4.7 Number of countries that the Internet covered from 1991 to 1997 [63]

Month/year	Number of countries
09/91	31
12/91	33
02/92	38
04/92	40
08/92	49
01/93	50
04/93	56
08/93	59
02/94	62
07/94	75
11/94	81
02/95	86
06/95	96
06/96	134
07/97	171

For the MLW model, it is quite natural to let a local-world in the model to represent a country that has connected to the global Internet in the world. From September 1991 to July 1997, the Internet had spread from 31 countries to 171 countries, as shown in Table 4.7 [63]. Although it was unknown as to how many countries the Internet had spread to in 2004, it is reasonable to assume that all countries in the world had been covered by the Internet due to the rapid growth of the Internet since 1999 as witnessed by Figure 4.36. Therefore, the MLW model takes $m = 186$ local-worlds, which is equal to the number of countries in the world in 2004, with the parameter $p = 0$ in the model. For each local-world, in the simulation it is assumed that the initial local-world consists of only $m_0 = 2$ nodes and $e_0 = 1$ edge, for simplicity.

On the other hand, assume that when a new AS joined the Internet, it had one or two edges to the existing nodes in most cases. Also, the nodes with degree 1 or 2 were removed from the network with higher probability than the others. Thus, one may reasonably set $m_1 = 2$ and $m_3 = 2$, and for simplicity also set $m_2 = m_4 = 2$, in the MLW model.

In the MLW model, the number of nodes, on average, is

$$N = mm_0 + qt \tag{4.24}$$

and the number of edges, on average, is

$$E = me_0 + t(pe_0 + qm_1 + rm_2 - sm_3 + um_4). \tag{4.25}$$

On the other hand, the degree exponent in the MLW model is

$$\gamma = 1 + 1/a, \tag{4.26}$$

Where

$$a = \frac{qm_1}{c} + \frac{rm_2(q + m_0 p - p)}{(q + m_0 p)c} + \frac{sm_3 p}{(q + m_0 p)c} + \frac{2um_4}{c},$$

$$c = 2(pe_0 + qm_1 + rm_2 - sm_3 + um_4) + q\alpha.$$

Let the degree exponent be $\gamma = 2.2$, as in the real data. Then, one has $s = 0.04$ and $u = 0.57$ by combining (4.24)–(4.26) together under the setting of $\alpha = 0$, $q = 0.28$ and $r = 0.11$.

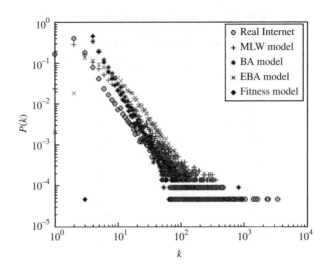

Figure 4.38 Comparison of the degree distributions between the real Internet and the four scale-free models [63].
Source: Courtesy of Z. P. Fan

Figure 4.38 [63] shows the comparison of the degree distributions between the real Internet and the four (BA, EBA, Fitness, and MLW) scale-free models with the parameters given above.

Obviously, the BA model is not a good candidate to model the AS-level Internet topology since it can only generate a scale-free network with the degree exponent exactly being 3. Yet it is not surprising to see the EBA and MLW models generated scale-free networks with the precise degree exponent $\gamma = 2.2$, identical to the actual exponent value of the Internet.

The basic small-world features exist in all the models, since the average shortest-path lengths are all small compared to their sizes. For example, in the MLW model, the average shortest-path length is only 3.4, which is very small comparing to its size $N = 21,999$. However, the distance distributions of these models are quite different, as shown in Figure 4.38 [63].

Some finer results at the distance distributions of the Internet and the BA, EBA, Fitness and MLW models are shown in Figure 4.39 [63]. From this figure, one can see that the BA, EBA and Fitness models have similar distance distributions. In these models, most nodes are separated by a distance d_0, which is near the average shortest-path length. Once the distance between a pair of nodes exceeds this value, the probability $P(d)$ with which a randomly selected pair of nodes is separated by the distance d will decrease dramatically. For example, in the Fitness model, 62.5% of nodes are separated by distance 4, which is near the average shortest-path length 3.7. However, only 6.5% of nodes are separated by distance 5. In the real Internet and the MLW model, most nodes are separated by a distance d_0, which is slightly smaller than the average distance. When the distance between any pair of nodes exceeds d_0, the probability $P(d)$ decreases slowly. For instance, in the MLW model, 53.1% of nodes are separated by distance 3 while 41% of nodes are separated by distance 4, which is quite different from the BA, EBA, and Fitness models.

On the other hand, the clustering coefficients in the BA, EBA, and Fitness models are very small. For example, the value of the clustering coefficient is 0.009 in the EBA model. However, the clustering coefficient in the real Internet is very large although it is still much smaller than 1. Among the BA, EBA, Fitness, and MLW models, only the MLW model can reproduce a large clustering coefficient, comparable to that of the real Internet. More importantly, the MLW model can capture the essential feature of the distribution of clustering coefficients of the Internet, while the BA, EBA and Fitness models fail, as shown in Figure 4.40 [63].

Therefore, after all, the MLW model is better to fit the Internet topology data than the BA, EBA, and Fitness models in terms of essential small-world features of the generated networks.

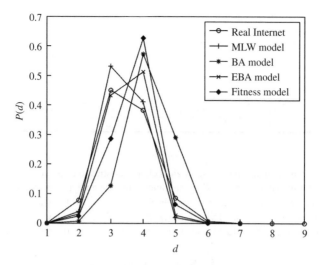

Figure 4.39   Distance distributions of the Internet and the four scale-free models [63]. *Source*: Courtesy of Z. P. Fan

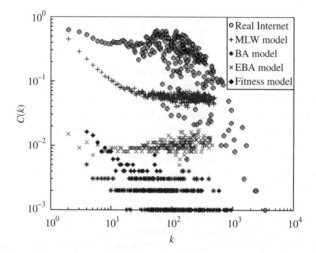

Figure 4.40   Clustering coefficients $C(k)$ as functions of the degree k for the real Internet and the four models [63]. *Source*: Courtesy of Z. P. Fan

A detailed comparison of some statistical results obtained from the BA, EBA, Fitness, and MLW models against the real AS-level Internet topology is summarized in Table 4.8 [63], where N is the number of nodes, C the average clustering coefficient, and L the average shortest-path length.

One can clearly see from Table 4.8 that the BA model cannot be used to describe the AS-level Internet topology since they cannot reproduce the same scale-free features as the real Internet. The EBA and Fitness models can capture the power–law characteristic of the real Internet, but they do not satisfy several basic statistical properties. Fox example, for the average clustering coefficient, the EBA model gives 0.009 while the MLW model gives 0.238, which has a much smaller error in comparison against 0.457 of the real Internet. Thus, the MLW model is better than the BA, EBA, and Fitness models in representing the Internet AS-level topology, since it can capture both the scale-free and small-world features of the real Internet.

Table 4.8 Comparison results for the four models against the real Internet [63]

	BA model	EBA model	Fitness model	MLW model	Real Internet (15 May 2005)
N	21 999	21 999	21 999	21 999	21 999
C	0.003	0.009	0.012	0.238	0.457
L	4.154	3.533	3.731	3.410	3.493
γ	3	2.2	2.26	2.2	2.2

One may also apply more measures of topological characteristics to evaluate and differentiate Internet models [67]. In so doing, a combination of the canonical variable analysis and Bayesian decision theory is desirable [68]. Suppose that the feature vector is $X = (x_1, x_2, \cdots, x_p)^T$, where x_i is a scalar measure used to classify N networks which are divided into M classes. The objective is to maximize the interclass dispersion while minimizing the intraclass scattering, where the intraclass matrix is defined by

$$S_{\text{intra}} = \sum_{k=1}^{M} \sum_{\zeta \in C_k} \left(X_\zeta - \overline{X}_k \right) \left(X_\zeta - \overline{X}_k \right)^T,$$

while the interclass matrix by

$$S_{\text{inter}} = \sum_{k=1}^{C} N_k \left(\overline{X}_k - \overline{X} \right) \left(\overline{X}_k - \overline{X} \right)^T,$$

where X_ζ is the feature vector of network ζ, $\overline{X}_k$ is the average feature vector of class C_k, $\overline{X}$ is the average feature vector of N networks, and N_k is the number of networks in class C_k, $k = 1, 2, \ldots, M$. The original higher-dimensional feature measures can then be projected into a two-dimensional feature space by using a linear transformation $Y = TX_\zeta$, where matrix T is constructed by the eigenvectors associated with the first two largest eigenvalues of the matrix $S_{\text{intra}}^{-1} S_{\text{inter}}$. Finally, in the two-dimensional feature space, a network with unknown classification can be determined as belonging to which class, on the basis of the Bayesian decision theory and method. For example, if the average clustering coefficient, the average distance, and the first largest eigenvalue of the adjacency matrix are involved in the evaluation and comparison of the Internet models in interest, one can find that the MLW model is indeed the most compatible one to the real Internet.

It is also possible to apply the hierarchical clustering algorithm [69] to classify various Internet models. This method builds a hierarchy by treating every network as a single cluster. Then, in each successive iteration, according to the predefined distance between clusters, the closest pair of clusters are merged, until only one cluster remains. In such a procedure, the sooner the two networks are merged, the more similar they are. Again, if the average clustering coefficient, the average distance, and the first largest eigenvalue of the adjacency matrix are used to classify the Internet models, one can see that the MLW model is closer to the real Internet than all other models in comparison.

In summary, the MLW model is the best candidate model to represent and describe the Internet, than all other models in consideration, in the sense of capturing most significant topological characteristics of common interest [70].

4.6.3 Performance Comparison

Although it has been shown, in the above, that the MLW model is better than the BA, EBA, and Fitness models in capturing the structural features of the Internet, one may still want to know what would happen to the performances of the MLW model in comparing to the real Internet and the other models, particularly in terms of the important and interesting "robust yet fragile" characteristics of the Internet.

On the Internet, local failures and errors often occur due to some hardware and software problems. Therefore, the ability to resist random failures or errors is quite important for a reliable Internet. Here, the "robustness yet fragility" property of the Internet is used as an evaluating indicator to compare the MLW model with the BA, EBA, and Fitness models against the real Internet topology.

To investigate the robustness and fragility of a network, it is natural to study S_f, the size of the largest component after a fraction of nodes, f, in the network are randomly removed from the network, such that the remaining network is undamaged (e.g., remains to be connected). Therefore, the ratio S_f/S_0 measures the capability of the network in which nodes can still communicate each other after the f portion of nodes has been randomly selected and removed. Obviously, if $S_f/S_0 \approx 1$, it means that the remaining network can still function as the original network; but if $0 < S_f/S_0 \ll 1$, then it indicates that the network has been broken into several clusters while a giant component still exists; yet, if $S_f/S_0 \approx 0$, it means that the network has been broken into several components and each component contains no meaningful networked nodes, namely, the network has collapsed.

Another metric to characterize the Internet's tolerance to random failures is L_g, the average shortest-path length of the largest component after the f portion of nodes has been randomly removed.

Figure 4.41 shows the ratios S_f/S_0, as functions of the portions of the randomly removed nodes, f, for different models. From the figure, one can clearly see that the Internet is quite resilient to random damages. For example, when 30% of nodes on the Internet have been randomly removed, the giant component of the network has a size close to 56.2% of that of the original network; even when 70% of nodes in the network have been randomly removed, the giant component still contains 15.7% of nodes of the original network.

Figure 4.42 shows the change of the average shortest-path length in the giant component of the Internet as a function of the portion of randomly removed nodes. In the beginning, with the increase of the portion of randomly removed nodes, the average shortest-path length on the Internet increases slightly because only some nodes and edges attached to these nodes on the Internet are removed but the Internet can still maintain a large component. With the further increase of the portion of randomly removed nodes, the Internet is finally broken into several small clusters, and consequently the average shortest-path length is drastically decreased.

Clearly, one can see from Figures 4.41 and 4.42 that the MLW model yields a smallest error in comparison with other models against the real Internet. For example, when 70% of nodes have been removed from the network, the size of the resulting giant component relative to the size of the original undamaged

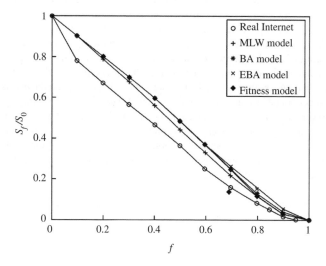

Figure 4.41 Comparison of the ratios S_f/S_0 for the Internet and the four models [63]. *Source*: Courtesy of Z. P. Fan

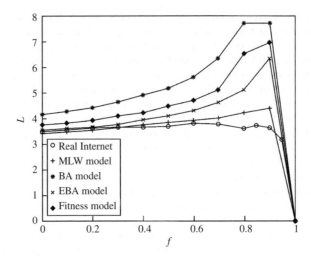

Figure 4.42 Comparison of the average shortest-path lengths in the giant component for the real Internet and the four models [63]. *Source*: Courtesy of Z. P. Fan

network is 21.6% while the average shortest-path length is 4.01 in the MLW model. However, the corresponding values are 24.9% and 6.3 in the giant component of the BA model, which gives larger errors than the MLW model against the real Internet.

In summary, one may conclude that the MLW model is the best as compared to the BA, EBA, and Fitness models in describing the AS-level Internet topology, since it can capture the basic structural features of the Internet and can also maintain the robust performance of the Internet in resisting random failures [70].

4.7 HOT Model

It has been observed lately that the preferential attachment scheme, which leads to power–law degree distributions of scale-free network models, is consistent with the favorable *cooperation* behaviors among the nodes in networks. When *competition* dominates a network, however, preferential attachment becomes less convincing. As it is intuitively clear, competitors usually try to optimize their own advantages and strengths in competitions and do not prefer to attach to giant nodes who have already had most benefits that may actually become threats to new comers and small entities (nodes) of the network.

With such a view in mind, an Internet model by Fabrikant *et al.* [71], called the *heuristically optimized trade-off* (HOT) model, found its place to step in. This model elaborates on the highly optimized tolerance mechanism for power–law distributions in designing a network, proposed by Carlson and Doyle [72], and suggests a new way to produce power laws by an intrinsic trade-off mechanism. More precisely, in designing a network, typically there will be some conflicting objectives; therefore, trade-off among them is usually necessary, while various optimizations toward the objectives are being performed.

Taking this approach, the HOT model suggests a growing network in which, at every step of its growth, a new node is being added and placed at a randomly selected position on a unit square in the partition of a planar region. The new node i is connected to an existing node j according to the minimization of a cost function, say of the form

$$\Phi(i,j) = a(N)d_E(i,j) + \phi(j), \tag{4.27}$$

where $a(N)$ is a constant depending only on the network size N, $d_E(i,j)$ is the Euclidean distance between node i and node j, and $\phi(j)$ is a measure of a certain centrality of node j such as one of the following [71]:

1. the average shortest-path length from j to all the other nodes in the network;
2. the maximum shortest-path length from j to any other node in the network;
3. the shortest-path length from j to a fixed "central" node.

Clearly, the first term in (4.27) aims to limit the cost of establishing the physical connection between the new node i and the existing node j by minimizing their Euclidean distance, while the second term there attempts to minimize the hop distance of node j to the "centrally located" node, so as to maximize the information transmission efficiency.

Figure 4.43 shows a representative simulated network [20], generated from a simulation of the HOT model with $N = 1000$ and $a(N) = 25$, where the "central" node is the one near the center of the figure. This simulated example of the HOT network has a power–law degree distribution, with $\gamma = 1.8$ [20].

The Abilene backbone network, illustrated by Figure 4.44 [73], was often used for illustration in the discussion of the HOT model (see, for example, [74–78]).

Finally, worth noticing are some consideration of the economics and evolution aspects in understanding and modeling the Internet [78] and a recent survey on Internet topology generators at the AS level [79], which are quite informative.

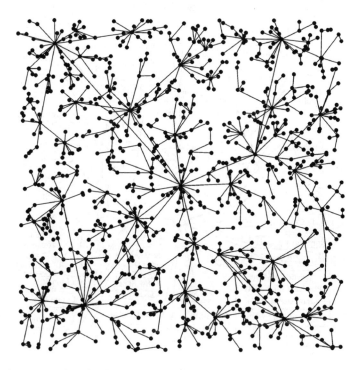

Figure 4.43 A representative simulated HOT network [20]. *Source*: Reproduced with permission from Pastor-Satorras, R. and Vespignani, A. (2004) *Evolution and Structure of the Internet: A Statistical Physics Approach*, Cambridge University Press, Cambridge

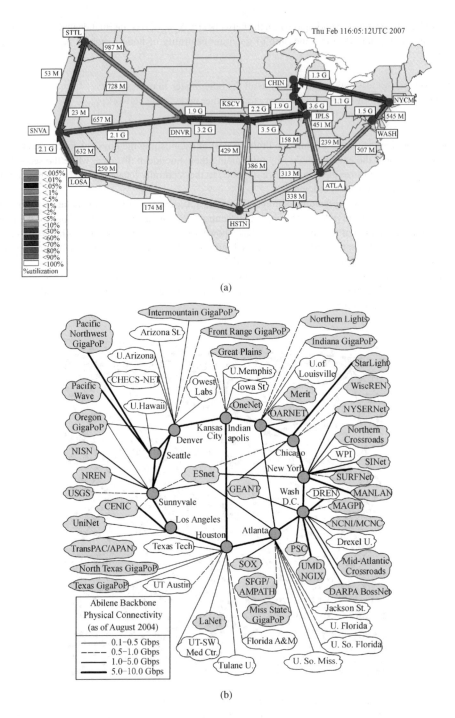

Figure 4.44 The Abilene network [73]: (a) network utilization; (b) network backbone

4.8   Dynamical Behaviors of the Internet Topological Characteristics

At present, topological characteristics have been extensively used to evaluate and differentiate Internet models. In most cases, however, such comparisons are based only on one set of snapshot data of the Internet. As an open network, the Internet continuously evolves with new nodes and new links joining the network while some existing nodes and links disappear from the network from time to time. As a result, the topological characteristics of the Internet also evolve with time. Recent work [78] suggested that the dynamical behaviors of topological characteristics can be useful when comparing and evaluating Internet models. Typically, due to the essential role of nodes on the Internet core, the evolving behavior of the Internet core should be taken into serious consideration.

Figure 4.45 [70] shows the number of nodes as a function of time from January 2004 to October 2010. From this figure, one can see that the number of nodes on the Internet core increases almost linearly, albeit with some fluctuations.

Figures 4.46 and 4.47 [70] show the average clustering coefficient and distance, respectively, for the nodes on the Internet core. One can see that the value of clustering coefficient is very high while the value of average distance is remarkably small, showing a typical small-world feature. It implies that the nodes on the Internet core are not loosely but tightly connected, rather different from a previous observation [80].

If such dynamical behaviors of the Internet core are involved in the comparison of Internet models, it will seemingly lead to a belief that no existing models can well capture such dynamical features. This demonstrates that the task of modeling the Internet is still quite far from being complete, greatly challenging future investigations.

4.9   Traffic Fluctuation on Weighted Networks

Regarding the dynamical behaviors of the Internet, data traffic and its fluctuation problem are particularly important thereby receiving considerable attention [81]. It is associated with an additive quantity representing the volume of traffic traversing through a node (or an edge) during a certain time window, and also with the dependence between its mean and standard deviation [82]. Knowledge on traffic fluctuation is relevant to the design and management of communication systems especially the Internet, for example how to deploy network resources, how to route traffic efficiently and how to mitigate congestion.

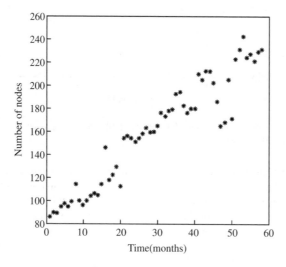

Figure 4.45   Number of nodes on the Internet core [70]. *Source*: Reproduced from Computers & Mathematics with Applications (2012) Elsevier

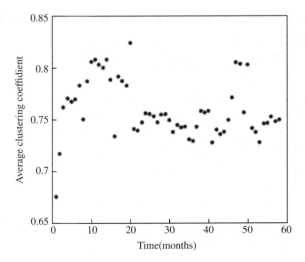

Figure 4.46 Clustering coefficient for nodes on the Internet core [70]. *Source*: Reproduced from Computers & Mathematics with Applications (2012) Elsevier

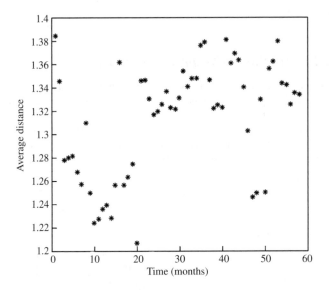

Figure 4.47 Average distance for nodes on the Internet core [70]. *Source*: Reproduced from Computers & Mathematics with Applications (2012) Elsevier

In recent years, there has been increasing research interest in understanding and analyzing the traffic fluctuation problem, which is key to a wide range of applications in various networked systems [83–87]. In particular, interest is in the relation between the mean and the standard deviation of the traffic on a given node or edge, which govern realistic conditions for various problems of immediate social and economical impacts, to the extent that the assignment of resources well matches the supplies and demands.

On the Internet, data traffic fluctuations are typically affected by specific physical properties of network components, such as the bandwidth of a cable or the computational power of a router. This is much better to be described by a weighted network, where the physical properties of the network components are represented as edge weights and node strengths. An early discovery [83] was that the average volume of traffic traveling through a node, $\langle f \rangle$, and the fluctuation (standard deviation) of the traffic, σ, follow a power–law form $\sigma \sim \langle f \rangle^{\alpha}$, where the exponent α has two universal values, 0.5 and 1.

Subsequently, it was shown [84], albeit numerically, that there is a wide spectrum of possible values within the range of [0.5, 1] for α in real systems. Then, an analytical law was derived [85], showing the dependence of fluctuations on the mean traffic over unweighted networks, where physical properties of edges and nodes are simply ignored. In reality, however, edges have different physical properties (e.g., bandwidths, delays, costs) and naturally traffic tends to choosing a path that can achieve better performance, higher efficiency, or lower cost. Therefore, it is very important to study data traffic fluctuation on weighted networks, especially as the Internet is in every sense a weighted network. For weighted networks, the critical questions include "What is the impact of different capacities of nodes and edges on the fluctuations of data traffic passing through them?", "Can we predict the fluctuations?", "What are their implications for network resource assignment?" and so on.

4.9.1   Weighted Networks

As reviewed in Chapter 2 on weighted graphs, in a weighted router network, edge weight can represent the bandwidth of a cable and node strength can represent the processing power of a router [88].

4.9.1.1   Edge Weights

To model a weighted network, the weight of an edge can be defined via the degrees of its two end-nodes, k_i and k_j, as

$$w_{ij} = w_{ji} = (k_i k_j)^{\theta}, \tag{4.28}$$

for all nodes $i, j = 1, 2, ..., N$, where θ is the weightiness parameter of the network, which characterizes the dependence between the edge weight and the node degrees [89, 90]. The weightiness parameter determines the level of edge heterogeneity in a weighted network. When $\theta = 0$, there is no dependence between the edge weight and the node degree, thus the network becomes an unweighted one. When $\theta > 0$, however, it is a weighted network where edges have different weights. The larger the θ, the wider the difference between different edges.

4.9.1.2   Node Strengths

The strength of node i can be defined as

$$s_i = \sum_{j \in \Gamma_i} w_{ij} = \sum_{j \in \Gamma_i} (k_i k_j)^{\theta}, \tag{4.29}$$

where Γ_i is the neighborhood of node i, $i = 1, 2, ... , N$. In an unweighted network, which has $\theta = 0$, node strength $s_i = k_i$. In a weighted network, where $\theta > 0$, two nodes with the same degree may have different strength values depending on the weights of their edges.

4.9.2   GRD Model

Random walk is a mathematical description of a trajectory taking successive random steps, which has been used to model dynamic processes on complex networks [91, 92], such as such as navigation and search of information on the World Wide Web and routing on the Internet [93–95]. Data traffic fluctuation on networks was studied by means of random walkers traveling on unweighted networks, where the choice of a route is at random [26, 84, 85, 96], or by means of a single random walker traveling on a weighted network [97, 98].

Here, a general random walk model on weighted networks is introduced [81].

On a given network, consider a random walker starting from node i at time $t = 0$ and let $P_{im}(t)$ be the probability that the walker arrives at node m at time $t > 0$. The probability that the walker is at node j at the next time step, after leaving the current node m, is given by $P_{ij}(t + 1) = \sum_m a_{mj} \Pi_{m \to j} P_{im}(t)$, where a_{mj} is an element of the network adjacent matrix $A = [a_{ij}]$, and $\Pi_{m \to j}$ is defined to be w_{mj}/s_m. Thus, the probability $P_{ij}(t)$ for the walker to travel from node i to node j in t time steps is

$$P_{ij}(t) = \sum_{m_1,\dots,m_{t-1}} \frac{a_{im_1} w_{im_1}}{s_i} \cdot \frac{a_{m_1 m_2} w_{m_1 m_2}}{s_{m_1}} \cdots \frac{a_{m_{t-1}j} w_{m_{t-1}j}}{s_{m_{t-1}}}$$

$$= \sum_{m_1,\dots,m_{t-1}} P_{im_1} P_{m_1 m_2} \cdots P_{m_{t-1}j}. \tag{4.30}$$

Comparing the expressions for P_{ij} and P_{ji}, one can see that $s_i P_{ij}(t) = s_j P_{ji}(t)$, for all $t \geq 0$. This is due to the undirectedness of the network. For a stationary solution, one obtains $P_i^\infty = s_i/\sum_i s_i$. Hence, the stationary distribution is, up to normalization, equal to the strength s_i of node i. This implies that the higher strength a node has, the more often it will be visited by a walker.

Next, the general random diffusion (GRD) model is introduced, which describes the traffic fluctuation problem as a large number of independent random walkers traveling simultaneously on a weighted network, whereby every walker's choice of paths is based on the rules defined above.

The GRD model is constituted by several measures: size of time window, preferential choice of path, and average traffic, which are described as follows.

4.9.2.1 Size of Time Window

Data traffic arriving at a node (or passing through an edge) is observed in a sequence of time windows of an equal size. Each time, a window consists of M time units, which is defined as the interval of steps for a random walker to hop from one node to another.

4.9.2.2 Preferential Choice of Path

A walker at node i chooses edge (i,j), which connects node i and node j, as the next leg of travel according to the following preferential probability:

$$\Pi = \frac{w_{ij}}{\sum_{j \in \Gamma_i} w_{ij}} = \frac{w_{ij}}{s_i}, \tag{4.31}$$

which is proportional to the weight of the edge.

4.9.2.3 Average Traffic

The data traffic arriving at node i during a time window of length M is $f_i = \sum_{m=1}^M \Delta_i(m)$, where $\Delta_i(m)$ is a random variable representing the number of walkers arriving at node i at the mth time step. The average traffic, $\langle f_i \rangle$, is the mean traffic volume at node i over all time windows. Similarly, f_{ij} is the traffic passing through edge (i,j) between node i and node j within a time window, and $\langle f_{ij} \rangle$ is the average edge traffic of edge (i,j).

4.9.3 Data Traffic Fluctuations

The traffic standard deviation σ_i indicates the fluctuation of traffic volume around the average traffic $\langle f_i \rangle$ at node i over all time windows. Similarly σ_{ij} is the fluctuation of edge traffic f_{ij} on edge (i,j).

The present interest on the traffic fluctuation problem is the relation between the average traffic $\langle f \rangle$ (of a node or an edge) and the corresponding fluctuation σ, and the impact of relevant parameters (i.e., time window size M, weightiness parameter θ, and node degree k) on this relation.

Next, the traffic fluctuations on nodes and edges are discussed, respectively.

4.9.3.1 Node Traffic Fluctuation

Analytic Solutions

According to the GRD model described above, the preferential choice of path (4.31), in the stationary status the number of walkers visiting node i at a single time step can be estimated by

$$\Phi_i(r) = r \cdot \frac{s_i}{\sum_{i=1}^{N} s_i}, \tag{4.32}$$

where r is the number of random walkers traveling on the weighted network and N is the network size, i.e., number of nodes in the whole network. In the GRD model, random walkers are independent variables and the arrival of walkers at a node is a Poisson process. Thus, the mean number of walkers visiting node i within a time window of length M is

$$\langle f_i \rangle = M\Phi_i(r), \tag{4.33}$$

and the probability that exactly n walkers arrived at node i within a time window is

$$P_i(n) = e^{-M\Phi_i(r)} \frac{[M\Phi_i(r)]^n}{n!}. \tag{4.34}$$

In a more general case, the number of walkers, r, observed from time window to time window, is uniformly distributed in $[R - \delta, R + \delta]$, $0 < \delta \leq R$, where R is the average number of arriving walkers and constant δ describes its variation. The probability of having r walkers within a time window is $1/(2\delta + 1)$. Thus, (4.34) becomes

$$P_i(n) = \sum_{j=0}^{2\delta} \frac{e^{-\left(s_i / \sum_{i=1}^{N} s_i\right)(R - \delta + j)M}}{2\delta + 1} \cdot \frac{\left[\left(s_i / \sum_{i=1}^{N} s_i\right)(R - \delta + j)\right]^n}{n!}. \tag{4.35}$$

Calculating the first and second moments of f_i yields

$$\langle f_i \rangle = \sum_{n=0}^{\infty} nP_i(n) = \frac{s_i}{\sum_{i=1}^{N} s_i} RM \tag{4.36}$$

and

$$\langle f_i^2 \rangle = \sum_{n=0}^{\infty} n^2 P_i(n) = \langle f_i \rangle \cdot \left(1 + \frac{\delta^2 + \delta}{3R^2}\right) + \langle f_i \rangle. \tag{4.37}$$

Consequently, the standard deviation as a function of $\langle f_i \rangle$ is obtained as

$$\sigma_i^2 = \langle f_i \rangle \cdot \left(1 + \langle f_i \rangle \frac{\delta^2 + \delta}{3R^2}\right). \tag{4.38}$$

This indicates that the relation between the traffic at nodes and its scale does not depend on the weightiness parameter θ. The traffic fluctuation at node i is determined by $\sigma_i^2 = (\sigma_i^{int})^2 + (\sigma_i^{ext})^2$, where $\sigma_i^{int} = \sqrt{\langle f_i \rangle}$ is the internal randomness of the diffusion process and $\sigma_i^{ext} = \langle f_i \rangle \sqrt{(\delta^2 + \delta)/(3R^2)}$ is the change in the external environment, i.e., the fluctuation of the number of walkers on the network in different time windows.

Numerical Simulations

Numerical simulations were run to verify the above analytical solutions, to examine the impact of model parameters, such as window size M and node degree k, on the scaling of the traffic fluctuation function, and to compare unweighted networks ($\theta = 0$) with weighted networks ($\theta > 0$).

The simulations are run on a BA scale-free network of 5000 nodes and 25 000 edges, with a power–law degree distribution $P(k) \sim k^{-3}$. Assign edge weights and node strengths as defined in (4.28) and (4.29), respectively. Initially, disperse $r = R \pm \delta = 10,000 \pm 1000$ random walkers uniformly at the nodes on the BA network. All walkers travel one hop at a time step according to (4.31). For a given and fixed time window size M, observe traffic fluctuation at each node over a large number of time windows.

Simulations on 10 BA networks of the same size on the same setting were performed for each given value of time window size M or weightiness parameter θ, and is repeated for 50 times (with different random seeds) on each BA network. Finally, results are plotted by averaging $10 \times 50 = 500$ simulation trials.

Power–Law Relation: Figure 4.48 (a) shows the relation between traffic fluctuation σ_i and average traffic $\langle f_i \rangle$ for different time window sizes M, with $\theta = 0.5$, which is a power–law $\sigma_i \sim \langle f_i \rangle^\alpha$. The simulation results well overlap with the analytical solutions. Both the average traffic and the traffic fluctuation increase as M increases. It can be seen that when M is small, the power–law exponent α is close to 0.5; when M increases, α approaches 1.

Figure 4.48 (b) shows an enlargement of the traffic fluctuation function when the window size $M = 100$, as circled out in Figure 4.48 (a). For high-degree nodes, large values of σ_i and $\langle f_i \rangle$ are observed. For low-degree nodes (e.g. $k = 5$), the power–law exponent α is close to 0.5, whereas for high-degree nodes (e.g. $k = 18$), α approaches 1. Figure 4.49 shows traffic fluctuation σ_i as a function of average traffic $\langle f_i \rangle$ for different values of weightiness parameter θ [81].

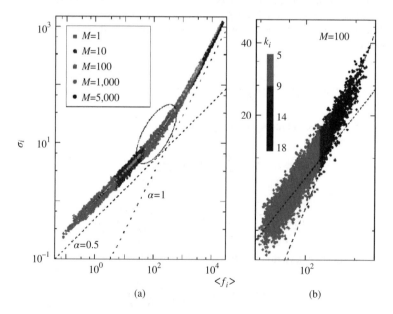

(a)   (b)

Figure 4.48   (a) Traffic fluctuation σ_i as a function of average traffic $\langle f_i \rangle$ [81]; (b) enlargement when window size $M = 100$ (as circled out in (a)). *Source*: Reprinted with permission from Zhang, Y.C., Zhou, S., Zhang, Z.Z., *et al.* (2012) Traffic fluctuations on weighted networks. *IEEE Circuits and Systems Magazine*, **1**: 33–44. Copyright (2012) IEEE

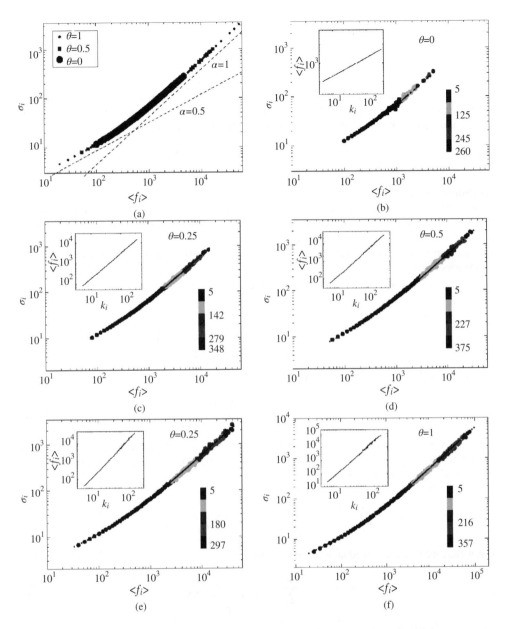

Figure 4.49 Traffic fluctuation σ_i as a function of average traffic $\langle f_i \rangle$ for different values of weightiness parameter θ [81]; (a) illustrates solutions of (4.38) for weightiness parameter values of $\theta = 0$, 0.5 and 1, with time window size fixed as $M = 100$; (b), (c), (d), (e) and (f) show simulation results for $\theta = 0$, 0.25, 0.5, 0.75, and 1, respectively. *Source*: Reprinted with permission from Zhang, Y.C., Zhou, S., Zhang, Z.Z., *et al.* (2012) Traffic fluctuations on weighted networks. *IEEE Circuits and Systems Magazine*, **1**: 33–44. Copyright (2012) IEEE

Impact of the Weightiness Parameter: It can be observed that for different θ values, the traffic fluctuation curves overlap with each other, and in all cases high-degree nodes are concentrated at the upper-right ends of the curves whereas low-degree nodes are dispersed near the lower-left parts of the curves.

A remarkable difference, however, is that with the increase of θ, the value ranges of σ_i and $\langle f_i \rangle$ expand significantly towards both directions. This shows that, comparing with an unweighted network, traffic fluctuation in a weighted network is more acute at high-degree nodes and more stable at low-degree ones. That is because, in a weighted network, the node strength $s_i \sim k_i^\theta$ (see (4.29)) therefore high-degree nodes deprive more traffic from low-degree ones than in an unweighted network.

4.9.3.2 Edge Traffic Fluctuation

Analytic Solutions

In the GRD model, random walkers on a weighted network travel independently and, therefore, the number of walkers passing through an edge is a Poisson process. As given in (4.31), the probability that a walker at node i chooses edge (i,j) as the next leg of travel is w_{ij}/s_i. Thus, for r random walkers, the average number of walkers passing through edge (i,j) on both forward and backward directions during a time window of length M is

$$\langle f_{ij} \rangle = \Psi_{ij}(r)M,$$

where

$$\Psi_{ij}(r) = r\left(\frac{s_i}{\sum_{i=1}^N s_i} \cdot \frac{w_{ij}}{s_i} + \frac{s_j}{\sum_{i=1}^N s_i} \cdot \frac{w_{ij}}{s_j} \right) \tag{4.39}$$

and the probability of $f_{ij} = n$ in a time window is

$$Q_{ij}(n) = e^{-\Psi_{ij}(r)M} \frac{[\Psi_{ij}(r)M]^n}{n!}. \tag{4.40}$$

Similarly, as the above analysis on node traffic fluctuation, for a more general case where the number of random walkers r from time window to time window is distributed in $[R-\delta, R+\delta]$, and the probability of $f_{ij} = n$ in a time window is given by

$$\Gamma_{ij}(n) = \sum_{j=0}^{2\delta} \frac{1}{2\delta+1} e^{2w_{ij}(R-\delta+j)M/(\langle k^{\theta+1}\rangle^2 N)} \times \frac{1}{n!} e^{2w_{ij}(R-\delta+j)M/(\langle k^{\theta+1}\rangle^2 N)} \tag{4.41}$$

Calculating the first and second moments of f_{ij} yields

$$\langle f_{ij} \rangle = \sum_{n=0}^{\infty} n\Gamma_{ij}(n) = \frac{2w_{ij}}{\sum_{i=1}^N s_i} RM \tag{4.42}$$

and

$$\langle f_{ij}^2 \rangle = \sum_{n=0}^{\infty} n^2\Gamma_{ij}(n) = \langle f_{ij}^2 \rangle \cdot \left(1 + \frac{\delta^2+\delta}{3R^2}\right) + \langle f_{ij} \rangle. \tag{4.43}$$

Consequently, the standard deviation as a function of the average traffic is obtained as

$$\sigma_{ij}^2 = \langle f_{ij} \rangle \cdot \left(1 + \frac{\delta^2+\delta}{3R^2}\right). \tag{4.44}$$

This also shows that the relation between the traffic on edges and its scale is irrelevant to the weightiness parameter θ.

Numerical Simulations

The simulation setting is same as the above in the study of node traffic fluctuation.

Power–Law Relation: Figure 4.50 shows the relation between the traffic fluctuation σ_{ij} and the average traffic $\langle f_{ij} \rangle$ on edge (i, j) for three different values of the time window size M. The simulation results are in good agreement with the analytical solutions. As predicted by (4.42) and (4.44), the average traffic $\langle f_{ij} \rangle$ and the fluctuation σ_{ij} increase with the value of M, and they are related through a power–law scaling, $\sigma_{ij} \sim \langle f_{ij} \rangle^{\alpha}$, where the exponent α is 0.5 for small values of M and approaches 1 as M increases. Such behavior is similar to the traffic fluctuation on nodes discussed above.

Impact of Weightiness Parameter: Figure 4.51 (a) shows that the range of scaling for $\theta = 1$ is [0.5031, 0.9602], while for $\theta = 0$ it is nearly 0. When $\theta = 0$, the edges form a dense group on the plot, representing almost identical fluctuation properties. This unaccounted fact can be explained by the solutions of (4.42) and (4.44). The dashed lines are drawn for reference, corresponding to $\sigma_{ij} \sim \langle f_{ij} \rangle^{\alpha}$ with $\alpha = 0.5$ and $\alpha = 1$, respectively. A comparison between unweighted networks ($\theta = 0$) and weighted ones ($\theta >$) can be clearly seen from Figure 4.51 (b), which shows that the differences of σ_{ij} and f_{ij} for different node pairs crop up when $\theta = 1$.

Node Degree: Figures 4.51 (c) and (d) show the middle case with $\theta = 0.5$ for different node pairs. In Figure 4.51 (c), the plots are the results obtained for pairs of k_i and k_j, with $k_i > k_j > 10$ in this simulation. One can easily observe that f_{ij} is directly proportional to $k_i k_j$ when $\theta > 0$, while they are almost constant when $\theta = 0$. Likewise, σ_{ij} is directly proportional to $k_i k_j$ when $\theta = 0.5$, but they are rather stable when $\theta = 0$, as also seen from Figure 4.51 (b).

To summarize the above study on traffic fluctuation on data communication networks, such as part of the Internet, one simple observation is that the traffic on different roads differs, the wider of which can allow more traffic but meanwhile the traffic on roads with heavy loads fluctuates more dramatically, depending on the road conditions such as peaktime of traffic.

Generally speaking, after all, the intrinsic relationships between network topology and dynamics are very important and yet also very challenging, which need more effort to understand and further investigate.

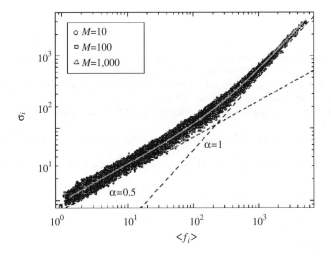

Figure 4.50   Traffic fluctuation σ_{ij} as a function of average traffic $\langle f_{ij} \rangle$ on edge (i, j) [81]. *Source:* Reprinted with permission from Zhang, Y.C., Zhou, S., Zhang, Z.Z., *et al.* (2012) Traffic fluctuations on weighted networks. *IEEE Circuits and Systems Magazine*, **1**: 33–44. Copyright (2012) IEEE

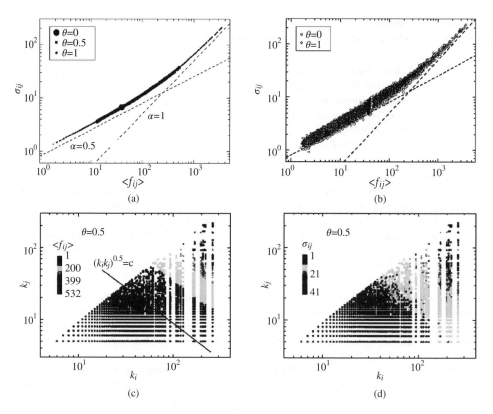

Figure 4.51 Traffic fluctuation σ_{ij} as a function of average traffic $\langle f_{ij} \rangle$ for different values of weightiness parameter θ [81]: (a) range of scaling; (b) difference curves; (c) difference curve, middle case 1; (d) difference curve, middle case 2. *Source*: Reprinted with permission from Zhang, Y.C., Zhou, S., Zhang, Z.Z., *et al*. (2012) Traffic fluctuations on weighted networks. *IEEE Circuits and Systems Magazine*, **1**: 33–44. Copyright (2012) IEEE

References

[1] http://www.internetworldstats.com/ (last accessed August 9, 2014); see also http://www.internetlivestats.com /total-number-of-websites/#trend (last accessed August 13, 2014).

[2] Faloutsos, M., Faloutsos, P. and Faloutsos, C. (1999) On power–law relationships of the Internet topology. *ACM SIGCOMM Computer Communication Review*, **29**(4): 251–62.

[3] Waxman, B-M. (1988) Routing of multipoint connections. *IEEE Journal of Selected Areas in Communication*, **6**(9): 1617–22.

[4] Doar, M.B. (1996) A better model for generating test networks. *Proceedings of IEEE Global Internet*, London, 86–93.

[5] Calvert, K., Doar, M. and Zegura, E. (1997) Modeling Internet topology. *IEEE Communication Magazine*, **35**(6): 160–3.

[6] Medina, A, Lakhina, A, Matta, I. and Byers, J. (2001) BRITE: An approach to universal topology generation. *Proceedings of MASCOTS*, Washington, 346–53.

[7] http://topology.eecs.umich.edu/inet/(last accessed August 9, 2014).

[8] Albert, R, and Barabási, A-L. (2000) Topology of evolving networks: Local events and universality. *Physical Review Letters*, **85**(24): 5234–7.

[9] Barabási, A-L. (2002) *Linked: How Everything is Connected to Everything Else and What It Means for Business, Science, and Everyday Life*, Plume, New York.

[10] Chen, Q., Chang, H., Govindan, R. and Jamin, S. (2002) The origin of power laws in Internet topologies revisited. *Proceedings of IEEE INFOCOM*, 608–17.

[11] Siganos, G., Faloutsos, M., Faloutsos, P. and Faloutsos, C. (2003) Power laws and the AS-level Internet topology. *IEEE/ ACM Transactions on Networking*, **11**(4): 514–24.
[12] Mahadevan, P., Krioukov, D., Fomenkov, M. *et al.* (2005) Lessons from three views of the Internet topology. *arXiv:cs.NI/0508033.*
[13] Jaiswal, S., Rosenberg, A.L. and Towsley, D. (2004) Comparing the structure of power–law graphs and the Internet AS graph. *Proceedings of the 12th IEEE International Conference on Network Protocols*, 294–303.
[14] http://www.routeviews.org/ (last accessed August 9, 2014); see also Claffy, K., Monk, T. and McRobb, D.(1999) Internet tomography. *Nature, 7* January.
[15] http://irl.cs.ucla.edu/topology/ (last accessed August 9, 2014).
[16] http://www.caida.org/tools/measurement/skitter/ (last accessed August 9, 2014).
[17] http://www.irr.net/ (last accessed August 9, 2014).
[18] RIPE: http://www.ripe.net/ (last accessed August 9, 2014) and http://en.wikipedia.org/wiki/RIPE (last accessed August 9, 2014).
[19] Zhang, B., Liu, R., Massey, D. and Zhang, L. (2005) Collecting the Internet AS-level topology. *ACM SIGCOMM Computer Communication Review*, **35**: 53–61.
[20] Pastor-Satorras, R. and Vespignani, A. (2004) *Evolution and Structure of the Internet: A Statistical Physics Approach*, Cambridge University Press, Cambridge.
[21] Cai, S.L., Gao, L.X., Gong, W.B. and Xu, W.Q. (2004) On generating Internet hierarchical topology. *Proceedings of the 43rd IEEE Conference on Decision and Control.*
[22] Zhou, S. and Mondragon, R-J. (2004) The rich-club phenomenon in the Internet topology. *IEEE Communications Letters*, **8**(3): 180–2.
[23] Zegura, E.W., Calvert, K.L. and Donahoo, M.J. (1997) A quantitative comparison of graph-based models for Internet topology. *IEEE/ACM Transactions on Networking*, **5**: 770–83.
[24] http://www.traceroute.org/ (last accessed August 9, 2014).
[25] Zhou, S. and Mondragon, R-J. (2004) Accurately modeling the Internet topology. *Physical Review E*, **70**: 066108.
[26] Newman, M.E.J. (2002) Assortative mixing in networks. *Physical Review Letters*, **89**(20): 208701.
[27] Gaertler, M. and Patrignani, M. (2004) Dynamic analysis of the autonomous system graph. *Proceedings of Inter-Domain Performance and Simulation*, 13–24.
[28] Feeman, L.C. (1977) A set of measures of centrality based on betweenness. *Sociometry*, **40**: 35–41.
[29] Newman, M.E.J. (2005) A measure of betweenness centrality based on random walks. *Social Networks*, **27**: 39–54.
[30] Latora, V. and Marchion, M. (2001) Efficient behavior of small-world networks. *Physical Review Letters*, **87**: 198701, 1–4.
[31] Fortunato, S., Latora, V. and Marchiori, M. (2004) Methods to find community structures based on information centrality. *Physical Review E*, **70**: 056104, 1–13.
[32] Govindan, R. and Tangmunarunkit H. (2000) Heuristics for Internet map discovery. *Proceedings of the 19th Annual Joint Conference of IEEE Computer and Communication Societies*, **3**: 1371–80.
[33] Qian, C., Chang, H., Govindan. R. *et al.* (2002) The origin of power laws in Internet topologies revisited. *Proceedings of 21st Annual Joint Conference of IEEE Computer and Communication Societies*, **2**: 608–17.
[34] Vazquez, A., Pastor-Satorrs, R. and Vespignani, A. (2002) Large-scale topological and dynamical properties of the Internet. *Physical Review E*, **65**: 066130, 1–12.
[35] http://www.traceroute.org/ [monthly updating list of online traceroutes] (last accessed August 9, 2014).
[36] Pansiot, D.G. (1998) On routes and multicast trees in the Internet. *ACM SIGCOMM Computer Communication Review*, **28**(1): 41–50.
[37] Govindan, R. and Tangmunarunkit, H. (2000) Heuristics for Internet map discovery. *Proceedings of IEEE INFO-COM*, **3**(1): 1371–80.
[38] Phillips, G., Tangmunarunkit, H. and Shenker, S. (1999) Scaling of multicast trees: comments on the Chuang-Sirbu scaling law. *Proceedings of ACM SIGCOMM.*, Boston, MA.
[39] Faloutsos, C., Faloutsos, M. and Faloutsos, P. (1999) What does Internet look like? Empirical laws of the Internet topology. *Proceedings of ACM SIGCOMM.*, Boston, MA.
[40] Danesh, A., Trajkovic, L., Rubin, S.H. and Smith, M.H. (2001) Mapping the Internet. *Proceedings of IFSA World Congress and 20th NAFIPS International Conference*, **2**: 687–92
[41] Burch, H. and Cheswick, B. (1999) Mapping the Internet. *IEEE Computer*, **32**(4): 97–8
[42] Spring, N., Mahajan, R., Wetherall, D. and Anderson, T. (2004) Measuring ISP topologies with rocketfuel. *IEEE/ACM Transactions on Networking*, **12**(1): 2–16.
[43] Yook, S., Jeong, H. and Barabási, A-L. (2002) Modeling the Internet's large-scale topology. *Proceedings of the National Academy of Sciences*, **99**(21): 13382–6.
[44] http://www.caida.org/tools/utilities/netgeo/ (last accessed August 9, 2014).

[45] http://sedac.ciesin.org/plue/gpw/ (last accessed August 9, 2014).

[46] Lakhina, A., Byers, J.W., Crovella, M. and Matta, I. (2002) On the geographic location of Internet resources. *Proceedings of ACM SIGCOMM Internet Measurement Workshop*, Marseilles.

[47] IxMapper. http://www.ixiacom.com/products/ (last accessed August 9, 2014).

[48] Akamai Inc. http://www.akamai.com (last accessed August 9, 2014).

[49] Doar, M. and Leslie, I. (1993) How bad is nave multicast routing. *Proceedings of IEEE INFOCOM*, **1**: 82–9.

[50] Medina, A., Matta, I. and Byers, J. (2000) On the origin of power laws in Internet topologies. *Computer Communication Review*, **32**(2): 18–28.

[51] http://topology.eecs.umich.edu/inet/ (last accessed August 9, 2014).

[52] Chen, J., Chen, Q. and Jamin, S. (2000) Inet: Internet topology generator. *Technical Report CSE-TR443 -00*, Dept of EECS, University of Michigan, USA.

[53] Medina, A., Lakhina, A., Matta, I., Byers, J. (2000) BRITE: An approach to universal topology generation. *Technical Report*, Dept of Computer Science, Boston University, USA.

[54] Di Fatta, G., Lo Presti, G. and Lo Re, G. (2001) Computer network topologies: Models and generation tools. *Technical Report n. 5/2001*, University of Palermo, Italy.

[55] Bu, T. and Towsley, D. (2002) On distinguishing between Internet power law topology generators. *Proceedings of INFOCOM*, **2**: 638–47.

[56] Albert, R. and Barabasi, A-L. (2000) Topology of evolving networks: Local events and universality. *Physical Review Letters*, **85**(24): 5234–7.

[57] Zhou, S. and Mondragon, R-J. (2003) Towards modeling the Internet topology-the interactive growth model. *Teletraffic Science and Engineering*, **5**: 121–30.

[58] Bar, S., Gonen, M. and Wool, A. (2004) An incremental super-linear preferential Internet topology model. *Proceedings of 5th Annual Passive and Active Measurement Workshop*, LNCS **3015**, 53–62.

[59] Bar, S., Gonen, M. and Wool, A. (2005) A geographic directed preferential Internet topology model. *Proceedings of 31st IEEE International Symposium on Modeling, Analysis, and Simulation of Computer and Telecommunication Systems*, 325–8.

[60] Chen, G., Fan, Z.P. and Li, X. (2005) Modeling the complex Internet topology. In G. Vattay, L. Kocarev (eds), *Complex Dynamics in Communication Networks*, Springer-Verlag, Berlin, 213–34.

[61] Pan, Z.F, Li, X. and Wang, X.F. (2006) Generalized local-world models for weighted networks. *Physical Review E*, **73**: 056109.

[62] Peng, G., Ko, K.T., Tan, L. and Chen, G. (2006) Router-level Internet as a local-world weighted evolving network. *Dynamics of Continuous, Discrete and Impulsive Systems*, **13**: 681–92.

[63] Fan, Z.P. (2006) *Complex Networks: From Topology to Dynamics*. PhD Thesis, Dept of Electronic Engineering, City University of Hong Kong, May.

[64] Fan, Z.P., Chen, G. and Zhang, Y. (2009) A comprehensive multi-local-world model for complex networks. *Physical Review A*, **373**: 1601–5.

[65] Chang, H., Govindan, R., Jamin, S. and Shenker, S.J. (2004) Towards capturing representative AS-level Internet topologies. *Computer Networks*, **44**: 737–55.

[66] Goh, K.I., Kahng, B. and Kim, D. (2002) Fluctuation-driven dynamics of the Internet topology. *Physical Review Letters*, **88**(10): 108701.

[67] Spatharis, A., Foudalis, I. and Sideri, M. (2009) Comparing trade-off based models of the Internet. *Fundamenta Informaticae*, **92**: 363–72.

[68] Costa, L.F., Rodrigues, F.A., Travieso, G. and Boas, P.R.V. (2007) Characterization of complex networks: A survey of measurements. *Advances in Physics*, **56**: 167–242.

[69] Costa, L.F., Boas, P.R.V., Silva, F.N. and Rodrigues, F.A. (2010) A pattern recognition approach to complex networks. *Journal of Statistical Physics*, **11**: P11015.

[70] Fan, Z.P., Chen, G. and Zhang, Y.N. (2012) Differentiating complex network models: An engineering perspective. *Computers & Mathematics with Applications*, **64**: 840–8.

[71] Fabrikant, A., Koutsoupias, E. and Papadimitriou, C.H. (2002) Heuristically optimized trade-off: A new paradigm for power law in the Internet. *Proceedings of 29th International Colloquium on Automata, Languages, and Programming* (ICALP), Malaga, Spain.

[72] Carlson, J.M. and Doyle, J. (1999) Highly optimized tolerance: A mechanism for power laws in designed systems. *Physical Review E*, **60**: 1412–27.

[73] http://abilene.internet2.edu/ (last accessed August 9, 2014) and http://en.wikipedia.org/wiki/Abilene_Network (last accessed August 9, 2014).

[74] Li, L., Alderson, D., Willinger, W. and Doyle, J. (2004) A first-principles approach to understanding the Internet's router-level topology. *Proceedings of ACM SIGCOMM Conference on Applications, Technologies, Architectures, and Protocols for Computer Communication*, 3–14.

[75] Doyle, J., Alderson, D, Li L *et al.* (2005) The "robust yet fragile" nature of the Internet. *Proceedings of National Academy Sciences*, **102**(41): 14497–14502.

[76] Willinger, W., Alderson, D. and Doyle, J. (2009) Mathematics and the Internet: A source of enormous confusion and great potential. *Notice of AMS*, **56**: 586–99.

[77] Serrano, M.A., Boguna, M. and Diaz-Guilera, A. (2006) Modeling the Internet. *European Physical Journal B*, **50**: 249–54.

[78] Wang, X. and Loguinov, D. (2010) Understanding and modeling the Internet topology: Economics and evolution perspective. *IEEE/ACM Transactions on Networking*, **18**(1): 257–70.

[79] Huang, L. (2007) Survey on generators for Internet topologies at the AS level. http://i11www.iti.uni -karlsruhe.de/_media/teaching/theses/files/studienarbeit-huang-07.pdf (last accessed August 9, 2014).

[80] Zhang, G.Q., Zhang, G.Q., Yang, Q.F. *et al.* (2008) Evolution of the Internet and its cores. *New Journal of Physics*, **10**: 123027.

[81] Zhang, Y.C., Zhou, S., Zhang, Z.Z., *et al.* (2012) Traffic fluctuations on weighted networks. *IEEE Circuits and Systems Magazine*, **1**: 33–44.

[82] Taylor, L.R. (1961) Aggregation, variance and the mean. *Nature*, **189**: 732–5.

[83] de Menezes, M.A. and Barabási, A-L. (2004) Fluctuations in network dynamics. *Physical Review Letters*, **92**: 028701.

[84] Duch, J. and Arenas, A. (2006) Scaling of fluctuations in traffic on complex networks. *Physical Review Letters*, **96**: 218702.

[85] Meloni, S., Gòmez-Gardeñes, J., Latora, V. and Moreno, Y. (2008) Scaling breakdown in flow fluctuations on complex networks. *Physical Review Letters*, **100**: 208701.

[86] Tadić, B., Rodgers, G.J. and Thurner, S. (2007) Transport on complex networks: Flow, jamming and optimization. *International Journal of Bifurcation and Chaos*, **17**: 2363.

[87] Eisler, Z., Bartos, I. and Kertèsz, J. (2008) Fluctuation scaling in complex systems: Taylor's law and beyond. *Advances in Physics*, **57**: 89–142.

[88] Kim, D.H. and Motter, A.E. (2008) Fluctuation-driven capacity distribution in complex networks, *New Journal of Physics*, **10**: 053022.

[89] Barrat, A., Barthèlemy, M., Pastor-Satorras, R. and Vespignani, A. (2004) The architecture of complex weighted networks. *Proceedings of the National Academy of Sciences*, **101**: 3747–52.

[90] Wang, W.X., Wang, B.H., Hu, B, *et al.* (2005) General dynamics of topology and traffic on weighted technological networks, *Physical Review Letters*, **94**: 188702.

[91] Noh, J.D. and Rieger, H. (2004) Random walks on complex networks. *Physical Review Letters*, **92**: 118701.

[92] Shi, D.H. (2011) *Theory of Network Degree Distribution* (in Chinese). Higher Education Press, Beijing.

[93] Adamic, L.A., Lukose, R.M., Puniyani, A.R. and Huberman, B.A. (2001) Search in power–law networks. *Physical Review E*, **64**: 046135.

[94] Guimerá, R, Díaz-Guilera, A., Vega-Redondo, F. *et al.* (2002) Optimal network topologies for local search with congestion. *Physical Review Letters*, **89**: 248701.

[95] Lee, S., Yook, S-H. and Kim, Y. (2006) Diffusive capture process on complex networks, *Physical Review E*, **74**: 046118.

[96] de Menezes, M.A. and Barabási, A-L. (2004) Separating internal and external dynamics of complex systems. *Physical Review Letters*, **93**: 068701.

[97] Kwon, S., Yoon, S. and Kim, Y. (2008) Condensation phenomena of a conserved-mass aggregation model on *weighted complex networks*. *Physical Review E*, **77**: 066105.

[98] Fronczak, A. and Fronczak, P. (2009) Biased random walks in complex networks: The role of local navigation rules. *Physical Review E*, **80**: 016107.

5

Epidemic Spreading Dynamics

5.1 Introduction

In a retrospective look at human history, one can easily realize that human civilization has always been accompanied with epidemics, such as malaria, orthopoxvirus variola, measles, pestis, typhoid fever, AIDS, SARS, avian flu, etc. The networking of human society greatly improves the public healthcare system, thereby reducing the threat of various diseases, and yet ironically it also enhances the wide spread of epidemics due to frequent individual contacts through the human relationship network.

Compared to biological epidemics, computer viruses are much easier to spread over the huge Internet worldwide, and have much longer lifetimes [1]. Major computer viruses may be roughly classified into (1) boot-sector viruses which infect the boot sectors of floppies and hardware devices, (2) file viruses which infect application programs, and (3) macro viruses which infect data files directly, as well as (4) some hybrid types of viruses in a certain combination of these basic ones.

The first serious virus capable of infecting PCs was perhaps the Brain virus developed in Pakistan in 1986. Many viruses have been born since then, and just in the year 2000 alone it was estimated that there were more than 48 000 identified viruses on the Internet [2]. Statistics show that more than 80% of computers were contaminated by viruses in China in 2004, and in that year the infamous "Worm Sasser" attacked several hundred thousands of computers over the world within just a couple of weeks.

Digital viruses seem quite capable of reaching their long-lasting and almost endemic steady states, regardless of the virus strains, in a fast and easy manner. Experts have warned that, if not extremely carefully protected, the whole Internet could totally collapse in seconds! Countless incidents of these kinds have already provoked some very serious rethinking: given the seemingly effective and advanced medical and electronic prevention and management systems today, how could biological diseases and computer viruses spread so fast and so wide? It turns out that the complex networks theory may provide some sensible analysis on, or even a meaningful solution to, this commonly concerned question.

A biological system (species, population, or cell) or a computer unit (AS, router, or PC) can be defined as a node in a network, connected together by certain edges (contact or linkage), in a particular topology. A conventional theory believes that only if the spreading speed is increasing to pass a relatively large positive threshold can a virus outbreak become possible. However, a study of Pastor-Satorras and Vespignani [2, 3] reveals that a scale-free network can well model such a virus spread and, on the contrary, that as the network size increases the threshold tends to zero, which means that a small source of virus is sufficient to cause a wide prevalence over the entire huge network. On the other hand, human societies have prominent small-world features which normally make diseases quite easy to propagate as well.

In this chapter, the network-based *epidemic threshold theory* for epidemics, as well as its immunization strategies and spread dynamics, are studied using computer virus propagation as typical examples.

Fundamentals of Complex Networks: Models, Structures and Dynamics, First Edition.
Guanrong Chen, Xiaofan Wang, Xiang Li.
© Higher Education Press. All rights reserved. Published 2015 by John Wiley & Sons Singapore Pte Ltd.
Companion Website: www.wiley.com/go/chen/complex

5.2   Epidemic Threshold Theory

The study of epidemics has a fairly long history, with several successful mathematical models available in the literature [4–6].

In a typical epidemic propagation model, the states of all individuals in a population are classified into:

- S (Susceptible) – healthy state (can be infected by others);
- I (Infected) – infected state (can infect others);
- R (Recovered) – recovered state (cannot be infected by others again).

Different combinations of these three states lead to different models, such as SIS and SIR models.

Recently, the classical theories of epidemic spread and threshold have been revisited for various community structures within such as random-graph, small-world and scale-free network frameworks. In a network, if two nodes are connected then they are considered to have "contact." Thus, if one node is "infected" by virus and the other is "susceptible," then with a certain probability the latter may become infected through contact. Throughout a virus spreading process, if an infected node is cured at some instant so it will become susceptive again, otherwise it may die or have permanent immunity. In the latter case, this node becomes "recovered" and may be removed from the network in the consequent discussion of further virus spreading over the network.

5.2.1   Epidemic (SI, SIS, SIR) Models

Consider a population of N connected individuals, described by a network of N nodes. Let the number of healthy nodes be $S(t)$, infected nodes be $I(t)$, and recovered nodes be $R(t)$ at time $t \geq 0$, initially with $S(0) = S_0, I(0) = I_0, R(0) = R_0 = 0$. For convenience in computation, one may normalize the three variables by dividing them with N, and in so doing they also have the meaning of "density" (percentage), with $S(t) + I(t) + R(t) = 1$ for all $t \geq 0$. Or, more precisely, one may introduce three corresponding density functions $\rho_S(t), \rho_I(t), \rho_R(t)$, satisfying $0 \leq \rho_S(t), \rho_I(t), \rho_R(t) \leq 1$ and $\rho_S(t) + \rho_I(t) + \rho_R(t) = 1$ for all $t \geq 0$.

Assume that the lifetime of virus or disease is much shorter than the lifetime of the nodes in the population; therefore, birth and death of nodes are not taken into consideration in the following study.

Suppose that the rate (in terms of probability) of a node becoming "infected" from "susceptible" is v, and the rate (probability) of an infected node being cured and becomes "susceptible" again is δ. Then, define the virus *effective spreading rate* as

$$\lambda = \frac{v}{\delta}. \tag{5.1}$$

One extreme case is that all cured nodes immediately become susceptible again, which corresponds to $\delta = 1$, thus $\lambda = v =$ rate (probability) of a node becomes infected.

5.2.1.1   SI Model

Suppose $R(t) = 0$ for all $t \geq 0$. Consider the rate of increase in the density of infected nodes, from time t to time $t + \Delta t$, given by

$$\frac{\rho_I(t + \Delta t) - \rho_I(t)}{\Delta t} \approx [\lambda \rho_S(t)] \rho_I(t).$$

In the limit $\Delta t \to 0$, one obtains $\frac{d\rho_I(t)}{dt} = \lambda \rho_S(t) \rho_I(t)$. Since $\rho_S(t) = 1 - \rho_I(t)$, this becomes the so-called Logistic model:

$$\frac{d\rho_I(t)}{dt} = \lambda[1 - \rho_I(t)]\rho_I(t), \quad \rho_I(0) = \rho_{I,0}. \tag{5.2}$$

This equation has a solution

$$\rho_I(t) = \frac{1}{1 + \left(\rho_{I,0}^{-1} - 1\right) e^{-\lambda t}}. \tag{5.3}$$

Clearly, $\rho_I(t) \to 1$ as $t \to \infty$, meaning that all nodes are infected eventually. This is true if no infected nodes are cured to become recovered in the process.

5.2.1.2 SIS Model

Again, consider the case of $R(t) = 0$. But, now, suppose that the rate of recovery from "infected" back to "susceptive" is δ, namely, $\rho_S(t) = \delta\rho_I(t)$. Then, it follows from (5.2) that

$$\frac{d\rho_I(t)}{dt} = \lambda[1 - \rho_I(t)]\rho_I(t) - \delta\rho_I(t), \quad \rho_I(0) = \rho_{I,0}. \tag{5.4}$$

This equation has a solution

$$\rho_I(t) = \begin{cases} \left\{ \left[\dfrac{1}{1 - \dfrac{\delta}{\lambda}} + \left(\rho_{I,0}^{-1} - \dfrac{1}{1 - \dfrac{\delta}{\lambda}} \right) e^{-\left(1 - \frac{\delta}{\lambda}\right)\lambda t} \right] \right\}^{-1}, & \delta \neq \lambda \\[4ex] \dfrac{1}{\lambda t + \rho_{I,0}^{-1}}, & \delta = \lambda \end{cases}. \tag{5.5}$$

There are two cases:

1. $\delta \geq \lambda$: This means that recovering is faster than infecting. It follows from (5.5) that $\rho_I(t) \to 0$ as $t \to \infty$, implying that the virus will die out eventually.
2. $\delta < \lambda$: This means that recovering is slower than infecting. It follows from (5.5) that $\rho_I(t) \to \left(1 - \dfrac{\delta}{\lambda}\right)$ as $t \to \infty$, implying that a certain portion of nodes will remain being infected, though not always the same nodes. In particular, if $\delta \ll \lambda$ then $\rho_I(t) \sim 1$ as $t \to \infty$, implying that almost all nodes will be infected eventually.

5.2.1.3 SIR Model

Now, suppose $R(t) > 0$, namely, some nodes will be cured therefore be recovered and cannot be infected by the others again. In this case, one can similarly establish the following model:

$$\begin{cases} \dfrac{d\rho_I(t)}{dt} = \lambda\rho_S(t)\rho_I(t) - \delta\rho_I(t) \\[2ex] \dfrac{d\rho_S(t)}{dt} = -\lambda\rho_S(t)\rho_I(t) \\[2ex] \dfrac{d\rho_R(t)}{dt} = \delta\rho_I(t) \\[2ex] \rho_I(0) = \rho_{I,0}, \quad \rho_S(0) = \rho_{S,0}, \quad \rho_R(0) = 0 \end{cases}. \tag{5.6}$$

By qualitative analysis or numerical solutions, one can find the following:

1. $\rho_{S,0} > \dfrac{\delta}{\lambda}$: virus will spread out for some time, but eventually die out.
2. $\rho_{S,0} \leq \dfrac{\delta}{\lambda}$: virus will die out quickly.

The condition in (ii) implies that more and more nodes will be cured, therefore finally the whole population will be recovered (namely, become healthy).

5.2.2 Epidemic Thresholds on Homogenous Networks

Furthermore, consider the situation where the network topology is homogeneous (such as a random-graph network or a small-world network). In such a network, the node-degree distribution has a peak at its average value $\langle k \rangle$, and then decays exponentially fast for both small $k \ll \langle k \rangle$ and large $k \gg \langle k \rangle$. Thus, based on the homogeneity, one may assume that each node has degree $k_i \approx \langle k \rangle$, $i = 1, 2, \ldots, N$. For simplicity, moreover, assume that all cured nodes immediately become susceptible again, which corresponds to $\delta = 1$ in (5.1).

If the node-degree correlations are neglected, the infected node density function $\rho_I(t)$ satisfies (5.4), namely

$$\frac{d\rho_I(t)}{dt} = \lambda \langle k \rangle [1 - \rho_I(t)]\rho_I(t) - \rho_I(t), \quad \rho_I(0) = \rho_{I,0}, \tag{5.7}$$

where the second term indicates that the infected node is recovered at a rate of unity, namely, always recovered immediately; the first term represents the average fraction of nodes being infected by an infected node, which depends on the effective spreading rate λ and the number of contact namely node degree $\langle k \rangle$. Since only the situation with $\rho_I(t) \ll 1$ is concerned, all possible higher-order terms in $\rho_I(t)$, due to the use of the approximation $\langle k \rangle$, are neglected on the right-hand side of this equation.

By setting the right-hand side of (5.7) be equal to zero, one obtains the steady density of infected nodes, as

$$\rho_I(\infty) = \begin{cases} 0, & \lambda < \lambda_c \\ 1 - \dfrac{\lambda_c}{\lambda}, & \lambda \geq \lambda_c \end{cases}, \tag{5.8}$$

where the *epidemic threshold* is

$$\lambda_c = \frac{1}{\langle k \rangle}. \tag{5.9}$$

This implies that there is a finite epidemic threshold $\lambda_c = \langle k \rangle^{-1} > 0$. There are two cases:

(i) Over this threshold, $\lambda = \lambda_0 > \lambda_c$ the infected node can propagate the disease to the whole network, eventually leading to an equilibrium state, $\rho_I(\infty) = 1 - \lambda_c/\lambda_0$, and in this situation the network is said to be in the active phase.

(ii) Under this threshold, the number of infected nodes decays exponentially. Since physically $\rho_I(\infty)$ cannot be negative, so for long enough time $t \to \infty$, $\rho_I(t) = 0$, therefore disease will not be able to spread out, and in this situation the network is said to be in the absorbing phase, as illustrated by Figure 5.1 [7].

The above analysis was based on homogeneous networks. Some real data on computer networks, however, show quite different behaviors. This implies that computer networks are likely inhomogeneous, as further discussed below.

5.2.3 Statistical Data Analysis

Define the *virus prevalence* to be the ratio of the average number of computers infected by virus versus the total number of all computers in a network of concern, and define the *virus surviving probability* $P_s(t)$ to be the percentage of nodes that are alive since birth till the current time t.

Figure 5.2 shows the computer virus prevalence in the 50 months from February 1996 to March 2000, with respect to the boot-sector, file, and macro viruses [3]. It can be seen that after a sharp initial drop, there is an exponential decay with an associate characteristic time τ (months), which depends on the given strain of the computer virus.

The above statistical data show that computer viruses on the real Internet actually did not propagate as fast and wide as one may suspect. If these strains of viruses were propagating over a homogeneous network, then the prevalence has to be happening at a virus effective spreading rate lower than the epidemic threshold since the surviving probabilities are so low (see Figure 5.2). On the other hand, however, the virus effective spreading rate should be higher than this epidemic threshold since the lifetimes of these viruses are so long (see Figure 5.1). These two contradictory phenomena together implies that computer networks must be inhomogeneous instead.

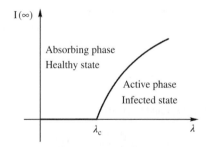

Figure 5.1 Phase transition of the SIS model on a homogeneous network [7]

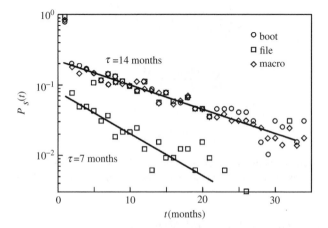

Figure 5.2 Virus surviving probabilities for three main strains of computer viruses [3]. *Source*: Reprinted with permission from Pastor-Satorras, R and Vespingnani, A. (2001) Epidemic spreading in scale-free networks. *Physical Review Letters*, **86**(4): 3200–3. Copyright (2001) American Physical Society

5.2.4 Epidemic Thresholds on Heterogeneous Networks

Now, consider the epidemic thresholds of some heterogeneous networks, typically scale-rich and scale-free networks.

Denote the relative density of infected degree-k nodes in a population of N by $\rho_{I,k}(t)$. Its mean-field equation is [8]

$$\frac{\partial \rho_{I,k}(t)}{\partial t} = -\rho_{I,k}(t) + \lambda k \left[1 - \rho_{I,k}(t)\right] \Theta\left(\rho_{I,k}(t)\right). \tag{5.10}$$

Here, $\Theta\left(\rho_{I,k}(t)\right)$ is the probability of an edge connecting to an infected degree-k node, λ is the effective spreading rate, but higher-order terms have been neglected assuming that $\rho_{I,k}(t) \ll 1$.

Let $\rho_{I,k}(t) \to \rho_{I,k}$ as $t \to \infty$, and assume $\Theta(\rho_{I,k}) \to \Theta < \infty$. Then, by setting the right-hand side of (5.10) be zero, one obtains

$$\rho_{I,k} = \frac{k\lambda\Theta}{1 + k\lambda\Theta}. \tag{5.11}$$

This implies that higher-degree nodes have higher probabilities to be infected.

It should be noted that Θ depends on the heterogeneity of the network. For uncorrelated heterogeneous networks, namely, there is no correlation between any pair of nodes with different degrees, since the probability of an edge connecting to a node with degree s is given by $sP(s)/\langle k \rangle$, one has

$$\Theta = \frac{1}{\langle k \rangle} \sum_{k=1}^{N} kP(k)\rho_{I,k}. \tag{5.12}$$

Thus, solving (5.11) and (5.12) for $\rho_{I,k}$ and Θ yields

$$\Theta = \frac{1}{\langle k \rangle} \sum_{k=1}^{N} kP(k)\frac{\lambda k\Theta}{1 + \lambda k\Theta}, \tag{5.13}$$

which has a trivial solution $\Theta = 0$. The epidemic threshold λ_c should be determined such that when $\lambda > \lambda_c$ the probability Θ has a nonzero solution. In so doing, the following condition must be satisfied:

$$\frac{d}{d\Theta}\left(\frac{1}{\langle k \rangle} \sum_{k=1}^{N} kP(k)\frac{\lambda k\Theta}{1 + \lambda k\Theta} \right)\Bigg|_{\Theta=0} \geq 1,$$

namely,

$$\sum_{k=1}^{N} \frac{kP(k)\lambda k}{\langle k \rangle} = \frac{\langle k^2 \rangle}{\langle k \rangle}\lambda \geq 1,$$

which yields

$$\lambda_c = \frac{\langle k \rangle}{\langle k^2 \rangle}. \tag{5.14}$$

For growing heterogeneous networks, as $N \to \infty$ one has $\langle k^2 \rangle \to \infty$, therefore $\lambda_c \to 0$. This means that diseases can easily break out because the epidemic thresholds are so low in such networks.

5.2.5   Epidemic Thresholds on BA Networks

As a typical heterogeneous network example, consider the BA network. Since its average degree and degree distribution are (Chapter 3)

$$\langle k \rangle = \int_{m}^{\infty} kP(k)dk = 2m , \; P(k) = 2m^2 k^{-3},$$

it follows from (5.12) that

$$\Theta = m\lambda\Theta \int_{m}^{\infty} \frac{1}{k}\frac{dk}{1 + k\lambda\Theta} = m\lambda\Theta \ln\left(1 + \frac{1}{m\lambda\Theta} \right),$$

so that

$$\Theta = \Theta(\lambda) = \frac{e^{-1/m\lambda}}{\lambda m}\left(1 - e^{-1/m\lambda}\right)^{-1}. \tag{5.15}$$

Next, calculate ρ as follows: as $N \to \infty$ and $t \to \infty$,

$$\rho = \sum_{k=1}^{\infty} P(k)\rho_{I,k}$$

$$= 2m^2\lambda\Theta(\lambda)\int_{m}^{\infty} \frac{1}{k^2}\frac{dk}{1 + k\Theta(\lambda)} \tag{5.16}$$

$$= 2m^2\lambda\Theta(\lambda)\left[\frac{1}{m} + \lambda\Theta(\lambda)\ln\left(1 + \frac{1}{m\lambda\Theta(\lambda)} \right)\right].$$

Then, substituting (5.15) into (5.16) gives [8]

$$\rho \sim 2e^{-1/(m\lambda)}. \qquad (5.17)$$

The right-hand side of the above is nonnegative, and it becomes zero if and only if $\lambda = 0$, implying that the epidemic threshold of the BA scale-free networks is $\lambda_c = 0$.

Figure 5.3 shows a comparison of the relationships between ρ and λ in the SIS model on a WS small-world network and a BA scale-free network, respectively [7]. It shows that the effective spreading rate λ on the BA network tends to zero continuously and smoothly, implying that it virtually has no positive threshold λ_c, so for any $\lambda > 0$ virus can easily propagate throughout the network and finally reach a steady state. This demonstrates the fragility of heterogeneous networks against virus spreading.

In the last chapter, it was shown that the Internet is rapidly growing with the degree distribution in a power-law form. Therefore, it is not surprising to see that computer viruses can spread all over the Internet easily and quickly. Yet, fortunately, on the real Internet, it is also found that the λ value is very small ($\lambda \ll 1$), leading to a low propagation speed. This is also consistent with the observation that the epidemic threshold of a scale-free network vanishes fairly slowly, while the size of the network expands even more quickly.

Figure 5.4 shows a semi-logarithmic plot of the relation between the density of infected nodes ρ and the effective spreading rate λ in a BA scale-free network model with different sizes, where "+" corresponds to $N = 10^5$, small squares to $N = 5 \times 10^5$, "×" to $N = 10^6$, and small circles to $N = 5 \times 10^6$. It implies that $\rho(\lambda) \sim e^{-c/\lambda}$ for a constant $c > 0$, independent of the size of the network.

Figure 5.5 shows the virus surviving probability $P_s(t)$ versus time t for the same four networks shown in Figure 5.4, from small to large (top down) in sizes. It indicates that on any finite-sized scale-free network,

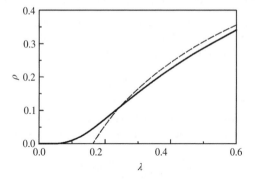

Figure 5.3 Relations between ρ and λ in an SIS model: WS network (dash curve) and BA network (solid curve) [7]
Source: Reproduced by permission of Wiley-VCH Verlag GmbH & Co. KGaA

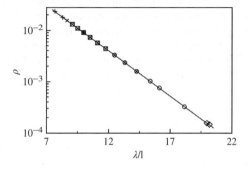

Figure 5.4 Relation between ρ and λ in a BA network [7]. *Source*: Reproduced by permission of Wiley-VCH Verlag GmbH & Co. KGaA

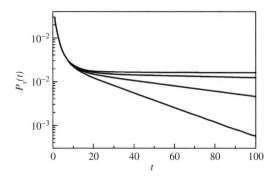

Figure 5.5   Relation between $P_s(t)$ and t in a BA network [7]. *Source*: Reproduced by permission of Wiley-VCH Verlag GmbH & Co. KGaA

epidemic will eventually die out. This is reasonable because there is a finite probability for the nodes to be cured from infection at the same time as epidemic propagates over the network. Moreover, the bigger the network is, the slower the disease dies out. Theoretically, the lifetime is infinite only in the limiting case of $N \to \infty$, a well-known feature of the virus surviving probability in finite-sized absorbing-state networks poised about a critical point [7].

5.2.6   Epidemic Thresholds on Finite-Sized Scale-Free Networks

For a finite-sized scale-free network, introduce a maximum connectivity k_c, which depends on the size N of the network. An SIS model, established on a scale-free network with node-degree distribution $P(k) \sim k^{-\gamma} \exp(-k/k_c)$, has a nonzero epidemic threshold [9]:

$$\lambda_c \sim \left(\frac{k_c}{m}\right)^{\gamma-3}, \tag{5.18}$$

where m is the number of edges being added to the network (i.e., the new edges brought in by the new nodes) during the formation of the scale-free network. The limit $\gamma \to 3$ corresponds to a logarithmic divergence, described by

$$\lambda_c \sim \frac{1}{m \ln(k_c m)} \text{ (for } \gamma \to 3). \tag{5.19}$$

Figure 5.6 shows a comparison, λ_c versus λ_c^H, of the epidemic threshold values on a finite-sized scale-free network and on a homogeneous network of the same size [7]. It can be seen that in a scale-free network with $\gamma = 2.5$, even for relatively small k_c, its threshold is only about 1/10 of the homogeneous network. It can also be seen that as k_c increases or $N \to \infty$, the threshold of the scale-free network can still tend to zero, implying the fragility of a finite-sized scale-free network against virus spreading.

It is interesting to point out that the above conclusions about the SIS model hold also for the SIR model in general, namely, the epidemic spreading threshold properties are not affected by the differences of the two epidemic models. The SIR model will be briefly introduced below in Section 5.2.9.

5.2.7   Epidemic Thresholds on Correlated Networks

The above discussions were mainly restricted on uncorrelated scale-free networks, namely, there is no connectivity correlation between any pair of nodes with different degrees in the network. Many networks, scale-free or not, such as the Internet are actually correlated networks (Chapter 2), and on a correlated network the epidemic threshold turns out to be quite different [10].

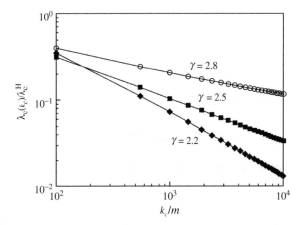

Figure 5.6 Comparison of epidemic threshold values on two types of networks [7]. *Source*: Reproduced by permission of Wiley-VCH Verlag GmbH & Co. KGaA

In a correlated network of size N, let $P(k'|k)$ be the conditional probability of a degree-k' node connecting to a given degree-k node. If this probability is independent of k, then the situation reduces to the uncorrelated case discussed above. Suppose that the degree distribution $P(k)$ and this $P(k'|k)$ satisfy the following normalized balance conditions:

$$\sum_{k=1}^{N} P(k) = \sum_{k'=1}^{N} P(k'|k) = 1$$

and

$$kP(k'|k)P(k) = k'P(k|k')P(k') \equiv \langle k \rangle P(k, k'),$$

where the symmetric function $(2 - \delta_{kk'})P(k, k')$ describes the joint probability of the connectivity of degree-k and degree-k' nodes, in which $\delta_{kk'} = 1$ if $k = k'$ or $= 0$ otherwise. Further, define a connectivity matrix $C_{kk'} = [kP(k'|k)]$. Then, it can be verified [10] that

$$\lambda_c = \lambda_{max}^{-1}, \tag{5.20}$$

where λ_{max} is the maximum eigenvalue of matrix $C_{kk'}$. For uncorrelated networks, $\lambda_{max} = \langle k^2 \rangle / \langle k \rangle$, leading to the same conclusion drawn for uncorrelated networks before, in (5.14). Therefore, the epidemic threshold on a network, correlated or not, is essentially determined by the maximum eigenvalue of the connectivity matrix $C_{kk'}$.

It was shown, however, that in an SIS model, the epidemic incidence on a correlated network is smaller than that on an uncorrelated network with the same node-degree distribution [11]. Although the basic properties of the epidemic threshold do not vary according to the node-degree correlations, the spreading lifetime on a corrected network is generally longer than that on an uncorrelated network. Therefore, on a finite-sized correlated network, the epidemic threshold usually is larger than that on an uncorrelated network, indicating that correlated networks are more robust than uncorrelated networks in resisting virus propagation.

5.2.8   SIR Model of Epidemic Spreading

So far, the discussions have been restricted to the SIS model. In this subsection, the SIR model will be introduced.

Consider a population of N networked individuals (nodes), each is either in the Susceptible (S), or Infected (I), or Recovered (R) state. Let $\rho_{S,k}(t)$, $\rho_{I,k}(t)$ and $\rho_{R,k}(t)$ be the densities of the S, I and R states of nodes of degree k at time t, respectively. Then, these densities are related by

$$\rho_{S,k}(t) + \rho_{I,k}(t) + \rho_{R,k}(t) = 1, \text{ for all } t \geq 0.$$

Define the total number of recovered nodes at time t by

$$R(t) = \sum_{k=1}^{N} P(k)\rho_{R,k}(t),$$

where $P(k)$ is the node-degree distribution of the network. Denote its steady-state prevalence by

$$R_\infty = \lim_{t \to \infty} R(t).$$

For an undirected random-graph type of uncorrelated network, similar to the above-discussed models, in average the three densities here satisfy the following system of differential equations:

$$\frac{d\rho_{I,k}(t)}{dt} = -\rho_{I,k}(t) + \lambda k \rho_{S,k}(t)\Theta(t)$$

$$\frac{d\rho_{S,k}(t)}{dt} = -\lambda k \rho_{S,k}(t)\Theta(t) \qquad , \qquad (5.22)$$

$$\frac{d\rho_{R,k}(t)}{dt} = \rho_{I,k}(t)$$

where λ is the effective spreading rate and $\Theta(t)$ represents the average density of infected nodes pointing to this node of degree k through a particular edge. In general, the probability that an edge points to an infected node with degree k is proportional to $kP(k)\rho_{I,k}(t)$. Notice that the infected node pointed by the edge has previously received virus through an edge that should not be counted for virus transmission again. Hence, the above probability should be modified to be $(k-1)P(k)\rho_{I,k}(t)$, so that

$$\Theta(t) = \frac{1}{\langle k \rangle} \sum_{k=1}^{N} (k-1)P(k)\rho_{I,k}(t). \qquad (5.23)$$

A combination of system (5.22) and (5.23), along with the natural initial conditions

$$\rho_{R,k}(0) = 0, \ \rho_{I,k}(0) = \rho_k^0 \text{ and } \rho_{S,k}(0) = 1 - \rho_k^0$$

completely defines the SIR model of virus spreading on a random-graph type of uncorrected network with node-degree distribution $P(k)$.

To investigate the asymptotic dynamical behavior of the model [12], assume that initially infected nodes are uniformly distributed, namely, $\rho_k^0 = \rho^0$ for all k at time $t = 0$. In this case, in the limit $\rho^0 \to 0$, namely, starting from infection-free nodes, one has $\rho_{I,k}(0) \approx 0$ and $\rho_{S,k}(0) \approx 1$. Under these initial conditions, the second and third equations in system (5.22) can be directly integrated, yielding

$$\rho_{S,k}(t) = e^{-\lambda k \phi(t)} \text{ and } \rho_{R,k}(t) = \int_0^t \rho_{I,k}(\tau)d\tau, \qquad (5.24)$$

where

$$\phi(t) = \int_0^t \Theta(\tau)d\tau = \frac{1}{\langle k \rangle} \sum_{k=1}^{N} (k-1)P(k)\rho_{R,k}(t),$$

which, accounting for (5.24), gives

$$\frac{d\phi(t)}{dt} = \frac{1}{\langle k \rangle} \sum_{k=1}^{N} (k-1)P(k)\rho_{I,k}(t)$$

$$= \frac{1}{\langle k \rangle} \sum_{k=1}^{N} (k-1)P(k)[1 - \rho_{R,k}(t) - \rho_{S,k}(t)]$$

$$= 1 - \frac{1}{\langle k \rangle} - \phi(t) - \frac{1}{\langle k \rangle} \sum_{k=1}^{N} (k-1)P(k)e^{-\lambda k \phi(t)}. \qquad (5.25)$$

If (5.25) can be solved, then one can obtain the steady-state epidemic prevalence $\rho_{S,k}(\infty)$ as a function of $\phi_\infty = \lim_{t \to \infty} \phi(t)$. Notice that in the steady state, $\rho_{I,k}(\infty) = 0$, since nodes are either all infected or all recovered, so the infection density will not change any more. Thus, $\rho_{R,k}(\infty) = 1 - \rho_{S,k}(\infty)$, so that

$$R_\infty = \sum_k P(k) \left[1 - e^{-\lambda k \phi_\infty} \right].$$

However, for a general node-degree distribution $P(k)$, (5.25) cannot be solved. Nevertheless, one can still obtain some useful information about the asymptotic behavior of the virus spreading. Indeed, since $\rho_{I,k}(\infty) = 0$ and consequently $\lim_{t \to \infty} d\phi(t)/dt = 0$, from (5.25) one has the following steady-state equation:

$$\phi_\infty = 1 - \frac{1}{\langle k \rangle} - \frac{1}{\langle k \rangle} \sum_{k=1}^{N} (k-1)P(k)e^{-\lambda k \phi_\infty}.$$

This equation has a fixed-point solution $\phi_\infty = 0$. In order to have a nonzero solution for ϕ_∞, which would mean a prevalence $R_\infty > 0$, it is necessary that

$$\frac{d}{d\phi_\infty} \left[1 - \frac{1}{\langle k \rangle} - \frac{1}{\langle k \rangle} \sum_{k=1}^{N} (k-1)P(k)e^{-\lambda k \phi_\infty} \right]\Bigg|_{\phi_\infty=0} \geq 1.$$

This condition implies that

$$\frac{\lambda}{\langle k \rangle} \sum_{k=1}^{N} k(k-1)P(k) \geq 1,$$

yielding the epidemic threshold

$$\lambda_c = \frac{\langle k \rangle}{\langle k^2 \rangle - \langle k \rangle}, \qquad (5.26)$$

below which $R_\infty = 0$ and above which $R_\infty > 0$.

5.2.9 *Epidemic Spreading on Quenched Networks*

As seen from (5.26), for the SIR model, the activity threshold λ_c vanishes when the maximum node degree $k_{max} \to \infty$ ash the network size $N \to \infty$. It is noted [13] that the vanishing of the threshold is not determined by the scale-free nature of the network, but rather, due to from the existence of largest hub in the network being active for any spreading rate $\lambda > \lambda_c \sim 1/\sqrt{k_{max}}$, as can be deduced from (5.26), particularly if this hub plays the role of a self-sustained source of virus that spreads to the rest of the network. Here, the existence of a largest hub implies that the network is heterogeneous, therefore likely follows a power-law form of node degree distribution. Therefore, in this subsection, the threshold of

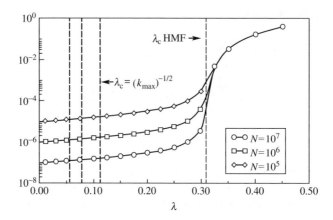

Figure 5.7 Total number of infected individuals versus the spreading rate [13]. *Source*: Reprinted with permission from Castellano, A. and Pastor-Satorras R. (2010) Thresholds for epidemic spreading in networks. *Physical Review Letters*, **105**: 218701. Copyright (2010) American Physical Society

epidemic models in heterogeneous networks with degree distribution following a power-law is further discussed.

For SIS network models, based on (5.14) and (5.20), which implies $\lambda > \lambda_c \sim 1/\sqrt{k_{max}}$ as just mentioned, by taking into account the exponent γ in the power law $k^{-\gamma}$, one has [13]

$$\lambda_c \sim \begin{cases} 1/\sqrt{k_{max}} & \gamma > 5/2 \\ \langle k \rangle / \langle k^2 \rangle & 2 < \gamma < 5/2 \end{cases}, \tag{5.27}$$

where the cut-off number 5/2 was determined via simulations.

For SIR network models, (5.26) should be used instead of (5.14). From a heterogeneous mean-field (HMF) approach, it was found [13] that $\lambda_c^{SIR} = 0.31$ independent of the network size on networks with a fixed $k_{max} = \langle k_{max} \rangle$, the so-called quenched networks, as shown in Figure 5.7 where the vertical line is the number of finally infected individuals (in the unit of the given population N) for $\gamma = 4.5$.

It was conjectured in [13] that on quenched scale-rich networks the threshold of generic epidemic models is vanishing if the network dynamics has a stead state, or is a finite value otherwise.

5.3 Epidemic Spreading on Spatial Networks

A mathematical graph basically represents the topology of a physical network, with a trivial metric defined on it: if two nodes are connected then their distance is one. A real network, however, usually has geographical distance that cannot be ignored. Examples include various (air, grand, ocean) transportation networks, social networks in which people live in different cities or countries, power grids and the Internet, and so on. Therefore, epidemic spreading over spatial networks is an important subject to study [14].

5.3.1 Spatial Networks

Spatial networks have their nodes located in a space equipped with a nontrivial metric. In the two-dimensional space, for example, the metric used typically is the Euclidean distance. This implies that the probability of finding a connection between two nodes generally decreases with the geographical distance between them. In fact, the GeoBA model for the Internet, discussed in Chapter 4, is established based on this observation. Moreover, many infrastructure networks are two-dimensional, such as highways, railways, city streets, and ocean transportation networks alike. In fact, many of them are planar networks. There are, of course, many nonplanar networks such as airline passenger networks, where geographical airports are connected through air-flights.

A few typical examples of spatial networks are the following:

5.3.1.1 Airline Networks

According to the database of the International Air Transportation Association (IATA), the airline network had $N = 3880$ nodes and $M = 18\,810$ edges in 2002, which displays both small-world and scale-free features [15]. In particular, the shortest average path length in the trivial metric, namely number of edges between the two connected nodes of concern, is only $\langle L \rangle = 4.37$. The node degree distribution is heavy-tailed with a cut-off, in the form of $P(k) = k^{-\lambda}f(k)$, where $\gamma \approx 2.0$ and $f(k)$ is an exponential cut-off function in terms of the degree k. In addition, the network is weighted, with weights representing the number of passengers on the edge connection, while the weight strength distribution also follows a power law $\sim k^{1.7}$ and similarly the distance strength distribution $\sim k^{1.4}$. Data show that the network is assortative (hubs are directly connected internationally) as well as disassortative (hubs are connected to small airports domestically), thereby showing also large clustering coefficients.

5.3.1.2 Highways, Railways and Subways

On the contrary to airline networks, highways, railways and subways are much more homogeneous in structure. As a simple example [16], the Switzerland railway network has $N = 1613$ nodes and $M = 1680$ edges, appearing as a homogeneous network with average node degree $\langle k \rangle = 2.1$, average shortest path length $\langle L \rangle = 47.0$, and node degree distribution is peaked and exponentially decays on both sides.

5.3.1.3 Power Grids

In a power grid network model, nodes represent power plants and transmission stations, and edges correspond to transmission lines. Power grids are planar graphs with a peaked node-degree distribution in general. For example, the degree distributions of Southern Californian and North American power grids decrease in an exponential form of $P(k) \sim e^{-k/\langle k \rangle}$, where $\langle k \rangle$ is of order 3 in Europe and 2 in the US. Also, as expected, the clustering coefficients of power grids typically are large and even independent of the node degree k [17].

5.3.2 Spatial Network Models for Infectious Diseases

During transmission of seasonal endemic diseases, such as avian influenza, spatial waves of infection have been observed even among populations in long distances. Even at the initial stages of an outbreak, infected individuals were distributed in spatial communities. Spatial models were developed for characterizing such large-scale disease spreading patterns and for evaluating the impact of human contact.

The well-known foot-and-mouth disease outbreaks provide a good example of spatial network model for distance-transmission spreading. Foot-and-mouth disease (FMD) virus infects cloven-hoofed animals, especially cows and pigs. The FMD virus has been eliminated in Europe, the Pacific Nations, the Caribbean, and North and Central America, while the last reported outbreak of FMD in the USA was in 1929. In 2001, however, there was outbreak of FMD in the UK, spatially distributed among many farms in the region, resulted in the slaughter of 4.2 million animals with a severe negative economic impact in the affected districts [18].

Precise location data are available for both affected and unaffected farms, and furthermore the number of infected premises during 2001 was sufficient to permit accurate modeling of spreading processes and

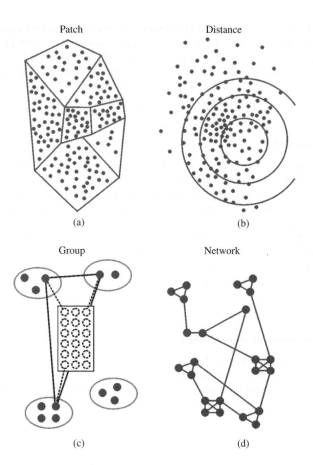

Figure 5.8 Four common patterns of spatial transmission of infectious diseases [18]: (a) patch; (b) distance; (c) group; (d) network. *Source*: Reprinted with permission from Riley, S. Large-scale spatial-transmission models of infectious disease. Science. Copyright (2007) AAAS

estimation of transmission parameters, ultimately suggesting effective farm-culling and immunization polices. More precisely, the available spatially-resolved farm census data enables to formulate a spatially explicit distance-transmission model, as shown in Figure 5.8. The figure shows four common patterns of spatial transmission of infectious diseases, where nodes are farms as the individual units of infection, with infected nodes in red [18], described as follows:

Pattern A. This is a patch transmission, in which all members of the same patch (residents of a town, for example) receive the same force of infection (FOI), namely the hazard of infection experienced by susceptible individuals, which is a function of the distance from their home patch to other patches, with prevalence of infection in all patches.

Pattern B. Every farm is assigned a precise location. Distance transmission is explicitly based on individual nodes. It is assumed that any infectious node can infect all susceptible nodes within the range defined by a distance. The pairwise probability of infection is typically a monotonically decreasing function of the distance. The absolute FOI experienced by each susceptible node due to a single infectious node is low.

Pattern C. In a pure multi-group model, the FOI is determined entirely by the group membership. For example, if an infectious node shares a household with a susceptible node (oval in the figure), then there will be a high probability of transmission between them. However, if an infectious node does not share with a particular susceptible node in a group, then transmission between them will not occur. The spatial spreading pattern is determined by the locations of households and workplaces (rectangle in the figure) and also by the typical distribution of journeys between them. In the figure, dashed lines indicate group membership and solid lines are potentially infectious links between nodes.

Pattern D. This is a network transmission pattern, which is similar to cluster transmission in that the FOI experienced by susceptible nodes is zero, unless they share a link with an infectious node. For directly transmitted respiratory pathogens, it is assumed that not all members of a group are equally well connected (e.g., colleagues in the same workplace do not have contacts). This kind of network transmission may be considered as a refinement of an implicit grouping structure, in which more than one component of transmission is possible.

It has been observed that the FMD virus spreads effectively in dense populations, as is intuitively true. Therefore, it is desirable to proactively cull at-risk nodes (farms) rather than waiting for them to be infected. This is a strategy of disconnecting edges from a graph, which was known to be beneficial for traffic control under certain circumstances [19], by appropriately doing so the overall number of infected and culled farms can be minimized. Of course, overly aggressive culling will lead to a greater loss than necessary but overly conservative culling will lead to a greater epidemic impact giving way to increasing outbreak.

It should be noticed that none of the above patterns or strategies considers the birth, death, and aging of nodes over time. Although such modeling will introduce substantial additional complexity, spatially resolved census data and projections are available today, which should allow for better modeling and parameter estimation. If one uses the network paradigm to describe infectious disease transmission, then these datasets should provide sufficient empirical evidence to determine the network topology, such as the average neighborhood size. In this regard, it is suggested that detailed micro-simulation models might be used to obtain estimates of spatial-network topologies for different pathogens [18].

5.3.3 Impact of Spatial Clustering on Disease Transmissions

Spatial heterogeneity and spatial separation of disease hosts have been considered as key factors in epidemics and pathogens spreading. It is desirable to determine how accurate or how coarse the resolution of the spatial data can be to build a mathematical model, based on which useful information can be generated for informing control policies [20].

Again, consider the foot-and-mouth disease (FMD) spreading among farms during the epidemic spreading in UK in 2001, discussed above. A model was developed by Keeling [21] especially for this FMD incidence, with the rate at which an infectious farm i infects a susceptible farm j given by

$$\rho_{ij} = \left(\sum_{s \in \Gamma} [N_{s,j}]^{p_s} S_s \right) \times \left(\sum_{s \in \Gamma} [N_{s,i}]^{q_s} T_s \right) \times K(d_{ij}), \qquad (5.28)$$

where $N_{s,i}$ is the number of livestock species s (in a certain category Γ) recorded on node (farm) i, S_s and T_s are the species-specific susceptibility and transmissibility, p_s and q_s account for the increase in susceptibility and transmissibility for species s as the animal number on a farm increases, d_{ij} is the distance between node i and node j, and K is the contact-based distance-dependent transmission function. This spatial transmission model has been shown [21] to provide an accurate and robust description of the UK 2001 outbreak of FMD, which captured very well the national, regional, and individual-level patterns of infection.

Typically, the ring-culling policy is adopted to prevent disease from wide spreading. In [20], a spatial clustering approach was taken by introducing an average farm-centered density distribution $D(r)$, which is the number of farms per unit area at a ring-cull distance $r > 0$ from an indexed farm and then averaged over all possible indexed farms in the population:

$$D(r) = S_{\text{inf}} + (S_0 - S_{\text{inf}})e^{-\alpha r}, \qquad (5.29)$$

where S_{inf} defines the long-distance asymptotic density, S_0 defines the average local density around a farm, and $\alpha > 0$ is a constant determined by fitting to the real data.

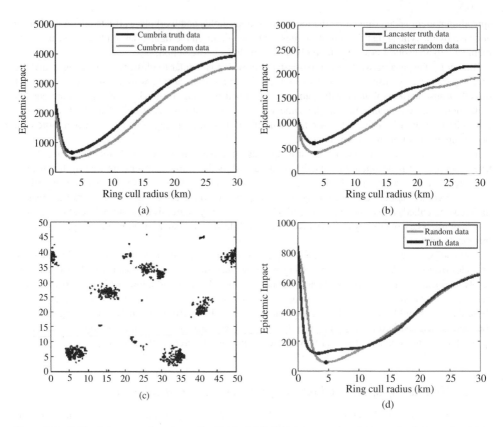

Figure 5.9 Epidemic impact against ring-cull radius for MFD [20]: (a) comparison between simulation and real data from Cumbria County, UK; (b) from Lancaster County; (c) farm network; (d) mean epidemic impact against ring-cull radius for random data (grey line) and true data (dark line). *Source*: Reprinted with permission from Tildesley, M.J., House, T.A. and Bruhn, M.C. *et al.* (2010) Impact of spatial clustering on disease transmission and optimal control. *Proceedings of the National Academy of Sciences*, **107**(3): 1041–6. Copyright (2002) National Academy of Sciences, USA

Numerical simulations were carried out on a farm network of $N = 1000$ nodes (farms) within a 50×50 km^2 area according to a given density distribution, which generated the results on epidemic impact of ring-culling policy shown in Figure 5.9. In the simulations, one farm is randomly seeded with infection. The heterogeneity in farm size and composition are ignored, and the transmission rate of infection between infectious and susceptible farms is highly simplified $\rho_{ij} = K(d_{ij})$ from (5.28), and each plot is a smooth data fit of 10 000 simulation trials.

In Figure 5.9, (a) is the comparison between simulation and real data from Cumbria County in UK, and (b) is from Lancaster County; (c) Farm network; and (d) mean epidemic impact against ring-cull radius for the random data (red line) and the true data (blue line). For (c) and (d), $S_0 = 4$ and $\alpha = 0.4$. In (a), (b), and (d), the black dots show the minima of each line. It has been observed that it is usually better to over-target control (i.e., bias control more toward high-risk hosts) than to under-target, hence it is better to ring cull using a radius that is slightly larger than the one calculated from (5.29).

It was shown [20] that, although spatial structure is critically important in predicting the emergent population-scale behavior from the knowledge of individual-level dynamics, such structure is mostly subsumed in the parameterization to allow making policy predictions in the absence of high-quality spatial information, which is beneficial if data are only available at intermediate spatial scales.

5.3.4   Large-Scale Spatial Epidemic Spreading

The above studies of epidemic spreading on spatial networks may be extended to the situations of an even much larger scale, e.g., the world scale, which is meaningful and important where global epidemics are concerned, such as SARS, AIDS and avian flus.

Characterizing to what extent spatial epidemics are spread out, especially at the outbreak stage, is important for controlling the evolution of a disease. At the outbreak, the number of infected individuals is typically small, so it is commonly assumed that the SIR model is good to use, where the locations of infected individuals can be modeled by Brownian motions if long-range movements and network interactions are negligible, such as in the case of animal epidemics [22].

When the network size is very large, it is found [23] that at the outbreak, the epidemic spreading patterns typically follow Zipf's law and Heaps' law, which coexist as had been widely observed before. As the process evolves, however, Heaps' law gradually takes over Zips' law and becomes dominant, until even right before saturation. This was supported by empirical data from pandemic diseases regardless of the biological details. More precisely, with the confirmed empirical data of A(H1N1) provided by the World Health Organization (WHO), the probability rank distribution (PRD), denoted $P_t(r)$, of the cumulative confirmed number (CCN) can be analyzed for every infected country in different time windows (typically, two weeks). Let $C_j(t)$ be the CCN in node (country) j at time t. Since it grows with time, its distributions in different dates are normalized by the global CCN, denoted $C_T(t) = (1/N)\sum_{j=1}^{N} C_j(t)$, which will be used for comparison.

Figure 5.10 (a) shows the Zipf-plots of the PRD of the confirmed cases in infected countries, with every $C_j(t)/C_T(t) > 0$ arranged in a descending order for each specimen. The maximal rank, $r_{t,\max}$ on the x-axis, for each specimen indicates the total number of infected countries in a given date, which grows as the epidemics spread. It can be observed that in the early stage (the period between April 30 and June 1, 2009), $P_t(r) \sim r^{-\theta}$ is in a power law form, which indicates the emergence of Zipf's law. Figure 5.10 (b) shows the Zipf-plots of $P_t^{US}(r)$ on several datasets sampled about every two weeks, where the data were provided by the Centers for Disease Control and Prevention (CDC), USA.

The temporal evolution of the power law exponent is shown in the left part of Figure 5.10 (c). About 60 countries were affected by the A(H1N1) on June 1, and most of them are countries with large population and/or economic power, e.g., USA, Mexico, Canada, Japan, Australia, and China. After June 1, the disease swept many more countries in a short period of time, and the WHO announcement on June 11 raised the pandemic level to its highest phase, phase 6, which implied that the global pandemic flu was taking place worldwide. After June 1, 2009, $P_t(r)$ gradually displayed a power-law distribution with an exponential cutoff, $P_t(r) \sim r^{-\theta}e^{-r/r_c}$, where r_c is the parameter controlling the cutoff effect, and the exponent gradually reduces to around $\theta \approx 1.7$, as shown in Figure 5.10 (C). As time evolves, however, $P_t(r)$ saturates. Figure 5.10 (d) shows the temporal evolution of the estimated exponent θ_{US} of the normalized distribution $P_t^{US}(t)$ during the period after May 15.

Figure 5.10 (e) shows a sublinear relation between the number of infected countries, $M(t)$, and the cumulative number of global confirmed cases $C_T(t)$, data collected by the World Health Organization (WHO), United Nations. Figure 5.10 (f) shows a sublinear relation between the number of infected states $M^{US}(t)$ and the cumulative number of national confirmed cases $C_T^{US}(t)$, based on the data collected by the CDC, USA.

In Figure 5.10, the shaded areas highlighted in (c), (e), and (f) correspond to different evolution stages, respectively.

By employing USA domestic air transportation and demographic data, a metapopulation model was constructed in [23] to simulate some pandemic spreading in a large scale at the country level, revealing that the broad heterogeneity of the infrastructure plays a key role in the evolution of scaling emergence. The analyses of large-scale spatial epidemic spreading help understand the temporal evolution of scaling, indicating that the coexistence of Zipf's law and Heaps' law depends on the collective dynamics of an epidemic process, and the heterogeneity of epidemic spread indicates the importance of performing targeted immunization or containment strategies at the early stage of a pandemic disease.

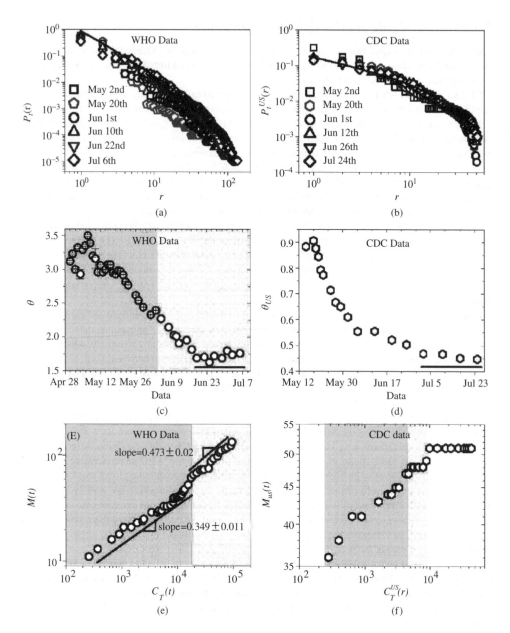

Figure 5.10 Empirical A(H1N1) data analysis [23]: (a) Zipf plot of PRD; (b) Zipf plot on sampled data; (c) temporal power-law; (d) power-law exponent; (e) sublinear relation between number of countries and number of cases; (f) sublinear relation between infected states and number of cases. *Source*: Reproduced with permission from Wang, L., Li, X., Zhang, Y.Q. *et al.* Evolution of scaling emergence in large-scale spatial epidemic spreading. *PLoS ONE* (2011)

5.3.5   Impact of Human Location-Specific Contact Patterns

To study the spatial transmission of epidemics in human society, many works have demonstrated the impact of human mobility on the epidemic threshold, assuming that the contact pattern of individuals is homogeneously mixed in the social network. A recent investigation shows, however, that location-related factors in reality are important in spatial network models for epidemics [24]. It was found that if location-specific heterogeneous human contact patterns are introduced into the phenomeno-logical models based on the commuting and contagion processes, then the epidemic threshold can be significantly reduced, thus favoring the outbreak of diseases.

More precisely, it was found [24] that a monotonic mode presents for the variance of disease preva-lence in dependence on the contact rates under the destination-driven contact scenario; while under the origin-driven scenario, enhancing the contact rate could counter-intuitively weaken the disease preva-lence in some parametric regimes of the model. Therefore, increasing the heterogeneity in human contacts seems to be beneficial in providing valuable support to public health implications.

5.4   Immunization on Complex Networks

Since heterogeneous networks are fragile to virus attacks, which cause serious and wide outbreaks, immu-nization (vaccination) becomes especially important for this type of networks. This section introduces three typical effective immunization strategies, namely, Random Immunization (or, Uniform Immuniza-tion), Targeted Immunization (or, Selected Immunization), and Acquaintance Immunization.

5.4.1   Random Immunization

Random immunization means to randomly select a fraction of nodes from the network to immune. In so doing, although large nodes have higher risk to be infected and small nodes are relatively safe, each of them has an equal chance to be chosen for immunization.

Consider heterogeneous networks. It is intuitively clear that generally random immunization for het-erogeneous networks is inefficient because such a network have a small fraction of large-degree nodes (hubs) while the majority of nodes have small degrees, thus a random immunization approach will likely immune only small-degree nodes which have less effect on the whole network. This observation is sup-ported by the following analysis.

Let the density of immunized nodes be g. Then, the threshold of the corresponding random immuniza-tion strategy is given via the epidemic threshold λ_c as

$$g_c = 1 - \frac{\lambda_c}{\lambda}. \tag{5.30}$$

Substituting the epidemic threshold formula (5.14) into (5.30) gives

$$g_c = 1 - \frac{\langle k \rangle}{\lambda \langle k^2 \rangle}. \tag{5.31}$$

Clearly, as the size of the network grows, one has $\langle k \rangle / \langle k^2 \rangle \to \infty$ so that the immune threshold for the heterogeneous network $g_c \to 1$, implying that almost every node in the network has to be immunized. This means that random immunization for homogeneous networks is inefficient, but nevertheless it is cost-effective due to its simplicity.

5.4.2   Targeted Immunization

By taking advantage of the heterogeneity of the scale-free networks, one may adopt a targeted immu-nization strategy, in which one progressively immunes the most highly connected nodes that are likely received the diseases from, and also spread the diseases to many other nodes in the network. Once these big nodes are immunized, conceptually their edges are removed, loosing connections with the other nodes thereby reducing or even completely blocking the way of virus spreading over the network.

Figure 5.11 shows a comparison between the two, targeted versus random, immunization strategies on a BA scale-free network model, where g is the density of immunized nodes, ρ_0 is the steady infection

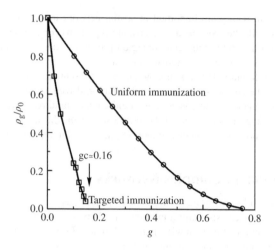

Figure 5.11 Comparison of two immunization strategies on a BA network [7]. *Source*: Reproduced by permission of Wiley-VCH Verlag GmbH & Co. KGaA

density before immunization, ρ_g is the steady infection density after immunization, and the ratio of ρ_g/ρ_0 indicates the effect of the immunization. It can be seen that the two immunization strategies have different efficiencies: for random immunization, the ratio decreases slowly and becomes zero only when $g \to 1$, and yet for the targeted immunization this is achieved for $g_c \approx 0.16$, which is very small as compared to 1. It implies that much less nodes are needed to be immunized by the targeted strategy than the random strategy to achieve a perfect immunization of the entire network.

Applying the targeted immunization strategy to an SIS-type model of the Internet at the AS level, similar results can be obtained as shown in Figure 5.12 [1]. The figure clearly demonstrates that random (uniform) immunization does not give a rapid decrease of the prevalence of the ratio ρ_g/ρ_0, but the targeted immunization with a small effort (only 2% of total population is immunized) can lead to a drastic reduction of the ratio.

It should be remarked that while the targeted immunization strategy is very effective on heterogeneous networks, it requires precise knowledge of the network structure in order to identify and immunize the

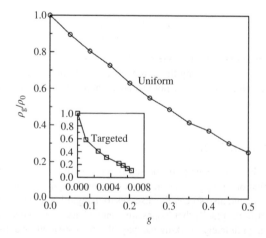

Figure 5.12 Comparison of two immunization strategies on the AS-level Internet [1]

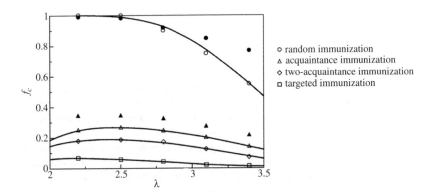

Figure 5.13 Comparison of immunizations: threshold f_c versus λ [27]. *Source*: Madar, N., Kalisky, T. and Cohen, R. *et al.* (2004) Immunization and epidemics dynamics in complex networks. *European Physical Journal B*, **38**: 269–76. figure 1, With kind permission from Springer Science and Business Media

big nodes with large numbers of connections. This is obviously not practical, at least not desirable, in large-scale network applications. Some remedies were therefore proposed, to use only local information available on the networks [25, 26]. In the case of the Internet, users frequently install and upgrade their anti-virus software, so that their PCs can immune to the new computer viruses, which by nature is a localized immunization strategy. From a global point of view, however, due to the heterogeneity of the Internet, even when a large number of small nodes (PCs) have been immunized by their local antivirus software, computer viruses spreading over the whole network still cannot be completely terminated in general.

5.4.3   Acquaintance Immunization

Acquaintance immunization is a localized strategy. The basic idea of acquaintance immunization is to randomly select a fraction f of nodes from the population of N nodes and then randomly select one of its neighbors [27], or select the bigger node among its neighbors, for immunization. This scheme only requires information about the randomly selected node and its neighbors, but not the global network. In a scale-free network, it is more likely a small node would be first selected at random, but then since most small nodes are connected to big nodes it is relatively easier to find a big node from among its neighbors to immunize. As a result, the immunization is quite efficient.

Figure 5.13 shows a comparison of the immunization threshold f_c in terms of the fraction f of nodes versus λ, for random, targeted and acquaintance immunization schemes on a scale-free network model [27], where the network size is $N = 10^6$. In the figure, empty circles correspond to random immunization; empty triangles, acquaintance immunization; empty diamonds, two-acquaintance (randomly select two neighbors) immunization; empty squares, targeted immunization. It can be seen that targeted immunization is better than acquaintance immunization, while they both are better than the random scheme. In the figure, solid circles and solid triangles represent the corresponding assortative networks, which show some but insignificant effects on the immunization strategies over the corresponding networks (marked by empty circles and empty triangles).

5.5   Computer Virus Spreading over the Internet

Computer viruses spreading over the Internet are in many ways similar to biological viruses spreading across human society.

Computer viruses are usually referred to as some small computer programs which can reproduce themselves by infecting other programs and computers, and continuously grow and spread out thereby damaging or even completely destroying the regular functioning of the computers and their programs. When a virus is active inside a computer, it is able to copy itself in many different ways into the codes of programs on the computer. When the infected computer program is run into another computer, typically the code of the virus is executed first thus continues to infect other programs in the new computer. This process repeats endlessly, leading to the collapse of a local or even global network of computers eventually, causing tremendous technological and economical disasters. Reportedly, the first virus capable of infecting PCs was the Brain virus developed in Pakistan in 1986.

Computer worms, on the other hand, are highly aggressive cyber-organisms (larger and more sophisticated programs) with much more powerful abilities to attack computers. The first worm was created by Robert Morris Jr., on November 2, 1988, then a graduate student in Computer Science at Cornell, who wrote an experimental, self-replicating, self-propagating program called a Worm and injected it into the Internet [28]. The first active worm of this kind was found in 1999, named Melissa, which shut down the Internet email systems that got clogged with infected emails propagating from the worm. In general, a worm is capable of sending itself to all email addresses in the email address book of the computer which received an infected email. The worm will then be sent out by this computer in every e-mail. This makes worms very effective in spreading. One of the infamous worms was the I-Love-You bug, first discovered in Hong Kong, which infected more than 78 million computers worldwide in just four days in year 2000. Another extremely virulent worm is the Nimda worm found in 2001, which used multiple methods of infection to spread among both Windows server and user machines, including file infections, massive numbers of infected emails attachments, web-server attacks, and even LAN propagation via network sharing. At about the same time, many more worms appeared, such as the well-known Lover Letter in 2000 and Sircam in 2001, which were among the most damaging ones.

Computer viruses and worms are extremely dangerous to all kinds of computers and the Internet as a whole. Active worms, for example, do not rely on any user intervention to propagate, but can "guess" IP addresses to attack. In 2004, the infamous Worm Sasser attacked several hundred thousands of computers over the world within just a couple of weeks. In 2009, worm Conficker remotely installed software on infected machines. Worm Koobface attached Facebook, also in 2009, and another malware worm spread on Facebook in January 2012, stealing more than 45 000 passwords. These are just a few incidents. More recently, a modular computer malware named Flame, also known as Flamer, sKyWIper, or Skywiper, was discovered in 2012, which attacked computers running the Microsoft Windows operating system. Reportedly, the program was being used for targeted cyber espionage (spy) in some Middle Eastern countries.

Today, many computer worms can quickly spread over different networks and make use of different protocols, which attack the Internet almost every day [29]. Therefore, understanding how computer viruses and worms are propagating over the Internet and various computer networks is extremely important for their prevention and control.

5.5.1 Random Constant-Spread Model

The so-called random constant-spread (RCS) model [30] is used to describe the outbreak of the code-red worm, found in 2001, which attacked computers running Microsoft's IIS web servers.

The RCS model assumes that the worm had a good random number of generator which is properly seeded, and the network size is fixed by ignoring both patching of systems during the worm spreading and normal deployment and removal of systems or turning on-off of systems at nights, and by ignoring any spread of the worm behind firewalls on private Intranets.

Let K be the initial infection rate per hour, namely, the number of susceptible hosts (nodes) which an infected node can reach at the start of the process. Assume that at the start, a few nodes were infected and, for simplicity, assume that K is a constant independent of the processor speed, bandwidth, network topology, and the locations of the infected nodes in the network, etc. Moreover, it is assumed that an

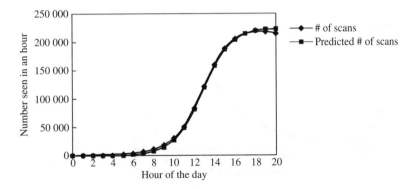

Figure 5.14 Hourly probe rate data during the reemergence of Code-Red-I [30]. *Source*: Reproduced by permission of Staniford, S., Paxson, V. and Weaver, N.

infected node randomly picks another node to attack and that any node, once infected, will stay as is but cannot be infected again.

Let N be the number of susceptible nodes, which is also assumed to be constant, and $a = a(t)$ be the proportion (percentage) of infected nodes at time t. Then, since the rate of infection is K, an infected node will reach and infect a total of $K(1 - a)$ nodes each time. Also, since the total number of infected nodes is Na, the rate of all nodes to be infected in the next short time duration will be $(Na)K(1 - a)$. Consequently, one has

$$\frac{d(Na)}{dt} = (Na)K(1 - a).$$

Or, since N is a constant,

$$\frac{da}{dt} = Ka(1 - a), \tag{5.32}$$

which is the Logistic equation, with solution

$$a = \frac{e^{K(t-t_0)}}{1 + e^{K(t-t_0)}}, \tag{5.33}$$

where t_0 is the initial time of the process. It is clear from (5.33) that the infection rate $a \to 1$ as $t \to \infty$, implying that all nodes will eventually be infected.

Figure 5.14 [30] shows the hourly probe rate data for the inbound port 80 at the Chemical Abstracts Service in the USA, during the reemergence of the Code-Red-I on August 1, 2002. It is clear that the above Logistic model can quite well capture and predict the real situations.

5.5.2 A Compartment-Based Model

Many new types of worms propagate extremely fast on the Internet, such as those named Flash, Warhol and Slammer found in 2003 which, within the first 10 minutes, already attacked 90% of vulnerable hosts running Microsoft's SQL servers or MSDE (MS Desktop Edition) 2000 that had buffer overflow vulnerability. In comparison, Code Red would need about 37 minutes to damage the same number (about 75 000) of hosts.

Since the spread of the Slammer worm is based on random scanning, in theory the RCS model discussed in the previous subsection should be appropriate for its description. However, as can be seen from Figure 5.15 [31], real data on July 19, 2001 show that the model is good only in the beginning stage of the process but then significantly differs from the data after some time because the data are saturated. More precisely, Figure 5.15 shows the total number of times that Slammer scanned the network. In about three

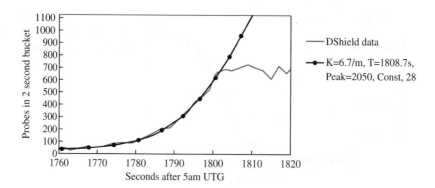

Figure 5.15 Slammer worm growth: real data versus model prediction [31]. *Source*: Serazzi, G. and Zanero, S. (2004) Computer virus propagation models. *Performance Tools and Applications to Networked Systems, Lecture Notes in Computer Science*, **2964**: Q1 26–50, figure 6, With kind permission from Springer Science and Business Media

minutes, the worm reached its maximum scanning speed but then suddenly slowed down. One explanation is that the majority of computers on the real network do not have enough bandwidths for the worm to continue to propagate exponentially, thus eventually it became saturated.

Notice that the Slammer distinguishes itself from the Code Red in the transmission mechanism: the exploit used by Slammer was based on the UDP (User Datagram Protocol) while Code Red is based on the TCP (Transition Control Protocol). The former offers a limited amount of services when messages are exchanged between computers (network limited); while the latter is a connection-oriented which creates and maintains connections until the time at which the messages to be exchanged by the application programs at each end have been exchanged (latency limited).

In order to better describe the spreading pattern of worms like Slammer, a model that can reflect the bandwidth limitation on the real Internet is desirable. This consideration led to a new compartment-based mode [31].

Suppose that inside a densely connected region of several AS on the Internet a worm propagates unhindered, for which the RCS model discussed in the previous subsection could be used as the basic framework. Let N_i be the number of susceptible hosts in the ith AS, denoted as AS_i, and a_i be the proportion (percentage) of the infected hosts among them. Also, let K be the average rate of spreading spread, which is assumed a constant in each AS_i, and let $P_{IN,i}$ be the probability of a node (host) infecting another node inside the same AS_i and $P_{OUT,i}$ be the probability of a node in AS_i infecting a node in another AS. The following equation describes the internal and external worm infection on AS_1 in a simple network with only two AS:

$$N_1 da_1 = \left[\underbrace{N_1 a_1 K P_{IN,1} dt}_{Internal} + \underbrace{N_2 a_2 K P_{OUT,2} dt}_{External} \right] (1 - a_1).$$

The equation about AS_2 is similar. Thus, the network describing both of the two AS can be established by combining them together, as

$$da_1/dt = \left[a_1 K P_{IN,1} + \frac{N_2}{N_1} a_2 K P_{OUT,2} \right] (1 - a_1)$$

$$da_2/dt = \left[a_2 K P_{IN,2} + \frac{N_1}{N_2} a_1 K P_{OUT,1} \right] (1 - a_2).$$

Assuming that the worm randomly selects a node from the network to attack, one has $P_{IN,i} = N_i/N$ and $P_{OUT,i} = 1 - P_{IN,i} = N_j/N, j \neq i$, yielding

$$da_i/dt = \left[a_i K \frac{N_i}{N} + \sum_{\substack{j=1 \\ j \neq i}} \frac{N_j}{N_i} a_j K \frac{N_i}{N} \right] (1 - a_i), \ i = 1, \ldots, N,$$

namely,

$$da_i/dt = \left[a_i K \frac{N_i}{N} + \sum_{\substack{j=1 \\ j \neq i}} \frac{N_j}{N} a_j K \right] (1 - a_i), \ i = 1, \ldots, N. \tag{5.34}$$

This system of nonlinear ordinary differential equations shows that in AS_i, the worm spreading inside AS_i follows the RCS model for a certain period of time, until it reaches out to infect another AS.

System (5.34) can be solved numerically, which has saturation along the ending part of the simulation curve shown in Figure 5.15, generated by model (5.32), matching the real data very well.

5.5.3   Spreading Models of Email Viruses

Email is the most common service and application of the Internet. In fact, most Internet hosts run email services that manage the addresses in their respective domains, therefore any email service can use the domain-name system of the Internet to retrieve the IP address of any other email server, connect to that server, and then transfer emails to the intended receivers in that domain through some standard communication protocols.

The wide connection of the Internet and convenience of email communications, on the other hand, enable viruses to spread out extremely easily by attaching themselves to emails. Since emails are private matters and email users usually trust their partners and therefore keep and forward most if not all emails that they have received to other partners, email viruses have broken out frequently and severely in the past. Typical examples include the Melissa (1999), I-Love-You (2000), Nimda (2001), Win32/Sircam (2001), the Chinese versions of Worm.Klez.cn.b (2002), Worm.SoBig.c and Worm.Mimail.C (2003), as well as SCO bomb (2004), among many others.

To understand the topological characteristics of the email networks, a report on the investigation of the email service in the Kiel University, Germany in 2002 shows that this campus email network with $N = 59\,812$ nodes (including 5 165 student accounts) has an average degree $\langle k \rangle = 2.88$, one giant cluster with 56 969 nodes and several small clusters with 150 nodes or less, following a power-law degree distribution of the form $k^{-\gamma}$ with exponent $\gamma = 1.81$, as shown in Figure 5.16 [32].

In another study of modeling a local email network [33], let T_i be the email checking time of user i, $i = 1, 2, \ldots, N$, which itself is a random variable denoted by T, and let P_i be the probability of opening the incoming email attachment, $i = 1, 2, \ldots, N$, which itself is a random variable denoted by P, where N is the total number (volume) of emails, which is a very large integer in general. Assume, moreover, that all users behave independently, for example, they are checking emails independently; each checking time T_i of user i is exponentially distributed with a mean $E[T_i]$; and T and P are independent Gaussian random variables: $T \sim N(\mu_T, \sigma_T^2)$ and $P \sim N(\mu_P, \sigma_P^2)$.

An email is said to be infected once the user opens a virus-infected email attachment. Let N_0 be the number of initially infected users who send out virus-contaminated emails to their neighbors. Let N_t be the number of infected users at time t during the virus propagation process, thus $N_0 \leq N_t \leq N$ for $t \geq 0$. Assume that the email transmission time is neglected.

In simulations, consider an email network model with $N = 100\,000$ and $\langle k \rangle = 8$. Using $T \sim N(40\,400)$, $P \sim N(0.5, 0.09)$, $N_0 = 2$ to perform some simulations on a set of real data with 800 000 Yahoo

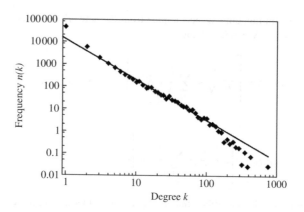

Figure 5.16 Node-degree distribution of email network in Kiel University in 2002 [32]. *Source*: Reprinted with permission from Ebel, H., Mielsch, L-I. and Bornholdt, S. (2002) Scale-free topology of e-mail networks. *Physical Review E*, **66**: 035103. Copyright (2002) American Physical Society

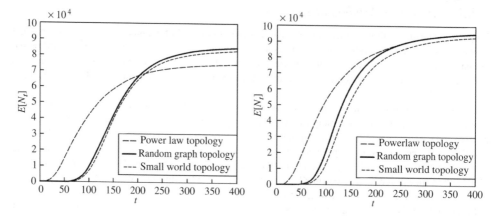

Figure 5.17 Comparison of $E[N_t]$ between networks in different topologies [33]. *Source*: Reproduced by permission of Cliff C. Zou

emails, which as a local network has a power-law node-degree distribution with exponent $\gamma = 1.7$. The simulations are concerned with the average number of infected users, $E[N_t]$, which is obtained by averaging 100 repeated simulations.

Figure 5.17 [33] compares the behaviors of email virus propagation over networks with different topologies: random-graph, small-world and scale-free networks, all on networks of 100 000 nodes with the same average degree $\langle k \rangle = 8$. In this study, the power-law network has the highest degree 1833 and lowest degree 3, with exponent $\gamma = 1.7$. Figure 5.17 shows that email virus propagation patterns over random-graph and small-world networks are similar, implying that the main factor on the propagation is the short average path-length characteristic but not the clustering coefficient of the network. On the other hand, email viruses seem to propagate much faster in scale-free networks than the other two, because an infected large node will send out more virus-contaminated emails. Since in the scale-free network, most nodes have a degree lower than the average value, they are not easy to be infected, therefore eventually the scale-free network has less nodes being infected as compared to the other two models.

5.5.4 Effects of Computer Virus on Network Topologies

It has been seen that network topologies significantly affect the virus spreading patterns over the networks. On the contrary, when a computer virus propagates over a network, it traverses part of the network therefore could affect the topology of this part of the network as the medium of virus spreading [34]. The main reason is that when a node (computer) is infected then it will not function well and therefore should be considered as being removed along with its edges from the network, thereby changing the effective network topology. Of course, another part of the network over which the virus never travels will be left unchanged. In most cases, the topology of the virus-traveling network is determined by the spread and replication of the virus. Most viruses and worms spread through the network in different formats at different rates to different extents, which often change the spreading-path and functional topologies of the underlying networks quite significantly.

For a more precise discussion, consider the following four types of technological networks, all vulnerable to attacks:

A. a network of computers connected via Internet Protocol (IP);
B. a network of shared administrator accounts for desktop computers;
C. a network of email address books;
D. a network of email messages mutually sending among different users.

Network A is the IP network, where each computer has a 32-bit IP address and there is a routing infrastructure that supports communications between any two addresses. Consider IP addresses as nodes on the network. It is known that many computer worms such as Nimda and Slammer can spread over such an IP network.

Network B is a product of the common operating-system feature that allows computer system administrators to read and write data on the disks of networked machines. Some worms like Nimda and Bugbear can spread by self-copying from disk to disk over such a network.

Network C is a directed graph with nodes representing users and a connection between two users exists if one user's email address appears in another's address book. Many email viruses such as I-Love-You use address books to spread, so can spread over such a network.

Network D is an undirected version of network C, in which nodes represent computer users and two users are connected if they have exchanged emails recently. Some viruses like Klez can spread over this type of network.

Figure 5.18 (a) shows the node-degree distributions of networks A and B on a system with 518 users and 382 machines, while (b) shows the cumulative degree distributions of networks C and D, with data collected from a large university and plotted in log–log scale. In network A, all nodes have the same degree, so its distribution is a discrete delta (the highest histogram), while in network B the distribution consists of several discrete peaks corresponding to different classes of computers, administrators, or administrative strategies (the short histograms). It can be seen that networks C and D do not follow power-laws but instead have long tails showing the heterogeneity of their topologies. This implies that targeted immunization may be effective for these two types of email networks. In fact, calculation shows that the epidemic threshold of targeted immunization is 0.1 on network C and 0.8 on network D.

In the above four types of networks, different virus replication and spreading patterns may lead to their different traveling-path and effective-functioning network topologies of the underlying networks. Therefore, it is desirable to have a control strategy that is immune to the change in network topology and thus does not require any knowledge of infections before an outbreak. Such a control strategy has to be highly effective against malicious infections but harmless to normal activities. The so-called throttling scheme is one of such control strategies [35], which limits the number of new connections a computer can make to other computers in a given period of time, thereby limiting the spreading rates of the viruses if they appear. Although this scheme does not completely eliminate infections, it works quite well to render a virus harmless or reduces its effect by other means.

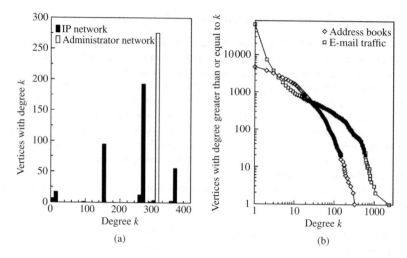

Figure 5.18 Four types of networks [34]: (a) node-degree distributions of A, B; (b) cumulative degree distributions of C, D. *Source*: Reprinted with permission from Balthrop, J., Forrest, S., Newman, M.E.J. and Williamson, M.M. (2004) Technological networks and the spread of computer viruses. Science. Copyright (2004) AAAS

To summarize the studies in this chapter, it is noted that the spreading threshold theory only considers the steady state, namely the asymptotic behaviors, of the spreading process, leaving alone the complex dynamics existing in the process such as oscillations, bifurcations and even chaos [36–38]. These complex dynamics and their regulation and control are oftentimes very important in understanding and controlling virus spreading over complex networks [39], therefore have been extensively studied in the literature [40].

References

[1] http://www.avira.com/en/threats/section/wildlist_intro/index.html (last accessed August 10, 2014).

[2] Pastor-Satorras, R. and Vespignani, A. (2004) *Evolution and Structure of the Internet*. Cambridge University Press, Cambridge.

[3] Pastor-Satorras, R. and Vespingnani, A. (2001) Epidemic spreading in scale-free networks. *Physical Review Letters*, **86**(4): 3200–3.

[4] Bailey, N.T.J. (1975) *The Mathematical Theory of Infectious Diseases and Its Applications*. Hafner Press, New York.

[5] Anderson, R.M. and May, R.M. (1992) *Infectious Diseases in Humans*. Oxford University Press, Oxford.

[6] Diekmann, O. and Heesterbeek, J.A.P. (2000) *Mathematical Epidemiology of Infectious Disease: Model Building, Analysis and Interpretation*. Wiley, New York.

[7] Pastor-Satorras, R. and Vespignani, A. (2003) Epidemics and immunization in scale-free networks. In Bornholdt, S., Schuster, H.G. (eds), *Handbook of Graphs and Networks*, Wiley-VCH, Berlin.

[8] Pastor-Satorras, R. and Vespignani, A. (2001) Epidemic dynamics and endemic states in complex networks. *Physical Review E*, **63**: 066117.

[9] Pastor-Satorras, R. and Vespignani, A. (2002) Epidemic dynamics in finite size scale-free networks. *Physical Review E*, **65**: 035108.

[10] Boguñá, M. and Pastor-Satorras, R. (2002) Epidemic spreading in correlated complex networks. *Physical Review E*, **66**: 047104.

[11] Moreno, Y., Gómez, J.B. and Pacheco, A.F. (2003) Epidemic incidence in correlated complex networks. *Physical Review E*, **68**: 035103.

[12] Moreno, Y., Pasto-Satorres, R. and Vespignani, A. (2002) Epidemic outbreaks in complex heterogeneous networks. *European Physical Journal B*, **26**: 521–9.

[13] Castellano, A. and Pastor-Satorras R. (2010) Thresholds for epidemic spreading in networks. *Physical Review Letters*, **105**: 218701.

[14] Barthélemy, M. (2011) Spatial networks. *Physics Reports*, **499**: 1–101.

[15] Barrat, A., Barthélemy, M., Pastor-Satorras, R. and Vespignani, A. (2004) The architecture of complex weighted networks. *Proceedings of the National Academy of Sciences*, **101**: 3747–52.

[16] Kurant, M. and Thiran, P. (2006) Extraction and analysis of traffic and topologies of transportation networks. *Physical Review E*, **74**: 036114.

[17] Ravasz, E. and Barabási, A-L. (2003) Hierarchical organization in complex networks, *Physical Review E*, **67**: 026112.

[18] Riley, S. (2007) Large-scale spatial-transmission models of infectious disease. *Science*, **316**: 1298–1301.

[19] Yin, Y.C., Wang, W.X., Chen, G. and Wang, B.H. (2006) Decoupling process for better synchronizability on scale-free networks, *Physical Review E*, **74**: 047102.

[20] Tildesley, M.J., House, T.A. and Bruhn, M.C. *et al.* (2010) Impact of spatial clustering on disease transmission and optimal control. *Proceedings of the National Academy of Sciences*, **107**(3): 1041–6.

[21] Keeling, M.J., Woolhouse, M.E.J., Shaw, D.J. *et al.* (2001) Dynamics of the 2001 UK foot and mouth epidemic: Stochastic dispersal in a heterogeneous landscape. *Science*, **294**: 813–17.

[22] Dumonteil, E., Majumdar, S.N., Rosso, A. and Zoia, A. (2013) Spatial extent of an outbreak in animal epidemics. *Proceedings of the National Academy of Sciences*, **110**(11): 4239–44.

[23] Wang, L., Li, X., Zhang, Y.Q. *et al.* (2011) Evolution of scaling emergence in large-scale spatial epidemic spreading. *PLOS ONE*, **6**: e21197.

[24] Wang, L., Wang, Z., Zhang, Y. and Li, X. (2013) How human location-specific contact patterns impact spatial transmission between populations? *Scientific Reports*, **3**: 1468.

[25] Dezsö, Z. and Barabási, A-L. (2002) Halting viruses in scale-free networks. *Physical Review E*, **65**: 055103.

[26] Cohen, R., Havlin, S. and Ben-Avraham, D. (2003) Efficient immunization strategies for computer networks and populations. *Physical Review Letters*, **91**: 247901.

[27] Madar, N., Kalisky, T. and Cohen, R. *et al.* (2004) Immunization and epidemics dynamics in complex networks. *European Physical Journal B*, **38**: 269–76.

[28] http://en.wikipedia.org/wiki/Robert_Tappan_Morris (last accessed August 10, 2014).

[29] http://en.wikipedia.org/wiki/List_of_computer_viruses (last accessed August 10, 2014).

[30] Staniford, S., Paxson, V. and Weaver, N. (2002) How to own the Internet in your spare time. *Proceedings of the 11th USENIX Security Symposium*, August, 149–67.

[31] Serazzi, G. and Zanero, S. (2004) Computer virus propagation models. *Performance Tools and Applications to Networked Systems, Lecture Notes in Computer Science*, **2964**: 26–50 Springer, Berlin.

[32] Ebel, H., Mielsch, L-I. and Bornholdt, S. (2002) Scale-free topology of e-mail networks. *Physical Review E*, **66**: 035103.

[33] Zou, C.C., Towsley, D. and Gong, W.B. (2003) Email virus propagation modeling and analysis. Technical Report TR-CSE-03-04, University of Massachusetts, Amherst.

[34] Balthrop, J., Forrest, S., Newman, M.E.J. and Williamson, M.M. (2004) Technological networks and the spread of computer viruses. *Science*, **304**: 527–9.

[35] Williamson, M.M. (2004) Resilient infrastructure for network security. *Complexity*, **9**: 34–40.

[36] Ramani, A., Carstea, A.S., Willox, R. *et al.* (2004) Oscillating epidemics: a discrete-time model. *Physica A*, **333**: 278–92.

[37] Li, X., Chen, G., Li. C G. (2004) Stability and bifurcation of disease spreading in complex networks. *International Journal of Systems Science*, **35**: 527–36.

[38] Li, X., Chen, G. (2006) Models, dynamics, and control of spreading in complex networks: A survey. *Dynamics of Continuous, Discrete and Impulsive Systems, Series B*, **13**: 109–16.

[39] Li, X. and Wang, X.F. (2006) Controlling the spreading in small-world evolving networks: Stability, oscillation, and topology. *IEEE Transactions on Automatic Control*, **51**(3): 534–40.

[40] Fu, X.C., Small, M. and Chen, G. (2013) *Propagation Dynamics on Complex Networks: Models*, Analysis and Stability. Higher Education Press, Beijing.

6

Community Structures

6.1 Introduction

The degree distribution of a network is an important topological characteristic which, however, cannot be used as a unique measure of the essence of a network because two networks with the same degree distribution can have very different properties and behaviors. For instance, Figures 6.1 (a) and (b) show two networks with the same degree sequence (hence the same degree distribution), yet (a) contains a closed triangle but disconnected while (b) does not contain any closed triangle but is connected.

The simple examples shown in Figures 6.1 and 6.2 demonstrate that the first-order topological property (the degree distribution) is not sufficient to determine the topological properties of a network; therefore, higher-order measures are needed [1–4]. One natural measure is the second-order degree distribution characteristic, namely the degree–degree correlation, which was introduced in Chapter 2, where the related concept of (dis)assortativity was also introduced.

6.1.1 Various Scenarios in Real-World Social Networks

It has been found and verified, based on large-scale real databases, that many biological networks such as protein reaction networks and many technological networks such as the Internet and WWW are disassortative, while many social networks such as scientific cooperation networks and movie-actor networks are assortative. Table 6.1 shows some real examples. However, most online social networks display various assortative, disassortative and even neutral characteristics. For example, the largest Korean online social network Cyworld has more than 100 million users, which is disassortative with assortativity coefficient $r = -0.13$, but Facebook with more than 700 million users is assortative with $r = 0.226$ [5].

There are several opinions about the assortativity of social networks. From the social and psychological points of view, in real life most people generally tend to connect to famous and well-established persons and yet the latter tend to connect to persons of the same categories, which creates positive correlations of node degrees thereby leading to assortativity. As to professional cooperation, politicians and movie stars tend to work with even more famous partners so as to further promote themselves. In academia, scientists work together due to some non-replaceable roles of their collaborators because of their specialties in research. Furthermore, the assortativity of real social networks also depends on the special properties of various organizations and societies [6, 7].

Recently, the rapid development of various online social networks has gradually filled the gaps between common people and famous ones, especially high profile people on the Internet, since it is much quicker and easier than traditional daily-life encounters. Knowing the differences between the two social contact scenarios will be helpful for understanding the formation and evolution of online social networks. As an

Fundamentals of Complex Networks: Models, Structures and Dynamics, First Edition.
Guanrong Chen, Xiaofan Wang, Xiang Li.
Companion Website: www.wiley.com/go/chen/complex

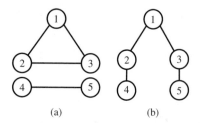

Figure 6.1 Two networks with the same degree sequence: (a) disconnected; (b) connected

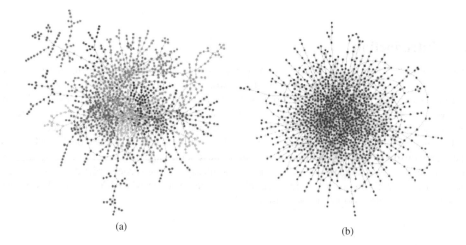

Figure 6.2 Two networks with the same degree sequence [1]: (a) metabolic network; (b) random network. *Source*: Reproduced from Amaral, L.A.N. and Guimera, R. Complex networks: Lies, damned lies and statistics. *Nature Physics* (2006) Macmillan Pub. Ltd.

example, consider the Chinese online social network displayed in Figure 6.3, which shows the evolution of the network during its first 27 months (from June 11, 2005 to August 11, 2007) [8]. Figure 6.3 (a) shows the evolution of nodes and edges, where the network grew slowly in the first 10 months but then accelerated rapidly for a short period of time and finally developed rather steadily. Noticeably, the network had a change from being assortative to disassortative, as shown in Figure 6.3 (b). To explain what happened, one possibility is that at the beginning of the development users were interconnected only to their close friends, namely only life friends were connected online, which yielded an assortative structure of the network. Gradually, low-degree users started to connect to some high-degree users for their greater influence and impact in the social network, which finally reverted the assortativity.

6.1.2   Generalization of Assortativity

From a more general point of view, assortativity means that nodes with similar characteristics will connect to each other with higher tendency. Here, basic characteristics can be node degrees, but can also be professions, ages, races, religions, etc. In social studies, this refers to homophily [9, 10]. Figure 6.4 shows a friendship network in a middle-high school [10], where every node is a student. If student A considers student B as a friend then there is an edge from A pointing to B. In the figure, while nodes represent Caucasians, dark nodes represent Blacks, and grey nodes represent students of other races. It can be seen from the figure that students of the same race more often tend to be friends. In the figure, the

Table 6.1 Assortativity coefficients of some real networks

Type	Network	N	r
Technological network	Internet	10 697	−0.189
	WWW	269 504	−0.065
Biological network	Protein-protein reactions	2115	−0.156
	Neuronal networks	307	−0.163
Online social network	Cyworld	120 481 860	−0.13
	Facebook	700 000 000	0.226
	MySpace	100 000	0.02
	Orkut	100 000	0.31
	RenRen	396 836	−0.0036
	Gnutella P2P(SN6)	191 679	−0.109
	LiveJournal	5 284 457	0.179
	YouTube	1 157 827	−0.033
Real social network	ArXiv cooperation	52 909	0.36
	Cond-mat cooperation	16 264	0.18
	Mathematicians cooperation	253 339	0.12
	Neural scientists cooperation	205 202	0.60
	Biologists cooperation	1520 251	0.13
	Movie actors cooperation	449 913	0.21
	TV-actors cooperation	79 663	0.53
	Council members network	7673	0.28

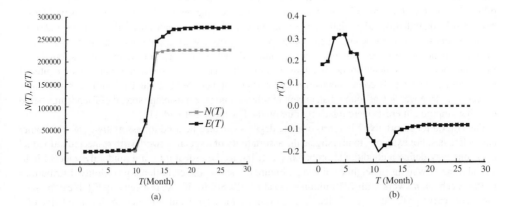

Figure 6.3 Evolution of an online Chinese social network [8]: (a) evolution of nodes and edges; (b) assortativity. *Source*: Reprinted from Hu, H. and Wang, X. (2009) Evolution of a large online social network. *Physics Letters A*, **373**(12–13): 1105–10. Copyright (2009) Elsevier

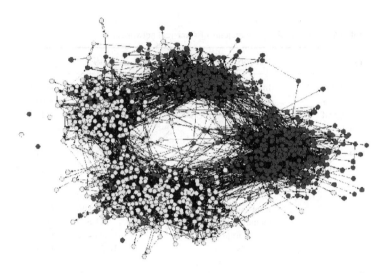

Figure 6.4 The friendship network in a middle-high school [10]. *Source*: Race, M.J. (2001) School integration, and friendship segregation in America. *American Journal of Sociology*, **107** (3): 679–716. Reproduced with permission from The University of Chicago Press

upper and lower levels represent middle and high school levels of students, respectively, showing that students of the same level are more likely to be friends with each other.

There are two opinions about assortativity in social networks: one is selection, that is, people tend to find friends in the same category; the other is influence, namely people are affected by their own friends. As such, one of the greatest challenges in social studies is how to distinguish the effects of selection and influence; more precisely, through the evolution process of a social network, which factor plays a more important role? The difficulty lies in the fact that it requires real-time evolving data about both individual properties and social relationships as well as an accurate evolving model of both factors. This problem is being resolved gradually and partially today, since more and more real data are available online and some good models such as the stochastic actor-based modeling framework enables us to adequately describe the interdependence between network topology and node behaviors [11]. For instance, it was found that, in a group of college students on the Facebook network, the chance for two students with the same interest in movies and music to become friends was higher than that between two students with the same habits in reading. Moreover, it was found that, except for classic and jazz music, the spread of friendships based on other common interests were relatively rare on the Facebook network [12].

The criteria for assortativity in terms of node degrees can also be used for assortativity of some other characteristics. For example, to investigate the assortativity of a social network with respect to individual ages, one may define a conditional probability $P_c(t'|t)$, as the probability of a randomly selected individual of age t who has a neighbor of age t'. Figure 6.5 shows the conditional probability distributions of the Facebook network with 721 million users at $t = 20, 30, 40, 50, 60$, respectively [5]. It can be seen that every curve peaks at $t = t'$, which decays faster on the right-hand side than the left-hand side of a peak. This implies that Facebook network has age-based assortativity: users tend to be friends of similar ages, particularly young people, while elder people have more friends in a wider spectrum of ages.

The concept of assortativity can also be extended to some other cases in network studies. Consider a network with a coupling matrix $A = [a_{ij}]$. Assume that the network has M edges, and let x_i be a scale parameter representing a certain property of node i in the network. Since every edge has two end nodes, thus

$$\mu = \frac{\sum_{i,j} a_{ij} x_i}{\sum_{i,j} a_{ij}} = \frac{\sum_i k_i x_i}{\sum_i k_i} = \frac{1}{2M} \sum_i k_i x_i \tag{6.1}$$

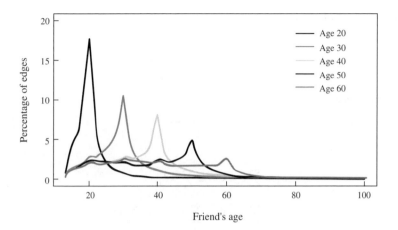

Figure 6.5 User friendships versus ages on Facebook [5]. *Source*: Courtesy of Ugander, J., Karrer, B. and Backstrom, L. *et al.* (2011)

represents the average value of the parameters x_i over the network. Since a node of degree k_i is the end node of k_i edges, the above formula is given in terms of k_i. Furthermore, considering that the two end nodes, i and j, of edge (x_i, x_j) have covariance given by

$$\mathrm{cov}(x_i, x_j) = \frac{\sum_{i,j} a_{ij}(x_i - \mu)(x_j - \mu)}{\sum_{i,j} a_{ij}}$$

$$= \frac{1}{2M} \sum_{i,j} a_{ij}(x_i x_j - \mu x_i - \mu x_j + \mu^2)$$

$$= \frac{1}{2M} \sum_{i,j} a_{ij} x_i x_j - \mu^2$$

$$= \frac{1}{2M} \sum_{i,j} a_{ij} x_i x_j - \frac{1}{(2M)^2} \sum_{i,j} k_i k_j x_i x_j$$

$$= \frac{1}{2M} \sum_{i,j} \left(a_{ij} - \frac{k_i k_j}{2M} \right) x_i x_j. \tag{6.2}$$

In the above, letting $x_i = x_j$ yields the variance of x_i, as follows:

$$\sigma_x^2 = \frac{1}{2M} \sum_{i,j} \left(a_{ij} - \frac{k_i k_j}{2M} \right) x_i^2$$

$$= \frac{1}{2M} \sum_{i,j} \left(k_i \delta_{ij} - \frac{k_i k_j}{2M} \right) x_i x_j. \tag{6.3}$$

The corresponding assortativity coefficient, thus, is given by the normalized variance, namely the Pearson correlation coefficient

$$r = \frac{\mathrm{cov}(x_i, x_j)}{\sigma_x^2} = \frac{\sum_{i,j} \left(a_{ij} - \frac{k_i k_j}{2M} \right) x_i x_j}{\sum_{i,j} \left(k_i \delta_{ij} - \frac{k_i k_j}{2M} \right) x_i x_j}. \tag{6.4}$$

Furthermore, if this particular property x_i is degree k_i, then the assortativity value is

$$r = \frac{\sum_{i,j}\left(a_{ij} - \frac{k_i k_j}{2M}\right)k_i k_j}{\sum_{i,j}\left(k_i \delta_{ij} - \frac{k_i k_j}{2M}\right)k_i k_j}. \tag{6.5}$$

This can be simplified to

$$r = \frac{S_1 S_e - S_2^2}{S_1 S_3 - S_2^2}, \tag{6.6}$$

where

$$S_e = \sum_{i,j} a_{ij} k_i k_j = 2 \sum_{(i,j)\in E} k_i k_j$$

$$S_1 = \sum_i k_i \,, \ S_2 = \sum_i k_i^2 \,, \ S_3 = \sum_i k_i^3 \,.$$

6.2   Community Structure and Modularity

6.2.1   Community Structure

A close look at Figure 6.4 reveals that the network has four communities and each of them are intra-connected relatively densely while the interconnections among communities are relatively sparse. As a matter of fact, many real networks have such community structures, as illustrated by Figure 6.6, including some real examples to be further discussed later.

Network community structures have close relationships with graph partitions (also known as graph cuts) in computer science and with hierarchical clustering in social science. Regarding graph partitions, one case is parallel computing. Suppose that there are n mutually communicating computers sharing their operation on g processors. The programs are interconnected and thus form a network, in which a node is a program and an edge represents a relation of directly connected pair of programs. Now, the question is: How to assign the n programs to the g processors so that every processor has about the same number of programs and the total number of edges is minimized? This means that the data flow is minimized, since the data communications on such edges are relatively slow. Generally, this is an NP-hard computational problem, for which there is no efficient algorithm available to solve very large-scale networks.

Hierarchical clustering is a classical algorithm of searching for community structures in social networks. It naturally divides a network into subgroups based on some similarities or strengths among the edges. According to additions or removals of network edges, it can be further classified into two categories: agglomerative methods and divisive methods [14].

6.2.2   Modularity

Modularity is a measure of the level or degree to which a network's communities may be separated and recombined, which is a commonly used criterion for determining the quality of network partitions.

For a given network, a random-graph model which possesses some common properties (e.g., the same number of edges or same degree distribution) is called a null model of the given network. In the study of network community structures, null models are important to consider. The lowest-order (zero-order) null model of a network is an ER random graph with the same number of edges as the given network. The ER random graph has a homogeneous degree distribution, while many real networks are heterogeneous. Therefore, it is common to compare the community structure of a given network with that of a first-order null model, which is a random graph with the same degree distribution as the given network.

As an example, consider a protein–protein interaction (PPI) network of rat proteome [14]. In this example, the proteins interact very frequently with each other. Communities correspond to functional

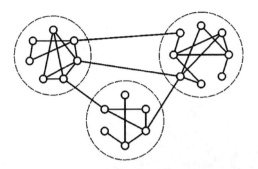

Figure 6.6   A small network with a community structure

groups of proteins that have the same or similar functions, which therefore can be classified into the same community. Figure 6.7 is the PPI network which clearly shows a community structure, but on the contrary a random network with exactly the same node-degree sequence does not [16].

Now, the concept of modularity is further discussed in more detail.

For a given real network, suppose a partition of communities has been found. Then, the total number of edges inside all communities is given by

$$Q_{real} = \frac{1}{2} \sum_{i,j} a_{ij} \delta(C_i, C_j),$$

where $A = [a_{ij}]$ is the adjacency matrix of the network, C_i is the community to which node i belongs, and if node i and node j belong to the same community then $\delta = 1$ otherwise $\delta = 0$.

Consider a null model of the same size for this network, and divide the null model with the same community structure. Then, the total expectation number of edges inside all communities is given by

$$Q_{null} = \frac{1}{2} \sum_{i,j} p_{ij} \delta(C_i, C_j),$$

where p_{ij} is the expectation value of the number of edges between node i and node j.

Then, the modularity of the above real network is defined to be the proportion of the difference between the real total number of edges and the expected total number of edges, defined above, over the total number of existing edges in the given network, M, namely

$$Q = \frac{Q_{real} - Q_{null}}{M} = \frac{1}{2M} \sum_{i,j} (a_{ij} - p_{ij}) \delta(C_i, C_j). \qquad (6.7)$$

In theory, for a null model with the same node-degree sequence as the given network, one has $p_{ij} = k_i k_j / M$, where k_i is the degree of node i in the given network, therefore

$$Q = \frac{1}{2M} \sum_{i,j} b_{ij} \delta(C_i, C_j), \qquad (6.8)$$

where $b_{ij} = a_{ij} - \frac{k_i k_j}{2M}$, and $B = [b_{ij}]$ is called the modularity matrix.

In practice, if only the information about the edges but not about the node degree sequence is available, the following formula is more useful: Let e_{vw} be the percentage of the number of edges between community v and community w over the number of edges of the whole network. Then,

$$e_{vw} = \frac{1}{2M} \sum_{i,j} a_{ij} \delta(C_i, v) \delta(C_j, w).$$

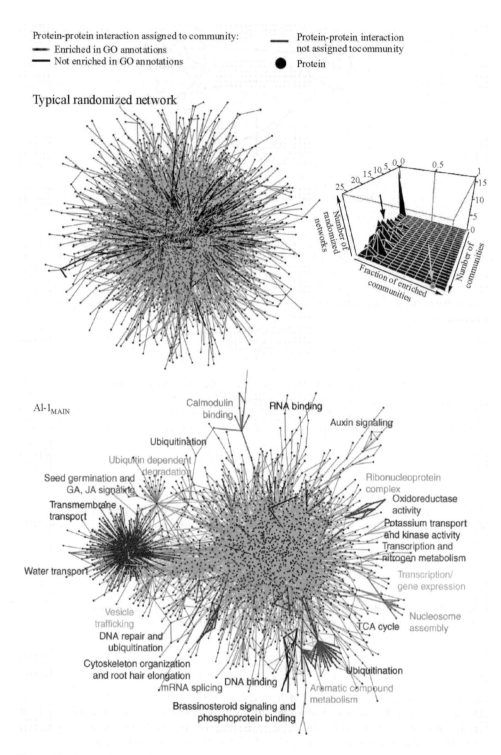

Figure 6.7 Community structure of the PPI network of rat proteome [16]. *Source*: From Arabidopsis Interactome Mapping Consortium (2011) Evidence for network evolution in an Arabidopsis interactome map, *Science*, **333** (6042): 601–7. Reprinted with permission from AAAS

Also, let a_v be the percentage of the number of edges with one end-node in community v over the number of edges of the whole network. Then,

$$a_v = \frac{1}{2M} \sum_i k_i \delta(C_i, v).$$

Note that

$$\delta(C_i, C_j) = \sum_v \delta(C_i, v)\delta(C_j, v).$$

Equation (6.8) can be rewritten as

$$Q = \frac{1}{2M} \sum_{ij} \left(a_{ij} - \frac{k_i k_j}{2M}\right) \sum_v \delta(C_i, v)\delta(C_j, v)$$

$$= \sum_v \left[\frac{1}{2M} \sum_{ij} a_{ij} \delta\left(C_i, v\right) \delta(C_j, v) - \frac{1}{2M} \sum_i k_i \delta(C_i, v) \frac{1}{2M} \sum_j k_j \delta(C_j, v) \right]$$

$$= \sum_v [e_{vv} - a_v^2] \qquad (6.9)$$

This implies that one only needs to compute e_{vw}, the percentage of the number of edges between community v and community w over the number of edges of the whole network, and a_v, the percentage of the number of edges with one end-node in community v over the number of edges of the whole network, then one can obtain the network modularity Q.

Here, the quantity a_v^2 has a clear meaning as the expectation value of the percentage of the number of edges in a first-order null model (called configuration model) over the total number of edges of the whole network.

It is noted that formula (6.9) can be equivalently expressed as

$$Q = \sum_{v=1}^{n_c} \left[\frac{l_v}{M} - \left(\frac{d_v}{2M}\right)^2 \right], \qquad (6.10)$$

where n_c is the number of communities, l_v is the number of edges in community v, and d_v is the sum of all node degrees inside community v.

For a given network, different community partitions usually yield different modularity values. Two extreme cases are: (1) considering the whole network as one community, thus the modularity value is zero; (2) considering every node as one community, thus the modularity value is always a negative value (this can be seen from (6.10), where $l_v \equiv 0$ in this case). Note that, between the modularity values and the number of communities in a network, their relation is not proportional. One important measure is the maximum modularity, or the largest possible modularity value of a given network, which is called the maximum cut of the network. It is denoted as Q_{max}, satisfying $0 \leq Q_{max} < 1$. Note also that although a larger-sized network usually has a larger Q_{max} value, which cannot be used as an absolute measure of the quality of the community partition for networks of different sizes, due to the nonlinear nature of Q as can be seen from formula (6.10).

6.2.3   Modularity of Weighted and Directed Networks

The modularity formula (6.8) can be extended to weighted and directed networks. To do so, it suffices to replace the number of edges by the sum of the weights and to replace the node degrees by the node strengths, which leads to

$$Q_w = \frac{1}{2W} \sum_{ij} \left(w_{ij} - \frac{s_i s_j}{2W}\right) \delta(C_i, C_j) = \sum_{c=1}^{n_c} \left[\frac{W_c}{W} - \left(\frac{S_c}{2W}\right)^2 \right], \qquad (6.11)$$

where w_{ij} is the weight value on the edge (i,j), W is the sum of all these weights, s_i is the strength of node i, namely the sum of all weights on the edges that connect to node i, $s_i s_j /(2W)$ is the expectation value of the weight on the edge (i,j) in its corresponding null model, W_c is the sum of all the weights inside community C, and S_c is the sum of all the weights on those edges that have one end-node belonging to community C.

Observe that, in an undirected network with M edges, its adjacency matrix has $2M$ nonzero elements, and its total degree is also $2M$. For a directed network with M edges, however, its adjacency matrix has only M nonzero elements, and its total in- (or out-)degree is also M. Thus, the modularity formula (6.8) for directed networks is modified to be the following:

$$Q_d = \frac{1}{M} \sum_{ij} \left(a_{ij} - \frac{k_i^{out} k_j^{in}}{M} \right) \delta(C_i, C_j), \qquad (6.12)$$

where k_i^{in} and k_i^{out} are the in- and out-degrees of node i, respectively. Note, however, that this straightforward generalization might not always be appropriate [16].

Nevertheless, combining (6.11) and (6.12) gives a general formulation for modularity of weighted and directed networks:

$$Q_{wd} = \frac{1}{W} \sum_{ij} \left(w_{ij} - \frac{s_i^{out} s_j^{in}}{W} \right) \delta(C_i, C_j), \qquad (6.13)$$

where s_i^{in} and s_i^{out} are the in- and out-strengths of node i, respectively.

6.3 Modularity-Based Community Detecting Algorithms

6.3.1 CNM Scheme

As mentioned above, searching for maximum modularity of a large-scale network is NP-hard computationally. Thus, some fast approximate algorithms were developed, such as greedy type of techniques, simulated annealing method, extremal optimization and spectral optimization algorithms, and so on [14].

Here, a greedy-type algorithm – CNM (Clauset-Newman-Moore) scheme [17] – for detecting community structures is introduced. This algorithm has computational complexity of $O(n \log^2 n)$, and is one of the few algorithms that can be used to estimate the maximum modularity of large-scale networks, with up to 10^6 nodes, and its codes are available online [17].

The CNM scheme is as follows:

1. Initialization: Suppose every node in the given network is a community; thus, the initial modularity value is $Q = 0$.
2. Compute:

$$e_{ij} = \begin{cases} 1/(2M) & \text{if } i \text{ and } j \text{ are connected} \\ 0 & \text{otherwise} \end{cases}$$

$$a_i = k_i /(2M)$$

and the incremental matrix of the modularity matrix $[\Delta Q_{ij}]$, with

$$\Delta Q_{ij} = \begin{cases} e_{ij} - a_i a_j & \text{if } i \text{ and } j \text{ are connected} \\ 0 & \text{otherwise} \end{cases}.$$

Then, use the maximum element of its very row to form an array, called the max-heap H.

3. In H, pick the maximum ΔQ_{ij}, and combine the two corresponding communities i and j, labeled the resulting community by j; then, repeat Step 2 to update ΔQ_{ij}, H, and $a = [a_1, \ldots, a_N]$. More precisely,

3.1 replace ΔQ_{ij} by

$$\Delta Q'_{jk} = \begin{cases} \Delta Q_{ik} + \Delta Q_{jk} & \text{if community } k \text{ connects to both } i \text{ and } j \\ \Delta Q_{ik} - 2a_j a_k & \text{if community } k \text{ connects only to } i, \text{ but not } j \\ \Delta Q_{jk} - 2a_i a_k & \text{if coomunity } k \text{ connects to only } j, \text{ but not } i \end{cases}$$

3.2 update the maximum elements in H.

3.3 update vector a as follows:

$$a'_i = 0, a'_{ij} = a_i + a_j$$

The new modularity value is $Q = Q + \Delta Q_{ij}$.

4. Repeat Steps 2 and 3, until all nodes are combined into one community. Then, stop.

Throughout the computational process, there was only one maximum value of Q, $0 \le Q_{max} < 1$. After all elements of the incremental modularity matrix has become negative, Q will continue to decrease monotonically. Therefore, as soon as this happens, the program can be stopped, and the network community structure is obtained at the situation with $Q = Q_{max}$.

As an example, consider Amazon network with 409 687 nodes and 2 464 630 edges at a time [17]. Figure 6.8 shows the node-combining process and the corresponding changes of modularity values, where $Q_{max} = 0.745$, corresponding to a partition of 1684 communities. Notice that the top 10 largest communities already contain 87% of nodes, while the largest one has 114 538 nodes. Figure 6.9 displaces the cumulative distribution of these 1684 communities, showing nearly a power law with exponent 1, which means that the community distribution of the network is nearly a power law with exponent 2.

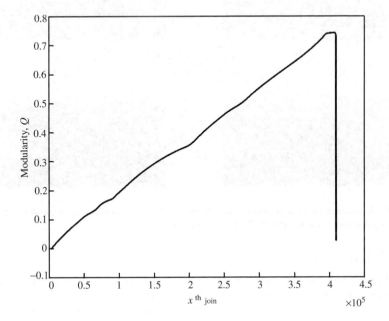

Figure 6.8 Changes of modularity in Amazon network computed by CNM scheme [17]. *Source*: Reprinted with permission from Clauset, A., Newman, M.E.J, and Moore, C. (2004) Finding community structure in very large networks. *Physical Review E*, **70**(6): 066111. Copyright (2004) American Physical Society

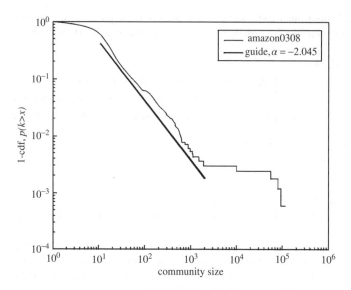

Figure 6.9   Accumulative distribution of communities in Amazon network [17]. *Source*: Reprinted with permission from Clauset, A., Newman, M.E.J, and Moore, C. (2004) Finding community structure in very large networks. *Physical Review E*, **70**(6): 066111. Copyright (2004) American Physical Society

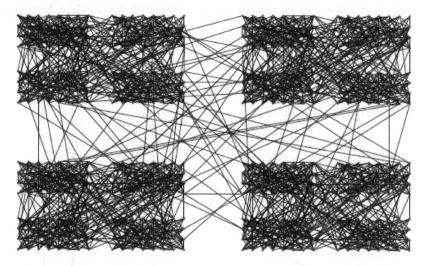

Figure 6.10   Hierarchical structure of a large-scale network [14]. *Source*: Reproduced by permission from Fortunato, S. Community detection in graphs. Physics Reports (2010) Elsevier

6.3.2   BGLL Scheme

Many real large-scale networks have hierarchical structures, and a large community may also contain many smaller communities, as illustrated by Figure 6.10 [14].

To detect the hierarchical structure of a given large-scale network, the BGLL scheme [18] works as follows:

1. Initialization: Suppose every node in the given network is a community; thus, the initial modularity value is $Q = 0$.

2. For every node i, consider all its neighboring nodes and compute the increment of the modularity value of neighboring node j's community C after node i joined into it:

$$\Delta Q = \left[\frac{W_c + s_{i,in}}{2W} - \left(\frac{S_c + s_i}{2W} \right)^2 \right] - \left[\frac{W_c}{2W} - \left(\frac{S_c}{2W} \right)^2 - \left(\frac{s_i}{2W} \right)^2 \right],$$

where $s_{i,in}$ is the weight sum of edges between node i and the nodes in community C.

3. Select the maximum value of all such increments: if this value is positive then move node i into this particular community; otherwise, node i stays in the original community. Repeat this process until no more combination of communities can be done. This yields the first layer of the hierarchy of communities.

4. Construct a new network, whose nodes are the communities obtained in Step 3, where the weight of each edge is the sum of all edge-weights inside the previous two communities. Then, partition the new network following Steps 2 and 3, until the second hierarchy of communities is obtained.

5. When no more higher-level hierarchy can be obtained, stop.

Figure 6.11 shows the partition process of a 15-node network into a community hierarchical structure using the BGLL scheme: the first layer has 4 communities and the second has 2.

Figure 6.12 shows the result of a network of 2 million mobile phone users, where each node represents a community. The sizes of the nodes are proportional to the number of users (but the figure shows only those with at least 100 users). Grey nodes are French-speaking users and white ones are German-speaking, while the others speak both or other languages.

6.3.3   Multi-Slice Community Detection

The concept of modularity can be extended to time-dependent networks, multiplex networks and multi-scale networks. A unified approach is to express such a network as a multi-slice network [19], as

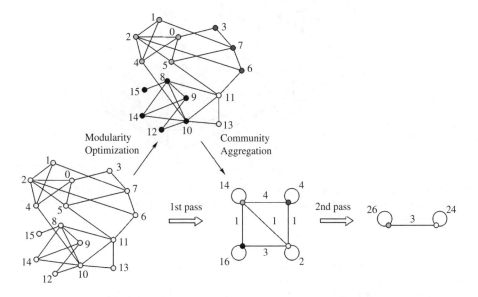

Figure 6.11   Partition of hierarchical structure of a community network [18]. *Source*: Copyright SISSA Medialab Srl. Reproduced by permission of IOP Publishing

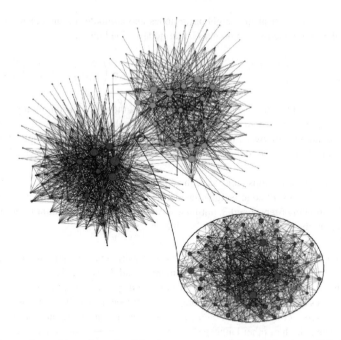

Figure 6.12 Community partition of a real mobile phone-user network by BGLL scheme [18] Copyright SISSA Medialab Srl. Reproduced by permission of IOP Publishing

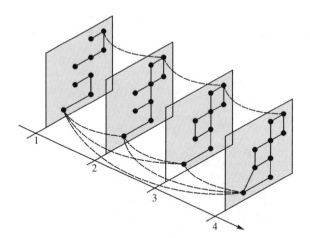

Figure 6.13 Structure of a multi-slice network [19]. *Source*: From Mucha, P.J., Richardson, T., Macon, K. *et al.* (2010) Community structure in time-dependent, multiscale, and multiplex networks. *Science*, **328** (5980): 876–8. Reprinted with permission from AAAS

shown in Figure 6.13, where nodes located on the same slice are connected by solid edges while those in between two slices are connected by dashed edges.

Now, a modularity formula is derived for such weighted multi-slice networks.

Let the edge weight between node i and node j on slice p be $w_{ij,p}$, and the edge weight between node i on slice p and node i on slice q be $w_{i,pq}$. Similarly, one can also define $w_{ij,pq}$ if needed. Moreover, define three strengths for node i on slice p as follows: its strength on slice p is defined by $s_{ip} = \sum_j w_{ij,p}$, its strength between slide p and slice q by $c_{ip} = \sum_q w_{i,pq}$, and its total strength by $w_{ip} = s_{ip} + c_{ip}$. On slice p, the total strength of all nodes is $W_p = \sum_i s_{ip}$ and the total strength on all slices of the whole network is $\Sigma := 2\mu = \sum_{i,p} w_{ip}$. Using these notations, the modularity formula for a weighted multi-slice network is given by

$$Q_{multi-slice} = \frac{1}{2\mu} \sum_{i,j,p,q} \left[\left(w_{ij,p} - \gamma_p \frac{s_{ip} s_{jp}}{2W_p} \right) \delta_{pq} + c_{j,pq} \delta_{ij} \right] \delta(c_{ip}, c_{jq}), \tag{6.14}$$

where γ_p is a control parameter distinguishing the numbers and sizes of the communities on slice p of the network, $\delta_{ij} = 1$ if $i = j$ otherwise $\delta_{ij} = 0$, and $c_{j,pq} = 0$ if there is no connection between slices p and q, otherwise $c_{j,pq} = \omega$ for some value $\omega > 0$.

According to the relations among the slices, the multi-slice networks can be classified into two, as follows.

One is the multi-slice networks in which the slices have ordering, such as a member network in an organization where the members' relationships are changing and evolving with time. As an example, consider the rollcall voting in the USA Senate from the first Congress in 1789 to the 110th in 2008, including 1884 distinct senators [19]. Define the weighted connections between each pair of senators by the similarity between their voting, independently for each two-year Congress. Thus, a multi-slice collection of 110 networks are obtained, with each individual node (senator) coupled to itself when appearing in two consecutive Congresses, which is similar to the dashed edges shown in Figure 6.13. The multi-slice community detection method [19] can uncover some subtle details about the continuity of individual and group voting trends over time, which cannot be captured by the union of the 110 independent partitions of separate Congresses.

Another is the multi-slice networks in which the slices have no ordering, such as a society where people have various relationships that are not in any ordering. As an example, consider a multiplex network of 1640 college students in a northeastern American university who had several relationships [19]: (1) Facebook friendships, (2) picture friendships, (3) roommates, and (4) housing-group preferences. Thus, a network with four slices can be constructed based on the above four types of relationships. The natural inter-slice couplings connect a node (student) in one network slice to itself in each of the other three slices, as shown by the dashed edges of each node on the bottom of Figure 6.13.

Table 6.2 shows the results of the multi-slice partition of the student network, where $\gamma_p = 1$ is fixed. As ω increases, the number of communities in the network decreases. On the right-hand side of the table, the four columns are various percentages of communities to which a node belongs: when $\omega = 0$ there are no connections between any pair of slices; therefore, on different slices, the same node belongs to different communities; as the ω value increases, the probability that nodes located on different slices with the same index belonging to a same community also increases; when $\omega = 1$, all nodes on different slices with the same index belong to a same community.

Table 6.2 Community partition of college students on a multi-slice network [19]

ω	Number of communities	Number of communities a node belongs to (%)			
		1	2	3	4
0.0	1036	0	0	0	100
0.1	122	14.0	40.5	37.3	8.2
0.2	66	19.9	49.1	25.3	5.7
0.3	49	26.2	48.3	21.6	3.9
0.4	36	31.8	47.0	18.4	2.8
0.5	31	39.3	42.4	16.8	1.5
1.0	16	100	0	0	0

6.3.4 Detecting Spatial Community Structures

Many real networks are embedded into the Euclidean space, such as the Internet and various online social networks and transportation networks.

To study the influence of spatial node-edge distributions on network topological and dynamical properties, first recall the modularity formula (6.7), where p_{ij} is the expectation value for the edge number between node i and node j in the null model with the same node-degree sequence as the given network, satisfying

$$p_{ij} = \frac{k_i k_j}{2M}. \tag{6.15}$$

Now, taking into account the effect of space, the above formula is modified to [20]

$$p_{ij}^{spa} = N_i N_j f(d_{ij}), \tag{6.16}$$

where N_i indicates the importance of node i and d_{ij} is the physical distance between node i and node j. Assuming that the edge-weight value is invariant with respect to the distance (length of the edge), one has

$$\sum_{i,j|d_{ij}=d} p_{ij}^{spa} = \sum_{i,j|d_{ij}=d} a_{ij}.$$

Consequently,

$$f(d) = \frac{\sum_{i,j|d_{ij}=d} a_{ij}}{\sum_{i,j|d_{ij}=d} N_i N_j}. \tag{6.17}$$

For distinction, in the following, the modularity based on (6.15) will be denoted as Q_{NG} which was suggested by Newman and Girvan [13], while that based on (6.16) will be denoted by Q_{spa}.

As an example, consider a mobile-phone network of 571 towns in Belgium [21]. Figure 6.14 (upper panel) shows the results of community partition obtained by using Q_{NG}, which contains 19 communities. Figure 6.14 (lower panel) shows the results obtained based on Q_{spa}, which has 31 communities. In these two figures, the importance value N_i of a town is defined to be the number of users therein, which is proportional to the size of the node (town) shown in the figures. In Belgium, people speak two major languages: French and Flemish. It can be seen that the community partition based on Q_{spa} well reflects this languages distribution: in the lower panel the light grey and dark grey colored nodes represent these two languages, respectively, and they cover 75% of the total number of towns in Belgium.

6.4 Other Community Partitioning Schemes

6.4.1 Limitations of the Modularity Measure

For a given network, its maximum modularity satisfies $0 \leq Q_{max} < 1$, as discussed at the end of Section 6.2.2. If one considers the whole network as a single community, then $Q_{max} = 0$. However, $Q_{max} > 0$ does not necessarily mean that the network has a clear community structure, because a randomly generated network will satisfy $Q_{max} > 0$ in general. So, a natural question to ask is, for example, if you have a real network with $Q_{max} = 0.45$, what can you say about its community structure, prominent or not? One reasonable approach to answering this question is to compare it with a suitable randomized network model. Usually, one can generate many randomized networks with the same sequence of node degrees, using for instance a random rewiring method, and then compute the mean (denoted by $\langle Q \rangle_{NM}$) and variance (denoted by δ_Q^{NM}) of the modularity values of these networks. Based on that, one can further compute the so-called z-value of the maximum modularity Q_{max} of the given network:

$$z_Q = \frac{Q_{max} - \langle Q \rangle_{NM}}{\delta_Q^{NM}}. \tag{6.18}$$

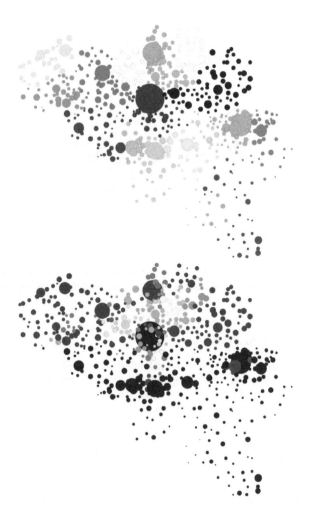

Figure 6.14 Community partition of the mobile-phone network in Belgium [21]. *Source*: Reprinted with permission from Expert, P., Evans, T.S., Blondel *et al.* (2011) Uncovering space-independent communities in spatial networks. *Proceedings of the National Academy of Sciences USA*, **108**(19): 7663–8. Copyright (2002) National Academy of Sciences, USA

This z-value quantifies statistically the significance of the modularity: if $z_Q > 0$, then one concludes that the given network has a community structure, and the bigger this value, the more prominent the community structure.

Note, however, that this measure also has its limitations and sometimes can yield wrong results: there are real datasets showing that some networks, being commonly recognized as having nonprominent community structures, can have large z_Q values, while some other networks, being commonly recognized as having prominent community structures, have small z_Q values.

More importantly, a concerned issue is the limitation in the resolution of modularity [22]: it is very difficult or even impossible to identify small-sized communities in a large network. For example, consider Figure 6.15, where each node labeled K_m is a clique (fully connected subgraph) composing of m nodes. If there are n_c such cliques, then intuitively the best partition of the network is to classify every such clique as a community especially when $m \gg 1$. However, if n_c is sufficiently large, by connecting two neighboring cliques into one community as shown by dashed circles in the figure will make the resulting

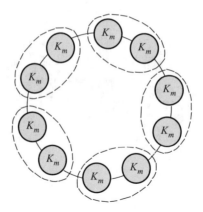

Figure 6.15   Limitation in the resolution of modularity of a network

modularity value even bigger! The main problem is that it is impossible to determine beforehand the sizes and the distribution of all actual communities in a real network; therefore, it is impossible to identify the true resolution of the network modularity.

6.4.2   Clique Percolation Scheme

In all the above-discussed algorithms, every node can be clearly classified into one community. In real networks, however, communities often have overlapping nodes which belong to more than one community.

In Figure 6.16 (a), the center node belongs to 4 different communities, and there are many such nodes in Figure 6.16 (b). The so-called clique percolation (CP) scheme with software CFinder1 [23, 24] was designed to partition such networks.

6.4.2.1 k-Clique Community Structure

A k-clique is a fully connected subgraph of k nodes. Two k-cliques are said to be adjacent if they share $k - 1$ nodes. A k-clique community is defined as the union of all k-cliques that can be reached from each

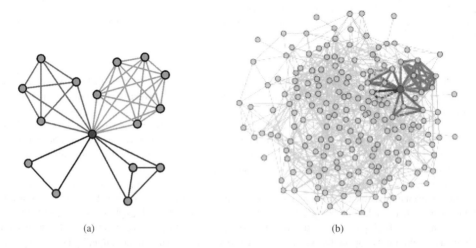

(a)   (b)

Figure 6.16   Networks with overlapping nodes in community partition: (a) center node belongs to 4 different communities; (b) many such nodes

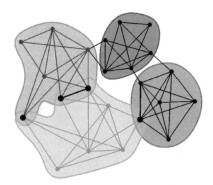

Figure 6.17   A network with overlapping 4-cliques

other through a series of adjacent k-cliques. Two k-cliques are k-clique connected if they are parts of a k-clique chain which is defined as the union of a sequence of adjacent k-cliques. For example, a 3-clique community in a network is given by the union of triangles that can be reached from one to another through a series of shared edges.

In a network, a single node can belong to several communities. Figure 6.17 shows an example of overlapping 4-clique communities, where the light-grey community has three and one overlapping node with the mid-grey community and a dark-grey community, respectively.

6.4.2.2   Searching for Cliques on a Network

The CP scheme searches cliques in a given network iteratively.

First, it is possible to find a largest possible clique, with size s, based on the information of the node-degree sequence from the given network. Thus, starting from any node in the given network, search for all possible s-cliques that contain this initial node. If no such s-clique is found then move to another node; if there are some such s-clique(s) then remove this initial node and all its adjacent edges (this can avoid finding the same clique again later on). Then, move to another node and repeat the above process, until no more nodes are left in the network. This iteration finds all s-cliques from the network. Next, repeat the above process to find all $(s-1)$-cliques, then all $(s-2)$-cliques, and so on.

In the CP scheme, the key step is to find all s-cliques starting from an initial node v. To do so, define two sets of nodes in the network, A and B, where A is the set of all connected pairs of nodes including node v and B is the set of nodes that are connected to all the nodes in A. To avoid repeatedly choosing a same node, list all nodes in A and B in the ordering that corresponds to the node indexes. Briefly, the scheme is designed as follows:

> Initialization: Let $A = \{v\}$, $B = \{$neighbors of $v\}$;

Step 1: Move one node from B to A, and then delete all those nodes from B that are no longer connected to all nodes in A.

Step 2: If B becomes empty before A reaches size s, or if both A and B have become subsets of an already found (larger) clique in the network, then stop and return to the previous step; otherwise, whenever the size of A reaches s, a new clique is found. After recording this clique, return to the previous step and then continue to search for new cliques that contain v.

6.4.2.3   Searching for k-Clique Communities

After finding all cliques, a clique–clique overlapping matrix can be obtained. Similar to the adjacency matrix of a network, this overlapping matrix is a symmetrical square matrix, in which every row (column) corresponds to one clique, and every diagonal element describes the size of the corresponding clique (i.e.,

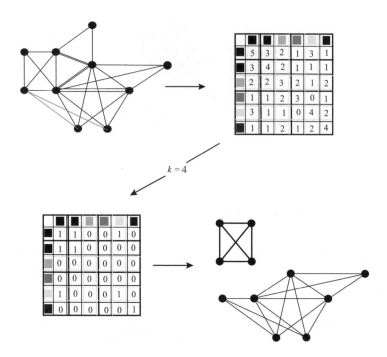

Figure 6.18 Searching for a community of 4-cliques [23]. *Source*: Reprinted by permission from Macmillan Publishers Ltd: [Nature] (Palla, G., Derenyi, I., Farkas, I. and Vicsek, T. (2005) Uncovering the overlapping community structure of complex networks in nature and society. *Nature*, **435** (7043): 814–18), copyright (2005)

the number of nodes in that clique), while each nondiagonal element indicates the number of overlapping nodes between two corresponding cliques. In this overlapping matrix of cliques, by setting those diagonal elements that are less than k to be 0 and also those nondiagonal elements that are less than $k - 1$ to be 0, respectively, the adjacency matrix for the community of the corresponding k-cliques can be obtained, in which every connected portion represents a k-clique.

Figure 6.18 shows an example of searching for 4-clique communities, where the upper-left panel is the given network, upper-right panel is its overlapping matrix, lower-left panel is the adjacency matrix of the 4-clique, and the lower-right panel shows two 4-clique communities.

Many real networks are evolving in time, so are their community structures. Specifically, both the number and sizes of communities in a network may change in time, thus small communities may be combined together to become large and likewise a large community may be split into a few smaller ones, as shown in Figure 6.19.

By applying the CP scheme to detect the community structures of a scientists' cooperation network and a mobile-phone users' network, it was found [24] that the changes in a larger community will maintain the community for a longer time, while members in a smaller community would try to keep unchanged so as to maintain the stability of the community.

6.4.3 Edge-Based Community Detection Scheme

A sensible idea to partition a network is based on the edges rather than the nodes [25], since many communities are connected through massive edges where the role of nodes is not as important. One advantage of using edges is that every edge belongs to one and only one particular community, but a node may belong to different communities defined by different categories such as organizations, families,

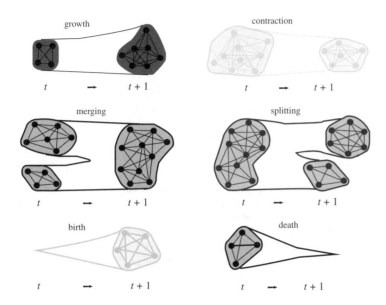

Figure 6.19 Evolution of community structures [24]. *Source*: Reprinted by permission from Macmillan Publishers Ltd: [Nature] (Palla, G., Barabási, A-L. and Vicsek, T. (2007) Quantifying social group evolution. *Nature*, **446** (7136): 664–7), copyright (2007)

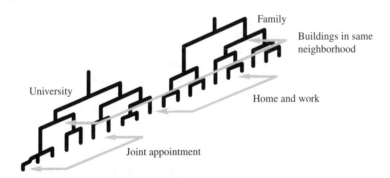

Figure 6.20 A tree with a hierarchical community structure [25]. *Source*: Reprinted by permission from Macmillan Publishers Ltd: [Nature] (Ahn, Y-Y., Bagrow, J.P. and Lehmann, S. (2010) Link communities reveal multiscale complexity in networks. *Nature*, **466** (7307): 761–4.), copyright (2010)

colleagues or friends. Based on edges to partition networks, less confusion will arise and communities can be classified through suitable thresholds.

Consider a tree network, for instance. If every leave represents a node then a tree cannot reflect the hierarchical structure of a complex network, as illustrated by Figure 6.20. For this example, however, if every leave represents an edge then each branch can be classified as a community. Since each edge in this edge-based tree is uniquely determined, it belongs to one and only one community. Moreover, since a node can be connected to several edges, if these edges belong to different communities then this node naturally belong to all of these various communities. This representation of a network effectively solves the node-overlapping problem in community partitions. Furthermore, partitioning a network according to different predefined threshold values can clearly detect the hierarchical structure of a tree.

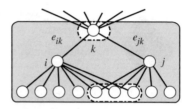

Figure 6.21   Similarity of two edges

Edge-based community detection scheme combines similar edges into the same community. In so doing, the so-called similarity needs to be precisely defined and quantified. To do so, initially every edge is considered as a community in the given network. To combine two edges into a new community, it is necessary that these two edges are connected with a common node. Notice that the similarity $S(e_{ik}, e_{jk})$ between two edges, e_{ik} and e_{jk}, which shares a common node k, can be measured in different ways. One common measure is to use the number of their common neighbors:

$$S(e_{ik}, e_{jk}) = \frac{|n_+(i) \cap n_+(j)|}{|n_+(i) \cup n_+(j)|}, \tag{6.19}$$

where $n_+(i)$ is the set of node i along with all its neighbors. For example, in Figure 6.21, the edge similarity is $S(e_{ik}, e_{jk}) = 4/12 = 1/3$.

According to the above definition of edge similarity, one can use a multilevel clustering method to detect the community structure of a given network, as follows:

0. Initialization: Each edge is a community.
1. Compute the similarity for every connected edge pair (with at least one common node), and arrange all such edge pairs in the decreasing order of their similarity values.
2. Following the order of the above arrangement, the pairs of edges with the largest similarity value are chosen and their respective communities are merged. Record the result as a tree (called partition tree).
3. Pairs of the same similarity values are grouped into to the same clique (or called tier). Then, cliques are agglomerated simultaneously.
4. This process is repeated until all edges belong to a single community.

Figure 6.22 shows a simple network with 9 nodes, its community partition, its edge partition tree and the similarity matrix (the darker the color, the closer the similarity). Figure 6.22 (a) indicates the nodes in the same community using the same color, where Node 4 belongs to different communities therefore its color is mixed; Figure 6.22 (b) indicates the edges in the same community using the same grey level of color.

In the above multilevel clustering process, the similarity value at which two communities merge is called the strength of the merged community, which corresponds to the high of the branch in the tree shown in Figure 6.22 (c).

To obtain the best result of the community structure, it amounts to determining the best position of the edge partition tree, namely, determining when to stop during the community merging process. For this purpose, define a natural cost function based on the edge density inside a community, D, called the partition density, as follows.

Suppose that a network with M edges are partitioned into C communities, $\{P_1, \dots, P_c\}$, where community P_c contains m_c edges and n_c nodes. A normalized density of this community is defined by

$$D_c = \frac{m_c - (n_c - 1)}{[n_c(n_c - 1)/2] - (n_c - 1)}, \tag{6.20}$$

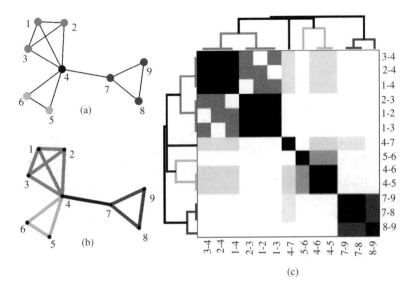

Figure 6.22 Detecting the community structure of a simple network [25]: (a) nodes in same community using same color; where Node 4 belongs to different communities, color is mixed; (b) edges in same community using same grey level of color; (c) the strength of the merged community

where $n_c - 1$ is the minimum number of edges needed to connect the n_c nodes together inside the community, while $n_c(n_c - 1)/2$ is the maximum number of possible edges therein. Here, if $n_c = 2$ then define $D_c = 0$. The partition density of the whole network is then defined as

$$D = \frac{1}{M} \sum_c m_c D_c = \frac{2}{M} \sum_c m_c \frac{m_c - (n_c - 1)}{(n_c - 1)(n_c - 2)}. \tag{6.21}$$

Note that every term in the summation of this formula corresponds to an edge within the same community, which avoid the above-mentioned limitation of modularity resolution. By computing the partition density of every level of the edge partition tree, or by directly optimizing the partition density, one can obtain the best partition of community structure of the given network.

Note also that the maximum value of D is 1, which corresponds to a network with all fully connected cliques, and $D = 0$ when every community is a tree. If an edge community is less dense than a tree (e.g., when it has disconnected components), then that community will give a negative contribution to D, so $D < 0$ is possible. Indeed, the minimum value of D is $-2/3$, for a community with only two disconnected edges.

Figure 6.23 shows a community partition of a relationship network among all the main characters in Victor Hugo's novel *Les Misérables*, where an edge means that the two end-nodes (characters) appear in the same chapter. The lower panel in the figure shows the edge partition tree and the corresponding partition density, calculated based on edge similarity values obtained during the community merging process, where the vertical axis is the edge similarity and the right-hand curve presents the partition density values, while the dashed partition corresponds to the optimal (maximum) partition density.

One advantage of using edge tree representation is that it can detect meaningful community structures not only according to the maximum partition density but also according to an appropriate level of the partition tree, which reveals the hierarchical structure of the community partition of the network [25].

Figure 6.24 shows the detected community structure of a word-network with central word "Newton," obtained based on partition density optimization. In this figure, the edges between various communities are marked by using different colors. It correctly identified subcommunity "clever, wit" from the community "smart/intellect." It should be noted that, although the edges connecting the words "Newton" and

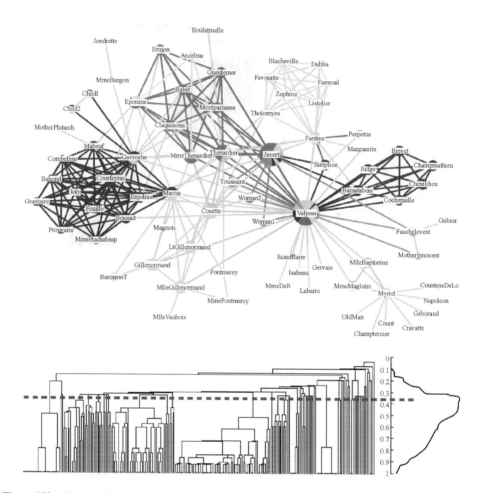

Figure 6.23 Merging process and the corresponding partition density values [13]. *Source*: Reproduced by permission from Newman, M.E.J. and Girvan, M. Finding and evaluating community structure in networks. *Physical Review E* (2004) American Physical Society

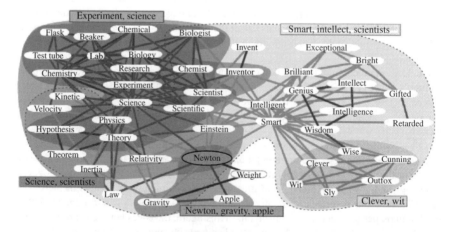

Figure 6.24 Community structure of a word-Newton network [25]. *Source*: Reproduced with permission from Ahn, Y-Y., Bagrow, J.P. and Lehmann, S. Link communities reveal multiscale complexity in networks. Nature (2010) Macmillan Pub. Ltd.

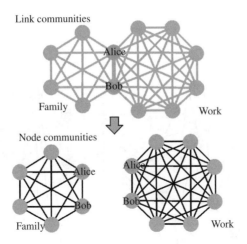

Figure 6.25 Re-viewing an edge community as a node community reveals multi-relationships between two nodes [25]. *Source*: Reproduced with permission from Ahn, Y-Y., Bagrow, J.P. and Lehmann, S. Link communities reveal multiscale complexity in networks. Nature (2010) Macmillan Pub. Ltd.

"Gravity" belong to the same community, these two words belong to three different node communities named "smart/intellect," "weight" and "apple."

In general, after obtaining an edge community partition, by reexamining it as a node community, one can further identify the overlapping nodes in the community partition. Even if the two end-nodes of an edge belong to two different communities, one can identify the multiple meanings of the edge despite the fact that one edge belongs to only one edge community.

Figure 6.25 shows one simple such example. Alice and Bob are wife and husband at home, but they are also partners at work. In edge community partition, they are naturally grouped into the family community. However, by re-viewing the edge community partition to be in the node community partition, it is clear that they are also partners at work. This successfully detects the multiple relationships between the two nodes in a same network.

6.4.4   Evaluation Criteria for Community Detection Algorithms

6.4.4.1   Benchmark Graph Method

When an algorithm is applied to detect the community structure of a real-world network, its quality is judged by two basic requirements:

1. Performance (i.e., quality of detection): whether or not the algorithm can correctly detect the real community structure of the given network.
2. Computational time (i.e., computational complexity): whether or not the algorithm can provide the expected result within acceptable time limit.

So far, computational complexity is studied on a case-by-case basis, but there is no general guideline for general community detection algorithms. One reasonable approach is to apply the concerned algorithm to a benchmark graph model, to see how well it works, with the expectation that a good algorithm should be good at least for the benchmark model.

A commonly-used benchmark model is Zachary's karate club network. In 1970–72, W.W. Zachary investigated the karate club of a university in USA to observe the relationship of their members, thereby constructing a network with 34 nodes and 78 edges where a node is a member of the club and an edge

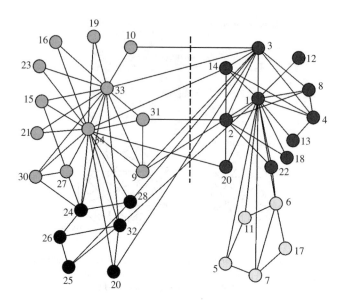

Figure 6.26 Zachary's karate club network [Internet]

indicates the two connected nodes also get together in other activities outside the karate club. Zachary found that the manager John (Node 34) and coach Hi (Node 1) had a conflict due to their disagreement on the tuition fees. Hi wished to raise the fee since he believed that, as the coach, he had the right to do so. However, John wished to maintain the stability in fee charges since he felt he had the responsibility to do so as manager. As the conflict became more serious, John fired Hi from the club. However, Hi's supporters resigned from the club and formed a new one led by Hi. As a result, the club was split into two, centered at John (Node 34) and Hi (Node 1), respectively. This is depicted by the vertical dashed line in Figure 6.26. Clearly, when applied to this example, a good algorithm should be able to distinguish these two communities.

Observe that Node 3 and Node 9 overlap the two communities, namely they both have connections to two different communities. Some algorithms would classify them as common nodes of the two communities. The fact is that Node 9 was only a weak supporter of John, and he join Hi's club after the split. Of course, classifying him as a common member of the two separated clubs is quite reasonable.

Zachary's club is quite small in size after all. Being able to partition it well is only necessary for an algorithm to be considered as a good scheme, but still far from being sufficient. Thus, to find large-scale meaningful benchmark models, one has to resort to some artificially constructed network models.

Recently, a planted l-partition model becomes popular to use, which is constructed as follows. The network has $N = g \cdot l$ nodes, distributed in l groups each having g nodes. Two nodes within the same group are connected with probability p_{in}, while two nodes in two different groups are connected with probability p_{out}. This means that every group is an ER random graph, and the average degree of the network is then given by

$$\langle k \rangle = p_{in}(g - 1) + p_{out}(l - 1).$$

If $p_{in} - p_{out} > 0$, then the density within each groups is higher than that between two different groups, implying that the network has a community structure. Furthermore, the larger the $p_{in} - p_{out} > 0$, the more prominent the community structure.

As an example, consider the following parameter set: $l = 4$, $g = 32$, $\langle k \rangle = 6$, so that $N = 128$ and $p_{in} + 3p_{out} \approx 0.5$. These yield the inner average degree $z_{in} = p_{in}(g - 1) = 31p_{in}$ and outer average degree $z_{out} = p_{out}g(l - 1) = 96p_{out}$ with respect to the groups. Figures 6.27 (a)–(c) show this benchmark model,

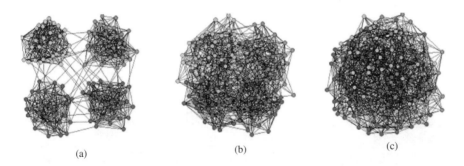

Figure 6.27   Benchmark model with three sets of inner parameter values [35]: (a) $z_{in} = 15$; (b) $z_{in} = 11$; (c) $z_{in} = 8$. *Source*: Reproduced with permission from Guimerà, R. and Amaral, L.A.N. Functional cartography of complex metabolic networks. Nature (2005) Macmillan Pub. Ltd.

with $z_{in} = 15$, 11 and 8, respectively. A good algorithm should be able to detect the community structure accurately for network (a) and relatively accurately for (b).

Although simple, the above benchmark model differs significantly from the real-work networks. For example, a real network usually has nonuniform degree distribution, with many triangular motifs, etc., but the benchmark model shows quite the opposite. To improve or to avoid such defects, some other benchmark models have also been proposed and discussed [14].

6.4.4.2   Metadata Method

In many real networks, usually the description of a node not only shows the basic structural data but also provides some other related information such as the node function and its similarity to other nodes. For instance, when someone is doing Internet shopping, the relevant website will inform them about the sale history of the product which they are interested in, show them some information about other consumers of the same product, and even recommend some other related products for his consideration. In addition, the website may also provide them with such information as classification of products and the tags of the products, etc., which are referred to as metadata. For such a commercial application, one can construct a network based on the following rule: if two products are purchased together, then connect them by an edge.

Figure 6.28 shows a webpage of amazon.com about books, where the right-bottom block shows the similarity between two books while the right-top block shows a book which may belong to different categories (communities).

To quantitatively evaluate and compare the performances of various community detection algorithms, the following four measures (see Figure 6.29) may be considered:

1. **Community quality**: Based on the intuition that similar nodes should share more metadata, the enrichment of two similar nodes is defined as

$$\frac{\langle \mu(i,j) \rangle_{i,j \ in \ same \ community}}{\langle \mu(i,j) \rangle_{i,j \ in \ whole \ network}},$$

where $\mu(i,j)$ is the similarity value between node i and node j based on metadata, which may be defined differently for different networks. Roughly, the enrichment is the average metadata-based average similarity of all node pairs within a community: the large the enrichment value, the closer the nodes in the community.

2. **Overlap quality**: For each node i in a network, define a value based on the available metadata set, as the number of the real communities in the network to which node i belongs. For example, in a word

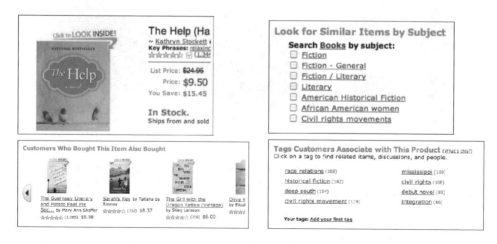

Figure 6.28   Webpage of amazon.com about a book [Internet]

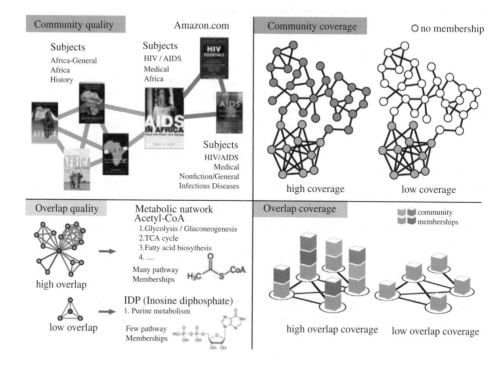

Figure 6.29   Four measures for comparing community detection algorithms [Internet]

association network, every community corresponds to a group of words that associate with a same topic. If a word has more meanings, it is expected to have more associated topics and therefore belongs to more communities. As another example, in a metabolism network, the number of reaction pathways that a metabolite participates in corresponds to the number of communities (contexts or roles) of this metabolite. Thus, the mutual information can be used to relate the number of communities and the overlapping metadata, which indicates how much information about the true overlap of a node is gained by knowing or learning the number of communities that a particular method has assigned to the node.

3. **Community coverage**: To count the fraction of nodes that belong to at least one community having three (or more) nodes, where three is the smallest nontrivial community size.

4. **Overlap coverage**: To count the average number of nontrivial communities to which each node belongs. Two different algorithms may yield the same overlap coverage, but one method may extract more information than the other, by finding many more densely overlapping communities. Note, however, that for nonoverlapping community methods, their coverage measures will be the same.

The above four measures can be normalized, so that each has maximum value 1 and minimum value 0. The sum of these four normalized values can then be used as a single unified measure, called composite performance index, for measuring and comparing the performances of different algorithms. Based on this measure, it was shown in [25], by testing on 11 real-world networks, that the edge-based community partition method introduced above via optimizing the partition density is better than other algorithms.

6.5   Some Recent Progress

Finally in this chapter, some recent progress in the research on community detection methods and algorithms is briefly discussed.

Recently, some techniques for robust detection of community structures in some classes of time-dependent networks were proposed, by using statistical null models to facilitate the principled identification of structural modules in semi-decomposable systems [36]. As introduced above, null models can be used to statistically validate various identified community structures. However, how sensitive are such methods to the model parameters and how comparisons to null models can help identify system scales remain to be concerned. In [36], the variances of network diagnostics over optimizations and over randomizations of network structures were quantified and analyzed, where a method to construct representative partitions was suggested from a null model approach.

It should be pointed out that other than the methods and approaches discussed above in this chapter, there are other techniques for community detection and graph partitioning, such as spectral methods, which can also produce efficient community detection algorithms [37].

More information about the theory, methods and applications of community partition can be found in, for example, the survey papers [14, 28, 34, 38].

References

[1] Amaral, L.A.N. and Guimera, R. (2006) Complex networks: Lies, damned lies and statistics. *Nature Physics*, **2**: 75–6.

[2] Maslov, S. and Sneppen, K. (2002) Specificity and stability in topology of protein networks. *Science*, **296**(5569): 910–13.

[3] Newman, M.E.J. (2002) Assortative mixing in networks. *Physics Review Letters*, **89**(20): 208701.

[4] Maslov, S. (2007) Complex networks: Role model for modules. *Nature Physics*, **3**(1): 18–19.

[5] Ugander, J., Karrer, B. and Backstrom, L. *et al.* (2011) The anatomy of the Facebook social graph. http://arxiv.org/abs/1111.4503 (last accessed August 10, 2014).

[6] Backstrom, L., Boldi, P., Rosa, M. *et al.* (2011) Four degrees of separation. http://arxiv.org/abs/1111.4570 (last accessed August 10, 2014).

[7] Feld, S (1991) Why your friends have more friends than you do. *American Journal of Sociology*, **96**(6): 1464–77.

[8] Hu, H. and Wang, X. (2009) Evolution of a large online social network. *Physics Letters A*, **373**(12–13): 1105–10.

[9] McPherson, M., Smith-Lovin, L. and Cook, J.M. (2001) Birds of a feather: Homophily in social networks. *Annual Review of Sociology*, **27**(1): 415–44.

[10] Race, M.J. (2001) School integration, and friendship segregation in America. *American Journal of Sociology*, **107**(3): 679–716.

[11] Snijders, T.A.B., van de Bunt, G. and Steglich, C.E.G. (2010) Introduction to stochastic actor-based models for network dynamics. *Social Networks*, **32**(1): 44–60.

[12] Lewis, K., Gonzalez, M. and Kaufman, J. (2012) Social selection and peer influence in an online social network. *Proceedings of the National Academy of Sciences USA*, **109**(1): 68–72.

[13] Newman, M.E.J. and Girvan, M. (2004) Finding and evaluating community structure in networks. *Physical Review E*, **69**(2): 026113.

[14] Fortunato, S. (2010) Community detection in graphs. *Physics Reports*, **486**(3–5): 75–174.

[15] Jonsson, P.F., Cavanna, T., Zicha, D. and Bates, P.A. (2006) Cluster analysis of networks generated through homology: Automatic identification of important protein communities involved in cancer metastasis. *BMC Bioinformatics*, **7**: 10.1186/1471-2105-7-2.

[16] Arabidopsis Interactome Mapping Consortium (2011) Evidence for network evolution in an Arabidopsis interactome map, *Science*, **333**(6042): 601–7.

[17] Clauset, A., Newman, M.E.J, and Moore, C. (2004) Finding community structure in very large networks. *Physical Review E*, **70**(6): 066111. Codes for downloading: http://cs.unm.edu/~aaron/research/fastmodularity.htm (last accessed August 10, 2014).

[18] Blondel, V.D., Guillaume, J. L., Lambiotte, R. and Lefebvre, E. (2008) Fast unfolding of community hierarchies in large networks. *Journal of Statistical Mechanics*, **10**: 10008.

[19] Mucha, P.J., Richardson, T., Macon, K. *et al.* (2010) Community structure in time-dependent, multiscale, and multiplex networks. *Science*, **328**(5980): 876–8.

[20] Barthelemy, M. (2010) Spatial networks. *Physics Reports*, **499**(13): 1–101.

[21] Expert, P., Evans, T.S., Blondel *et al.* (2011) Uncovering space-independent communities in spatial networks. *Proceedings of the National Academy of Sciences USA*, **108**(19): 7663–8.

[22] Fortunato, S. and Barthélemy, M. (2007) Resolution limit in community detection. *Proceedings of the National Academy of Sciences USA*, **104**(1): 36–41.

[23] Palla, G., Derenyi, I., Farkas, I. and Vicsek, T. (2005) Uncovering the overlapping community structure of complex networks in nature and society. *Nature*, **435**(7043): 814–18.

[24] Palla, G., Barabási, A-L. and Vicsek, T. (2007) Quantifying social group evolution. *Nature*, **446**(7136): 664–7.

[25] Ahn, Y-Y., Bagrow, J.P. and Lehmann, S. (2010) Link communities reveal multiscale complexity in networks. *Nature*, **466**(7307): 761–4.

[26] Zachary, W.W. (1977) An information flow model for conflict and fission in small groups. *Journal of Anthropological Research*, **33**: 452–73.

[27] Newman, M.E.J. (2012) Communities, modules and large-scale structure in networks. *Nature Physics*, **8**(1): 25–31.

[28] Coscia, M., Giannotti, F. and Pedreschi, D. (2011) A classification for community discovery methods in complex networks. *Statistical Analysis and Data Mining*, **4**(5): 512–46.

[29] Karrer, B. and Newman, M.E.J. (2011) Stochastic block models and community structure in networks. *Physical Review E*, **83**(1): 016107.

[30] Guimerà, R. and Sales-Pardo, M. (2009) Missing and spurious interactions and the reconstruction of complex networks. *Proceedings of the National Academy of Sciences USA*, **106**(52): 22073–8.

[31] Clauset, A., Moore, C. and Newman, M.E.J. (2008) Hierarchical structure and the prediction of missing links in networks. *Nature*, **453**(7191): 98–101.

[32] Wang, F., Li, T., Wang, X. *et al.* (2011) Community discovery using nonnegative matrix factorization. *Data Mining and Knowledge Discovery*, **22**(3): 493–521.

[33] Chen, Y., Wang. X., Shi, C. *et al.* (2011) Phoenix: A weight-based network coordinate system using matrix factorization. *IEEE Transactions Network and Service Management*, **8**(4): 334–47.

[34] Newman, M.E.J. (2012) Communities, modules and large-scale structure in networks. *Nature Physics*, **8**(1): 25–31.

[35] Guimerà, R. and Amaral, L.A.N. (2005) Functional cartography of complex metabolic networks. *Nature*, **433**: 895–900.

[36] Bassett, D.S., Porter, M.A., Wymbs, N.F. *et al.* (2013) Robust detection of dynamic community structure in networks. *Chaos*, **23**: 013142.

[37] Newman, M.E.J. (2013) Spectral community detection in spare networks. arXiv:1308.6494v1.

[38] Newman, M.E.J. (2011) Communities, modules and large-scale structure in networks. *Nature Physics*, **8**: 25–31.

7

Network Games

7.1 Introduction

Cooperation, which means individuals working together, is ubiquitous in nature and human society. For example, genes cooperate in genomes and bees cooperate in colonies. Humans, in particular, work side by side or help each other to achieve goals together in many different ways: for instance, when facing natural disasters, such as floods and earthquakes, people group together to survive. In fact, there were evidences showing that cooperation leads to the start of life on earth.

Throughout a cooperation process, on the one hand, there is one kind of individual, a cooperator (C), who pays a cost to help the others; on the other hand, there is another type of individual, a defector (D), who tries to gain benefit without providing help to the others. As a result, an individual may tend to choose defection to maximize its payoff and to avoid paying a cost of cooperation, although a group of cooperators should bring higher social welfare than that of defectors. In such a situation, clearly there exists a conflict of interest between an individual and the group, resulting in a social dilemma. Hence, understanding the emergence and evolution of cooperation is a challenging problem, which has drawn much attention from various disciplines today.

Game theory, which originated from understanding the behaviors of individuals playing parlor games like poker and chess, provides a unified and powerful framework for studying and analyzing decision making in cases of social dilemma. Through game theory, economists analyze how people make choices about money; biologists explain the origin of altruism; anthropologist disclose the diversity of human nature; neuroscientists reveal how individuals' strategies influence others' emotions and behaviors. A game usually consists of a set of individuals, the players, who can choose one from a set of strategies, e.g., cooperation or defection. Through interacting with the others, an individual will obtain payoff that can also be seen as its fitness.

Game Theory was invented by von Neumann and Morgenstern [1], when they planned to build a mathematical theory to investigate human decisions. Lately, Nash [2] proposed a simple but important concept in game theory, referred to as the *Nash equilibrium* today, which characterizes a state that no individual can increase his payoff by changing his own strategy unilaterally. In order to characterize the social dilemma and explain the interactions of conflicts among egoistic individuals, many significant and interesting game-theoretic models had been proposed thereafter, among which Prisoner's Dilemma game is one of the most well-known models that are commonly used today.

Consider a scenario where two thieves had committed a joint crime. One day, they are arrested by police. But the police have no sufficient evidence to punish them. Thus, the thieves have two choices: confess the crime and become a witness, or reject the charge of crime. In this situation, if both thieves refuse to talk to the police, they are considered as cooperators and will be put in jail for 2 year only.

Fundamentals of Complex Networks: Models, Structures and Dynamics, First Edition.
Guanrong Chen, Xiaofan Wang, Xiang Li.
© Higher Education Press. All rights reserved. Published 2015 by John Wiley & Sons Singapore Pte Ltd.
Companion Website: www.wiley.com/go/chen/complex

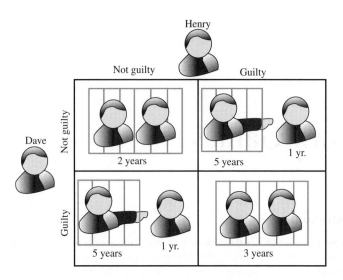

Figure 7.1   The payoff matrix of Prisoner's Dilemma game [investopedia.com]. *Source*: Reprinted by permission from Macmillan Publishers Ltd: [Nature] (Nowak, M.A. and May, R. (1992) Evolutionary games and spatial chaos. *Nature*, **359**: 826–9), copyright (1992)

But, if every thief confesses thereby becoming a witness, both of them are considered as defectors and will be put in jail for 3 years instead. Moreover, if one confesses but the other does not talk, the former is a cooperator and will be jailed for 5 years and yet the latter as a defector will stay in jail for only 1 year because the police has no reason to further punish him. The interactions between these two thieves, as shown in Figure 7.1, can be described by a *payoff matrix*:

$$\text{player 1} \begin{array}{c} \\ \text{C} \\ \text{D} \end{array} \overbrace{\begin{bmatrix} R & S \\ T & P \end{bmatrix}}^{\text{player 2}} \quad \text{C} \quad \text{D} \tag{7.1}$$

The element in the payoff matrix means the payoff of player 1 when he meets player 2. Specifically, if both of them are cooperators, player 1 can gain a reward, R, for mutual cooperation, but if both of them are defectors, then he will get a punishment, P, for mutual defection. However, if he chooses cooperation while his opponent defects him, he will receive sucker's payoff, S, but his opponent will gain a temptation to defect, T. In the situation discussed above, $R = -2, P = -3$ and $T = -1$.

   Given the above game rules, what should the two thieves do if they know the payoff matrix?

   Game theory provides a perspective that an individual should think over his behavior by standing at his opponent's side. The strategy can be analyzed as follows: assuming that the opponent will cooperate with you, you have the choice of cooperation or defection, for which you will receive −2 or −1, respectively. It is clear that the best choice for you would be to choose defection. Similarly, if your opponent is a defector, you can get −5 to be a cooperator and −3 to be a defector. The best choice for you is also defection. Hence, whatever the opponent will do, a selfish player will always choose defection. However, if both prisoners choose to be a defector, then they will both get a lowest payoff; on the contrary, they can receive highest payoff by mutual cooperation. This situation is referred to *Prisoner's Dilemma* (PD).

   One always arrive at this situation, when the ranking of the four payoff values is a simple sequence of $T > R > P > S$, for which mutual defection is the Nash equilibrium in such a PD game. The cost or benefit can be measured as fitness by biologists. Defectors have a higher fitness when meeting cooperators. Therefore, from the viewpoint of evolution, natural selection favors defectors.

   What kind of mechanism can help rational individuals jump out of the dilemma?

It is difficult to maintain cooperation if the PD game takes place only once between two individuals. Whereas the situation may change when the same two individuals can play PD game repeatedly, since each player considers his behavior may affect the choice of the opponent at the next round, which may eventually lead to cooperation. What will be a good strategy in this repeated game? A political scientist, Axelrod, addressed this question by conducting a PD game competition [3]. He invited people from all over the world to submit strategies for such a repeated PD game. Through two rounds of computer tournaments, Axelrod found that the so-called "Tit-for-tat" (TFT) rule, as the simplest one of all, is the best therefore wins the champion. This rule starts with cooperation, and then always imitates what his opponent did in the previous round. Through carefully analysis, Axelrod found that TFT is the winner since it captures three key factors, i.e., it is a "nice" rule in the sense that one is never to first defect, it can quickly "punish" its opponent's defection, and it can immediately "forgive" his opponent who defected him before but still selects cooperation at the new round. However, TFT has a shortcoming in that it cannot correct any mistake. As a remedy, Nowak and Sigmund proposed two other now-well-known rules to overcome the weakness of TFT. The first one is "Generous tit-for-tat" (GTFT) [4], which let an individual cooperate with this cooperative opponent, and even cooperate with the defected opponent in a certain probability. GTFT is a stochastic rule that leads to the emergence of forgiveness. The second one is "Win–stay, lost–shift" (WSLS) [5], which means that a player can insist on his choice if he is satisfied with it, whereas changing it if he feels lost. TFT can defeat defection while TFT can be replaced by GTFT in noisy environment, while WSLS can efficiently correct mistakes and is stable against TFT and GTFT [6].

Traditional game theory analyzes the interactions between two players and assumes that they are rational. Selfish individuals tend to maximize their payoffs and fall into Nash equilibrium using common knowledge. However, individuals cannot make the best decision in a complex environment, where they have only limited information, and thus they do not behave rationally [7]. Smith and Price [8] introduced the common idea of evolutionary biology into game theory, thereby developed an Evolutionary Game (EG) theory which does not rely on individuals' rationality and only assumes a population of individuals interacting in the game. In EG, an individual randomly interacts with other individuals and adds up his payoff from all the encounters. Payoff can be seen as fitness. The individual with better strategy can reproduce faster, while the loser disappears from the population. Natural selection plays a crucial role in EG and finally becomes an evolutionarily stable strategy, which cannot be invaded by other strategies in an infinitely large population.

Now, consider a population with two kinds of individuals, cooperators and defectors, in fractions x and y, respectively. If individuals randomly interact and play a game by following rules set by (7.1), then the payoffs of cooperators and defectors are:

$$\begin{cases} P_C = Rx + Sy \\ P_D = Tx + Py \end{cases}. \tag{7.2}$$

Taylor and Jonker [9] described the strategy selection through replicator dynamics, i.e., the frequency of changes of a strategy depends on both the strategy and the payoff, in the following form:

$$\begin{cases} \dot{x} = x\left(P_C - \phi\right) \\ \dot{y} = y\left(P_D - \phi\right) \end{cases}, \tag{7.3}$$

where the average payoff of population is $\phi = xP_C + yP_D$. Therefore, the above replicator equation implies the strategy that performs better than the population on average can increase in abundance.

Consider the situation of $x + y = 1$. The replicator equation of cooperators becomes

$$\dot{x} = x(1 - x)[(R - S - T + P)x + S - P]. \tag{7.4}$$

For the PD game, the ranking of $T > R > P > S$ still holds. In this case, observe that $P_C - \phi = (R - T)$ $x + (S - P)(1 - x) < 0$, so the number of cooperators decreases over time and finally become extinct in the well-mixed population, rendering $x^* = 0$ be the only stable fixed point.

The PD game depicts the case that defector can beat cooperator. On the other hand, there exist other situations which characterize the relationships among individuals, and the Snowdrift Game (SG) describes one of them.

Consider the scenario where two drivers are stuck on their way home by trapping on either side of a big snowdrift. Thus, they can choose either shovel the snowdrift (cooperation) or stay in the car (defection). If both cooperate, they obtain benefit b for getting home earlier but share the cost of shoveling $-c$. Thus, $R = b - c/2$. If both defect, then they do nothing thus $P = 0$. If one shovels but another does nothing, then they both can return home yet the defector had only the benefit, thereby the former has $S = b - c$ while the latter gets $T = b$. In this case, if $b > c > 0$, the situation falls into the case of SG, namely, a player's best choice depends on his co-player: it is best to defect when the other player cooperates. This leads to a stable coexistence of cooperators and defectors in a well-mixing population by the equilibrium of frequency of cooperators, as $x^* = (S - P)/(S - P + T - R) = 1 - r_{SG}$, where $r_{SG} = (T - R)/(S - P + T - R) = c/(2b - c)$ is the cost-to-benefit ratio of mutual cooperation.

The SG always exists if the ranking of the four payoff values is $T > R > S > P$. It should be noted, however, that the average population payoff at an evolutionary equilibrium is smaller than that of having only cooperation, thus a paradox of cooperation also exists in the SG. The similar Hawk-Dove game [8] and Chicken game [10] also depict the situation where it is best to always adopt the opposite strategy of the opponent.

Stag-hunt game [11] characterizes the third case of the two-player/two-strategy game. Consider two individuals going out on a hunt. There are two preys, stag and hare. Each individual can get a hare by himself, but they have to cooperate to hunt a stag. Two small hares are worth less than one large stag. Therefore, hunting a stag is desirable but needs social cooperation. However, if a player prepares to hunt a stag with his partner but the partner chooses to only hunt a hare, then the former may get nothing. Hence, hunting hare is a safe choice for both players, although the social welfare is less than that of hunting a stag. The corresponding payoff matrix with $R > T > P > S$ characterizes the Stag-hunt game, where choosing the same strategy with another player is the best choice. Thus, mutual cooperation and mutual defection are bi-stable, and both of them belong to the Nash equilibrium, while mutual defection (hunting hare only) is a risk-dominant equilibrium. In selection dynamics within a population of many players, the outcome relates with the initial condition and $x^* = (P - S)/(R - S - T + P)$ is an unstable equilibrium. The coordination game [12] is one variant of the Stag-hunt game.

The celebrated game models discussed above disclose various social dilemmas in two-player/two-strategy games. Under the governance of two fundamental principles of evolution, namely mutation and nature selection, cooperative behaviors will eventually become extinct. It is quite counterintuitive, given that so many cooperative behaviors in nature. Therefore, there may be the third principle which motivates selfish individuals to cooperate and work together. In deed, this is the so-called natural cooperation proposed by Nowak [13]. There are five rules for the evolution of cooperation: kin selection, direct reciprocity, indirect reciprocity, group selection and network reciprocity. Kin selection implies that cooperation can emerge among relatives. For example, a mother can jump into the river to save her child although she may not be able to swim. But cooperation can emerge among unrelated individuals as well. Therefore, there are some other mechanisms for cooperation. Direct reciprocity means that you may like to help others who helped you before, and TFT-related rules play important roles in such direct reciprocity. Cooperation may also occur between strangers, where indirect reciprocity takes effect. It means that if you often help others and build a good reputation, some strangers may help you as return when you are in need. The fourth rule, the group selection, means that cooperation can emerge in a group.

In the rest of this chapter, network reciprocity, also called spatial reciprocity, will be introduced, which addresses the central question: if individuals can interact with only a small number of others in a population, how the spatial structure of the population affects the emergence and evolution of the individuals' cooperation?

7.2   Two-Player/Two-Strategy Evolutionary Games on Networks

7.2.1   Introduction to Games on Networks

Usually, each individual cannot interact with all other individuals in a large population. Following the evolution, however, they can make friends, thereby forming a social structure in the population. For example, animals create hierarchical societies and humans form different community networks. Various relationships in the population can be represented by networks. Therefore, exploring the relationships between game dynamics and population structure is not only theoretically interesting but also practically important.

Networked (or spatial) game theory, first formally proposed by Nowak and May [14], considers individuals located at nodes of a network (e.g., a square lattice). The network characterizes who interacts with whom. These individuals play a game (e.g., PD game) with their immediate neighbors and obtain payoffs according to the payoff matrix of the game. Based on the payoff from the previous rounds, individuals update their strategies, C or D, so as to maximize their future payoff. Therefore, the structure of the population can be represented by a network, which not only describes who plays the game with whom, but also shows who learns behaviors from whom. The game model, the network structure and the update rules are the three components of the spatial game theory [15, 16].

In social and biological systems, each individual i tends to select the more successful behaviors from its immediate neighbors. Therefore, after playing the game and obtaining an accumulated payoff P_i, this individual with strategy S_i will compare its payoffs with the neighbors and learn successful behaviors. A widely used update rule in networked game theory is the replicator dynamics [17], namely, an individual i randomly selects a neighbor j; if they have different strategies, i imitates the strategy of j with a probability proportional to their payoff difference:

$$W(S_i \leftarrow S_j) = f(P_j - P_i). \tag{7.5}$$

7.2.2   Two-Player/Two-Strategy Games on Regular Lattices

There are four parameters in the payoff matrix of the two-player/two-strategy game (2×2 game) according to (7.1). In order to simplify the payoff matrix, Nowak and May [14] proposed a weak PD game, with $R = 1$, $P = S = 0$ and $T = b$, where b is the only parameter and the player has a higher temptation to choose defection when $b > 1$. The weak PD game is widely adopted in networked game theory.

In a well-mixed population, defectors will diffuse and cooperators will extinct. However, as shown in Figure 7.2 (a), due to the fact that an individual only interacts with local neighbors on the network, cooperators playing the weak PD game can form tight clusters to defend invasion of the defectors. Figure 7.2 shows some typical snapshots of (a) weak PD game and (b) SG, on a 100×100 square lattice, with the fraction of cooperators around 35%. Usually, it is set at the beginning an equal percentage of cooperation and defection strategies which are randomly distributed among individuals on the network. After a transient state, the percentage of cooperators fluctuates around a static value and the network reaches a steady state. Figure 7.2 (a) shows that the cooperators in light grey playing a weak PD game with $b = 1.1$ can form compact clusters to defend the invasion of the defectors in dark grey. However, Figure 7.2 (b) shows that for the SG with $r_{SG} = 0.5$ the cooperators compose a small crosslike structure that restrains the persistence of cooperation. These individuals update their behavior with replicator dynamics [14].

Figure 7.3 (a) shows a time series of the frequency of cooperators, f_C, for different values of b, (b) shows the frequency of cooperators, f_C, as a function of b on a square lattice, where individuals update their strategy according to the replicator dynamics.

It can be seen from Figure 7.3 (a) that cooperation playing the weak PD game is sustained on a regular graph (e.g., square lattice) and thus the spatial structure promotes the emergence of cooperation by

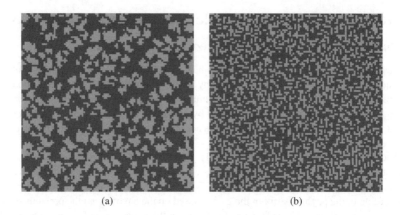

Figure 7.2 Typical snapshots of (a) weak PD game and (b) SG [14]. *Source*: Reprinted from Amaral, L.A.N. and Guimera, R. (2006) Complex networks: Lies, damned lies and statistics. *Nature Physics*, **2**: 75–76. Reproduced by permission of Macmillan Pub. Ltd.

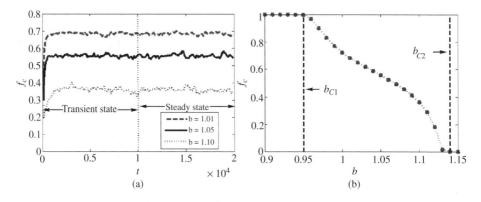

Figure 7.3 (a) Time series of f_C versus b; (b) f_C as a function of b. Courtesy of Z.H. Rong

limiting the interactions among individuals. The emergence frequency of cooperators, f_C, which is the average percentage of cooperators in the steady state, is a key index for measuring the cooperative level on the network. Moreover, it can be seen from Figure 7.3 (b) that, as the temptation to defection increases, described by b, there are three phases: one is the situation with all cooperators (ALLC), where $f_C = 1$; another is the situation with defectors appearing on the network; the last is that there is a range of coexistence with cooperators and defectors. Finally, the cooperators disappear and all individuals are defectors (ALLD), where $f_C = 0$. There are two important thresholds, the appearance of defector, b_{C1}, and the extinction of cooperators, b_{C2}, which are also key indexes for measuring the emergence of cooperation in the network.

Furthermore, one can understand the evolution of cooperation on a network through analyzing some typical subgraphs. Consider the subgraph with overlapping triangles shown in Figure 7.4. Each individual i plays the weak PD game with its neighbors and updates its strategy as follows: it randomly selects a neighbor j, and if j's payoff is higher than i, then i learns j's strategy; otherwise, i holds on its current strategy. Initially, there are only three cooperators (white circles) composing a triangle and others are defectors (black circles), as shown in Figure 7.4 (a). Therefore, the payoffs of cooperators (nodes 3, 4 and 5) are 2, since they each has two cooperative neighbors, and the payoffs of defectors 1 and 2 are b,

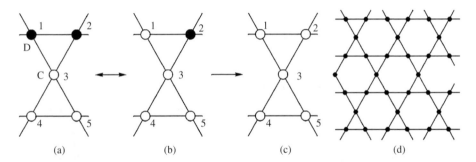

Figure 7.4 (a)–(c) Diffusion of cooperators (white circles) in the sea of defectors (black circles) on a subgraph with one-site overlapping triangles; (d) two-dimensional Kagome lattice with overlapping triangles [15]. *Source:* Reprinted from Szabó, G. and Fath, G. (2007) Evolutionary games on graphs. *Physics Reports*, **446**(46): 97–216. Copyright (2007) Elsevier

since they each meet a cooperator (node 3). Others have nothing, since they interact only with defectors. When $1 < b < 1.5$, the payoff of defective nodes 1 and 2 is less than their cooperative neighbor (node 1). If node 1 compares its payoff with node 3, it will turn to become a cooperator. Therefore, at the second generation, shown in Figure 7.4 (b), the payoffs of nodes 1, 2 and 3 are 1, 2b and 3, respectively. For the case of $1 < b < 1.5$, the payoff of defective node 2 is higher than that of cooperative node 1 but less than that of node 3. If node 1 compares its payoff with node 2 in this generation, it will become a defector again, so that the state of the subgraph will turn to that shown in Figure 7.4 (a). While if node 1 holds on its cooperative behavior and node 2 compares its payoff with node 3, then node 2 will become a cooperator, so that the state of the subgraph will turn to that shown in Figure 7.4 (c). The overlapping triangles in the subgraph can be extended to a two-dimensional Kagome lattice (Figure 7.4 (d)), whose clustering coefficient is 1/3, where cooperative behaviors can efficiently diffuse for $b < 1.5$ [15].

There are distinct cooperative behaviors on different regular lattices. Still consider the weak PD game, with another update rule, i.e., the Fermi dynamics, which is also widely used in networked game [19]: In each generation, an individual i randomly selects a neighbor j and learns j's behavior with a probability calculated in terms of the Fermi function:

$$W(S_i \leftarrow S_j) = \frac{1}{1 + \exp[(P_i - P_j)/\kappa]}, \tag{7.6}$$

where S_i represents individual i's strategy and P_i is its payoff in the current generation, and the parameter κ represents the temperature in terms of statistical physics, which characterizes the stochastic uncertainties (noise) of the irrational choices. For $\kappa = 0$, individuals are rational and player i will determinately learn a selected neighbor j's behavior if $P_j > P_i$. Following the increase of κ, individuals tend to become irrational and an individual may learn from a neighbor even if the payoff of this neighbor is less than its payoff. As $\kappa \to \infty$, there is a noisy environment and individuals randomly update their behavior regardless of the payoffs.

Figure 7.5 illustrates the relationship between the threshold of cooperation extinction and the parameter κ on different regular lattices, where individuals have the same degree $\langle k \rangle = 4$. As $\kappa \to 0$, the cooperative behavior is difficult to exist on a square lattice, but it can sustain on the Kagome lattice when $b < b_{C2} = 1.5$. The triangle subgraph cannot always promote the emergence of cooperation. For the four-site-clique lattice, whose clustering coefficient is 1/2, the cooperative behavior is similar with the square lattice. This is because each triangle shares one edge with another triangle, a defector can interact with many cooperators thereby the defective behavior is easy to invade into a cooperative cluster. Furthermore, it is shown in Figure 7.5 that the parameter κ plays a nontrivial role for the cooperative behaviors on the square lattice and the four-site-clique lattice: cooperation can be enhanced for proper values of κ. Also, the threshold of cooperation extinction, b_{C2}, of the Kagome lattice monotonously

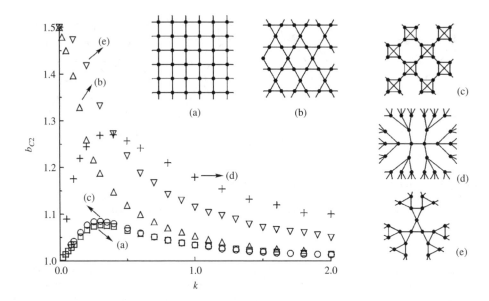

Figure 7.5 Threshold of cooperation extinction, b_{C2}, as a function of parameter κ, on five regular graphs with average degree $\langle k \rangle = 4$: (a) square lattice, (b) the Kagome lattice, (c) four-site-clique lattice, (d) bethe lattice, and (e) regular graph of overlapping triangles [15]. *Source*: Reprinted from Szabó, G. and Fath, G. (2007) Evolutionary games on graphs. *Physics Reports*, **446**(46): 97–216. Copyright (2007) Elsevier

decreases with the increase of κ, since an irrational cooperator may learn from the defective behavior. Furthermore, through observing the thresholds of cooperation extinction on bethe lattice and the regular graph of overlapping triangles, it can be seen that the cooperative behavior can be promoted by comparing with square lattice and the Kagome lattice. This indicates that cooperation is easier to exist if the loops of a regular graph become longer [15]. Hence, the topology has significant influence on cooperation.

The above discussions reveal that a suitable spatial structure can promote the emergence of cooperation for the weak PD game. Hauert and Doebeli further showed [21] that the cooperation may be inhibited for the networked snowdrift game (SG). In a well-mixed population, cooperators can coexist with defectors, and the equilibrium frequency of cooperators is $1 - r_{SG}$. Through observing Figure 7.6, where individuals update their strategies in terms of replicator dynamics, it can be seen that the cooperator's frequencies, f_C, are lower than $1 - r_{SG}$ for different regular lattices. This indicates that the spatial structure may inhibit the emergence of cooperation for SG. It is due to the fact that individuals tend to choose the opposite behavior in the SG. Therefore, on a lattice, different from the compact cooperator clusters observed from the networked PG game, the cooperators playing a networked SG game can only compose a small cross-like structure that inhibits the persistence of cooperation (Figure 7.6 (b)). Therefore, for larger values of the cost-to-benefit ratio r_{SG}, defectors are easy to invade in a cooperator cluster, which results in the decrease of the frequency of cooperators. This phenomenon leads to some rethinking over the influence of network topology on game dynamics.

7.2.3   Two-Player/Two-Strategy Games on BA Scale-Free Networks

The cooperative behaviors of a two-player/two-strategy game on the Barabási-Albert (BA) scale-free network model were studied by Santos and his collaborators [22–24]. They found that the scale-free feature can provide a universal framework for the emergence of cooperation.

Consider a BA network, on which each individual i plays the PD game with its neighbors and its payoff is accumulated as P_i in each generation (as shown by Figure 7.7). When updating its strategy,

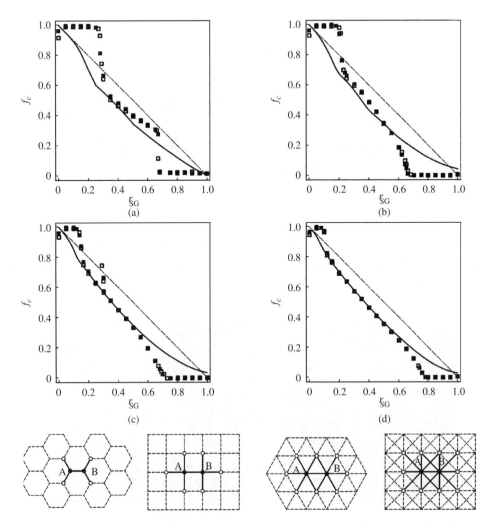

Figure 7.6 Frequency of cooperators, f_C, as a function of the cost-to-benefit r_{SG} on various regular lattices: (a) triangle lattice with $\langle k \rangle = 3$, (b) square lattice with $\langle k \rangle = 4$, (c) hexagonal lattice with $\langle k \rangle = 6$, (d) Moore lattice with $\langle k \rangle = 8$ [21]. *Source*: Reprinted by permission from Macmillan Publishers Ltd: [Nature] (Hauert C, Doebeli M. Spatial structure often inhibits the evolution of cooperation in the snowdrift game. *Nature*, 2004, **428**: 643–646.), copyright (2004)

each individual i will randomly select a neighbor j and adopts its strategy according to the replicator dynamics:

$$W(S_i \leftarrow S_j) = \frac{P_j - P_i}{\max(k_i, k_j)[\max(T, R) - \min(S, P)]}, \tag{7.7}$$

where k_i is individual i's degree. The denominator is used to normalize the probability. Therefore, the higher payoff the j has, the more likely the i will adopt j's strategy in the next round. Comparing with ER random graphs, where cooperators can only maintain a low temptation to defect, the cooperators dominate all ranges on a BA scale-free network (as shown in Figure 7.8) [23].

The mechanism of cooperation domination on a heterogeneous scale-free network can be revealed through the diffusion of defective hub (D-hub) on the scale-free network [24]. Consider the scenario

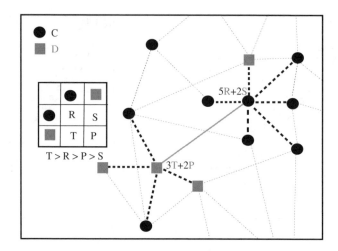

Figure 7.7 Two-player/two-strategy game on a heterogeneous network [24]. *Source*: Reproduced by permission of John Wiley & Sons, Inc.

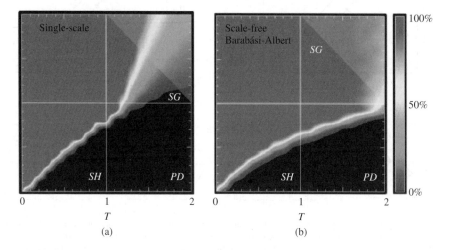

Figure 7.8 Cooperation in a two-player/two-strategy game on (a) ER random-graph network, and (b) BA scale-free network. Here, $R = 1$ and $P = 0$. The four regions in the figure corresponds to four cases: C domination, C and D coexistence (SG), C and D bi-stability (SH), and D domination (PD) [23]. *Source*: Santos, F.C., Pacheco, J.M. and Lenaerts, T. (2006) Evolutionary dynamics of social dilemmas in structured heterogeneous populations. *Proceedings of the National Academy of Sciences USA*, **103** (9): 3490–4. Copyright (2006) National Academy of Sciences, USA

on a BA network, where the max-degree hub is the only single defector in the world of cooperators. When considering the accumulating payoff, the D-hub has higher payoff than all those low-degree nodes (leaves) because the former plays more rounds of the game with its neighbors, thus the leaves tend to learn the D-hub's strategy. It is shown in Figure 7.9 that, initially the D-hub can efficiently diffuse its behaviors to neighbors, leading to the decrease of the cooperators' frequency around the D-hub, denoted by f_C^{D-hub}, as well as its payoff. Since, on the BA network, the D-hub not only has neighbors with low-degrees, but also links with some other hubs. Therefore, the D-hub on the BA network always has some hub-neighbors who persist on their initial behavior. After some transient time, the C-hub's payoff is higher than that of

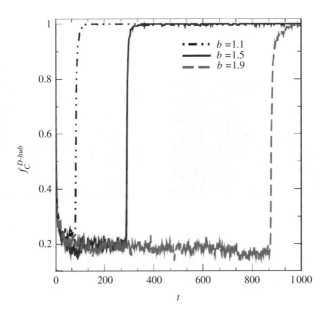

Figure 7.9 Evolution of frequency of cooperators around the max-degree hub on a BA network. Initially there is only one defector located on the max-degree hub [24]. *Source*: Reproduced by permission of John Wiley & Sons, Inc.

the D-hub, thus the max-degree hub will learn the good strategies to become a cooperator and, with the increase of its frequency, the cooperators will increase again. Therefore, hubs have a sustainability of cooperation on the BA network.

Furthermore, the evolution of cooperation on a networked system can be understood through dynamical organization of cooperators/defectors [25]. During the steady state, the individuals can be divided into three kinds: pure cooperator (Pc), pure defector (Pd) and fluctuating individual (Fi). Pc/Pd are the individuals who always hold on C/D strategies at the steady state, and Fi represents the individuals who never change their strategies during the steady state. Therefore, the hubs on a heterogeneous network are Pc who compose a steady cooperative core. On an ER random-graph network with weak degree heterogeneity, the steady cooperation core is quickly divided into several clusters in a flood of fluctuating individuals as the temptation to defect, b, increases. Therefore, the cooperation is difficult to sustain on the ER random-graph network, as shown in Figure 7.10 (a). On the contrary, there exists a steady cooperation core on BA scale-free network, which slowly decreases with the increase of b, due to the strong degree heterogeneity. Therefore, the cooperative hubs on the BA network can efficiently protect themselves from the invasion of defectors, as shown in Figure 7.10 (b) [25].

7.2.4 Two-Player/Two-Strategy Games on Correlated Scale-Free Networks

There are many different mixing patterns according to the node degrees in real-world networked systems. To measure the degree-mixing of a network, the concept of assortativity coefficient, r_k, introduced in Section 2.1.4 of Chapter 2, may be used. When a network is assortatively (disassortatively) mixed by degree, r_k is positive (negative) and the highly-connected nodes tend to choose those nodes with similar (dissimilar) degrees as neighbors. An uncorrelated network exhibits the neutral degree-mixing pattern $r_k = 0$. Generally, social networks are assortatively mixed, while many technological and biological networks exhibit disassortatively-mixing patterns. A simple algorithm proposed by Xulvi-Brunet and Sokolov (referred to as the XS algorithm) can generate different degree-mixing network [26].

The degree correlation significantly influences the collective dynamical behaviors of complex networks. In fact, there are distinct cooperative behaviors on different correlated networks [27]. To reveal

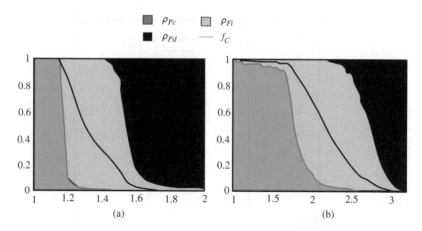

Figure 7.10   Fraction of cooperators, f_C, pure cooperators ρ_{Pc}, pure defectors ρ_{Pd}, and fluctuating individuals ρ_{Fi}, as a function of temptation to defect, b, on ER random-graph and BA scale-free networks [25]: on ER network; on BA network. *Source*: Reprinted with permission from Gómez-Gardeñes, J., Campillo, M. and Floria, L.M. *et al.* (2007) Dynamical organization of cooperation in complex topologies. *Physical Review Letters*, **98**(10): 108103. Copyright (2007) American Physical Society

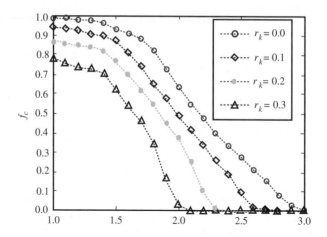

Figure 7.11   Frequency of cooperators, f_C, as a function of the temptation to defect, b, on assortative scale-free networks, obtained on a BA network [27]. *Source*: Reproduced with permission from Rong, Z.H., Li, X. and Wang, X.F. (2007) Roles of mixing patterns in cooperation on a scale-free networked game. Physical Review E (2007) American Physical Society

how the frequency will change when a network becomes assortative, Figure 7.11 shows that, comparing with uncorrelated networks, the cooperation on assortative networks is significantly inhibited. This is because, not only the frequency of cooperators in assortative networks is lower than that in uncorrelated networks, but also the cooperators are earlier to disappear in the former case than in the latter.

Now, the role of assortative mixing in the extinction threshold of cooperators is discussed. On a BA scale-free network, the hubs uniformly select nodes with high-degrees or low-degrees as their neighbors. Therefore, on the one hand, hubs can directly communicate with each other; on the other hand, they share a small number of common neighbors, so a defector is hard to invade a hub of cooperators, called a C-hub. However, when a scale-free network becomes more and more assortatively mixing, the high-degree nodes tend to compose a core group sharing more neighbors than before. This promotes the diffusion of defectors and inhibits the emergence of cooperation on assortatively-mixing networks.

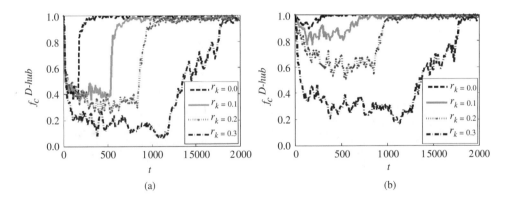

Figure 7.12 Frequency of cooperation of hubs' neighbors as a function of generation when the assortative coefficients r_k of a group of scale-free networks vary from 0.0 to 0.3 [27]: (a) around D-hub; (b) around C-hub. *Source*:
Reproduced with permission from Rong, Z.H., Li, X. and Wang, X.F. (2007) Roles of mixing patterns in cooperation
on a scale-free networked game. Physical Review E (2007) American Physical Society

Consider a subgraph on which two hubs share m lowly-connected neighbors. At the initial state, only
one hub is a defector and all the other nodes are cooperators. The C-hub has a tendency to become
defector because its payoff $\rho_C m$ is always less than the D-hub's payoff $\rho_C mb$, where ρ_C is the percentage
of neighbors of the cooperator in the two hubs. Thus, the rest cooperators (lowly-connected nodes) will
vanish on the network with two D-hubs.

Figure 7.12 shows the frequency of cooperation of hubs' neighbors as a function of the generation
when the assortative coefficients r_k of a group of scale-free networks vary from 0.0 to 0.3. Initially only
the max-degree node is the defector and all the others are cooperators. The temptation to defect is $b = 1.5$.
Evolution of cooperators are plotted around: (a) the max-degree defector (D-hub) with 149 connections,
and (b) the second max-degree cooperator (C-hub) with 147 neighbors.

In order to understand this mechanism more clearly, it is now to further consider how the defective
behavior diffuses on scale-free networks with different mixing patterns. Initially set the max-degree node
as the unique D-hub and all the others as cooperators. Let the system relax to the equilibrium. Figure 7.12
(a) and (b) show the time series of the number of cooperative neighbors around the D-hub, and that of
the C-hub, respectively. For an uncorrelated network with $r_k = 0$, since at the very beginning the D-hub
receives the highest payoff, its cooperator neighbors (especially those with very low degrees) will imitate
its strategy. This, in turn, decreases the D-hub's payoff in the subsequent steps. Since there are only a few
common neighbors shared by the two hubs on the uncorrelated network, the payoff of the C-hub will not
decrease by too much (only decrease about 10% under the influence of the D-hub in Figure 7.12 (b)).
The payoff of the D-hub will, after some transient time, be far lower than its C-hub neighbors, which will
turn it to be a cooperator, sooner or later. When a scale-free network becomes assortatively mixing by
degrees, however, the hubs are themselves neighbors each other, composing a compact core and resulting
in even more common neighbors among them. In such a case, the D-hub with the highest degree will
greatly impact the payoff of other hubs, so that defection will be more easily to diffuse on assortative
networks. From Figure 7.12, it can be observed that, as the network becomes assortative, the fraction of
cooperators around the two hubs decrease more and more notably.

Another indicator of assortative network suppressing cooperation is the increasing relaxation time to
the steady state with the increment of r_k. For $r_k = 0$, after the D-hub with the max-degree changes to a
cooperator, its defective neighbors with low degrees are very easy to change their strategies. As a result,
it will form a positive feedback loop: the more payoff the max-degree node obtains, the more attractable
its strategy will become, which in turn gives rise to even more payoff for the hub. This is what can be
observed from Figure 7.12 (a), where the frequency of cooperators around the D-hub ascends rapidly
after it becomes a cooperator, and the transient time to the equilibrium on the uncorrelated network is
quite short. In contrast, as the network becomes more assortative, it would be more difficult for the C-hub
to efficiently migrate its strategy to others, and as a result, the network needs longer time to attain the

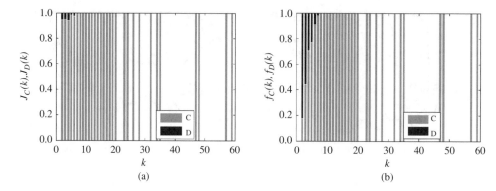

Figure 7.13 Distribution of stationary strategies on a scale-free network [27]: (a) relative distribution = 0.0; (b) relative distribution = 0.3. *Source*: Reproduced with permission from Rong, Z.H., Li, X. and Wang, X.F. (2007) Roles of mixing patterns in cooperation on a scale-free networked game. Physical Review E (2007) American Physical Society

equilibrium. Thus, the positive feedback effect is restrained, and the cooperation is easier to become extinct on the assortative networks as compared to uncorrelated networks.

Figure 7.13 shows the distribution of stationary strategies on a scale-free network with (a) $r_k = 0$, (b) $r_k = 0.3$, where $b = 1.5$. Cooperators (C) and Defectors (D) are denoted by light-grey (green) bars and dark-grey (blue) bars, respectively. Each bar adds up to a total fraction of 1 per degree, and the light-grey and dark-grey fractions are directly proportional to the relative percentage of the respective strategy for each degree k.

Moreover, when b is less than the threshold of cooperation extinction, the frequency of cooperators on an assortative network is also lower than that of an uncorrelated network. To show this, Figure 7.13 plots the relative strategy distribution per degree of the networks with $r_k = 0$ and $r_k = 0.3$ at the steady states, respectively. There exist more defectors with low degrees on an assortative network than that on an uncorrelated network, and the C-hubs sustain in both networks. On an assortative network, nodes with similar degrees tend to be interconnected, thus the lowly-connected nodes tend to select nodes with low degrees rather than hubs as their neighbors. Therefore, the influence of the hubs on low-degree nodes is weaker on assortative networks, and defection is easier to diffuse among the low-degree nodes. Hence, the assortatively-mixing pattern inhibits the emergence of cooperation.

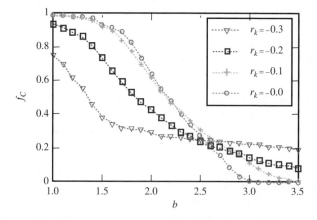

Figure 7.14 Frequency of cooperators, f_C, as a function of b on scale-free networks, with $r_k = -0.3, -0.2, -0.1, 0.0$, respectively [27]. *Source*: Reproduced with permission from Rong, Z.H., Li, X. and Wang, X.F. (2007) Roles of mixing patterns in cooperation on a scale-free networked game. Physical Review E (2007) American Physical Society

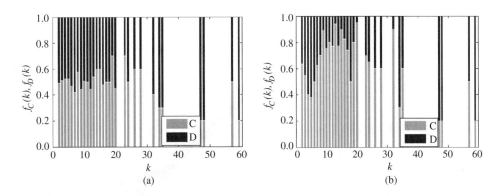

Figure 7.15   Distribution of strategies on a disassortative network with $r_k = -0.3$, $b = 1.5$: (a) initial strategies distribution; (b) stationary strategies distribution, where the distribution of strategies of hubs at the end are unchanged comparing with the initial case [27]. *Source*: Reproduced with permission from Rong, Z.H., Li, X. and Wang, X.F. (2007) Roles of mixing patterns in cooperation on a scale-free networked game. Physical Review E (2007) American Physical Society

Similarly, to investigate how the emergence of cooperation is affected by the degree-mixing pattern on disassortative networks, Figure 7.14 shows that the frequency of cooperators on some disassortative networks is lower than that on uncorrelated networks for a wide range of b. On a disassortative network, there are few interconnections among hubs, and the sustainability of cooperation among hubs is destroyed, so a hub can only influence the actions of its local neighbors. In Figure 7.15 (a), nodes were initialized with one half being cooperators and the other half being defectors. Figure 7.15 (b) shows that at the steady state the hubs still hold on their initial strategies and only those low-degree nodes change their strategies. Therefore, the frequency of cooperators in disassortative networks is lower than that of uncorrelated networks. Furthermore, as shown in Figure 7.14, the extinction threshold of cooperators becomes higher when r_k decreases, which implies that the cooperators can be sustained due to their larger temptation on disassortative networks. That is, due to the fact that a C-hub is only surrounded by low-degree neighbors, it is easy to retain its initial strategy, and is composed of a cluster of cooperators with its neighbors so as to withstand the invasion of defectors. Thus, the disassortative mixing pattern destroys the communication among hubs. This, on the one hand, leads to the disappearance of cooperation sustainability among hubs and the decrease of frequency of cooperators, and, on the other hand, protects the cooperation from becoming extinction for a large range of temptation.

7.2.5   Two-Player/Two-Strategy Games on Clustered Scale-Free Networks

The clustering phenomenon, which implies that two friends of an individual are usually also friends, is common in real-world scale-free networks. Holme and Kim (HK) proposed a simple model to obtain a scale-free network with a tunable clustering coefficient [28]. The HK network is constructed as follows. Starting from an initial core of m_0 fully-connected nodes. At each time step, a new node i is added to the network which links to m existent nodes. The first edge follows a preferential attachment rule, i.e., node i connects to node j with a probability proportional to the degree k_j of node j. The remaining $m - 1$ edges connect to existing nodes in two different ways: (i) with probability p, node i connects to a randomly-chosen neighbor of node j, one by one; (ii) with probability $1 - p$ the same preferential attachment rule is used again for node i to connect to an existing node, one by one. With such a procedure, one obtains a scale-free network, and all such networks have average connectivity $\langle k \rangle = 2m$ and degree distribution $P(k) \sim k^{-3}$. In particular, for $p = 0$, HK network reduces to the BA model.

Figure 7.16 shows the degree distribution of HK networks. The upper-right inset shows the clustering coefficient and the lower-left inset is the degree correlation coefficient r_k versus p. From the upper-right inset, it can be observed that, as p increases, the clustering coefficient CC is ascending, from 0.0 to 0.6, on HK scale-free networks.

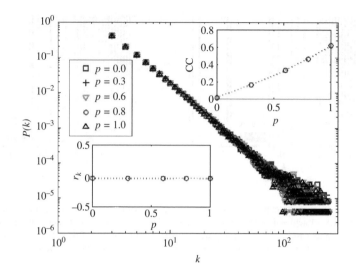

Figure 7.16 Degree distribution of HK scale-free networks [37]. *Source*: Reprinted with permission from Rong, Z., Yang, H-X. and Wang, W-X. (2010) Feedback reciprocity mechanism promotes the cooperation of highly clustered scale-free networks. *Physical Review E*, **82**: 047101. Copyright (2010) American Physical Society

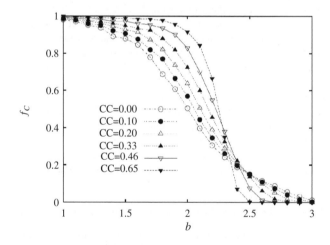

Figure 7.17 Frequency of cooperators, f_C, as a function of temptation, b, to defect on clustered scale-free networks [29]. *Source*: Reprinted with permission from Assenza, S., Gómez-Gardeñes, J. and Latora V. (2008) Enhancement of cooperation in highly clustered scale-free networks. *Physical Review E*, **78**: 017101. Copyright (2008) American Physical Society

Assenza *et al.* [29] investigated the cooperative behavior of two-player PD game on the HK clustered scale-free networks. As shown in Figure 7.17, it was found that the cooperators are flourishing on highly-clustered scale-free networks when the temptation to defect is below a threshold value, after which the cooperative behavior is easy to disappear. This is due to the fact that for low temptations, the hubs on highly-clustered scale-free networks are more resistant to defection, which thereby boosts cooperation. Whereas, for high temptations, the defectors can spread across all degree classes and cooperation is easily suppressed on higher-clustered scale-free networks.

7.3 Multi-Player/Two-Strategy Evolutionary Games on Networks

7.3.1 Introduction to Public Goods Game

Multiple individuals usually work together to reach a target and share a limited public resource. Public goods game (PGG) is a multi-player PD game that depicts the group interaction of individuals where the defective free-rider may exploit the cooperator to gain high fitness.

Consider N individuals participating in the PGG. Each player may or may not invest some money, c, into a common pool. Thus, an investor is a cooperator and a free-rider is a defector. The total invested money is then multiplied by a fact r and divided equally among the N players. For example, if there are x cooperators and the rest are defectors, then the payoff of a defector is $P_D = rcx/N$ and a cooperator receives $P_C = P_D - c$. Since the profit gained by a cooperator is always smaller than that by a defector, all selfish individuals tend to becoming free-riders and invest nothing into the common pool, which however leads to a dilemma that there is no benefit for anyone. Therefore, PGG characterizes such a phenomenon that exists in social systems today.

For example, currently the greatest public good dilemma is perhaps the global warming problem. For the climate, it is best if everyone does not consume any energy. However, if only a few individuals waste energy, it does not make the climate any worse but the life will become better for those individuals. Yet, when a lot of people consume a lot of energy, the climate certainly becomes worse which, in turn, downgrade or even completely ruin everyone's life quality. Therefore, humans are facing a collective-risk social dilemma. Through a controlled human experiment on the threshold of the PGG, research showed that communications based on the fact of high risk of collective failures, and by eliminating inequality among individuals, can convince the majority of people to invest enough for life quality while protecting the climate at a safe level [30–32].

PGG is widely used by economists and sociologists to study cooperation. Recently, researchers investigated the hunter-gatherers social network of the Hadza through a PGG donation, and found that the hunter-gatherers social network has many important structural properties, such as skewed degree distribution, assortativity among cooperators, high clustering, and homophily, indicating that the structural properties may have been present at the early stage of human evolution and may contribute to the emergence of social cooperation all along [33]. Hence, investigating the networked PGG and disclosing the evolution of cooperation among group interactions are of practical importance [34].

7.3.2 Multi-Player/Two-Strategy Evolutionary Games on BA Networks

In the networked PGG, each individual takes part in the game centered on it and its neighbors, and this individual can decide whether or not to invest some money into a common pool. Santos *et al.* [35] considered the situation that individuals have limited resources, and proposed the networked PGG with a fixed contribution per individual, where a cooperator i with degree k_i contributes a fixed amount of money (e.g., $c = 1$) to its neighborhood, which is equally shared among all $k_i + 1$ individuals. Thereafter, the contribution of a cooperator in one PGG is multiplied by a factor r and divided equally among all participators. On the contrary, the defector invests nothing to its neighborhood. Therefore, the payoff of individual i, who participates in the PGG centered on individual j with degree k_j, is

$$P_i^j = \frac{r}{k_j + 1} \sum_{x \in \Gamma_j} \frac{c}{k_x + 1} \delta_x - \frac{c}{k_i + 1} \delta_i, \qquad (7.8)$$

where Γ_j denotes the set of nodes containing $k_j + 1$ individuals and $\delta_x = 1$ or 0 if the individual i is a cooperator (defector). The total benefit P_i of individual i is the accumulated payoff obtained from all such PGGs which it participates in.

Figure 7.18 [35] shows the frequency of cooperators, f_C, as a function of the normalized multiplication factor, $r/(\langle k \rangle + 1)$, on the nearest-neighbor lattice (grey lines with open squares) and on a BA scale-free network (black lines with filled circles). The inset is the influence of the networked PGG with fixed contribution per individual.

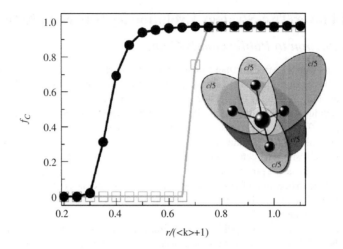

Figure 7.18 Frequency of cooperators, f_C, on the nearest-neighborand on a BA scale-free network [35]. *Source*: Reprinted by permission from Macmillan Publishers Ltd: [Nature] (Santos, F.C., Santos, M.D., Pacheco, J.M. Social diversity promotes the emergence of cooperation in public goods games. *Nature*, 2008, **454**: 213–216), copyright (2008)

Figure 7.19 A simple network of three nodes

From the perspective of networked games, the two-player PD game is essentially different from the multi-player PGG in the sense that the former describes pairwise interactions but the latter depicts the multi-interactions among groups of individuals. To see the subtle differences, consider a simple network of three nodes shown in Figure 7.19.

For the networked PD game, which describes the pairwise interaction, every individual plays the game with its immediate neighbor(s). Therefore, the payoff of node 1 is

$$P_1 = \delta_1\delta_2 R + \delta_1(1 - \delta_2)S + (1 - \delta_1)\delta_2 T + (1 - \delta_1)(1 - \delta_2)P.$$

The gain of node 1 is only related with its immediate neighbor node 2. However, for the spatial PGG that captures group interactions, every individual takes part in the game centered on it and its neighbors. The payoff of node 1, in this case, is

$$P_1 = \frac{r}{k_1 + 1}\sum_{x=1}^{2}\frac{c}{k_x + 1}\delta_x + \frac{r}{k_2 + 1}\sum_{x=1}^{3}\frac{c}{k_x + 1}\delta_x - c\delta_1.$$

The first and second terms are the gains of node 1, obtaining from the PGG centered on nodes 1 and 2. It can be observed from the second term that the payoff of node 1 not only is related with its immediate neighbor (the first neighbor), but also depends on its neighbor's neighbor (the second neighbor). Therefore, the behavior of an individual playing the PGG will affect more individuals' payoff, in comparison with the PD game. Therefore, the main difference between PD game with pairwise interactions and the PGG with group interactions is that, for the former an individual will play the PD game with its immediate neighbors one by one; however, for the latter, an individual and its immediate neighbors will simultaneously participate in the PGG game centered on it or on its neighbors. Therefore, in the latter case, the behavior of an individual will affect not only the payoff of its neighbor, but also its neighbor's

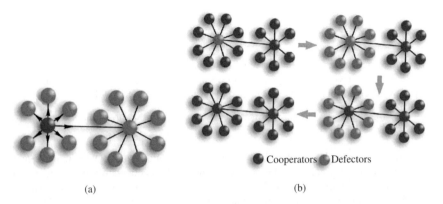

Figure 7.20 (a) A double-star subnetwork; (b) evolution of a D-hub [35]. *Source*: Reprinted by permission from Macmillan Publishers Ltd: [Nature] (Santos, F.C., Santos, M.D., Pacheco, J.M. Social diversity promotes the emergence of cooperation in public goods games. *Nature*, 2008, **454**: 213–216), copyright (2008)

neighbor, since both of them will participate in the PGG game centered on their common neighbor, which does not exist in the pairwise interactions.

Now, the PGG on scale-free networks is further discussed. Consider a network evolving in terms of replicator dynamics, described by (7.5), namely, in each step, each individual randomly selects one neighbor and adopt this neighbor's strategy with a probability proportional to their accumulated payoff difference. Santos *et al.* [35] addressed the issue of social diversity through an investigation of heterogeneous scale-free networks. Comparing with regular lattices, it was found that cooperation is promoted by the diversity associated with the number and size of the PGG groups on BA scale-free networks. This is due to the distinguished feedback mechanisms of cooperative/defective hubs (C-hub/D-hub) on heterogeneous networks. This is illustrated by Figure 7.20: (a) a double-star subnetwork; (b) evolution of a D-hub on this double-star subnetwork [35].

Specifically, consider the double-star subnetwork shown in Figure 7.20, where all nodes are connected with two hubs (V and W). The hubs V and W are connected with each other, and have m and n neighbors, respectively. All the low-degree nodes (leaves, L) that are connected with only one hub have the same degree, k. In the extreme case where there is only one cooperator, located on the left star V, and the others are defectors, as shown in Figure 7.20 (a). The payoff of C-hub (P_V^C) is

$$P_V^C = \frac{rc}{(m+1)^2} + (m-1)\frac{rc}{(k+1)(m+1)} + \frac{rc}{(n+1)(m+1)} - c, \tag{7.9}$$

where the first, second, and third terms on the right-hand side correspond to the gains from the game centered on the C-hub, leaves and D-hub, respectively. Similarly, the payoffs of a defective leaf (P_L^D) and D-hub (P_W^D) are

$$P_L^D = \frac{rc}{(m+1)^2} + \frac{rc}{(k+1)(m+1)} \tag{7.10}$$

$$P_W^D = \frac{rc}{(m+1)^2} + \frac{rc}{(n+1)(m+1)}. \tag{7.11}$$

From (7.9)–(7.11), it can be found that in the networked PGG, an individual acquires profit not only from its immediate (or first) neighbors, but also from its second neighbors, which is different from the spatial PD game where the payoff of an individual comes only from its immediate neighbors.

Next, consider the payoff difference between C-hub and its defective leaves:

$$P_V^C - P_L^D = (m-2)\frac{rc}{(k+1)(m+1)} + \frac{rc}{(n+1)(m+1)} - c > (m-2)\frac{rc}{(k+1)(m+1)} - c. \tag{7.12}$$

Therefore,

$$P_V^C - P_L^D > 0 \text{ if } r > \frac{(k+1)(m+1)(n+1)}{(k+1)+(m-2)(n+1)} = \alpha_1,$$

which is a decreasing function of m and indicates that the C-hub can become more advantageous therefore efficiently spread its behavior from hub to leaf as the its degree m increases. Moreover, through comparing with the payoff difference between the C-hub and the D-hub, it can be found that

$$P_V^C - P_W^D = (m-1)\frac{rc}{(k+1)(m+1)} - c > 0 \text{ if } r > \frac{(k+1)(m+1)}{m-1} = \alpha_2.$$

Since $\alpha_2 < \alpha_1$ when $k < n$, the C-hub is easier to invade the D-hub than the leaves to the C-hub. There exists a positive feedback mechanism between the C-hub and its cooperative neighbors, i.e., as more neighbors become cooperators, the payoff of the C-hub will increase, thereby becoming easier to induce more neighbors to learn its behavior. On the contrary, the feedback mechanism of the D-hub is negative, as can be illustrated by Figure 7.20 (b), which shows how a D-hub is taken over by a C-hub. As the leaves learn more about the defective strategy, the payoff of the D-hub will decrease and, after some time, the payoff of the D-hub will become lower than that of the C-hub. Thus, it will change its strategy and become a C-hub, since the two hubs are interconnected with each other. As a result, all the hubs playing PGGs tend to become cooperators, which promote the emergence of cooperation on the BA scale-free network.

7.3.3 Multi-Player/Two-Strategy Evolutionary Games on Correlated Scale-free Networks

It can be seen from (7.8) that the larger size the neighborhood $k_j + 1$ is, the less payoff the individual i will gain. This suggests that the degree correlation plays a nontrivial role in the PGG on heterogeneous networks.

Consider the evolutionary PGG on assortative networks. Figure 7.21 shows the frequency of cooperators, f_C, as a function of the multiplication factor r for different values of r_k. It can be seen that on the uncorrelated network with $r_k = 0$, the cooperators can sustain on a nonzero level until r becomes less than a threshold value, $r_c \approx 2.0$, below which the defectors dominate the network. The cooperation, however, is inhibited as the network becomes assortative, which is reflected not only by the fact that r_c

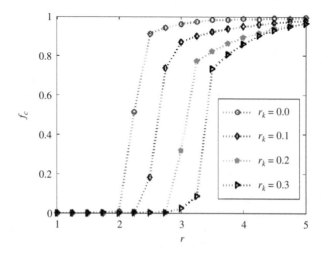

Figure 7.21 Frequency of cooperators f_C vs. r on the scale-free networks [36]. *Source*: Reproduced by permission of *Europhysics Letters*

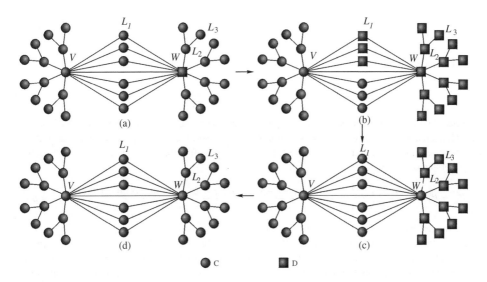

Figure 7.22 Illustration of a D-hub's demise on a double-star network [36]: (a) initial stage; (b) evolving stage 1; (c) evolving stage 2; (d) final stage. *Source*: Reproduced by permission of *Europhysics Letters*

increases as r_k increases, but also by the fact that f_C decreases as r_k increases for a given multiplication factor r.

Now, consider what would be happen if the game is played on a double-star network. The double-star network shown in Figure 7.20 has no common neighbors between the two stars, which are actually abundant in real-world networks. For this reason, some common neighbors are added to the double-star network, as shown in Figure 7.22, where there are two connected hubs, V and W, with m neighbors. The two hubs have l common neighbors (denoted by L_1), and each of their remaining $m - l - 1$ neighbors (denoted by L_2) has k leaves (denoted by L_3). In this figure, $m = 10$, $l = 6$. Initially, the hub W is set to be D (dark-grey, or red) and all the others to be C (light-grey, or green), as seen in Figure 7.22 (a). In this case, the payoff of W is

$$P_W^D = \frac{2rc}{m+1}\left(\frac{1}{m+1} + \frac{l}{3} + \frac{m-l-1}{k+1}\right) + \frac{rcl}{3}\left(\frac{1}{m+1} + \frac{1}{3}\right) + \frac{rc(m-l-1)}{k+1}\left(\frac{1}{k+1} + \frac{k-1}{2}\right)$$

(7.13)

where the first, second, and third terms on the right-hand-side correspond to the gains from the game centered on the two hubs, L_1 - and L_2-neighborhoods, respectively. Due to the symmetry of the position of the two hubs and the fact that the C-hub has contribution c to its neighbors while the D-hub does not, one can obtain the payoff of the C-hub, as

$$P_V^C = P_W^D + \frac{rc(m-l-1)}{(k+1)(m+1)} - c$$

Clearly, as the degree k of those neighbors in L_2 increases, this payoff of the C-hub will drop.

The payoff difference between the C-hub V and the D-hub W in Figure 7.22 (a) is

$$P_V^C - P_W^D = \frac{rc(m-l-1)}{(k+1)(m+1)} - c := \beta_1 c.$$

(7.14)

It can be seen that, for a given value of m, parameter β_1 decreases with the increase of either l or k, namely, the presence of some more common neighbors between the hubs or some higher-degree neighbors around the C-hub would weaken the capability of competition of the C-hub against the D-hub. In this stage of the game, the payoff gained by the D-hub is far greater than those low-degree neighbors. As a consequence, in the next step, many of them would change their strategies to follow D; hence, the number of cooperative neighbors around the D-hub will rapidly decrease. As a result, the network will evolve to a state as shown in Figure 7.22 (b). Since those common neighbors can learn from either the C-hub or the D-hub, one may expect that a half of them will become C and the other half become D. Thus, the payoff difference between the two hubs is

$$P_V^C - P_W^D = \frac{rc(m-l-1)}{k+1}\left(\frac{1}{m+1} + \frac{1}{k+1}\frac{k-1}{2}\right) - c := \beta_2 c. \tag{7.15}$$

Compared with (7.14), it is clear that $\beta_2 > \beta_1$ and the payoff of the C-hub is larger than that of the D-hub. In such a situation, sooner or latter W will imitate V's cooperative strategy, and the network will evolve to a state as shown in Figure 7.22 (c). In this case, the payoff difference between W and its defective neighbors among L_2 is

$$P_W^C - P_{L_2}^D = \frac{rc}{m+1}\left(\frac{2}{m+1} + \frac{l}{3} + \frac{m-l-1}{k+1}\right) + \frac{rcl}{3}\left(\frac{2}{m+1} + \frac{1}{3}\right) + \frac{rc(m-l-2)}{m+1} - c := \beta_3 c, \tag{7.16}$$

where the profit of W comes from the C-hub, their shared common neighbors, and the L_2-neighborhoods, respectively. In such a situation, the hub W's cooperative behavior will diffuse in its neighborhood, as shown in Figure 7.22 (d). Nonetheless, it should be noted that as k increases, β_3 decreases, which indicates that the more connections the neighbors in L_2 have, the more difficult the hub W changes its strategy. Taken altogether, if these hubs share many neighbors with other hubs and their immediate neighbors also possess high degrees, i.e., having an assortative degree correlation, then it would be difficult for the cooperative behavior to diffuse, leading to inhibition of cooperation.

Looking back at Figure 7.21, one can notice that in the coexistence region of C and D, f_C decreases as r_k increases. To gain a better understand of this phenomenon, consider the fraction of cooperators per degree, $f_C(k)$, and the distribution of the average payoffs per degree, $\rho(k)$, on the networks with $r_k = 0$ and $r_k = 0.3$, respectively, as shown in Figures 7.23 and 7.24. It can be seen that, for both assortative and uncorrelated networks, the hubs are always C. According to the above analysis, this is expected (otherwise the negative feedback effect on D-hubs would push them back to C). By comparing these two figures, one can notice that the payoffs of the hubs are lower on the assortative network than on the uncorrelated network with the same given r. This is due to the fact that the high-degree neighbors around the hubs on the assortative network dilute their contributions to each other, since in such a case the nodes with similar degrees are likely interconnected to each other, which weakens the hubs' ability to affect the behaviors of the leaves. For the same reason, on the assortative network, the low-degree nodes tend to adopt the defective strategy (Figure 7.24), because there are less chances for them to learn from the hubs. Consequently, as k decreases, $f_C(k)$ monotonously descends. Besides, the nodes with low degrees are abundant on scale-free networks, so the fraction of cooperators on the assortative network is less than that on the uncorrelated network.

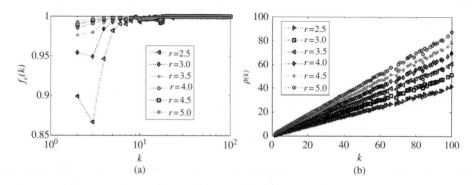

Figure 7.23 (a) Fraction of cooperators per degree, $f_C(k)$; (b) distribution of average payoffs per degree, $\rho(k)$, on the uncorrelated network [36]. *Source*: Reproduced by permission of *Europhysics Letters*

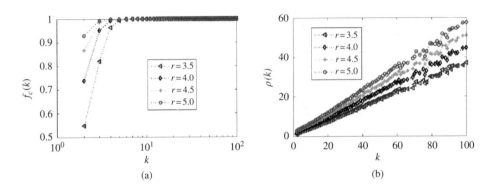

Figure 7.24 (a) Fraction of cooperators per degree, $f_C(k)$; (b) distribution of average payoffs per degree, $p(k)$, on the assortative network [36]. *Source*: Reproduced by permission of *Europhysics Letters*

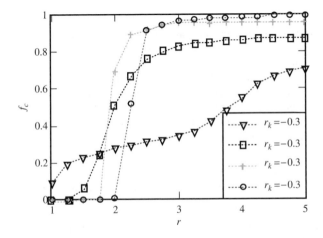

Figure 7.25 Frequency of cooperators, f_C, as a function of r for different values of r_k [36]. *Source*: Reproduced by permission of *Europhysics Letters*

Now, consider the evolution of cooperative behavior in the PGG on disassortative networks. Figure 7.25 shows f_C as a function of r when the assortative coefficient r_k decreases from 0.0 to -0.3. Compared with the uncorrelated network, f_C is smaller in the case of large r, while is bigger in the case of small r (the cooperation is easier to sustain). To further understand this phenomenon, as before Figure 7.26 here plots the distribution of cooperation and average fitness per degree on the network with $r_k = -0.3$ for different values of r. It can be observed that, unlike the uncorrelated and assortative networks on which all the hubs are C at the steady states, only one half of hubs are C but the other half are D on this disassortative network. The main reason is that, on the disassortative network, the hubs are likely connected to those low-degree nodes, and there are very few connections among themselves. As a result, the cooperative or defective behaviors are difficult to spread among hubs, so the hubs always maintain their initial strategies. Furthermore, the hubs can easily attract low-degree neighbors to follow their behaviors. Consequently, those leaf-nodes of the C-hubs (D-hubs) will be C (D), while those low-degree nodes located between the hubs with different strategies will intermittently alter their strategies. This enables the hubs to gain higher fitness than their leaf-nodes, as shown in Figure 7.26.

The behaviors of the nodes with medium degrees turn out to be quite complicated. For $r_k = -0.3$, for example, almost all medium-degree nodes (here, degrees 4–8) select those nodes with lower

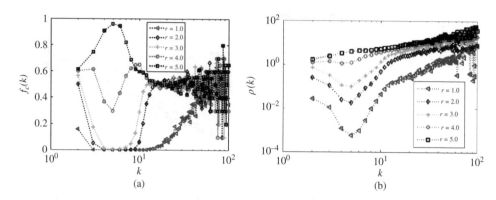

Figure 7.26 (a) Frequency of cooperators per degree, $f_C(k)$; (b) distribution of average payoffs $\rho(k)$ on the disassortative network with $r_k = -0.3$ [36]. *Source*: Reproduced by permission of *Europhysics Letters*

degrees as their neighbors. Accordingly, for a small multiplication factor, such as $r = 1.0$ or 2.0, these medium-degree nodes cannot gain sufficient benefit from their neighborhood and so have very low fitness, which makes them fragile to the invasion by defectors. As r increases, there are more nodes with lower degrees (e.g., $k = 2$ and 3) becoming C under the influence of the hubs, which in turn improves the fitness of the medium-degree nodes. For sufficiently large values of r, it would be better for the medium-degree nodes to choose C so as to obtain higher fitness. This leads to a high level of f_C, as shown in Figure 7.25. Therefore, the strategies of medium-degree nodes are more sensitive to the magnitude of r than those high-degree nodes.

7.3.4 Multi-Player/Two-Strategy Evolutionary Games on Clustered Scale-free Networks

The PD game is essentially different from the PGG in the sense that the former is a two-person game but the latter is played by groups of individuals. The difference between these two kinds of games leads to their distinctive cooperative behaviors on clustered scale-free networks. In this subsection, the effects of clustering coefficient on cooperation in scale-free PGG are examined, and the feedback reciprocity mechanism of triangles in the games played by groups of people is revealed [37].

Consider a networked PGG on a scale-free network with a tunable clustering coefficient, generated by the HK algorithm [28], where individuals update their strategies according to the Fermi dynamics (7.6). Figure 7.27 shows f_C as a function of the multiplication factor r for the scale-free network with different clustering coefficients. It is observed that f_C is an increasing function of r, which means that cooperators are easy to survive for large values of r. More importantly, as shown by Figure 7.27, cooperation can sustain for small values of r on the scale-free network with high clustering, which is different from the pairwise interactions of the PD game shown in Figure 7.17.

The two typical star subnetworks shown in Figure 7.28 are used to represent a scale-free network without (with) clustering, where k_i denotes the degree of nodes at the ith layer (denoted as L_i, $i = 0, 1, 2, \ldots$). In the figure, light-grey (green) disk denotes a cooperator and dark-grey (red) square denotes a defector, respectively. In Figure 7.28 (b), called starlike-II, the hub at L_0 and two nodes at L_1 together compose a triangle. In order to characterize the degree heterogeneity of this scale-free network, assume that $k_0 > k_1$. For simplicity, let the other nodes have the same degree, k_1. Figure 7.28 (a), called starlike-I, can be obtained by reshuffling an edge that links nodes at L_1 with an edge randomly chosen from a layer far-away on starlike-II. Since the nodes, excluding the hub, have the same degree, the reshuffling operation will not change the degree heterogeneity and the degree correlation of the original subnetwork. And, for a

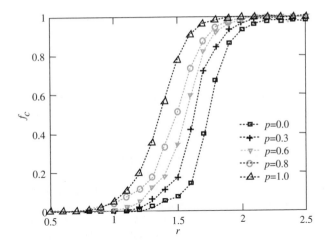

Figure 7.27 Frequency of cooperators, f_C, as a function of r [37]. *Source*: Reprinted with permission from Rong, Z., Yang, H-X. and Wang, W-X. (2010) Feedback reciprocity mechanism promotes the cooperation of highly clustered scale-free networks. *Physical Review E*, **82**: 047101. Copyright (2010) American Physical Society

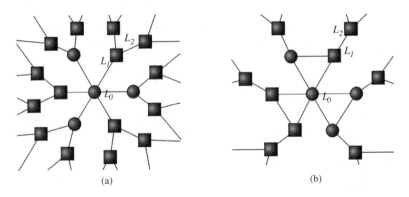

Figure 7.28 Two typical subnetworks: (a) starlike-I subnetwork without any triangle around the hub; (b) starlike-II subnetwork with triangles around the hub [37]. *Source*: Reprinted with permission from Rong, Z., Yang, H-X. and Wang, W-X. (2010) Feedback reciprocity mechanism promotes the cooperation of highly clustered scale-free networks. *Physical Review E*, **82**: 047101. Copyright (2010) American Physical Society

large network, the randomly-selected edge is far from the hub, so one can obtain a starlike-I subnetwork, as shown in Figure 7.28 (a).

Next, consider the influence of the triangle structure on the evolution of cooperation in PGG. Initially, let only the central hub at L_0 and its n_c neighbors at L_1 be cooperators and the others be defectors. Then, conditions for cooperation diffusion in the two subnetworks can be derived by considering the payoff difference between cooperators and defectors. Although the underlying networks are very simple, and quite regular, they are helpful for revealing the effect of the triangular structure on cooperation, to some extent, due to the presence of a hub at the center and a treelike structure that excludes loops. As will be demonstrated below, this simple network indeed can provide some insights into the understanding of the role of the clustering structure on scale-free networks, especially for the triangles around hubs.

First, the payoff difference between cooperators and defectors is studied on the starlike-I subnetwork shown in Figure 7.28 (a). Consider the C-hub at L_0, which will contribute $1/(k_0 + 1)$ for each PGG centered on itself and its L_1 neighbors, and the n_c cooperative neighbors at L_1 will contribute $1/(k_1 + 1)$ for each PGG centered on themselves and the C-hub. The payoff $P_{L_0}^C$ of the C-hub is

$$P_{L_0}^C = \frac{rc}{k_0 + 1}\left(\frac{1}{k_0 + 1} + \frac{n_c}{k_1 + 1}\right) + \frac{rc}{k_1 + 1}\left(\frac{k_0}{k_0 + 1} + \frac{n_c}{k_1 + 1}\right) - c. \tag{7.17}$$

Since the defector at L_1 can obtain benefit from the C-hub through the PGG centered on itself and on the C-hub, respectively, the payoff difference between the C-hub and its defective neighbor at L_1 can be obtained, as follows:

$$P_{L_0}^C - P_{L_1}^D = \frac{rc(k_0 - 1)}{(k_0 + 1)(k_1 + 1)} + \frac{rcn_c}{(k_1 + 1)^2} - c := \gamma_1 c, \tag{7.18}$$

where $rc/[(k_0 + 1)(k_1 + 1)]$ and $rc/(k_1 + 1)^2$ correspond to the contributions of the C-hub and the cooperators at L_1 for the PGG centered on the nodes at L_1. Similarly, compared with the defector at L_2, the cooperator at L_1 can gain additional benefits from the PGG centered on the C-hub and the $k_1 - 2$ defective neighbors at L_2, respectively. Therefore, the payoff difference between the cooperator at L_1 and its defective neighbor at L_2 is

$$P_{L_1}^C - P_{L_2}^D = \frac{rc}{k_0 + 1}\left(\frac{1}{k_0 + 1} + \frac{n_c}{k_1 + 1}\right) + \frac{rc(k_1 - 2)}{(k_1 + 1)(k_2 + 1)} - c := \gamma_2 c. \tag{7.19}$$

Next, the payoff difference between a cooperator and its defective neighbors on the starlike-II subnetwork is investigated. The results are shown in Figure 7.28 (b). Due to the existence of triangles, the C-hub can obtain the contribution of a cooperative L_1-neighbor i, not only from the PGG centered on i, but also from the common neighbor with i. As a result, the payoff of the C-hub on the starlike-II subnetwork is obtained as follows:

$$P_{L_0}^C = \frac{rc}{k_0 + 1}\left(\frac{1}{k_0 + 1} + \frac{n_c}{k_1 + 1}\right) + \frac{rc}{k_1 + 1}\left(\frac{k_0}{k_0 + 1} + \frac{2n_c}{k_1 + 1}\right) - c. \tag{7.20}$$

It should be noted that compared with (7.17), the C-hub on the starlike-II subnetworks can gain additional $rcn_c/(k_1 + 1)^2$ payoff, since the L_1-cooperators can feedback their contributions to the C-hub through the triangle.

Further, consider the worst case where the C-hub and its defective L_1-neighbor j share one cooperator i. The defector j can get benefits from the PGG centered on the C-hub, on i and on j, respectively, and thus the payoff difference between the C-hub and j is

$$P_{L_0}^C - P_{L_1}^D = \frac{rc(k_0 - 2)}{(k_0 + 1)(k_1 + 1)} + \frac{2rc(n_c - 1)}{(k_1 + 1)^2} - c := \gamma_3 c. \tag{7.21}$$

Moreover, the payoff difference between the cooperator i and its defective neighbor at L_2 can be obtained, as

$$P_{L_1}^C - P_{L_2}^D = \frac{rc}{k_0 + 1}\left(\frac{1}{k_0 + 1} + \frac{n_c}{k_1 + 1}\right) + \frac{rc}{k_1 + 1}\left(\frac{1}{k_0 + 1} + \frac{1}{k_1 + 1}\right) + \frac{rc}{k_2 + 1}\frac{k_1 - 3}{k_1 + 1} - c := \gamma_4 c, \tag{7.22}$$

where the first, second and third terms correspond to the gains of i obtaining from the PGG centered on the C-hub, on the L_1- and L_2-neighbors with the defective strategy, respectively.

Furthermore, to reveal the distinction between the two subnetworks regarding their ability of cooperation diffusion from L_0 to L_1, compare (7.21) with (7.18) and obtain

$$\gamma_3 - \gamma_1 = \frac{r}{k_1 + 1}\left(\frac{n_c - 2}{k_1 + 1} - \frac{1}{k_0 + 1}\right).$$

This implies that if $n_c > 2$ and $k_0 > k_1$, the reciprocity between the C-hub and its L_1-cooperators can be enhanced through the feedback loops of the triangle; therefore, $\gamma_3 - \gamma_1 > 0$ and the invasion from C-hub

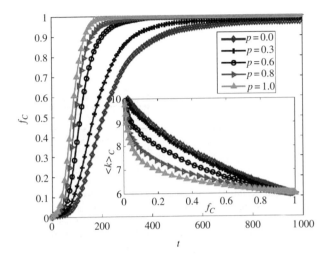

Figure 7.29 Diffusion of cooperation on a scale-free network with different clustering coefficients [37]. *Source*: Reprinted with permission from Rong, Z., Yang, H-X. and Wang, W-X. (2010) Feedback reciprocity mechanism promotes the cooperation of highly clustered scale-free networks. *Physical Review E*, **82**: 047101. Copyright (2010) American Physical Society

to the L_1-defectors is easy to occur on the starlike-II subnetwork than on the starlike-I subnetwork. This is a positive feedback, so that if there are more cooperators around the C-hub, then it can gain more payoff and the cooperative behavior is easier to diffuse from L_0 to L_1. Furthermore, comparing (7.22) with (7.19), and considering the case of $k_1 = k_2$, one can obtain the ability distinction of cooperation diffusion from L_1 to L_2, as

$$\gamma_4 - \gamma_2 = \frac{r}{(k_0 + 1)(k_1 + 1)} .$$

It can be observed that since the C-hub can feed back the contribution to its cooperative neighbor through the triangle, $\gamma_4 - \gamma_2 > 0$, and so the L_1-cooperators are easier to diffuse their behaviors to the L_2-neighbors on the starlike-II subnetwork than on the starlike-I subnetwork. This also leads to the increase of C-hub's payoff and speeds up the diffusion of cooperation on the network. Therefore, the triangle clustering on the scale-free network can form a kind of feedback reciprocity that promotes the diffusion of cooperation.

Although all the above analysis is carried out from a C-hub initially, the scenario of starting from a D-hub can be discussed by the same analysis. It is known that the D-hub will trigger a negative feedback due to the diffuse of its defection strategy to the leaves. A D-hub will likely turn to C, if it is connected to some C-hubs [35]. After a strategy switch of the D-hub, the next evolution phase with an initial C-hub can be analyzed similarly as above.

Finally, to check the feedback reciprocity mechanism on the clustered scale-free networks, consider a scale-free network as shown in Figure 7.29, where averagely each node has 6 neighbors. Initially there are only 10 cooperators (the highest-degree node and its 9 low-degree neighbors) and the others are defectors. The multiplication factor is $r = 3.0$. The figure shows the frequency of cooperators, f_C, versus the generation time t, and the average degree of cooperators, $\langle k \rangle_C$ versus f_C (inset). The figure shows how the cooperation diffuses on the scale-free network with different clustering coefficients.

It is interesting to see that the higher clustering the network has, the earlier the frequency of cooperators reaches an equilibrium state and the easier the cooperation diffuses. Furthermore, it is interesting to observe from the inset figure that for the same f_C, the average degree of cooperators, $\langle k \rangle_C$, decreases as C increases. This implies that the low-degree nodes are easier to become cooperators on a highly-clustered scale-free network than on a lower one, which further accelerates the diffusion of cooperation. The results corroborate the above analysis about the feedback reciprocity mechanism of the triangle on the subnetworks.

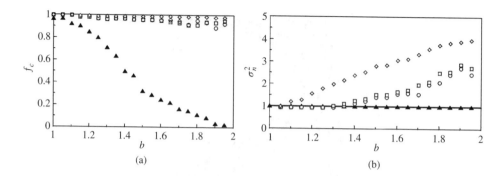

Figure 7.30 (a) Frequency of cooperators, f_C; (b) normalized variance of degree, σ_n^2, as a function of temptation to defect, b, when $p = 0$ (full triangles), 0.01 (circles), 0.1 (squares) and 1.0 (diamonds) [40]. *Source*: Reprinted with permission from Zimmermann, M.G., Eguiluz, V.M, and Miguel, M.S. (2004) Coevolution of dynamical states and interactions in dynamic networks. *Physical Review E*, **69**(6): 065102. Copyright (2004) American Physical Society

7.4 Adaptive Evolutionary Games on Networks

The relationship among individuals in a real-world system is usually not steady but changing over time. People often make some new friends and lost some old friends. Therefore, a social network typically evolves in which individuals adjust their social ties adaptively. Such adaptive networks, which combine the network topological evolution with the dynamics of individuals, characterize the behavioral evolution in many social and biological systems [38, 39]. Through a proper feedback mechanism between individuals' behaviors and their social ties, individuals can shape their neighborhoods, which may promote the emergence of cooperation to a new level.

Zimmermann *et al.* [40] studied an adaptive networked game model, in which the interaction of individuals coevolves with their strategies. Consider an individual occupying a node on a network plays the PD game with his current neighbors and obtains an accumulated payoff. The coevolutionary rule is defined as follows: An individual i will compare his payoff P_i with his neighbor j, who has the highest payoff in the neighborhood. If $P_i > P_j$, the individual i is satisfied; otherwise, he is unsatisfied. The alteration of social ties only occurs between defector-defector pairs, i.e., an unsatisfied defector may remove his edge with another defector with a probability p and rewire it to a randomly selected new node instead. Following this coevolutionary rule, the average degree of the network is constant but defectors can become satisfied through interacting only with cooperators, while unsatisfied cooperators always imitate other cooperators. Thus, a winning defector may lose neighbors as a punishment for his defection, while a winning cooperator may attract more social ties. As shown in Figure 7.30, for low values of p, the cooperation is dramatically enhanced as the network becomes heterogeneous when the initial configuration was a random network. The cooperative hierarchical interaction structure can be formed, where cooperators occupy on the center nodes, which supports the stability of a high-cooperation state on the adaptive network.

A multi-adaptive game model was studied in [41], where the payoff matrix of the PD game evolves over time, in that the temptation to defect which an individual adapts is dependant on the fraction of cooperation in the network. Each individual has a free edge that can be connected to a long-range neighbor, creating an adaptive network where if an individual i adopts a strategy of an neighbor j with the highest payoff, then i rewires its free edge to connect himself to j. Therefore, individuals tend to build long-range connections with other individual who have high payoffs, and the coevolutionary cooperation at multi-levels generates an interaction network having a scale-free property as well as a hierarchical structure.

Recently, some controlled experiments with human subjects have validated that dynamic social networks promote cooperation. Rand *et al.* [42] invited 785 human subjects participating in a repeated PD game experiments. The subjects were randomly assigned into 40 groups and each took part in one of four experiments, where the average network size is 19.6. Initially, 20% edges were randomly connected among the subjects, thus a social network was initialized with an average degree $\langle k \rangle \approx 4.0$. Then, three kinds of conditions were considered: random edge updating, fixed edges, and strategic edge updating. In the experiment of random edge updating, the network is randomly altered after each round of the game, which creates a well-mixed population. For the setting of fixed edges, the network maintains unchanged as its initial state during the experiment. In the strategic edge updating, after one round of the game, a rewiring round occurs where the subjects are permitted to change their social ties. For each rewiring round, $f\%$ of subject pairs are randomly selected. If an edge exists between them, then one of them is randomly selected to offer a chance to break the edge. If no edge between them, a new edge is created. Before breaking or creating an edge, the deciding subject is informed of his opponent's action in the

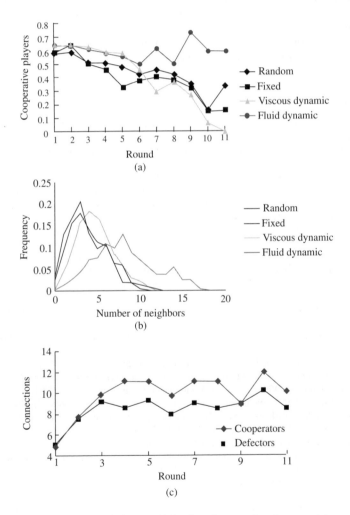

Figure 7.31 Results of human game experiments: (a) fraction of cooperative players evolving over one round in four experiments; (b) fraction of the number of neighbors that a player has across all sections and rounds; (c) average connections of cooperators or defectors on the fluid network [42]. *Source*: Rand, D.G., Arbesman, S. and Christakis, N.A. (2011) Dynamic social networks promote cooperation in experiments with humans. *Proceedings of the National Academy of Sciences USA*, **108** (48): 19193–8. Copyright (2011) National Academy of Sciences, USA

preceding round. But the subjects do not have global information, such as the structure of the network or the number of neighbors. For the strategic edge updating, two cases are considered: the viscous dynamic ($f\% = 10\%$) and the fluid dynamic ($f\% = 30\%$) cases.

In the above controlled human experiments, cooperation decays over time in the well-mixed, fixed, and viscous networks, while cooperation can maintain at a high level on the fluid network, as shown in Figure 7.31 (a). The degree distribution becomes more heterogeneous on the fluid network than on the viscous network, as shown in Figure 7.31 (b). On the dynamic networks, edge reciprocity works well, i.e., individuals tend to connect with those who cooperated in the previous round and, meanwhile, cut the existing edges with defectors. Therefore, the cooperator–cooperator pairs are more stable than the cooperator–defector pairs, and the latter are more stable than the defector–defector pairs. As time evolves, cooperators attract more connections than defectors, as shown in Figure 7.31 (c). More interestingly, an individual who never defected in the last rounds is more likely to turn into a cooperator, if other individuals cut their edges with him. This leads to the emergence of stable cooperation on the fluid network. Hence, the experiments have actually conformed to the theoretical results that an adaptive network can enhance the sustainment of cooperation.

A similar human experiment was carried out in [43], with about the same conclusions. Recently, some experimental results of human cooperation have been reviewed in [44].

References

[1] von Neumann, J. and Morgenstern, O. (1944) *Theory of Games and Economic Behavior*. Princeton University Press, Princeton, NJ.

[2] Nash, J.F. (1950) Equilibrium points in n-person games. *Proceedings of the National Academy of Sciences USA*, **36**(1): 48–9.

[3] Axelrod, R. (2006) *The Evolution of Cooperation*. Basic Books, New York; 1984, revised 2006.

[4] Nowak, M.A. and Sigmund, K. (1992) Tit for tat in heterogeneous populations. *Nature*, **355**(6357): 250–3.

[5] Nowak, M.A. and Sigmund, K. (1993) A strategy of win-stay, lose-shift that outperforms tit-for-tat in the Prisoner's Dilemma game. *Nature*, **364**: 56–8.

[6] Nowak, M.A. (2006) *Evolutionary Dynamics: Exploring the Equations of Life*. Harvard University Press, Cambridge, MA.

[7] Fudenberg, D. and Levine, D.K. (1998) *The Theory of Learning in Games*. MIT Press, Cambridge, MA.

[8] Smith, J.M. and Price, G.R. (1973) The logic of animal conflict. *Nature*, **246**(5427): 15–18.

[9] Taylor, P.D, and Jonker, L. (1978) Evolutionarily stable strategies and game dynamics. *Mathematical Biosciences*, **40**: 145–56.

[10] Rapoport, A. and Chammah, A.M. (1966) The game of chicken. *American Behavioral Scientist*, **10**: 10–14, 23–8.

[11] Skyrms, B. (2004) *The Stag Hunt and the Evolution of Social Structure*. Cambridge University Press, Cambridge, UK.

[12] Cooper, R. (1998) *Coordination Games*. Cambridge University Press, Cambridge, UK.

[13] Nowak, M.A. (2006) Five rules for the evolution of cooperation. *Science*, **314**(5805): 1560–3.

[14] Nowak, M.A. and May, R. (1992) Evolutionary games and spatial chaos. *Nature*, **359**: 826–9.

[15] Szabó, G. and Fath, G. (2007) Evolutionary games on graphs. *Physics Reports*, **446**(46): 97–216.

[16] Killingback, T. and Doebeli M. (1996) Spatial evolutionary game theory: hawks and doves revisited. *Proceedings of the Royal Society: Biological Sciences*, **263**(1374): 1135–44.

[17] http://en.wikipedia.org/wiki/Replicator_equation (last accessed August 10, 2014).

[18] Vukov, J., Szabó, G. and Szolnoki, A. (2006) Cooperation in the noisy case: Prisoner's dilemma game on two types of regular random graphs. *Physical Review E*, **73**(6): 067103.

[19] Szabó, G. and Toke, C. (1998) Evolutionary prisoner's dilemma game on a square lattice. *Physical Review E*, **58**(1): 69–73.

[20] Hauert, C. and Szabó, G. (2005) Game theory and physics. *American Journal of Physics*, **73**(5): 405–14.

[21] Hauert, C. and Doebeli, M. (2004) Spatial structure often inhibits the evolution of cooperation in the snowdrift game. *Nature*, **428**: 643–6.

[22] Santos, F.C. and Pacheco, J.M. (2005) Scale-free networks provide a unifying framework for the emergence of cooperation. *Physical Review Letters*, **95**(9): 098104.

[23] Santos, F.C., Pacheco, J.M. and Lenaerts, T. (2006) Evolutionary dynamics of social dilemmas in structured heterogeneous populations. *Proceedings of the National Academy of Sciences USA*, **103**(9): 3490–4.

[24] Santos, F.C. and Pacheco, J.M. (2006) A new route to the evolution of cooperation. *Journal of Evolutionary Biology*, **19**(3): 726–33.

[25] Gómez-Gardeñes, J., Campillo, M. and Floria, L.M. *et al.* (2007) Dynamical organization of cooperation in complex topologies. *Physical Review Letters*, **98**(10): 108103.

[26] Xulvi-Brunet, R. and Sokolov, I.M. (2004) Reshuffling scale-free networks: From random to assortative *Physical Review E*, **70**(6): 066102.

[27] Rong, Z.H., Li, X. and Wang, X.F. (2007) Roles of mixing patterns in cooperation on a scale-free networked game. *Physical Review E*, **76**(2): 027101.

[28] Holme, P. and Kim, B.J. (2002) Growing scale-free networks with tunable clustering. *Physical Review E*, **65**: 026107.

[29] Assenza, S., Gómez-Gardeñes, J. and Latora V. (2008) Enhancement of cooperation in highly clustered scale-free networks. *Physical Review E*, **78**: 017101.

[30] Dreber, A. and Nowak, M.A. (2008) Gambling for global goods, *Proceedings of the National Academy of Sciences USA*, **105**: 2261–2.

[31] Milinski, M., Sommerfeld, R.D. and Krambeck, H-J. *et al.* (2008) The collective-risk social dilemma and the prevention of simulated dangerous climate change, *Proceedings of the National Academy of Sciences USA*, **105**: 2291–4.

[32] Tavonia, A., Dannenberg, A. and Kallis, G. *et al.* (2008) Inequality, communication, and the avoidance of disastrous climate change in a public goods game, *Proceedings of the National Academy of Sciences USA*, **108**: 11825–9.

[33] Apicella, C.L., Marlowe, F.W. and Fowler, J.H. *et al.* (2012) Social networks and cooperation in hunter-gatherers. *Nature*, **481**(7382): 497–501.

[34] Gómez-Gardeñes, P.M., Szolnoki, J. and Floría, A. *et al.* (2013) Evolutionary dynamics of group interactions on structured populations: A review, *Journal of the Royal Society Interface*, **10**: 20120997.

[35] Santos, F.C., Santos, M.D. and Pacheco, J.M. (2008) Social diversity promotes the emergence of cooperation in public goods games. *Nature*, **454**: 213–16.

[36] Rong, Z. and Wu, Z-X. (2009) Effect of the degree correlation in public goods game on scale-free networks. *Europhysics Letters*, **87**: 30001.

[37] Rong, Z., Yang, H-X. and Wang, W-X. (2010) Feedback reciprocity mechanism promotes the cooperation of highly clustered scale-free networks. *Physical Review E*, **82**: 047101.

[38] Gross, P.T. and Blasius, B. (2008) Adaptive coevolutionary networks: A review. *Journal of the Royal Society Interface*, **5**: 259–71.

[39] Perc, M. and Szolnoki, A. (2010) Coevolutionary games – A mini review. *BioSystems*, **99**: 109–25.

[40] Zimmermann, M.G., Eguiluz, V.M, and Miguel, M.S. (2004) Coevolution of dynamical states and interactions in dynamic networks. *Physical Review E*, **69**(6): 065102.

[41] Lee, S., Holme, P. and Wu, Z-X. (2011) Emergent hierarchical structures in multiadaptive games. *Physical Review Letters*, **106**: 028702.

[42] Rand, D.G., Arbesman, S. and Christakis, N.A. (2011) Dynamic social networks promote cooperation in experiments with humans. *Proceedings of the National Academy of Sciences USA*, **108**(48): 19193–8.

[43] Wang, J., Suri, S. and Watts, D.J. (2012) Cooperation and assortativity with dynamic partner updating. *Proceedings of the National Academy of Sciences USA*, **109**(36): 14363–8.

[44] Rand, D.G. and Nowak, M.A. (2013) Human cooperation, *Trends in Cognitive Sciences*, **17**(8): 413–25.

8

Network Synchronization

8.1 Introduction

The term *synchronization* is bound with the name Christiaan Huygens (April 14, 1629–July 8, 1695), a Dutch mathematician, astronomer and physicist. Huygens worked on the construction of accurate clocks, suitable for naval navigation, over a long period of his lifetime. His invention, the pendulum clock, was a breakthrough in timekeeping, which was patented in 1657. Then, in 1658, he published a book entitled *Horologium* on this subject. The most important work of Huygens relating to the concept of synchronization was his observation that two pendulums mounted on the same beam would come to swing in perfectly opposite directions, a phenomenon he referred to as odd sympathy.

Another interesting discovery was the observation of fireflies' synchronous flashing by another Dutch, a tourist named Kempfer. When he traveled through the River Naenam in Thailand in 1680, Kempfer found that those little insects could flash together fairly accurately in time.

If attention is paid, one can easily find many synchronization phenomena in different forms in nature as well as man-made systems. For example, an audience expresses appreciation for a good performance by its applause: the tumultuous applause can transform itself into waves of synchronized clapping quickly and this synchrony can also disappear and then reappear several times during the applause. This common social harmony and its generation mechanism may be studied from a complex dynamics point of view [1]. The rhythm in the human heart certainly is another well-known incident. In mammals, as another example, a small group of neurons in the brain stem, named pre-Bötzinger complex, is responsible for generating a regular rhythmic output to motor calls that initiate a breath [2]. In computer science, especially in parallel computing, synchronization means the coordination of simultaneous threads or processes to complete a task of obtaining a correct runtime order while avoiding unexpected race conditions. There are many types of synchronizations there: barrier, lock/semaphore, nonblocking synchronization, synchronous communication operations, and file synchronization, and so on. There are simply too many examples to list. In fact, in science and technology, synchronization has become a focal subject for study today [3, 4].

Yet, synchronization can be harmful. On June 10, year 2000, when the London Millennium Footbridge over the River Thames was first opened to the public, thousands of people walked on it for celebration but unexpectedly lateral vibration (resonant structural response) caused this 690-ton steal bridge to sway severely. This swaying motion earned it a nickname the Wobbly Bridge afterwards. Although the resonant vibrational modes have been well understood in bridge design after the famous event of collapse of the Tacoma Narrows Bridge in 1940, not much attention had been given to pedestrian-excited lateral motion, which was responsible for the big vibration of the millennium bridge. An extensive analysis was conducted thereafter, but it took more than one year and costed about £5 million to finally fix the problems and then reopen the bridge on February 22, 2002.

Fundamentals of Complex Networks: Models, Structures and Dynamics, First Edition.
Guanrong Chen, Xiaofan Wang, Xiang Li.
© Higher Education Press. All rights reserved. Published 2015 by John Wiley & Sons Singapore Pte Ltd.
Companion Website: www.wiley.com/go/chen/complex

Internet is another phenomenal example for which synchronization could be harmful. On the Internet, many apparently independent periodic processes such as routers can inadvertently become synchronized. In particular, the synchronization of periodic routing messages can emerge, which have a harmful effect on other network traffics. Notably, the transition from unsynchronized to synchronized traffic is not a gradual degradation but has a very abrupt phase transition where the addition of a single router can literally convert a completely unsynchronized traffic stream into a completely synchronized one. The danger is that this kind of inadvertent synchronization of periodic processes is likely to become an increasing problem in the Internet [5].

Research reveals that all these seemingly independent events of synchronizations can be described under a unified mathematical framework. Suppose that each individual in a population is a dynamical system oscillating periodically and they are connected as a network. Winfree [6] showed that if each oscillator is strongly coupled with its finitely many neighbors then the amplitudes of these oscillators may be neglected thereby transforming the concerned issue into a phase synchronization problem. From this point of view, by completely ignoring oscillatory amplitudes, Kuramoto [7] further suggested that a network of finitely many coupled oscillators could be described by a simple phase equation, no matter how weak the coupling strength is among them.

This formulation facilitates the discussion of the synchronization problem in a finite population of connected oscillators. Since these earlier investigations, various synchronization phenomena on networks have evoked a lot of interests in theoretical as well as practical research studies. In the last century, the main research efforts were focused on regular networks, such as Coupled Map Lattices (CML) [8] and Cellular Neural Networks (CNN) [9]. This kind of simplification on the network structures may have the advantage of studying only the complex dynamics caused by the nonlinearity of the individual systems by ignoring the effects of the complex network topologies.

However, network topology certainly has significant effects on the network dynamics particularly synchronous behaviors. For example, as intuitively clear, a strong enough coupling strength can lead to the synchrony of a network [10], but this does not help explain why a weakly coupled network still have very strong tendency towards synchronization. One answer was revealed by the recent discoveries of small-world and scale-free features of various complex network topologies, which have dragged increasing attention to the relationship between the network topology and network synchronous behaviors, as discussed below.

8.2   Complete Synchronization of Continuous-Time Networks

A general continuous-time dynamical network and its synchronization problem can be formulated as follows.

Consider a network of N identical nodes, in which node i is described by

$$\dot{x}_i = f(x_i) + c \sum_{j=1}^{N} a_{ij} H(x_j), \qquad i = 1, 2, \ldots, N, \tag{8.1}$$

where $f(\cdot)$ is generally a nonlinear function satisfying a local or global Lipschitz condition (which guarantees that the function will not diverge too quickly before synchronization takes time to achieve), $x_i = [x_i^{(1)}, x_i^{(2)}, \ldots, x_i^{(n)}]^T \in R^n$ is the state vector, constant $c > 0$ is the coupling strength, $H : R^n \to R^n$ is the *inner coupling* matrix connecting different components of a state vector, and $\widetilde{A} = [a_{ij}] \in R^{N \times N}$ is the *outer coupling* matrix defined as follows: if there is a connection between node i and node j, $i \neq j$, then $a_{ij} = a_{ji} = 1$; otherwise, $a_{ij} = a_{ji} = 0, i \neq j$; the diagonal elements with indices $i = j$ are defined as

$$a_{ii} = -\sum_{j=1, j\neq i}^{N} a_{ij} = -\sum_{j=1, j\neq i}^{N} a_{ji} = -k_i, \qquad i = 1, 2, \ldots, N, \tag{8.2}$$

where k_i is the degree of node $i, i = 1, 2, \ldots, N$. Thus, the outer coupling matrix is actually the negative Laplacian matrix discussed in Chapter 2, namely $L = -\widetilde{A}$, which describes an undirected and unweighted network topology.

In view of (8.2), the Laplacian matrix $L = [l_{ij}]$ of network (8.1) satisfies

$$\sum_{j=1}^{N} l_{ij} = -\sum_{j=1}^{N} a_{ij} = 0, \qquad i = 1, 2, \ldots, N, \tag{8.3}$$

which is referred to as a *diffusive condition*, describing a kind of energy-balance situation; conceptually, it is similar to the well-known Kirchhoff's law in circuits theory.

If the network is wholly connected without separate subnets, then its Laplacian matrix L is an irreducible matrix, i.e., it cannot be reduced to an upper-triangular form by a similar transformation, thus by matrix theory [11], matrix L has a zero eigenvalue of multiplicity 1, associated with the eigenvector $[1, 1, \ldots, 1]^T$, which may be normalized by dividing by $\sqrt{N}$, and the other eigenvalues of matrix L are all positive:

$$0 = \lambda_1 < \lambda_2 \leq \cdots \leq \lambda_N. \tag{8.4}$$

Here, $\lambda_2 > 0$ is called the *algebraic connectivity* of the network. Moreover, the set of corresponding n-dimensional eigenvectors of all the nonzero eigenvalues span an $(N-1)n$-dimensional subspace, transversal to the eigenvector vector $[1, 1, \ldots, 1]^T$ of the zero eigenvalue.

To verify the algebraic connectivity $\lambda_2 > 0$ for a connected network, let x be a nonzero eigenvector associated with the eigenvalue $\lambda_1 = 0$ of its Laplacian matrix L. Then, $Lx = 0$, so that $x^T L x = \sum_{(u,v) \in E} (x_u - x_v)^2 = 0$. Consequently, $x_u = x_v$ for every pair of nodes (u, v) in the network since the network is connected. This implies that $x = a [1, 1, \ldots, 1]^T$ for some constant $a \neq 0$, namely, the eigenvalue $\lambda_1 = 0$ has multiplicity 1; therefore $\lambda_2 \neq 0$. By the semi-positiveness of the Laplacian matrix L, one has $\lambda_2 > 0$.

Spectral analysis in graph theory [11] shows that if the network is composed of two components, then $0 = \lambda_1 = \lambda_2 < \lambda_3 \leq \cdots \leq \lambda_N$, and so on, namely the number of zeros eigenvalues equals the number of components, and in the extreme case when the network is a set of N isolated nodes then $0 = \lambda_1 = \lambda_2 = \cdots = \lambda_N$.

Mathematically, network synchronization is defined as follows.

Definition 8.1 *Network (8.1) is said to achieve complete (asymptotic) synchronization, if*

$$\lim_{t \to \infty} \| x_i(t) - x_j(t) \| = 0 \quad \text{for all } i, j = 1, 2, \ldots, N, \tag{8.5}$$

where $\| \cdot \|$ is the Euclidean norm.

Furthermore, the set $\{x_1 = x_2 = \cdots = x_N\}$ is referred to as the *synchronization manifold* in the state space $R^{n \times N}$. To achieve complete synchronization of network (8.1) is equivalent to guaranteeing its synchronization manifold be an *(asymptotically) stable invariant synchronization manifold* in the sense that, for all network orbits in $R^{n \times N}$, if they are moving to be close enough to this synchronization manifold then they will be attracted to the manifold and then stay inside forever.

Physically, throughout the synchronization process all node states will evolve continuously governed by the differential equations of the node dynamical systems, therefore if all node states finally reach synchrony then the synchronized state must be one of the evolving states of the node system, namely one solution orbit of the node system. For this reason, synchronization may also be defined as

$$\lim_{t \to \infty} \| x_i(t) - s(t) \| = 0 \quad \text{for all } i = 1, 2, \ldots, N, \tag{8.6}$$

for some $s(t)$ satisfying $\dot{s}(t) = f(s(t))$, $s(t) \in R^n$. It is noted that for synchronization, this $s(t)$ is not specified, since (8.6) always leads to (8.5); but if this $s(t)$ is specified then (8.6) becomes a typical "tracking" problem in classical control systems theory.

Actually, Definition 8.1 (8.5) is equivalent to the following definition:

$$\lim_{t \to \infty} \| x_i(t) - \bar{x}(t) \| = 0 \quad \text{for all } i = 1, 2, \ldots, N, \tag{8.7}$$

where $\bar{x}(t) = \sum_{i=1}^{N} \beta_i x_i(t)$ was first introduced in [47, 48] and later used in [49, 50], with $[\beta_1, \beta_2, \ldots, \beta_N]^T$ being the left eigenvector of the zero eigenvalue of the network Laplacian matrix $L \equiv -\tilde{A}$. In fact,

$$0 \leq ||x_i - \bar{x}|| = \left\| x_i - \sum_{j=1}^{N} \beta_j x_j \right\| = \left\| \sum_{j=1}^{N} \beta_j x_i - \sum_{j=1}^{N} \beta_j x_j \right\|$$

$$= \left\| \sum_{j=1}^{N} \beta_j \left(x_i - x_j\right) \right\| \leq \sum_{j=1}^{N} \beta_j ||x_i - x_j|| \to 0 \quad (t \to \infty),$$

for all $i = 1, 2, \ldots, N$. Therefore, (8.5) implies (8.8). On the other hand,

$$||x_i - x_j|| = ||x_i - \bar{x} + \bar{x} - x_j|| \leq ||x_i - \bar{x}|| + ||\bar{x} - x_j|| \leq 2 \max_{1 \leq i \leq N} ||x_i - \bar{x}||,$$

which, by taking limits on both sides, shows that (8.8) implies (8.5).

Now, it can also be shown that Definition (8.6) is equivalent to (8.5) for two general cases: (i) $f(\cdot)$ is linear homogeneous in the sense that $f\left(\sum_{j=1}^{N} \alpha_j x_j\right) = \sum_{j=1}^{N} \alpha_j f(x_j)$ for any constants α_i, $i = 1, 2, \ldots, N$, which includes all linear systems; (ii) $f(\cdot)$ satisfies a local or global Lipschitz condition, as indicated in the network model (8.1), in the sense that $||f(x) - f(y)|| \leq \rho ||x - y||$ for some constant $\rho > 0$ and for all x, y confined in their domain in R^n. For these two cases, it is shown [46] below that the two definitions (8.5) and (8.6) are indeed equivalent:

(i) If $f(\cdot)$ is linear homogeneous then it can be shown that $\bar{x}(t) = s(t)$, namely, $\dot{\bar{x}}(t) = f(\bar{x}(t))$. Indeed, one has [46]

$$\dot{\bar{x}} = \sum_{j=1}^{N} \beta_j \dot{x}_j = \sum_{j=1}^{N} \beta_j \left(f\left(x_j\right) + c \sum_{k=1}^{N} a_{jk} H(x_k) \right)$$

$$= \sum_{j=1}^{N} \beta_j f(x_j) + c \sum_{j=1}^{N} \sum_{k=1}^{N} \beta_j a_{jk} H(x_k)$$

$$= f\left(\sum_{j=1}^{N} \beta_j x_j \right) + c [\beta_1, \beta_2, \ldots, \beta_N] \tilde{A} \begin{bmatrix} H\left(x_1\right) \\ H(x_2) \\ \vdots \\ H(x_N) \end{bmatrix}.$$

Since $[\beta_1, \beta_2, \ldots, \beta_N]^T$ is the left eigenvector of the zero eigenvalue of matrix $L \equiv -\tilde{A}$, one has $[\beta_1, \beta_2, \ldots, \beta_N] \tilde{A} = 0$, so that $\dot{\bar{x}} = f\left(\sum_{j=1}^{N} \beta_j x_j \right) = f(\bar{x})$. This means that $\bar{x}$ is indeed a solution $s(t)$ of a single node discussed above.

(ii) If $f(\cdot)$ satisfies the local Lipschitz condition, then [46]

$$\| \dot{\bar{x}} - f(\bar{x}) \| = \left\| \sum_{j=1}^{N} \beta_j \dot{x}_j - f\left(\bar{x}\right) \right\|$$

$$= \left\| \sum_{j=1}^{N} \beta_j \left(f\left(x_j\right) + c \sum_{k=1}^{N} a_{jk} H(x_k) \right) - f(\bar{x}) \right\|$$

$$= \left\| \sum_{j=1}^{N} \beta_j f\left(x_j\right) + c \sum_{j=1}^{N} \sum_{k=1}^{N} \beta_j a_{jk} H(x_k) - f(\bar{x}) \right\|$$

$$= \left\| \sum_{j=1}^{N} \beta_j f\left(x_j\right) + c[\beta_1, \beta_2, \ldots, \beta_N] \tilde{A} \begin{bmatrix} H\left(x_1\right) \\ H(x_2) \\ \vdots \\ H(x_N) \end{bmatrix} - f(\bar{x}) \right\|$$

$$= \left\| \sum_{j=1}^{N} \beta_j \left(f\left(x_j\right) - f(\overline{x}) \right) \right\| \le \sum_{j=1}^{N} \beta_j \| f(x_j) - f(\overline{x})) \|$$

$$\le \rho \sum_{j=1}^{N} \beta_j \|x_j - \overline{x}\|.$$

Therefore, by taking limits on both sides, one has $\lim_{t\to\infty} \|\dot{\overline{x}}(t) - f(\overline{x}(t))\| = 0$. Note that the definitions of synchronization only concern the limiting behaviors of the node dynamics.

It is remarked that for a very special case of network (8.1), if the network is synchronized to a constant state vector $\overline{s}$, then by taking the time limit on both sides of (8.1), due to the diffusive coupling condition (8.3) of the network, one has

$$\dot{\overline{s}} = f(\overline{s}). \tag{8.8}$$

Here, since s is a constant vector, one has $\dot{\overline{s}} = 0$, so $f(\overline{s}) = 0$, namely, this constant state vector $\overline{s}$ is an equilibrium of the node dynamical system.

8.2.1   Complete Synchronization of General Continuous-Time Networks

Linearizing equation (8.1) at the synchronized state $s(t)$ and then letting ζ_i be the variation of the state vector of node i lead to

$$\dot{\zeta}_i = \partial f(s)\zeta_i + \sum_{j=1}^{N} ca_{ij}\partial H(s)\zeta_j, \quad i = 1, \dots, N,$$

where $\partial f(s)$ and $\partial H(s)$ are the Jacobi matrices of $f(s)$ and $H(s)$ evaluated at s, respectively. Now, setting $\zeta = [\zeta_1, \dots, \zeta_N]$ transforms the above to the following matrix equation:

$$\dot{\zeta} = \partial f(s)\zeta + c\partial H(s)\zeta\widetilde{A}^T.$$

Furthermore, by diagonalizing $\widetilde{A}^T = S\Lambda S^{-1}$ with a diagonal matrix $\Lambda = diag(\lambda_1, \dots, \lambda_N)$, where $\{\lambda_k\}_{k=1}^{N}$ are eigenvalues of matrix $\widetilde{A} = [a_{ij}]$ with $\lambda_1 = 0$, and by denoting a new vector $\eta = [\eta_1, \dots, \eta_N] = \zeta S$, one has

$$\dot{\eta} = \partial f(s)\eta + c\partial H(s)\eta\Lambda,$$

which is equivalent to

$$\dot{\eta}_k = [\partial f(s) + c\lambda_k \partial H(s)]\eta_k, \quad k = 2, \dots, N. \tag{8.9}$$

Since the function $f(\cdot)$ is Lipschitz, it is possible to make the term $c\lambda_k \partial H(s)$ dominant over the Jacobi matrix $[\partial f(s)]$. To this end, a criterion for the synchronization manifold to be locally stable is that all the transversal Lyapunov exponents of the variational equation (8.9) are strictly negative [13–16], where the Lyapunov exponent is defined by (2.113) in Chapter 2. Clearly, these Lyapunov exponents depend on the node dynamics $f(\cdot)$, the network coupling strength c and the coupling matrices $\widetilde{A}$ and H.

Note that in (8.9), each equation has the same form and only η_k and λ_k depend on k. For the case of $k = 1$, the variational equation (not shown in (8.9)) corresponds to the synchronization manifold associated with $\lambda_1 = 0$; for all other $k = 2, \dots, N$, they correspond to the transversal eigenvectors that span some subspaces, referred to as transversal modes.

Note also that when matrix A is asymmetric (for directed networks), its eigenvalues can have complex values, so it is natural to replace $c\lambda_k$ by a complex parameter $(\alpha + i\beta)$, which is a function of $c\lambda_k$ where the eignvalues are generally complex, in each equation. Then, define the following so-called *master stability equation* for all $k = 2, \dots, N$:

$$\dot{y} = [\partial f(s) + (\alpha + i\beta)\partial H(s)]y. \tag{8.10}$$

Since this may be a time-varying system, particularly if $s(t)$ is a time function, its eigenvalues may not be useful for determining the stability. Thus, the maximum Lyapunov exponent L_{max} of the system will be used instead, which is a function of α and β, and is called the *master stability function* [15]. Similarly, these Lyapunov exponents depend on the node dynamics $f(\cdot)$, the network coupling strength c and the coupling matrices A and H.

For a given and fixed coupling strength c, one can find a point $c\lambda_k$ on the parameter plane (α, β), at which the sign of L_{max} indicates the stability of the corresponding transversal mode: a negative sign means stability and a positive sign means instability of the transversal mode. Thus, it is necessary to require all transversal modes of λ_k be stable, $k = 2, \dots, N$, so that the synchronization manifold of the original network (8.1) is stable, implying that the network achieves synchronization. In other words, the negative master stability function is a convenient (necessary) condition for testing the (undirected or directed) network synchronization.

Example 8.1 Consider a network of N Rössler oscillators, in which the ith node is described by (2.128), namely,

$$\dot{x}_i^{(1)} = -(x_i^{(2)} + x_i^{(3)})$$
$$\dot{x}_i^{(2)} = x_i^{(1)} + ax_i^{(2)}$$
$$\dot{x}_i^{(3)} = b + x_i^{(3)}(x_i^{(1)} - c).$$

This is the function $f(\cdot)$ in network (8.1). When $a = 0.2$, $b = 0.2$, $c = 5.7$, this Rössler oscillator has a chaotic attractor as shown in Figure 2.48, or Figure 8.1.

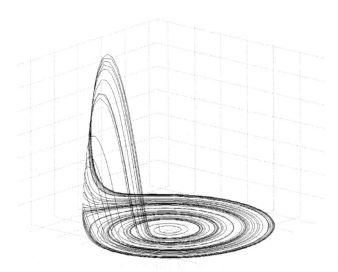

Figure 8.1 Rössler chaotic attractor. *Source*: Reprinted from Chen, G. and Dong, X. (1998) From Chaos to Order: Methodologies, Perspectives and Applications. World Scientific Pub. Co., Singapore. Copyright (1998) World Scientific Pub. Co.

Suppose that all nodes are coupled through the first components $x_i^{(1)}$ of their state vectors, $i = 1, 2, \dots, N$. This means that the inner coupling matrix $H = \begin{bmatrix} 1 & 0 & 0 \\ 0 & 0 & 0 \\ 0 & 0 & 0 \end{bmatrix}$ in network (8.1). The master stability function of a ring network of 10 Rössler oscillators is shown in Figure 8.2 [15], where dash curves are negative Lyapunov exponents, solid curves are positive Lyapunov exponents, and black dots

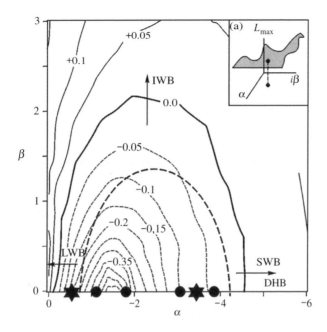

Figure 8.2 Master stability function of the $x^{(1)}$-coupled Rössler network [15]. *Source*: Reprinted with permission from Pecora, L.M. and Carroll, T.L. (1998) Master stability functions for synchronized coupled systems. *Physical Review Letters*, **80**: 2109. Copyright (1998) American Physical Society

are the (α, β) values, with LWB, IWB and SWB indicating long-wavelength, intermediate-wavelength and short-wavelength bifurcations, respectively. The inset (a) shows a typical master stability function surface, from which it can be seen that corresponding to $\alpha = \beta = 0$, i.e., corresponding to the coupling strength $c = 0$ (uncoupled), one has $L_{max} > 0$, implying that each individual Rössler is chaotic before being coupled together. For fixed $\beta = 0$, as α decreases (correspondingly, c increases), after a threshold value, L_{max} will decrease to become negative; as α continues to decrease, however, after another threshold value, L_{max} will return to become positive. This example demonstrates that too strong or too weak a coupling strength c will lead the synchronization manifold of the coupled network to become unstable, i.e., desynchronized.

For undirected and unweighted networks, the eigenvalues of their outer coupling matrix A are all real, as shown in (8.3) above. In this case, the corresponding master stability equation (8.10) can be simplified to

$$\dot{y} = [\partial f(s) + c\lambda_k \partial H(s)]y \tag{8.11}$$

and the corresponding L_{max} is a function of $c\lambda_k$, $k = 2, \dots, N$. The range of $c\lambda_k$, $k = 2, \dots, N$, which guarantees L_{max} be negative is called a *synchronized region*, denoted by S, on which network (8.1) achieves synchronization. It is clear that this region is determined not only by the real parameter α, which depends on the outer coupling strength c, but also by the node dynamics $f(\cdot)$ and the inner coupling function $H(\cdot)$. Hence, the synchronized region can be restricted onto a one-dimensional set with respect only to α as shown by Figure 8.3 [31]. Thus, if the nonzero Laplacian eigenvalues (as shown in (8.4)) satisfy

$$c\lambda_k \in S, \quad k = 2, \dots, N, \tag{8.12}$$

then the synchronization manifold will be stable, i.e., the network will synchronize.

According to its different synchronized regions S, the dynamical network (8.1) is classified into the following types (see Figure 8.3, [31, 51, 52]):

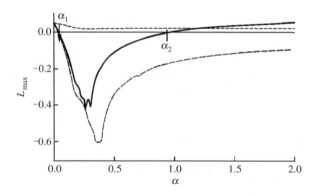

Figure 8.3 Master stability functions of different types of networks [31]. *Source*: Reprinted with permission from Barahona, M. and Pecora, L.M. (2004) Synchronization in small-world systems. *Physical Review Letters*, **89**(5): 054101. Copyright (2004) American Physical Society

Type-I: Synchronized region is $S_1 = (\alpha_1, \infty)$, where constant $\alpha_1 > 0$ is determined by the given network. For this type of networks, if

$$c\lambda_2 > \alpha_1 \tag{8.13}$$

or

$$c > \frac{\alpha_1}{\lambda_2} > 0, \tag{8.14}$$

then the synchronization manifold of the network will be stable. Therefore, the synchronizability of Type-I networks is determined by the smallest nonzero eigenvalue λ_2 of its Laplacian matrix L. The larger the λ_2, the smaller the c is needed, so the better or stronger the synchronizability of the network. The inequality (8.13) or (8.14) is the basic criterion for the Type-I network synchronizability, where unfortunately the constant α_1 is not explicitly given.

Type-II: Synchronized region is $S_2 = (\alpha_2, \alpha_3) \subset (0, \infty)$, where constants $\alpha_3 > \alpha_2 > 0$. For this type of networks, if

$$\frac{\alpha_2}{\lambda_2} < c < \frac{\alpha_3}{\lambda_N} \tag{8.15}$$

or

$$c > \frac{\alpha_2}{\alpha_3} \frac{\lambda_N}{\lambda_2} > 0, \tag{8.16}$$

then the synchronization manifold of the network will be stable. Similarly, the inequality (8.15) or (8.16) is the basic criterion for Type-II network synchronizability, which can be simply written as $0 < \frac{\lambda_N}{\lambda_2} < c\alpha$ for some constant $\alpha > 0$. In this case, (8.12) becomes

$$\frac{\lambda_N}{c\lambda_2} \in S. \tag{8.17}$$

Thus, the synchronizability of Type-II networks is characterized by the ratio λ_N/λ_2 of the largest and smallest nonzero eigenvalues of the Laplacian matrix L. The criterion $0 < \frac{\lambda_N}{\lambda_2} < c\alpha$ implies that the smaller the ratio λ_N/λ_2, the smaller the c is needed, so the stronger the synchronizability of the network.

Type-III: Synchronized region is a union of several intervals from (α_1, ∞), (α_2, α_3), and so on; for instance, in the form of $(\alpha_2, \alpha_3) \cup (\alpha_1, \infty)$ or $(\alpha_2, \alpha_2) \cup (\alpha_4, \alpha_5)$ or $(\alpha_2, \alpha_3) \cup (\alpha_4, \alpha_5) \cup (\alpha_1, \infty)$, etc. [51, 52].

Type-IV: Synchronized region does not exist, i.e., it is an empty set. For this type of networks, any coupling strength and coupling matrices will not be able to lead the network to synchronize, unless external control input is inserted, a topic to be studied in the next chapter.

As mentioned, the synchronized region is determined by the node dynamics $f(\cdot)$ and the inner coupling matrix H, and is characterized by the outer coupling matrix $\tilde{A}$ and coupling strength c. For a connected network, if the coupling strength c is large enough, a Type-I network will always synchronize; but only if c is inside a certain value range will a Type-II or Type-III network synchronize, for which too small or too large a coupling strength c will not be desirable.

In applications, to determine the synchronized region for a given network, those thresholds $\alpha_1, \alpha_2, \dots,$ are usually estimated via numerical simulations. Only for some special inner coupling function H may these thresholds be derived via theoretical analysis, as further discussed below.

8.2.2   Complete Synchronization of Linearly Coupled Continuous-Time Networks

When the inner coupling matrix H is a linear function, it is simply an $n \times n$ matrix. In this case, network (8.1) reduces to [17–21]:

$$\dot{x}_i = f(x_i) + c \sum_{j=1}^{N} a_{ij} H x_j, \quad i = 1, \dots, N, \tag{8.18}$$

where typically $H = diag(r_1, r_2, \dots, r_n)$, which describes the way of the coupling among components of the state vectors. In Example 8.1, for instance, $n = 3$, $r_1 = 1$, $r_2 = 0$, $r_3 = 0$.

The following result is a consequence of the above discussion, where the concepts of exponential stability and Lyapunov function were introduced in the last part of Chapter 2.

Theorem 8.1 *[18] For network (8.18), if the following system of n-dimensional linear time-varying systems*

$$\dot{w} = [\partial f(s) + c\lambda_k H]w, \quad k = 2, \dots, N \tag{8.19}$$

are exponentially stable about zero, then the synchronization manifold of network (8.18) is also exponentially stable. Consequently, the network synchronizes.

Theorem 8.2 *[18] For network (8.18), if there exist an n × n diagonal matrix $\Gamma > 0$ and two constants $\bar{d} > 0$ and $\tau > 0$, such that*

$$c\lambda_2 \geq \bar{d} \tag{8.20}$$

And

$$[\partial f(s) + dH]^T \Gamma + \Gamma[\partial f(s) + dH] \leq -\tau I_n \tag{8.21}$$

for all $d \geq \bar{d}$, where I_n is the identity matrix, then the synchronization manifold of network (8.18) is exponentially stable about zero. Consequently, the network synchronizes.

Proof. It follows from (8.20) and (8.3) that

$$c\lambda_k \geq \bar{d}, \quad k = 2, \dots, N. \tag{8.22}$$

Substituting it into (8.21) gives

$$[\partial f(s) + c\lambda_k H]^T \Gamma + \Gamma[\partial f(s) + c\lambda_k H] \leq -\tau I_n, \quad k = 2, \dots, N.$$

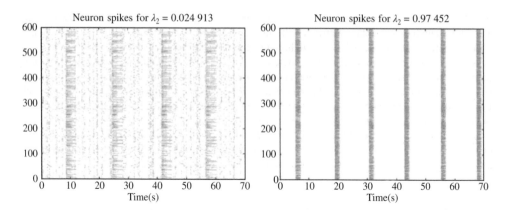

Figure 8.4 Rhythmic output of two neural networks with different Laplacian eigenvalue [2]. *Source:* Reproduced by permission of John Wiley & Sons, Inc.

Then, by defining Lyapunov functions of the form $V_k = \zeta^T \Gamma \zeta$, $k = 2, \ldots, N$ one can easily show that system (8.19) is exponentially stable about its zero equilibrium. To this end, Theorem 8.1 implies that the synchronization manifold of network (8.18) is exponentially stable. ∎

Next, recall the theory of chaos discussed in Section 2.3.3 of Chapter 2. For a network of chaotic node systems, the following synchronization criterion can be obtained.

Theorem 8.3 *[23] For a network (8.18) with identical chaotic nodes, if the inner coupling matrix H is an identity matrix, and if the maximum Lyapunov exponent $h_{\max}$ of every individual node described by $f(\cdot)$ satisfies*

$$c\lambda_2 \geq h_{\max}, \tag{8.23}$$

then the synchronization manifold of network (8.18) is exponentially stable about zero. Consequently, the network synchronizes.

It is clear from (8.20) and (8.23), or $c \geq \alpha/\lambda_2$ where $\alpha = \bar{d}$ or $\alpha = h_{\max}$, that the larger the λ_2, the smaller the coupling strength c is required to achieve the network synchronization, so the better the synchronizability of the network.

As an example, in mammals a small group of neurons in the brain stem, named pre-Bötzinger complex, is responsible for generating a regular rhythmic output to motor calls that initiate a breath [2]. Figure 8.4 shows simulation results on such a neural network, where the rhythmic output from the network with Laplacian engenvalue $\lambda_2 = 0.025$ is ragged with fuzzy bursting while that with $\lambda_2 = 0.974$ displays clear regular bursting [2].

Suppose that one wants to stabilize network (8.18) onto a state $\bar{x}$, for example the one defined in (8.7), satisfying

$$\dot{\bar{x}} = f(\bar{x}).$$

To achieve the goal, one applies the pinning control strategy on a small fraction $\delta(0 < \delta \ll 1)$ of the nodes in network (8.18). Suppose that nodes $1, 2, \ldots, l$ are selected, where $l = [\delta N]$ stands for the largest integer smaller than the real number δN. This controlled network can be described by

$$\dot{x}_i = f(x_i) + c\sum_{j=1}^{N} a_{ij} H x_j + cd_i H(x_i - \bar{x}), \qquad i = 1, \ldots, l,$$

$$\dot{x}_i = f(x_i) + c\sum_{j=1}^{N} a_{ij} H x_j, \qquad i = l, \ldots, N, \tag{8.24}$$

where the feedback gains $d_i > 0$, and let $D = diag(d_1, d_2, \ldots, d_l, 0, \ldots, 0) \in R^{N \times N}$.

Definition 8.2 *[24] A function* $\phi : R^n \times R \to R^n$ *is V − uniformly decreasing if there exists a square matrix V and a constant* $\rho > 0$ *such that for all* $z, y \in R^n$ *and all* $t \geq 0$,

$$(z - y)V[\phi(z, t) - \phi(y, t)] \leq -\rho\|z - y\|^2.$$

Theorem 8.4 *Consider controlled network (8.24). Suppose that H is symmetrical and positive semi-definite. Let T be a matrix such that* $f(x_i) + Tx_i$ *is V-uniformly decreasing for some symmetrical and positive definite matrix V and for all* $x_i \in R^n$, $i = 1, 2, \ldots, N$. *If there exists a positive definite diagonal matrix U such that*

$$(U \otimes V)[\rho(A + D) \otimes H + I \otimes T] > 0, \qquad (8.25)$$

then the controlled network (8.24) is globally stable about the state $\bar{x}$ *which satisfies* $\dot{\bar{x}} = f(\bar{x})$.

Proof. Construct a Lyapunov function

$$W(\tilde{x}) = \frac{1}{2}\tilde{x}^T(U \otimes V)\tilde{x},$$

where $\tilde{x} = [\tilde{x}_1^T, \tilde{x}_2^T, \ldots, \tilde{x}_N^T]^T \in R^{Nn}$ with $\tilde{x}_i = x_i - \bar{x}$, $i = 1, 2, \ldots, N$. The derivative of $W(\tilde{x})$ along the trajectories of the network is

$$\dot{W}(\tilde{x}) = \tilde{x}^T(U \otimes V)\dot{\tilde{x}}$$

$$= \tilde{x}^T(U \otimes V)[f(x) - f(\theta \otimes \bar{x}) + (I \otimes T)\tilde{x} - [\rho(A + D) \otimes H + I \otimes T]\tilde{x}]$$

$$\leq \tilde{x}^T(U \otimes V)[f(x) - f(\theta \otimes \bar{x}) + (I \otimes T)\tilde{x}], \qquad (8.26)$$

where $\theta = [1, 1, \ldots, 1]^T \in R^N$ and $x = [x_1^T, x_2^T, \ldots, x_N^T]^T \in R^{Nn}$, and the last inequality follows from (8.25). Since $f(x_i) + Tx_i$ is V-uniformly decreasing and $U = diag[u_1, u_2, \ldots, u_N]$ is positive definite, it follows from (8.26) that

$$\dot{W}(\tilde{x}) = \tilde{x}(U \otimes V)[f(x) - f(\theta \otimes \bar{x}) + (I \otimes T)\tilde{x}]$$

$$= (x - \theta \otimes \bar{x})(U \otimes V)[f(x) + (I \otimes T)x - f(\theta \otimes \bar{x}) - (I \otimes T)(\theta \otimes \bar{x})]$$

$$= \sum_{i=1}^{N} u_i(x_i - \bar{x})V[f(x_i) + Tx_i - f(\bar{x}) - T\bar{x})]$$

$$\leq -\sum_{i=1}^{N} u_i\rho\|x_i - \bar{x}\|^2.$$

Hence, by Lyapunov's direct method the theorem is proved. ∎

Theorem 8.4 corrects some errors in Theorem 1 in [24], by strengthening the requirement on matrix U as stated above and by simply changing (8.25) from originally "positive semi-definite" to presently "positive definite" and replacing D with cD therein.

8.3   Complete Synchronization of Some Typical Dynamical Networks

Recall that the synchronized region S of a network (8.1) is determined by the node dynamics $f(\cdot)$ and the inner coupling matrix H, and is characterized by the outer coupling matrix $\tilde{A}$ and coupling strength c. Therefore, depending on the different node dynamics $f(\cdot)$, the same structural network (8.1) can be of Type-I, Type-II, Type-III or even Type-IV. This can be easily understood; for example, if $f(\cdot)$ is a highly unstable dynamical system then a network of it can hardly synchronize.

In this section, the study is to set aside the node dynamics by assuming it well behaved (e.g., satisfying a certain Lipschitz condition), and to focus on the effects of the network topology on the network synchronizability.

8.3.1   Complete Synchronization of Regular Networks

First, recall the concept of complete synchronization from Definition 8.1, and the classification of synchronized regions from Section 8.2.1.

8.3.1.1   Type-I Networks

Recall also that the synchronizability of Type-I networks is determined by the smallest zero eigenvalue $\lambda_2 > 0$ of the Laplacian matrix L.

A nearest-neighbor coupled network of N nodes with an even degree K has a Laplacian matrix L_{nc} in the following circulant form:

$$L_{nc} = \begin{bmatrix} K & -1 & \cdots & -1 & 0 & \cdots & 0 \\ -1 & K & -1 & \cdots & -1 & 0 & \vdots \\ \vdots & -1 & K & -1 & \cdots & -1 & 0 \\ -1 & \cdots & -1 & \ddots & & \vdots & -1 \\ 0 & -1 & \vdots & & K & -1 & \vdots \\ \vdots & 0 & -1 & \cdots & -1 & K & -1 \\ 0 & \cdots & 0 & -1 & \cdots & -1 & K \end{bmatrix},$$

with the smallest nonzero eigenvalue

$$\lambda_{2nc} = 4 \sum_{j=1}^{K/2} \sin^2(j\pi/N).$$

Clearly, for any fixed K, $\lambda_{2nc} \to 0$ monotonically as $N \to \infty$, implying that it is difficult for such a nearest-neighbor coupled network to achieve synchronization if its size is too large.

A fully-coupled network of N nodes has a Laplacian matrix L_{gc}, with

$$L_{gc} = \begin{bmatrix} N-1 & -1 & \cdots & \cdots & -1 \\ -1 & N-1 & -1 & \cdots & -1 \\ \vdots & & \ddots & & \ddots & \vdots \\ -1 & \cdots & -1 & N-1 & -1 \\ -1 & \cdots & & \cdots & -1 & N-1 \end{bmatrix},$$

which has a single zero eigenvalue of multiplicity 1 and all the other eigenvalues are equal to $\lambda_{gc} = N$. Thus, as $N \to \infty$, its smallest nonzero eigenvalue $\lambda_{2gc} = N \to \infty$ monotonically, implying that a fully-coupled network can easily achieve synchronization if its size is large enough.

A star-shaped network of N nodes has a Laplacian matrix:

$$L_{sc} = \begin{bmatrix} N-1 & -1 & -1 & \cdots & -1 \\ -1 & 1 & 0 & \cdots & 0 \\ \vdots & & \ddots & & \vdots \\ -1 & 0 & \cdots & 1 & 0 \\ -1 & 0 & 0 & \cdots & 1 \end{bmatrix}.$$

Its smallest nonzero eigenvalue $\lambda_{sc2} = 1$, which is independent of the network size. Hence, the synchronizability of a star-shaped network is independent of the network size.

In summary, for Type-I linearly and diffusively coupled networks (8.1):

1. For a fixed coupling strength $c > 0$, no matter how strong it is, when the size of a nearest-neighbor coupled network is too large, the network is difficult to achieve synchronization.
2. For a fixed coupling strength $c > 0$, no matter how weak it is, when the size of a fully-coupled network is large enough, the network will synchronize.
3. For a star-shaped network, the network synchronizability is independent of the network size; namely, when the coupling strength $c > 0$ is larger than a threshold, which is independent of the network size, the network will synchronize.

8.3.1.2 Type-II Networks

Recall that the synchronizability of Type-II networks is determined by the ratio of the largest and the smallest nonzero eigenvalues, λ_N/λ_2, of the Laplacian matrix L.

For a nearest-neighbor coupled network of N nodes with even degree K, its eigenratio satisfies [31]

$$\frac{\lambda_{Nnc}}{\lambda_{2nc}} \approx \frac{(3\pi + 2)N^2}{2\pi^2(K+1)(K+2)} \quad \text{for } 1 < K \ll N.$$

Therefore, $\lambda_N/\lambda_2 \to \infty$ as $N \to \infty$, implying that the synchronizability of the network is very weak.

A fully-coupled network has all nonzero Laplacian eigenvalues $\lambda_2 = \cdots = \lambda_N = N$, so that $\lambda_N/\lambda_2 \equiv 1$, which cannot become any smaller. Therefore, as long as the coupling strength $c > 0$ is large enough, the network will synchronize.

A star-shaped network has $\lambda_1 = 0, \lambda_2 = \cdots = \lambda_{N-1} = 1, \lambda_N = N$. Hence, $\lambda_N/\lambda_2 \equiv N$, so $\lambda_N/\lambda_2 \to \infty$ as $N \to \infty$, implying that it is generally difficult for the network to achieve synchronization.

In summary, for Type-II linearly and diffusively coupled networks (8.1):

1. For a fixed coupling strength $c > 0$, no matter how strong it is, when the size of a nearest-neighbor coupled network and the size of a star-shaped network are too large, these two types of networks are difficult to achieve synchronization.
2. For a fully-coupled network, the network synchronizability is independent of the network size; if the coupling strength $c > 0$ is large enough, then the network will synchronize.

8.3.2 Synchronization of Small-World Networks

Now, consider an NW small-world network (8.1) of N dynamical systems. Only Type-I networks are discussed here [17].

Notice that in the NW small-world network model, the process of adding an edge with probability p means that in the outer coupling matrix $\tilde{A}$, the corresponding 0 element is to be replaced by 1 with probability p.

In simulating a nearest-neighbor coupled network, in its outer coupling matrix A_{nc}, one may first replace its zero elements $a_{ij} = a_{ji} = 0$ by $a_{ij} = a_{ji} = 1$ with probability p, then recalculate its diagonal elements by using formula (8.2) to obtain a new outer coupling matrix, hence a new Laplacian matrix $L_{nw} = -A_{nw}(p, N)$, and finally calculate its eigenvalues to obtain the smallest nonzero eigenvalue $\lambda_{2nw}(p, N)$.

Simulations on the NW small-world network model of sizes (a) $N = 200$ and (b) $N = 500$, respectively, with different probabilities p, are shown in Figure 8.5 [14]. It can be seen that the nearest-neighbor coupled network (with $p = 0$) has $\lambda_{2nm}(p, N) \approx 0$, therefore its synchronizability is very weak. As more new edges are being added to the network (i.e., as p is increased from 0 to 1), $\lambda_{2nm}(p, N) \to N$, showing that the synchronizability of the network is increasing. This implies that for any fixed coupling strength $c > 0$, if the network has a large enough number of nodes so that condition (8.20) is satisfied, i.e., $N > \bar{d}/c$, then as the probability p becomes larger than a threshold $\bar{p}, \bar{p} \leq p \leq 1$, the network will synchronize.

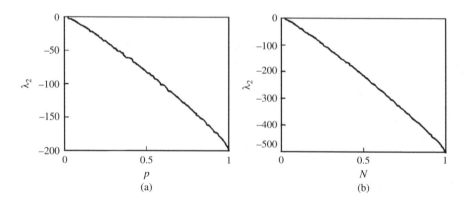

Figure 8.5 Changes of the smallest nonzero eigenvalue of A_{nw} versus p [17]: (a) $N = 200$; (b) $N = 500$. *Source*: Reprinted with permission from Wang, X.F. and Chen, G. (2002) Synchronization in small-world dynamical networks. *International Journal of Bifurcation Chaos*, **12**(1): 187–92. Copyright (2002) World Scientific Pub. Co.

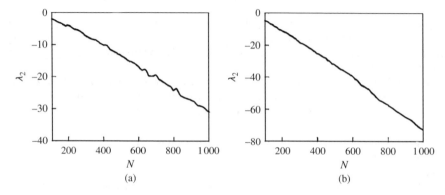

Figure 8.6 Changes of the smallest-indexed nonzero eigenvalue of A_{nw} versus N [17]: (a) $p = 0.05$; (b) $p = 0.1$. *Source*: Reprinted with permission from Wang, X.F. and Chen, G. (2002) Synchronization in small-world dynamical networks. *International Journal of Bifurcation Chaos*, **12**(1): 187–92. Copyright (2002) World Scientific Pub. Co.

Figure 8.6 [17] shows the changes of the smallest-indexed nonzero eigenvalue of the matrix A_{nw} versus N in an NW small-world network, with (a) $p = 0.05$ and (b) $p = 0.1$, respectively. It can be seen that for the same p, the larger the N, the stronger the synchronizability of the network.

8.3.3 Synchronization of Scale-Free Networks

8.3.3.1 BA Scale-Free Networks

Now, consider a BA scale-free network in the form of (8.1) with N dynamical systems. Only Type-I networks are discussed here [18].

In constructing the BA model, let $m_0 = m = \hat{m}$ and denote its outer coupling matrix by $A_{sf}(\hat{m}, N)$, hence its Laplacian matrix by $L_{sf} = -A_{sf}(\hat{m}, N)$, with the smallest nonzero eigenvalue $\lambda_{sf2}(\hat{m}, N)$.

Simulations show that, as N increases, $\lambda_{sf2}(\hat{m}, N)$ also increases and

$$\lim_{N \to \infty} \lambda_{sf2}(\hat{m}, N) = \hat{\lambda}_{sf2}(\hat{m}) > 0.$$

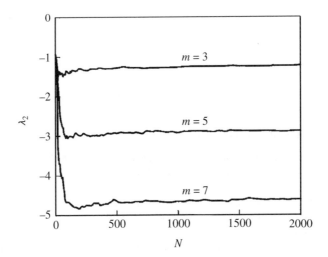

Figure 8.7 Changes of $\lambda_2 = -\lambda_{sf2}(\hat{m}, N)$ versus N (modified from [18]). *Source*: Reprinted with permission from Wang, X.F, and Chen, G. (2002) Synchronization in scale-free dynamical networks: robustness and fragility. *IEEE Transactions on Circuits and Systems Part I,* **49**(1): 54–62. Copyright (2002) IEEE

Figure 8.7 (modified from [18]) shows the changes of $\lambda_2 = -\lambda_{sf2}(\hat{m}, N)$ versus different values of $\hat{m}$ and N: when $m_0 = m = 3, 5, 7$, $\lambda_2 \approx -1.2, -2.9, -4.6$, respectively. It can be seen that the network synchronizability will saturate, namely, for large enough N, continuously increasing the number of new nodes does not change the network synchronizability significantly.

8.3.3.2 Synchronization-Optimal Networks

Intuitively, a network with a larger number of edges should have a stronger synchronizability. Indeed, this is generally true for typical regular networks, random networks, small-world networks, and scale-free networks. A natural question is: if the number of edges is given and fixed, what kind of network has the strongest synchronizability? One possible answer is given by the following so-called synchronization-optimal network model [41]:

1. Start with a small fully-connected network of m_0 nodes.
2. *Growth*: In each step, add one new node to the network, with m ($m \leq m_0$) edges connecting to m randomly selected existing nodes simultaneously.
3. *Optimal Attachment*: The way of a new edge connecting to an existing node is to maximize the synchronizability of the resulting network, i.e., making the smallest nonzero eigenvalue of the resulting network outer coupling matrix as large as possible.

After t steps, the network has $N = t + m_0$ nodes and $mt + m_0(m_0 - 1)/2$ edges, which has the strongest synchronizability as compared to other networks.

Similar to the BA network discussed above, as $N \to \infty$, the smallest nonzero eigenvalue will approach a positive constant value, $\lambda_{so2}(m)$. For example, when $m = m_0 = 3, 5, 7$, one has $\lambda_{so2}(m) \approx 2.0, 4.0, 5.9$, respectively. Compared with the BA network model discussed above, however, these three eigenvalues are all much bigger, implying significant improvement of the network synchronizability.

Analysis further shows that the topology of this synchronization-optimal network model is similar to a multi-center network: a few nodes are connected to big nodes (hubs), while the majority of nodes have small degrees. This structural characteristic helps increase the network synchronizability, yet it also makes the network more vulnerable to attacks, i.e., less robust, leaving an important issue for future research. Recently, it has been found that some compensatory structures hidden within a network can be very important for the network synchronization; for example, appropriately reverse or even remove some edges (i.e., using negative interactions or removals to compensate overreactions) can actually facilitate the collective synchronization as well as the robustness of the whole network thereby achieving certain optimality [42].

8.3.3.3 Synchronization-Preferred Network

To balance better synchronizability and stronger robustness against attacks, the following synchronization-preferred network model may be considered [43]:

1. Start with a small fully connected network of $m_0 > 0$ nodes.
2. *Growth*: In each step, add one new node to the network, with m ($m \leq m_0$) edges connecting to randomly selected existing nodes simultaneously.
3. *Preferential Attachment*: A new edge is connecting to an existing node i with the following probability:

$$\Pi_i = \lambda_{i2} / \sum_j \lambda_{j2}$$

where λ_{i2} is the smallest nonzero eigenvalue of the outer coupling matrix of the network when the new node had just been added to node i.

After t steps, the network has $N = t + m_0$ nodes and $mt + m_0(m_0 - 1)/2$ edges, with a preferred synchronizability.

For a fixed m, as $N \to \infty$, the smallest nonzero eigenvalue will approach a constant value, $\lambda_{sp2}(m)$. For example, for $m = m_0 = 3, 5, 7$, $\lambda_{sp2}(m) \approx 1.3, 2.9, 4.6$, respectively.

Now, in the case of $m_0 = m = 3$, Figure 8.8 [43] compares the simulation results on the smallest nonzero eigenvalues of the BA network (solid curve with small circles), synchronization-optimal network (dash curve with diamonds), and synchronization-preferred network (dot-dash curve with small squares), where $\lambda_2 = \lambda_{sp2}(m)$.

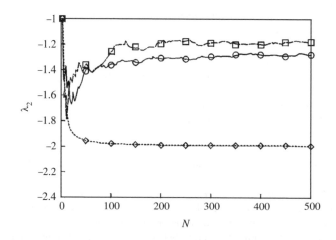

Figure 8.8 Comparison of synchronizability of three network models [43]. *Source*: Reprinted from Fan, J., Li, X. and Wang, X.F. (2005) On synchronous preference of complex dynamical networks. *Physica A*, **355**: 657–66, Copyright (2005) Elsevier

It is clear that the last two models have about the same synchronizability. However, it will be shown in the next subsection that the synchronization-preferred network model significantly improves the network robustness against attacks.

8.3.3.4 Robustness and Fragility of Scale-Free Networks against Attacks

The robustness and fragility of scale-free networks were analyzed in Section 3.5.2, Chapter 3. This issue is revisited here from a synchronization point of view.

Consider a scale-free network in the form of (8.1), with N nodes and an outer coupling matrix $A_{sf} \in R^{N \times N}$. Suppose that the network is now being attacked, so a small fraction f of nodes have been destroyed therefore removed, where $0 < f < 1$. Let the removed nodes be denoted by $i_1, i_2, \ldots, i_{[fN]}$, where $[fN]$ is the integer part of real number fN. Accordingly, the elements of A_{sf} on the $i_1, i_2, \ldots, i_{[fN]}$ rows and the $i_1, i_2, \ldots, i_{[fN]}$ columns become zero, so A_{sf} reduces to $\overline{A}_{sf}$. Consequently, the diagonal elements of $\overline{A}_{sf} = [\overline{a}_{ij}]$ also need to be recalculated, by formula (8.2), resulting in a new outer coupling matrix, $\widetilde{A}_{sf} = [\widetilde{a}_{ij}]$. To this end, let λ_{2sf} and $\widetilde{\lambda}_{2sf}$ be the smallest nonzero eigenvalues of Laplacian matrices $L_{sf} = -A_{sf}$ and $\widetilde{L}_{sf} = -\widetilde{A}_{sf}$, and denote $\lambda_2 = \lambda_{sf2}$ and $\widetilde{\lambda}_2 = \widetilde{\lambda}_{sf2}$, respectively.

In the case of random attacks or random failures, due to the heterogeneity of the scale-free networks, the nodes being removed are generally small-degree nodes; therefore, $\lambda_{sf2} \approx \widetilde{\lambda}_{sf2}$, so the synchronizability of the resulting network will remain basically unchanged. A simulation on a BA scale-free network with $N = 2000$ and $m_0 = m = 3$ shows that after 5% of nodes have been removed, the network remains being connected, with $\widetilde{\lambda}_2 < -0.5$, as seen in Figure 8.9 [43]. In this figure, four different types of networks are compared: the random-graph network (solid curve with small stars), the BA network (solid curve with small circles), the synchronization-optimal network (dash curve with diamonds), and the synchronization-preferred network (dot-dash curve with small squares).

It can be seen from Figure 8.10 [43], where $\lambda_{LC2} = \lambda_2$ here, that under an intentional attack to a scale-free network, some largest-degree nodes were removed, so the network topology had a drastic change and even became unconnected, which results in $\lambda_{sf2} \gg \widetilde{\lambda}_{sf2}$. Consequently, the synchronizability of the network is significantly reduced. In the simulation, even only 0.7% of hub nodes (largest-degree ones) were removed, the network became unconnected, leading to $\widetilde{\lambda}_{BA2} = 0$, as shown by the dash curve in the figure. The inset in Figure 8.10 shows the percentage of the remaining connected subnets in the

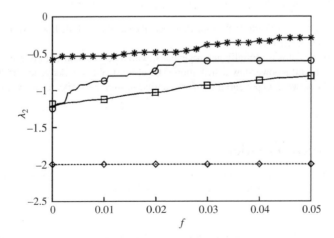

Figure 8.9 Comparison of synchronization robustness for four types of networks [43]. *Source*: Reprinted from Fan, J., Li, X. and Wang, X.F. (2005) On synchronous preference of complex dynamical networks. *Physica A*, **355**: 657–66. Copyright (2005) Elsevier

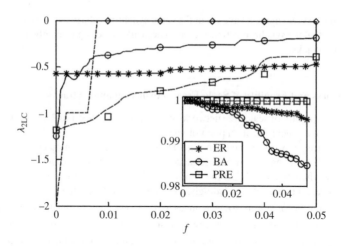

Figure 8.10 Comparison of synchronization fragility for four types of networks [43]. *Source*: Reprinted from Fan, J., Li, X. and Wang, X.F. (2005) On synchronous preference of complex dynamical networks. *Physica A*, **355**: 657–66. Copyright (2005) Elsevier

whole network after a fraction f of nodes (the horizontal axis) had been removed. It can be seen that if 5% of largest-degree nodes were removed, even in the largest connected subnet, its synchronizability had a significant decrease. It is notable that for synchronization-optimal networks, since it has a multi-center structure, it is more vulnerable to intentional attacks: after as less as m_0 largest-degree nodes were removed, the whole network was broken to be a set of isolated nodes. But, on the other hand, since the majorities of nodes in this kind of networks are small-degree nodes, they are very robust against random attacks.

It is noted that, in a worse case, if there is uncertainty in the network, then the so-called adaptive synchronization technique is needed to enhance the network robustness [44].

8.3.4 Complete Synchronization of Local-World Networks

Consider the so-called Local-World (LW) model, a special case of the Multi-Local-World (MLW) model studied in Section 3.6.5, Chapter 3.

The LW network model is essentially heterogeneous, with a degree distribution in between the exponential distribution and the power-law distribution. Therefore, LW networks generally have robustness and fragility also in between exponential networks and scale-free networks, as shown by Figures 8.11 and 8.12 [25].

8.4 Phase Synchronization

Consider two coupled dynamical systems with oscillatory behaviors, referred to as oscillators, where the oscillations are completely characterized by their amplitudes and phases.

Definition 8.3 *If the phases ϕ_1 and ϕ_2 of two coupled oscillators has a certain ratio $n : m$, where n and m are integers, ideally $|n\phi_1 - m\phi_2| = 0$ or practically $|n\phi_1 - m\phi_2| \leq \varepsilon$ (a small constant), then these two oscillators are said to achieve (ideal or practical) phase synchronization.*

Clearly, phase synchronization is a kind of weak synchronization, since when phase synchronization is achieved, the phases of the oscillators are locked but their amplitudes may be different.

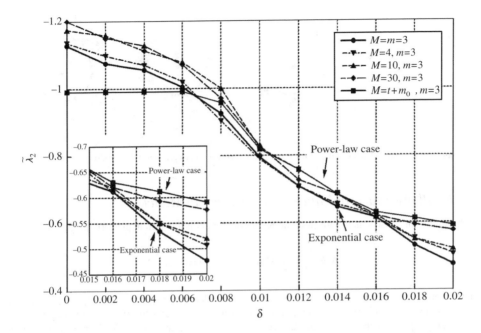

Figure 8.11 Comparison of synchronization robustness [25] (inset is an enlargement of segment $0.015 \leq \delta \leq 0.02$). *Source*: Reprinted from Li, X. and Chen, G. (2003) A local-world evolving network model. *Physica A*, **328**: 274–86. Copyright (2003) Elsevier

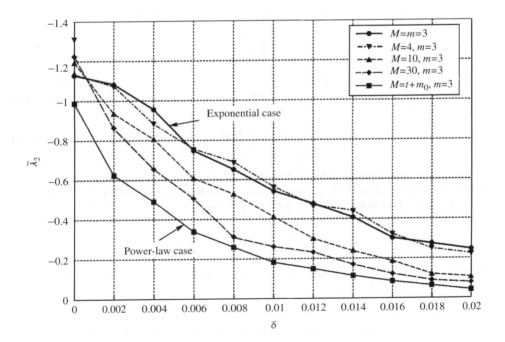

Figure 8.12 Comparison of synchronization fragility [25]. *Source*: Reprinted from Li, X. and Chen, G. (2003) A local-world evolving network model. *Physica A*, **328**: 274–86. Copyright (2003) Elsevier

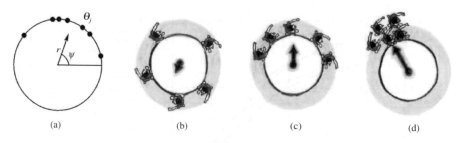

Figure 8.13   Geometric meaning of the order parameter: (a) order parameter; (b) $r{\approx}0$; (c) $0{\ll}r{\ll}1$; (d) $r{\approx}1$

8.4.1   Phase Synchronization of the Kuramoto Model

In the studies of phase synchronization, the Kuramoto model is a common platform [7, 53, 54]:

$$\dot{\theta}_i = \omega_i + \sum_{j=1}^{N} \Gamma_{ij}(\theta_j - \theta_i), \qquad i = 1, \dots, N. \tag{8.27}$$

Here, θ_i and ω_i are the phase and natural frequency of oscillator i, $i = 1, 2, \dots, N$, respectively, in which all ω_i have the same probability distribution $g(\omega)$. For simplicity, assume that $g(\omega)$ is a symmetric function with a single peak, such as Gaussian, satisfying $g(\omega) = g(-\omega)$, and $g(\omega)$ is nonincreasing on interval $[0, \infty)$. Moreover, for fully coupled equally-weighted networks, consider the simple case

$$\Gamma_{ij}(\theta_j - \theta_i) = \frac{c}{N} \sin(\theta_j - \theta_i),$$

where $c \geq 0$ is a constant coupling strength. In this case, (8.27) can be rewritten as

$$\dot{\theta}_i = \omega_i + \frac{c}{N} \sum_{j=1}^{N} \sin(\theta_j - \theta_i). \tag{8.28}$$

To better understand the dynamical behaviors of the phases during the process of synchronization, imagine a group of nodes moving along a circular path, as illustrated by Figure 8.13. Introduce an *order parameter* defined by

$$re^{i\psi} = \frac{1}{N} \sum_{j=1}^{N} e^{i\theta_j}, \tag{8.29}$$

where $\mathbf{i} = \sqrt{-1}$ and $r = r(t)$ measures the coherence of the group of moving nodes with $\psi = \psi(t)$ representing their average phase. Here, r can be used to describe the ratio of the number of the synchronous nodes over the total number of nodes, as illustrated by Figure 8.13.

Using the order parameter, (8.26) can be rewritten as

$$\dot{\theta}_i = \omega_i + Kr \sin(\psi - \theta_i), \qquad i = 1, 2, \dots, N, \tag{8.30}$$

which has a mean-field characteristic, with an effective coupling strength Kr. When synchronized, all $\theta_i \to \psi$ as $t \to \infty$, $i = 1, 2, \dots, N$.

Now, assume that $g(\omega)$ is Gaussian. Figure 8.14 [51] shows that when $K < K_c$, a threshold, all nodes will oscillate according to their individual natural frequencies, independent of their initial phases, in a way just like they are uncoupled. Moreover, $r(t)$ decreases exponentially fast, to be about $O(N^{-1/2})$. The figure also shows that when $K > K_c$, $r(t)$ increases exponentially fast, implying that a subgroup of the nodes start to synchronize, finally approaching a saturated value $r_\infty < 1$, and all nodes are synchronized.

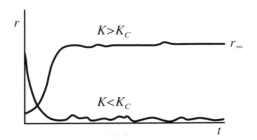

Figure 8.14 Evolution of $r(t)$ in the Kuramoto model [53]. *Source*: Reprinted from Strogatz, S.H. (2000) From Kuramoto to Crawford: exploring the onset of synchronization in populations of coupled oscillators. *Physica D*, **143**: 1–20. Copyright (2000) Elsevier

Next, without loss of generality, assume $\psi \equiv 0$. Then, (8.30) becomes

$$\dot{\theta}_i = \omega_i - Kr \sin \theta_i, \qquad i = 1, 2, \dots, N. \tag{8.31}$$

For this coupled network, the threshold K_c can be more precisely characterized, as explained below.

The group of nodes can be classified into two subgroups according to the relative values of $|\omega_i|$ and Kr: for the nodes with $|\omega_i| \leq Kr$, since $\dot{\theta}_i \approx 0$, their natural frequencies will be "phase-locked":

$$\omega_i = Kr \sin \theta_i, \qquad i = 1, 2, \dots, N. \tag{8.32}$$

For those nodes with $|\omega_i| > Kr$, however, they will be "phase-drifted" in an uneven manner.

Now, let $\rho(\theta, \omega)d\theta$ be the portion of nodes with natural frequencies ω in the interval $[\theta, \theta + d\theta]$:

$$\rho(\theta, \omega) = \frac{C}{|\omega - Kr \sin \theta|},$$

where $C = \sqrt{\omega^2 - (Kr)^2}/(2\pi)$, which normalizes $\int_{-\pi}^{\pi} \rho(\theta, \omega)d\theta = 1$.

Since all nodes are classified into two groups, by assuming $\psi \equiv 0$ and setting

$$\langle e^{i\theta} \rangle = \langle e^{i\theta} \rangle_{lock} + \langle e^{i\theta} \rangle_{drift},$$

where $\langle \cdot \rangle$ means taking an average, one has $\langle e^{i\theta} \rangle = re^{i\psi} = r$, which gives

$$r = \langle e^{i\theta} \rangle_{lock} + \langle e^{i\theta} \rangle_{drift}.$$

For the phase-locked group, all nodes with $|\omega| \leq Kr$ satisfy $\sin \theta = \omega/(Kr)$. Moreover, since $g(\omega) = g(-\omega)$, all locked phases are symmetrically distributed around $\theta = 0$, so that $\langle \sin \theta \rangle_{lock} = 0$ and

$$\langle e^{i\theta} \rangle_{lock} = \langle \cos \theta \rangle_{lock} = \int_{-Kr}^{Kr} \cos \theta(\omega)g(\omega)d\omega.$$

It then follows from (8.31) that

$$\langle e^{i\theta} \rangle_{lock} = \int_{-\pi/2}^{\pi/2} \cos \theta g(Kr \sin \theta)Kr \cos \theta d\theta = Kr \int_{-\pi/2}^{\pi/2} \cos^2 \theta g(Kr \sin \theta)d\theta.$$

For the phase-drifted group, $\langle e^{i\theta} \rangle_{drift}$ decays, so

$$r = Kr \int_{-\pi/2}^{\pi/2} \cos^2 \theta g(Kr \sin \theta)d\theta.$$

It is clear that this equation has a zero solution $r = 0$ for any K, which corresponds to a completely incoherent motion. For any θ and ω, $\rho(\theta, \omega) = 1/2\pi$. A nonzero solution is given by

$$1 = c \int_{-\pi/2}^{\pi/2} \cos^2\theta g(cr\sin\theta)d\theta,$$

which corresponds to the synchronization of parts of the nodes. It follows that the synchronization threshold is given by

$$K_c = \frac{2}{\pi g(0)} \tag{8.33}$$

and the order parameter is given by

$$r \approx \sqrt{\frac{16}{\pi K_c^3} \frac{\mu}{(-g''(0))}}, \tag{8.34}$$

where $\mu = (K - K_c)/K_c$.

8.4.2 Phase Synchronization of Small-World Networks

Consider a small-world network of coupled oscillators [55]:

$$\dot{\theta}_i = \omega_i + c\sum_{i\in\Lambda_i} \sin(\theta_j - \theta_i), \quad i = 1, 2, \dots, N, \tag{8.35}$$

where Λ_i is the neighborhood of node i, and phases θ_i and natural frequencies ω_i have zero-mean uniform distributed initial conditions on $(-1/2, 1/2)$ and $(-\pi, \pi)$, respectively. Similarly, define the average order parameter by

$$r = \left[\left\langle \frac{1}{N}\sum_{j=1}^{N} \cos(\theta_j - \theta_i)\right\rangle\right], \tag{8.36}$$

where $\langle\cdot\rangle$ and $[\cdot]$ represent time average and frequency average, respectively.

Different small-world models generated by different coupling strengths c generally have different phase synchronization characteristics. Figure 8.15 [55] shows the relationship of r versus c for different small-world networks. It can be seen that when the coupling strength is weak, $c \to 0$, all nodes are uniformly distributed in the interval $[0, 2\pi]$, so $r = O(1/\sqrt{N})$. This corresponds to the uniform distribution shown in Figure 8.13 (b), for which no synchronous group exists. As c increases, synchronous group is formed and then grows. As $c \to \infty$, one has $r = 1$, implying that the whole group of nodes synchronize in phase, regardless of the network topology.

It can also be seen from Figure 8.15 that phase synchronization in a small-world network depends on the edge-addition probability p: when $p = 0$, no long-range edges are added, so no synchronization occurs; as p increases, even for a very small $p = 0.05$, synchronous group emerges and then grows, thereby global synchronization takes place gradually. On the other hand, it is quite interesting to see that for $p > 0.5$, phase synchronization saturates, indicating that a small-world network and a fully connected network behave similarly in phase synchronization. This once again demonstrates the advantage of having a small-world topology for achieving (phase) synchronization, since a small-word network has very few long-range edges as compared to a fully connected network.

8.4.3 Phase Synchronization of Scale-Free Networks

Consider a BA scale-free network of N oscillators, with degree distribution $P(k) \sim k^{-3}$, described also by (8.35), namely [56]

$$\dot{\theta}_i = \omega_i + c\sum_{i\in\Lambda_i} \sin(\theta_j - \theta_i), \quad i = 1, 2, \dots, N, \tag{8.37}$$

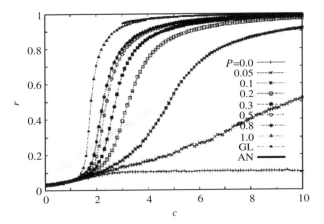

Figure 8.15 Relationship of r versus c for different small-world networks [55]. *Source*: Reprinted with permission from Hong, H., Choi, M.Y. and Kim, B.J. (2002) Synchronization on small-world networks. *Physical Review E*, **65**: 026139. Copyright (2002) American Physical Society

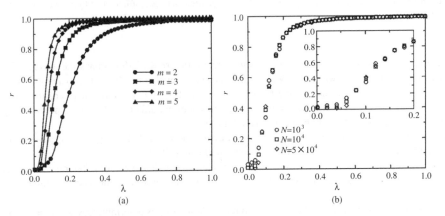

Figure 8.16 Relationship of r versus c for different small-world networks [56]: (a) different m; (b) $m = 3$. *Source*: Reproduced by permission of *Europhysics Letters*

where Λ_i is the neighboring set of node i, and phases θ_i and natural frequencies ω_i have zero-mean uniform distributed initial conditions on $(-1/2, 1/2)$ and $(-\pi, \pi)$, respectively. Similarly, define the average order parameter by

$$r = \left[\left\langle \frac{1}{N} \sum_{j=1}^{N} \cos(\theta_j - \theta_i) \right\rangle \right], \tag{8.38}$$

where $\langle \cdot \rangle$ and $[\cdot]$ represent time average and frequency average, respectively.

For this scale-free network model, when the coupling strength $c \to 0$, all nodes are oscillating according to their own natural frequencies. As c increases, synchronous group is formed and then grows. After c passes a threshold, the whole network of nodes synchronize in phase. For various BA networks of different sizes (determined by the number m of added new edges), their phase synchronization behaviors are similar, as shown in Figure 8.16 [56], where $N = 10000$ and $\lambda = c$.

Due to the different heterogeneities of degree distributions in these scale-free networks, their robustness against perturbations are varied. When a scale-free network is slightly perturbed, it may lose global

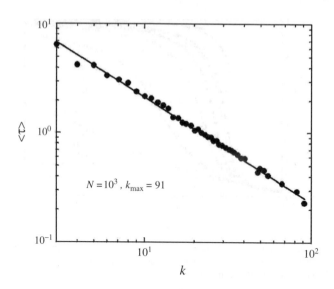

Figure 8.17 Time needed to resynchronize a perturbed scale-free network [56]. *Source*: Reproduced by permission of *Europhysics Letters*

synchrony for some time but then resynchronize again. Figure 8.17 [56] shows the average time $\langle \tau \rangle$ needed for a perturbed network to resynchronize. It can be seen that the data fall into a power-law curve with $\langle \tau \rangle \sim k^{-0.96}$. This means that the bigger the degree of a node, the more stable of the node. It is interesting to see that the instability of a big node (hub) does not affect much on its synchronous group; instead, the neighbors of this hub "help" it restabilize itself.

For a scale-free network having a node-degree distribution $k^{-\gamma}$ with $2 < \gamma \le 3$, its phase synchronization can be carried out analytically with some approximations [57].

Consider again network (8.37), and let $P(k)$ denote the node-degree distribution and $\rho(k, \omega, t, \theta)$ be the density of nodes with phase θ at time t. Assume, moreover, the normalization condition $\int_0^{2\pi} \rho(k, \omega, t, \theta)d\theta = 1$.

When all nodes synchronize, $d\rho/dt = 0$, and the evolution of ρ is determined by $\partial\rho/\partial t = -\partial(\rho v)/\partial\theta$, where v is a constant. Since the probability of randomly selecting a node with degree k, frequency ω and phase θ is

$$kP(k)N(\omega)\rho(k, \omega, t, \theta) / \int dkkP(k),$$

the density $\rho(k, \omega, t, \theta)$ must satisfy

$$\frac{\partial\rho(k, \omega, t, \theta)}{\partial t} = -\frac{\partial}{\partial\theta}\left[\rho(k, \omega, t, \theta)\left(\omega + \frac{ck \int d\omega' \int dk' \int d\theta' g(\omega') P(k')\rho(k', \omega', t, \theta')\sin(\theta' - \theta)}{\int dk' P(k')k'}\right)\right],$$

where, as before, $g(\omega_i)$ is the probability distribution of frequency ω_i, $i = 1, 2, \dots, N$.

Defining the order parameter

$$re^{i\psi} = \frac{\int d\omega \int dk \int d\theta g(\omega)P(k)k\rho(k, \omega, t, \theta)e^{i\theta}}{\int dkP(k)k}$$

and substituting it into the above gives

$$\frac{\partial \rho(k,\omega,t,\theta)}{\partial t} = -\frac{\partial(\rho(k,\omega,t,\theta)(\omega + ckr\sin(\psi - \theta)))}{\partial \theta}.$$

It then follows from $d\rho/dt = 0$ that

$$\frac{\partial(\rho(k,\omega,t,\theta)(\omega + ckr\sin(\psi - \theta)))}{\partial \theta} = 0.$$

Now, without loss of generality, assume that $\psi \equiv 0$. In order to have the same conclusion as the case of a fully coupled network of Kuramoto oscillators studied before, assume that a solution of the above equation is

$$\rho = \begin{cases} \delta\left(\theta - \arcsin\left(\omega/ckr\right)\right) & if \quad |\omega/ckr| \le 1 \\ \dfrac{C(k,\omega)}{|\omega - ckr\sin\theta|} & otherwise \end{cases},$$

where $C(k,\omega)$ is a normalized constant. It then follows that

$$r = \frac{\displaystyle\int d\omega \int dk \int d\theta g(\omega)P(k)k\rho(k,\omega;\theta)e^{i\theta}}{\displaystyle\int dkP(k)k} = \frac{cr\displaystyle\int dkk^2 P(k)\int_{-1}^{1} d\omega' g(ckr\omega')\sqrt{1-\omega'2}}{\displaystyle\int dkP(k)k}. \tag{8.39}$$

If $r \neq 0$, then

$$\int dkP(k)k = c\int dkk^2 P(k)\int_{-1}^{1} d\omega g(ckr\omega)\sqrt{1-\omega^2}.$$

It can be seen that the left-hand side is independent of r. However, the right-hand side depends on r, which is denoted as $f(r)$. When $r = 1$, one has

$$\int dkk^2 P(k)\int_{-1}^{1} d\omega g(ckr\omega)\sqrt{1-\omega^2} \le \int dkk^2 P(k)\int_{-1}^{1} d\omega g(ckr\omega)$$

$$\le \int dk\frac{1}{ckr}k^2 P(k)\int_{-\infty}^{\infty} d\omega'' g(\omega'')$$

$$= \frac{1}{cr}\int dkkP(k).$$

Thus, $f(r) \le \int dkkP(k)$. Consequently, for $0 < r \le 1$, (8.39) has a solution only if $r = 0$ implies $f(r) > \int dkkP(k)$, namely,

$$\frac{cg(0)\pi\displaystyle\int dkk^2 P(k)}{2\displaystyle\int dkP(k)k} > 1. \tag{8.40}$$

This is a sufficient condition for the network to achieve phase synchronization.

If $P(k) \sim k^{-\gamma}$, with $2 < \gamma \le 3$, then

$$\frac{\displaystyle\int dkk^2 P(k)}{\displaystyle\int dkP(k)k} \gg 1,$$

implying that hubs are very robust against perturbations.

Therefore, for any coupling strength $c > 0$, condition (8.40) is always satisfied, so the threshold for such a scale-free network is almost zero. This is similar to the virus spreading process on an SIS model, where for a BA scale-free network the epidemic threshold is zero (see Section 5.2.4, Chapter 5).

8.4.4   Phase Synchronization of Nonuniformly Coupled Networks

In all the network models discussed above, every edge has the same coupling strength. In this subsection, one type of nonuniformly coupled network model is discussed [45]:

$$\dot{\theta}_i = \omega_i + \frac{c}{k_i} \sum_{j=1}^{N} a_{ij} \sin(\theta_j - \theta_i), \tag{8.41}$$

where the coupling strength $c > 0$ is a constant; k_i is the degree of node i with a distribution $P(k)$; ω_i is the natural frequency with a distribution $g(\omega)$ as before, satisfying $g(\omega) = g(-\omega)$; $a_{ij} = 1$ if node i and node j are connected, $a_{ij} = 0$ otherwise, $i, j, = 1, 2, \dots, N$. Clearly, if all $a_{ij} = N$, the network becomes a fully connected network and the model reduces to the standard Kuramoto model discussed before.

Define an order parameter

$$re^{i\psi} = \frac{\int d\omega \int dk \int d\theta g(\omega) P(k) k \rho(k, \omega, t, \theta) e^{i\theta}}{\int dk P(k) k}.$$

Then,

$$\frac{\partial \rho(k, \omega, t, \theta)}{\partial t} = -\frac{\partial}{\partial \theta} \left[\rho(k, \omega, t, \theta) \left(\omega + \frac{c}{k} \frac{k \int d\omega' \int dk' \int d\theta' g\left(\theta'\right) P(k') \rho(k', \omega', t, \theta') \sin(\theta' - \theta)}{\int dk' P(k') k'} \right) \right]$$

$$= -\frac{\partial}{\partial \theta} [\rho(k, \omega, t, \theta)[\omega + cr \sin(\psi - \theta)]].$$

In order for $\rho(k, \omega, t, \theta)$ to be a constant, let

$$\rho = \begin{cases} \delta\left(\theta - \arcsin\left(\omega/ckr\right)\right) & \text{if } \ |\omega/ckr| \leq 1 \\ \dfrac{C(k, \omega)}{|\omega - ckr \sin \theta|} & \text{otherwise,} \end{cases}$$

where $C(k, \omega)$ is a normalized constant. It then follows that

$$r = cr \int_{-\pi/2}^{\pi/2} d\theta \cos^2 \theta g(cr \sin \theta),$$

which eventually gives the following threshold, consistent with (8.33):

$$c^* = \frac{2}{\pi g(0)}. \tag{8.42}$$

This means that the threshold of phase synchronization is independent of the coupling strength, verifying once again that a weakly coupled oscillator network may have strong tendency towards synchronization.

Similarly, introduce the average order parameter:

$$r_{av} = \left\langle \left[\frac{\sum_{i=1}^{N} k_i e^{i\theta_i}}{\sum_{i=1}^{N} k_i} \right] \right\rangle,$$

where $\langle \cdot \rangle$ and $[\cdot]$ represent time average and frequency average, respectively.

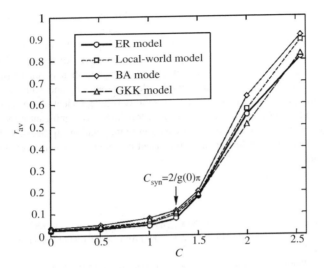

Figure 8.18 Comparison of average order parameter of four network models [45]. *Source*: Reprinted from Li, X. (2006) Uniform synchronous criticality of diversely random complex networks. *Physica A*, **360**: 629–36. Copyright (2006) Elsevier

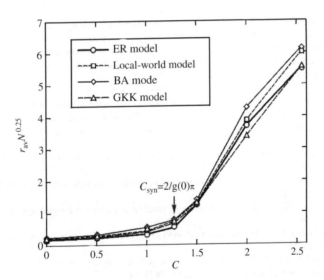

Figure 8.19 Comparison of average value $r_{av}N^{0.25}$ of four network models [45]. *Source*: Reprinted from Li, X. (2006) Uniform synchronous criticality of diversely random complex networks. *Physica A*, **360**: 629–36. Copyright (2006) Elsevier

In the following simulation, r_{av} is the average of 10 groups of networks with the same node-degree distribution $P(k)$, where each network takes the average of 5 times of simulations based on the same probability distribution $g(\omega)$, where

$$g(\omega) = \begin{cases} 0.5 & if \quad -1 < \omega < 1 \\ 0 & otherwise. \end{cases}$$

It follows from (8.42) that $c^* \approx 1.273$.

Figures 8.18 and 8.19 [45] compare the phase synchronizations of ER random-graph network (dash curve with small circles), BA scale-free network with $P(k) \sim k^{-\gamma}, \gamma = 6$ (solid curves with small diamonds), modified scale-free model (GKK model) [56] (dot-dash curve with small triangles), and local-world (LW) model (dot-dash curves with small squares). All networks have the same size $N = 2048$ and average node-degree $\langle k \rangle = 6$. It can be seen that all network phase synchronization thresholds match (8.42). When $c > c^*$, the average order parameter r_{av} and average value $r_{av}N^{0.25}$ both increase prominently, showing that phase synchronizability is independent of the network topology.

To summarize, one main issue is that the network topology has significant effects on the network dynamics. Lately, this has attracted increasing attention to the relationship between the network topology and network synchronous behaviors in different settings of complex networks [12–44, 56–64, and references cited therein].

References

[1] Neda, Z., Ravasz, E. and Brechet, Y et al. (2000) The sound of many hands clapping. *Nature*, **403**: 849–50.
[2] Kincaid, R.K., Alexandrov, N. and Holroyd, M.J. (2008) An investigation of synchrony in transport networks. *Complexity*, **14**: 34–43.
[3] Blekhman, I.I. (1988) *Synchronization in Science and Technology*. ASME Press.
[4] Strogatz, S.H. (2003) *Sync: The Emerging Science of Spontaneous Order*. Hyperion, New York.
[5] Floyd, S. and Jacobson, V. (1993) The synchronization of periodic routing messages. *ACM SIGCOMM Computer Communication Review*, **23**: 33–44.
[6] Winfree, A.T. (1967) Biological rhythms and the behavior of populations of coupled oscillators. *Journal of Theoretical Biology*, **16**: 15–42.
[7] Kuramoto, Y. (1984) *Chemical Oscillations, Waves and Turbulence*. Springer, Berlin.
[8] Kaneko, K. (1992) *Coupled Map Lattices*. World Scientific, Singapore.
[9] Chua, L.O. (1993) *CNN: A Paradigm for Complexity*. World Scientific, Singapore.
[10] Wu, C.W. and Chua, L.O. (1995) Synchronization in an array of linearly coupled dynamical systems. *IEEE Transactions on Circuits and Systems Part I*, **42**: 430–47.
[11] Chung, F. (1992, 1997) *Spectral Graph Theory*. AMS Press, New York.
[12] Wu, C.W. and Chua, L.O. (1995) Application of graph theory to the synchronization in an array of coupled nonlinear oscillators. *IEEE Transactions on Circuits and Systems Part I*, **42**: 494–7.
[13] Heagy, J.F., Carroll, T.L. and Pecora, L.M. (1994) Synchronous chaos in coupled oscillator systems. *Physical Review E*, **50**(3): 1874–85.
[14] Ding, M.Z. and Yang, W.M. (1997) Stability of synchronous chaos and on-off intermittency in coupled map lattices. *Physical Review E*, **56**(4): 4009–16.
[15] Pecora, L.M. and Carroll, T.L. (1998) Master stability functions for synchronized coupled systems. *Physical Review Letters*, **80**: 2109.
[16] Rangarajan, G. and Ding, M.Z. (2002) Stability of synchronized chaos in coupled dynamical systems. *Physics Letters A*, **296**: 204–9.
[17] Wang, X.F. and Chen, G.. (2002) Synchronization in small-world dynamical networks. *International Journal of Bifurcation Chaos*, **12**(1): 187–92.
[18] Wang, X.F. and Chen, G. (2002) Synchronization in scale-free dynamical networks: robustness and fragility. *IEEE Transactions on Circuits and Systems Part I*, **49**(1): 54–62.
[19] Wang, X.F. (2002) Complex networks: topology, dynamics and synchronization. *International Journal of Bifurcation Chaos*, **12**(5): 885–916.
[20] Wang, X.F. and Chen, G. (2003) Complex networks: small-world, scale-free and beyond, *IEEE Circuits and Systems Magazine*, **3**: 6–20.
[21] Wang, X.F. and Chen, G. (2003) Synchronization in complex dynamical networks, *Journal of Systems Science and Complexity*, **16**: 1–14.
[22] Li, X., Wang, X.F. and Chen, G. (2003) Synchronization in complex dynamical networks and its applications, *Proceedings of Conference on Growing Networks and Graphs in Statistical Physics, Finance, Biology and Social Systems*, Rome, Italy.
[23] Li, X, and Chen, G. (2003) Synchronization and desynchronization of complex dynamical networks: an engineering viewpoint. *IEEE Transactions on Circuits and Systems Part I*, **50**(11): 1381–90.
[24] Li, X., Wang, X.F. and Chen, G. (2004) Pinning a complex dynamical network to its equilibrium. *IEEE Transactions on Circuits and Systems Part I*, **51**: 2074–87.

[25] Li, X. and Chen, G. (2003) A local-world evolving network model. *Physica A*, **328**: 274–86.

[26] Chen, G., Wang, X., Li, X. and Lu, J. (2009) Some recent advances in complex networks synchronization. In K. Kyamakya (ed.), *Recent Advances in Nonlinear Dynamics and Synchronization*, Springer, Berlin, pp. 3–16.

[27] Nishikawa, T., Motter, A.E. and Lai Y-C. *et al.* (2003) Heterogeneity in oscillator networks: are smaller worlds easier to synchronize? *Physical Review Letters*, **91**: 014101.

[28] Wu, C.W. (2003) Perturbation of coupling matrices and its effect on the synchronizability in arrays of coupled chaotic systems. *Physics Letters A*, **319**: 495–503.

[29] Hong, H., Kim, B.J. and Choi, M.Y. *et al.* (2004) Factors that predict better synchronizability on complex networks. *Physical Review E*, **69**: 067105.

[30] Atay, F.M. and Jost, J. (2004) Delays, connection topology, and synchronization of coupled chaotic maps. *Physical Review Letters*, **92**: 144101.

[31] Barahona, M. and Pecora, L.M. (2004) Synchronization in small-world systems. *Physical Review Letters*, **89**(5): 054101.

[32] Li, C. and Chen, G. (2004) Phase synchronization in small-world networks of chaotic oscillators. *Physica A*, **341**: 73–9.

[33] Li, C. and Chen, G. (2004) Synchronization in general complex dynamical networks with coupling delays. *Physica A*, **343**: 236–78.

[34] Lu, J., Yu, X., Chen, G. and Cheng, D. (2004) Characterizing the synchronizability of small-world dynamical networks. *IEEE Transactions on Circuits and Systems Part I*, **51**: 787–96.

[35] Lu, J. and Chen, G. (2005) A time-varying complex dynamical network model and its controlled synchronization criteria. *IEEE Transactions on Automatic Control*, **50**: 841–6.

[36] Lu, J, Yu, X. and Chen, G. (2004) Chaos synchronization of general complex dynamical networks. *Physica A*, **334**: 281–302.

[37] Motter, A.E., Zhou, C. and Kurths, J. (2005) Enhancing complex-network synchronization. *Europhyics Letters*, **69**: 334–40.

[38] Motter A E, Zhou C, Kurths, J (2005) Network synchronization, diffusion, and the paradox of heterogeneity. *Physical Review E*, **71**: 016116.

[39] Chavez, M., Hwang, D-U. and Amann, A. (2005) *et al.* Synchronization is enhanced in weighted complex networks. *Physical Review Letters*, **94**: 218701.

[40] Kocarev, L. and Amato, P. (2005) Synchronization in power-law networks. *Chaos*, **15**: 024101.

[41] Fan, J, and Wang, X.F. (2005) On synchronization in scale-free dynamical networks. *Physica A*, **349**: 443–51.

[42] Nishikawa, T. and Motter, A.E. (2010) Network synchronization landscape reveals compensatory structures, quantization, and the positive effect of negative interactions. *Proceedings of the National Academy of Sciences USA*, **107**: 10342–7.

[43] Fan, J., Li, X. and Wang, X.F. (2005) On synchronous preference of complex dynamical networks. *Physica A*, **355**: 657–66.

[44] Zhou, J., Lu, J.A. and Lu, J.H. (2006) Adaptive synchronization of an uncertain complex dynamical network. *IEEE Transactions on Automatic Control*, **51**: 652–6.

[45] Li, X. (2006) Uniform synchronous criticality of diversely random complex networks. *Physica A*, **360**: 629–36.

[46] Chen, J., Lu, J-A. and Zhou, J. (2013) On relations between synchronous state and solution of single node in complex networks (in Chinese). *ACTA Automatica Sinica*, **39**(12): 2111–20.

[47] DeGroot, M.H. (1974) Reaching a consensus, *Journal of the American Statistical Association*, **69**(345): 118–21.

[48] Olfati-Saber, R, and Murray, R.M. (2003) Consensus protocols for networks of dynamic agents. *American Control Conference*.

[49] Olfati-Saber, R. and Murray, R.M. (2004) Consensus problems in networks of agents with switching topology and time-delays. *IEEE Transactions on Automatic Control*, **49**(9): 1520–33.

[50] Lu, W. and Chen, T. (2006) New approach to synchronization analysis of linearly coupled ordinary differential systems. *Physica D*, **213**: 214–30.

[51] Stepanski, A., Perlikowski, P. and Kapitaniak, T. (2007) Ragged synchronizability of couplied oscillators. *Physical Review E*, **75**: 016210.

[52] Liu, C., Duan, Z.S., Chen, G. and Huang, L. (2007) Synchronization regions in complex networks: analysis and control. *Physica A*, **386**: 531–42.

[53] Strogatz, S.H. (2000) From Kuramoto to Crawford: exploring the onset of synchronization in populations of coupled oscillators. *Physica D*, **143**: 1–20.

[54] Acebrón, J.A., Bonilla, L. and Vicente, C.J.P. *et al.* (2005) The Kuramoto model: A simple paradigm for synchronization phenomena. *Reviews of Modern Physics*, **77**: 137–86.

[55] Hong, H., Choi, M.Y. and Kim, B.J. (2002) Synchronization on small-world networks. *Physical Review E*, **65**: 026139.

[56] Moreno, Y., Pacheco, A.F. (2004) Synchronization of Kuramoto oscillators in scale-free networks, *Europhysics Letters*, **68**: 603–9.

[57] Ichinomiya, T. (2004) Frequency synchronization in random oscillator network. *Physical Review E*, **70**: 026116.

[58] Belykh, I., Hasler, M. and Belykh, V.N. (2007) When symmetrization guarantees synchronization in directed networks. *International Journal of Bifurcation and Chaos*, **17**(10): 3387–95.

[59] Duan, Z.S., Chen, G. and Huang, L. (2007) Complex network synchronizability: Analysis and control, *Physical Review E*, **76**: 056103.

[60] Duan, Z.S., Chen, G. and Huang, L. (2008) Network synchronizability analysis: The theory of subgraphs and complementary graphs. *Physica D*, **237**:1006–12.

[61] Chen. G. and Duan, Z.S. (2008) Network synchronizability analysis: A graph-theoretic approach. *Chaos*, **18**: 037102.

[62] Boccaletti, S., Latora, V., Moreno Y *et al.* (2006) Complex networks: Structure and dynamics. *Physics Reports*, **424**: 175–308.

[63] Arenas, A., Diaz-Guilera, A. and Kurths, J, *et al.* (2008) Synchronization in complex networks. *Physics Report*, **469**: 93–153.

[64] Wu, C.W. (2007) *Synchronization in Complex Networks of Nonlinear Dynamical Systems*. World Scientific, Singapore.

9

Network Control

9.1 Introduction

Since the pioneering work of Wiener [1], automatic control theory and technology have been rapidly developed, and are recently being further extended from a single (albeit higher-dimensional) dynamical system to a network of many (higher- dimensional) dynamical systems mutually connected in various topologies.

Chaos theory was introduced in Section 2.3.3 of Chapter 2. Chaos control, as a special subject in general control theory and engineering, aims at utilizing the extreme sensitivity of chaotic dynamics to system initial conditions to achieve significant effects by tiny control actions [2, 3]. Synchronization of two coupled chaotic oscillators, or a network of coupled chaotic oscillators thereafter, have been investigated, as briefly discussed in Chapter 8. When a given network of dynamical systems is not synchronizable, control becomes a necessary means for guiding or forcing the network to synchronize. In the past, regarding the special structures of complex networks, a simple and effective control strategy named "pinning control" was commonly used [4, 5]. The pinning control technique was at the beginning to add a constant control to a small fraction of nodes in the network, where the constant control input remains unchanged (just like a "pin") until the end of the control process when the control objective such as synchronization is achieved. Lately, this constant control input had been extended to a general controller such as state-feedback, time-delay feedback, nonlinear feedback, etc., which in a broader sense can be any kind of conventional controllers [6–11]. No matter what kind of controllers are used, pinning control differs from many other control strategies such as switching control and impulsive control in that pinning controllers will not be disconnected or turned off throughout the entire control process after being put at a fraction of nodes of the network.

Noticeably, network control via local injections, a kind of pinning control, was studied under a network framework for multiple connected chaotic oscillators earlier. One representative example is first reviewed below as a motivation to the present discussion. In this chapter, only undirected networks are discussed.

9.2 Spatiotemporal Chaos Control on Regular CML

Consider a continuous-time nearest-coupled network of the form [12]

$$
\begin{cases}
\dot{x}_i = f\left(x_i\right) + \dfrac{\varepsilon}{2}(x_{i+1} + x_{i-1} - 2x_i) + \dfrac{r}{2}(x_{i-1} - x_{i+1}), & i = 1, 2, \ldots, N-1 \\
\dot{x}_0 = f(x_0) + \dfrac{\varepsilon}{2}(x_1 + x_{N-2} - 2x_0) + \dfrac{r}{2}(x_{N-2} - x_1) - \lambda x_0
\end{cases}
\tag{9.1}
$$

where $f : R \to R$ is a chaotic map with state variable $x_i \in R$ of node i, satisfying $f(0) = 0$ for simplicity, $\varepsilon > 0$ is the coupling strength, and $r \geq 0$ and $\lambda \geq 0$ are the control gains of the state-feedback controllers

---

Fundamentals of Complex Networks: Models, Structures and Dynamics, First Edition.
Guanrong Chen, Xiaofan Wang, Xiang Li.
© Higher Education Press. All rights reserved. Published 2015 by John Wiley & Sons Singapore Pte Ltd.
Companion Website: www.wiley.com/go/chen/complex

$\frac{1}{2}(x_{i-1} - x_i)$ and $-x_0$, respectively, with periodic boundary conditions as described by the second equation in (9.1), $i = 1, 2, \ldots, N$.

The objective is to stabilize the network to its zero equilibrium, in the sense that

$$\lim_{t \to \infty} ||x_i|| = 0, \qquad i = 1, 2, \ldots, N,$$

or, to achieve network synchronization, in the sense that

$$\lim_{t \to \infty} ||x_i - x_j|| = 0, \qquad i, j = 1, 2, \ldots, N,$$

where $|| \cdot ||$ is the Euclidean norm of the state vector.

Simulations show [12] that for $r = 0$, it is impossible to achieve control, as shown by Figure 9.1 (a) [12], where λ_m is the maximum Lyapunov exponent ($\lambda_m > 0$ means the network is chaotic, $\lambda_m = 0$ means the network is oscillatory, $\lambda_m < 0$ means the networked can be stabilized to its equilibrium). As $r > 0$ is increased to be larger than a threshold value $r_c > 0$, the network is being controlled to its equilibrium, as shown by Figure 9.1 (c) [12].

The above investigation can be easily extended to the discrete-time setting. Consider a discrete-time Coupled Map Lattice (CML) of the form [4]

$$x_{n+1}(i) = (1 - \varepsilon)f[x_n(i)] + \frac{\varepsilon}{2}\{f[x_n(i-1)] + f[x_n(i+1)]\} \tag{9.2}$$

or, when pinning control is added,

$$x_{n+1}(i) = (1 - \varepsilon)f[x_n(i)] + \frac{\varepsilon}{2}\{f[x_n(i-1)] + f[x_n(i+1)]\} + \sum_{k=0}^{L/I} \delta(i - Ik - 1)g_n, \tag{9.3}$$

where same notations are defined as above; L is the total number of nodes; I is the distance between two controlled nodes; g_n is a controller; δ determines if a controller is to be added: $\delta(j) = 1$ for $j = 0$, and $\delta(j) = 0$ otherwise. Clearly, in this controlled CML, there are a total of L/I controllers used.

Research shows that in order to effectively control a CML, to its equilibrium for example, one must use a large enough number of pinning controllers [4]. Also, this pinning control strategy can be applied to achieve network synchronization [13], where numerical simulations show that for this

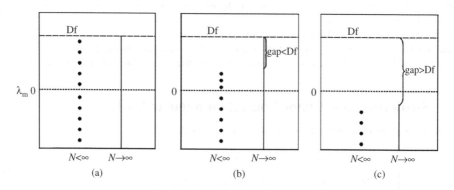

Figure 9.1 Control performance of pinning a nearest-coupled network [12]: (a) $r=0$; (b) $0<r<r_c$ (c) $r>r_c$.
Source: Reprinted with permission from Hu, G., Xiao, J.H. and Gao, J.H. *et al.* (2000) Analytic study of spatiotemporal chaos control by applying local injections. *Physical Reviews E*, **62**(3): 3043–6. Copyright (2000) American Physical Society

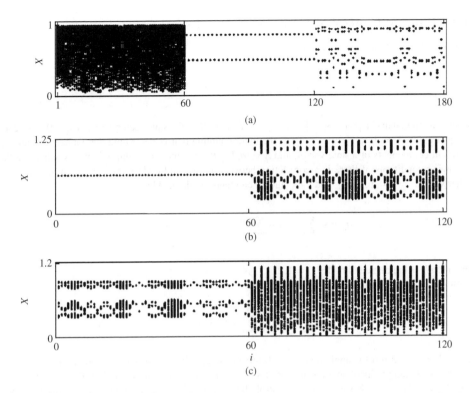

Figure 9.2 Chaos control and anti-control of CML network by pinning [16]: (a) $r = 3.95$; (b) $r = 2.8$; (c) $r = 3.6$.
Source: Courtesy of Santa Fe Institute

kind of discrete-time regular CML, the fraction of controllers used depends on the control gains of the controllers: the smaller the control gains are, the more the pinning controllers will be needed in general.

The above pinning controller is of closed-loop state-feedback type. One may also consider using open-loop pinning controllers such as the following [14]:

$$x_{n+1}(i) = (1 - \varepsilon)f(x_n(i)) + \frac{\varepsilon}{2}[f(x_n(i - 1)) + f(x_n(i + 1))] + p_n(i), \qquad (9.4)$$

where $p_n(i)$ represents the pinning input strength of node i at time n, with $p_n(i) = \delta(i - i_p)p$, in which $p > 0$ is a constant, and $\delta(j) = 1$ for $j = 0$ and $\delta(j) = 0$ otherwise, therefore only nodes i_p are pinned by $p_n(i_p) = p$ and the other nodes receive $p_n(i) = 0$.

Simulations show [14] that both uniformly and randomly distributed pinning control input strengths p can stabilize the spatiotemporal network to its equilibrium, and that the number of controllers and the control input strength both have significant effects on the control performance.

As seen above, when controlling a network (or a system) from a chaotic state to a nonchaotic or even an equilibrium state, it is referred to as "control of chaos," while the opposite task, i.e., controlling a network (or system) from a regular state to a chaotic state, is called "anti-control of chaos" [3, 15].

Some studies [16] show that pinning can also achieve anti-control of chaos in the above CML network (9.4), with $f(\cdot)$ being a logistic map. Figure 9.2 (a) [16] shows that the spatiotemporal chaotic CML (left) is controlled to a periodic state (middle) and nonchaotic state (right); while Figures 9.2 (b) and (c) [16] show that the CML is controlled to chaotic and strongly chaotic states, respectively, all by means of pinning.

9.3   Pinning Control of Complex Networks

Consider the following linearly and diffusively coupled scale-free network [6]

$$\dot{x}_i = f(x_i) - c \sum_{j=1}^{N} a_{ij} \Gamma x_j, \qquad i = 1, 2, \cdots, N, \tag{9.5}$$

where, as studied in Chapter 8, $x_i = [x_i^{(1)}, x_i^{(2)}, \cdots, x_i^{(n)}]^T \in R^n$ is the state vector, constant $c > 0$ is the coupling strength, $\Gamma = diag\{r_1, r_2, \ldots, r_n\}$ is the inner coupling matrix describing the connections among different components of a state vector, and $\widetilde{A} = [a_{ij}] \in R^{N \times N}$ is the outer coupling matrix satisfying the following conditions: if there is a connection between node i and node j, for $i \neq j$, then $a_{ij} = a_{ji} = 1$; otherwise, $a_{ij}a_{ji} = 0$, for $i \neq j$; and the diagonal elements are defined by

$$a_{ii} = - \sum_{\substack{j=1 \\ j \neq i}}^{N} a_{ij} = - \sum_{\substack{j=1 \\ j \neq i}}^{N} a_{ji} = -k_i, \qquad i = 1, 2, \cdots, N, \tag{9.6}$$

in which k_i is the degree of node i, $i = 1, 2, \ldots, N$.

Now, consider the corresponding controlled network

$$\dot{x}_i = f(x_i) - c \sum_{j=1}^{N} a_{ij} \Gamma x_j - c \sum_{j=1}^{N} b_{ij} H_j(x_j - s), \qquad i = 1, 2, \cdots, N. \tag{9.7}$$

Here, $b_{ij} = 1$ if control is applied but $b_{ij} = 0$ otherwise, and H_j is a constant control gain matrix to be designed. For simplicity of notation and discussion, let $H_j = h_j I$, where $h_j > 0$ and I is the identity matrix, for all $j = 1, 2, \ldots, N$. Assume that the control objective here is to guide all the state vectors x_i to track a particular solution trajectory of the node system $\dot{s} = f(s)$ in the sense that

$$||x_i(t) - s(t)|| \to 0, \qquad as \qquad t \to \infty, \tag{9.8}$$

for all $i = 1, 2, \ldots, N$.

9.3.1   Augmented Network Approach

The augmented network approach [7] is to extend the controlled network (9.7) to a network of $N + 1$ nodes, having state vectors denoted by y_i, with $y_i = x_i$ for $i = 1, 2, \ldots, N$ and $y_{N+1} = s$. Thus, the controlled network (9.7) can be rewritten as an "uncontrolled" network of the form

$$\dot{y}_i = f(y_i) - c \sum_{j=1}^{N} M_{ij} \Gamma y_j, \qquad i = 1, 2, \cdots, N, N + 1, \tag{9.9}$$

where $M = [M_{ij}]$ is an $(N + 1) \times (N + 1)$ matrix, with

$$M_{ij} = \begin{bmatrix} a_{11} + \sigma_1 h_1 & a_{12} & \cdots & a_{1N} & -\sigma_1 h_1 \\ a_{21} & a_{22} + \sigma_2 h_2 & & a_{2N} & -\sigma_2 h_2 \\ \vdots & \vdots & \ddots & \vdots & \vdots \\ a_{N1} & a_{N2} & \cdots & a_{NN} + \sigma_N h_N & -\sigma_N h_N \\ 0 & 0 & \cdots & 0 & 0 \end{bmatrix},$$

where $\sigma_i = \sum_{j=1}^{N} b_{ij}$ is the number of pinning controllers used at node i, $i = 1, 2, \ldots, N$.

Note that the matrix M is asymmetric but still has zero row-sum with positive diagonal elements. Since the coupling matrix $\widetilde{A} = [a_{ij}]$ is symmetrical, M is diagonalizable and its eigenvalues satisfy $0 = \mu_1 < \mu_2 \leq \cdots \leq \mu_{N+1}$.

Recall the master stability function approach studied in Section 8.2.1, Chapter 8, which is applicable to network (9.9). As a result, a necessary condition for network (9.9) to synchronize to the manifold $y_1 = y_2 = \cdots = y_N = y_{N+1}$ is that all $c\mu_i \in S$, where S is the network synchronized region discussed in Section 8.2.1, Chapter 8, $i = 1, 2, \ldots, N, N + 1$. Consequently,

$$x_1 = y_1 \rightarrow x_2 = y_2 \rightarrow \cdots \rightarrow x_N = y_N \rightarrow s = y_{N+1},$$

namely, the control objective (9.8) is achieved.

9.3.2   Pinning Control of Scale-Free Networks

Now, return to network (9.5). The objective here is, once again, to control the network to its equilibrium $\bar{x}$, which satisfies $f(\bar{x}) = 0$:

$$x_1 = x_2 = \cdots = x_N = \bar{x}. \tag{9.10}$$

Assume that only a fraction of nodes are pinned and, for notational simplicity, let these nodes be labeled as $1, 2, \ldots, l$, where $1 \leq l \leq N$ and l can actually be as small as one. Thus, the controlled network can be written as

$$\begin{cases} \dot{x}_k = f\left(x_k\right) - c\sum_{j=1}^{N} a_{kj}\Gamma x_j - cd\Gamma(x_k - \bar{x}), & k = 1, 2, \cdots, l \\ \\ \dot{x}_k = f(x_k) - c\sum_{j=1}^{N} a_{kj}\Gamma x_j, & k = l+1, l+2, \cdots, N, \end{cases} \tag{9.11}$$

where $d > 0$ is the control gain of the linear state-feedback controller $(x_k - \bar{x})$, $k = 1, 2, \ldots, l$.

Linearizing network (9.11) around its equilibrium $\bar{X} = \begin{bmatrix} \bar{x}^T & \bar{x}^T & \cdots & \bar{x}^T \end{bmatrix}^T$ gives the following linear matrix equation:

$$\dot{\eta} = \eta[Df(\bar{x})] - cB\eta\Gamma, \tag{9.12}$$

where $Df(\bar{x})$ is the Jacobi matrix of $f(x)$ evaluated at $\bar{x}$, $\eta = (\eta_1, \eta_2, \cdots, \eta_N)^T$, $\eta_i(t) = x_i(t) - \bar{x}$, matrix $B = \widetilde{A} - D$ and matrix $D = diag(d_1, d_2, \cdots, d_N)$, in which for $1 \leq k \leq l$, $d_k = d$, and for $l + 1 \leq k \leq N$, $d_k = 0$.

Thus, the problem of controlling the network (9.11) to its equilibrium $\bar{x}$ is studied locally around $\bar{x}$, which is transformed to be a stabilization problem for system (9.12). Consequently, the classical linear stability theory can be applied, leading to the conclusion that if there exists a constant $\rho < 0$ such that $[Df(\bar{x}) + \rho\Gamma]$ is Hurwitz stable and that

$$c \geq \left| \frac{\rho}{\lambda_1(B)} \right|, \tag{9.13}$$

then the dynamical system (9.11) will be controlled to its equilibrium $\bar{x}$, where $\lambda_1(B)$ is the largest eigenvalue of matrix B.

Notice that as $d \rightarrow \infty$, one has $\lim_{d \rightarrow \infty} \lambda_1(B) = \lambda_1(\widetilde{A}_0)$, where the matrix $\widetilde{A}_0$ is obtained from the outer coupling matrix $\widetilde{A}$ by removing those rows and columns that correspond to the controlled nodes $1, 2, \ldots, l$. When $d \rightarrow \infty$, the stability of the equilibrium of network (9.11) is equivalent to the stability of the following dynamical systems:

$$\begin{cases} \dot{x}_k = \bar{x}, & k = 1, 2, \cdots, l \\ \\ \dot{x}_k = f\left(x_k\right) - c\sum_{j=1}^{N} a_{kj}\Gamma x_j, & k = l+1, l+2, \cdots, N \end{cases} \tag{9.14}$$

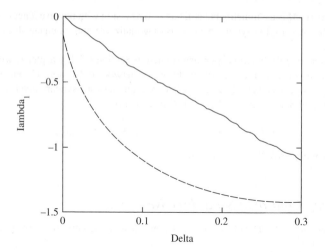

Figure 9.3 Comparison of two pinning schemes on scale-free networks [6]. *Source*: Reprinted from Wang, X.F. and Chen, G. (2002) Pinning control of scale-free dynamical networks. *Physica A*, **310**: 521–31. Copyright (2002) Elsevier

In this case, the stability condition (9.13) becomes

$$c \geq \left| \frac{\rho}{\lambda_1\left(\widetilde{A}_0\right)} \right|. \tag{9.15}$$

For scale-free networks, the pinning control strategy can be classified into two different types, *random pinning* and *selective pinning*, where the former means to randomly pin l nodes among the N nodes of the network while the latter means to successively pin the l big nodes with the largest degree, second largest degree, and so on.

   To evaluate the control performance, according to condition (9.15), one may compare different control schemes by examining their corresponding largest eigenvalues $\lambda_{1r}(\widetilde{A}_0)$ and $\lambda_{1s}(\widetilde{A}_0)$ versus δ (i.e., versus l). In a BA scale-free network (9.11) with $N = 3000$, simulation shows that it suffices to control only a few large-degree nodes to stabilize such a network, as shown in Figure 9.3 [6], where the solid curve corresponds to random pinning and the dashed curve to selective pinning. It can be seen that selective pinning is much more effective than random pinning for scale-free networks, consistent with the experience about the robustness and fragility of this kind of network.

Example 9.1 Consider a scale-free network of Chua's circuits, defined by (2.131a) and (2.131b) in Chapter 2, shown in Figure 9.4(a), with dynamical equations

$$C_1 \dot{v}_{C_1} = R^{-1}(v_{C_2} - v_{C_1}) - f(v_{C_1})$$
$$C_2 \dot{v}_{C_2} = R^{-1}(v_{C1} - v_{C2}) + i_L \quad ,$$
$$L\dot{i}_L = -v_{C_2} \tag{9.16}$$

where L is a conductor, i_L is the current through L, C_1 and C_2 are two capacitors, v_{C_1} and v_{C_2} are the voltages across C_1 and C_2, respectively, R is a resistor, and R_N is a nonlinear resistor described by $f(\cdot)$ in (9.16) with expression

$$f(v_{C_1}) = m_0 v_{C_1} + \frac{1}{2}(m_1 - m_0)(|v_{C_1} + 1| - |v_{C_1} - 1|),$$

in which the two constants $m_0 < 0$ and $m_1 > 0$, as shown in Figure 9.4(b).

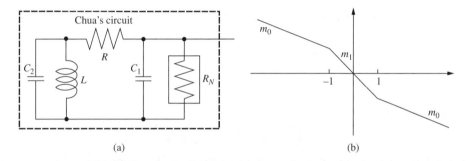

(a)   (b)

Figure 9.4 Chua's circuit and its nonlinear resistor: (a) Chua's circuit; (b) piecewise linear function *Source*: Reprinted from Wang, X.F. and Chen, G. (2002) Pinning control of scale-free dynamical networks. *Physica A*, **310**: 521–31. Copyright (2002) Elsevier

This circuit can produce complex chaotic behaviors, as shown in Figure 2.51 or Figure 9.5.

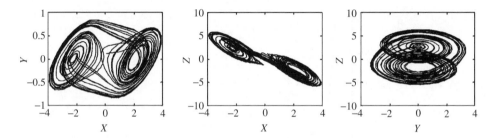

Figure 9.5 Chaotic attractor of Chua's circuit. *Source*: Reprinted from Chen, G. and Dong, X. (1998) *From Chaos to Order: Methodologies, Perspectives and Applications*. World Scientific Pub. Co., Singapore. Copyright (1998) World Scientific Pub. Co.

The circuit equation (9.16) can be rewritten in a dimensionless form via a simple linear nonsingular transformation, as follows:

$$
\begin{pmatrix} \dot{x}_{i1} \\ \dot{x}_{i2} \\ \dot{x}_{i3} \end{pmatrix} = \begin{pmatrix} \alpha\left(x_{i1} - x_{i2} + f\left(x_{i1}\right)\right) - c\sum_{j=1}^{N} a_{ij} x_{i1} \\ x_{i1} - x_{i2} + x_{i3} \\ -\beta x_{i2} + \gamma x_{i3} \end{pmatrix}, \quad i = 1, 2, \cdots, N
$$

where

$$
f(x_1) = \begin{cases} -bx_1 - a + b & x_1 > 1 \\ -ax_1 & |x_1| < 1 \\ -bx_1 + a - b & x_1 < -1 \end{cases}
$$

and, with parameters

$$
\alpha = 10, \quad \beta = 15, \quad \gamma = 0.0385, \quad a = -1.27, \quad b = -0.68,
$$

the circuit has three unstable equilibrium points:

$$
x^{\pm} = \begin{bmatrix} \pm 1.8586 & \pm 0.0048 & \mp 1.8539 \end{bmatrix}^{T}, \quad x^{0} = \begin{bmatrix} 0 & 0 & 0 \end{bmatrix}^{T}.
$$

The objective here is to control the circuit to its equilibrium x^+ by pinning:

$$
\begin{pmatrix} \dot{x}_{i1} \\ \dot{x}_{i2} \\ \dot{x}_{i3} \end{pmatrix} = \begin{pmatrix} \alpha\left(x_{i1} - x_{i2} + f\left(x_{i1}\right)\right) - c\sum_{j=1}^{N} a_{ij}x_{i1} + u_i \\ x_{i1} - x_{i2} + x_{i3} \\ -\beta x_{i2} + \gamma x_{i3} \end{pmatrix}, \quad i = 1, 2, \cdots, N,
$$

where the controllers are

$$
u_i = \begin{cases} cd\left(x_1^+ - x_{i1}\right) & i = i_1, \, \ldots \,, i_l \\ 0 & otherwise \end{cases}.
$$

It follows from condition (9.15) that $\rho = -4.71$. Under the two pinning control schemes, the results are compared in Figure 9.6, where the dash curve corresponds to random pinning while the solid curve to selective pinning.

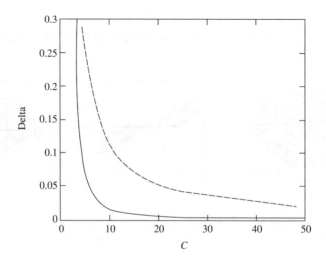

Figure 9.6 Comparison of two pinning schemes on a network of Chua's circuit [6]. *Source*: Reprinted from Wang, X.F. and Chen, G. (2002) Pinning control of scale-free dynamical networks. *Physica A*, 310: 521–31. Copyright (2002) Elsevier

9.4 Pinning Control of General Complex Networks

9.4.1 *Stability Analysis of General Networks under Pinning Control*

Consider a general network

$$
\dot{x}_i = f(x_i) - \sum_{\substack{j=1 \\ j\neq i}}^{N} c_{ij}a_{ij}\Gamma(x_j - x_i), \quad i = 1, 2, \cdots, N, \tag{9.17}
$$

where all notations are defined as above, and $c_{ij} > 0$ is the coupling strength of the connection between node i and node j, with $i, j = 1, 2, \ldots, N$.

In order to pin this network to its equilibrium $\bar{x}$, consider the following pinning controlled model:

$$
\begin{cases} \dot{x}_k = f\left(x_k\right) - \sum c_{kj}a_{kj}\Gamma(x_j - x_k) - c_{kk}d_k\Gamma(x_k - \bar{x}), & k = 1, 2, \ldots, l \\ \dot{x}_k = f(x_k) - \sum c_{kj}a_{kj}\Gamma(x_j - x_k), & k = l+1, l+2, \ldots, N \end{cases}, \tag{9.18}
$$

where the control gains $d_k > 0$, assuming the diffusive condition

$$c_{kk}a_{kk} + \sum_{\substack{j=1 \\ j \neq k}}^{N} c_{kj}a_{kj} = 0, \qquad k = 1, 2, \dots, l; \qquad j = 1, 2, \dots, N.$$

Define

$$D = diag\{d_1, \dots, d_l, 0, \dots, 0\} \in R^{N \times N}$$

$$D' = diag\{c_{11}d_1, \dots, c_{ll}d_l, 0, \dots, 0\} \in R^{N \times N}$$

Moreover, using the Kronecker notation, one can write

$$\dot{x} = f(x) - [(G+D) \otimes \Gamma]x + (D' \otimes \Gamma)\overline{X} = I_N \otimes f(x_i) - [(G+D) \otimes \Gamma]x + (D' \otimes \Gamma)\overline{X}, \qquad (9.19)$$

where $G = [g_{ij}] \in R^{N \times N}$ is a symmetric and semi-positive definite matrix, with $g_{ij} = -c_{ij}a_{ij}$, $i, j = 1, 2, \dots, N$, and $G + D$ is positive definite, with the smallest eigenvalue $\lambda_{\min}(G+D) > 0$.

Theorem 9.1 [10] *Suppose that $f(x)$ is Lipschitz continuous with Lipschitz constant $L_c^f > 0$, and matrix Γ is symmetric and positive definite. If*

$$\lambda_{\min}(G+D) > \alpha \equiv \frac{L_c^f}{\lambda_{\min}(\Gamma)}, \qquad (9.20)$$

where $\lambda_{\min}(\Gamma)$ and $\lambda_{\min}(G+D)$ are the smallest eigenvalues of matrices Γ and $G+D$, respectively, then the equilibrium $\bar{x}$ of the pinning controlled network (9.18) is globally and asymptotically stable.

Condition (9.20) reveals a sufficient condition that the coupling strength matrix $C_{couple} = [c_{ij}]^{N \times N}$ needs to satisfy in order to guarantee the equilibrium of network (9.18) to be globally and asymptotically stable. In the special case where $c_{ij} = c$ and $d_i = cd$, condition (9.20) reduces to

$$c > \frac{L_c^f}{\lambda_{\min}(-\tilde{A} + diag(d, \dots, d, 0, \dots, 0)) \cdot \lambda_{\min}(\Gamma)} \qquad (9.21)$$

and, if $\Gamma = [\tau_{ij}] \in R^{n \times n}$ is a 0-1matrix, then the above condition furthermore reduces to

$$c > \frac{L_c^f}{\lambda_{\min}(-\tilde{A} + diag(d, \dots, d, 0, \dots, 0))}. \qquad (9.22)$$

For a pinning controlled chaotic network (9.18), the Lyapunov exponent of each isolated node $\dot{x}_i = f(x_i)$ can characterize the local stability of the network, as follows.

Theorem 9.2 [10] *Consider the pinning control network (9.18) of chaotic nodes described by $\dot{x}_i = f(x_i), i = 1, 2, \cdots, N$, with the maximum Lyapunov exponent $h_{\max} > 0$. If $c_{ij} = c$, $d_i = cd$, $\Gamma = I_m$, and*

$$c > \frac{h_{\max}}{\lambda_{\min}(-\tilde{A} + diag(d, \dots, d, 0, \dots, 0))}, \qquad (9.23)$$

then the network equilibrium is locally asymptotically stable.

It can be seen that in many cases the constant ρ in conditions (9.13) and (9.15) can be taken to be the Lipschitz constant $L_c^f > 0$ or the maximum Lyapunov exponent $h_{\max} > 0$, but in general the condition (9.23) has to be satisfied by choosing some appropriate coupling strengths $C_{couple} = [c_{ij}]^{N \times N}$.

9.4.2   Pinning and Virtual Control of General Networks

Consider the simple case where $c_{ij} = c$ and $d_i = cd$ in the network (9.18), and rewrite it as

$$
\begin{aligned}
\dot{x}_i &= f(x_i) - c\sum_{j=1}^{N} a_{ij}\Gamma x_j - cd\Gamma(x_i - \bar{x}), \qquad i = 1, 2, \ldots, l \\
\dot{x}_i &= f(x_i) - c\sum_{j=1}^{N} a_{ij}\Gamma x_j, \qquad i = l+1, l+2, \ldots, N
\end{aligned}
\tag{9.24}
$$

According to the above analysis, if

$$
\begin{cases}
\Gamma = I_m \\
c > \dfrac{c}{\lambda_{\min}\left(-\tilde{A} + diag(d, \ldots, d, 0, \ldots 0)\right)}
\end{cases}
\tag{9.25}
$$

then the equilibrium of network (9.24) is globally asymptotically stable when $C = L_c^f$ and is locally asymptotically stable when $C = h_{\max}$.

Recall also from the last subsection that as the control gain $d \to +\infty$, the network can be stabilized to its equilibrium by choosing appropriate nodes to pin. Notice that

$$
a_{ii} = -\sum_{\substack{j=1 \\ j \neq i}}^{N} a_{ij} = -\left(\sum_{\substack{j=l+1 \\ j \neq i}}^{N} a_{ij} + \sum_{j=1}^{l} a_{ij} \right), \qquad i = l+1, l+2, \ldots, N;
$$

therefore, as $d \to +\infty$, network (9.24) becomes [10]

$$
\begin{cases}
x_i = \bar{x}, \qquad i = 1, 2, \ldots, l \\
\dot{x}_i = f(x_i) - c\sum_{j=l+1}^{N} \tilde{b}_{ij}\Gamma x_j + \tilde{u}_i, \qquad i = l+1, l+2, \ldots, N
\end{cases}
\tag{9.26}
$$

where $\tilde{B} = [\tilde{b}_{ij}] \in R^{(N-l)\times(N-l)}$ with

$$
\tilde{b}_{ij} = a_{ij}, \qquad j \neq i, j = l+1, \ldots, N, i = l+1, l+2, \ldots, N
$$

$$
\tilde{b}_{ii} = -\sum_{\substack{j=l+1 \\ j \neq i}}^{N} a_{ij}
$$

Note that $\tilde{u}_i$ here are not real controllers being added to the nodes, therefore they are referred to as *virtual control*, which are give by

$$
\tilde{u}_i = -c\tilde{d}_i(x_i - \bar{x}), \qquad i = l+1, l+2, \ldots, N,
\tag{9.27}
$$

where $\tilde{d}_i = \sum_{j=1}^{l} a_{ij}$. It can be verified that $\tilde{A} = \tilde{B} + diag(\tilde{d}_{l+1}, \tilde{d}_{l+2}, \cdots, \tilde{d}_N)$.

Theorem 9.3 [10]   *If $\tilde{A}$ is irreducible, $\Gamma = I_m$, and*

$$
c > \frac{c}{\lambda_{\min}(-\tilde{A})},
\tag{9.28}
$$

then the equilibrium of the virtually controlled network (9.26) is globally stable when $C = L_c^f$ and is locally asymptotically stable when $C = h_{\max}$.

If $\widetilde{A}$ is reducible, then $\widetilde{A}$ can be decomposed into a sequence of irreducible sub-matrices, $\widetilde{A}_1, \cdots \widetilde{A}_m$, so condition (9.28) becomes

$$c > \frac{C}{\max\{\lambda_{\min}(-\widetilde{A}_j)|j = 1, 2, \cdots, m\}}. \tag{9.29}$$

In this case,

$$0 = \lambda_{\min}(-\widetilde{A}) < \lambda_{\min}(-\widetilde{A} + diag\{d, \cdots, d, 0, \cdots, 0\})$$

$$< \lim_{d \to +\infty} \lambda_{\min}(-\widetilde{A} + diag\{d, \cdots, d, 0, \cdots, 0\})$$

$$\le \max\{\lambda_{\min}(-\widetilde{A}_j)|j = 1, 2, \cdots, m\}. \tag{9.30}$$

It should be pointed out that condition (9.30) actually is a sufficient condition for network (9.26) to synchronize. Therefore, during the process of virtual control, those uncontrolled nodes in the network are being "controlled" through synchronization to those controlled nodes. This reflects the close relationship between control and synchronization from another point of view.

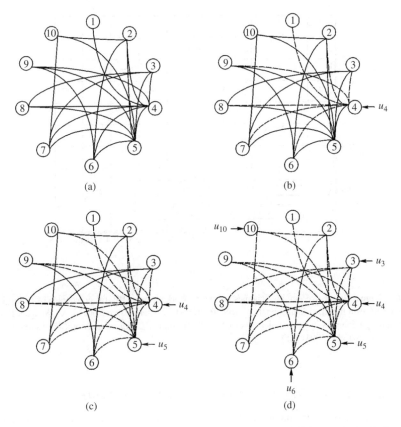

Figure 9.7 Illustration of virtual control by selective pinning scheme [10]: (a) initial network; (b) pinning one node; (c) pinning two nodes; (d) pinning five nodes. *Source*: Reprinted with permission from Li, X., Wang, X.F. and Chen, G. (2004) Pinning a complex dynamical network to its equilibrium. *IEEE Transactions on Circuits and Systems Part I*, 51: 2074–87. Copyright (2004) IEEE

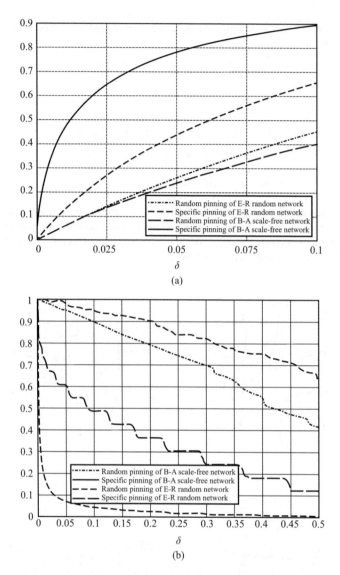

Figure 9.8 Comparison of two pinning schemes on two network models [10]: (a) percentage of controlled nodes; (b) percentage of resulting maximum subnets. *Source*: Reprinted with permission from Li, X., Wang, X.F. and Chen, G. (2004) Pinning a complex dynamical network to its equilibrium. *IEEE Transactions on Circuits and Systems Part I*, 51: 2074–87. Copyright (2004) IEEE

9.4.3 Pinning and Virtual Control of Scale-Free Networks

As discussed above, selective pinning is more effective than random pinning for scale-free networks, and if the number of pinned nodes is relatively small comparing to the network size, all the uncontrolled nodes are being virtually controlled to the network equilibrium via synchronizing to the controlled nodes.

To better describe the virtual control principle under selective pinning control scheme, consider a small network of 10 nodes, as shown in Figure 9.7 [10]. First, 4 nodes are pinned to the network equilibrium $\bar{x}$. Then, through coupling (dash curves) they indirectly affect those uncontrolled nodes. In this case, the

network is divided into two parts: node 1 and the rest nodes on the right are separated (Figure 9.7(b)). As
the selective pinning scheme controls more nodes, the network is further divided into more and smaller
subnets. Finally, the entire controlled network as shown in Figure 9.5(d), in which there are 5 nodes being
pinned and the other 5 are being virtually controlled.

The virtual control performances of different pinning schemes are generally not the same, which
depend on the percentage of virtually controlled nodes in the network and the maximum subnets divided
by pinning control.

Figure 9.8 (a) [10] shows the percentages of controlled nodes on a BA scale-free network and an ER
random-graph network under selective and random pinning schemes, respectively. Both network models
have 3000 nodes and 9000 edges. It can be seen from the simulation results depicted in this figure that
for the BA model, selectively pinning 5% big nodes can virtually control 80% of other nodes over the
network, while randomly pinning 5% nodes can only virtually affect less than 30% other nodes; while
for the ER model, the two pinning schemes do not have significant differences, as expected.

Figure 9.8 (b) [10] compares the percentage of the resulting maximum sub-nets on both BA and ER
models under the two pinning control schemes. For the BA model, selectively pinning 5% big nodes
rapidly reduces this percentage to be below 10%. Since, according to conditions (9.28) and (9.29), the
coupling strengths required by this scheme are much smaller than that required by the random pinning scheme, it once again shows the advantage of utilizing the heterogeneity of scale-free networks for
control. Similarly, for the ER model, the two pinning schemes have about the same performance.

The above analysis is now illustrated and visualized by an example of a scale-free chaotic network.

Example 9.2 Consider the chaotic Chen system, defined by (2.125) in Chapter 2, or

$$\begin{pmatrix} \dot{x}_1 \\ \dot{x}_2 \\ \dot{x}_3 \end{pmatrix} = \begin{pmatrix} p_1 \left(x_2 - x_1 \right) \\ (p_3 - p_2)x_1 - x_1 x_3 + p_3 x_2 \\ x_1 x_2 - p_2 x_3 \end{pmatrix}.$$

When the constant parameters $p_1 = 35, p_2 = 3, p_3 = 28$, this system has some very complex dynamical
behaviors: for example, it produces a chaotic attractor, as shown in Figure 2.45 or Figure 9.9. In this case,
the system has three unstable equilibria, among which one is $x^+ = \begin{bmatrix} 7.9373 & 7.9373 & 21 \end{bmatrix}^T$.

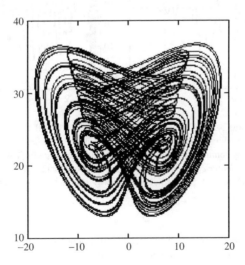

Figure 9.9 Chen's chaotic attractor (projection on x_1-x_3 plane). *Source*: Reprinted from Chen, G. and Dong, X.
(1998) *From Chaos to Order: Methodologies, Perspectives and Applications*. World Scientific Pub. Co., Singapore.
Copyright (1998) World Scientific Pub. Co.

Now, consider the following scale-free network of N Chen systems:

$$
\begin{pmatrix} \dot{x}_{i1} \\ \dot{x}_{i2} \\ \dot{x}_{i3} \end{pmatrix} = \begin{pmatrix} p_1\left(x_{i2} - x_{i1}\right) - c\sum_{j=1}^{N} a_{ij}x_{j1} + u_{i1} \\ (p_3 - p_2)x_{i1} - x_{i1}x_{i3} + p_3 x_{i2} + c\sum_{j=1}^{N} a_{ij}x_{j2} + u_{i2} \\ x_{i1}x_{i2} - p_2 x_{i3} + c\sum_{j=1}^{N} a_{ij}x_{j3} + u_{i3} \end{pmatrix}, \qquad i = 1, 2, \cdots, N.
$$

The objective is to stabilize it to the unstable equilibrium $\bar{x}$, shown above, by virtually controlling the network through the pinning controllers

$$
u_{ij} = \begin{cases} -cd\left(x_{ij} - x_j^+\right) & i = i_1, \ \ldots, i_l, j = 1, 2, 3 \\ \\ 0 & otherwise \end{cases}.
$$

It follows from condition (9.28) that $c = 2.01745$, and in this case $d = 1000$ (high gain controllers).

Simulations on a BA network of $N = 50$ nodes, each node is a Chen system, show that pining only the biggest node needs a much larger coupling strength than pinning two biggest nodes, and the virtual control process is much slower, as shown in Figure 9.10, where solid curves correspond to the biggest node and the dash curves to the smallest node.

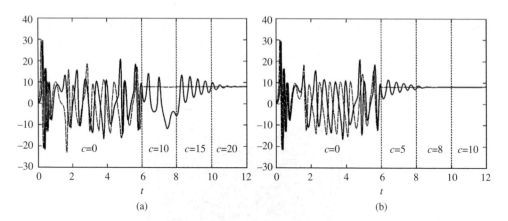

Figure 9.10 Selective pinning control of a BA network of chaotic Chen systems [10]: (a) pinning the biggest node; (b) pinning two biggest nodes. *Source of (b)*: Reprinted with permission from Li, X., Wang, X.F. and Chen, G. (2004) Pinning a complex dynamical network to its equilibrium. *IEEE Transactions on Circuits and Systems Part I*, 51: 2074–87. Copyright (2004) IEEE

Simulations also show that a selective pinning control scheme requires a much smaller coupling strength and a small number of nodes to pin, as compared to random pinning control. Figure 9.11 shows the performance by selectively controlling 2 biggest nodes (solid curves) and randomly pinning 2 or 5 nodes, under different coupling strengths (other curves).

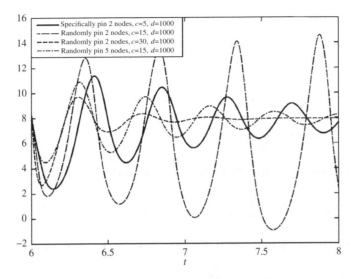

Figure 9.11 Orbits of the smallest node under selective and random pinning schemes [10]. *Source*: Reprinted with permission from Li, X., Wang, X.F. and Chen, G. (2004) Pinning a complex dynamical network to its equilibrium. *IEEE Transactions on Circuits and Systems Part I*, 51: 2074–87. Copyright (2004) IEEE

9.5   Time-Delay Pinning Control of Complex Networks

Consider once again a linearly and diffusively coupled network

$$\dot{x}_i = f(x_i) - c\sum_{j=1}^{N} a_{ij}\Gamma x_j, \qquad i = 1, 2, \cdots, N, \tag{9.31}$$

where all notations are defined as before. The objective is to stabilize the network onto the equilibrium $\bar{x} \in R^n$ of the network, in the sense that

$$x_1(t) \to x_2(t) \to \cdots \to x_N(t) \to \bar{x}, \; as \; t \to \infty,$$

where for simplicity it is assumed that $f(0) = 0$, so $\bar{x} = 0$. Without loss of generality, suppose that nodes $1, 2, \cdots, l$, are selected for pinning control. Thus, the controlled network can be written as

$$\begin{cases} \dot{x}_i = f\left(x_i\right) - c\sum_{j=1}^{N} a_{ij}\Gamma x_j + u_i, & i = 1, 2, \cdots, l \\ \dot{x}_i = f(x_i) - c\sum_{j=1}^{N} a_{ij}\Gamma x_j, & i = l+1, l+2, \cdots, N \end{cases}, \tag{9.32}$$

in which u_i is the controller which pins node i, $i = 1, 2, \ldots, l$.

By using the identity matrix $I \in R^{l\times l}$ and zero matrix $\Omega \in R^{(N-l)\times(N-l)}$, which has all elements $\Omega_{i,j} = 0$, and defining matrix $B = [b_{ij}] = diag\{I, \Omega\} \in R^{N\times N}$, network (9.32) can be rewritten as

$$\dot{x}_i = f(x_i) - c\sum_{j=1}^{N} a_{ij}\Gamma x_j + b_{ii}u_i, \qquad i = 1, 2, \cdots, N, \tag{9.33}$$

where b_{ii} are the diagonal elements of matrix B, satisfying $b_{ii} = 1$ if node i is pinned, and $b_{ii} = 0$ otherwise.

Now, the following time-delay feedback controller is applied for pinning:

$$u_i = -k_i \Gamma(x_i(t) - x_i(t - \tau)), \tag{9.34}$$

where k_i is a constant control gain and τ is the constant delay time. Then, network (9.33) becomes

$$\dot{x}_i = f(x_i) - c \sum_{j=1}^{N} a_{ij} \Gamma x_j - b_{ii} k_i \Gamma(x_i(t) - x_i(t - \tau)), \qquad i = 1, 2, \cdots, N. \tag{9.35}$$

Let $e_i(t) = x_i(t) - \bar{x}$ be the control errors, $i = 1, 2, \ldots, N$. Then, one has

$$\dot{e}_i = f(\bar{x} + e_i(t)) - f(\bar{x}) - c \sum_{j=1}^{N} a_{ij} \Gamma e_j - b_{ii} k_i \Gamma(e_i(t) - e_i(t - \tau)), \qquad i = 1, 2, \cdots, N. \tag{9.36}$$

Assume that f is continuously differentiable. Then, linearizing the above equation at its zero equilibrium gives

$$\dot{e}_i = (J(t) + b_{ii} k_i \Gamma) e_i(t) - c \sum_{j=1}^{N} a_{ij} \Gamma e_j - b_{ii} k_i \Gamma e_i(t - \tau), \qquad i = 1, 2, \cdots, N. \tag{9.37}$$

Theorem 9.4 [17] *The equilibrium point of the controlled network (9.35) is locally asymptotically stable if there are symmetrical and positive-definite matrices $W, X, Z \in R^{n \times n}$ such that the following Linear Matrix Inequality (LMI) holds:*

$$M = \begin{bmatrix} \widehat{A} & ca_{i1}\Gamma W & \cdots & ca_{iN}\Gamma W & 0 & \cdots & -b_{ii}\Gamma X & \cdots & 0 \\ ca_{i1} W\Gamma & Z & & & & & & & \\ \vdots & & \ddots & & & & & & \\ ca_{iN} W\Gamma & & & Z & & & & & \\ 0 & & & & -Z & & & & \\ \vdots & & & & & \ddots & & & \\ -b_{ii}X\Gamma & & & & & & & & \\ \vdots & & & & & & & & \\ 0 & & & & & & & & -Z \end{bmatrix} < 0,$$

where $\widehat{A} = WJ^T + JW + b_{ii}X\Gamma + b_{ii}\Gamma X$.

Example 9.3 Consider a BA scale-free network consisting of N cellular neural nodes, with $\Gamma = diag(1, 1, 1, 1)$ and each isolated node described by

$$\begin{cases} \dot{x}_1 = -x_3 - x_4 \\ \dot{x}_2 = 2x_2 + x_3 \\ \dot{x}_3 = 14x_1 - 14x_2 \\ \dot{x}_4 = 100x_1 - 100x_4 + 100\left(|x_4 + 1| - |x_4 - 1|\right) \end{cases}$$

The entire network is described by

$$
\dot{x}_i = \begin{pmatrix} \dot{x}_{i1} \\ \dot{x}_{i2} \\ \dot{x}_{i3} \\ \dot{x}_{i4} \end{pmatrix} = \begin{pmatrix} -x_{i3} - x_{i4} + c\sum_{j=1}^{N} a_{ij}x_{j1} \\[2ex] 2x_{i2} + x_{i3} + c\sum_{j=1}^{N} a_{ij}x_{j2} \\[2ex] 14x_{i1} - 14x_{i2} + c\sum_{j=1}^{N} a_{ij}x_{j3} \\[2ex] 100x_{i1} - 100x_{i4} \\ + 100\left(|x_{i4}+1| - |x_{i4}-1|\right) \\[1ex] + c\sum_{j=1}^{N} a_{ij}x_{j4} \end{pmatrix}, \qquad i = 1, 2, \cdots N.
$$

To stabilize this network with $N = 60$ to its zero equibrium, choose the coupling strength $c = 8.2$ and the number of controlled nodes $l = 15$. In the selective pinning control scheme, set $b_{ii} = 1$ for the first 15 nodes of largest degrees. The control gains are found to be $k_i = 29.76$ according to the condition given in Theorem 9.4. For comparison, the control gains $k_i = 513.37$ are needed by the random pinning scheme, which pins also $l = 15$ randomly selected nodes.

Figure 9.12 shows plots of the first state components of the largest node in the network, using the selective pinning control scheme versus the random pinning control scheme. It can be seen that the random pinning control scheme not only uses higher gains, about 17 times larger than the selective pinning scheme, but also takes doubly longer time, to achieve the same control performance.

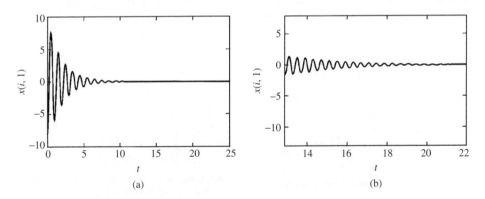

Figure 9.12 Comparison of two pinning control schemes [17]: (a) selective pinning; (b) random pinning. *Source:* Courtesy of Z. P. Fan

9.6   Consensus and Flocking Control

Cooperative and collective behaviors in a group of multiple autonomous agents, who are communicating thereby forming a wired or wireless network, such as synchronization, consensus (rendezvous), swarming and particularly flocking, have received considerable attention in recent years due to their broad applications to biological systems, sensor networks, unmanned air vehicle formations, robotic cooperation teams, mobile communication systems, and so on.

The goal of group *consensus* is similar to network synchronization, but usually is put in a slightly more general setting in the sense that it requires all agents converge together within a small neighborhood of radius $\varepsilon > 0$:

$$\lim_{t\to\infty} ||x_i - x_j|| \le \varepsilon, \quad i,j = 1, 2, \dots, N. \tag{9.38}$$

One reason for doing this is not to require all states to crash together in the end of the group motion. Clearly, when $\varepsilon = 0$, this is exactly the objective of network synchronization studied in Chapter 8. Flocking control, on the other hand, typically has some other specific requirements such as keeping a certain minimum distance between any pair of agents (called *collision avoidance*), forming a certain position-orientation pattern during the motion (called *formation control*), and so on.

In a flock of autonomous agents, to coordinate with other agents, everyone needs to share information with its neighboring peers and they together need to agree on a common objective of interest. When a flock is being modeled, the asymptotic behavior of the agent group is usually the main concern, for which typical coordination such as synchronization and consensus is of particular importance [18, 19]. More precisely, with a model established, the main tasks in studying collective behaviors of a flock of autonomous agents are to analyze how coordinated group behaviors emerge as a result of distributed local interactions among the multiple agents and how to guide them with the smallest possible amount of control and management efforts towards a pre-desired goal. In other words, the aims are to understand and study flocks of interconnected multiple dynamical agents with respect to such fundamental issues as mathematical modeling, dynamics analysis, behavioral prediction, and distributed control.

To describe flocking motion and evolvement, three heuristic rules to animate flocking behaviors were proposed by Reynolds using the Boids model in 1987 [20], though similar ideas had already emerged even earlier [21]: (i) alignment – to head to the same direction; (ii) separation – to avoid collision; (iii) cohesion – to move together, as illustrated by Figure 9.13.

Based on the three basic rules of the Boids model, Vicsek *et al.* [22] developed a simple programmable model for a system of self-driven particles, considered here as agents. This model describes a flock of discrete-time multiple autonomous agents moving in the plane with the same speed but different headings (directions). Specifically, consider a flock of N dynamical agents moving on the plane and let $x_i(t)$ and $\theta_i(t)$ be respectively the state and heading of agent i at discrete time $t \ge 0$, $i = 1, 2, \dots, N$. Then, by the

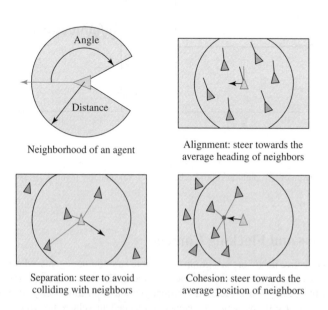

Neighborhood of an agent

Alignment: steer towards the average heading of neighbors

Separation: steer to avoid colliding with neighbors

Cohesion: steer towards the average position of neighbors

Figure 9.13   Three basic rules of the Boids model [Internet]

basic law of motion, one can write

$$x_i(t + 1) = x_i(t) + v(\cos \theta_i(t + 1), \sin \theta_i(t + 1))^T, \quad i = 1, 2, \dots, N, \quad (9.39)$$

where v is a constant and the headings satisfy

$$\theta_i(t + 1) = \arctan \left\{ \sum_{j \in \Omega_i(t)} \frac{\cos \theta_j(t)}{\sum_{j \in \Omega_i(t)} \cos \theta_j(t)} \tan \theta_i(t) \right\}, \quad (9.40)$$

in which $\Omega_i(t)$ is the neighborhood of agent i at time t defined by

$$\Omega_i(t) = \{j : \|x_i(t) - x_j(t)\| < r\}, \quad 0 < r < \infty. \quad (9.41)$$

Through numerical simulations, it was shown that by using a distributed averaging rule of neighboring agents' headings, without any centralized coordination or control, the whole flock will eventually converge on the same direction as $t \to \infty$.

More specifically [22], in simulating this model for example with $N = 300$, $v = 0.03$, $r = 1$, and various population densities $\rho = N/L^2$ ($L > 0$ is a planar lattice size), starting from a random initial situation of all agents (with positions and headings randomly placed), as shown in Figure 9.14(a), it was found that three outcomes are possible (see Figure 9.14): (b) with low density and low noise, the agents tend to

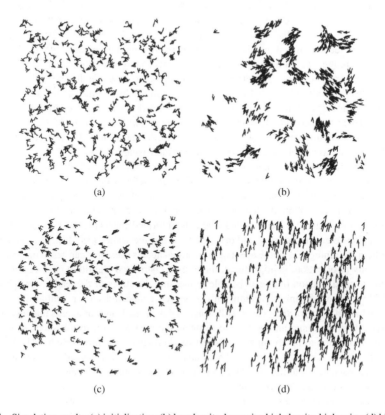

(a)   (b)

(c)   (d)

Figure 9.14   Simulation results: (a) initialization; (b) low density, low noise;high density, high noise; (d) high density, low noise [22]. *Source*: Reprinted with permission from Vicsek, T., Cziok, A., Jacob, E.B. *et al.* (1995) Novel type of phase transition in a system of self-driven particles. *Physical Review Letters*, **75**(6): 1226–9. Copyright (1995) American Physical Society

form groups moving coherently in random directions, (c) with high density and high noise, the agents move randomly with some correlation, and (d) with high density and low noise, the motion of all agents becomes orderly.

To simplify the analysis, the Vicsek model may be linearized:

$$
\begin{cases}
x_i(t+1) = x_i(t) + v(\cos\theta_i(t+1), \sin\theta_i(t+1))^T \\
\\
\theta_i(t+1) = \dfrac{1}{|\Omega_i(t)|} \displaystyle\sum_{j\in\Omega_i(t)} \theta_j(t)
\end{cases}
\tag{9.42}
$$

where $|\Omega_i(t)|$ is the number of agents within the neighborhood of agent i at time $t \geq 0$. In [23], this linearized discrete-time Vicsek model and its continuous-time version were both theoretically analyzed, showing that consensus can be reached in a network with a dynamically changing topology if the time-varying network structures are jointly connected within a moving time window.

The results of [22, 23] were then extended to the case of directed networks, proving that consensus can be reached if the union of the time-varying network structures contains a spanning tree frequently enough as the flock evolves in time [24–26]. In particular, in [27], a relation between the speed of convergence and the algebraic connectivity (also called the spectral gap or the Fiedler eigenvalue [28]) was established, for balanced directed networks, revealing that the algebraic connectivity of a network is key to ensuring consensus of a flock of dynamical agents.

In the literature concerned with the consensus problem, agents are usually considered to be governed by first-order dynamics due to the basic law of motion. Meanwhile, there is a growing interest in consensus algorithms where all agents are governed by second-order dynamics based on a more accurate law of motion. It was shown in [29] that, in sharp contrast to the first-order consensus setting, consensus may fail for agents with second-order dynamics even if the network topology contains a directed spanning tree.

In the case where the whole group of autonomous agents cannot reach collective behaviors by themselves, control becomes necessary. Regarding control, of course, it is literally impossible to equip with one controller to each node, especially for large-scale networks of high-dimensional node systems. Thus, to be energy- and/or cost-effective, it is very desirable to apply local-feedback controllers only to a small fraction of nodes in the network. This strategy is known as *pinning control* [6, 30, 31], as discussed above. The pinning control methodology in complex networks and systems has proved to be an efficient strategy; therefore it has recently received continuously increasing interest [32–35].

A conventional flocking algorithm consists of two terms: the gradient of the collective potential between the agent of concern and all its neighbors, and their velocity consensus errors [36–40]. For the leader–follower setting, where one agent is the *leader* who knows what to do or where to go and all the others (*followers*) simply follow the leader, an additional term about the navigation feedback from the leader to the informed agents is incorporated where the informed agents are those followers who receive some information (e.g., the position and/or velocity) from the leader [38, 39]. In a leader–follower flocking system, assuming that all the agents are informed agents (i.e., they can sense the leader about its position-velocity information) is impractical, therefore a distributed algorithm is more desirable which requires only a small fraction of agents be able to measure the states of the leader through the motion process. A distributed flocking algorithm with preserved connectivity on potential energy functions was developed in [40]. In practical cases, still, some states of the leader or agents may not be available to the others. Thus, designing an observer to estimate the missing information such as velocity states is an effective approach to resolving the information shortages for control design [41–43]. Recently, based on adaptive technique, several distributed adaptive laws were designed for estimating network parameters, for instance, coupling strengths [44], connection weights [45], and control gains [46], for flocking control in uncertain environments.

In many real-world networks such as biological and communication networks, time delays are inevitable due to slow processing of information transmission among agents. It has been observed, both numerically and experimentally, that flocking and consensus algorithms without accounting for time delays may lead to unexpected instability for some complex networks [47]. Moreover, information transmission may not be continuous or accurate due to technological limitations such as short sensing ranges and external disturbances or internal malfunctioning. Thus, flocking and consensus under intermittent measurements and random environments has also attracted increasing attention recently [48].

On the other hand, a new network characterization index was introduced in [49], called *generalized connectivity* and used to derive some sufficient conditions for reaching first-order local or global consensus in directed networks of mobile agents with nonlinear dynamics. In addition, some necessary and sufficient conditions for ensuring second-order consensus in a linear multi-agent system with or without time delays were established in [49]. It was found that both the real and imaginary parts of the eigenvalues of the Laplacian matrix of the network play key roles in reaching second-order consensus [50, 54]. Based on these results, consensus in multi-agent systems with second-order nonlinear dynamics and directed topologies were further investigated, and the generalized connectivity concept was applied to establishing some simple sufficient conditions in [51]. More recently, the consensus problem of multi-agent systems with time-invariant topologies was considered and some distributed observer protocols were developed in [52].

A framework under a Lyapunov stability concept was introduced to design some effective pinning schemes in [53, 54], where each node is associated with a passivity degree. An extension of this result was also carried out, via a renormalization approach to a cascaded model in networks with layer structures. In addition, network synchronization subject to a linear feedback pinning scheme by using adaptive tuning of the coupling strengths was studied in [55]. Rather surprisingly, it was found that the nodes with low degrees should be pinned first, when the coupling strength is small, which is contrary to the common view that the nodes with high degrees should be pinned first. Furthermore, a lower-dimensional condition without involving the pinning controller parameters was derived in [55], which significantly reduces the computational complexity of the established criteria.

A rendezvous protocol for multi-agent systems with second-order dynamics was proposed in [56], which can preserve the network connectivity during the evolution. The approach employs a special bounded potential energy function. A distributed leader-follower flocking control scheme was designed in [57] for multi-agent systems using pinning navigation feedback with nonlinear dynamics, where nonlinear self-dynamics are added to determine the final asymptotic time-varying velocities of the mobile agents. To avoid an impractical common assumption that the informed agents can sense all the states of the leader, observer-based pinning navigation feedback was used to allow informed agents to use only partial information about the leader, while the velocity of the whole group can converge on that of the leader and the centroid of those position-informed agents can follow the trajectory of the leader asymptotically. Interestingly, it was found that the local minima of the potential function may not form a commonly-believed lattice as reported in [38].

A connectivity-preserving flocking algorithm was designed in [58] for multi-agent systems based only on information about the position states of the flocking agents. Moreover, a linear consensus protocol was designed in [59] for multi-agent systems with second-order dynamics, whereby information about both current and delayed positions was utilized. On this basis, a necessary and sufficient condition was derived for reaching second-order consensus, which can be achieved if and only if the time delay is less than a critical value depending on the control gains and the largest eigenvalue of the Laplacian matrix of the network. It was found, again surprisingly, that time delays can actually induce consensus without measuring and utilizing the agents' velocity information [59].

Furthermore, in [60], an adaptive leader–follower flocking algorithm was developed on both the weights of the velocity navigation feedback and the coupling strengths from the leader to the informed agents with nonlinear dynamics, by using some connectivity-preserving potential functions. Also, the commonly concerned robust flocking control problem for nonlinear agents with asymmetrically perturbed coupling weights was studied in [61]. It was found that flocking pattern formation can be achieved if the topology of the updated connection weights forms a spanning tree.

Based on control systems theory and algebraic graph theory, some distributed consensus filters were designed for flocking from the pinning control approach [62], where only a small fraction of sensors were used to measure partial states of the leader or target. As an example of applications, an adaptive filter was designed in [63] to estimate the unknown parameters and states in a delayed genetic regulatory network with uncertain stochastic disturbances using only partial information from the genetic regulatory network, namely, the concentrations of the proteins.

References

[1] Wiener, N. (1948) *Cybernetics or the Control and Communication in the Animal and the Machine.* MIT Press, Cambridge, MA.
[2] Ott, E., Grebogi, C. and Yorke, J.A. (1990) Controlling chaos. *Physical Review Letters,* **64**: 1196–9.
[3] Chen, G. and Dong, X. (1988) *From Chaos to Order: Methodologies, Perspectives and Applications.* World Scientific, Singapore.
[4] Hu, G. and Qu, Z.L. (1994) Controlling spatiotemporal chaos in coupled map lattice systems. *Physical Review Letters,* **72**(1): 68–71.
[5] Roy, R., Murphy, T.W., Maier Jr, T.D. *et al.* (1992) Dynamical control of a chaotic laser: Experimental stabilization of a globally coupled system. *Physical Review Letters,* **68**: 1259–62.
[6] Wang, X.F. and Chen, G. (2002) Pinning control of scale-free dynamical networks. *Physica A,* **310**: 521–31.
[7] Sorrentino, F., di Bernardo, M., Garofalo, F. and Chen, G. (2007) Controllability of complex networks via pinning, *Physical Reviews E,* **75**: 046103.
[8] Li, X. and Wang, X.F. (2003) Pinning control of scale-free Chen's networks. *Proceedings of 2nd Asia-Pacific Workshop on Chaos Control and Synchronization,* Shanghai, China.
[9] Li, X. and Wang, X.F. (2004) Feedback control of scale-free coupled Henon maps. *Proceedings of 8th International Conference on Control, Automation, Robotics and Vision* (ICARCV), Kunming, China, 574–8.
[10] Li, X., Wang, X.F. and Chen, G. (2004) Pinning a complex dynamical network to its equilibrium. *IEEE Transactions on Circuits and Systems Part I,* **51**: 2074–87.
[11] Fan, Z.P. and Chen, G. (2005) Pinning control of scale-free complex networks. *Proceedings of IEEE International Symposium on Circuits and Systems,* Kobe, Japan, May 23–26: 284–7.
[12] Hu, G., Xiao, J.H. and Gao, J.H. *et al.* (2000) Analytic study of spatiotemporal chaos control by applying local injections. *Physical Reviews E,* **62**(3): 3043–6.
[13] Hu, G., Yang, J.Z. and Liu, W.J. (1998) Instability and controllability of linearly coupled oscillators: Eigenvalue analysis. *Physical Reviews E,* **58**(4): 4440–7.
[14] Parekh, N., Parthasarathy, S. and Sinha, S. (1998) Global and local control of spatiotemporal chaos in coupled map lattices. *Physical Review Letters,* **81**(7): 1401–4.
[15] Chen, G. and Wang, X.F. (2006) *Anti-Control of Chaos: Theory and Applications* (in Chinese), Shanghai Jiao Tong University Press, Shanghai, China.
[16] Parekh, N. and Sinha, S. (2000) Controlling spatiotemporal dynamics in excitable systems. *SFI Working Paper,* No. 00-06-031.
[17] Fan, Z.P. (2006) *Complex Networks: From Topology to Dynamics.* PhD Thesis, Dept of Electronic Engineering, City University of Hong Kong, May.
[18] Ren, W. and Beard, R.W. (2008) *Distributed Consensus in Multi-vehicle Cooperative Control.* Springer-Verlag, London.
[19] Arenas, A., Diaz-Guilera, A., Kurths, J. *et al.* (2008) Synchronization in complex networks. *Physics Reports,* **468**(3): 93–153.
[20] Reynolds, C.W. (1987) Flocks, herds, and schools: A distributed behavior model. *Computer Graphics,* **21**: 25–34. See: http://www.red3d.com/cwr/boids/ (last accessed August 11, 2014).
[21] Aoki, I. (1982) A simulation study on the schooling mechanism in fish. *Bulletin of Japanese Society of Scientific Fisheries,* **48**(8): 1081–8.
[22] Vicsek, T., Cziok, A., Jacob, E.B. *et al.* (1995) Novel type of phase transition in a system of self-driven particles. *Physical Review Letters,* **75**(6): 1226–9.
[23] Jadbabaie, A., Lin, J. and Morse, A.S. (2003) Coordination of groups of mobile autonomous agents using nearest neighbor rules. *IEEE Transactions on Automatic Control,* **48**(6): 985–1001.
[24] Cao, M., Morse, A.S. and Anderson, B.D.O. (2008) Reaching a consensus in a dynamically changing environment: A graphical approach. *SIAM Journal on Control and Optimization,* **47**(2): 575–600.
[25] Ren, W. and Beard, R.W. (2005) Consensus seeking in multiagent systems under dynamically changing interaction topologies. *IEEE Transactions on Automatic Control,* **50**(5): 655–61.
[26] Moreau, L. (2005) Stability of multiagent systems with time-dependent communication links. *IEEE Transactions on Automatic Control,* **50**(2): 169–82.
[27] Olfati-Saber, R. and Murray, R.M. (2004) Consensus problems in networks of agents with switching topology and time-delays. *IEEE Transactions on Automatic Control,* **49**(9): 1520–33.
[28] Fiedler, M. (1973) Algebraic connectivity of graphs, *Czechoslovak Mathematical Journal,* **23**: 298–305.
[29] Ren, W. and Atkins, E. (2007) Distributed multi-vehicle coordinated control via local information exchange. *International Journal of Robust and Nonlinear Control,* **17**(10–11): 1002–33.

[30] Wang, X.F. and Chen, G. (2003) Complex networks: small-world, scale-free, and beyond. *IEEE Circuits and Systems Magazine*, **3**: 6–20.

[31] Wang, X.F., Li, X. and Chen, G. (2006) Complex Networks Theory and Its Applications *(in Chinese)*, Beijing: Tsinghua University Press.

[32] Lu, W., Li, X. and Rong, Z.H. (2010) Global stabilization of complex directed networks with the local pinning algorithm. *Automatica*, **46**: 116–21.

[33] Porfiri, M. and di Bernardo, M. (2008) Criteria for global pinning-controllability of complex networks. *Automatica*, **44**: 3100–6.

[34] Wu, C. (2008) On the relationship between pinning control effectiveness and graph topology in complex networks of dynamical systems. *Chaos*, **18**: 037103.

[35] Chen, T.P., Liu, X. and Lu, W.L. (2007) Pinning complex networks by a single controller. *IEEE Transactions on Circuits and Systems Part I*, **54**: 1317–26.

[36] Tanner, H.G., Jadbabaie, A. and Pappas, G.J. (2003) Stable flocking of mobile agents, part I: Fixed topology. *Proceedings of 42nd IEEE Conference on Decision Control*, 2010–15.

[37] Tanner, H.G., Jadbabaie, A. and Pappas, G.J. (2003) Stable flocking of mobile agents, part II: dynamic topology. *Proc. 42nd IEEE Conference on Decision Control*, 2003, 2016–21.

[38] Olfati-Saber, R. (2006) Flocking for multi-agent dynamic systems: Algorithms and theory. *IEEE Transactions on Automatic Control*, **51**: 401–20.

[39] Su, H.S., Wang, X.F. and Lin, Z.L. (2009) Flocking of multi-agents with a virtual leader. *IEEE Transactions on Automatic Control*, **54**(2): 293–307.

[40] Zavlanos, M.M., Jadbabaie, A. and Pappas, G.J. (2007) Flocking while preserving network connectivity. *Proceedings of 46th IEEE Conference on Decision Control*, 2919–24.

[41] Hong, Y.G., Chen, G. and Bushnell, L. (2008) Distributed observers design for leader-following control of multi-agent networks. *Automatica*, **44**: 846–50.

[42] Hong, Y.G., Hu, J.P. and Gao, L. (2006) Tracking control for multi-agent consensus with an active leader and variable topology. *Automatica*, **42**: 1177–82.

[43] Ren, W. (2008) On consensus algorithms for double-integrator dynamics. *IEEE Transactions on Automatic Control*, **58**(6): 1503–9.

[44] Zhou, C.S. and Kurths, J. (2006) Dynamical weights and enhanced synchronization in adaptive complex networks. *Physical Review Letters*, **96**: 164102.

[45] De Lellis, P., di Bernardo, M. and Garofalo, F. (2009) Novel decentralized adaptive strategies for the synchronization of complex networks. *Automatica*, **45**: 1312–18.

[46] Lu, W. (2009) Adaptive dynamical networks via neighborhood information: Synchronization and pinning control. *Chaos*, **17**: 023122.

[47] Tian, Y and Liu, C. (2008) Consensus of multi-agent systems with diverse input and communication delays. *IEEE Transactions on Automatic Control*, **53**: 2122–8.

[48] Li, T. and Zhang, J. (2009) Mean square average consensus under measurement noises and fixed topologies: Necessary and sufficient conditions. *Automatica*, **45**(8): 1929–36.

[49] Yu, W.W., Chen, G. and Cao, M. (2011) Consensus in directed networks of agents with nonlinear dynamics. *IEEE Transactions on Automatic Control*, **56**(6): 1436–41.

[50] Yu, W.W., Chen, G. and Cao, M. (2010) Some necessary and sufficient conditions for second-order consensus in multi-agent dynamical systems. *Automatica*, **46**(6): 1089–95.

[51] Yu, W.W., Chen, G., Cao, M. *et al.* (2010) Second-order consensus for multi-agent systems with directed topologies and nonlinear dynamics. *IEEE Transactions on Systems Management and Cybernetics, Part B*, **40**(3): 881–91.

[52] Li, Z.K., Duan, Z.S., Chen, G. and Huang, L. (2010) Consensus of multiagent systems and synchronization of complex networks: A unified viewpoint. *IEEE Transactions on Circuits and Systems Part I*, **57**(1): 213–24.

[53] Xiang, J. and Chen, G. (2007) On the V-stability of complex dynamical networks. *Automatica*, **43**: 1049–57.

[54] Xiang, J. and Chen, G. (2009) Analysis of pinning-controlled networks: a renormalization approach. *IEEE Transactions on Automatic Control*, **54**(8): 1869–75.

[55] Yu, W.W., Chen, G. and Lu, J.H. (2009) On pinning synchronization of complex dynamical networks. *Automatica*, **45**(2): 429–35.

[56] Su, H.S., Wang, X.F. and Chen, G. (2010) Rendezvous of multiple mobile agents with preserved network connectivity. *Systems & Control Letters*, **59**(5): 313–22.

[57] Yu, W.W., Chen, G. and Cao, M. (2010) Distributed leader-follower flocking control for multi-agent dynamical systems with time-varying velocities. *Systems & Control Letters*, **59**(9): 543–52.

[58] Su, H.S., Wang, X.F. and Chen, G. (2009) A connectivity-preserving flocking algorithm for multi-agent systems based only on position measurements. *International Journal of Control*, **82**(7): 1334–43.

[59] Yu, W.W., Chen, G. and Ren, W. (2010) Delay-induced quasi-consensus in multi-agent dynamical systems. *Proceedings of 29th Chinese Control Conference*, Beijing, China, 4566–71.

[60] Su, H.S., Chen, G., Wang, X.F. *et al.* (2010) Adaptive flocking with a virtual leader of multiple agents governed by nonlinear dynamics. *Proceedings of 29th Chinese Control Conference*, Beijing, 5827–32.

[61] Yu, W.W. and Chen, G. (2010) Robust adaptive flocking control of nonlinear multi-agent systems. *Proceedings of 2010 IEEE Multi-Conference on Systems Control*, Yokohama Japan.

[62] Yu, W.W., Chen, G., Wang, Z. *et al.* (2009) Distributed consensus filtering in sensor networks. *IEEE Transactions on Systems Management and Cybernetics, Part B*, **39**(6): 1568–77.

[63] Yu, W.W., Lu, J. and Chen, G. *et al.* (2009) Estimating uncertain delayed genetic regulatory networks: An adaptive filtering approach. *IEEE Transactions on Automatic Control*, **54**(4): 892–7.

10

Brief Introduction to Other Topics

10.1 Human Opinion Dynamics

Human opinion dynamics refer to a kind of human behavioral dynamics, a subject of study generally concerning with the behaviors, actions and interactions of human individuals, groups, communities, and various social organizations, regarding their opinions formation, evolution, separation and consensus, as well as other related issues such as effects and impacts of media and government policies on opinion-based decision making and behavioral consequences.

Human opinion dynamics are driven and influenced by many important factors like cultures, economics, politics and religions. Unlike other dynamics such as mechanical dynamics, electronic dynamics, chemical dynamics, etc., human opinion dynamics involve many invisible and immeasurable human emotional and psychological factors, and therefore are extremely difficult to precisely quantify. Nevertheless, statistically describing and evaluating human opinion dynamics is still possible. In fact, there has been a persistent trend in quantitatively studying different kinds of human behavioral dynamics, including opinion dynamics in particular, first from a behavioral analysis approach in sociology [1], then from a statistical analysis viewpoint in mathematics [2, 3], and recently from a complex-network perspective in network science [4–6].

The main stream of human opinion dynamics creates order from disorder, and preserves order after it is in place. Here, order in social opinion means agreement, consensus, uniformity, self-organized decisional activities, converging patterns, etc. Its study includes spontaneous emergence of opinion consensus, which can often be directly extended to include other human behavioral dynamics such as generation of languages, self-organized migration, and formation of mobility patterns. Human opinion dynamics theory generally concerns questions like how an initially disordered opinion distribution can eventually become orderly through interactions among the large number of interrelated agents. It is well agreed that, in human opinion dynamics, agent-wise interactions are so important that all the macroscopic properties are not due to the behaviors of isolated individual agents, no matter how complex they are, but to the nontrivial collective effects of their intensive and intermitted interactions, typically discussions and debates. This is known as the "$1 + 1 > 2$" phenomenon in complex systems and networks.

On the other hand, qualitative properties of a large-scale social system generally do not depend on the microscopic details of the underlying evolutionary process, but on higher-level features such as attraction, cooperation, synchrony, and even competition and repulsion. The driving force behind the transition from disorder to order is the tendency of interactive agents to becoming more alike to each other, known as the "social influence" which guides the majority of agents to accept some existing differences among diverse peers, at least to some extent, for any two of them cannot be too far apart when living within the same community (the so-called "bounded confidence" [7]). This eventually leads to global or clustering consensus and synchrony, namely, order.

Fundamentals of Complex Networks: Models, Structures and Dynamics, First Edition.
Guanrong Chen, Xiaofan Wang, Xiang Li.
© Higher Education Press. All rights reserved. Published 2015 by John Wiley & Sons Singapore Pte Ltd.
Companion Website: www.wiley.com/go/chen/complex

The most interesting topics include social network topologies and sociodynamics. To represent and model human opinion dynamics, a natural way is to put the framework into a complex network setting, in which a node represents an individual or a community and an edge represents the interaction between two of them [8].

For quite a long time, social network analysis had already been a focus in social science studies, where social network metaphor was used to represent various complex relationships between related agents within a social system at different scales, from interpersonal to interregional, even to international [9–11]. Spurred by the recent rapid development in the studies of technological networks, social networks are also compared to technological networks in many aspects. It is found that social networks generally differ from the technological networks in many measures such as their inherent assortative property, namely, there usually is a positive correlation between two adjacent nodes in social networks, attributed to human nature, while technological networks typically are disassortative. Moreover, social networks show more prominent large clustering coefficients, well above those in technological networks, indicating that the small-world network model or its variant is appropriate to be used as a basic framework for studying social dynamics. In addition, social networks are usually hierarchical, with a small number of leaders and a large number of followers, at several different layers of the society. Noticeably, social networks have many special structural and dynamical features different from any other networks particularly technological networks [12].

Many network-based models have been developed and analyzed for studying human opinion dynamics: their modeling, simulation and analysis. The aim is to reveal the underlying mechanism of human opinion formation, evolution and convergence, hoping to gain a better understanding of human social behaviors particularly their opinion dynamics. Change and consensus of opinions and decisions are very important aspects in human behavioral dynamics in social activities. There are many recent examples of public opinion changes and consensus; for example, the rejection of the Maastricht treaty in Ireland, the negative vote in France against the European constitution, the switch in the belief of the authorship of the terrorist attacks in Madrid, Spain on March 11, 2004, the rumors concerning the September 11 opinions in France, and so on [13].

To describe human opinion formation, changes, split, evolution, opposition or consensus, mathematical modeling is useful. In a typical mathematical model of a social opinion formation and its associated dynamics, every opinion is a variable which can change in time. In such a model, different opinions may be labeled by different numbers for distinction: in the discrete case, it is common and convenient to use binary values, ± 1, for yes or no, support or against; in the continuous case where opinion is not so crispy but fuzzy (such as strongly agree, agree, partially agree, somewhat agree, not agree, strongly against, etc.), a real value has to be adopted for quantification.

A typical model of the discrete case is the voter model, which is an important social activity in human life, where voters' opinions determine the outcome of an election or a decision. Voters' behavioral dynamics were first studied in [14], where a model for species competition was established which was referred to as a "voter model" in [15], including the so-called direct voter model and reverse voter model. On a general complex network, voter behavioral dynamics are far more complicated and indeed quite intrinsic. On heterogeneous networks such as scale-free networks, direct voter model and reverse voter model behave very differently. This is essentially due to the fact that the first random pick from a scale-free network will likely be a small-degree node while the send pick from its neighbors can be a hub-node with a very high probability. On the contrary, for homogeneous networks the two models show similar behaviors simply because the node-picking order does not make much difference due to the near uniform nature of their degree distributions.

The Galam model [16], on the other hand, considers a fully connected network of agents. At each step, a group of agents are selected at random to have discussion about their opinions. Suppose that in the end of discussion every agent will take the opinion of the majority in the discussion group, thus the majority will keep their original opinion while the minority will change their opinion to be opposite. Lately, the Galam majority rule model has also been extended, for example, to a dynamical model of agents with variable numbers of neighbors [17], the case with three opinions [18], and multistate opinions with a plurality rule [19], where the plurality rule is meaningful only if each agent can have more than two opinions.

The Latané social impact theory is also important in the study of opinion dynamics. The psychological theory of social impact addresses the concerns of how a person feels his/her peers and how he/she influences the others as a return [20]. Social impact theory predicts that, as the strength and immediacy increase within a group of agents, conformity of every of its members will also increase. The theory also explains that, the more important a group is and the more involved an individual into the group, the more likely the individual will conform to the normative pressures of the group. Moreover, the theory shows that, as the size of a group increases, an individual has less effect on the others and, as a result, if one feels pressures from a group then any addition of new members to the minority in a small group will make a much bigger difference than the case in a large group.

In [20], Latané constructed a mathematical model of the effects of strength, immediacy, and number in social systems. The model was applied to several conformity studies and it accurately predicted the actual level of conformity that occurred within social groups. More precisely, the theory states that the likelihood that a person will respond to social influence will increase with several factors: *Strength* (how important the influencing group of people is to you); *Immediacy* (how close the group is to you in both space and time); *Number* (how many people are there in the group who influence you). For instance, as has been widely experienced, increasing the number has a decreasing incremental effect on each group member (e.g., increasing from 2 to 3 has more effect than changing from 99 to 100). As another example, the effect is most powerful when a large number of members other than you clearly agree upon a certain opinion (e.g., it is not unusual that in a meeting you will not feel comfortable to speak out if your opinion differs from the majority).

Along the same lines, the Sznajd model deserves special attention. The Sznajd model has found applications in voting dynamics [21, 22], interaction between economics and individual attitudes [23], competition in open markets [24], opinion spreading in trading [25], and generation of new complex networks [26].

Note that the above social impact theory does not take into consideration of some realistic features of social interactions, for example individual's past experience and learning, physical space limitation and communication time constraints. These issues have been accounted for in some related studies lately [27].

Finally, it is noticed that all the opinion formation models discussed above are binary, namely with two opinions, $s_i = \pm 1$, for all individuals who can only hold either "agree" or "disagree" ("yes" or "no") opinions. In reality, however, oftentimes people have fuzzy but not crispy opinions like "strongly agree", "somewhat oppose", or "not sure." In such situations, the so-called continuous opinion models [28–30] with real values to quantify opinions appear to be more realistic albeit more difficult to model.

The bounded confidence model [31] is a representative model used to study the continuous opinion dynamics. In a network of multiple agents, initially every agent is randomly assigned an opinion described by a real value within some intervals. Agents interact (namely, have discussions) only if they are sufficiently close to each other in opinion, a situation referred to as *bounded confidence*. In such a multi-opinion situation, if interactions lead to convergence of opinions then the final opinion clusters within the network can be one (consensus), two (polarization) or more (fragmentation). In fact, the statistical asymptotic behaviors of this bounded confidence model are quite rich and complicated.

It has been experienced that on any network topology, the Deffuant model [32] with a wide range of parameter values has dynamics always evolving to a steady state with one or two clusters. As a tolerance parameter becomes smaller, however, every agent has a smaller neighborhood; therefore more clusters will emerge generating a large number of fragments in the population. On scale-free networks, for example, the number of clusters with converging opinions is found to be proportional to the number of agents in the population for a fixed tolerance parameter [33]. In particular, agents with few connections have a significantly high probability to keep their original opinions unchanged because of receiving less external influence [34].

For continuous opinion dynamics, there are other models, such as the Hegselmann-Krause model [35], which is similar to the Deffuant model but each agent takes the average opinion of its compatible neighbors, so the dynamic evolution is completely determined by the tolerance parameter. A variant of this and the Deffuant model is for each agent to pick the opinion of a randomly selected neighbor [32]. In another model, opinions are considered being also affected by environmental factors such as social imitation, majority rules, media, and individual uncertainties [36]. The Deffuant model may also be combined with an opinion diffusion process [37].

Some other models for opinion formation are variants of the classical Ising model [38], which is a mathematical model of ferromagnetism in statistical mechanics where the discrete variables called spins can be in one of two states and each spin interacts only with its nearest neighbors.

Interestingly, binary and continuous opinions may also be combined together to establish a dynamical opinion spreading model [39], in which two agents can declare the same binary opinion but actually holding in mind somewhat different continuous opinions respectively. Some rules can then be set up allowing agents to vary their opinions based on both their own and that of their peers. Multi-agent interactions in this model can show complex dynamics with various clustering patterns.

Recently, the two main stochastic process models, namely the voter model [23, 24] and the cultural model [40], were revisited in [41]. For a generalized model that combines confidence threshold and social influence together, some rigorous analytical results were obtained. Recently, a bounded confidence plus random selection model is proposed in [42], in which each agent has several long-distant neighbors outside the bound who are selected based on a similarity probability.

10.2   Human Mobility and Behavioral Dynamics

Albert Einstein published five research papers in 1905, which all turned out to be fundamental in modern natural science; one was devoted to the theory of relativity [43] and one discussed "unexplained motion" of tiny particles suspended in a fluid, better known today as Brownian motion reported by botanist Robert Brown in 1828 [44].

Humans, on the other hand, have strong desire to move, from place to place and from time to time, driven by our daily life, jobs, responsibilities or leisure. To many, especially those who do not know our motion routine and patterns, our mobility trajectory might look just as Brownian motion. It is therefore reasonable to assume that human also moves randomly in general studies of their motion behaviors. Differing from particles, however, human motions are strongly influenced by the transportation and mobility infrastructures such as vehicles which create large numbers of travelers, their wide interconnectivity and far reachability, and massive intermixing, in different geographical regions all over the world, significantly reshaping our modern daily life.

Noticeably, although these achievements facilitate people's mobility and interactions, they sometimes lead to troubles and problems such as pandemic disease spreading, where mobility is a key [45–48]. Since it is possible that the advanced modern transportation system merely speeds up and facilitates a faster and wider human motion pattern, but has no fundamental differences from the random motion of particles, it is very natural for one to ask: Is Einstein's theory about randomness still valid for today's human mobility?

The *Where's George* website [49] tracks the path of each spent dollar bill registered on it, and thousands of citizens of the USA participated in the activities of this interesting website [50]: First, a registered user types in the serial number of an individual dollar bill with his/her zipcode, effectively recording the bills' current location. Then, the user marks the bill and then enters it to circulation (e.g., for banking or shopping). Anyone noticing the mark might be curious hence likely would visit the website, on which he/she can register and report the bill's new location via the corresponding zipcode. Successive reports of a bill can thereby yield its spatiotemporal trajectory, thus the bills' travel history can be traced.

Dirk Brockmann from the Northwestern University in USA noticed this website provides an opportunity of tracing human movement because money travels with humans so such data can be a proxy of human mobility. Dirk compiled the banknote trajectories and found that the distance covered by the bills did not follow the Poisson distribution, which Einstein predicted, but followed a power law [50, 51] which indicates that the bills' trajectory is best described by the Lévy flight. A Lévy flight is a random walk in which the step-lengths have a heavy-tailed probability distribution.

Similarly to a random walk of a particle, a person on a Lévy flight randomly alters the motion direction after each jump, while the jump-size distribution also follows a power law. As it turns out, the probability that Lévy flight walker will return to a previously visited location decreases. This observation may seem to be leading to a contradiction that if a person follows the Lévy flight then he/she will likely be unable to return home. Fortunately, with the exploding usage of mobile phones, GPS, and all kinds of handheld devices, humans are capable of tracking their mobility. For example, each time one makes a call on a mobile phone, his/her location is being effectively recorded. These records are not very accurate, yet such data offer an exceptional occasion to explore the mobility of millions of individuals.

Marta González and Cesar Hidalgo [52], with access to a large database of mobile phones usage records, observed every user's movement in nearly real time. They reconstructed a user's trajectory and then drew a circle around it, sizing up the neighborhoods the user frequented, thus found that a power law emerged again among a hundred thousand users' radii of neighborhoods. It indicated that most people are highly localized and commonly confine their daily life to very small circles in distance, typically within only a few miles, moving back and forth with high regularity among several nearby locations. This majority of people coexist with some who move dozens of miles and a few who travel more than hundreds of miles each day. They found no people taking occasional trips, unlike us who travel for vacation or make business trips sometimes. Marta discovered that the observed jump-size distribution is the convolution between the statistics of individual trajectories and the population heterogeneity. Analyzing mobile phone data at the city level, they found that the trip-length distribution can be well fitted by various distributions [53].

By analyzing a large GPS database for single-vehicle mobility in the Florence urban area, Italy, Armando Bazzani *et al.* [54] found that the statistical law of path lengths for individual trajectories follows an exponential distribution. They also analyzed the activity downtime and the distribution of the monthly activity degree. Under assumptions like the existence of "individual mobility energy" and "individual mobility time" that define the daily agenda of the travelers, they found in the equilibrium state all individuals seem to have tendency to behave independently trying to minimize interactions with the others.

There are many interesting issues for further investigation. For example, human migration patterns and contact behavior play critical roles in pandemic spreading therefore are important for study. Migration is a characteristic of human mobility in a large-scale space. There are two viewpoints on the intrinsic mechanisms of human migration patterns. One is to argue that migration is directly deterred by the costs (time and energy) associated with the physical distances. In analogy with Newton's law of gravity, the flow of individuals is predicted to decrease with the physical distance between two locations, typically as a power-law of the distance variable [46, 55]. Another is to argue that there is no direct relation between mobility and distance, while distance is merely a surrogate for the effect of intervening opportunities [56]. In [57], the migration from the origin to the destination is assumed to depend on the number of opportunities closer than this destination. A person thus tends to search for destinations so as to satisfy the need giving rise to its journey, but the absolute value of their distance is irrelevant.

At regional spatial scale, people always have some fashion of interactions, e.g., conversations, conferences, meetings, etc., and they inevitably contact with each other. Ciro Cattuto *et al.* [58] built a flexible contact-sensing platform, utilizing the distributed active Radio Frequency Identification (RFID) technology to track people's face-to-face social interactions, with tunable spatial and temporal granularities. They uncovered similarities in the way the individuals interact within different contexts, and identified some patterns of a superconnector's behavior. Marcel Salathé *et al.* [59] applied wireless sensors to assess the risk of virus transmission through person-to-person interactions among the members of an American high school.

In summary, Einstein's randomness hypothesis seems to be infused in all fields of science today, from the spread of ideas, information or virus to the dispersion of drug component in our stomach, where the randomness and diffusion impact almost everything.

10.3   Web PageRank, SiteRank and BrowserRank

Page importance is perhaps the most concerned factor for the World Wide Web search using contemporary search engines, in terms of crawling, indexing, and ranking etc. Conventionally, link analysis was used to calculate the page importance using information from the hyperlink graph of the Web. Two typical examples are PageRank [60, 61] and HITS [62].

To date, many algorithms have been developed for computing page importance, which can roughly be classified into two categories: one is based on the structure of the edge graph, called edge (or link) analysis, and the other introduces extra information into the calculation process, such as users' web-search behaviors.

10.3.1   Methods Based on Edge Analysis

Representative edge analysis algorithms include PageRank [60, 61] and HITS [62]. The basic idea of PageRank is based on the assumption that if many popular pages are linking to a page on the edge graph, then this page is likely to be important, and such importance information can be propagated along the hyperlinks. A discrete-time Markov chain model, which simulates a web surfer's random walk on the hyperlink graph, is defined and page importance is calculated as the stationary probability distribution of the Markov chain. HITS, on the other hand, is based on the concepts of hub and authority to model the two aspects of importance of a webpage. A hub page is one which many pages are linking to, while an authority page is one which many pages are linked from. In principle, good hubs tend to link to good authorities, and vice versa. A previous study has shown that HITS performs comparably with PageRank [63].

In addition to PageRank and HITS, many other algorithms have also been proposed. Some of these methods focus on speeding up the computation of PageRank and HITS [64, 65], while some others focus on the refinement and enrichment of PageRank and HITS algorithms such as the Topic-sensitive PageRank [66] and query-dependent PageRank [67]. The basic idea of these two algorithms is to introduce topics into the page importance model, assuming that the endorsement from a page with the same topic is larger than that from a page with a different topic. In addition, there are some other algorithms, which either modify the "personalized vector" [68, 69], change the "damping factor" [70], or introduce different weights to inter-domain and intra-domain edges [71]. Moreover, there are also theoretical studies of the PageRank algorithm [68, 69, 72] (see also the good survey [71]).

Edge-analysis-based algorithms that are robust against edge spam have also been proposed recently, including the TrustRank [73, 74]. In TrustRank, a set of reliable pages are first identified as seed pages and then the trust of the seed pages is propagated to other pages along hyperlinks. Since the propagation starts from reliable pages, TrustRank can be more spam-resistant than the original PageRank.

10.3.2   Methods Using Users' Behavior Data

There are several methods aiming at leveraging users' behavior data in the calculation of page importance, for example, by combining the hyperlink graph with the usage graph obtained from web logs so as to adjust the transition weights between two pages [75]. In this scheme, the weights of existing hyperlinks may be adjusted and meanwhile some new edges may be created according to the usage data. Another approach [76] is to utilize the usage data, i.e., the visiting frequency by previous users when amending the transition probability. The main difference is that the latter only trusts the usage data but ignores the web structural information. The two approaches both emphasize that real users' behavior data are essential for page importance calculation.

On the other hand, even the browsers can be and have been ranked, where the motivation was to overcome some limitations of the PageRank algorithms. Recently, an algorithm called BrowseRank was developed in [77, 78], which computes the page importance based only on the users' behavior data. A significant difference between BrowseRank and PageRank is that they use different data bases and take different actions in evaluating the page importance. More precisely, PageRank algorithm relies solely on the data of the edge graph of the web, where the page importance is evaluated by the votes of web content creators who create or delete hyperlinks. BrowseRank algorithm, on the contrary, collects the users' behavior data in web surfing and builds a user browsing graph, which contains both user transition information and user staying time information. In this way, the importance of pages relies on the browsing behavior of a large number of users, and is evaluated by hundreds of millions of users' implicit votes. There are also some other distinctions, as discussed in [78–81].

Further to webpages, even websites can be ranked and have been ranked. In the literature of website ranking, it is common to apply those technologies proposed for ranking webpages, e.g., the PageRank algorithm [82, 83], to rank the websites as well. In doing so, a HostGraph was constructed, where the nodes denote websites and there is an edge between two nodes if there are hyperlinks from the webpages in one website to the webpages in the other. According to the different definitions of the edge weights, HostGraphs can be classified into two categories: one defines the weight of an edge between two websites to be the number of hyperlinks between the two sets of webpages in these sites [84], while the other simply sets the weight of an edge to 1 [85]. Afterwards, it was pointed out in [82, 83] that these methods were not as reasonable as PageRank because they are not in accordance with the browsing behaviors of the web surfers. Typical real-world web surfers have two basic ways to access the web, one is to type the URL in the address edit of the web browser, using for instance the My Favorite folder, and the other is to click a hyperlink in the current loaded webpage. These two manners can be well represented and described by the PageRank algorithm. As a remedy, the so-called AggregateRank algorithm was proposed in [86, 87], which ranks the importance of a website by the mean frequency of a surfer's visiting to the site.

In conclusion, Web PageRank, SiteRank and BrowserRank clearly show that complex network theory finds a great opportunity in Internet applications.

10.4   Recommendation Systems

The exponential growth of the Internet and World Wide Web confronts people with information overloading: there is a too large amount of data and sources to cope with in order to find relevant messages. It has been well experienced that it is not unusual for one to choose what he needs from thousands of movies, millions of books and billions of web pages today. The amount of information is increasing faster than the growth of our data-processing ability. As a result, evaluating all these alternatives and then making choices becomes literally infeasible.

A landmark for information filtering is the use of a search engine [88], by which users could find relevant objects with the help of some properly chosen keywords. However, the search engine has two essential disadvantages. On the one hand, it does not take into account personal preference thus returns the same results to different people who may have very different expectations and desires. As such, if a user has different demands from that of the majority, "right keywords" do not help him to find out what he is looking for the seemingly countless searched results. On the other hand, some flavors and tastes, such as personal feelings of music and paintings, cannot be expressed by keywords, not even languages. The search engine, based on text matching alone, thereby will lose its effectiveness in such situations.

To date, the most promising way to efficiently filter out the unneeded information is to provide personalized recommendations [89]. That is, using some personal information of a user (i.e., the historical track of this user's activities and possibly his personal profile) to identify his styles and habits so as to incorporate them into the recommendations when he browses the web next time. In fact, these techniques have already found significant applications in e-commerce. For example, Amazon.com uses one's purchase record to recommend books, AdaptiveInfo.com uses one's reading history to recommend news, and the TiVo digital video system recommends TV shows and movies on the basis of users' viewing patterns and ratings.

A simplest version of a recommender system can be described by a bipartite network consisting of users and objects, where an object is connected with a user if and only if this object has been collected by this user. A recommender system needs to rank all those objects that have not yet been collected by a target user and then recommend the top-ranked objects to this user. Real systems may include user profiles, object attributes, tags, ratings, comments, etc.

While originally a field occupied by computer scientists, recommendation calls for contributions from various directions and is now a topic of interest also for mathematicians, physicists, psychologists and, above all, business personnel. Representative recommending techniques include collaborative filtering [90], dimensionality reduction (e.g., singular value decomposition [91], latent semantic models [92], latent Dirichlet allocation [93], Beyesian clustering [94], principle component analysis [95]), diffusion-based algorithms (e.g., heat conduction [96] and mass diffusion [97]), content analysis [98] and hybrid algorithms [99].

Several challenges remain, which pose potential threats to the use and to the performances of recommendation algorithms. Major issues include: (i) How to make recommendations based on very sparse data [100]; (ii) How to recommend items to cold-start users [101]; (iii) How to guarantee the recommendations be both accurate and diverse [102]; (iv) How to make use of tags [103]; (v) How to design scalable algorithms for large-scale incremental systems [104]; (vi) What is the value of time [105]? (vii) Do social relationship work in recommendation systems [106]? (viii) How to build a robust system against malicious attacks [107]. And so on.

10.5   Network Edge Prediction

Edge prediction, or link prediction, refers to the estimation of the possibility of a new edge creation between two existing nodes which do not have linkage currently, based on the present network structure and available information on the network [108]. It commonly refers to predicting both "exists yet unknown edges" and "future edges."

In many biological networks such as food webs, protein–protein interaction networks and metabolic networks, whether an edge between two nodes exists requires extensive and expensive laboratorial experiments, where our knowledge of these networks is very limited. To predict possible future interactions, based on known network topology and node interactions, hence to focus only on those emerging edges that are most likely to exist can be very valuable in the sense of, for instance, reducing the experimental costs if the predictions are accurate enough. Social networks, as another example, usually provide vague and incomplete data, where edge prediction plays an important role for study.

For an undirected network $G(V, E)$, where V is the set of N nodes and E the set of edges, it has $U := N(N - 1)/2$ pairs of nodes. Given an edge prediction algorithm, for every unconnected node pair $(x, y) \in U \backslash E$, associate with it a value S_{xy}, which has a certain meaning of proximity, proportional to the probability of having an edge between this node pair. Then, arrange all such proximity values in decreasing order, in which the first one has the largest probability of receiving a new edge in the next step of the algorithm. Moreover, divide the known set of existing edges into two parts: training set E^T and test set E^P, thus $E = E^T \cup E^P$ and $E^T \cap E^P = \phi$. Here, those edges in U but not in E are called nonexisting edges.

To evaluate edge prediction algorithms, three criteria are commonly used: (i) Area Under (the receiver operating characteristic) Curve (AUC), (ii) Precision, and (iii) Ranking Score [109]. Among them, AUC is a global measure and is of the most popular [110], while Precision considers only the first few with larger probabilities [111] and Ranking Score emphasizes on the ranking of the predicted edges [112].

(i) AUC: Given a ranking of all nonobserved edges, the value of AUC is calculated, which can be interpreted as the probability that a randomly chosen missing edge (i.e., an edge in E^P) is given a higher score than a randomly chosen nonexistent edge (i.e., an edge in $U \backslash E$). In implementing the algorithm, the score of each non-observed edge is calculated, instead of giving the ordered list since the latter task is more time consuming. Then, at each time, one randomly picks a missing edge and a nonexistent edge to compare their scores. If, among n independent comparisons there are n' times where the missing edge has higher scores and n'' times they have the same score, then the AUC value is $AUC = (n' + 0.5n'')/n$. If all such scores are generated from an independent and identical distribution, then the AUC value should be about 0.5. Therefore, the degree to which the value exceeds 0.5 indicates how much better the algorithm performs as compared to a purely random picking scheme.

(ii) Precision: Given a ranking of all nonobserved edges, the precision is defined as the ratio of relevant items selected against the number of items selected. That is, if one takes the top-L edges from the given ranking as the predicted ones, among which L_r edges are right (i.e., there are L_r edges in the probe set E^P), then the precision equals L_r/L. Clearly, higher precision means higher prediction accuracy.

(iii) Ranking Score: Given a ranking of all nonobserved edges, simply use the scores of the ordered edges in decreasing order. This is a simple and efficient method but not very accurate as compared to the above two.

Edge prediction as a frontier research direction has been extensively studied in the field of computer science, where a basic approach is based on Markov chains [113] and machine leaning. Lately, this idea was extended to adaptive websites [114]. Noticeably, the earlier approaches were based on node information [115–117], while recently there are proposals of new methods based on network topological information [118, 119]. In particular, for networks with layer structures, an effective edge prediction scheme was developed in [120]. On the other hand, edge prediction methods based on random block models [121] and based on reconstruction of network due to missing or incorrect data [122] were proposed, where the latter introduced a new concept of spurious edges which occurs in many real applications. Moreover, there are some other related studies with various edge prediction methods proposed [123–126].

Clearly, the studies of edge prediction and network science are mutually beneficial, because an in-depth understanding of network structure can enhance the design of effective edge prediction algorithms and the results and performances of edge prediction algorithms can provide good estimation of network topological evolution and suggest guidelines for real network applications. For example, for highly clustered networks, the common-neighbor-based algorithms should be desirable because they can provide good predictions with low computational complexity. However, if not so then some other schemes using the local path index and local random walk index [126], which make use of more available information, will be more preferable.

To date, the studies of edge prediction have been devoted to unweighted undirected networks. For directed networks, even the ternary relations are quite complicated, thus the simple common-neighbor-based similarity indices have to be modified to take into account the local motif structure [127]. Otherwise, even one can predict the existence of an edge between two nodes, it is still impossible to determine its direction. In addition, the path-dependent similarity indices should also be extended to take into account the edge direction [128].

Some basic tasks of edge prediction for weighted networks, on the other hand, have already been considered [129, 130], where the former suggests that the edges with higher weights are more important in predicting missing edges while the latter shows a completely opposite conclusion: the weak edges play a more significant role, leaving some more investigation to the future.

There are other related and challenging issues about edge prediction for weighted directed networks, such as to predict the weights of the edges, to deal with multidimensional networks, networks with different kinds of nodes in different clusters (e.g., with users, URLs and tags on a web), and so on.

Most of current approaches rely only on a single snapshot of a network to predict the missing or future edges. Extensive experiments have shown that these methods can well predict the existence of an edge, but unable to predict any repeated edge occurrence, especially for evolving networks such as online social networks. Although these questions have been addressed to some extent, to develop more effective edge prediction algorithms to thoroughly handle such difficult issues, one needs further comprehensive understanding of network science theory such as the temporal effects of human behaviors on the network topological evolution.

10.6 Living Organisms and Bionetworks

A living organism can be modeled by a huge-scale nonlinear biochemical reaction system, which is generally represented through the intermittent interactions of biomolecules including genes, RNAs, proteins and metabolites, thereby forming various types of biomolecular networks [131, 132]. It has been commonly recognized that a complex living organism cannot be fully understood by merely analyzing its individual components, but the networks of these components are ultimately responsible for the organism's form and they rein the organism's behaviors. Such complex networks indispensably exist in biological systems and play fundamental roles to give rise to life and maintain the homeostasis in living organisms. In addition, biological processes are governed by various complex networks ranging from gene regulation to signal transduction. These processes are required to be modeled at the molecular level to accurately reflect their essential characteristics and properties.

To elucidate the basic principles of biological systems, studying biomolecular networks has attracted increasing attention from not only biology but also science and engineering communities [127, 133]. One of major challenges in life science is to understand how genes, proteins and small molecules interact thereby forming biomolecular networks and how these interactions achieve functions and complexity of the living organisms. High-throughput experimental methods in molecular biology have produced an enormous amount of data, including interactions, networks and pathways. Hence, it is highly desirable and, in fact, demanded that mathematicians and computer scientists provide efficient computational tools to help reveal the essential biological information and mechanisms from a system perspective. In other words, instead of analyzing individual components or partial aspects of the organism, there are strong desire and urgent need to study an organism from the perspective of a dynamical network of genes, proteins and biochemical reactions, which lead to the call for helpful complex network theory and technology.

A molecular network naturally has a hierarchical structure with such main ingredients as molecules (e.g., gene, mRNA, protein, metabolite, and complex), interactions, local structures (e.g., network motif, network module, pathway, subnetwork) and, after all, networks. Their hierarchical structure is formed conceptually from individual molecules, to pairwise interactions, to local structures, and eventually to the global network as a whole. In other words, basic components in a cellular system are individual molecules, which affect each other by their pairwise interactions. A cascade of such pairwise interactions forms a local structure which transforms local perturbations into a functional response. All local structures including linear pathways or subnetworks are then assembled into a global biomolecular network, which eventually generates global behaviors and holds responsibility for life in a living organism. Depending on pairwise interactions, molecular networks can be categorized into the following different types [131]:

1. transcription regulatory network: TF-DNA interactions;
2. gene regulatory network: gene-gene interactions (or genetic interactions);
3. protein interaction network: protein-protein interactions;
4. metabolic network: enzyme-substrate interactions;
5. signaling network: molecule-molecule interactions.

From a computational point of view, modeling biomolecular networks (e.g., gene regulatory network or signal transduction network) by proper mathematical models will enable and enhance the understanding of biological systems in general. Main research topics on biomolecular networks are rich and diverse, for example:

1. huge deposit of gene expression profiles and protein-DNA interaction data makes it possible to quantitatively study the regulatory relationships between genes;
2. reverse engineering of regulatory networks is one of the main computational problems in this field – given a large amount of gene expression data from microarray techniques, one needs to identify gene–gene interactions and signaling pathways, which is by no means a trivial task;
3. protein interaction data from high-throughput techniques are highly noisy and mostly incomplete, so one is required to systematically integrate these data and further estimate their confidence by statistical techniques, which is known as the difficult protein interaction or protein network prediction problem;
4. it is commonly believed that interacting proteins tend to have similar functions, therefore the annotation of proteins is currently far from being complete, which can be enhanced by employing protein

interaction data and other biological sources, known as the challenging problem of protein function prediction;

5. with the current technologies, the experiment cost to determine protein complexes and functional modules is not only extremely high but also very time-consuming, and the result is not so reliable, thus it would be desirable to accomplish the task by mining the data from protein interaction networks so as to provide a rough estimation for biologists, which is the so-called functional module detection problem.

6. given some protein interaction networks or metabolic networks from multiple species, how to compare such networks and extract important information and knowledge related to evolution, or likewise for a given concerned pathway how to find a similar one in a protein interaction network, is an important question, known as network alignment and query;

7. in order to understand the structure and function of a living cell, the structure and dynamics of such biological networks have to be carefully investigated, leading to the problem of dynamical modeling or quantitative simulation of biomolecular networks.

In addition to the above computational problems, one is interested in the question whether biomolecular networks have similar topological properties to some particular types of complex networks, and whether the topological patterns (e.g., network motifs, modules or hubs) of biomolecular networks are related to specific biological functions? Moreover, how to reconstruct metabolic pathways and how to identify active subnetworks from a large set of biochemical reactions? How to detect signal transduction pathways or drug targets from the available data from perturbed biological experiments? Can one design or construct a synthetic biological network representing the whole or some part of a cellular system (referred to as forward engineering of biomolecular networks)? All these problems are expected to be answered at least by means of computational biology, which heavily relies on complex network theory and technology.

Life is dynamically evolving and dynamics exist in living organisms at every level. To study the dynamics of a biological system, one typically model it a nonlinear dynamical system such as a system of ordinary differential equations, or a stochastic process, based on the mass action law or the enzyme reaction kinetics alike. From the viewpoint of network dynamics, there are many important topics on the subject [132], such as stability analysis of steady states, bifurcation analysis of phase transitions, robustness, sensitivity, perturbations, synchronization of multiple subnetworks, controllability, stochasticity, and oscillatory and switching behaviors, etc.

Based on the increasingly-accumulated huge amount of data measured from high-throughput technologies, biomolecular networks and their functional roles have been studied extensively on various aspects of living organisms. These studies not only help scientists understand complex biochemical phenomena but also reveal fundamental mechanisms of living organisms from a systematic perspective. The investigation on biomolecular networks is anticipated to enhance our understanding of cellular systems by integrating the available comprehensive data of molecular components in different layers of the networks to study how the multitudes of interactions can facilitate the complicated biological functions within a cell. In particular, by investigating the relationships and interactions among different parts of a biological system, such as gene regulatory systems, protein interaction networks, metabolic pathways, organelles, cells, physiological systems and organisms, it can be expected to develop an understandable model of a biological system [133]. This is critical for a deeper understanding of the essential mechanisms in life, for which complex networks theory and technology can and will continue to contribute.

10.7 Cascading Reactions on Networks

The phenomena of *cascading reactions* and, in particular, *cascading failures* are quite similar to virus spreading over various complex networks. In many real-world networks, intentional attacks or unexpected failures on a few nodes may cause severe chain reactions through the connections among nodes, leading to collapse of a large portion of the network or even the entire network. This is also

Fundamentals of Complex Networks

called *avalanche*. One example in point is the Internet, where attacks on a few routers can cause overloading of some nearby routers which consequently redistribute their loads to other routers; this eventually lead to data-traffic congestion of some parts of the network. In electric power grids, as another example, failures of some local facilities or devices such as generators and transmission lines can lead to blackout of a large area of residence and industry. The well-known Northeast Blackout in 2003 was a massive power outage that occurred throughout a large region of the northeastern United States and Ontario Canada on Thursday 14 August 2003, the largest blackout in North America's history, which reportedly affected about 10 million people in the province of Ontario (about 1/3 of the population of Canada) and 40 million people in eight U.S. states (about 1/7 of the population of USA) and caused financial losses of about $6 billion USD. To prevent such disasters from happening, understanding how cascading failures are propagating over complex networks is extremely important and also very urgent.

To study the cascading reactions over complex networks, some network models have been developed and analyzed, based on node dynamics, edge dynamics and node-edge dynamics.

Node-based models include the fiber-bundle model is a conceptual graph framework for cascading failure analysis on networks [134] and node-betweenness-based model [135]. In these models, loads are distributed over the network according to certain distributions. When overloading occurs on some nodes, it causes failures of these nodes, which will then be removed from the network, along with their adjacent edges. The loads of these nodes will then be further distributed to their neighbors according to some pre-set rules, which leads to more nodes to fail. Such a model describes how the failure propagates through cascading of overloads.

Another model [136] assumes that on a network the load of a node is measured by its node betweenness, similar to the above, but the maximum-load capacity of the node is defined by two different measures: (i) the maximum-load capacity increases linearly as the number of nodes increases; (ii) the maximum-load capacity is constant. Regarding the network, if it grows according to the BA power law, then when nodes and edges increase to a certain number, respectively, some nodes will be overloaded because the node-betweenness will be higher than its maximum-load capacity. Thus, these nodes and their connecting edges will be removed, and consequently the betweenness of the remaining nodes will have to be recalculated. Repeat this process until no overloaded nodes remaining on the network. Simulations [136] show that in case (ii) cascading failures are basically unavoidable, because the capacity of each node is fixed. Also, comparing a scale-free network with the BA preferential attachment scheme to a scale-free network with a random attachment scheme, the former is faster to encounter cascading failures. Another similar cascading failure model is based on the BA model with load redistribution from the failed node [137].

On the other hand, there are models established based on edge dynamics [138]. Since the edge dynamics can also affect the cascading failure processes, actually often quite significantly, it is very reasonable to take into account the edge characteristics in network failure modeling. Some models also take node and edge capacities into consideration [139].

Comparing the overloading of nodes and the overloading of edges, one can see that in the former case there will be mutually disconnected clusters after cascading failures have occurred, while in the latter case there will be large cluster(s) left out in the network. Moreover, scale-free networks with the random attachment scheme are more robust against traffic congestion due to node or edge overloading.

Furthermore, it is also possible to take into account both node and edge dynamics in a cascading failure model.

For example, one model [140] uses an undirected weighted network to model a communication or transportation system. After a node failed and so being removed, all the relevant efficiency-optimal paths will be changed, leading to a redistribution of loads which may cause overloading to some nodes. This, in turn, may lead to another round of load-redistribution, eventually leading to cascading failures.

A power grid can be viewed as a network with nodes being power generators and edges being power lines. It has been observed that the North America's power grid, for example, approximately follows a power-law node distribution. In fact, if the betweenness is used as the loading measure, then the North America's power grid has a precise power-law distribution in terms of load distribution [141].

Further analysis reveals that node removal due to failures may be classified into three types according to their effects on the network efficiency: (i) nodes with small degrees and loads, which do not significantly affect the network efficiency after being removed, constitute about 60% of the total; (ii) nodes with large degrees or loads, which will significantly affect the network efficiency after being removed, constitute about 20% of the total and are typically dependent on the tolerance parameter; (iii) nodes have effects on network efficiency when the tolerance parameter is small but the effects are fading out as the tolerance parameter becomes large [142].

There is a so-called binary influence model is a special case of a general influence model [143], which can be applied to analyzing the mechanisms and effects of cascading failures [144]. It is found that the heterogeneity of network connectivity has mixed effects on the network stability. On one hand, increasing the heterogeneity of the individual node-failing thresholds can easily cause global failures; on the other hand, increasing the heterogeneity of the node-degree distribution can decrease the possibility of global failures.

The now-well-known sand-pile model was proposed by three physicists, Bak, Tang and Wiesenfeld, at the US Brookhaven National Lab in 1987 [145]. This is the first example of a dynamical system displaying self-organized criticality. The model is by nature a cellular automaton. At each site on the lattice there is a value that corresponds to the slope of the pile. This slope builds up as grains of sand are randomly placed onto the pile, until the slope exceeds a specific threshold value and, at that moment, this site collapses thereby transferring the sand into its adjacent sites, which increases their slopes. This random placement of sand may have no effect on an individual site but it may cause cascading reactions that can affect every site on the lattice, finally leading to avalanche.

A study of sand-pile model dynamics on ER random-graph networks shows that the distribution of avalanches follows a power-law distribution, with exponent 1.5 [146] or 1.65, under a slightly different model [147, 148].

Specified for power grids, the so-called OPA model is the ORNL-PSerc-Alaska model used to study the blackout dynamics in power transmission grids, where ORNL stands for Oak Ridge National Laboratory and PSerc for Power Systems Engineering Research Center, both in the USA. The model represents transmission lines, loads and generators with the usual DC load flow assumptions. Blackouts are initiated by a random line outage. When a transmission line is outaged, the generation and loads are re-dispatched using standard linear programming. If any lines were overloaded during the optimization then these limes are outaged with a certain probability. The process of re-dispatch and testing for outages is iterated until there are no outages. Thus, the OPA model can represent generic cascading outages (failures), which are consistent with network and operational constraints [149–153].

The OPA model involves two intrinsic time scales. There is a slow time scale, of the orders of days to years, over which load-power demand slowly increases and the network is upgraded in engineering responses to blackouts. Both the slow process opposing load increase and slow network upgrade will self-organize the system to a dynamic equilibrium. On the other hand, there is a fast time scale, of the order of hours or even minutes, over which cascading failures occur and propagate fairly quickly.

As power demand increases, power-served on the network will reach the maximum, around which the probability of failures (blackouts) follows a power-law form, and the probability of blackout will increase rapidly, so that in this case the power demand arrives at a threshold value [150].

Power grid blackouts occur typically due to power-served or power-overloading of transmission lines. In the OPA model, these two types of failures correspond to two different thresholds, depending on the operational conditions and the distance between the two threshold values [150]. As the power demand continues to increase, the model has several transition points, representing the changes of the network characters: one is the load shed, in which the power demand cannot be met by the generators due to insufficient capacity or transition line outage; another is the number of line outages. Near a transition point, the probability of failure follows a power law and so it will rapidly increase around the transition point, leading to a sudden change of the power-served [150].

From the above discussion on the OPA model, it can be seen that the increase of power loading is the main cause of large-scale blackouts on power grids. In order to better understand the cascading frequency and the distribution of failure probability, the so-called CASCADE model was created [151]. Compared to the OPA model, the CASCADE model is simpler and can be used to study the distribution of cascading failure probability.

There are some other models for cascading reactions or failures over complex networks. Representative models include: a fluid model and a birth-death model for router networks [152]; a hybrid differential-algebraic equations model [153], a Monte Carlo model [154] and a Markov-chain model [155] for power networks, etc.

Recently, cascading failures of interdependent networks attract a great deal of interest and attention. A large-scale complex network in the real world typically is a network of networks, namely an integrated network of many different kinds of interdependent networks. For example, the human mobility network consists of short-range interconnected flows by cars, trains and other means of transportation networks, interconnected with long-range commuting flows like airline flights. On top of them, there are communication networks such as mobile phone calls and Internet message exchanges [156].

As reported in [157], in such a tightly interconnected network infrastructure, the failure of nodes in one network not only can lead to consequent failures of some other nodes in the same network but also can lead to failures of nodes in another network, which in turn can cause further failures in the first network, ultimately leading to collapse of the entire networked system.

As an example based on the real data collected from the Italy blackout on September 28, 2003 [157], the cascading failures of an interdependent power network (located on the map of Italy) and Internet network (lifted above the map) took place, where every Internet server is connected to a geographically nearest power station. As a result of alternating failures in between the two interdependent networks, the entire infrastructural network in the Southern Italy finally collapsed.

Another finding reported in [157] is that a broader degree distribution increases the vulnerability of interdependent networks to random failures of nodes, which is opposite to the scenario in a single heterogeneous network. This reveals the need to consider interdependence among different networks in an integrated network in designing its strong and robust ability against random attack and failures.

Some recent progress on network of interdependent networks can be found in [158] (and references therein).

References

[1] Seagal, S. and Horne, D. (1997) *Human Dynamics: A New Framework for Understanding People and Realizing the Potential in Our Organizations*. Pegasus Inc., Waltham, MA.

[2] Chow, S.M, Ferrer, E. and Hsieh, F. (eds) (2008) *Statistical Methods for Modeling Human Dynamics: An Interdisciplinary Dialogue*. Psychology Press, Sussex, UK.

[3] Castellano, C., Fortunato, S. and Loreto, V. (2009) Statistical physics of social dynamics. *Reviews of Modern Physics*, **82**: 591–646.

[4] Barabási, A.L. (2005) The origin of bursts and heavy tails in human dynamics. *Nature*, **435**: 207–11.

[5] Oliveira, J.G. and Barabási, A.L. (2005) Human dynamics: The correspondence patterns of Darwin and Einstein. *Nature*, **437**: 1251–4.

[6] Vazquez, A., Oliveira, J.G., Dezso, Z. *et al.* (2006) Modeling bursts and heavy-tails in human dynamics. *Physical Review E*, **73**: 036127.

[7] Festinger, L., Schachter, S. and Back, K. (1950) *Social Pressures in Informal Groups: A Study of Human Factors in Housing*. Harper, New York.

[8] Castellano, C., Fortunato, S. and Loreto, V. (2009) Statistical physics of social dynamics, *Reviews of Modern Physics*, **81**: 591–646.

[9] Moreno, J.L. (1934) *Who Shall Survive? A New Approach to the Problem of Human Interrelations*. Nervous and Mental Disease Pub. Co., Washington DC.

[10] Wasserman, S. and Faust, K. (1994) *Social Network Analysis*. Cambridge University Press, Cambridge, UK.

[11] Freeman, L. (2004) *The Development of Social Network Analysis: A Study in the Sociology of Science*. Book Surge Pub., Vancouver, Canada.

[12] Roehner, B. (2007) *Driving Forces in Physical, Biological and Socio-Economic Phenomena*. Cambridge University Press, Cambridge, UK.

[13] Toral, R. and Tessone, C.J. (2006) Finite size effects in the dynamics of opinion formation. *Communications in Computational Physics*, **1**: 1–19.

[14] Clifford, P. and Sudbury, A. (1973) A model for spatial conflict, *Biometrika*, **60**: 581–8.

[15] Holley, R. and Liggett, T. (1975) Ergodic theorems for weakly interacting systems and the voter model, *Annals of Probability*, **3**: 643–63.

[16] Galam, S. (2002) Minority opinion spreading in random geometry, *European Physical Journal B*, **25**(4): 403–6.

[17] Tessone, C.J., Toral, R. and Amengual, P, *et al.* (2004) Neighborhood models of minority opinion spreading, *European Physical Journal B*, **39**: 535–44.

[18] Gekle, S., Peliti, L. and Galam, S. (2005) Opinion dynamics in a three-choice system, *European Physical Journal B*, **45**: 569–75.

[19] Chen, P. and Redner, S. (2005) Consensus formation in multi-state majority and plurality models, *Journal of Physics A*, **38**: 7239–52.

[20] Latané, B. (1981) The psychology of social impact, *American Psychologist*, **36**: 343–56.

[21] Bernardes, A.T., Stauffer, D. and Kertész, J. (2002) Election results and the Sznajd model on Barabasi network, *European Physical Journal B*, **25**: 123–7.

[22] González, M.C., Sousa, A.O. and Herrmann, H.J. (2004) Opinion formation on a deterministic pseudo-fractal network, *International Journal of Modern Physics C*, **15**: 45–57.

[23] Sznajd-Weron, K. and Sznajd, J. (2005) Who is left, who is right? *Physica A*, **351**: 593604,

[24] Schultz, C. (2004) Advertising, consensus, and aging in multilayer Sznajd model, *International Journal of Modern Physics C*, **15**: 569–73.

[25] Sznajd-Weron, K. and Sznajd, J. (2002) A simple model of price formation, *International Journal of Modern Physics C*, **13**: 115–23.

[26] Da Fontoura Costa, L. (2005) Sznajd complex networks, *International Journal of Modern Physics C*, **16**: 1001–16.

[27] Nowak A, Szamrej J and Latané B. (1990) From private attitude to public opinion: A dynamic theory of social impact. *Psychological Review*, **97**: 362–76.

[28] Stone M (1961) The opinion pool, *The Annals of Mathematical Statistics*, **32**: 1339–42.

[29] Chatterjee, S. and Seneta, E. (1977) Toward consensus: some convergence theorems on repeated averaging, *Journal of Applied Probability*, **14**: 89–97.

[30] Cohen, J.E., Hajnal, J. and Newman, C.M. (1986) Approaching consensus can be delicate when positions harden, *Stochastic Processes and Their Applications*, **22**: 315–22

[31] Gómez-Serrano, J., Graham, C, Le Boudec, J.Y. (2012) The bounded confidence model of opinion dynamics, *Mathematical Models and Methods in Applied Sciences*, **22**(2): 1150007.

[32] Deffuant, G., Neau, D., Amblard, F. and Weisbuch, G. (2000) Mixing beliefs among interacting agents, *Advances in Complex Systems*, **3**: 87–98.

[33] Stauffer, D. and Meyer-Ortmanns, H. (2004) Simulation of consensus model of Deffuant *et al.* on a Barabási-Albert Network, *International Journal of Modern Physics C*, **15**: 241–6.

[34] Weisbuch, G. (2004) Bounded confidence and social networks, *European Physical Journal B*, **38**: 339–43.

[35] Hegsemann, R, and Krause, U. (2002) Opinion dynamics and bounded confidence: Models, analysis and simulation, *Journal of Artificial Societies and Social Simulation Index*, **5**(2).

[36] Kuperman, M.N. and Zanette, D.H. (2002) Stochastic resonance in a model of opinion formation on small world networks, *European Physical Journal B*, **26**: 387–91.

[37] Toscani, G. (2006) Kinetic models of opinion formation, *Communications in Mathematical Sciences*, **4**: 481–96.

[38] Jiang, L.L., Hua, D.Y. and Zhu, Z.F. *et al.* (2008) Opinion dynamics on directed small-world networks, *European Physical Journal B*, **65**: 251–5.

[39] Martins, A.C.R. (2008) Mobility and social network effects on extremist opinions, *Physical Review E*, **78**: 036104.

[40] Axelrod, R. (1997) The dissemination of culture: A model with local convergence and global polarization, *Journal of Conflict Resolution*, **41**: 203–26.

[41] Lanchier, N. (2010) Opinion dynamics with confidence threshold: an alternative to the Axelrod model, *ALEA*, **7**: 1–18.

[42] Liu, Q. and Wang, X.F. (2013) Opinion dynamics with similarity-based random neighbors. *Scientific Reports*, **3**: 2968, doi: 10.1038/srep02968.

[43] Stachel, J. (2005) *Einstein's Miraculous Year: Five Papers that Changed the Face of Physics*, Princeton University Press, Princeton, NJ.

[44] Barabási, A-L. (2010) *BURSTS: The Hidden Pattern behind Everything We Do*, Dutton Books, New York.

[45] Colizza, V., Barrat, A., Barthélemy, M. and Vespignani, A. (2006) The role of the airline transportation network in the prediction and predictability of global epidemic. *Proceedings of the National Academy of Sciences USA*, **103**: 2015–20.

[46] Balcan, D., Colizza, V., Gonçalves, B. *et al.* (2009) Multiscale mobility networks and the spatial spreading of infectious diseases. *Proceedings of the National Academy of Sciences USA*, **106**: 21484–9.

[47] Hufnagel, L., Brockmann., D. and Geisel, T. (2004) Forecast and control of epidemics in a globalized world. *Proceedings of the National Academy of Sciences USA*, **101**: 15124–9.

[48] Wang, L., Li, X. and Zhang, Y-Q. *et al.* (2011) Evolution of scaling emergence in large-scale spatial epidemic spreading. *PLoS ONE*, **6**: e21197.

[49] http://www.wheresgeorge.com/ (last accessed August 12, 2014).

[50] Brockmann, D. and Theis, F. (2008) Money circulation, trackable items, and the emergence of universal human mobility patterns. *IEEE Pervasive Computing*, **7**: 28–35.

[51] Brockmann, D., Hufnagel, L. and Geisel, T. (2006) The scaling laws of human travel. *Nature*, **439**: 462–5.

[52] González, M.C., Hidalgo, C.A. and Barabási, A-L. (2008) Understanding individual human mobility patterns. *Nature*, **453**: 779–82.

[53] Noulas, A., Scellato, S., Lambiotte, R. *et al.* (2012) A tale of many cities: Universal patterns in human urban mobility, *PLoS One*, DOI: 10.1371/journal.pone.0037027.

[54] Bazzani, A., Giorgini, B., Rambaldi, S. *et al.* (2010) Statistical laws in urban mobility from microscopic GPS data in the area of Florence, *Journal of Statistical Mechanics: Theory and Experiment*, P05001.

[55] Barrat, A., Barthélemy, M., Pastor-Satorras, R. and Vespignani, A. (2004) The architecture of complex weighted networks. *Proceedings of the National Academy of Sciences USA*, **101**: 3747–52.

[56] Stouffer, S.A. (1940) Intervening opportunities: A theory relating mobility and distance, *American Sociological Review*, **5**: 845–67.

[57] Noulas, A., Scellato, S., Lambiotte, R. *et al.* (2011) A tale of many cities: universal patterns in human urban mobility. *arXiv*: 1108.5355v1.

[58] Cattuto, C., Van den Broeck, W., Barrat, A. *et al.* (2010) Dynamics of person-to-person interactions from distributed RFID sensor networks. *PLoS ONE*, **5**: e11596.

[59] Salathé, M., Kazandjieva, M., Lee, J.W. *et al.* (2010) A high-resolution human contact network for infectious disease transmission. *Proceedings of the National Academy of Sciences USA*, **107**: 22020–5.

[60] Brin, S. and Page, L. (1998) The anatomy of a large-scale hypertextual Web search engine. *Computer Networks and ISDN Systems*, **30**(1–7): 107–17.

[61] Page, L., Brin, S., Motwani, R. and Winograd, T. (1999) The pagerank citation ranking: Bringing order to the Web. *Technical Report* 1999-66, Stanford InfoLab, Nov.

[62] Kleinberg, J.M. (1998) Authoritative sources in a hyperlinked environment. *Proceedings of SODA98*, Philadelphia, USA, 668–77.

[63] Amento, B., Terveen, L. and Hill, W. (2000) Does "authority" mean quality? *Proceedings of ACM SIGIR'00*, 296–303.

[64] McSherry, F. (2005) A uniform approach to accelerated PageRank computation. *Proceedings of ACM WWW'05*, 575–82.

[65] Haveliwala, T. (1999) Efficient computation of PageRank. *Technical Report* 1999-31, Stanford InfoLab.

[66] Haveliwala, T. (2002) Topic-sensitive PageRank. *Proceedings of ACM WWW'02*, 517–26.

[67] Richardson, M. and Domingos, P. (2002) The intelligent surfer: Probabilistic combination of link and content information in PageRank. In Becker, S., Thrun, S., Obermayer, K. (eds), *Advances in Neural Information Processing Systems*, Vol. 14, MIT Press, Cambridge, MA, 1441–8.

[68] Haveliwala, T. and Kamvar, S. (2003) The second eigenvalue of the google matrix. *Technical Report* 2003-20, Stanford InfoLab.

[69] Haveliwala, T., Kamvar, S. and Jeh, G. (2003) An analytical comparison of approaches to personalizing PageRank. *Technical Report* 2003-35, Stanford InfoLab.

[70] Boldi, P., Santini, M. and Vigna, S. (2004) PageRank as a function of the damping factor. *Proceedings of ACM WWW'05*, 557–66.

[71] Langville, A.N. and Meyer, C.D. (2004) Deeper inside pagerank. *Internet Mathematics*, **1**(3): 335–400.

[72] Bianchini, M., Gori, M. and Scarselli, F. (2005) Inside PageRank. *ACM Transactions on Internet Technology*, **5**(1): 92–128.

[73] Gyöngyi, G. and Garcia-Molina, H. (2004) Web spam taxonomy. *Technical Report* 2004-25, Stanford University.

[74] Gyöngyi, G., Garcia-Molina, H. and Pedersen, J. (2004) Combating web spam with trustrank. *Proceedings of VLDB'04*, 576–87.

[75] Oztekin, B., Ertoz, L., Kumar, V. and Srivastava, J. (2003) Usage aware PageRank. *Technical Report* 03-010, University of Minnesota.

[76] Eirinaki, M. and Vazirgiannis, M. (2005) Usage-based PageRank for web personalization. *Proceedings of ICDM'05*, 130–7.

[77] Liu, Y., Gao, B., Liu, T-Y. *et al.* (2008) BrowseRank: letting web users vote for page importance. *Proceedings of ACM SIGIR'08*, 451–8.

[78] Liu, Y., Liu, T-Y., Gao, B. *et al.* (2010) A framework to compute page importance based on user behaviors. *Journal of Information Retrieval*, **13**(1): 22–45.

[79] Liu, Y. and Ma, Z. (2010) Comparison of two algorithms for computing page importance. *Proceedings of AAIM'2010, Lecture Notes in Computer Science*, **6124**: 1–11.

[80] Gao, B., Liu, T-Y., Liu, Y. *et al.* (2009) A general Markov framework for page importance computation. *Proceedings of CIKM'09*, 1835–8.

[81] Gao, B., Liu, T-Y., Liu, Y. *et al.* (2010) Page importance computation based on Markov processes. *Journal of Information Retrieval*, **14**(5): 488–514.

[82] Eiron, N., McCurley, K.S., Tomlin, J.A. (2004) Ranking the web frontier. *Proceedings of the 13th International World Wide Web Conference*, 309–18.

[83] Wu, J. and Aberer, K. (2004) Using SiteRank for P2P web retrieval. *EPFL Technical Report*, IC/2004/31.

[84] Bharat, K., Chang, B.W., Henzinger, M. and Ruhl, M. (2001) Who links to whom: Mining linkage between websites. *Proceedings of ICDM'01*, 51–8.

[85] Dill, S., Kumar, R., McCurley, K. *et al.* (2001) Self-similarity in the Web. *Proceedings of International Conference on Very Large Data Bases*, 69–78.

[86] Bao, Y., Feng, G., Liu, T-Y. *et al.* (2006) Ranking websites: a probabilistic view. *Internet Mathematics*, **3**(3): 295–320.

[87] Feng, G., Liu, T-Y., Wang, Y. *et al.* (2006) AggrerateRank: bringing order to web sites. *Proceedings of ACM Conference on Research and Development on Information Retrieval*, 75–82.

[88] Langville, A.N. and Meyer, C.D. (2008) *Google's PageRank and Beyond: The Science of Search Engine Rankings*. Princeton University Press, Princeton, NJ.

[89] Ricci, F., Rokach, L., Shapira, B., Kantor, P.B (eds) (2011) *Recommender Systems Handbook*, Springer, New York.

[90] Su, X. and Khoshgoftaar, T.M. (2009) A survey of collaborative filtering techniques. *Advanced Topics in Artificial Intelligence*, 421425.

[91] Ren, J., Zhou, T. and Zhang, Y-C. (2008) Information filtering via self-consistent refinement. *Europhysics Letters*, **82**: 58007.

[92] Hofmann, T. (2004) Latent semantic models for collaborative filtering. *ACM Transactions on Information Systems*, **22**: 89–115.

[93] Blei, D.M., Ng, A.Y. and Jordan, M.T. (2003) Latent Dirichlet allocation, *Journal of Machine Learning Research*, **3**: 993–1022.

[94] Zhang, Y. and Koren, J. (2007) Efficient Bayesian hierarchical user modeling for recommendation systems, *Proceedings of SIGIR'07*, Amsterdam, 47–54.

[95] Goldberg, K., Roeder, T., Gupta, D. and Perkins, C. (2001) Eigentaste: A constant time collaborative filtering algorithm, *Information Retrieval*, **4**: 133–51.

[96] Zhang, Y-C., Blattner, M., Yu, Y-K. (2007) Heat conduction process on community networks as a recommendation model, *Physical Review Letters*, **99**: 154301.

[97] Zhou, T., Ren, J., Medo, M., Zhang, Y-C. (2007) Bipartite network projection and personal recommendation, *Physical Review E*, **76**: 046115.

[98] Pazzani, M. and Billsus, D. (2007) Content-based recommendation systems, *Lecture Notes in Computer Sciences*, **4321**: 325–41.

[99] Burke, R. (2002) Hybrid recommender systems: survey and experiments, *User Modeling and User-Adapted Interaction*, **12**: 331–70.

[100] Huang, Z., Chen, H. and Zeng, D. (2004) Applying associative retrieval techniques to alleviate the sparsity problem in collaborative filtering, *ACM Transactions on Information Systems*, **22**: 116–42.

[101] Zhang, Z.K., Liu, C., Zhang, Y-C. and Zhou, T. (2010) Solving the cold-start problem in recommender systems with social tags, *Europhysics Letters*, **92**: 28002.

[102] Zhou, T., Kuscsik, Z., Liu, J-G. *et al.* (2010) Solving the apparent diversity-accuracy dilemma of recommender systems, *Proceedings of the National Academy of Sciences USA*, **107**: 4511–15.

[103] Zhang, Z.K., Zhou, T., Zhang, Y-C. (2010) Tag-aware recommender systems: A state-of-the-art survey, *Journal of Computer Science and Technology*, **26**: 767–77.

[104] Sarwar, B., Konstan, J. and Riedl, J. (2002) Incremental singular value decomposition algorithms for highly scalable recommender systems. *Proceedings of International Conference on Computer Information Science*.

[105] Min, S.H. and Han, I. (2005) Detection of the customer time-variant pattern for improving recommender systems, *Expert Systems with Applications*, **28**: 189–99.

[106] Zhou, T., Medo, M., Cimini, G. *et al.* (2011) Emergence of scale-free leadership structure in social recommender systems. *PLoS One*, **6**: e20648.

[107] Mobasher, B., Burke, R., Bhaumik, R. and Williams, C. (2007) Toward trustworthy recommender systems: An analysis of attack models and algorithm robustness, *ACM Transactions on Internet Technology*, **7**: 23(1–38).

[108] Getoor, L. and Diehl, C.P. (2005) Link mining: A survey. *ACM SIGKDD Explorations Newsletter*, **7**(2): 3–12.

[109] Lu, L.Y. and Zhou, T. (2010) Link prediction in complex networks: a survey. *Physica A*, **390**: 1150–70.

[110] Hanely, J.A. and McNeil, B.J. (1982) The meaning and use of the area under a receiver operating characteristic (ROC) curve. *Radiology*, **143**: 29–36.

[111] Herlocker, J.L., Konstann, J.A., Terveen, K. *et al.* (2004) Evaluating collaborative filtering recommender systems. *ACM Transactions on Information Systems*, **22**(1): 5–53.

[112] Zhou, T., Ren, J., Medo, M. *et al.* (2007) Bipartite network projection and personal recommendation. *Physical Review E*, **76**: 046115.

[113] Sarukkai, R.R. (2000) Link prediction and path analysis using Markov chains. *Compnet*, **33**(1–6): 377–86.

[114] Zhu, J., Hong, J. and Hughes, J.G. (2002) Using Markov chains for link prediction in adaptive web sites. *Lecture Notes in Computer Science*, **2311**: 60–73.

[115] Popescul, A. and Ungar, L. (2003) Statistical relational learning for link prediction. *Proceedings of Workshop on Learning Statistical Models from Relational Data*. ACM Press, New York, 81–7.

[116] O'Madadhain, J., Hutchins, J. and Smyth, P. (2005) Prediction and ranking algorithms for even-based network data. *Proceedings of ACM SIGKDD 2005*. ACM Press, New York, 23–30.

[117] Lin, D. (1998) An information-theoretic definition of similarity. *Proceedings of 15th International Conference on Machine Learning*. Morgan Kaufman Pub., San Francisco, 296–304.

[118] Liben-Nowell, D. and Kleinberg, J. (2007) The link-prediction problem for social networks. *Journal of American Society for Information Science and Technology*, **58**(7): 1019–31.

[119] Zhou, T., Lu, L.Y., Zhang, Y.C. (2009) Predicting missing links via local information. *European Physical Journal B*, **71**(4): 623–30.

[120] Clauset, A., Moore, C. and Newman, M.E.J. (2008) Hierarchical structure and the prediction of missing links in networks. *Nature*, **453**: 98–101.

[121] Holland, P.W., Laskey, K.B, and Leinhard, S. (1983) Stochastic blockmodels: First steps. *Social Networks*, **5**: 109–37.

[122] Guimera, R. and Sales-Pardo, M. (2009) Missing and spurious interactions and the reconstruction of complex networks. *Proceedings of the National Academy of Sciences USA*, **106**(52): 22073–8.

[123] Pan, Y., Li, D.H., Liu, J.G. *et al.* (2010) Detecting community structure in complex networks via node similarity. *Physica A*, **389**(14): 2849–57.

[124] Wang, Y.L., Zhou, T., Shi, J.J. *et al.* (2009) Empirical analysis of dependence between stations in Chinese railway network. *Physica A*, **388**(14): 2949–55.

[125] Lu, L.Y., Jin, C. H. and Zhou, T. (2009) Similarity index based on local paths for link prediction of complex networks. *Physical Review E*, **80**(4): 046122.

[126] Liu, W.P., Lu, L.Y. (2010) Link prediction based on local random walk. *Europhysics Letters*, **89**(5): 58007.

[127] Alon, U. (2007) Network motifs: theory and experimental approaches, *Nature Rev. Genetics*, **8**: 450–61.

[128] Mantrach, A., Yen, L., Callut, J. *et al.* (2010) The sum-over-paths covariance kernel: a novel covariance measure between nodes of a directed graph, *IEEE Transactions On Pattern Analysis and Machine Intelligence*, **32**: 1112–26.

[129] Murata, T. and Moriyasu, S. (2007) Link prediction of social networks based on weighted proximity measure. *Proceedings of IEEE/WIC/ACM International Conference on Web Intelligence*, ACM Press, New York.

[130] Lu, L.Y. and Zhou, T. (2010) Link prediction in weighted networks: the role of weak ties, *Europhysics Letters*, **89**: 18001.

[131] Chen, L., Wang, R. and Zhang, X (2009) *Biomolecular Network: Methods and Applications in Systems Biology*. John Wiley & Sons, Inc., New York.

[132] Chen, L., Wang, R., Li, C. and Aihara, K. (2010) *Modelling Biomolecular Networks in Cells: Structures and Dynamics*. Springer, New York.

[133] Barabási, A-L. and Oltvai, Z.N. (2004) Network biology: Understanding the cell's functional organization, *Nature Review Genetics*, **5**: 101–13.

[134] Moreno, Y., Gómez, J.B. and Pacheco, A.F. (2002) Instability of scale-free networks under node-breaking avalanches. *Europhysics Letters*, **58**(4): 630–6.

[135] Motter, A.E., Nishikawa, T. and Lai, Y-C. (2002) Cascade-based attacks on complex networks. *Physical Review E*, **66**: 065102(R).

[136] Holme, P., Kim, B.J., Yoon, C.N. and Han, S.K. (2002) Attack vulnerability of complex networks. *Physical Review E*, **65**: 056109.

[137] Wang, J., Rong, L., Zhang, L. and Zhang, Z. (2008) Attack vulnerability of scale-free networks due to cascating failures. *Physica A*, **387**: 6671–8.

[138] Moreno, Y., Pastor-Satorras, R., Vázquez, A. and Vespignani, A. (2003) Critical load and congestion instabilities in scale-free networks. *Europhysics Letters*, **62**: 292–8.

[139] Holme P, Kim B J. Vertex overload breakdown in evolving networks. *Physical Review E*, **65**: 066109.

[140] Crucitti, P., Latora, V. and Marchiori, M. (2004) Model for cascading failures in complex networks. *Physical Review E*, **69**, 045104(R).

[141] Albert, R., Albert, I. and Nakarado, G.L. (2004) Structural vulnerability of the North American power grid. *Physical Review E*, **69**: 025103(R).

[142] Kinney, R., Crucitti, P., Albert, R. *et al.* (2004) Modeling cascading failures in the north American power grid. cond-mat/0410318.

[143] Asavathiratham, C. (2000) *The Influence Model: A Tractable Representation for the Dynamics of Networked Markov Chains*, Dissertation, Electrical Engineering and Computer Science Department, MIT, Cambridge, MA.

[144] Watts, D.J.A. (2002) simple model of global cascades on random networks. *Proceedings of the National Academy of Sciences USA*, 2002, **99**: 5766-5771

[145] Bak P, Tang C, Wiesenfeld K. Self-organized criticality: An explanation of the 1/f noise. *Physical Review Letters*, **59**: 381−4.

[146] Bonabeau, E. (1995) Sandpile dynamics on random graphs. *Journal of the Physical Society of Japan*, **64**: 327−8.

[147] Lise, S. and Paczuski, M. (2002) Nonconservative earthquake model of self-organized criticality on a random graph. *Physical Review Letters*, **88**: 228301.

[148] Olami, Z., Feder, H.J.S. and Christensen, K. (1992) Correlation functions in the fully frustrated 2D XY model. *Physical Review Letters*, **68**: 1224−7.

[149] Dobson, I., Chen, J., Thorp, J.S. *et al.* (2002) Examining criticality of blackouts in power system models with cascading events. *Proceedings of 35th Hawaii International Conference on System Sciences*, 63−72.

[150] Carreras, B.A, Lynch, V.E., Dobson, I. *et al.* (2002) Critical points and transitions in an electric power transmission model for cascading failure blackouts. *Chaos*, **12**(4): 985−94.

[151] Dobson, I, Carreras, B.A., Newman, D.E. (2002) A probabilistic loading-dependent model of cascading failure and possible implications for blackouts. *Proceedings of 35th Hawaii International Conference on System Sciences*, 1−8.

[152] Coffman Jr,, E.G., Ge, Z., Misra, V. *et al.* (2002) Network resilience: Exploring cascading failures within BGP. *Proceedings of 40th Annual Allerton Conference on Communications, Computing and Control*, 1−10.

[153] Parrilo, P.A., Lall, S., Paganini, F. *et al.* (1999) Model reduction for analysis of cascading failures in power systems. *Proceedings of American Control Conference*, **6**: 4208−12.

[154] Rios, M.A., Kirschen, D.S., Jawayeera, D. *et al.* (2002) Value of security: modeling time-dependent phenomena and weather conditions. *IEEE Transactions on Power Systems*, **17**(3): 543−8.

[155] Pepyne, D.L., Panayiotou, C.G. and Cassandras, C.G. (1999) Vulnerability assessment and allocation of protection resources in power systems. *Proceedings of American Control Conference*, **6**: 4705−10.

[156] Vespignani A (2010) The fragility of interdependency. *Nature*, **464**: 984−5.

[157] Buldyrev, S.V., Parshan, R., Paul, G. *et al.* (2010) Catastrophic cascade of failures in interdependent networks. *Nature*, **464**: 1025−8.

[158] Gao, J., Buldyrev, S.V., Stanley, H.E. and Havlin, S. (2012) Networks formed from interdependent networks. *Nature Physics*, **8**: 40−8.

Index

Fundamentals of Complex Networks: Models, Structures and Dynamics, First Edition.
Guanrong Chen, Xiaofan Wang, Xiang Li.
© Higher Education Press. All rights reserved. Published 2015 by John Wiley & Sons Singapore Pte Ltd.
Companion Website: www.wiley.com/go/chen/complex